'. . . a brave, insightful book. Bren
and his discussion on the Christia
is superb.'

weekend Australian

'*Acting on Conscience* . . . demonstrates the constructive contribution a religious person can make to public debate, even if one does not agree with the arguments.'

The Age

'Father Frank Brennan has been called a "meddling priest" by Paul Keating and been attacked by John Howard and Peter Costello. I think this means he is probably right most of the time.'

Sydney Morning Herald

'Well written and argued, *Acting on Conscience* is an important piece in the nation's debate on politics and public life.'

Australian Bookseller & Publisher

'. . . clear, sober and sensible. [*Acting on Conscience*] argues with measure, its tome mercifully free from hectoring and sanctimony.'

The Australian

'. . . a distinguished and courageous reflection on the meaning of conscience in both our religious and civic identities that will be of great assistance to all those who share a commitment to the common good.'

Australasian Catholic Record

Father Frank Brennan SJ AO, a Jesuit priest and lawyer, is professor of Law at the Australian Catholic University and professor of Human Rights and Social Justice at the University of Notre Dame, Australia. His books include *Legislating Liberty* and *Tampering with Asylum.*

In 2002 he was awarded the Humanitarian Overseas Service Medal for his work in East Timor and was a recipient of the Australian Centenary Medal in 2003 for his service with refugees and for human rights work in the Asia–Pacific region.

Other books by Frank Brennan

Too Much Order with Too Little Law
Land Rights Queensland Style
Sharing the Country
One Land, One Nation
Legislating Liberty
The Wik Debate
Tampering with Asylum

Frank Brennan

ACTING ON CONSCIENCE

How can we responsibly mix law, religion and politics?

UQP

First published 2007 by University of Queensland Press
PO Box 6042, St Lucia, Queensland 4067 Australia
This edition 2007

www.uqp.uq.edu.au

Typeset by Post Pre-press Group, Brisbane
Printed in Australia by McPherson's Printing Group

Cataloguing in Publication Data
National Library of Australia

Brennan, Frank, 1954-.
Acting on conscience: how can we responsibly mix law, religion and politics?

ISBN 978 0 7022 3674 7.

1. Church and state – Australia. 2. Religion and state – Australia.
3. Australia – Politics and government. I. Title.

322. 10994

To Mirinda, Shannon, Bridget, Patricia and Angela

CONTENTS

ACKNOWLEDGMENTS

Before departing for the United States in 2004, I dined with five of my nieces: Mirinda, Shannon, Bridget, Patricia and Angela. They not only asked that this book be dedicated to them (as it now is) but that it be readable and appealing to them (as I hope it is). With the dedication comes the hope that young Australians – of all faiths and none – might find the book a helpful tool for deciding responsibly how to mix law, religion and politics in the future public debates which will shape our national response to big moral questions. Together we might then enact values appropriate for the public square.

I thank the Jesuit Institute at Boston College for the opportunity to reflect on these issues at leisure. I especially thank Fr Bryan Hehir at Harvard and the Jesuit and Franciscan community at Roberts House, who showed me things old and new in the pantry for dealing with these perennial questions.

INTRODUCTION

A meddling priest's search for answers

Like-minded, liberal-minded atheists who agreed to live together on a remote island could decide to maximise their individual liberties and minimise government interference with their lifestyle choices. They might succeed in maximising personal choice and liberty for a short time – until there was a need to reach agreement on shared community obligations to assist those who could no longer help themselves. Over time, differences of opinion would emerge. Debates about law, politics and morality would occur. Eventually there would be passionate arguments and a need for compromise.

The scenario becomes more complex when you move from the fairytale island to the reality of a nation state like Australia where there are people of all faiths and none, individual libertarians, communal idealists and strong state interventionists. In the past, we assumed that the Judeo-Christian religious backgrounds and the post-Enlightenment rationalism of most Australians were fairly consonant with the Australian way of doing things. When it came to discussing law or public policy, a person's religious views were judged to be irrelevant in the public forum unless they could be translated into language comprehensible to the secular humanist. Law, civic discourse, and respect for the other were needed to keep religion and politics in check.

This task became more urgent and more apparent after 11 September 2001. Muslims in Australia, like all other persons on our shores, deserve a fair go. Many of us wonder how we can accommodate Islamic perspectives in our public life. Many of us are awkward in hearing public expression of religious views, no matter what the religion. We often doubt that religious views should have any place at the table of public deliberation. In an age of heightened security, we readily presume that government will act in the public interest without unwarranted interference with civil liberties. But those of us who are not Muslim nor of Middle Eastern appearance probably have little to fear from increasing police powers.

The night the Australian Senate voted to remove Health Minister Tony Abbott's veto power over the importation of the abortion drug RU486, Abbott said:[1]

> Many people were saying as a Catholic I couldn't be trusted with this power. Obviously I do have some views which I have expressed. But my views on abortion are pretty much in sync with the views that have been expressed over the years by such diverse people as the Dalai Lama and Mohandas K. Ghandi. There's nothing necessarily Catholic about my views on abortion. But in any event as a minister of the Crown, any decision that I make is based on ordinary rational principles of Government.

The parliamentary debate had been complex. Senators with a conscience vote needed to discuss not only the morality of abortion. They also had to consider the appropriate checks and balances in the exercise of state power, resolving whether the decision to approve RU486 should rest with the minister for Health or the Therapeutic Goods Administration. In debates of this sort, there is a need to set down the place and the limits of religion in government decision making. There is also a need to have in place appropriate checks and balances for the responsible exercise of government power. Conscience, civic discourse, the right checks and balances, and community values such as tolerance (which requires respect for minority viewpoints) are needed to keep religion and politics in place. Checks and balances are those constitutional arrangements in a nation state which ensure that the legislature (both houses of Parliament), executive (government ministers and the public service) and judiciary (the courts) have sufficient power to keep one another in check, balancing the will of the majority and the rights and entitlements of the individual and those minority groups who disagree with the majority view.

In the same week that the Senate took a conscience vote on the abortion drug, Danish embassies burned and western media proprietors debated whether to publish cartoons of the prophet Mohammed which had first appeared in the Danish press. The cartoons caused grave offence to many Muslims. Conceding the right to freedom of speech, many community leaders urged that the right not be exercised on this occasion out of respect for the religious sensibilities of others, and with a concern for law and order. In these situations, rights are not trumps and neither are religious sensibilities. Though religious views should be respected and given their place in the public forum, there are limits on how far religious views (whether of a minority or majority) can be invoked to restrict the lawful actions of others.

We need appropriate checks and balances on state power and on the rhetoric of our mass media and elected politicians. We need a tradition of civic discourse respectful of the views of all people, including those with passionately held religious views. We need a commitment to mutual tolerance accommodating the utterances and actions of others who think differently from the majority. We need to have a special care for the most vulnerable in our diverse society without unduly curbing the liberty and opportunities for those less vulnerable and those with few or no religious sensibilities. We need to prize the individual conscience. We need to value the dissenter. With appropriate checks and balances, and respect for the argued positions of our fellow citizens (even if those positions are premised on religious or other world views foreign to us), we can work together for laws and policies that provide the social order necessary for all citizens to achieve their human flourishing, despite their contentious and argumentative differences.

Having spent twenty years in the public forum calling attention to what I regard as democratically responsible religious views on vexed moral, political and legal questions, I want to unpack some of the complexities of law, religion and politics in contemporary Australia. I have now returned to Australia after living in the United States for a year, including the latter stages of the 2004 presidential election, and seeing how another, very different, western society deals with the mix of religion and politics. I make no claim that my religious views or public policy preferences on particular controversial issues are more correct or preferable to the views and preferences of any other citizen. I do claim that the appropriate resolution of public conflicts would be more achievable and certain if we accorded greater respect to the conscience of each person. We need to better understand the limits on any individual exercising power in the name of the state, to place better checks and balances on those exercising state power, and to engage in more respectful public dialogue being attentive to religious and other world views. We need to distinguish between the public forum (in which all citizens are entitled to share) and the various communal spaces in the social life of citizens (in which people voluntarily opt in or out of sharing common interests, including religious beliefs and practice). In the public forum, there is a need to distinguish our personal morality from the social mores and laws that are to be imposed on all.

I was a first-year law and politics student at the University of Queensland in 1971. Joh Bjelke-Petersen declared a state of emergency during the Springbok rugby tour so the government could more ruthlessly repel the protests of those demonstrating against the apartheid regime in South Africa. The university's vice-chancellor, Sir Zelman Cowen, walked a fine, judicious line questioning the need for government to suspend the rule of law and scrutinising the actions of the Queensland Police as they clashed with the protesters. The protesters called attention to racist laws and policies in Queensland as well as in South Africa. For the first time in Australian history, a court had just ruled – in August 1971 – that Aborigines who had come to court seeking recognition of their traditional rights had no land rights that had survived the assertion of British sovereignty. Young agitators from Aboriginal communities came onto the university campus telling horror stories of human rights violations on the Queensland reserves. Church leaders took a stand, urging a fair consideration of grievances in South Africa and Queensland. Many on the left of the political spectrum, regardless of their own religious background or practice, praised the church leaders. Others, including Sir Joh, wondered aloud why church leaders wanted to consort with communists.

My study of politics and law was complemented by a growing religious sensibility. By 1975, I had completed my initial university studies and entered the Jesuit order of the Catholic Church. Ever since, with a mission from my religious superiors, I have been involved in legal and political issues which have a strong moral edge and which invite attention and comment by citizens with religious convictions, sometimes resulting in formal statements and joint action by church leaders. Over the years, I have wondered whether there are rules, principles or prudential guidelines to offer for those involved in public controversies with religious, legal and political elements. I had cause to wonder aloud whether I had breached any of those rules, principles or guidelines in 1998, when Paul Keating labelled me a meddling priest during the *Wik* debate which followed the High Court's decision that Aborigines might still have native title rights on pastoral leases in outback Australia. This was the time when the Howard government needed to pass its legislation restricting Aboriginal rights through the Senate, while the staunchly Catholic Senator Brian Harradine held the balance of power.

Keating wrote in the *Sydney Morning Herald*, 'Talk about meddling priests! When Aborigines see Brennan, Harradine and other professional Catholics coming they should tell them to clear out.' He claimed that Harradine and I had 'saved Howard from paying the price of his folly, and made the Aborigines pay instead'. Keating thought Howard was 'beatable' at the polls. He not only thought that Harradine and I had no right to make and act on predictions about the government's prospects at the polls. He thought Harradine and I were demonstrably wrong in any predictions we might have made. He said:[2]

> Harradine and Brennan have taken the view that Labor, which would take a different approach to Wik, cannot win the election. They have second guessed the electorate. They are like a lot of people in and out of politics: they talk loudly and often about principle, and when the weights are on and permanent interests are at stake they look for a way to slide out.
>
> Unwilling to let the electorate play out the issue – and play out this Government's role in it – they have done their best to take the pressure off.

If *Wik* had been left unresolved, Howard would have had no option but to return to the matter after an election in which his proposed legislation would have been an electoral issue, at least in the bush. Howard would have won the election, and Pauline Hanson's One Nation Party would have obtained a handful of seats in the Senate. One way or another, Howard would have passed his legislation – either with support from One Nation in the Senate, or by a joint sitting of the houses if there were a double dissolution. In hindsight, no-one has seriously suggested that Kim Beazley could have won an election in 1998 with *Wik* unresolved.

The prudential choice was simple. Aborigines and their supporters had the choice of a bird in the hand and none in the bush. The bird in the hand was Howard's original legislation, with some added benefits for Aborigines stipulated by Harradine as the precondition for his giving the legislation passage through the Senate. The none in the bush would have been John Howard's unamended original legislative proposal passed after an election without the Harradine top-up. In theory, this was not a difficult political choice. The hard political choices are when there is a choice of a bird in the hand and two in the bush.

Seven years later, when Harradine was retiring from the Senate, Andrew Bartlett, deputy leader of the Democrats, made this acknowledgment of Harradine's acumen on *Wik*:[3]

> The agreement he reached on the Wik legislation was one of the few cases I would point to where John Howard was bested in negotiations.
>
> Whilst the legislative merits of the Wik agreement were less than ideal, the sort of race election, focused on Indigenous people, that our country would have faced in 1998 if that agreement had not been reached would have been far worse even than the one we endured in 2001.

These were complex political issues and I still have a strong self-interest in agitating a particular view of it all. But without resolving all the outstanding questions, we need to ask: Would it have been good enough in 1998 for someone in my position simply to critique the Howard legislation, without working to create the space for Harradine to effect a compromised outcome which was more beneficial to Aborigines – and at the same time avoiding the prospect of a race-based election? Having critiqued the Howard legislation, I could have withdrawn from the political fray arguing that the world of political controversy is no place for a religious person, especially when the controversy is marked by a sharp contest between political parties after all stakeholders have put their case to the public.

Whatever the internal contradictions of the High Court's *Wik* decision, I believed that the decision entitled Aborigines to the right to negotiate with mining companies wanting access to traditional lands that were also subject to pastoral leases. The government was wrongly claiming that equal treatment of Aboriginal native title holders and pastoralists required that native title holders have no right to put their case about the effects of mining on their sacred sites and other areas of land used for residence or traditional activities. The Aborigines' own lawyers had crafted a compromise on the right to negotiate.

Rather than withdrawing completely from the political process, I thought it right to create the space and pressure for government to accept that compromise, thereby avoiding the need for the legislation to be held over until a subsequent election, when a returned Howard government would have been more emboldened to legislate without the compromise crafted by lawyers for the National Indigenous Working Group (NIWG).

It was complex politics. It was complex law. The place of a church person who was not an Aborigine, a miner or a pastoralist was very fraught. I can understand Paul Keating's annoyance at a cleric's involvement in the process. Even if I was right in assessing the political outcome of any likely election, was I right to involve myself so intimately in the political process? Mind you, my involvement in the lead-up to the third and critical Senate debate was confined to a series of letters to government which I shared with a senior member of the NIWG. I then absented myself from the country and from the debate for the critical weeks of the final negotiations. That did not deter Paul Keating from telling the *Daily Telegraph* that the compromise had my 'fingerprints all over it'.[4] Ever since, I have had cause to reflect acutely on how to mix law, religion and politics responsibly.

Now, as a professor of Law at the two Australian Catholic universities, I have reason to contemplate the distinctive contribution of religion to Australian law and politics. Since 11 September 2001, these are not idle academic questions, nor are they questions confined to the Christian churches in Australia. We need to understand better the role of meddling priests, meddling imams and other meddling citizens who draw upon religious beliefs in their domestic and international political activity and their commitment to law reform.

Being a Christian, I am a member of the largest religious grouping in Australia. Given that discriminating between religious groups merely on account of their size would be unacceptable, any place we carve out as the appropriate realm for Christians bringing their religious beliefs to bear in the public forum, must also be an appropriate realm for all other religious believers. The same limits should be applied to all religious believers, regardless of their creed, and to those other citizens who hold comprehensive world views not shared by their fellow religious citizens.

Being a Catholic, I am a member of the Christian denomination whose leaders claim the most definitive authority to give answers to moral questions as well as questions about religious faith. If we can get the rules right for Catholics engaging in the public forum, especially setting the appropriate limits on the Catholic Church's involvement of its leaders in legal and political controversies, we will have gone a long way towards setting down limits appropriate for all religious authorities.

It is non-negotiable in the public forum of the democratic nation state that we accord primacy to the individual conscience of the citizen in the search for truth. In a moral political controversy, our fellow citizens are more likely to respect a position enunciated: 'In good conscience I believe that X is the situation and we should do Y and avoid Z'. There will always be room in a pluralist democracy for the citizen who says, 'I believe that we should do Y and avoid Z, not because I in good conscience have decided that this is the case. Rather my religious leaders have told me that we should do Y and avoid Z.' That may be a good enough reason for a religious believer of that particular group to do Y and avoid Z. It is no reason at all for other citizens who are not members of that religious group. Nor is it a sufficient reason to make a law or policy insisting that all citizens do Y and avoid Z.

In the light of my twenty years' experience in Australia and my one year's close observation of the United States during an election year, I argue that religion once again has a place at the table of public discussion on law and policy. All citizens are self-determining individuals who have the capacity and desire to seek the true and the good for themselves and for their fellow citizens in community. For many of these citizens, their religious view of life and the world contributes to their perception, understanding and search for the true and the good. That is why religion deserves a place at the table of public deliberation. However there will always be contested views about the true and the good. In a democracy, there will always be public dispute. That is why religion's place at the table must be rightly circumscribed.

We establish that place by first according primacy to the conscience of the individual who makes decisions about what is right and wrong. It is right and proper that citizens who unthinkingly repeat the moral claims of their religious leaders about contested legal and political questions will carry little weight in any public resolution of conflict. In raw political terms, they may make up a constituency that has to be accommodated. But where political debate is about contested moral questions, citizens or politicians who accord primacy to their religious leaders' declaration rather than to their own conscience formed and informed especially by the teaching authority of their own church will not be regarded as self-determining political actors. They will be sidelined as being accountable to external authorities who have no right to dictate the terms of public debate in the nation state.

We then set limits on religion's place at the table by asking what public trust is exercised by the person either as citizen, legislator, administrator or judge. That place is subject to constitutional constraints. The place of religion is subject to political and social constraints which require religious citizens and religious authorities to exercise caution in distinguishing principle from strategy and tactics. Right judgment, prudence and political savvy all have their place. That place is fraught by the public's mistrust of church statements that are not matched by church action and institutional arrangements which themselves fall short of the ideal espoused in the statement, whether it be self-determination for Aborigines or equal rights, due respect and dignified recognition of minorities. That place is fraught by the politics of compromise, including the self-interest of stakeholders suspicious of what Paul Keating during the *Wik* debate called 'the goody-goody brigade [who] display their Catholicism like a lamp'.[5]

That place is fraught by the lack of expertise, lack of specialist and confidential knowledge, and by the sensitivities of government at times of high security – as with the public controversy over the Iraq war or new anti-terrorism laws. That place is fraught by the morality of politics where a democratically elected government thinks it must do evil to some in order to do good for the majority, and where government is influenced by a utilitarian calculus, often embracing the Caiaphas principle that it is better that one person suffer for the people. In recent times that one person has included the asylum seeking child held in long-term detention so that a message might be sent to others not to breach our ordered migration barriers. That place is fraught by the emotion and rhetoric of politics, especially at election time. That place is fraught by the differing conceptions of morality and the common good. But we are fortunate to live in a society where we can mix law, religion and politics responsibly. We need to keep religion in its proper place in the Australian public forum of law and politics. We also need to ensure an adequate separation of powers, with workable checks and balances so that executive government does not trample the rights of unpopular and powerless minorities.

In 1998, I published *Legislating Liberty* in which I opposed the creation of a comprehensive constitutional bill of rights for Australia. In the United States, the Supreme Court has become very politicised with its modes of appointment and procedures. This is in part because the court has such political power to strike down laws which offend the very broad due process and equal protection clauses in the US bill of rights. These clauses give the judges the last 'say' in many political disputes that are controversial precisely because there is as yet no emerging moral consensus in the community. It is invidious for unelected judges to make such decisions. I did propose a statutory scheme for the recognition of specified rights and entitlements, permitting the Parliament specifically to infringe on a right or entitlement if Parliament adverted to the issue and decided that some greater good needed to be legislated. I thought this modest addition to Australia's constitutional machinery of rights would be adequate because, at the time, executive government was constrained by a number of factors which are no longer in play.

At that time, the government did not control the Senate. Control of the Senate by the Opposition together with the minor parties resulted in the government of the day having to be accountable to the Senate, providing compelling public rationales for the government's legislative program. As the *Mabo* debate in 1993 demonstrated, this fetter on the government could work to the government's advantage. When crafting the original *Native Title Act*, Prime Minister Paul Keating had to negotiate with all key stakeholders including Aborigines, mining companies, pastoralists and state governments. These stakeholders had access to the Senate, including the committee processes. They were able to put their case, exert influence and be heard. Early in the negotiations, the Aboriginal leaders rejected Keating's legislation on the basis that it was too favourable to the other interests. It was only because Keating did not control the Senate that it was possible to craft an outcome which was owned by the Aboriginal leaders, who hailed Keating a hero at the end of the legislative process.

By late 2005, John Howard controlled the Senate. It would have been easier for Howard to convince the broad spectrum of public opinion that he had struck the right balance with industrial relations legislation or anti-terrorism laws if he had run the gauntlet of a hostile Senate, where he would need to give a public account of the necessity for novel measures. Without such transparency in the parliamentary process, the public is left dependent on a handful of rebel backbenchers who have abandoned all hope of preferment in the ministry to call the government to account.

Prior to 1998, the Australian government had shown that it was committed to honouring the decisions of international tribunals that heard complaints from Australian citizens who had exhausted all domestic remedies, claiming an infringement of their rights set down in various international treaties to which Australia was a party. The Howard government reversed this commitment and has made a habit of disregarding the findings of international bodies that comment adversely on Australia's human rights record.

In those days prior to 1998, the High Court of Australia had also demonstrated a willingness to be guided by international human rights instruments to which Australia was a party, especially when there was an ambiguity in a statute or there was a need to develop the common law. Where there was a choice available to the judges, some of them were willing to exercise the choice consistent with the developing international jurisprudence. Since then, all equivalent countries including the United Kingdom have subscribed to their own bills of rights. The Australian judiciary is left isolated. The High Court is less assisted by other final courts of appeal which resolve difficult political challenges through the interpretation of their own bills of rights. In 2004, the High Court reached the stage of authorising the indefinite detention of a stateless person, without judicial review or supervision. Such detention could possibly be for life. One of the four judges in the majority said the result was tragic, but without a bill of rights he could do no other.

A government which is less constrained by the Senate, the High Court and international tribunals is a government that risks thwarting more readily the rights and entitlements of minorities and those who hold an unpopular view of the true and the good. With party machines that enforce tighter discipline than in other countries, such as the United States and the United Kingdom, we Australians then become more dependent on the magnanimity and vision of the prime minister and his advisers. In the long term, this is dangerous for democracy.

The terrorist threat, combined with the tight discipline of the government parties and the unwillingness of the parliamentary opposition to invest much political capital in protection of minority rights, contributes added potency to the call from the community for a statutory bill of rights. A bill of rights can consolidate the checks and balances needed in a modern democracy regardless of the strength of the government parties and the weakness of the opposition parties.

As we have seen recently in the United Kingdom, a statutory bill of rights provides no automatic right answer in striking the appropriate balance between security and liberty. But it does provide a template for public discussion which must precede any novel legislation interfering with long-cherished rights and freedoms. The ACT has now legislated a statutory bill of rights and the Victorian government has announced its intention to do likewise. There is a national community initiative led by John Menadue and Susan Ryan called New Matilda. They are proposing a national Human Rights Bill that would provide some practical checks and balances on executive power. This initiative ought to have appeal to any political party wanting to ensure that Osama Bin Laden does not make further incremental gains, by default or by proxy, in stripping away the freedoms we cherish. The New Matilda draft contains modest and sensible proposals, including a requirement that the attorney-general provide the House of Representatives with a compatibility statement assessing new legislation against the checklist of human rights in the Human Rights Bill.[6]

Our national fuel tank of checks and balances is running low. It needs to be topped up. In this realm, popularity cannot be equated with infallibility. Governors as well as the governed should welcome responsible checks and balances. In the legislative rush at the end of 2005, the Australian public was dependent on closed door assurances within the Coalition party room that the legislative outcomes in the new anti-terrorism laws struck the right balance, even when they could not withstand scrutiny before a parliamentary committee dominated by the government's own members. Then the government told the public that new sedition laws, which they admitted were not perfect, could be submitted for later review by the law reform commission.

Such shoddy lawmaking would be precluded by a Human Rights Act that required the attorney-general first to submit a compatibility statement of the sedition laws before passage of the legislation. We can credibly and dispassionately part company with the prime minister, who responded to the calls for a bill of rights: 'I regard a free press as more important to the maintenance of liberty in Australia than a bill of rights. I don't believe a bill of rights works.'[7] A free press with a bill of rights is a better protection than a free press without a bill of rights for those of us who cherish liberty as well as security.

Prior to the present threat of terrorism, we Australians could not accept any government's plea to 'Trust us' in setting the right balance between liberty and security. Confronting terrorism, we need to enhance the checks and balances so that government, police and security services will remain trustworthy. Government alone, unchecked and unfettered, sometimes makes mistakes, especially in the wake of populist sentiment and when the focus falls on an unpopular minority of outsiders. To any government pleading 'Trust us', we the people can reply, 'Maintain that trust with appropriate checks and balances. Provide us with a bill of rights as well as a free press.'

If our search for the true and the good, even in their unpopular guises, is to be pursued effectively in the Australian public forum we need to provide effective checks and balances on the various branches of government. We also need to ensure that politics and religion are kept in place in a more coherent way than they have been in recent years.

In this book I want to reflect on the appropriate place of religion in the public forum, investigating its relationship to law and policy and setting appropriate limits on the use to be made of religious ideas and the role of religious authorities participating in public debate about contested issues. The restrictions placed on Islamic ideas in the public square should be the same as the restrictions placed on Christian ideas and any other religious ideas. The restrictions and regulations imposed on religious authorities in the public square should be the same, regardless of their creed and the number of their followers in Australia.

After a brief overview in chapter 1 of the religious and political mix in Australia, I will argue strongly in chapter 2 for the primacy of the individual's conscience as the basis for engagement in the public forum in a pluralist democracy. In chapter 3, I will draw some lessons from the conduct of politicians and church leaders in the United States in election mode. After a general survey in chapter 4 of the relationship between religious leaders and politicians, and the ways in which Australian politicians play off politics and religion, I will make a particular study in chapter 5 of the actions of religious leaders and politicians over the recent Australian military intervention in Iraq. In chapter 6, I will move the focus from government and Parliament to the courts, investigating how we can keep political claims in place in our courts. Many disputes in society can be resolved only by access to the courts. Fundamental human rights should be protected by law. Without a bill of rights, Australian judges sometimes have difficulty in protecting such rights which are political claims rather than legal entitlements. In chapter 7, I will look at how religion can be kept in place in the courts. Religious leaders sometimes seek to achieve policy results through litigation when such results cannot be achieved through parliamentary action or in the court of public opinion. When courts are asked to resolve disputes about hotly contested issues, self-interested citizens have a heightened sensitivity about judges seeming to act on their religious impulses. In chapter 8 I will investigate how religion and politics can be kept in place as we deal with the vexed issue of same-sex marriage. This issue has occupied the minds of politicians and judges in Canada and the United States, while the Westminster Parliament has proceeded without court intervention to legislate for civil unions of same-sex partners. I will conclude with a plea and proposal as to how we Australians can enact values in times of moral controversy despite our social and institutional isolation.

In multicultural Australia, we need to keep religion and politics in place in the public forum – for the good of us all, including those who think and want to act differently from the majority; and for the common good, which is that combination of factors which renders life in community fulfilling for all.

CHAPTER ONE

THE AUSTRALIAN MIX OF POLITICS AND RELIGION

George Pell and Peter Jensen, the Catholic and Anglican archbishops of Sydney, issued statements in July 2005 expressing concerns about the Australian government's proposals to amend the industrial relations laws. Churchgoing government members questioned the competence and role of church leaders. Prime Minister John Howard said there was no such thing as a Catholic or Anglican view on anything. When asked to explain this statement during parliamentary question time, he said: 'There will be Catholics who will agree with us and disagree; there will be Anglicans who will agree and disagree. That is how it should be in a nation such as this, which has a proper regard for the respective roles of the government and the church.'[1] His deputy, Peter Costello, had earlier been very critical of Phillip Aspinall, the primate of the Anglican Church, on the basis that 'having a theological degree doesn't mean you are an IR expert'. Costello said he had no problem with church leaders speaking as freely as they wish on every issue: 'Whether it is a politician, whether it is a journalist or whether it is a church leader, every person has the right to freedom of speech and the right to be judged on the merit and content of their views'.[2]

The church leaders had confined themselves to general statements of principle about the proposed legislation, expressing particular concern for the weak and vulnerable workers who, without the benefits of collective bargaining, might forego their entitlements too easily in their negotiations with an employer. In Australia, the senior church leaders do not see a need to offer their own assessment of most issues requiring resolution by our elected politicians through parliamentary debate and legislation. When they do speak, it is usually in relation to issues which are contested on moral and religious grounds. There are coherent and morally defensible views about such issues on both sides of the parliamentary chamber and a plurality of views within any church community. Some of these issues even risk splits within a church community.

Basil Hume, the late archbishop of Westminster, said his greatest grief was 'the marginalization of the church' during his lifetime.[3] Hume thought he was not a bad politician. When asked what he meant, he replied: 'Well, you see, I think I know when to speak, and more importantly, I know when not to speak'.[4] In one of his last public addresses, he said:[5]

> It is important always to be strict concerning principles and endlessly compassionate and understanding of persons. It does happen that a person or group may take up a position on some issue against the teaching of the Church. How should the pastor act? A first instinct may be to exclude from the community those who dissent. We must rather keep them within the community and work – sometimes very hard – to lead them to take up positions consistent with the Church's teaching.

Amidst controversy within church communities and in society at large, we need to discern the role of religion in the public forum, keeping religion in its place. There has never been any risk that Australia would be a theocratic state with religious leaders dictating law and policy for all citizens. Many Australians think that religion is purely a private affair and it should be kept out of politics. They presume that religious beliefs have no relevance to law. They are not troubled by the occasional public claim that Australia's laws and policies are informed by values imbedded in the Judeo-Christian tradition. They are used to seeing church leaders making periodic appearances on contested moral questions such as abortion, euthanasia and stem cell research.

There is no problem with church leaders speaking to their church members even if they do it over the public airwaves, allowing non-members to overhear the church instruction and discussion. There is a problem when church leaders or key church members appear to be speaking for their church members in the public forum. They may speak about their church's tradition and teaching. But it is a bold claim in our pluralistic age for church leaders to claim that they speak for even the majority of their own members on any contested political question. Politicians know that on any contested issue there will be members of each church community on both sides of the debate, and on both sides of the parliamentary chamber.

Religious practice and attendance in most Christian churches has declined in Australia in recent years. The regular Sunday attendance in the Catholic, Anglican and Uniting churches has declined, while there are growing numbers attending evangelical and Pentecostal churches such as Hillsong in Sydney. Nonetheless the majority of Australians still identify with one of the three major Christian churches.

Small 'l' liberals have often argued that religion should be kept out of politics. They think that, in the public forum, only arguments comprehensible to non-religious persons should be used and only positions appealing also to non-religious persons should be espoused by advocates even if they happen to be religious. Some of these liberals would permit an exception where the religious persons were advocating only their own self-interest and where that self-interest would not impact on non-religious persons. For example, they would tolerate government funding for church schools which would be attended voluntarily by the children of church members, provided that such funding did not unjustly disadvantage the funding of non-religious schools which would be attended voluntarily by the children of citizens who had no interest in sending their children to church schools. But they would not tolerate church advocates arguing their distinctive religious position on a general law or policy such as euthanasia or abortion, unless that position could be translated comprehensibly into a position with reasons not drawing on the religious tradition.

In the past too much deference has been paid to the liberals arguing what religious people should and should not do in the public forum. The 'should' has been seen as a statement of political morality rather than a statement of political good sense. Some might still think it is wrong for a Catholic bishop to advocate publicly for a strict abortion law, quoting a string of Vatican documents in support of his position. But this might not be wrong, just not very sensible. His advocacy might be better aimed at his own church members, urging them to practise abortion less frequently, assisting women to explore other options, and proposing to his co-religionists that abortion is always a matter for regret, not the enjoyment of a civil liberty.

Gone are the days when the only proper arguments to be put in the public forum were those arguments comprehensible to the non-religious person. There is now a need to be more discriminating between principles to be applied and strategies and tactics which may be sensible or stupid, rather than right or wrong.

Since 11 September 2001, Australians have displayed an increased sensitivity to the demands of Muslim Australians that their perspective on pressing social and political questions be heeded. Though there is no public sympathy for incorporating Sharia law into the Australian legal system, Australians are interested in hearing their Muslim fellow citizens explain their aspirations for living a full religious life in the Australian community while continuing to honour the laws and policies of the nation state. There is much room for misunderstanding. Attorney-General Philip Ruddock upset some of the worshippers at the Lakemba mosque when he addressed them on the first day of Eid al-Adha in January 2006. In the wake of the Cronulla race riots, he said, 'I think it is important to acknowledge that when you are Australian, as all Australians, you have a responsibility to uphold the laws of this country. If we are able to live in a tolerant society, we have to offer tolerance to others.'[6] Even these measured remarks were interpreted as contempt for Muslim Australians. Keysar Trad, the founder of the Islamic Friendship Association of Australia, was not publicly contradicted by other Muslim leaders when he replied that Ruddock's comments indicated that 'he doesn't have as much respect for Australians of a Muslim background as he should'.[7]

While there are religious citizens in a democratic state, there will always be a place for religious arguments and positions in the public forum. Like their fellow citizens, they should be free to advocate peacefully their preferred policy positions as competently or foolishly as they are able or as they wish. They are free to vote as they wish and for whatever reasons they wish.

Some religious citizens will be elected or selected for public office. Like all other officeholders they have obligations to fulfil. They cannot abuse their office and simply implement their own religious view of the world if that would be inconsistent with the public trust that goes with their office. Members of parliament, public servants, government ministers, judges and governors take on formal state functions. They not only make policy decisions. They make law, interpret law and apply law. Their religious disposition may inspire them to fulfil their public function faithfully. Though religion is guaranteed its place in the public forum of a democracy of citizens including some religious persons living under the rule of law, its place and role will be circumscribed by legal, moral and prudential considerations relevant to the discharge of any public office.

It is not a matter of laying down a set of rules to follow. We are moving in a number of different worlds of discourse here. I might have religious reasons for thinking that some form of behaviour is wrong. At the very least, that would mean that I would not commit that act myself, or if I did I would consider it wrong. I might or might not give unsolicited advice to others, such as my friends, in urging them not to commit the act. Church officials might give advice to their co-religionists about the moral propriety of the activity. They might concede that their church's moral evaluation of the act was different from the prevailing public attitude to such behaviour. Even if a large number of religious persons thought some action immoral, they would not necessarily think it desirable that there be a law against it. For example, a religious group is very likely to think that lying is wrong in most circumstances. They would make an exception, as when the householder is asked by the Nazis whether he is sheltering Jews in his house. But like their non-religious, responsible fellow citizens, they would consider a law against lying only in special circumstances, such as when a person is under oath in court or when a person is a director of a corporation making statements to the market about the state of the corporation. The purpose of the law would not be to punish lying as such nor to try and enhance the public's general commitment to the truth, but rather to punish lying in those circumstances when it would impact directly on the rights and entitlements of other citizens and when the person has a duty to those other people or to a social institution.

Even if there is a law prohibiting some activity, there may be good reasons for implementing the law selectively. It may make good sense to leave some behaviour untried and unpunished even if technically it was against the law. So there are very different questions to consider:

– Is this action wrong?
– Would I do it myself?
– Would I counsel my friends not to do it?
– Would I counsel my fellow church members not to do it?
– Would I publicly urge my fellow citizens not to do it?
– Should there be a law against this action?
– If so, should there be some legal exceptions?
– Should the law be strictly enforced?
– Should a penalty be imposed on the wrongdoer?

We are confronted with a whole conundrum of law, morality, public policy and public administration. Even if we wanted to agitate for a law banning a particular activity, we would need to consider the different realms of principle, strategy and tactics. For example, a church leader might think that the cloning of human embryos is always wrong. His religious tradition teaches him that there can be no exceptions to this moral injunction. In good conscience, he may decide that he should be very upfront and even prophetic in declaring from the rooftops: 'The cloning of human embryos is wrong'. He might be speaking first to his own fellow church members but then to all his fellow citizens. But for whom is he speaking? He may be speaking authoritatively in the name of his church tradition. That means nothing more than he is one within the structure of his own church who has the authority to speak and he speaks in a manner consistent with his church's tradition and teaching on this particular issue. But in the public forum, he cannot claim to speak for all members or even the majority of that church's members who are citizens of the state.

Australia is a robust democracy. Though an increasingly secular society, Australia is home for believers from all the major religious traditions. The majority of citizens still have some religious affiliation, most of them being influenced by the Judeo-Christian tradition. Never an election goes by and rarely does a parliamentary session conclude without some public controversy erupting, spiced with moral outrage and religious overtones. Since 11 September 2001, we have had to become more attentive to the religious tradition of non-Christian Australians. Though a federation with a written Constitution, Australia does not have a bill of rights. This means that many controversies that would be resolved in part by judges in similar countries, such as the United States, the United Kingdom, Canada and New Zealand, are more likely to be resolved by elected politicians unhampered by unelected judges.

Australians have no desire to live in a theocratic state in which the religious views even of a majority would be imposed on everyone, including non-believers, with laws and government policies reflecting the opinions of religious leaders. But neither do we want to live in a country where the citizen's religious views are automatically ruled out of court in the public forum. Religious beliefs and practices are not just private matters which should influence the world view and practice only of fellow believers. It is not simply a matter of respecting the individual citizen's religious motivations and convictions while insisting that any political or legal action be based on non-religious motivations and convictions. In political debate about contested issues of law, government policy and public administration, religious beliefs are not trumps; but neither are they irrelevant.

The private domain of religious belief and practice poses few problems for us in Australia. But we are yet to work out how religion can be practised and professed by all citizens who so desire, in the public domain, paying due respect and regard to their religious sensibilities and to the sensibilities of those of other faiths, of other perspectives in the same faith, and of no religious belief at all.

It is very easy to cherry-pick, declaring that religion is relevant and appropriate when it supports our own policy or legal preference, while being convinced that it is irrelevant and easily discounted when it runs counter to our preferred outcome. The person gratified by the intervention of church leaders in the political debate about Aboriginal native title rights might be outraged by their daring to offer public positions on abortion or stem cell research. The person hoping that church leaders will speak up in support of asylum seekers might be rendered speechless by their declarations against same-sex marriage. The politician seeking church leaders' involvement in debate about euthanasia might also hope that they would remain silent during debate on the Iraq war or industrial relations reforms.

The citizen who is also a judge might have personal religious views about a whole variety of moral questions. Do those views ever have relevance when she sits in judgment? Usually the judge will be able to say that she simply interprets the law and applies it to the facts of the case. But there are times, especially in an ultimate court of appeal, when there is the opportunity to interpret an ambiguous statute or to develop the common law in a manner consistent with our religious beliefs rather than the contrary. The preferred interpretation or development may be consistent with philosophical positions and rules of interpretation and legal development independent of judicial religious beliefs.

The public servant charged with the implementation of a controversial law or policy is not just a state robot. Like all of us, public servants have consciences and they have to make decisions about what they will and will not do. Thankfully in Australia, they are not often confronted with the decision to resign rather than implement a law or policy in a manner inconsistent with their own conscience and which would result in other people being made to suffer unjustly. At the height of the controversy over the Australian treatment of asylum seekers, including the long-term detention of children, there were public servants who had to make decisions in good conscience. Some of them were guided by their own religious sensibilities and the teaching of their religious leaders.

There are some questions which arise in Parliament providing the members with the opportunity for a conscience vote. In the recent past these issues have included abortion, RU486, euthanasia, stem cell research, human cloning and same-sex marriage. Are politicians entitled to rely only or primarily on their religious views about the rightness or wrongness of the activity, or ought they confine themselves to views about rightness or wrongness which are verifiable or comprehensible to the citizen with no religious views or with different religious views? On closer examination, even the most religious politician may conclude that there is a difference between espousing a moral good for oneself and one's loved ones, prescribing a law which binds all citizens, and deciding to implement a law in a strict manner permitting no exceptions. Two equally religious politicians of the same religious faith may believe that abortion in even the earliest phase of pregnancy is morally wrong. One may be convinced that a law prohibiting all abortion would not be a good law, while the other thought it would be. Even the one who thought it could be a good law might espouse a policy of selective law enforcement by the police such that most early phase abortions went unpunished.

In a pluralist society like Australia, there is a changing range of issues to which people bring a religious perspective. It must always be acceptable for religious leaders to express public views about the morality of any particular war to which government wants to commit troops. We expect that religious leaders will have a concern for the poorest, the weakest and the voiceless in society. But there will be disagreement about how paternalistic, protective, redistributive or equalising the law or policy should be. There will be varying views on the appropriate tax structure, or on striking the appropriate balance in loosening up the labour market to maximise job creation in a globalised world and to maintain fair bargaining arrangements and decent working conditions for all workers, even if there is an increased risk of unemployment.

Prior to 11 September 2001, there was not much discussion in the public forum about the religious views of those from minority faiths. There was the occasional fracas about Jehovah's Witnesses denying blood transfusions to their children, young Aboriginal girls being given in traditional marriage to old men, and Muslims wanting to build mosques in built-up areas where they would call people to prayer before sunrise by means of invasive loudspeaker systems. Most members of the intellectual and power elites in Australia regarded religion as a non-rational component in any political calculus. They prided themselves in being free of religious prejudice or predisposition. The presumption was that a person's religious beliefs, practices and values were private matters that could provide the motivation for public action, but that such action could be justified or explained only by public reason which excluded consideration of religious convictions.

The standard unreflected consideration of the role of religion in international affairs was that it was not a factor, but simply an indicator or reflector of other differences (social, economic or ethnic); or it was a factor in societies which were regarded as 'less developed' in that they had not yet endured the full brunt of secularisation, thereby permitting periodic outbursts of fundamentalism.

Since the events of 11 September 2001, we have all been seeking a way to keep religion in its rightful place, subject to appropriate checks and balances. It used to be easier for anti-religious or non-religious persons to discount the relevance of religion in the public forum and in the political process. Now, any Australian government has to deal seriously with Muslims and their leaders though they number only 1.5 per cent of the Australian population (281,572 persons in the 2001 census – a sharp increase from 200,805 in the 1996 census).[8]

Seventy per cent of Australians describe themselves as Christian. It has become very easy to make the simplistic public assumption that Christianity is identified with western values and public goods such as democracy and individual human rights. Islam then becomes the foil or the cover for anti-western sentiment. Professor Abdullah Saeed makes the point that 'Muslims in Australia do not form a single homogeneous community' and that 'their attitudes, behaviours, ideas, values and perspectives reflect the sorts of cultures from which they originally came'. He observes:[9]

> In Australia, there is no inherent contradiction between being Christian and Australian, or being Jewish and Australian. Likewise, there is no contradiction between being Muslim and Australian.

However, Saeed does concede that there are some traditionalist and neo-revivalist Muslims in Australia who are 'likely to be hostile to the West and Western values, and by extension to fundamental Australian values'.[10]

Despite Henry Kissinger's capacity to write his massive 1995 tome *Diplomacy* without even mentioning the role of religion in international politics, all commentators would now accept that religion has a role to play in international relations in the wake of 11 September 2001. The problem is being able to invoke the utterances of religious leaders in a way that is equally comprehensible to those outside their circle of faith as to their followers and adherents.[11] It is essential that religious freedom and tolerance not be identified as western values or as Australian values, but as universal values.[12]

Religious freedom and tolerance are incontrovertible indicators of a government's commitment and a society's capacity for individual freedom and enjoyment of basic human rights. But what are the reasonable limits to place on religious freedom? How tolerant do we need to be? Given the religious indifference of many Australians and the Australian government's disinterest in any particular religion or in religion generally, we are in a strong position to advocate religious freedom for others, pointing out that tolerance rather than indifference or secularism is the answer to religious discrimination or persecution. Given that Australia is an increasingly secular society, we are in a strong position to insist that other countries should accord protection to those of minority faiths and also to indicate the advantages of a nation state refraining from establishing or preferring a particular religion. We could not be seen to be pushing a self-interested agenda nor a preference for a particular religious group.

Poverty, economic insecurity, ethnic difference, class conflict, political marginalisation and social instability are often contributing factors and obvious outcomes in situations of acute social unrest. Democracy is the best protection for any majority. The rule of law is the best protection for any minority, however they identify themselves and however they are identified by the majority.

Talk of Australian values should stop at the Australian low water mark.

Talk of Christian values should be addressed primarily to those who profess to be Christian, including those who might be inclined to commit unchristian acts on their Muslim neighbours. It is appropriate to conduct our dialogue in accordance with universal human rights, which are not externally imposed western constructs but voluntarily appropriated universal standards. It is appropriate that the non-government organisations (NGOs) in Australia (including church groups) give every assistance to foreign NGOs anxious to fortify their own civil society and to call their own governments to account by recourse to the UN reporting procedures.

In Australia, Muslims and other religious citizens of goodwill should be able to talk together, forming a bridge to their co-religionists in other countries, sharing the burden of the moral quandaries which these political and economic problems create. While governments will maintain pragmatic commitments to their national interest and good trading relations, private citizens and those in the NGO sector are the ones with greater latitude to espouse the primacy of human rights and individual liberty. Those with greatest freedom will carry the greatest responsibility for fostering a relationship which is productive for all.

The secularism and materialism of Australian society and the simple majoritarianism of Australian democracy can cloud the vision just as surely as the fundamentalism and poverty of other societies that lack the coverage of the rule of law.[13] Through dialogue, we can avoid the absurd situation of excluding or killing others in the name of God, creating a new situation of including others and prizing the other who is different in the name of God.

CHAPTER TWO

MAINTAINING THE CITIZEN'S FREEDOM OF CONSCIENCE

Religious views will enjoy an enhanced place at the table of public deliberation in a pluralist democracy if religious leaders encourage their members to participate in the life of the nation state, engaging in the controversies of the moment, forming and informing their consciences about the good and the true. Religious views will be less relevant, and even ruled ineligible for a place at the table of public deliberation, if religious leaders insist that their members simply follow hierarchical directives regardless of their own formed and informed conscientious view about the true and the good. Many religious citizens will look to their leaders for guidance about the applicable values, hierarchy of values and principles to be applied to policy, law and administration questions. But they will insist on their own self-determination as citizens and their own non-delegable duty to fulfil their public trust when they occupy public positions in the nation state. It is catastrophic when the individual's freedom of conscience is violated by a religious authority acting in the public forum beyond its competence.

The possible conflict between conscience and religious authority was highlighted in the dispute between British Prime Minister W. Gladstone and John Henry Newman, who had left the Anglican Church and joined the Roman Catholic Church. The First Vatican Council in 1870 taught that the Pope could define infallibly 'a doctrine of faith or morals'. Gladstone feared that 'no one can now become [a Catholic] without renouncing his moral and mental freedom, and placing his civil loyalty and duty at the mercy of another'.[1] Newman refuted this fear, conceding that there may be 'extreme cases in which conscience may come into collision with the word of a Pope, and is to be followed in spite of that word'.[2] He asserted that 'infallibility alone would block the exercise of conscience' but that 'the Pope is not infallible in that subject matter in which conscience is of supreme authority' and thus 'no dead-lock, such as is implied in the objection ... can take place between conscience and the Pope'.[3] Newman's confidence that there would be no prospect of an overlap, let alone a conflict, between the matters on which the pope would speak infallibly and the matters on which the citizen would have to decide political and moral questions accounts for his notorious declaration:[4]

> Certainly, if I am obliged to bring religion into after-dinner toasts, (which indeed does not seem quite the thing) I shall drink – to the Pope if you please, – still, to Conscience first, and to the Pope afterwards.

Neither Gladstone nor Newman perceived the extent to which the state might legislate in centuries to come about all manner of things. Newman had no idea about the range of issues on which subsequent popes would issue declarations not just on the faith but in relation to morals, and in considerable detail. Newman would have been surprised by some of the contemporary claims that popes have taught infallibly on a vast range of moral issues, including contraception.[5] He would have had no comprehension that the Vatican's Congregation for the Doctrine of the Faith would issue very detailed guidelines on law and policy, providing guidance for Catholic politicians having to vote on vexed moral and political questions. Newman was confident that there would be little overlap between the state's law and policy and church teaching. He thought there ought to be little overlap. He thought Gladstone was being censorious. But given that there now is overlap, there is a need to investigate the restrictions on conscience so as to determine if Gladstone's fears now have substance.

Here on the other side of the globe 130 years later, there has been some suggestion that there is a competition between conscience and truth, only one of which can enjoy primacy. Some Catholics like Cardinal Pell think other Catholics would do better if they stopped talking about the primacy of conscience. Others think there is a need for more emphasis on the primacy of the individual conscience over the directives, witness and actions of bishops and even the pope if we are to have any chance of discerning and living out the complex truth of our life project as citizens of a pluralist democracy. I am one of those others.

There is a conflict in the Australian Catholic community about the primacy of conscience. It may simply be a difference of perspective with some seeing the glass half-full and warning against the limits of conscience in coming to truth, while others see the glass half-empty and espouse the potential of conscience in living the truth. For some years now, Cardinal Pell has been eloquently blunt, suggesting that the notion be ditched. In his 1999 Acton Lecture, then Archbishop Pell said:

> Catholics should stop talking about the primacy of conscience. This has never been a Catholic doctrine (although this point generally cuts little ice). Moreover, such language is not conducive to identifying what contributes to human development. It is a short cut, which often leads the uninitiated to feel even more complacent while 'doing their own thing'.

Then in May 2003, Cardinal Pell took his assault on the primacy of conscience one step further when he said:[6]

> In the past I have been in trouble for stating that the so called doctrine of the primacy of conscience should be quietly dropped. I would like to reconsider my position here and now state that I believe that this misleading doctrine of the primacy of conscience should be publicly rejected.

The cardinal has been rightly anxious to avoid the situation in which 'conscience would become personal preference – a polite term for "doing it my way", and clear thinking and past wisdom would be repudiated and ridiculed'.[7]

We can espouse the primacy of conscience without abandoning a commitment to clear thinking and past wisdom. The human person is a moral agent who is shaped by his actions. By forming and informing her conscience, the human person is deciding not only what she wants to do but also who she wants to be. It is not only the mind or the will that acts morally but the whole person. As the person changes and grows, the conscience is formed and grows too. So each conscience is unique as each person is unique. In the Catholic tradition, the conscience is sacred ground where the person meets God; all others (including church authorities), unless invited in, are trespassers in this place. Pope Pius XII described conscience as 'a sanctuary on the threshold of which all must halt, even, in the case of a child, his father and mother'.[8] John Henry Newman had earlier defined conscience 'not as a fancy or an opinion, but as a dutiful obedience to what claims to be a divine voice, speaking within us'.[9] The Catholic view of conscience holds in tension the dignity and freedom of the human person, the teaching authority of the Church, and the search for truth and good. The tension arises because the Catholic concedes not only the possibility but also the common reality of the incompletely formed conscience, which may receive guidance from the Church's teaching authority. This tension accounts for the Catholic Church's unequivocal affirmation of the primacy of individual conscience against the state together with its occasional ambivalence about the role of conscience in relation to church authority.

Conscientious Catholics would deviate from church teaching on moral issues only with deep regret and after careful attention to the developing and changing situation, and only on condition that they are satisfied that they have a greater command of the facts or of their situation than the church authority issuing universal declarations faithful to a constant tradition. The Second Vatican Council in its Declaration on Religious Freedom said, 'In the formation of their consciences, the Christian faithful ought carefully to attend to the sacred and certain doctrine of the Church. For the Church is, by the will of Christ, the teacher of the truth'.[10] However, in changing times or particular personal circumstances, there may be true doubt about the certain doctrine of the Church and its application to the changing circumstances. Changes to church teaching about slavery and usury were preceded by persons of good conscience acting at variance with traditional teaching.

Conscience is engaged when the person looking ahead asks: 'What should I do or not do?', or when the person looking back asks: 'Should I have done that or not done that?' There are two extremes to be avoided in answering these questions. The person may be tempted simply to do his own thing, choosing according to his own preference on the basis that there is no objective truth or verifiable good. Or the agent may woodenly apply the prescriptions of authority, including church authority, without attending to the voice of conscience urging her to do the greater good or to be prophetic, not just complying with the mores of her society or church community. Ideally, the actor will follow her or his conscience.

We do not have to be natural law theorists to affirm a law implanted in the human heart commanding the person, in freedom, to seek the truth, to do good and to avoid evil. In the very act of seeking the truth and trying to do good, the person further forms and informs their conscience. But what is truth? What is the good in this particular situation? In the Catholic tradition, the person is guided and even directed in the formation and informing of conscience by the church authorities. Traditionally, the church authorities claim to teach not only that which is revealed in the scriptures but also that which can be derived from natural law by reflecting on the ends for which people were created. Many Catholics now share the contemporary era's pessimism about an all-embracing natural law based on a single static human nature that permits a wholesale determination of what is right and wrong in each and every situation. That pessimism is heightened when the church hierarchy's reading of what is natural differs from that of other people who in good faith reflect on their own human reality, concluding that what is natural to the church hierarchy is not self-evidently natural to them.

Ultimately every person is obliged to follow their conscience even if that conscience is erroneous. When making a decision to act or to refrain from an action, in good conscience, the Catholic actor is obliged to consider the church teaching on the matter at hand. Before becoming pope, Pope Benedict XVI provided a good rule of thumb on conscience: 'A man of conscience is one who never acquires tolerance, well-being, success, public standing, and approval on the part of prevailing opinion at the expense of the truth'.[11] Saint Augustine taught that 'there is no soul, however perverted . . . in whose conscience God does not speak'.[12] Thomas Aquinas taught that a person must always follow their conscience even if that conscience be erroneous. For 'when a reason which is in error proposes something as a command of God, then to dismiss the dictate or reason is just the same as dismissing the command of God'.[13]

The Second Vatican Council, in its Declaration on Religious Freedom in 1965, teaches:[14]

> In all his activity a man is bound to follow his conscience faithfully, in order that he may come to God, for whom he was created. It follows that he is not to be forced to act in a manner contrary to his conscience. Nor, on the other hand is he to be restrained from acting in accordance with his conscience, especially in matters religious.

Cardinal Pell insists that this Vatican Council declaration does not deal with the relationship between church members and the church authorities. He confines its scope to 'relationships between state and Church, and between state and individual'.[15] He does concede that John Courtney Murray SJ, who was a key adviser on the text of the declaration, predicted that the declaration would have a profound ripple effect and that: 'Inevitably, a great second argument will be set afoot now on the theological meaning of Christian freedom'.[16] The church teaching on conscience gives no consolation to the uninitiated, thinking they can simply do their own thing. But neither does it accord religious authorities the liberty of insisting upon wooden compliance with their instruction or view of the world. Some religious authorities like Cardinal Pell take a more restrictive approach. He says:[17]

> While we should follow a well-formed conscience, a well-formed conscience is hard to achieve. And if we suspect – as surely we all sometimes must – that our conscience is under-formed or malformed in some area, then we should follow a reliable authority until such time as we can correct our consciences. And for Catholics, the most reliable authority is the Church.

It is too simplistic to resolve the tension between conscience, authority and truth to urge: 'When in doubt, follow the bishops'. The bishops may be right; they often are. But then again, they may be wrong, as the Vatican authorities have been in dealing with the AIDS pandemic.

The official teaching by the Catholic hierarchy on AIDS is very problematic for people wanting to provide care and compassion to persons regardless of their religious identity and practice. Some of the most senior Catholic bishops responsible for healthcare issues insisted for years that it was intrinsically evil in all circumstances for a person to wear a condom during sexual intercourse, even if there were the risk of transmitting the AIDS virus. These bishops said that even a married couple, one of whom was infected with the virus, would be wrong to use a condom. Such couples were urged to forego sexual relations and embrace the fullness of the Cross! Very few bishops were prepared to speak out against this proclamation.

Cardinal Javier Lozano Barragan, the Vatican's official representative at the UN conference convened to discuss the AIDS crisis in June 2001, told the assembly:[18]

> Regarding the sexual transmission of the disease, the best and most effective prevention is training in the authentic values of life, love and sexuality. A proper appreciation of these values will inform today's men and women about how to attain full personal fulfilment through affective maturity and the proper use of sexuality, whereby couples remain faithful to each other and behave in a way that prevents them from becoming infected by HIV/AIDS. No one can deny that sexual licence increases the danger of contracting the disease. It is in this context that the values

> of matrimonial fidelity and of chastity and abstinence can be better understood. Prevention, and the education which fosters it, are realized in respecting human dignity and the person's transcendent destiny, and in excluding campaigns associated with models of behaviour which destroy life and promote the spread of the evil in question.

There was a public outcry and many persons made strong representations to the Vatican. The Catholic Church cares for twenty-five per cent of AIDS victims in Africa. Many campaigners were anxious that work to contain the virus would be hampered by the Catholic Church's refusal to distribute condoms. By November 2003, Cardinal Barragan had been appointed president of the Pontifical Council for Health Care, and had been commissioned by the Pope to coordinate the Church's response to the AIDS crisis. He was now prepared to countenance a solitary exception to the 'no condoms' rule, but no official statement was to be issued. Though still urging both partners to refrain from sexual relations, he would approve a coerced partner's use of a condom:[19]

> The doctrine of the Catholic Church is very clear. To defend one's life against an aggressor, one can even kill. So a wife, whose husband is infected with AIDS and who insists on marital relations with her, and might therefore pass on the virus which would kill her, can defend her life by using a condom.

By February 2005, Cardinal Barragan was still confining his attention to the case of the married couple with the infected male partner forcing himself on the unwilling, uninfected female partner. He granted a rare interview to a church news service. Once again, no senior Vatican official was prepared to say anything to the contrary. Barragan said:[20]

> By the commandment 'Thou shalt not kill' we are obliged not to kill anyone but at the same time, not to let ourselves be killed, that is, to protect our life. So much so, that it is a traditional doctrine of the Church,

which has never changed, that to defend one's own innocent life, one can even kill an aggressor. If the aggressor has the Ebola virus, flu, or AIDS and wants to kill me, I must defend myself. If he wants to kill me with AIDS, I must defend myself from AIDS. How do I defend myself? With the most appropriate means. I must decide. If it is a club, with a club. If it is a pistol, with a pistol. And with a condom? Yes, if it is effective in defending me, in this case of unjust aggression.

The journalist pressed him saying, 'There is the impression in the media that the only message the Church can give today is whether or not condoms may be used. Is this so?' He refused to discuss condoms specifically and answered:

The remedy is abstinence and faithfulness. Why? Because the Sixth Commandment is the most sublime expression of love that God has given us. And it means vital love and life is total giving. Which means that sex between man and woman exacts that nothing is left over for a third.

Therefore, to really live out one's sexuality, one must do so only in a marriage that is one and permanent for life. To defend the preciousness of sex, God gave an absolute Commandment, enunciated in a negative way: 'Thou shalt not commit adultery'. He did not say, 'Do not have sexual relations'. Sexual relations are precisely the greatest expression of human love, which is fulfilled in marriage. Celibacy is still greater, but it is about divine love.

By keeping these two Commandments – 'Thou shalt not kill' and 'Thou shalt not commit adultery', life is protected. How do we defend ourselves from AIDS? By protecting life, in its sexual excellence and from its vicious aggression. If we are opposed to its vicious aggression, if we don't break that finest of crystals that is sex, we do not get AIDS.

In the end the journalist asked, 'So the Church does not give recipes, but proclaims the Ten Commandments?' He replied:

Let us be clear that in that sense, we are talking about the essence of Christianity, as it is about loving God above all things, and one's

> neighbour as oneself. What matters is abstinence, faithfulness and 'Thou shalt not kill'.

This wholly unsatisfactory 'teaching' about a pressing social, moral and political question highlights a major problem for those church leaders wanting to circumscribe the realm of conscience so that the 'simple faithful' might follow the wisdom of the bishops. In the Catholic Church there are numerous competent moral theologians who disagree with the statements of Cardinal Barragan. The religious believer gains more assistance from church authorities in the formation of conscience and the discovery of truth when he has confidence that the church authorities have actually considered the gravity of the issue and applied the Church's best theological acumen to the question at hand.

There can be no objection to a married couple using condoms when one of the couple is infected with the AIDS virus. Such a couple in good conscience together could decide to maintain sexual relations while ensuring by all means possible not to infect each other. Those in positions of authority ought be able to give clear guidance to perplexed couples in such circumstances. The provision of condoms is no panacea for the reduction of AIDS. There are not likely to be many couples who are put off using condoms or sexual relations because of incoherent Vatican pronouncements. But if church authorities want to be taken seriously in contemporary political and moral debates, they cannot insist on wooden compliance by their members with such ill-considered declarations.

Good conscience must always be accorded primacy even by bishops who would act differently in the circumstances, bearing in mind John Henry Newman's observation that 'conscience is not a judgment upon any speculative truth, any abstract doctrine, but bears immediately on conduct, on something to be done or not done';[21] and Aquinas's view that conscience is what I genuinely personally believe, even if mistakenly, that God is asking of me. As the Vatican Council said in its 1965 Pastoral Constitution on the Church in the Modern World (with some modification out of consideration for those offended by non-inclusive language):[22]

> In the depths of our conscience, we detect a law which we do not impose upon ourselves, but which holds us to obedience. Always summoning us to love good and avoid evil, the voice of conscience can when necessary speak to our hearts more specifically: do this, shun that. For we have in our hearts a law written by God. To obey it is the very dignity of the human person; according to it we will be judged.
>
> Conscience is the most secret core and sanctuary of a person. There we are alone with God, whose voice echoes in our depths.

We must always accord primacy to the conscientiously formed and informed conscience, regardless of the person's place in the church hierarchy. The Christians' contribution to the contemporary world would be greater if there were more attention to the formation of conscience and to the injunction: educate your conscience and to that conscience be true. For most people, the questions of conscience will not be: 'Am I to believe this church teaching?' but 'Am I to do this particular act or refrain from it?' That act may be one relating to personal relationships; it may be about political engagement and a commitment to make a difference in the public forum. It may even be the decision to endorse a war or to condemn it or to remain silent.

Each of us must ensure that we have a formed and informed conscience as we decide not only what we will believe, as that is probably the less problematic part, but also as we decide what we will do. Before acting we will search for the truth insofar as the truth is discoverable. But we will then make prudential decisions about what to do, having applied whatever moral principles may be appropriate to the matter under consideration. In his World Day of Peace Address in January 2002, Pope John Paul II said:

> Respect for a person's conscience, where the image of God himself is reflected, means that we can only propose the truth to others, who are then responsible for accepting it. To try to impose on others by violent means what we consider to be the truth is an offence against human dignity, and ultimately an offence against God whose image that person bears.

There are many complex issues in the world today which are not susceptible of unequivocal answers about what is true and what is good, or what is the greater good in terms of actions and outcomes. In these situations, I cannot acquit my conscience simply by pleading that I followed what the bishops said, did or failed to do. All of us, like the bishops, are obliged to play our respective roles in the societies of which we are a part, forming and informing our consciences, and acting according to our consciences. The Second Vatican Council's 1965 Pastoral Constitution on the Church in the Modern World made clear that often it is the laity and not the church leaders who are the experts about moral quandaries in the world. The laity were not to expect that the bishops would have all the answers. The council stated:[23]

> Laypeople should also know that it is generally the function of their well-formed Christian conscience to see that the divine law is inscribed in the life of the earthly city; from priests they may look for spiritual light and nourishment. Let the laypeople not imagine that their pastors are always such experts, that to every problem which arises, however complicated, they can readily give them a concrete solution, or even that such is their mission. Rather, enlightened by Christian wisdom and giving close attention to the teaching authority of the Church, let the laypeople take on their own distinctive role.
>
> Often enough the Christian view of things will itself suggest some specific solution in certain circumstances. Yet it happens rather frequently, and legitimately so, that with equal sincerity some of the faithful will disagree with others on a given matter. Even against the intentions of their proponents, however, solutions proposed on one side or another may be easily confused by many people with the Gospel message. Hence it is necessary for people to remember that no one is allowed in the aforementioned situations to appropriate the Church's authority for their opinion. They should always try to enlighten one another through honest discussion, preserving mutual charity and caring above all for the common good.

After the Second Vatican Council, many Catholics made decisions in conscience not to follow Pope Paul VI's teaching on birth control – a teaching which varied from the teaching of other Christian churches whose hierarchy, being free to marry, often had personal experience of married life. This teaching was also at variance from the recommendations made by the majority of theological experts and married persons appointed to advise the pope on the question.

Paul VI taught 'that each and every marital act must of necessity retain its intrinsic relationship to the procreation of human life'.[24] Many Catholics in good conscience accepted the position set out in the Papal Commission's majority report of 1966 that 'the morality of sexual acts between married people takes its meaning first of all and specifically from the ordering of their actions in a fruitful married life, that is one practised with responsible generous and prudent parenthood. It does not then depend upon the direct fecundity of each and every particular act.'[25] Their consciences are untroubled and even fortified by the fact that other Christian churches whose clergy are often married teach such an ethic. They find unconvincing Catholic hierarchical claims to superior insight into the natural law (as distinct from Revelation) when such insight is proclaimed to be available to every thinking person. Such claims are made with insufficient regard for the experience of married Catholics, and contrary to the considered reflection on that experience by competent moral theologians. Many Catholics are convinced that Pope Paul VI would not have overruled the majority of the commission but for his conviction that the Church's previous teaching on the natural law of marriage could not be changed.

In 1978, the theologian Fr John Ford SJ, who had been one of the minority on the Papal Commission in the 1960s urging no change to the 1930 church teaching on contraception, said, 'I remain utterly convinced that the teaching will never be changed precisely because it is a truth of faith'. He then revealed for the first time:[26]

> During an interview with Pope Paul he and I were discussing the positions being proposed in the Commission. The Pope was calm and composed

> while we talked about these. I did have the impression that he did not talk about the proponents of these new positions as though they were 'formati doctores' speaking about the faith. But when I said to Pope Paul, 'Are you ready to say that *Casti Connubii* (1930) can be changed?', Paul came alive and spoke with vehemence. 'No!' he said. He reacted *exactly* as though I was calling him a traitor to his Catholic belief.

Back in 1965, Ford had noted in his diary that he was troubled that the pope had indicated that the commission would still be free to 'discuss natural law and birth control on a broad basis'. His Roman diary for November 1965 notes: 'Here, I believe, there is an ambiguity or inconsistency in the Holy Father's attitude. It is not logical to insist in the strongest language that the solemn doctrine of *Casti Connubii* must be upheld and at the same time allow discussions to be conducted in his own commission which make sense only in the supposition that the doctrine can be rejected. I wonder if he realises the inconsistency of this position?'[27]

On the issue of contraception, it is now clear that Pope Paul VI in 1968 thought he had to maintain the consistency of the Church's teaching from 1930 regardless of any scientific advances, changed social conditions, and changing theological reflections on marriage by married Catholics and competent moral theologians. In good conscience, many married Catholics have practised contraception ever since, consistent with the theological arguments put by the majority of the commission appointed by Paul VI to investigate the matter. Even Cardinal Pell concedes that the arguments for individual judgment or private conscience on the matter of contraception were disputed 'with some justification' within the Catholic tradition prior to Paul VI's publication of *Humanae Vitae*. These arguments were unlikely to be resolved by a papal declaration known to be contrary to the recommendations of the papally-appointed committee of experts, and contrary to the lived experience of many married persons who did not find the pope's explanation of the self-evident natural law to be at all comprehensible. In good conscience, they chose to follow the view of the majority and the church hierarchy lost the unquestioned adherence of many Catholics who rightly thought that they knew more about the lived reality of the issue than the pope. In his 1993 encyclical *Veritatis Splendor*, John Paul II stated:[28]

> Like the natural law itself and all practical knowledge, the judgment of conscience also has an imperative character: man must act in accordance with it. If man acts against this judgment or, in a case where he lacks certainty about the rightness and goodness of a determined act, still performs that act, he stands condemned by his own conscience, the proximate norm of personal morality.

In his 1972 lecture 'Conscience in its Age', Joseph Ratzinger (now Pope Benedict XVI) took as his starting point for reflection Hermann Rauschning's *Conversations with Hitler*, in which Hitler pledged to liberate man 'from the filthy and degrading torments inflicted on himself by a chimera called conscience and morality, and from the claims of a freedom and personal autonomy that only very few can ever be up to'. The future Pope Benedict said:[29]

> The destruction of the conscience is the real precondition for totalitarian obedience and totalitarian domination. Where conscience prevails there is a barrier against the domination of human orders and human whim, something sacred that must remain inviolable and that in an ultimate sovereignty evades control not only by oneself but by every external agency. Only the absoluteness of conscience is the complete antithesis to tyranny; only the recognition of its inviolability protects human beings from each other and from themselves; only its rule guarantees freedom.

In his 1991 essay 'Conscience and Truth', Ratzinger says, 'It is of course undisputed that one must follow a certain conscience, or at least not act against it'.[30] Reflecting on the actions of the SS during World War II, Ratzinger distinguishes conscience from 'firm, subjective conviction and the lack of doubts and scruples' which do not justify man.[31] Though we are obliged to follow an erroneous conscience, 'conscience's reduction to subjective certitude betokens at the same time a retreat from truth'.[32] Ratzinger happily adopts Newman's approach to authority and conscience, noting that Newman embraced 'a papacy not put in opposition to the primacy of conscience but based on it and guaranteeing it'.[33] For Pope Benedict XVI:[34]

> The true sense of the teaching authority of the pope consists in his being the advocate of the Christian memory. The pope does not impose from without. Rather he elucidates the Christian memory and defends it. For this reason the toast to conscience indeed must precede the toast to the pope because without conscience there would not be a papacy.

On 21 September 2005, Cardinal Pell told the National Press Club:

> Recently I heard of a discussion between two Christian politicians (I am not sure both were Catholics) on how they would vote on destructive human embryo experimentation. One proposed to vote for it and the other to oppose, and the supporter of the legislation justified his position by claiming he had asked advice from a priest who told him to follow his conscience. At best the priest ducked the issue; at worst he disguised his dissent by advocating what his listener preferred.

A citizen agitating for law reform and a politician deciding how to vote are confronted with a whole conundrum of law, morality, public policy and public administration. Following our conscience can be a very demanding task, requiring detailed assistance and guidance from others. By following the formed and informed conscience, the politician and the priest do not necessarily duck the issue or opt for personal preference. Pope Benedict XVI is adamant that 'it is not the Church's responsibility to make [its] teaching prevail in political life':[35]

> Rather, the Church wishes to help form consciences in political life and to stimulate greater insight into the authentic requirements of justice as

> well as greater readiness to act accordingly, even when this might involve conflict with situations of personal interest.

Those agitating for a law banning a particular activity need to consider the different realms of principle, strategy and tactics. A church leader might think that the cloning of human embryos is always wrong. His religious tradition teaches him that there can be no exceptions to this moral injunction. In good conscience, he may decide that he should be very upfront and even prophetic in declaring from the rooftops: 'The cloning of human embryos is wrong'. He might be speaking first to his own fellow church members but then to all his fellow citizens. But for whom is he speaking? He may be speaking authoritatively in the name of his church tradition. That means nothing more than he is one within the structure of his own church who has the authority to speak and he speaks in a manner consistent with his church's tradition and teaching on this particular issue. But in the public forum, does he speak for all members or even the majority of that church's members who are citizens of the state? Who knows?

When making a submission to a government inquiry on human cloning in September 2005, Cardinal Pell spoke in the name of the 'Catholic Church in Sydney'. That may be a more user-friendly term in the mainstream media than the more cumbersome 'Catholic Archdiocese of Sydney'. But who or what is the 'Catholic Church in Sydney'? No politician would look at the submission presuming that it was a statement on behalf of the majority of Catholics living in the city of Sydney. Some local parishes also put in their own submissions. But not even they would claim to speak for all the people in their parish. There was also a submission by the Australian Catholic Bishops Conference, of which Cardinal Pell is a member.

There is not necessarily anything wrong with this duplication of submissions. It may just be not very sensible. Most bishops of the Catholic Church have taken the view that the state has a choice between treating human embryos as complete, living, though immature, human beings or treating them as biological material for research. But others, including many scientists and politicians, have decided that it is not such a stark choice.

Rather they see human embryos and foetuses on a spectrum, all deserving greater respect than non-human embryos and foetuses. In good faith, they no more see a human embryo as a human person than they would see a pig embryo as a pig. Just as they see good reasons for treating a pig embryo differently from a pig, they see good reason for treating a human embryo differently from a newborn baby or from an elderly person facing death. Some religious leaders see spectrums as slippery slopes and warn that if the embryo is at risk, the vulnerable old person or the newborn baby could be next. Their critics respond that the usefulness of a spectrum is that it does show differing gradations, allowing distinctions to be drawn.

The Catholic Church hierarchy has been the group most consistent in proclaiming the right to life of the embryo. If the embryo has a right to life, obviously it is in need of legal protection because it is the most vulnerable of the 'human family'. Vatican statements have been quite consistent in developing a coherent argument from this premise. But those who do not accept the premise are then troubled by the conclusions drawn by the Vatican. They are also fortified in their view that the Vatican's conclusions and formulae do not resonate with their own moral sense about the status of the human embryo. In light of the fact that the majority of human embryos do not successfully implant naturally, perishing promptly after their expulsion from the womb, these persons wonder whether you can postulate a morality or even a theology that countenances the immediate death of at least half the 'human family' within moments of conception. They question the presuppositions of a moral argument that leads to the Vatican's conclusion that: 'The corpses of human embryos and foetuses, whether they have been deliberately aborted or not, must be respected just as the remains of other human beings'.[36] Very few of us respect a three-day-old embryo which has succumbed *just as* they would respect the corpse of a 25-year-old person.

There are many people of goodwill, including many Catholics, who question tortured language which links 'corpse' and 'embryo', referring to 'his nature and identity' when speaking of an embryo, and describing 'a personal presence at the moment of this first appearance of a human life'.[37] There are many people who are philosophically competent and compassionate who argue that the disposal of a beaker of human embryos is not the moral equivalent of sending thousands of people to a gas chamber. Such people are not necessarily immoral or amoral. They do not identify an embryo as an individual or as a person. They respect a human embryo because it (not he or she) has the capacity to develop into an individual, a person, if successfully implanted and able to thrive. They do not set the precise moment at which the entity becomes recognisable as a person or individual. But in good faith they say that the embryo is not yet there. Given that nature disposes of the majority of embryos, they then do not lose any sleep over the loss of embryos that have been treated respectfully having been created as part of an IVF procedure so that one of their number might have the opportunity to thrive and become a person, an individual, a citizen with rights.

Writing in the *New England Journal of Medicine*, Professor Michael J. Sandel, who serves on the President's Council on Bioethics, says:[38]

> Defenders of in vitro fertilization point out that embryo loss in assisted reproduction is less frequent than in natural pregnancy, in which more than half of all fertilized eggs either fail to implant or are otherwise lost. This fact highlights a further difficulty with the view that equates embryos and persons. If natural procreation entails the loss of some embryos for every successful birth, perhaps we should worry less about the loss of embryos that occurs in in vitro fertilization and stem-cell research. Those who view embryos as persons might reply that high infant mortality would not justify infanticide. But the way we respond to the natural loss of embryos suggests that we do not regard this event as the moral or religious equivalent of the death of infants.

If over half the embryos naturally produced in the womb fail to implant, should we be in mourning that over half the human race never develop beyond a couple of cells? The Vatican says, 'In consequence of the fact that they have been produced *in vitro*, those embryos which are not transferred into the body of the mother and are called "spare" are exposed to an absurd fate, with no possibility of their being offered safe means of survival which can be licitly pursued'. Their fate is no more absurd than the fate of the majority of embryos which are never successfully implanted naturally.

True to my religious tradition, I am happy to view a human embryo respectfully as a human being in the earliest stages of development. I need to concede that in a democracy under the rule of law, the majority of citizens are entitled to work on the presupposition that a human embryo is not a human person but is an embryo deserving more respect than a pig embryo because it has at this stage only the potential to develop into a human being, into a human person.[39]

Some church authorities argue that the state should never produce excess embryos, even if the scientist is anxious to maximise the prospects of implantation of a healthy embryo. They need to counsel their own church members not to participate in IVF programs that produce excess embryos. They would know that many of their own church members do avail themselves of such programs because they are seeking life, seeking the fulfilment of their marriage, remembering the hope on their wedding day that they would be able to bear and nurture each other's children. Some of these church authorities may even tell such couples that what they have done is objectively wrong according to the church teaching. They may think they are being prophetic in urging their co-religionists to distance themselves from the individualist and consumerist mentality which leads contemporary couples to think they are entitled to have children. However other church authorities are unlikely to see such action as wrong when confronted with a couple who are seeking the best for a child of their own, though with the regret that some other embryos will succumb in the process. It is possible that no more embryos will have succumbed in their procedure than would have succumbed in the normal marital relations of a fertile couple who over the years have conceived momentarily before the embryo has failed to implant.

Religious leaders are entitled to agitate against laws and policies that would permit IVF procedures for infertile married couples when such procedures entail the knowing production of excess embryos. But there is little likelihood of such a position winning acceptance with many politicians, given that they are popularly elected and each of them would have in their own electorate couples who want to avail themselves of this procedure convinced that there is nothing immoral in the procedure. In proposing a ban on such a procedure, the church authorities would be wrong to claim that they speak for all their members. They would be unwise to claim that they speak even for a majority of their members. They need to make a prudential assessment about how hard to push their view publicly. They are probably better off trying to convince their own church members of the cogency of their moral case, while conceding publicly that community values or community standards would tolerate and even encourage the provision of IVF services to infertile married couples, even with the production of excess embryos provided only that the excess embryos were treated respectfully.

Church leaders then find themselves moving into a default position. Their own preference would be the banning of all IVF procedures that entailed the production of excess embryos. Some Australian Catholics, including some of the bishops convinced of the Vatican's position, would even oppose IVF procedures without the production of excess embryos. The Vatican objects to the creation of any embryo outside the act of sexual intercourse which thereby deprives 'human procreation of the dignity which is proper and connatural to it'. This is not a moral teaching which is very compelling for persons outside the inner Catholic circle. It would make no sense for Catholic bishops to urge a civil legal regime which reflected the Catholic Church's claim that 'procedures which assist the marital act to achieve its purpose are morally permissible, but those which substitute for it are not'.[40] While urging that Catholic healthcare facilities should not provide or refer for technological intervention such as IVF, the bishops would have no business in urging such a blanket policy for all healthcare facilities in Australia. They know that many Catholics will avail themselves of such services at non-Catholic facilities.

Religious leaders need to be prudent in their public declarations, urging their co-religionists in the moral life, enhancing their capacity to contribute to the common good of society through the development of laws and policies which uphold the rights and dignity of all citizens as well as those others within the jurisdiction and any others affected by the actions and decisions of the nation state. There is a need to set the limits for all religious traditions, ensuring that the nation state and the dignity and rights of its citizens are not threatened by the religious activity and beliefs of some, even if they are the majority.

It is an internal church matter whether a church authority can purport to bind the conscience of the individual believer about moral right and wrong action. Religious leaders have no special competence about how the civil law ought and can maximise the moral good and reduce the prospects of moral wrong in a society which is committed to self-determination for its members and legal protection for the vulnerable.

Political, legal and moral advice is needed to inform the citizenry about law reform and public administration. These are not primarily moral questions, but they require prudence and political savvy best practised by those who are imbued with the local culture and who are experienced in the law and politics of that society. For this very reason, religious leaders, and especially those from other countries, are less likely to be competent no matter what their place in the hierarchy of the religious community. The more expert they are in moral and political philosophy, the more they should be attuned to the limits of their competence and the prudence of silence in the wake of the local faithful trying not just to live the individual moral life but also to contribute to public life, true to their public trust and responsive to the cultural, political and legal ethos of their society. With prudence, religious authorities can ensure that Gladstone's fears remain groundless and Newman's defence sound, toasting conscience before religious authority without reservation. In the realm of law and social policy, all religious leaders would be well advised to follow Pope Benedict's caution against attempting 'to impose on those who do not share the faith ways of thinking and modes of conduct proper to faith'. According to Benedict, their aim should simply be 'to help purify reason and to contribute, here and now, to the acknowledgement and attainment of what is just'.[41]

CHAPTER THREE

LESSONS FROM THE UNITED STATES IN ELECTION AND SELECTION MODE

The United States engages in very robust discussion about the appropriate mix of law, religion and politics. But there is no right answer for all societies and for all occasions. We can only formulate guidelines for the responsible mix of law, religion and politics. The elements of the mix will vary from society to society and from time to time. In our post-11 September world, even the most hardened atheist and even the most intolerant liberal has to admit that religion does have a place in the mix. Keeping religion out of politics is neither a worthy ideal nor a practical objective in robust western democracies, because the subject matter of politics will inevitably include issues about which citizens care passionately and on which they disagree vehemently, some of them drawing their inspiration and vision from a religious tradition.

What is the role of church leaders in the political process, proclaiming the truth from their religious perspective, when that perspective is not necessarily shared by the majority? When should politicians vote for a law or social policy according to their religious convictions rather than according to the policy of their party or according to the opinion of the majority whom they represent?

In countries like Australia and the United States, these questions most often arise when Catholic bishops or Catholic politicians start talking about abortion, euthanasia or stem cell research. But they also arise when community leaders and politicians of all faiths and none buy into the question of tax reform and wealth redistribution, or ponder the morality of going to war, or wrestle with the right balance between border security and the dignity of asylum seekers. Americans become very focused on these questions when they are electing a president or selecting a new Supreme Court judge.

In preparation for the 2004 US presidential election, the Vatican took the extraordinary step of issuing a 'doctrinal note' setting out 'some principles proper to the Christian conscience, which inspire the social and political involvement of Catholics in democratic societies'.[1] Though some bishops like Cardinal Pell are fond of saying 'Catholics should stop talking about the primacy of conscience', this document from Cardinal Ratzinger mentioned conscience fifteen times, conceding that: 'It is not the church's task to set forth specific political solutions – and even less to propose a single solution as the acceptable one – to temporal questions'.[2] The document saw the formed and informed conscience of the politician and church leader as critical for getting at the truth. A century ago, the Catholic Church was opposed to all forms of liberalism and very suspicious of democracy. Now even its critics would accept that the Church is a leader in espousing the cause of democracy, though it rightly clings to the primacy of truth rather than the primacy of majority opinion.

The document refreshingly proclaimed, 'Living and acting in conformity with one's own conscience on questions of politics is not slavish acceptance of positions alien to politics or some kind of confessionalism, but rather the way in which Christians offer their concrete contribution, so that, through political life, society will become more just and more consistent with the dignity of the human person'.[3] At the time, this seemed good news for tolerant, liberal citizens living in a democracy, regardless of their religious beliefs. It did not resolve many of the old tensions which some religious believers, especially more conservative Catholics, encounter living in a society where their comprehensive view of the good and the true is not shared by the majority of their fellow citizens.

If I believe something is wrong, I would not do it, or if I did, I would regard myself as being in error. I would not commend this action to another person for whom I care. But does this necessarily mean that I would campaign for a law or social policy banning this practice, even invoking criminal sanctions of the state against others who would freely choose to do this thing? Cardinal Ratzinger was understandably concerned about those who 'yield to ephemeral cultural and moral trends, as if every possible outlook on life were of equal value'.[4] Not all outlooks on life are equal. But in a democracy where the dignity of each citizen is respected, the different outlooks on life are equally deserving of guaranteed non-interference and non-discriminatory agnosticism by the state, provided those enacting their outlooks on life do not interfere with the basic rights and dignity of others.

The Vatican Congregation said that political freedom could not be 'based upon the relativistic idea that all conceptions of the human person's good have the same truth and value'.[5] That is not to deny that political freedom in a diverse, tolerant democracy must be based on the idea that all conceptions of the good are entitled to an equal hearing before the bar of reason and public opinion when our lawmakers determine the law applicable to all citizens. For example, being a Catholic seeking to form and inform my conscience, I readily agree with the Vatican Congregation asserting that 'the family needs to be safeguarded and promoted'.[6] When it comes to the operation of the law rather than personal preference or moral encouragement at church, I do not see that it necessarily follows that 'in no way can other forms of cohabitation be placed on the same level as marriage, nor can they receive legal recognition as such'. What about the need to protect the dignity and rights of children born of a de facto union? A lawmaker could in good and informed conscience vote for a legal measure recognising the legal effects and benefits of de facto relationships while at the same time personally encouraging people to consider matrimony.

In the democratic spirit of the age, this Vatican note was authoritative as an invitation to discussion rather than an edict on faith and morals. It did not provide any politician, judge or administrator with the answers to the moral quandaries they confront in the faithful discharge of their public office. But it did provide useful guideposts for the decision maker wanting to govern in good conscience being true to her office, to her people and to her God.

In both the United States and Australia, the Catholic bishops publish a document well before the election setting out the issues that should be considered by candidates and electors wanting to inform themselves of the Catholic position on disputed questions. The document has two purposes: to provide accurate information on the Church's position on key social and moral questions, before the electoral heat is turned up; and to excuse the bishops from the need to walk the tightrope of comment on sensitive issues during the clamour of the election campaign. Usually, some issue will arise during the campaign that draws some of the bishops into debate. This then causes a flurry of speculation about the prudence and political motivation for such intervention.

As has been their practice for twenty years, the 281 US bishops issued *Faithful Citizenship: A Catholic Call to Political Responsibility* a year before the 2004 presidential election.[7] They had also chosen seven senior bishops to set up a task force on Catholic bishops and Catholic politicians. This task force was to spend the election year reflecting on church–state issues. Its mandate became very difficult once the Democrats had chosen the pro-choice Catholic John Kerry from Boston as the challenger to the pro-life Methodist George W. Bush. The abortion controversy has grown even more contested and political in the United States since the Supreme Court's 1975 decision *Roe* v *Wade*. It affects every presidential election and every nomination to the Supreme Court. Americans struggle to keep religion and politics in their place every time the abortion controversy is raised.

Making his own long-range preparation for the 2004 presidential election, Bishop Raymond Burke, a trained canon lawyer who had spent five years working in the church courts in Rome, sent letters to three Catholic legislators in his US diocese of La Crosse. He asked them to explain themselves on issues such as abortion. Receiving no adequate responses, he took the extraordinary step of signing a canonical declaration on 23 November 2003 calling on the legislators 'to uphold the natural and divine law regarding the inviolable dignity of all human life' and declaring that: 'To fail to do so is a grave public sin and gives scandal to all the faithful'. He decreed: 'Catholic legislators who are members of the faithful of the diocese of La Crosse and who continue to support procured abortion or euthanasia may not present themselves to receive Holy Communion. They are not to be admitted to Holy Communion, should they present themselves, until such time as they publicly renounce their support of these most unjust practices.'[8] Burke did not extend his edict to Catholic judges who supported abortion or euthanasia. A week later it was announced that Burke had been promoted and was to become Archbishop of St Louis in the New Year. Before his installation in St Louis, he formally published the decree in his diocesan newspaper. Later in the campaign he told reporters that he would refuse communion to John Kerry if he were to visit the diocese. Archbishop Sean O'Malley, Kerry's bishop in Boston, said that he would not take the same course of action. Things were getting messy.

Six months out from the presidential election, Archbishop Charles Chaput of Denver sent out his own warning shot:[9]

> Catholics have a duty to work tirelessly for human dignity at every stage of life, and to demand the same of their lawmakers. But some issues are jugular. Some issues take priority. Abortion, immigration law, international trade policy, the death penalty and housing for the poor are all vitally important issues. But no amount of calculating can make them equal in gravity. The right to life comes first. It precedes and undergirds every other social issue or group of issues.

From the outset, bishops Burke and Chaput turned the 2004 election into a test of Catholic candidates and Catholic voters such as had never occurred before in the United States. Their key issue was abortion, but others were euthanasia, stem cell research and same-sex marriage. The Iraq war and the death penalty, both strongly advocated by George Bush, did not rate a mention. These bishops were adamant that they were not making political choices. They were simply highlighting the moral issues which in their opinion should be of greatest concern to Catholic politicians and Catholic voters. On 1 May 2004, Bishop Michael Sheridan from Colorado Springs issued his own pastoral letter threatening not only errant Catholic politicians but also errant Catholic voters:

> Any Catholic politicians who advocate for abortion, for illicit stem cell research or for any form of euthanasia ipso facto place themselves outside full communion with the Church and so jeopardize their salvation. Any Catholics who vote for candidates who stand for abortion, illicit stem cell research or euthanasia suffer the same fateful consequences.

By the time the election had run its course, only a handful of bishops had said they would refuse communion to pro-choice candidates. But these few attracted much media attention. In the wake of the sexual abuse crisis in the Catholic Church, bishops seemed to be less listened to when it came to issues like the Iraq war and yet these few bishops were more visible in the 2004 presidential campaign than any of their fellow bishops during any previous campaign. They were definitely much more visible than the bishops in the 2004 Australian election.

In the United States, it had been difficult for the bishops to get any airplay in the publication of their considered views about the war in Iraq. Their condemnation of the war appeared on page 17 of the *New York Times*. But once the election was on, the bishops were even appearing on the front page of the *New York Times*, denying communion to those candidates for election who supported the Supreme Court's status quo on the abortion question, or who voted against Congress's *Partial-Birth Abortion Ban Act* which has already been struck down by three District Courts. It seemed that a good Catholic candidate would now be unselectable or unelectable in the United States. A Catholic candidate would be at a significant disadvantage to a non-Catholic opponent who would not usually expect such strict scrutiny from the leaders of his or her religious group. Some of the bishops' statements purported to rule out one candidate as being morally ineligible for office, leaving no room for the Catholic voter to determine for themselves the weight they wanted to give to a comparison of the moral worth and character of each candidate, and to any particular policy issue. This was all the more daunting because the presidential election comes down to a two-horse race, and the stakes are very high in all areas of public life and administration. As George Weigel says, 'Americans don't just elect a president; we elect a party and its people, who will fill the federal government for years – and the appellate benches for decades'.[10]

I am one of those Catholics who is always troubled when the Eucharist is politicised. I even cringe a little when I see national flags flown permanently in sanctuaries of churches. Some years ago, we had a stand-off between some gay rights activists and bishops when the activists presented themselves for communion wearing rainbow sashes and the bishops denied them communion. I expressed disquiet both with the wearing of the sashes and with the refusal of communion. All of us who take communion, bishop or not, gay or straight, approach the altar with the apprehension of any sinner declaring: 'Lord, I am not worthy to receive you, but only say the word and I shall be healed'. I would deny communion to totalitarian, murderous dictators who made a mockery of the Eucharist and of the table fellowship by presenting themselves for communion in the communities that they were terrorising. But usually, it is best that priests and communicants leave their political and moral differences at the door of the church, approaching the table of the Lord, not presuming to judge each other, and offering Eucharistic hospitality to those who do believe they are receiving the Body of Christ. There is a teaching role vested in the bishop, who is entitled to teach about the disposition of one who approaches the table of the Lord. But having taught, he is not commissioned to pass public judgment on a communicant while presiding at Eucharist. During his long pontificate, Pope John Paul II gave communion to a range of government leaders who supported laws permitting abortion in some circumstances. He was not taken as approving every action of such a communicant, any more than any priest is deemed to approve all things done by a communicant parishioner whose confession he hears regularly.

Future popes and bishops should continue to give communion to those who approach for reception unless the communicant is one who causes grave scandal to the community by actions which are totally offensive to the Eucharistic community. Those who approve war in some circumstances, or capital punishment in some circumstances, or abortion in some circumstances should not be denied communion if they come to the altar in good faith, not seeking some public showdown, and not wanting to display contempt for the Eucharistic community as would a tyrannical, murderous dictator seeking communion from a bishop or pope on a solemn occasion. It is no defence for the priest to claim that he is simply setting down the circumstances in which the communicant can come in good conscience. To do that during an election campaign, deciding that some moral issues rather than others are the determinative issues, is to politicise the Eucharist.

If the priest finds himself giving the Eucharist to a public official, with a heavy heart and with grave reservation, the priest is of course entitled to discuss the matter with the official, but he should not make a public display of his reservation about the worthiness of the official to receive communion. Such a public display during election time with inevitable attention by the national media is just as much a national political act as a parochial pastoral one.

If there were a choice of candidates or parties, one of which opposed the church position on all moral questions and one of which supported the church position on all moral questions, there may be a case for a church leader publicly urging a vote for the latter if he or she is also notoriously known to be the morally superior, more prudent and wise candidate. But given the unlikelihood of such a choice, church pastors are well advised not to campaign for one candidate or party. Who are they to determine which issue or issues are the litmus test for the conscientious religious voter?

In response to the Vatican's Doctrinal Note of November 2002, Cardinal McCarrick, Archbishop of Washington DC, suggested to his fellow bishops the establishment of a group who 'would consider the relationship that we as bishops and teachers in the Church should have with Catholic politicians who are not always with us on the major issues that face the Church in our time in our country'.[11] As chair of the Task Force on Catholic Bishops and Catholic Politicians, he gave the US Catholic Bishops Conference an interim report on 15 June 2004, plaintively noting:[12]

> In our view the battles for human life and dignity, and for the weak and vulnerable should be fought not at the communion rail but in the public square, in hearts and minds, in our pulpits and public advocacy, in our consciences and communities.

There had been a lot of work going on behind the scenes. A report had appeared on the Catholic News Service on 4 June 2004 that Cardinal Joseph Ratzinger was proceeding cautiously on the issue and that he would like Vatican officials to meet soon with the US bishops' task force. McCarrick told his fellow bishops on 15 June 2004:[13]

> In recent days, I have once again been in contact with Cardinal Ratzinger both by letter and telephone calls. He has offered some observations for our work which he specifically asked not be published, but which I wish to share with you.

Some bishops were surprised that Ratzinger's letter was not to be shared with all the bishops. McCarrick provided a summary of his dealings with Ratzinger, indicating that it was 'up to us as bishops in the United States to discern and act on our responsibilities as teachers, pastors and leaders in our nation'. According to McCarrick:

> Cardinal Ratzinger outlines HOW a bishop might deal with these matters, including a series of precautionary measures involving a process of meeting, instruction and warning.
>
> I would emphasize that Cardinal Ratzinger clearly leaves to us as teachers, pastors and leaders WHETHER to pursue this path. The Holy See has repeatedly expressed its confidence in our roles as bishops and pastors. The question for us is not simply whether denial of Communion is possible, but whether it is pastorally wise and prudent. It is not

> surprising that difficult and differing circumstances on these matters can lead to different practices. Every bishop is acting in accord with his own understanding of his duties and the law.

The US bishops decided that the task force should issue a statement clarifying the misunderstandings that had arisen about John Kerry's eligibility for communion. Bishop Chaput and a couple of other bishops were asked to assist the task force in its deliberations. They cobbled together a document, *Catholics in Political Life*, which conceded ground to all parties and was approved by the bishops 183 to six. The document noted:[14]

> Given the wide range of circumstances involved in arriving at a prudential judgment on a matter of this seriousness, we recognize that such decisions rest with the individual bishop in accord with the established canonical and pastoral principles. Bishops can legitimately make different judgments on the most prudent course of pastoral action. Nevertheless, we all share an unequivocal commitment to protect human life and dignity and to preach the Gospel in difficult times.
>
> The polarizing tendencies of election-year politics can lead to circumstances in which Catholic teaching and sacramental practice can be misused for political ends. Respect for the Holy Eucharist, in particular, demands that it be received worthily and that it be seen as the source for our common mission in the world.

No sooner had the bishops dispersed from their national meeting than the Italian press leaked Ratzinger's letter entitled 'Worthiness to Receive Holy Communion'. Ratzinger had not entertained the idea that it would be up to individual bishops to make pastoral and prudent decisions. He had counselled a uniform approach. His letter was quite consistent with the approach which had earlier been taken by Archbishop Burke. Ratzinger had said:[15]

> Not all moral issues have the same moral weight as abortion and euthanasia. For example, if a Catholic were to be at odds with the Holy

> Father on the application of capital punishment or on the decision to wage war, he would not for that reason be considered unworthy to present himself to receive Holy Communion.

But there is a difference between committing an abortion yourself and saying that it is not a matter for the civil law to try and deter others. Bush himself authorised the execution of 152 persons on death row, only once exercising clemency in his term as state governor.[16] He committed the United States to war. He was responsible for these acts. Kerry did not commit abortions, nor did he commit acts of euthanasia. He simply said that these were not issues in relation to which the state should interfere with the choice made by the individual.

As far as Ratzinger was concerned, if a pro-choice Catholic candidate had been counselled and warned 'and the person in question, with obstinate persistence, still presents himself to receive the Holy Eucharist, the minister of Holy Communion must refuse to distribute it'. According to Ratzinger's prescription, Burke had followed the right canonical prescriptions, first warning the politicians privately and then taking public action only once there was no satisfactory response.

Ratzinger was less sympathetic to the line being taken by bishops impugning voters who were minded to vote for a candidate who was pro-choice. After all, there were only two candidates. Some bishops were saying it would be sinful to vote for Kerry and therefore the voter who was a good Catholic was being told that the only choices they had were to vote for Bush or abstain. Ratzinger appreciated that a good Catholic might have reason for voting for Kerry regardless of his views on abortion. Ratzinger had written:

> A Catholic would be guilty of formal cooperation in evil, and so unworthy to present himself for Holy Communion, if he were to deliberately vote for a candidate precisely because of the candidate's permissive stand on abortion and/or euthanasia. When a Catholic does not share a candidate's stand in favour of abortion and/or euthanasia, but votes for that candidate

> for other reasons, it is considered remote material cooperation, which can be permitted in the presence of proportionate reasons.

Given the pro-Burke part of the Ratzinger advice, it is no wonder that McCarrick had not published it. It was political dynamite. Conservative elements in the US Church then got to work, expressing outrage that the episcopacy had been denied the wisdom of Cardinal Ratzinger's insights at a critical time in the US Church's history.

McCarrick went into damage control, as did Ratzinger. In response to the formal transmission of *Catholics in Political Life* to Rome, Ratzinger replied by letter to McCarrick. This time McCarrick published the letter immediately, pointing out that he and Ratzinger had engaged in numerous discussions on this question, and not just by letter. In this second letter, Ratzinger said:[17]

> The statement is very much in harmony with the general principles 'Worthiness to Receive Holy Communion', sent as a fraternal service – to clarify the doctrine of the Church on this specific issue – in order to assist the American Bishops in their related discussion and determinations.

If Ratzinger's first letter had been sent as a fraternal service to assist the US bishops, it is surprising that they were not given copies. It is even more surprising that Ratzinger had asked that it not be published, as McCarrick had advised the bishops in conference. The internal church politics of the issue were becoming very strained. As the presidential campaign grew more intense, the bishops once again started to break ranks. Diametrically opposed statements were issued, even by bishops working in the same state.

The bishops had publicly disgraced themselves with no prospect of reaching agreement. The Jesuit Cardinal Avery Dulles gave the right mix of pastoral concern, reverence for the Eucharist, political pragmatism and common sense in his observation: 'The church's prime responsibility is to teach and to persuade. She tries to convince citizens to engage in the political process with a well-informed conscience'. He cautioned against penalties, including a public banning of communion:[18]

> In the first place, the bishop may be accused, however unfairly, of trying to coerce the politician's conscience. Second, people can easily accuse the church of trying to meddle in the political process, which in this country depends on the free consent of the governed. And finally, the church incurs the danger of alienating judges, legislators, and public administrators whose goodwill is needed for other good programs such as the support of Catholic education and the care of the poor. For all these reasons, the church is reluctant to discipline politicians in a public way, even when it is clear that their positions are morally indefensible.

There were good grounds for suspicion about the public description of political parties and their policies permitting commentators to boldly assert, as George Weigel did: 'A second Bush administration will give Catholics an unprecedented opportunity to help create a new governing majority informed by the riches of Catholic social doctrine. That cannot be done in the Democratic Party.'[19]

Two months out from the poll, Archbishop Burke, by now well installed as the Archbishop of St Louis and buoyed by the publication of the Ratzinger correspondence with McCarrick, issued another pastoral letter answering his critics and urging Catholic voters to focus on those issues which entailed intrinsic evil. Even though a particular war might be wrong, not all wars were necessarily wrong. Even though most uses of capital punishment might be wrong, not all acts of capital punishment were necessarily wrong. Given that abortion is always wrong and given that homosexual genital activity is always wrong, he was suggesting that it was self-evident that Catholic voters would therefore focus exclusively on these issues if there were a difference between the two candidates on these issues, regardless of their political stance on other moral issues. Burke said:[20]

> Some Catholics have suggested that a candidate's position on the death penalty and war are as important as his or her position on procured abortion or same sex marriage. This, however, is not true. Procured abortion and homosexual acts are intrinsically evil and as such can never be justified in any circumstances. One cannot justify a vote for a candidate who promotes intrinsically evil acts which erode the very foundation of the common good, such as abortion and same-sex 'marriage', by appealing to that same candidate's opposition to war or capital punishment.

According to Burke, the conscientious Catholic did not have a choice between candidates in a presidential election if one candidate, unlike the other, supported the recognition of same-sex marriage, the constitutional right to abortion, and embryo experimentation in even very restricted circumstances. Questions of character, ability to lead, morality of commitment to a particular war, excessive reliance on the death penalty, and less equitable provision of education and health care were not relevant in these circumstances. You had no choice but to vote for Bush regardless of your view about his leadership ability or about the morality of the Iraq war.

After the US poll, twenty-two per cent of voters named 'moral values' as the issue that most mattered in the casting of a vote. Of that group, eighty per cent voted for Bush and eighteen per cent for Kerry. The conservative commentator Fr Richard Neuhaus claimed that 'all sensate voters understood that "moral values" referred to the candidates' clear differences on abortion, embryonic stem cell research, a marriage amendment, and, more generally the role of morality and religion in public life'.[21]

Abortion remains the big emblematic moral and political issue in the United States, which has now endured thirty years of controversy following the Supreme Court's decision in *Roe* v *Wade*.[22] With the court's 1992 decision in *Planned Parenthood* v *Casey*,[23] the court's jurisprudence of abortion was laid bare. Key members of the majority abandoned the strict trimester framework imposed by *Roe* over the objections of Justice Blackmun, who said it should not be disturbed. Chief Justice Rehnquist, a constant dissenter on the issue, observed that '*Roe* continues to exist, but only in the way a store front on a western movie set exists: a mere facade to give the illusion of reality'.[24] Justices O'Connor, Kennedy and Souter thought they were consolidating the court's task by calling upon 'the contending sides of a national controversy to end their national division by accepting a common mandate rooted in the Constitution'.[25] Twelve years on, the Americans were further from that than ever. While Supreme Court justices on both sides of the abortion controversy had distanced themselves from the reasoning in *Roe* v *Wade*, the Democratic Party had turned unquestioning adherence to *Roe* into a precondition for party participation. Ever since the exclusion of Governor Bob Casey from the speaker list at the 1992 Democratic National Convention, the Democratic Party has provided the opening for the Republicans to present themselves as the pro-life party, though there is little reason to expect that ultimately there would be fewer abortions in Republican states than in Democrat states, were the Supreme Court to deconstitutionalise the issue. By the time of the 2004 convention, the Democrats had politicised the issue and determined that *Roe* v *Wade* was 'sacred ground'.[26] The party platform declared:

> Because we believe in the privacy and equality of women, we stand proudly for a woman's right to choose, consistent with *Roe* v *Wade*, and regardless of her ability to pay. We stand firmly against Republican efforts to undermine that right.

Commencing his epic 1973 decision in *Roe*, Justice Blackmun had declared, 'Our task, of course, is to resolve the issue by constitutional measurement, free of emotion and predilection'.[27] Two decades later, in *Planned Parenthood*, he was lamenting: 'A woman's right of reproductive choice is one of [the] fundamental liberties. Accordingly that liberty need not seek refuge at the ballot box. I am eighty-three years old. I cannot remain on this court forever, and when I do step down, the confirmation process of my successor well may focus on the issue before us today.'[28] How right he was then about the confirmation process of judges; and even more right after the 2004 election as President Bush prepared the first round of Supreme Court appointments after a record eleven-year term of stability on the court.

There was more than a dose of emotion and predilection in Blackmun's last judicial utterance on the issue of abortion. It has now reached the stage, thirty years after *Roe*, that the limits of what some judges describe as a fundamental liberty depend not on the ballot box directly but on the view of the judges chosen and confirmed by those at the ballot box. By attempting to constitutionalise the issue of abortion, the Supreme Court has further politicised the issue and the court itself, such that abortion features in US election campaigns far more than it does in the elections of other western democracies where the abortion rate is similar.

In the last ten years, the US debate has focused on attempts to outlaw partial-birth abortion or D&X ('intact dilatation and extraction' as distinct from D&E 'dilatation and evacuation'). In *Stenberg* v *Carhart*, Justice Scalia observed:[29]

> I cannot understand why those who *acknowledge* that, in the opening words of Justice O'Connor's concurrence, '[t]he issue of abortion is one of the most contentious and controversial in contemporary American society,' persist in the belief that this Court, armed with neither constitutional text nor accepted tradition, can resolve that contention and controversy rather than be consumed by it. If only for the sake of its own preservation, the Court should return this matter to the people – where the Constitution, by its silence on the subject, left it – and let *them* decide, State by State, whether this practice should be allowed.

Not only has the Supreme Court been consumed by the issue. So too has the US political process at election time, and also the Catholic Church and the evangelical churches.

The jurisprudence of abortion has been rendered even more incoherent because Justice Kennedy, one of the three judges in the joint opinion in *Planned Parenthood* v *Casey*, has now split from the pack and insisted that *Planned Parenthood* permitted a state to outlaw partial-birth abortion, providing an exception only when such a mode of abortion was necessary to protect the life of the mother. He saw no need for an added exception permitting this style of abortion for the health of the mother. He acknowledged that some doctors did practise this form of abortion but he obviously had a fairly low opinion of their professional competence. At the time *Stenberg* v *Carhart* was decided, Kennedy was able to say:[30]

> Dr Carhart has no specialty certifications in a field related to childbirth or abortion and lacks admitting privileges at any hospital. He performs abortions throughout pregnancy, including when he is unsure whether the fetus is viable. In contrast to the physicians who provided expert testimony in this case (who are board certified instructors at leading medical education institutions and members of the American Board of Obstetricians and Gynecologists), Dr Carhart performs the partial birth abortion procedure (D&X) that Nebraska seeks to ban.

Since then the partial-birth abortion procedure has become the defined battleground for all those Americans agitating the abortion question. It has become a federal issue with Congress taking up where twenty-seven state legislatures had left off, seeking to limit the availability of the procedure. Defying the courts to challenge their fact-finding capacity, Congress has asserted: 'Partial-birth abortion is never necessary to preserve the health of a woman'.[31] Congress also asserts that partial-birth abortion 'poses serious risks to a woman's health, and lies outside the standard of medical care'.[32] Four Congresses have now conducted hearings on partial-birth abortion. President Clinton vetoed legislation passed by Congress criminalising the procedure. President George W. Bush signed into law a measure banning partial-birth abortion. Presidential aspirant John Kerry voted against proposed laws on partial-birth abortion at every turn. So by the time of the 2004 election, there was a clear split on party lines regarding attempts to limit partial-birth abortion.

Following the lead of Justice Kennedy, Congress has gone further in questioning the competence, impartiality and professionalism of those doctors who practise partial-birth abortion, asserting: 'No controlled studies of partial-birth abortions have been conducted nor have any comparative studies been conducted to demonstrate its safety and efficacy compared to other abortion methods. Furthermore, there have been no articles published in peer-reviewed journals that establish that partial-birth abortions are superior in any way to established abortion procedures.'[33]

Congress claimed that the legitimate state interests to be achieved by the banning of partial-birth abortion included the promotion of maternal health, and the drawing of 'a bright line that clearly distinguishes abortion and infanticide, that preserves the integrity of the medical profession, and promotes respect for human life'.[34]

The three District Courts which have already been asked to rule on the constitutionality of the Congress provision have pointed out: 'The congressional record, encompassing the views of individual physicians and medical associations on both sides of the debate surrounding D&X, and as supplemented by the trial testimony, evidences a division of medical authority over the issue of whether D&X is generally safer than the alternatives'.[35] Where there is a division of medical opinion, the lower courts have said they have no option but to strike down any provision that does not contain an exception for the procedure to be used when the medical practitioner thinks it is for the health of the mother. Obviously such an exception arms pro-choice doctors with the legal entitlement to use D&X whenever they choose, thinking it the more appropriate or convenient means. The American Medical Association (AMA) continues to state:[36]

> According to the scientific literature, there does not appear to be any identified situation in which intact D&X is the only appropriate procedure to induce abortion, and ethical concerns have been raised about intact D&X. The AMA recommends that the procedure not be used unless alternative procedures pose materially greater risk to the woman.

Whatever may have been its previous stand on the issue, the AMA cannot now be classed as an opponent of partial-birth abortion because it goes on to say, 'The physician must, however, retain the discretion to make that judgment, acting within standards of good medical practice and in the best interest of the patient'.

There is something surreal to this whole debate about partial-birth abortion. Even if the Bush administration succeeds in having the Supreme Court uphold the validity of the law, doctors like Dr Carhart will still be free to use the D&E procedure on foetuses who are very close to viability, and with a reckless disregard for the viability of the foetus. While all sorts of adverse descriptions can be proffered of the D&X technique, there is nothing more humane or moral about the dismembering of the foetus inside the womb before it is taken out piece by piece. What is the real point in being able to restrict Dr Carhart's choice to the D&E technique rather than his having the option of using D&X when he thinks this technique will be better for the health of the mother? Presumably pro-life advocates and the bishops have decided that the D&X abortion technique is a useful focus for the debate because it is so akin to infanticide, permitting the president and others to claim: 'A terrible form of violence has been directed against children who are inches from birth, while the law looked the other way. Today, at last, the American people and our government have confronted the violence and come to the defence of the innocent child.'[37] The tragic irony is that the result of this law is not that the innocent child is spared in these circumstances, but that he or she is dismembered in the womb rather than being partially delivered before death.

Why have the Catholic Church and some of the evangelical Protestant churches become so identified with a political campaign which does not reduce the number of abortions, but which, if successful, will simply mean death is administered in one way and not another, and in some of those cases, the death will be administered in a way that the treating doctor thinks would increase the risk to the health of the mother? Presumably the bishops and the evangelical leaders have made a political assessment that this is the best way to keep the issue before the courts, trying to exploit the Kennedy disillusionment with the *Planned Parenthood* reinterpretation, and the best way to focus the public on the barbarity of late-term abortions. But who are the church leaders to make these political judgments?

There could be some members of Congress who in good conscience oppose the partial-birth abortion law on the basis that it could adversely affect the health of some women while not saving the life of one near-viable foetus. Politics is a dirty business. What are the bishops doing getting into a situation where a law such as this becomes the litmus test for the moral appropriateness of election to office?

There is also something surreal to the pro-choice lobby crying foul at every attempt to limit the access to abortion when the foetus is very close to viability. Procedures such as D&E and D&X highlight that by the time the foetus has reached that stage of development, you are dealing with a defenceless being who is recognisably and tangibly a human being. You are no longer in the moral penumbra where there is still the possibility of twinning or where nature as a matter of course disposes of many embryos.

But with a late-term abortion, the abortionist beholds the bodily parts of a human being who is only days and inches away from life amongst us. The question for society is how best to draw the bright line, distinguishing the time when continued life of the embryo or foetus will be the prerogative of the mother, from the time when continued life will be the preserve of the state, which is positioned to protect the foetus despite the wishes of the mother. The smartest judges in the United States have now had over thirty years to craft an answer. They can't. They are the wrong people to decide. Such moral conflicts can be resolved only by compromise crafted by elected legislators in the various states. Resulting legislation will emerge from the legislators' attention to the qualms of citizens being revolted by the D&E and D&X procedures, rather than from fine judicial distinctions between levels of scrutiny and between classes of interest.

Justice Scalia made good sense when he observed in *Lawrence* v *Texas* that many persons wrongly assume that an overruling of *Roe* v *Wade* would result in abortion being made unlawful. He said:[38]

> It would not; it would merely have *permitted* the States to do so. Many States would unquestionably have declined to prohibit abortion, and others would not have prohibited it within six months (after which the most significant reliance interests would have expired). Even for persons in States other than these, the choice would not have been between abortion and childbirth, but between abortion nearby and abortion in a neighbouring State.

When you strip away the heat of the argument in the United States, as it was played out during the 2004 election campaign, the debate is largely about symbolic issues. Those who are pro-life need to dedicate their energies to the support and encouragement of mothers during the time that life in their womb is solely their prerogative, and to the design of law and policy which in part reflects, and in part contributes to, an emerging moral consensus that late-term abortions fill us with dread because they are wrong. In a democratic society, the law will always permit some access to abortion if only because there is no moral consensus about the status of the embryo. As soon as the election was over, President Bush admitted as much in a post-election interview in the *New York Times*:[39]

> I think the goal ought to be to convince people to value life. But I fully understand our society is divided on the issue and that there will be abortions. That's reality. It seems like to me my job is to convince people to make right choices in life, to understand there're alternatives to abortion, like adoption, and I will continue to do so.

John Kerry could have said the same thing! Whatever the moral arguments, the criminal law is too blunt an instrument to use even on the doctor alone when a woman wants to decide what is for the best before the new life in her womb is recognisable, tangible and viable.

After the 2004 presidential election, Cardinal William Keeler, who chairs the bishops' pro-life committee, wrote to all US Senators in relation to the mode of judicial appointments especially to the Supreme Court. He wrote:[40]

> Insisting that judicial nominees support abortion throughout pregnancy is wrong. By any measure, support for the Supreme Court's 1973 *Roe* v *Wade* decision is an impoverished standard for assessing judicial ability. For over three decades, *Roe* has sparked more informed criticism and public resistance than any other court decision of the late 20th century. Even legal scholars who support abortion have criticized *Roe* for not being grounded in the U.S. Constitution. Further, in 2000, the Supreme Court relied on *Roe* to rule that the gruesome and inhumane practice of partial-birth abortion must be constitutionally protected. When considering nominees the Senate should not allow itself to be held captive to such an unfair and unreasonable standard.

In Australia, we do not have a bill of rights. We do not have any *Roe* v *Wade.* Our abortion rate is similar. In his 2004 address to the Acton Institute, Cardinal Pell compared abortion rates in the United States and Australia and said that in Australia 'proportionately they are just as alarming – averaging out at approximately ten abortions for every twenty-five live births'. He said, 'There are approximately 100,000 abortions performed in Australia each year. In 2003, there were 252,000 live births registered.'[41] On 1 November 2004, Mr Tony Abbott, the Australian health minister told ABC Radio:

> We have something like 100,000 abortions a year, 25 per cent of all pregnancies end in abortion and even the most determined pro-choice advocates these days seem to be rightly concerned at the way that the abortion epidemic has developed. But certainly the Government has no plans to change existing policy at this time.

This would amount to an abortion rate of twenty-eight per cent, three-quarters of which are funded by Medicare. After the 2004 election, Tony Abbott, a strong Catholic, announced a desire to limit the availability of taxpayer-funded abortion. The prime minister vetoed the suggestion and Cardinal Pell announced that the Church would devote greater resources to the support of pregnant women who thought they had no option but abortion. Recently the Australian Institute of Health and Welfare has estimated there were 84,218 induced abortions in Australia in 2003.[42] Tony Abbott now says:[43]

> For the record, I would not support withdrawing Medicare funding from abortion, let alone trying to re-criminalise it. With former US president Bill Clinton, I think there's much to be said for ensuring that abortion is 'safe, legal and rare'.

In some dioceses of the United States, Tony Abbott would find himself refused communion for these remarks. If he were standing for election in the United States, he would be publicly criticised by some bishops, who would tell Catholics not to vote for him. And yet he is well known as a politician who is a conservative and faithful Catholic, knowing that in politics you have to make compromises seeking what is achievable, and realising that your personal morality is not necessarily the template for good law and administration applied to a diverse community that does not share your own moral perspective.

The Australian experience attests the correctness of Justice Scalia's assertion. If *Roe* v *Wade*, *Planned Parenthood* v *Casey* and *Stenberg v Carhart* were all overruled tomorrow, there would be no significant change in the national abortion rate of the United States. The political debate would move to the states and the crunch question would be: 'Which abortions do we want to criminalise so that a doctor will face a jury with a real risk that the jury will record a verdict of guilty requiring the doctor to be sent to prison?' Education and support will be far more determinative than the criminal law. Even if pro-life groups were to succeed in their political campaigns in some states by criminalising abortion from the moment of conception, except when the life of the mother was in danger, the net result would be a negligible decrease in the number of abortions or a politicisation of the criminal law and its mode of administration. This would undermine the integrity of the legal processes.

In a democratic society the law is not likely to be a significant determinant of the rate of abortions. At most, it might limit the time at which an abortion may be performed. It does not matter what the religious affiliation of the electors may be. The US National Survey of Religion and Politics, by the Bliss Institute, University of Akron, bears this out. In 2004, they surveyed 4000 Americans. Thirteen per cent of Catholics (compared with fifteen per cent of the overall sample) thought abortion 'should not be legal at all'. Thirty-five per cent of Catholics (and thirty-three per cent of the overall sample) thought abortion 'should be legal in only a few circumstances such as to save the life of the mother'. Seventeen per cent of Catholics (and seventeen per cent of the overall sample) thought abortion 'should be legal in a wide variety of circumstances'. Thirty-five per cent of Catholics (and thirty-five per cent of the overall sample) thought abortion 'should be legal and solely up to a woman to decide'.[44]

Pope John Paul II was tireless in teaching that all direct abortion was a grave moral disorder. He invoked scripture, natural law, church tradition and the Magisterium:[45]

> I declare that direct abortion, that is, abortion willed as an end or as a means, always constitutes a grave moral disorder, since it is the deliberate killing of an innocent human being. This doctrine is based upon the natural law and upon the written Word of God, is transmitted by the Church's Tradition and taught by the ordinary and universal Magisterium.

But the invocation of so many sources to conclude that something is a grave moral disorder does not help to determine whether there should be a law against it in all circumstances, especially when there is no equivalent moral consensus even amongst the faithful of the church community. At election time, we all need to distinguish three discrete questions: Is something a grave moral disorder? Should there be a law against it? Is this the best way to work for a change in public understanding and commitment, providing some prospect for legislative change leading to a change in people's thinking and actions?

For the majority of citizens, disposing of a beaker full of embryos is not the moral equivalent of committing thousands of partial-birth abortions on near viable foetuses. There are times when both sides of the debate want to insist that these actions are morally equivalent. Insisting that a partial-birth abortion is not morally different from the removal of an embryo (even one implanted against the wishes of the mother), the pro-choice lobby insists that partial-birth abortion is permissible, no matter what the tangible and visible effects, and no matter what the revulsion experienced by many nurses and doctors. The pro-life lobby argues that the community revulsion at the detail of partial-birth abortion should be translated into a blanket ban on all direct abortion. It then becomes a winner take all argument. Either all are permitted or none.

There are many religious people who believe that abortion is a grave moral disorder. But they do not believe that a law criminalising all direct abortion from the moment of conception is appropriate or enforceable in a society where the majority of citizens draw some distinction between the embryo, the non-viable foetus and the viable foetus. Or even if they believe such a law is ultimately achievable and desirable, they do not believe that making a party political issue of partial-birth abortion in the interim is helpful or warranted, given that not one life will be saved, and given that the health of some women may be placed at risk in the hands of less competent doctors. There is a case for an enforceable criminal law that prosecutes a doctor for terminating the life of a foetus with reckless disregard for the viability of the foetus or without due regard for the health of the mother. Beyond that, the criminal law is an inappropriate device to attempt further protection of the foetus. The criminal law has no role to play in attempting to protect the embryo which the mother wishes removed from her womb. There is neither deterrent value nor educative effect in passing a criminal statute which will never be enforced. Such a statute undermines the efficacy of the law and imperils the integrity and impartiality of the law enforcers. There are many citizens who think direct abortion is a grave moral disorder. But in democracies under the rule of law, such as Australia and the United States, not every grave moral disorder ought to be made unlawful with provision for criminal sanctions.

The law, politics and morality of this issue are so much more complex than the case of the notorious murderous, tyrannical dictator who presents himself for communion in the community which he is persecuting. The relationship between religion and politics is badly out of kilter when bishops announce publicly that they would deny communion to John Kerry, and even suggest that those who vote for him should examine their conscience. All voters should examine their consciences all the time. But singling out voters for Kerry from voters for Bush is so morally selective as to be political, being perceived to be partisan.

If fewer Americans were having abortions, if fewer Americans were performing abortions, if far fewer Catholics were having abortions, if far fewer Catholics were performing abortions, there would be a stronger case for a law limiting the availability of abortion in the United States. Even then, it is not likely that many, if any, jurisdictions would pass and implement a law criminalising all abortion from the moment of conception, except when the life of the mother was in danger. In part that is because we are a long way from a moral consensus that the withdrawal of an embryo from the womb is the equivalent of dismembering and killing a near viable foetus who is only days and inches from a life protected by law and respected by society. There are some citizens, including many Catholics, who are convinced of this moral equivalence and thus would urge a woman not to exercise her prerogative to control her own body by removing an embryo which would be dependent on her for survival and thriving. But there can be no legitimate expectation that a democratic government will criminalise such activity when the majority of citizens are not so convinced. That is why so many citizens are both revolted by the detail of D&X or D&E while being sanguine or regretful about the loss of an embryo which joins those many other embryos that leave the womb naturally.

During the 2004 campaign the unsuccessful candidate John Kerry had said that he would 'only nominate individuals to the federal bench whose records demonstrate . . . the right to choose'. Raymond Flynn, the former mayor of Boston and former ambassador to the Vatican under the Clinton administration, placed a full page advertisement in the *New York*

Times asking: 'Why do you, Senator Kerry, have a "litmus test" for judicial candidates that discriminates against Faithful Catholics?'[46] Two days later, Archbishop Charles Chaput was being quoted on the front page of the *New York Times* declaring that a vote for a candidate who supported abortion rights and stem cell research required absolution. He said, 'If you vote this way, are you cooperating in evil? And if you are cooperating in evil should you go to confession? The answer is yes.' Chaput denied that he was promoting the Republican Party. He said, 'We are not with the Republican party. They are with us.'[47]

Some Catholics like Mark Roche, dean of Arts at Notre Dame University, had pointed out that abortion was not the only life issue in the election. There was the Iraq war, the death penalty, universal health care and environmental protection. Even if one confined attention to abortion, Roche claimed there was a gulf between the Republican rhetoric and the outcomes with a Republican administration. His figures were not contested when he wrote an opinion piece in the *New York Times* pointing out that the number of legal abortions increased by five per cent during the Reagan presidency and dropped by thirty-six per cent during the Clinton presidency, presumably because Clinton provided a better safety net for poor women confronting the reality of single motherhood.[48]

Things had gone so badly off the rails at the end of the presidential campaign that a Vatican official had to inform the *New York Times* that Kerry was not a heretic. This after a layman seeking the excommunication of Kerry in the Diocese of Boston had visited the Congregation for the Doctrine of the Faith and then received a letter from a priest, ostensibly acting at the request of an official in the congregation, saying that 'if a Catholic publicly and obstinately supports the civil right to abortion, knowing that the church teaches officially against that legislation, he or she commits that heresy' and is 'automatically excommunicated'.[49]

The election is now well past but the bishops are no closer to reaching agreement on how to proceed on these vexed political and pastoral issues. In March 2005, McCarrick gave a public lecture in Boston and reviewed the last year's work on his task force. He concluded:[50]

> The denial of Holy Communion became the focal point of the discussion – not the defense of human life and the dignity of the human person. The bishops in their statement made it clear that you could not be accused of being less than Catholic if you did not deny Communion, nor should you be accused of being lacking of pastoral judgment if you did. The Church is called to be principled but not ideological. We cannot compromise our basic values or teaching, but we should be open to different ways to advance them.

The task force hopes to issue new guidelines in time for the next round of Congressional elections.

It is essential that all US bishops abandon the theocratic hope that the law reflects Catholic moral teaching in all its aspects. They should take the lead from Pope Benedict XVI who, in his first encyclical, insists that 'it is not the Church's responsibility to make [its social teaching] prevail in political life'.[51] The new pope may well have been reflecting on the actions of some of the US bishops like Burke who, during the 2004 presidential campaign, had insisted: 'Of course, the end in view for the Catholic must always be the total conformity of the civil law with the moral law'.[52] Bishops like Burke need to concede that there is a moral chasm between committing an immoral act and deciding that the law should leave the commission of an immoral act to the individual without state coercion or sanction. They need to abandon the simplistic hierarchy of political wrongs, giving a preference to politicians who favour the criminalisation of acts judged to be intrinsically evil while leaving out of calculation the direct actions of those same politicians who themselves commit immoral acts, such as sending large numbers of people to the gallows or committing the nation to war without just cause. They need to understand that their internal pastoral initiatives about the availability of the sacrament to politicians becomes a political lightning rod at election times and in the interests of church–state separation they should avoid public statements on such questions at election time.

It is quite inappropriate for religious leaders to express a political preference based on the distinction between acts which are intrinsically evil and those acts which are contingently evil, depending on the circumstances in which the acts are committed and on the resulting effects of the acts. Even if such a distinction be coherent, it does not follow that all intrinsically evil acts are more evil than all contingently evil acts. It is spurious for religious leaders to claim that a politician who permits others to commit intrinsically evil acts is less worthy than a politician who himself commits contingently evil acts. The moral calculus is far more complex. If bishops like Burke and Chaput were consistent, they would need to advise most political candidates to stay away from communion during election time, and they would need to advise their church members to abstain from voting for want of any worthy candidates. The Canadian bishops showed greater prudence, declining to comment on their Catholic prime minister Paul Martin's continued reception of communion despite his support for measures such as same-sex marriage and his instruction to his Catholic Cabinet colleagues that they had no choice but to support such measures. Martin lost office without being branded unworthy by his bishops.

Just as the abortion question haunted the presidential candidates in the 2004 election, it then taunted the new nominees for the Supreme Court. The president of the Catholic bishops in the United States took the extraordinary step of writing to President Bush on 6 July 2005, when Sandra Day O'Connor had announced her retirement, saying:

> [B]ecause of the Supreme Court's ability to affect both principles and policies, I urge you to consider for the Court qualified jurists who, pre-eminently, support the protection of human life from conception to natural death, especially of those who are unborn, disabled, or terminally ill. I would ask you to consider jurists who are also cognizant of the rights of minorities, immigrants, and those in need; respect the role of religion and of religious institutions in our society and the protections afforded them by the First Amendment; recognize the value of parental choice in education; and favour restraining and ending the use of the death penalty.

During the confirmation hearing for John Roberts as Chief Justice, the senators harked back to the 1960 address by the Catholic presidential aspirant John F. Kennedy. Addressing the Greater Houston Ministerial Association, Kennedy told his Protestant audience:[53]

> I believe in an America that is officially neither Catholic, Protestant nor Jewish – where no public official either requests or accepts instructions on public policy from the Pope, the National Council of Churches or any other ecclesiastical source – where no religious body seeks to impose its will directly or indirectly upon the general populace or the public acts of its officials – and where religious liberty is so indivisible that an act against one church is treated as an act against all.

He went on to declare:

> I am not the Catholic candidate for President. I am the Democratic Party's candidate for President who happens also to be a Catholic. I do not speak for my church on public matters – and the church does not speak for me.
>
> Whatever issue may come before me as President – on birth control, divorce, censorship, gambling or any other subject – I will make my decision in accordance with these views, in accordance with what my conscience tells me to be the national interest, and without regard to outside religious pressures or dictates. And no power or threat of punishment could cause me to decide otherwise.
>
> But if the time should ever come – and I do not concede any conflict to be even remotely possible – when my office would require me to either violate my conscience or violate the national interest, then I would resign the office; and I hope any conscientious public servant would do the same.

Kennedy was elected as the first Catholic president. Roberts became the first Catholic Chief Justice since the Civil War – on a court that now has a majority of Catholic members. It is this majority which in part informs some of the concern on Capitol Hill with recent nominations. At the very outset of questioning Roberts, Senator Specter, the chair of the committee, did not dally. He announced:[54]

> Judge Roberts, there are many subjects of enormous importance that you will be asked about in this confirmation hearing, but I start with the central issue which perhaps concerns most Americans, and that is the issue of the woman's right to choose and *Roe* v *Wade*.

Roberts assured the committee that 'there's nothing in my personal views based on faith or other sources that would prevent me from applying the precedents of the court faithfully under principles of *stare decisis*'. He went on to claim that 'my faith and my religious beliefs do not play a role in judging. When it comes to judging, I look to the law books and always have. I don't look to the Bible or any other religious source.'

Specter then asked whether Roberts subscribed to the Kennedy dictum 'I do not speak for my church on public matters and the church does not speak for me'. Roberts replied, 'I agree with that, Senator. Yes.' Despite Roberts' affability and judicious modesty, groups such as Planned Parenthood opposed his nomination because they presume he will not uphold the court's decisions on abortion. Presumably the White House is fairly confident that Roberts, like Rehnquist, would question the efficacy of the precedents on abortion.

When it came to filling the more crucial vacancy to replace the critical swing vote of O'Connor, Bush dropped the ball badly, displaying a complete nonchalance to those, including the Catholic bishops, who had campaigned strongly on the judicial nomination of strong anti-*Roe* candidates. He nominated his White House counsel, Harriet Miers, who had no judicial experience, a very slight paper trail, but a record of some very off-hand remarks indicating an in-principle acceptance of *Roe* and *Planned Parenthood*. She had told the Executive Women of Dallas in 1993:[55]

> The law and religion make for an interesting mixture but the mixture tends to evoke the strongest of emotions. The underlying theme in most

> of these cases is the insistence of more self-determination. And the more I think about these issues, the more self-determination makes the most sense. Legislating religion or morality we gave up on a long time ago. Remembering that fact appears to offer the most effective solutions to these problems once the easier cases are disposed of.

Once she withdrew, Bush proposed the more reliable and very judicious Samuel A. Alito. But the Miers nomination illustrates that, no matter what the pressure groups think they may have contributed to a presidential campaign, there are always other elements to the mix. This should be very troubling for bishops like Burke and Chaput as they try to impose their religious authority on election results.

The Senate Judiciary Committee focused again on the abortion question when Judge Alito appeared before them. Senator Specter wanted to nail Alito down to a commitment that *Roe* v *Wade* was the settled law of the land. He adopted the majority's approach in *Planned Parenthood* v *Casey* conceding that the soundness of the reasoning in *Roe* was no longer the issue but rather the precedential value of its holding. Alito, a Catholic like Roberts, replied judiciously:[56]

> I agree that in every case in which there is a prior precedent, the first issue is the issue of *stare decisis* and the presumption is that the court will follow its prior precedents. There needs to be a special justification for overruling a prior precedent.

A person's religious faith is irrelevant to the judicial determination of when an ultimate court of appeal is justified in overriding a prior precedent. US church leaders have appreciated the need to leave conscientious judges well alone in the performance of their judicial tasks. The Catholic bishops never led calls for Justice Kennedy to be denied communion, despite his pro-abortion ruling in *Casey*. They have realised what folly it would be to call for judicial nominees like Roberts and Alito to proclaim their personal preferences on abortion. It is time for some of this common sense and margin of appreciation to be extended to politicians and candidates for elected office who have to weigh conscientiously many diverse factors in determining their stand on law reform and law enforcement, regardless of their personal views on the morality of some acts committed by their fellow citizens who do not happen to be their co-religionists. Even those citizens who are their co-religionists are no more likely than other citizens to agree with the bishops on an issue like the desirable law on abortion. If conscientious persons with religious values are to be both selectable and electable in the United States, they need to be given the room to engage in the political process without church leaders at election time purporting to have the authority to name a hierarchy of moral issues. It is not the role of religious leaders to judge not only who is worthy to approach the communion table but also who is worthy to aspire to elected office while still claiming to be a citizen with religious beliefs which have to be lived privately and publicly in a compromised, fallen world.

CHAPTER FOUR

KEEPING POLITICS AND RELIGION IN PLACE WITH AUSTRALIAN POLITICIANS

By respecting the primacy of the individual conscience, ensuring adequate checks and balances to protect individual rights from interference by popular sentiment, and upholding the rule of law without undue religious influences, we are well on the way to confining religion and politics to their proper place. Religion and politics can play out appropriately in their respective places if politicians and religious actors establish a right relationship based on trust and civic discourse. Together they can determine the relevance of religious beliefs when it comes to participating in public life and contributing to the development of law and policy, whether as citizens or as public officials. We need to determine what role is appropriate for religious authorities participating in public life, wanting to contribute to the development of law and policy.

We need to distinguish principle, strategies and tactics. There are three distinct types of claim in public debate about legal and political issues. First, there are claims that some course of behaviour is immoral; second, claims that there should be a law banning or regulating some course of behaviour; and third, claims that the law banning or regulating some course of behaviour should be enforced or interpreted in a strict or lax way.

Happily we are leaving behind the era in which it was thought that we should all leave our religious beliefs at home when it came to participating in public life. Things may have been simpler for some public actors when it could be blithely asserted that religion was irrelevant to public life.

In a democracy, we must start with the presumption that the individual citizen is free to vote for the candidate or party of their choice for whatever collection of reasons or intuitions they wish. There is no point in political philosophers moralising about what factors ought and ought not to influence a prospective voter. Such philosophers may draw up a list of criteria which satisfy them and their circle in their assessment of the relative merits of voters. But in a democracy, we do not need to expend much energy on making moral assessments of voters and their voting intentions. Such energy is better directed at assessments of those who are elected and of those other citizens who are appointed to positions of public trust requiring them to act in the public interest.

The vote of the person who likes Mr Howard's smile is worth as much as the vote of the person who passionately agrees with Mr Beazley's view on the US alliance. In a democracy citizens are entitled to urge their fellow citizens to consider seriously the reasons they would vote for a candidate or a party. Some of these urgers may even occupy official positions in churches or other religious organisations. They may want to influence members of their own congregations to consider particular moral or religious issues before they cast their vote. They may even be so presumptuous as to urge other citizens, not members of their flock, to heed their message about such moral or religious issues. Being a free country, we can urge or be urged as much or as little as we choose.

In the past, there was a presumption that in the public forum religious leaders should speak about issues only in terms comprehensible to those with no religious faith, with the voice of public reason. There may be good pragmatic reasons for this. But once again there is no rule of political morality which would render religious urgings outside the church circle improper. Such urgings may simply be wasted breath, and even counterproductive. That does not make them wrong or improper.

In the past, some liberal atheists conducted themselves in the public forum as if the forum was their privileged place and the rest of us had to play by their rules, choosing only from the policy options they would countenance. Persons with religious views or religious motivations were treated not only as if they held no trump cards at the table. They were treated as if they had no cards at all. The only cards which could be played from the hand were cards which would be valued by liberal atheists. The religious person had the responsibility to translate his religious view or religious motivation into a comprehensible non-religious view or non-religious motivation. If complete translation were not possible, that which could not be translated was to be cast aside.

Now there is a greater mutuality in the public forum. In the name of equality, it has to be accepted that the religious person has no more obligation than the non-religious person to translate her views or motivations into propositions acceptable to the other. But given that we live in a very secular environment, it is sensible for the religious person to put in the work making their case comprehensible and appealing to the non-religious person. Religious authorities have to be especially careful because of the strong public suspicion and dislike of persons in religious authority. Mark Latham is not the only person to have been in public life and have a strong distrust of religious authorities. He has just been more public, bilious and blunt in the expression of his views. In his diaries, he took strong exception to Cardinal Pell's intervention during the 2004 federal election. He wrote:[1]

> If the parishioners were fair dinkum they would rise up and punt Big George. But they just cop it from this authoritarian institution. Hey, if they encouraged people to experience Christ's teachings as individuals, free from the pulpit, all the kiddie-fiddlers would be out of a job.

It is sensible for citizens who urge others to vote in a particular way or who urge others to exercise their public functions in a particular way to be prepared to give a public account of themselves, explaining their reasons and motivations. Once again there is no moral imperative for this. But if they are unwilling to do it, they may do their position and their cause some harm.

In a democracy like Australia, those elected to public office are expected to give a public account of themselves. In the interests of truth, they should be prepared to explain their reasons for voting legislation or policy up or down. In many instances, the member of parliament may simply invoke the party policy and the need to follow party discipline. But even on those occasions, the member will usually attempt to appropriate the party decision and reasons to herself. There may be occasions when the member has her own reasons and even own distinctive position on a law or policy. Very rarely, there could even be the time that the member's conscience dictates that she take a stand. In all cases, the member should be prepared to give an account of herself.

What if her stand depends not on a party decision, not on her own conscience, but on the dictates of her church? What would be the situation if a politician thought she should not only vote against her party's policy but also thought she should vote against her own conscience? Why? Because her church taught that the proposed law or policy was wrong. She would be obliged at the very least to declare to the voters and the Parliament that she was voting against the policy not because she believed the contrary to be the moral good or the greater good but because her church commanded her obedience. Presumably this would be electoral folly. Electors in a parliamentary democracy are entitled to have members of parliament who will vote either according to conscience or in conformity with their party policy. The electors would be ill-served by a member who thought he was compelled to vote against his party policy and against his own conscience simply because his church commanded a contrary position.

In a democracy, absolute primacy must be accorded the conscience of the voter and the elected politician. A church which questioned such absolute primacy would rightly be perceived as a threat to democracy, maintaining to itself the entitlement to interfere in the affairs of the state with decrees issued by persons not necessarily citizens of the state. Even the senior church authorities who happened to be citizens of the state would have to admit that their position and activity was not necessarily the result of their acting on their own conscience but rather the result of their implementing the church discipline imposed by their superiors who were not citizens of the state. There would be no way of escaping the charge of outside interference by pleading that local church hierarchs were themselves citizens. You would need to offer the assurance that the local hierarchs were free to act according to their consciences. If they could, why not the rest of us?

There can be no objection to church leaders participating in public life when there are moral issues to be discussed. The precondition for such participation is the acknowledgment of the absolute primacy of conscience in the public forum of the democratic nation state, regardless of the position adopted within the Church in the governance of its own affairs. Many citizens are elected or appointed to positions in the state, positions which carry obligations to the state and the citizens. To what extent can the religious views and motivations of these citizens affect or dictate their discharge of their public trust? To what extent is it proper for religious authorities to try and influence their co-religionists who happen to occupy these posts?

In Australia, there is no such thing, if there ever was, as the 'Catholic vote'. There is probably not a view on any contested political issue commanding the assent of most Catholics. There probably never was a regimented Catholic vote in Australia. There is definitely no such thing as an 'Anglican vote' or a 'Uniting Church vote'.

Though involved for years in public debate about issues such as Aboriginal rights, refugee rights, euthanasia and abortion, I would never pretend to speak for the Catholic Church or for the Catholics of Australia. However, I do think you can still responsibly argue for a Catholic position on some key moral and political questions, regardless of whether Catholic voters would be split on such questions in much the same way as the community generally.

In a liberal democratic society, you cannot expect to be taken seriously in the public square unless you are prepared to give an account of yourself and your convictions. It is not good enough to espouse a position just because some religious authority figure asks you to, or because that authority says it is the true position. Respecting our own integrity as citizens and the integrity of our fellow citizens, we can agitate only for proposals that command our real assent. Though we respect the authority of our church, we must accord absolute primacy to the conscience of the citizen engaged in public discourse about issues of law and policy, taking seriously our own conscience and the conscience of those charged with authority in the state.

How do we get to the situation where Prime Minister John Howard can say, 'There's no such thing as a Catholic or Anglican view on anything; it depends on individuals'?[2] More importantly, if the prime minister is wrong, when is it appropriate to speak of a Catholic or Anglican view on a moral or political issue?

Archbishops Pell and Jensen have been the preferred Catholic and Anglican church spokesmen for the government and its supporters. The cherry-picking of bishops was made easy for the government politicians and their supporters, given the frequent public disagreements between Archbishop Jensen and Archbishop Peter Carnley when he was primate of the Anglican Church.

The standing of Pell and Jensen with government members skyrocketed during the 2004 federal election, when they took the initiative and singled out Labor's education policy for adverse public moral assessment. Pell and Jensen were joined by their Melbourne colleagues while the bishops outside the two big cities were left out of the loop. The government was very happy to run with this timely moral assessment by senior church leaders. Archbishop Bathersby from Brisbane went public in response to his brother bishops' action, saying that if Catholic leaders 'were constructive in the matter' they would 'find flaws in both sides of an education policy'.[3]

Some in the government may even have thought that Pell and Jensen were sympathetic supporters of the Howard government. Thus the surprise when both these men, and not just the likes of Peter Carnley, came out and expressed some reservations about the government's proposed industrial relations changes. It was easy for the government to dispatch the new primate, Phillip Aspinall, to the sidelines, dismissing him because he was not an expert in industrial relations. But such a cheap trick could not be played on Pell and Jensen, whose expertise on war and education funding was not an issue for the government when in a corner.

When told that Pell and Jensen were 'worried about the impact [of the industrial relations changes] on family life',[4] the prime minister claimed this was an exaggeration. It was not. Jensen had said, 'This nation and its political leaders must be committed to ensuring optimum working conditions for the nation's workers; a living wage that will mean everyone has the ability to provide for themselves and their families the necessities of life; strong unions that will represent workers; and the preservation of leisure time for families to be together for rest and recreation and to maintain their relationships'.[5] Cardinal Pell told the *Sydney Morning Herald* that he was awaiting the details of the reforms but expressed the point of principle that 'civilised' conditions such as lunch breaks, annual leave, long service leave, superannuation, union access and family time should be preserved. He was 'not sure we should encourage foolish people to barter these things away too quickly'.[6]

Church leaders, like the rest of us, could be forgiven at that time for not knowing the detail of the industrial reforms and their impact. Even Andrew Robb, the chairman of the government's task force, speaking after the prime minister's observation about the churches, had to admit that 'we just simply don't know' whether Mr Howard's 1996 guarantee that no worker would be worse off under his workplace laws still applied. When asked about the stand taken by Pell and Jensen in support of powerless or ill-informed persons seeking to negotiate their employment conditions under the new arrangements, the government backbencher Malcolm Turnbull replied:[7]

> George Pell and Dr Jensen are [in] no doubt there are foolish people; and no doubt they're very concerned for them. But perhaps they would be better off trusting individuals' freedom and sense of independence and capacity to determine their own lives and make their own judgments and if they did that, people would make the decisions that suited them. The old sort of regime of telling people how to live their lives, be you a government or a churchman, is running out of time. Australians want

> to be free. They want to have independence. They want to have choice. And our side of politics, the Liberal Party, we are a party committed to freedom and choice and independent enterprise and that's what we seek to promote. Now there are some people that distrust human nature and believe that people won't make the right decisions and that others should make those decisions for them. We err on the side of respecting individual judgment and respecting individual's choices. Others may disagree, but that's our philosophy.

Jensen and Pell rightly confined themselves to statements of principle – statements consistent with their church traditions and teaching on economic matters. Archbishop Jensen is a strong evangelical Anglican rightly reputed for basing his public utterances on the scriptures and the tradition of his church. Cardinal Pell has been a strong supporter of the Catholic social teaching enunciated by Pope John Paul II, whose encyclical *Laborem Exercens* dealt with human labour and the rights of workers.

Though there is always room for disagreement about how the principles are to be applied in practice, it is far too cavalier for government or their supporters to dismiss church leaders who have restricted themselves to statements of principle. There may be room to debate how families are best protected in a more globalised economy. But it is not good enough for government simply to cherry-pick their church leaders, and then, when they find even their preferred church leaders expressing concerns based on the religious tradition, to dismiss their remarks on the basis that each individual will decide. Each individual will make a decision in good conscience about how best to apply the relevant moral principles in the particular situation. But a Catholic or Anglican should receive some guidance from church authorities who confine themselves to expressions of principle true to the religious tradition. This should even be the case for a Catholic or Anglican cabinet minister in an Australian government which has control of both houses of Parliament.

Maybe Mr Howard was concerned about the effect that the archbishops' remarks could have on some senators and members of the public not quite so convinced about the need to take the industrial reform package on trust. The prime minister was wrong on two counts. It was not an exaggeration to claim that the archbishops were worried about the impact on family life. There is such a thing as a Catholic or Anglican view on the morality of war or the morality of government funding for education or on the morality of industrial relations changes affecting families.

While the bishops confine themselves to statements of principle true to their faith traditions, they do express an Anglican or Catholic view. As for the application of the principles and the assessment of the detail of proposed laws or policy, there is much room for individual judgment made in good conscience.

After my first visit to the Woomera Detention Centre in 2002, I went to Canberra to meet with Minister Philip Ruddock. One of my government contacts warned me that they were sick of the moral outrage from the churches and other advocacy groups. I was urged to keep cool. I kept cool until Easter that year. I then wrote to the minister:[8]

> My three hours in the detention centre on the evening of Good Friday convinced me that it was time to put the message to you very plainly despite its public unpopularity and despite your government's immunity to moral outrage: 'Minister, this is no place for kids'. When children end up in the sterile zone against the razor wire with tear gas and batons around them in Australia, it is time for all parties including the Commonwealth government to stop blaming others and to effect policy changes so that it can never happen again.

If religious citizens are to maintain a passion for law with justice, there is no substitute for being able to eyeball the victims as well as the government decision makers. Religious citizens should never presume that the public are less moral than themselves. There is a need to take into account that other citizens have plenty of other worries on their mind and they are easily influenced by the prevailing public and media mindset, which can be changed over time.

In the end, the government did apologise to the mother of the seven-year-old boy whose bruises I had seen after he had been hit with a baton and tear gas. Finally, government decided that a detention centre is no place for kids. We have even been treated to the theatrical scene of Amanda Vanstone donning the gloves and goggles to begin the removal of razor wire at Villawood Detention Centre. Phillip Adams from A Just Australia has observed, 'We've seen the campaign broaden from just the left and the churches, creating divisions in the government to achieve change. But there's no guarantee that if another group of asylum seekers headed our way, we wouldn't do it all again.'[9]

It took fifteen years of community agitation, including strong representations from the churches and a courageous stand by a mere handful of government backbenchers, to have government reverse the policy and law of mandatory detention for all asylum seekers who came to Australia without a visa. Back in February 2004, Andrew Bolt, reflecting on the ABC *Lateline* debate he had with me after the baton assault on the child, told the Sydney Institute:[10]

> Why was it . . . that so many Australians did not accept the truth of what people like Frank [Brennan] were arguing – that the Howard government, contrary to what it claimed, was in fact treating asylum seekers monstrously in our detention centres? Frank argued strongly that all we needed was more debate about asylum seekers, more leadership by politicians, and then Australians would swing around and see the shameful truth.
>
> [The debate] is manic. It's incessant . . . The public has heard as much of the argument about asylum seekers as it is ever going to listen to. We must now, surely, agree that the public has heard you, Frank, but simply disagrees in the main with you and your many supporters on this one.

Because many citizens hung in, in season and out of season, the public and the government did come to see the 'shameful truth' about children in detention. The government backbencher Bruce Baird echoed much of the community outrage at mandatory detention of children when he told Parliament during debate on the Migration Amendment (Detention Arrangements) Bill 2005:[11]

> I am sure that all members from both sides of this chamber would absolutely endorse this as fundamental. Let us never again see children in detention in this country. They should not be behind barbed wire or razor wire. It is an indictment that we have let it happen. Both sides of the House have been involved in that but we are changing this process through the bill. I really stress the importance of these changes.

Unlike Messrs Howard and Ruddock, Mr Baird and his fellow Coalition members who agitated for the policy change had the opportunity to visit detention centres and look the children in the eye. They visited all the detention centres. Mr Baird told Parliament that these visits were the most confronting he had ever undertaken. The law has now changed and children are no longer to be held in mandatory detention.

There was a broad coalition of community groups that contributed to this belated change of government policy. Church groups played a significant and responsible role. Church leaders not only issued statements but made regular visits to people in detention. Local church groups worked tirelessly with other community groups, visiting remote detention centres and assisting people on temporary protection visas. When the rights of a despised minority are being trampled by government implementing a popular policy driven by fear, religious citizens are well placed to contribute to social and political change because their motivations are not purely political and because they see the contemporary political issues in a broader, even transcendental perspective.

Citizens and groups with religious convictions should not be too quick to bow to pressure from the contemporary majority arguing that the minority with strong religious views are simply wanting to impose their will in an undemocratic way. The minority may be espousing a truth about rights and entitlements to which the majority is temporarily blind or in which they are uninterested. Pope Benedict XVI says:[12]

> The State must inevitably face the question of how justice can be achieved here and now. But this presupposes an even more radical question: what is justice? The problem is one of practical reason; but if reason is to be exercised properly, it must undergo constant purification, since it can never be completely free of the danger of a certain ethical blindness caused by the dazzling effect of power and special interests.

History provides good examples of those who held a minority position fearlessly, thereby helping to form a more coherent political morality for the majority and for the society. Deputy Prime Minister John Anderson highlighted this in his contribution to the 2002 debate on cloning and embryo experimentation. He urged attention be given to the views of religious persons and others espousing the humanity of embryos and recalled the contribution made by the Catholic Church in particular at the time of the Myall Creek Massacre, when most citizens in New South Wales opposed the prosecution of white settlers for the murder of Aborigines. He told Parliament:[13]

> Here in Australia we ought not to forget that for a long time there were those who saw the Indigenous people as less than human. Indeed, I recall the debate in this place about the matter of our regret for things that happened in the past and I raised the issue of the Myall Creek massacre, which happened in the northern part of my electorate around 1840. Seven stockmen were apprehended. They were charged with the murder of over 30 Aboriginal women and children. The trial was aborted because of the view, widely expressed in Sydney, that a white man should not suffer for harming a black man. They were somehow – and the language was used – less than human. There was a vigorous debate at the time, led by the Catholic Church, which demanded a retrial on the basis that this was an unsatisfactory drawing of the boundaries of humanity. As you know and as is now well recorded, there was a retrial. Seven men died for their part in those murders on the basis that those who had been murdered were entitled to a full recognition of their humanity.

The majority in any society can have a strong self-interest in drawing the boundaries of humanity to exclude the weak, vulnerable and powerless. At such times, citizens with religious convictions and religious organisations professing universal values have every right to espouse equal treatment for those who are different or unrepresented in the national political processes.

Concluding the mammoth 2002 debate on human cloning in the House of Representatives, Attorney-General Daryl Williams told the house that all members who had participated in the debate 'unanimously agreed that a ban on human cloning and other unacceptable practices is crucial'.[14] Stephen Smith, leading the debate for the ALP, replied: 'A ban on human cloning is sensible, is necessary and, on the basis of the debate both here and in the Senate, has the universal and unanimous support of the parliament'.[15]

Just three years later, the Lockhart committee of two lawyers and four medico-scientific experts with their own research interests recommended legislative changes which would permit human cloning, provided the cloned embryos are not permitted to thrive beyond fourteen days and are not permitted to be implanted in any womb. Anna Lavelle, chief executive of AusBiotech, immediately declared, 'After considerable research, consultation and reflection, the independent umpire has laid out his decision. It is time to accept it and move on.'[16] She was anxious to avoid a return to the intense parliamentary debate of 2002.

The so-called independent umpire made it clear from the outset of its deliberations that it had no brief 'to revisit the underpinning community debate and rationale for the legislation'.[17] Rather, its role was to review the legislation 'in the light of any changes in the scientific or community understanding or standards since 2002, and any indications that the provisions are no longer appropriate and/or practical in their application'.[18]

The committee conceded that 'it is not known at this stage whether embryonic or adult stem cell research will provide greater benefits [if any]'.[19] It acknowledged that in 2005, as in 2002, embryonic stem cell research was 'mainly confined to preclinical (animal) studies because the cells are not yet characterised well enough for use in clinical trials and there are significant risks (such as tumour formation)'.[20]

The review committee found that there was strong community division about the acceptability of therapeutic cloning. Those less worried about the status of the embryo favoured the creation of embryos for research and experimentation by means of somatic cell nuclear transfer. Having removed the nucleus from an egg in this procedure, scientists are then able to transfer the nucleus from a patient's cell into the egg. This process creates an embryo unsatisfactory for implantation and growth. Lavelle says the egg in this instance 'is used purely as an incubator for copying the patient's own cells'.[21] There could be no objection to the destruction of an incubator once it had performed its task. But there is no getting away from the fact that it is an embryo, regardless of the 'creator's' intention.

Everyone wants cures for terrible diseases. There is agreement that embryonic stem cell research has not yet borne any results in the cure of disease. The continuing community disagreement focuses on the same question as it did in 2002. What respect is owed to an embryo regardless of its age, regardless of its mode of creation, and regardless of its intended use? Some, including many scientists, think that an embryo should be accorded some special 'human' status only if it be created by the union of an egg and sperm, be more than fourteen days old, and be intended by its 'creators' for implantation in a womb. Others think that an embryo should be accorded special respect from the moment of creation regardless of means, intention or age.

Given that some excess embryos remain when a couple have completed an IVF program, lawmakers have given approval to the parents permitting experimentation on the excess embryos produced by assisted reproductive technology (ART). Does that mean that we do not have a special, universal respect for human embryos? The committee sided with those who view this exception as an open door for the creation, experimentation and destruction of human embryos. They argued: 'To permit one [production and destruction of ART embryos] but not the other [production and destruction of nuclear transfer and other bioengineered embryos] would be inconsistent and appear to attach more importance to the treatment of infertility than to the treatment of other diseases and conditions that could be helped as a result of this activity'.[22]

Back in 2002, some opposed any experimentation on excess embryos because this would mean a lack of respect for the individual embryo. Many, but not all, of these opponents had a religious perspective on the respect and dignity due to a human embryo. Others were prepared to permit experimentation, given that the embryos already existed and were destined to succumb with no chance of implantation and development. These embryos would not suffer pain and would not know the indignity to which they were subjected. The unwilling supporters of this legislative compromise permitting limited experimentation on embryos would never have countenanced such experimentation if this permission were to open the door to the deliberate creation of embryos for experimentation and destruction with no prospect or intention of implantation.

The moral argument now is the same as it was in 2002. Some would want to maintain respect for all embryos by banning experimentation in all cases. Failing a total ban, we can still show some respect for all embryos, not just treating them as a means to an end, by giving every embryo created an opportunity to be selected for implantation and growth to term. At the end of an IVF procedure, we then have the choice of letting the excess embryos succumb or permitting experimentation for the good of humanity. We abandon universal respect for embryos, and simply use them as a means to an end, when we create some embryos with no intention of giving them the opportunity to be selected for implantation, creating them with the sole purpose of experimentation and destruction.

Our politicians saw the validity of this moral distinction between means and ends in 2002. Some of us hope they will continue to see it. To date, there is not even hard scientific evidence of utilitarian benefits from embryo creation, experimentation and destruction to cloud that moral vision. In 2002, our elected politicians decided that we would not permit the creation of embryos unless they were created with the possibility of implantation in a womb. To create embryos with no intention of permitting implantation is to cross a moral Rubicon. It should not be crossed by politicians simply endorsing the report of an unelected committee whose mandate was to report on scientific and moral changes in the community. The Lockhart committee was not mandated to make moral changes or leaps. Respecting our own humanity, we need good grounds to follow their recommendation that some embryos be made less equal than others.

Senator Nick Minchin, a strong opponent of the destruction of embryos says:[23]

> My views on this issue do not stem from any deep-seated religious conviction. (For the record, I would continue to describe myself as a disillusioned Anglican.) But it is fundamentally wrong, and dangerous, to let stand the idea that the only people uneasy about the march of science in this area are motivated by religious belief. All humans, regardless of their faith, should hold human life as sacred – and a secular pluralist society should never leave the defence of its values to institutional religion.
>
> Frankly, in an era when the intervention of many mainstream religious institutions in public debate is just as likely to be based on the political views of some of their adherents as the core spiritual teachings of their faith, the contribution of many churches to public policy debate has been particularly unedifying. In this debate, however, I do find myself in lock step with many colleagues who hold strong religious beliefs.

The Lockhart Review received over a thousand submissions, many of which came from religious authorities. The Catholic submissions were fairly consistent in proposing a ban on any further experimentation with embryos and opposing any possibility of cloning, including somatic cell nuclear transfer. But the committee was able to quote some Anglican and Uniting church authorities who left the door open to further experimentation. According to the committee, 'differences of opinion were evident within every professional and social group that came to the table'.[24] Recommending a permissive regulatory regime allowing cloning and experimentation on embryos maturing up to fourteen days, the committee drew support from a leading Anglican ethicist, John Morgan, who distinguished between cellular life and early human life:[25]

> Almost up until 14 days with the beginning of the primitive streak we are justified in observation at least and careful observation and at the earliest stage before the cells have moved very far, we possibly are justified in carrying out work which may lead to their destruction.

Ross Carter represented the Bioethics Committee of the Uniting Church in Australia and told the committee:[26]

> There are different opinions within the Christian Church (and over time). Some people within the church think that implantation is the point of personhood – there is diversity in the church and the church's tradition.

No doubt those agitating to restrict human cloning and human embryo experimentation would have been in a stronger position before the committee if they could credibly have argued unanimity of position by the major Christian churches. Some churches do not dedicate the same resources and give the same priority to these issues as do the Catholics. That is no reason for the Catholic position to enjoy priority in the public forum. A government-appointed body is entitled to gauge the variety of religious perspectives on such questions. The final decision on where to draw the moral line should rest with elected politicians voting according to conscience and not with unelected medico-scientific specialists. In reaching their decision in good conscience, politicians should have regard to the coherence of the moral arguments offered, permitting experimentation and destruction of embryos only in circumstances where human embryos are created and then treated respectfully as ends and not means.

Where religious groups themselves are divided on the ethical perspectives on proposed laws and policies, they cannot expect elected politicians to favour a particular approach simply because it is preferred by the leaders of one religious grouping claiming superior ethical insights to their fellow believers. Catholic special pleading on stem cell research, same-sex marriage or abortion will count for less when other Christian groups countenance more flexible moral positions. Catholics could do well to spend more time in ethical dialogue with the leaders of other Christian denominations seeking agreed terms of engagement, rather than invoking Vatican declarations to impress government with the coherence of their arguments. All mainstream Christian churches need to devote more energy to enlisting the support of evangelical groups which often do not expend many resources on researching ethical questions. With the growing diversity of religious belief in Australia, Christian leaders would also be well served by enlisting cooperation with the leaders of the other major faith traditions. Bridging the gaps of ethical understanding between different religious groups, religious leaders might then be better positioned to explain their moral case to fellow citizens who profess no religious beliefs or who see no correlation between religious faith, law and public policy.

Religious groups would have more influence on laws and policies in a pluralist democracy like Australia if they could agree on a universal ethic. The German theologian, Hans Kung, has established the Global Ethic Foundation in Tübingen to follow up on the 'World's Religions Declaration Toward a Global Ethic'. This was adopted by a parliament of the world's religions attended by 6,500 people in Chicago in 1993. But there is little prospect of such agreement. Cardinal Walter Kasper, president of the Pontifical Council for Promoting Christian Unity, has a reputation for being one of the more liberal, open Catholic leaders in the Vatican. He says, 'The dividing lines which have unfortunately become evident on ethical issues since the latter half of the last century are therefore not secondary or irrelevant for an understanding of the nature of the church'. He laments that in Europe and North America, 'the changed situation is evident in a new polarization and fragmentation exemplified by divergent and even conflicting verdicts on ethical problems'.[27]

CHAPTER FIVE

THE IRAQ WAR STAND-OFF BETWEEN POLITICIANS AND RELIGIOUS LEADERS

Our government was a member of the Coalition of the Willing in the 2003 Iraq war, helping to oil the wheels of negotiation in Washington for the implementation of the free trade agreement. Our government was adamant that there was only one justifiable reason for our joining the coalition: the disarming of Iraq. Our prime minister told us repeatedly that we had no interest in the issue of regime change. Humanitarian relief for the Iraqi people became a public objective only once the initial conflict was over and when no weapons of mass destruction (WMD) were found.

A majority of John Howard's senior Cabinet ministers are Anglicans or Catholics. They wear religious affiliation on their sleeves more readily than did the senior ministers of the Hawke and Keating governments. Yet they have pursued policies on asylum seekers and the Iraq war contrary to the position adopted by most of their church leaders. When John Howard committed Australian troops to the Coalition of the Willing in Iraq, most church leaders were very critical of his decision. However, he said that he found the views of Archbishops Peter Jensen and George Pell together with the detailed public explanation of the Anglican military bishop Tom Frame more helpful. Since then, Frame has formally and publicly retracted his support for the government position. Neither archbishop issued a formal retraction, but in interviews they did clarify that they had not unequivocally supported Australia's involvement in the Iraq conflict. Their even-handed statements provided support for the prime minister, who was attempting to deflect the more unambiguous church criticisms in Australia, the United States, the United Kingdom, and in the Vatican.

In September 2002, the United States National Security Council published *The National Security Strategy of the United States of America* asserting:[1]

> The United States has long maintained the option of pre-emptive actions to counter a sufficient threat to our national security. The greater the threat, the greater is the risk of inaction – and the more compelling the case for taking anticipatory action to defend ourselves, even if uncertainty remains as to the time and place of the enemy's attack. To forestall or prevent such hostile acts by our adversaries, the United States will, if necessary, act pre-emptively.

The invasion of Iraq was consistent with the previously published neo-conservative agenda of Mr Bush's key advisers. Regime change in Iraq was a centrepiece of that agenda. In Australia, the Defence Intelligence Organisation (DIO) told our parliamentary inquiry into the intelligence operations preceding the 2003 war: 'We made a judgement here in Australia that the United States was committed to military action against Iraq. We had the view that that was, in a sense, independent of the intelligence assessment.'[2] When tabling the unanimous, all-party report on Australian intelligence services, the senior government member of the Parliamentary Joint Committee on ASIO, ASIS and DSD told Parliament of the committee's conclusion 'that there was unlikely to be large stocks of weapons of mass destruction, certainly none readily deployable'.[3] In other words, the Australian intelligence service was convinced at the time that we went to war that WMD were not a pressing concern for the US administration. The governments of the United States and Australia thought war was warranted even though Iraq was most unlikely to have any WMD and even though Iraq was no direct, immediate threat to the United States.

We Australians did not go to war because there was an imminent threat to our own security. We went to war because the Americans asked us to. The reasons the Americans asked us to go to war have become a movable feast in the public square. Before the war, Prime Minister Howard insisted: 'Our goal is disarmament'.[4] He was anxious to explain to Parliament 'the government's belief that the world community must deal decisively with Iraq; why Iraq's continued defiance of the United Nations and its possession of chemical and biological weapons and its pursuit of a nuclear capability poses a real and unacceptable threat to the stability and security of our world'.[5] Later the head of our Defence Intelligence Organisation told the parliamentary inquiry that this 'was not a judgement that DIO would have made'.[6] They just weren't asked.

Back on 11 February 2003, our prime minister had a round of meetings in Washington and received a briefing from Hans Blix, the executive director of the UN Monitoring, Verification and Inspection Commission (UNMOVIC). According to Blix, Howard 'agreed with the US administration's line of reasoning regarding Iraq. He listened kindly to my briefing and the hope I voiced for assurance of Iraqi disarmament through inspection, but appeared convinced that the Iraqis were cheating.'[7] A month later, on 14 March, Howard told our National Press Club: 'I couldn't justify on its own a military invasion of Iraq to change the regime. I've never advocated that.' The problem was that George W. Bush's advisers had, and that is what they got.

On 14 March 2003, John Howard explained in detail to the National Press Club the reasons for joining the Coalition of the Willing and going to war:

> We believe that it is very much in the national interest of Australia that Iraq have taken from her chemical and biological weapons and [be] denied the possibility of ever having nuclear weapons. Not only is it inherently dangerous for a country such as Iraq with its appalling track record to have these weapons but if Iraq is allowed to get away with it other rogue States will believe they can do the same because they will have seen a world effectively stand by and allow it to happen.

He then added, 'Of course our alliance with the United States is also a factor, unapologetically so'.

Even if the United Nations Security Council were not considered formally to be the competent, relevant authority for deciding just cause for war, it remains a suitable sieve for processing the conflicting claims in determining whether there is 'a real and unacceptable threat to the stability and security of our world' and whether or not war is the only realistic resort. The French and Germans would have a mixture of motives for their stand, just as the English and the Americans would have for theirs. Given the mix of motives, the elusiveness of truth, and the now admitted unreliability of the intelligence, it would be better in future to have decisions made by a community of disparate nations united only by a common concern for international security against terrorism, rather than a coalition of allies who either share or are neutral about the strategic objectives of the US administration.

Our politicians have a difficult call to make when assessing intelligence about the likelihood of weapons of mass destruction being developed and handed on to terrorist organisations that have no respect for western nations. In times of crisis, we need to trust our leaders. But it becomes more difficult to grant that trust when the rationale for war is changed after the event. The belated emphasis on the humanitarian concern for the Iraqi people was rank hypocrisy coming from the United States, which had first given Saddam Hussein his WMD capacity for countering Iran, and from an Australian government which had punished Iraqis who had the temerity to seek asylum within our borders. In Australia, trust in government would be better maintained if Mr Howard simply admitted that his public rationale for war was the honouring of the US alliance. Australian government ministers were not much interested in making their own independent assessment of the wisdom of seeking Iraqi regime change without UN endorsement. Nor were they much concerned about the shortcomings in the intelligence relating to readily deployable weapons of mass destruction. On these matters, the Australian government was happy to follow the assessments made by the Americans.

A post-World War II settlement of the UN Security Council configuration, including allocated seats enjoying a permanent veto, cannot be determinative of any moral assessment about war. However, when prudential assessments of threats have to be made on intelligence against a backdrop of continual breaches of solemn undertakings by a rogue state, the security council does provide a useful sieve for getting willing combatants over the threshold of their own self-interest and ideology to a publicly reasoned rationale for military engagement. If western democratic members of the security council cannot be convinced of the need for war, there are good grounds for citizens to suspect that the conditions for a just war have not been fulfilled. If such members voted for war, there would still be a need to scrutinise the conditions for a just war.

There was a surprising unanimity of views amongst church leaders opposing the Iraq invasion on the grounds that it did not comply with the just war criteria. On the eve of war, Bishop Gregory, the head of the US Catholic Bishops Conference said:[8]

> Our bishops' conference continues to question the moral legitimacy of any pre-emptive, unilateral use of military force to overthrow the government of Iraq. To permit pre-emptive or preventive uses of military force to overthrow threatening or hostile regimes would create deeply troubling moral and legal precedents. Based on the facts that are known, it is difficult to justify resort to war against Iraq, lacking clear and adequate evidence of an imminent attack of a grave nature or Iraq's involvement in the terrorist attacks of September 11. With the Holy See and many religious leaders throughout the world, we believe that resort to war would not meet the strict conditions in Catholic teaching for the use of military force.

As early as September 2002, the US bishops had told the president: 'We fear that resort to force, under these circumstances, would not meet the strict conditions in Catholic teaching for overriding the strong presumption against the use of military force. Of particular concern are the traditional just war criteria of just cause, right authority, probability of success, proportionality and noncombatant immunity.'[9] The US Catholic bishops maintained that view.

The suspected capacity to produce weapons of mass destruction is not itself just cause for an attack. Even if a state or a coalition of states is able to claim that it is the right authority to make a decision about war, that authority must be able to produce credible evidence about the possession of such weapons and the distinctive threat they pose to those states wanting to launch an attack. If you cannot convince the western democratic members of the UN Security Council that there is a real threat to world peace or a real and unacceptable threat to particular states, it is very likely that you are not engaged in war for a just cause. Even if the coalition of willing states be the appropriate authority, they still need to demonstrate that all other avenues have been tried to disarm the rogue state. As the coalition of willing states provided the incentive for renewed inspections by pre-deploying troops, the coalition was entitled to put a reasonable limit on the terms of pre-deployment or to demand that other states opposed to war provide assistance with the pre-deployment simply to maintain the pressure for verifiable inspections. Even if the United States had established that it was a competent authority to determine that there was a just cause for war which was a last resort, there would still have been a need to consider the consequences of such an engagement.

The nonchalance and belated show of humanitarian concern by the Coalition of the Willing after it had failed to uncover large stockpiles of weapons of mass destruction confirmed the suspicion that the coalition's leader, the United States, had an alternative agenda; namely, regime change in Iraq, an attempted re-ordering of the Middle East, and an experiment with a new American project premised on preventive intervention.

Those who oppose such ideological experiments in the future will do better if they are able to articulate more clearly the margin of appreciation afforded governments which are privy to sensitive intelligence material. Even if such opponents fail to agree on whether the UN Security Council is the competent authority to determine the legitimacy of war, they could agree that the security council is the most appropriate sieve for sorting the conflicting claims made by nation states which may be the appropriate authority. The UN Security Council is well qualified to sift out those claims of nation states based only on ideology or national self-interest.

The Coalition of the Willing's failure to find any weapons of mass destruction, and its inability without UN endorsement and Arab acceptance to impose secular democracy on factionalised Iraq, give us good grounds to return to the orthodox theory of just war, adapting the application of the criteria to the contemporary situation.

Washington-based George Weigel, who was the biographer of Pope John Paul II, claims: 'There is a world of difference between recognising the serious failures of US public diplomacy since 9/11 and a foreign policy approach that imagines the impossible [French and German support for deposing Saddam Hussein] and proposes the imprudent [waiting for French and German permission to do what needs to be done – whether that be in Iraq, Iran, North Korea, Darfur or wherever].'[10] There is also a world of difference between a real threat to world peace, dictating no option but war, and a claimed threat to world peace, being acknowledged neither by France and Germany nor by an overwhelming majority of the UN Security Council.

Catholics in particular should have some caution in backing their government on such issues when the Vatican continues to express strong reservations. All citizens need to review their trust in government in light of the fact that the United States was confident that weapons of mass destruction would be discovered, and then took almost two years to admit that none would be found. Admittedly not even Hans Blix knew whether or not the Iraqis had disposed of all their WMD. He was happy to adopt Donald Rumsfeld's line that 'the absence of evidence is not the evidence of absence'. Not even Hans Blix could guarantee that Iraq was without WMD. In his book, *Disarming Iraq*, Blix said:[11]

> Could it have been argued that this uncertainty was intolerable and required elimination by armed action? It could, but I think it is unlikely that such an argument would have been endorsed by the legislatures of the US and the UK, let alone the UN Security Council. Presumably it was an awareness of this circumstance that led the US and UK governments to claim certainty that the weapons existed.

According to Blix it was most probable 'that the governments were conscious that they were exaggerating the risks they saw in order to get the political support they would not otherwise have had'. Blix conceded:[12]

> It is understood and accepted that governments must simplify complex international matters in explaining them to the public in democratic states. However, they are not just vendors of merchandise but leaders from whom some integrity should be asked when they exercise their responsibility for war and peace in the world.

As we look back over the Iraq war, all of us must concede that it does not make a good case for the so-called doctrine of pre-emption. The religious leaders did well in spelling out the principles and directing the public to the relevant questions. In a modern democracy, government needs to package the issue simply. It has reached the stage that a civil servant like Paul Wolfowitz can admit that weapons of mass destruction were chosen as the 'bureaucratic' reason for the war.[13] Government always acts out of a plurality of motives, not the least of which is national interest. Since 11 September 2001, US bases have been removed from Saudi Arabia and are now established in Iraq. Strategists in Washington would not have disregarded concerns about future oil supplies. Following 11 September, the American people had good grounds to fear further terrorist attack.

A democratic government in such a situation rightly and understandably gives first priority to the safety and the fears of the population. If a government can engage in action which it thinks guarantees the safety of its citizens while placing at risk only those under a tyrant regime which has failed to guarantee the removal of the threat, it will so act. As we have now seen, it will earn further electoral support and legitimacy from the people.

It is one thing to advocate the role of the UN Security Council. But once further inspections were contingent on the United States doing the lions' share of maintaining an army camped beside Iraq, the United States had a prerogative for determining how long it was prepared to wait. Those urging further delay had an obligation to commit troops to maintain the pressure. These prudential and strategic questions are well beyond the competence of religious leaders. But these leaders are entitled to maintain the pressure on the decision makers, urging greater transparency and honesty in decision making, highlighting the national self-interest and ulterior strategic objectives in any such unilateral, pre-emptive strike. Given all that we now know, Hans Blix is surely right in asserting, 'The action taken against Iraq in 2003 did not strengthen the case for a right of pre-emptive action'.[14]

What place was there for the religious leaders and religious thought in the lead-up to the 2003 Iraq war and in the subsequent debate about the morality of the war? In the lead-up to the war, the church leadership in the United States, the United Kingdom and Australia was remarkably united in its criticism of the public rationale offered for war. However, there was a variety of views about the margin for error to be afforded to government. There was a variety of responses from church leaders here in Australia when the prime minister claimed some church support for his decision to join the Coalition of the Willing. When asked about the clear opposition from church leaders such as the archbishop of Canterbury, the Anglican John Howard told the National Press Club:[15]

> There is a variety of views being expressed. I think in sheer number of published views, there would have been more critical than supportive. I thought the articles that came from Archbishop Pell and Archbishop Jensen were both very thoughtful and balanced. I also read a very thoughtful piece from Bishop Tom Frame, who is the Anglican Bishop

> of the Australian Defence Forces. The greater volume of published views would have been critical, but I think there have been some very thoughtful other views and the ones I have mentioned, I certainly include in them.

Once the war commenced, Archbishop Jensen said, 'For my own part I remain unpersuaded that we ought to have committed our military forces, but I recognise the limitations of my judgment and the sincerity of those who differ'.[16]

In the month before the war, Bishop Frame had said: 'I am now inclined to believe a campaign against Iraq during the next few months involving Australian Defence Force personnel would be just'.[17] Three months after the war, Bishop Frame said: 'If it is established that the weapons did not exist and the Coalition did or should have known this, the war will not have been justified and must be deemed immoral. A case for war against Iraq based solely on "regime change" would have been inadequate and I would have been obliged to share this conclusion with those for whom I have a pastoral responsibility.'[18] On Palm Sunday 2004 Bishop Frame announced his 'considered conclusion that the war against Iraq was neither just nor necessary'. He said:[19]

> My conclusion is simply that the war cannot be reconciled with just war principles nor, in my judgement, are there grounds for claiming it was strategically necessary.
>
> One year on, it would appear that no-one now seriously entertains the prospect that WMDs will ever be found in Iraq.
>
> I do not agree with those who say it is still too early to make ethical judgements about the war itself. Perhaps it is too early for political and strategic assessments but there is sufficient data to allow ethical determinations to be made.
>
> As I look back on the events of the last twelve months I continue to seek God's forgiveness for my complicity in creating a world in which this sort of action was ever considered by anyone to be necessary. Even so, come Lord Jesus. Amen.

It is helpful to quote Bishop Frame at some length for three reasons. He was the clearest public advocate for war in the Australian church hierarchies before the war. He is a senior military chaplain who was himself an officer in the services before his ordination. Most significantly, as he now tells us:

> In the weeks leading up to the commencement of hostilities on 20 March 2003 I had direct dealings with the Prime Minister and senior ADF officers concerning public anxieties over the prospect of Australian involvement in a US-led campaign against Iraq. I wrote two articles for *The Australian* newspaper concerning the matter because I was asked by many ADF members to assess ethically the case for war as it was presented by the Government.

Speaking on ABC Radio National on 14 April 2004, Bishop Frame said in light of the absence of weapons of mass destruction and the absence of means or motive for Iraq to have been a threat to its neighbours: 'It would be impossible for me to say now that the war in Iraq was just . . . I could not and cannot take that view now and that's something that sits very uneasily with me but it's the way my conscience has driven me when I've considered what's at stake here.'

Then on 18 June 2004, he published an opinion piece in the *Age* acknowledging:

> As the only Anglican bishop to have publicly endorsed the Australian Government's case for war, I now concede that Iraq did not possess weapons of mass destruction. It did not pose a threat to either its nearer neighbours or the United States and its allies. It did not host or give material support to al-Qaeda or other terrorist groups.

Despite the prime minister's fudging of the issue, Cardinal Pell had never given any public indication that the war was justified. However, unlike Jensen, Pell did not make any clarifying statement once the war commenced. He left stand his earlier caveat, 'The public evidence is as yet insufficient to justify going to war, especially without the backing of the UN Security Council',[20] as well as the statement of the Australian Catholic Bishops' Conference to which he was a signatory:[21]

> With the Holy See and many bishops and religious leaders throughout the world, we believe that the strict conditions of Christian teaching for the use of military force against Iraq have not been met. In particular, we question the moral legitimacy of a pre-emptive strike. Indeed, any action against Iraq without broad international support and the mandate of the United Nations Security Council would be questionable.

The prime minister's statements and the cardinal's later silence left many Catholics confused. Presumably the prime minister drew solace from the cardinal's pre-war observation: 'Decisions about war belong to Caesar, not the church'. Though Caesar makes the decision, the Church must discern and comment on the morality of that decision. Church leaders must publicly help their people make the moral assessment. It is not good enough to suspend the moral faculty and simply trust the government of the day. If we do that with war, then why not with any other moral issue?

Cardinal Pell did not clarify his position following the prime minister's misrepresentation of his position in March 2003. On 19 May 2004, he made a return visit to country Victoria and told ABC Radio in Ballarat:

> I never publicly endorsed the second war in Iraq. I wrote publicly about it and I said at that stage the case was not established. They said they were going to Iraq basically on two grounds: that there were weapons of mass destruction there; and that Saddam was actively supporting Al Qaeda. Neither of those two grounds has been established . . . I didn't endorse the war.

Presumably the cardinal was acting with a good conscience when he decided not to correct the public misperception about his position at such a crucial time. It may have been more prudent for him to have issued a correction at the time. Given the good working relationship between the two men, the cardinal would have had the opportunity to express his view privately to the prime minister many times between March 2003 and May 2004. As the prime minister was taking time to meet with Bishop Frame back in March 2003, there would have been an opportunity for discussion between the cardinal and the prime minister when the prime minister, at least by implication, was invoking Cardinal Pell as one of three church leaders giving him greater room to move in joining the Coalition of the Willing with arguably just cause.

Though the prime minister purported to distinguish those views of church leaders that were 'thoughtful and balanced' from those that were critical, we can now appreciate how misleading it was for the prime minister to group the Pell and Jensen comments together with the Frame comments. At no time did Pell and Jensen give the war the tick. Frame did but has since retracted, obviously having good reason to revise what he was told by the prime minister and senior advisers before the war.

We are still in turbulent waters assessing what is a moral response to the new world situation in which the Americans have put us all on notice that there is one rule for the United States and one rule for the rest of the world. Imagine, for example, if India and Pakistan were free to engage in pre-emptive strikes.

After the Iraq debacle, it is essential that we return to a more critical application of just war theory. If the western democracies on the UN Security Council are not unanimous about the international threat to peace and security posed by a rogue state, it is unlikely that such a state poses an imminent threat warranting armed intervention.

Given the mistakes made before and after the Iraq intervention, it is proper for citizens motivated by religious beliefs to pose two questions: Why is it so unthinkable that we Australians should become a little more like the New Zealanders and Canadians, rather than surrendering our consciences and subscribing to armed intervention whenever requested by the Americans? Why don't all our religious leaders assist our thinking in this regard? Catholics might ask why the public stance of our bishops is not seen to be more in harmony with the conscience of the pope than with the conscience of our prime minister.

UN Secretary-General Kofi Annan is right to seek clearer guidelines for the future, setting down criteria for humanitarian intervention. We Australians can constructively contribute to such a discussion if we abandon our recently acquired taste for bagging the United Nations. The Vatican's contribution to such a dialogue needs to be strongly backed by the bishops' conferences of those countries that signed on for the Coalition of the Willing.

Seeking to reclaim the place of conscience in these debates, we all need to admit that it is very easy for us to be swayed more by our ideology and preconceptions than by a dispassionate moral assessment of the issue. I must confess that I don't always quote the pope with such vigour on all social questions that he addresses. But I think that goes for all Catholics. After the Iraq war, a conservative Catholic friend told me that he was to attend a seminar by Professor Neuhaus, who he described as 'President Bush's adviser on gay marriage'. I observed: 'Isn't he the same man that Bush dispatched to the Vatican to try and convince the Pope about the morality of the war? He failed dismally.' My friend agreed, but indicated that President Bush and Pope John Paul II had come much closer at their meeting. I asked, 'Who moved?' He said they both did. In his address to President Bush, John Paul II said: 'Your visit to Rome takes place at a moment of great concern for the continuing situation of grave unrest in the Middle East, both in Iraq and in the Holy Land. You are very familiar with the unequivocal position of the Holy See in this regard, expressed in numerous documents, through direct and indirect contacts, and in the many diplomatic efforts which have been made since you visited me in 2001 and 2002.'[22] No movement there! John Paul II's view remained quite entrenched: this war was wrong. The Coalition of the Willing acted immorally in violating the just war principles.

Church leaders who take on government when war is contemplated have to be ready for some rough treatment, even from those politicians who are their co-religionists. Archbishop Peter Carnley, who was primate of the Anglican Church in Australia during the Iraq war, is a case in point.

On 8 August 2002, Carnley wrote on behalf of the Anglican bishops of Australia to Prime Minister John Howard expressing concern with Australia's endorsement of the US first strike policy of pre-emption. On 12 October 2002, the first Bali bombings killed 202 people, including eighty-eight Australian tourists. Next day, Carnley issued a statement expressing his horror at these murderous attacks and announcing that all Anglican parishes 'would offer prayers for the victims, their friends and families, regardless of their nationality or faith'. He called on members of the Anglican community to offer whatever support they could at the local level. He concluded the statement: 'My prayers are with the families and friends of those who are victims of this atrocity'.

On 18 October 2002, he presented his annual address to the WA Synod of the Anglican Church. He told the synod:

> Most of us now believe that such a well planned and strategic placing of a bomb speaks clearly enough for itself. Retaliation against America's allies has been verbally threatened for some months.
>
> The targeting of a nightclub, which is known to have been popular with young Australians on holiday, suggests that this terrorist attack was aimed both at Australia, as one of the allies of the United States of America and, at the same time, at what is seen by militant Muslims to be the decadence of western culture.

Tanya Nolan from the ABC's *AM* program interviewed him after the synod address. She asked: 'So are you therefore criticising the Howard government's vocal support of American-led action?' Carnley replied:

> No, I'm not wanting to criticise the Howard government's support. I think we did think earlier on that we were unwisely supporting unilateral action by the United States in Iraq. I think we've moderated that position. If anything I think the Howard government is to be commended for backing away from that and for supporting UN inspections.

In light of his earlier letter objecting to Australia's endorsement of the US first strike policy, Nolan asked him if this policy could be connected with the bombing. He replied:

> No; I wouldn't say the Howard government brought the bomb attack on Australian people. I think it was our lot in fact to suffer because of our close association with America anyway. I think any government with an alliance with America would have been in the firing line.

These remarks upset the government and some of its supporters. They were convinced that there was no specific targeting of Australians, or if there had been it was only because of Australia's noble action of coming to the defence of the East Timorese. Carnley issued a detailed explanation of his position to newspapers on 29 October 2002. He wrote:

> Some of your correspondents are apparently content to contend that the bombing was a reprisal for Australian support of independence for East Timor, or even that the large number of Australians killed or injured can be explained simply as a kind of geographical accident: the proximity of Australia to Bali means that naturally there would be a good number of Australians there.
>
> For many of us, however, such an explanation of a well planned and deliberate targeting of a nightclub when it was common knowledge that large numbers of Australians would be present, seems both too narrowly focused and at the same time too shallow. The shadow side of human motivation to hatred is surely much more complex.
>
> We will be whistling in the dark if we do not take note of the actual reasons expressed by the terrorist network itself. Within recent weeks there have been explicit reported threats against America and its allies. For this reason alone, it is entirely understandable that a Newspoll conducted last week for a Sydney newspaper found that 69% of respondents believed our support for the US was a factor in the Bali attack.
>
> Islamic fundamentalist invective against western culture – whose

> global intrusiveness is resented and hated – has been long sustained. The addressing of hatred is a religious and not just a political matter. You cannot bomb away hatred. That is why Christian leaders have a responsibility to enter into dialogue with moderate and peaceable Islam and work actively to overcome the deep seated alienation that so clearly exists at present between East and West.
>
> It is not by denial, but in owning up to some of the harsh and difficult realities of our situation, and in grappling with them together, that we will be able to move forward. By this means we will give ourselves the understandings to marginalise – and eventually neutralise and eliminate – the destructive forces of suspicion and hatred that feed world terrorism.

No-one now seriously doubts what Carnley was saying back then. But at the time the government and its supporters were very testy. Australians were being targeted both because we are identified with the decadent west by militant Muslims and also because of our close relationship to the United States. There may also have been other factors, including our intervention in East Timor. We know from horrific experience that not only do Australians face the same level of threat as any other people subject to indiscriminate terrorist attack but also, as was the case in Bali in October 2002, Australians can be specific targets.

Though there was spirited debate and cabinet resignations in the United Kingdom because of Mr Blair's ready membership of the Coalition of the Willing, Canberra compliance with prime ministerial directives was complete in the lead-up to the Iraq conflict in March 2003. It was very troubling to hear the mixed messages from Prime Minister John Howard and Minister Tony Abbott about the increased risks of terrorism to Australian citizens just days before the Iraq war commenced. Abbott, the leader of the government in the House, told Parliament: 'There is the increased risk of terrorist attack here in Australia'.[23] Next day, the prime minister told us: 'We haven't received any intelligence in recent times suggesting that there should be an increase in the level of security or threat alert'.[24] Regardless of who was right, their contradictory statements provided incontrovertible evidence that there was insufficient debate, discussion and discernment within our Cabinet and political party processes prior to making a commitment to war in such novel political circumstances. The thinking was done in Washington. We signed on, presuming that our national interest and the international common good would be served by alliance compliance. In these circumstances, there is a place for church leaders to speak out. If they are misunderstood and they then punctiliously correct the public record as Carnley did, that should be acknowledged by our very sensitive political leaders.

Once the Iraq war was over, the government was arguing in the Senate for an expansion of ASIO's powers. Government Senator Santo Santoro told the Senate:[25]

> We know from horrific experience that not only do Australians face the same level of threat as any other people but also, as was the case in Bali in October last year, they are very specific targets.

What Santoro said was quite consistent with Carnley's position. There was no public castigation of Mr Santoro by any government minister. Foreign Minister Alexander Downer, himself an Anglican, then decided to launch a concerted attack on Peter Carnley. Delivering the Sir Thomas Playford Lecture on 27 August 2003, he commenced:[26]

> Let me begin with a personal anecdote. Listening to the ABC's AM on Saturday morning 19th October I was dumbfounded to hear the announcer Hamish Robertson say 'well, the head of the nation's Anglican Church says the Bali Bomb attack was an inevitable consequence of Australia's close alliance with the United States . . . Dr Peter Carnley says terrorists were responding to Australia's outspoken support for the United States and particularly its preparedness to take unilateral action against Iraq.'
>
> Here was the head of my own church, reported by the ABC as rushing to judgment and blaming the Australian Government for bombing incidents in which so many of our people were killed or terribly injured.

> Whether this report was fair or not, it struck me hard. There was no concentration on comforting the victims and their families, no binding up of the broken-hearted while a shocked nation mourned.
>
> Yet surely that first and foremost is what was needed and what we were entitled to expect. It was a stark reminder of the tendency of some church leaders to ignore their primary pastoral obligations in favour of hogging the limelight on complex political issues – and in this case a national tragedy – in ways which would have been inconceivable in the Playford era. This is something that has troubled me for some time.

What was the problem? Were community leaders like Carnley not permitted to speculate on why Australians are very specific targets? Or is that no role for reflective church leaders? There is always need for caution when you have a senior politician with a team of researchers and speech writers ten months later deciding not to quote directly what his victim said. Carnley had offered comfort to the victims. It was just that such an offer did not rate a mention on the ABC *AM* program. He had not said that terrorists were responding to Australia's support for the US first strike policy. He was very nuanced and considered in his responses to Nolan's questions.

Downer's office declined to correct the speech before it was later published as a chapter of a book. John Howard himself then joined the fray in a broad ranging interview with the *Adelaide Advertiser* on 16 February 2004. He focused on Carnley's post-Bali remarks and said:

> I think church leaders should speak out on moral issues but there is a problem with that justification being actively translated into sounding very partisan. I don't deny the right of any church leader to talk about anything. But I think, from the point of view of the unity of the church, it stresses and strains when the only time they hear from their leaders is when they are talking about issues that are bound to divide their congregations.
>
> I know something of the composition of church congregations. There

> are a range of political views and you can offend. Particularly [when] some of the church leaders have been particularly critical of our side of politics, they end up offending a large number of their patrons.
>
> They can say what they like but, equally, they have to understand that if they say things that are unreasonable, a lot of people are going to have a go back.

It later transpired that Carnley's remarks were perfectly consistent with the candid observation of Federal Police Commissioner Mick Keelty after the Madrid bombing, when he answered Jana Wendt's question 'Could this happen here?':[27]

> If this turns out to be Islamic extremists responsible for this bombing in Spain, it's more likely to be linked to the position that Spain and other allies took on issues such as Iraq. And I don't think anyone's been hiding the fact that we do believe that ultimately one day, whether it be in one month's time, one year's time, or ten years' time, something will happen.

Peter Carnley had cause to reflect on the Howard–Downer head-butting when he received an honorary doctorate at the Melbourne College of Theology:[28]

> It would be an odd kind of approach to a prophetic ministry to keep silent because of the fear of alienating those who might disagree. Our responsibility is to articulate truth, and theological and moral truth is decided by cogent argument, not by a democratic head count.
>
> Sometimes the cry that Church leaders should stick to pastoral and spiritual things and be mute on issues of a political nature [is] argued on the basis of the so-called separation of Church and State . . . The fact is, however, that the separation of the Church and State really means that no Christian denomination or religious tradition is given a privileged place in society: and people are free to worship as they choose, or not to worship at all, for no particular religious observance is required by the State. But the so-called separation of Church and State is often expounded as though

> it were intended to eliminate the Church from the State. Christians have as much right to express an opinion on moral and political matters as anybody else in a democratic society.
>
> In the face of this I think that theology, if it is to retain its integrity, quite simply must engage with the world and Church leaders must firmly resist any attempt to intimidate and silence them or push them into a kind of mamby pamby pietism.

All Australians, and not just Anglicans, were assisted by the expression of different, considered views on the morality of the Iraq war by Anglican bishops Carnley and Frame. Frame got his fingers burnt, being taken too closely into the confidences of government. Carnley was head-butted by government ministers for being so fearless and independent in the expression of his views.

Years later, we are still left wondering why we went to war in Iraq. It is essential that religious leaders state clearly the theological and moral principles about just war, in season and out of season. The novel US doctrine of pre-emption does not pass moral muster, and it was wrongly applied in the Iraq case. There was not sufficient threat to US national security to warrant the Iraq war. Neither was there sufficient threat to international security. If there had been, there would have been agreement to invade amongst the governments of democratic nation states at the UN Security Council. Conceding the need for specialist expertise to assess terrorist threats to use weapons of mass destruction, we are still well served by church leaders remaining resolute in their insistence that the conditions for a just war – including just cause, right authority, probability of success, proportionality and noncombatant immunity – be fulfilled. The questions raised by the US Catholic bishops in their letter to George W. Bush six months before the Iraq war were never satisfactorily answered by the US administration or its supporters in the United States and in Australia:[29]

> Is there clear and adequate evidence of a direct connection between Iraq and the attacks of September 11th or clear and adequate evidence of

> an imminent attack of a grave nature? Is it wise to dramatically expand traditional moral and legal limits on just cause to include preventive or pre-emptive uses of military force to overthrow threatening regimes or to deal with the proliferation of weapons of mass destruction? Should not a distinction be made between efforts to change unacceptable behaviour of a government and efforts to end that government's existence?

At times of war, nationalism and loyal support of troops often demand a judicious quelling of residual doubts about the morality of war. But the nation and its troops are well served by religious leaders who state plainly their moral assessment of a proposed conflict, conceding their lack of expertise and access to military intelligence. Church leaders struck dumb once war is declared fail their religious communities and the nation. In war, religion has a place, and not just in providing pastoral solicitude to the troops.

CHAPTER SIX

KEEPING POLITICS IN PLACE IN THE AUSTRALIAN COURTS

The ballot box is a good means for protecting the rights and enhancing the life prospects of the majority in any society. The members of entrenched and unpopular minorities often find little consolation at the ballot box. In a democracy, it is only the rule of law which can guarantee the protection of the fundamental rights and liberties of all, including the minority or the person who the majority would prefer to marginalise. When receiving no satisfaction from elected legislators, citizens need access to the courts to agitate their claims. The citizen's dispute with government or with other citizens may be intensely political but if the dispute relates to fundamental human rights, the courts need to be able to respond by applying the rule of law. Prime Minister John Howard continues to oppose a bill of rights in any form for Australia. He asserts:[1]

> The strength and vitality of Australian democracy rests on three great institutional pillars: our parliament with its tradition of robust debate; the rule of law upheld by an independent and admirably incorruptible judiciary; and a free and sceptical press of the sort that we politicians simply adore.

For the protection of unpopular minorities, I doubt that parliamentary debate and the mass media can be adequately complemented by a judiciary having one arm tied behind its back, having no power to scrutinise laws against a bill of rights. Often it is the mob instinct of the parliamentary majority and the press that colludes against the interests of the unpopular minority group.

I have previously opposed the introduction of a constitutional bill of rights for Australia. Conceding the shortfall for the protection of rights in our constitutional machinery, I suggested in *Legislating Liberty* that the shortfall could be made up in the long term with four modest additions to our constitutional arrangements: the passage of a statutory bill of rights similar to that in New Zealand; a constitutional amendment guaranteeing no discrimination against any person, so that we could permanently fetter the Commonwealth Parliament and government from discriminating against people on the basis of race, gender or sexual orientation; continued access to the First Optional Protocol of the International Covenant on Civil and Political Rights, which provides for equal protection and a ban on arbitrary interference with privacy; and a High Court open to the influence of international norms of human rights on statutory interpretation and development of the common law.[2]

In the short term I suggested the creation of a Senate committee for rights and freedoms, which could complement and incorporate the existing Scrutiny of Bills Committee, the Regulations and Ordinance Committee and the Legal and Constitutional Committee by implementing a Commonwealth charter of espoused rights and freedoms as 'a precursor to a statutory bill of rights'. I conceded that 'bipartisan intransigence by our federal politicians confronted with violations against unpopular, powerless minorities would remain a problem'. But, I suggested, 'That intransigence presents an even greater obstacle to a more entrenched proposal such as a statutory bill of rights or a constitutional bill of rights'.[3]

I suggested that we had two distinctive Australian safeguards against majoritarianism: a Senate in which the balance of power will be held by minor parties whose political niche, in part, is carved from the espousal of individual and minority rights; and a judiciary shaping the common law and interpreting statutes while responding to international developments in human rights jurisprudence.

So what has changed in eight years? Even before we come to consider the contemporary challenge of balancing civil liberties and national security in the wake of terrorist attacks off shore and threats on shore, we must acknowledge the profound changes that have occurred to our checks and balances. The government now controls the Senate. The government no longer takes any notice of procedures under the first optional protocol. The High Court has become isolated from other final courts of appeal. With the passage of the UK *Human Rights Act*, even the UK courts (like the courts in the United States, Canada, South Africa and New Zealand) now work within the template of a bill of rights when confronting new problems, seeking the balance between civil liberties and public security. The isolated High Court has found itself unable to interpret a statute so as to avoid the possibility of stateless asylum seekers spending their lives in detention without a court order or judicial supervision.

In this chapter I will consider the increasing irrelevance of the UN's first optional protocol procedure and Australia's judicial isolation, which combine to render Australians and others within our jurisdiction less protected than we were from violations of our fundamental human rights.

It is now very difficult credibly to defend the rulings of the UN Human Rights Committee, which deals with communications from individuals complaining that domestic laws infringe the International Covenant on Civil and Political Rights. When countries signed up to the first optional protocol procedure they were assured that the international committee would not deal with any case unless all domestic remedies had been exhausted. Article 2 of the protocol could not be clearer. It requires that complaints be brought only by those 'who have exhausted all available domestic remedies'. Over time, the committee has whittled down this barrier to their jurisdiction, determining cases when they think that the complainant would have had no chance of winning relief even if they had pursued all domestic remedies. The committee purports to have developed 'its jurisprudence to the effect that a remedy which had no chance of being successful could not count as such and did not need to be exhausted for the purposes of the optional protocol'.[4]

In a recent case where a minor was refused authorisation for an abortion, the committee observed that there was no domestic judicial remedy 'functioning with the speed and efficiency required to enable a woman to require the authorities to guarantee her right to a lawful abortion', and therefore the committee found itself able to act, despite the complainant's failure to exhaust domestic remedies, in part because 'her financial circumstances and those of her family prevented her from obtaining legal advice'.[5] Three years and nine months after the birth of the child, the committee gave a decision requiring the state to provide the woman with 'an effective remedy, including compensation' for the state's failure to protect the minor without discrimination, for its cruel and degrading punishment of the girl, and for its arbitrary and unlawful interference with her privacy. The committee saw no need to investigate the availability of domestic remedies for a complainant seeking damages for wrongful birth, rather than a court order authorising an abortion. Given the lengthy time taken for the UN Human Rights Committee to process a complaint, it would be even more hamstrung than the domestic courts in being able to provide authorisation for an abortion. If the woman were to be eligible for compensation for wrongful birth, she would still need to pursue a remedy through the domestic courts.

One member of the committee was even prepared to find that the state had interfered with the girl's right to life because 'it is not only taking a person's life that violates Article 6 of the Covenant but also placing a person's life in grave danger, as in this case'.[6] Not surprisingly international pro-choice groups hailed this decision as a great victory for their cause. But the fuzzy jurisprudence, broad sweeping findings in the absence of any submissions from the state, and the peremptory exercise of the committee's jurisdiction render the committee suspect for resolving acute human rights claims. Such sweeping findings are founded more on ideology than law. It is no wonder that the Howard government has seen fit in recent years to disregard the committee findings without any political fallout domestically or internationally.

Two months before the committee gave its decision in the notorious

Bakhtiyari case, ordering Australia to pay compensation for the long-term detention of the asylum seeking children, the committee had delivered its opinion in the case of Edward Young, an Australian who claimed to be the same-sex partner of a war veteran who had died of war caused injuries in circumstances that would entitle Young to a pension if he had been of the opposite sex to the veteran. The committee found in Young's favour and said he was entitled to a reconsideration of his pension application without discrimination based on his sex or sexual orientation, 'if necessary through an amendment of the law'.[7] Back in Australia, Young could have appealed to the Administrative Appeals Tribunal and then through the courts, but the committee said that 'domestic remedies need not be exhausted if they objectively have no prospect of success'.[8] The Australian government had argued that this was not an appropriate case for the committee to intervene because, regardless of Young's sexual orientation, he would not have been eligible for a pension because there was insufficient evidence that the veteran's death was 'war caused' and Young had failed to provide the government department with probative evidence of his long-term cohabitation with the veteran. In the government's view, even if Young were the opposite sex of the veteran, he would not have been eligible for a pension and therefore the committee had no jurisdiction. The Australian government saw this as a case where the committee was prepared gratuitously to provide an advisory opinion on Australian law, using the artifice of a complaint without merit, regardless of the complainant's gender.

When pressed to respond to the committee decision in Parliament, Danna Vale, the minister for Veterans' Affairs, was dismissive, observing that the 'views adopted by the Human Rights Committee are not binding on Australia in domestic or international law'. She told Parliament: 'The Government does not acknowledge that Australia has failed to comply with international law'.[9] Then on the same day that the prime minister announced legislation ensuring that marriage was restricted to opposite sex couples, he was asked to justify the discrimination against Mr Young, whose same-sex partner of thirty-eight years had served in Borneo during World War II. He did not seek to justify the refusal of a pension on the grounds that the death was not war caused or that there was no probative evidence of a long-term relationship. He acknowledged the discrimination and noted:[10]

> It has been the longstanding policy of governments of both persuasions to pay a veteran's affairs entitlement according to criteria which apply in relation to relationships in the rest of the community – namely, married or de facto relationships as commonly understood. It has not been the disposition of governments of both persuasions over the years to change that.

At a press conference outside Parliament House on the same day, Mr Howard announced that tax concessions on superannuation benefits at death would be extended to any person in an interdependent relationship 'including of course members of same sex relationships'.

By giving an advisory opinion in the Young case, the UN Human Rights Committee indicated to government that it was prepared to cut corners. The committee's deliberations could be publicly dismissed by government, which viewed them as more political than legal, and their findings more like policy recommendations than judicial determinations. Though there were incremental changes to Australian law and policy minimising discrimination against same-sex couples, the Human Rights Committee ruling was at best an irrelevance, confirming the government's view that the committee runs a political agenda.

Since Young's case, the committee has decided four refugee and immigration cases against the Australian government, all of which have been disregarded by the government and none of which has been pursued by the Opposition in Parliament. In 2005, the committee gave a decision impugning Australia's work for the dole scheme as a possible instance of 'forced or compulsory labour'. This decision is probably the final nail in the coffin of the committee's utility in contributing to law reform and policy change in Australia. No member of parliament has bothered to call government to account for its failure to respond to the committee's request that the government provide information within ninety days about the measures taken to give effect to the committee's views.

Bernadette Faure left school, aged 16, whereupon she 'continuously drew unemployment benefits'.[11] After work for the dole was introduced in 1997, Ms Faure was referred to an 'intensive assistance' program. Then, on three occasions, she was asked to report for interviews with Mission Australia. She failed to attend and provided no explanations. Eventually she completed an 'initial employment placement' for three months in 2001, having been in receipt of unemployment benefits for four years. She then commenced a second employment placement, but within a week absented herself for a day. Another week later, she absented herself for two days, claiming to be too ill to attend, but being unable to produce any medical certificate. Her unemployment benefits were then suspended for more than two months. She unsuccessfully sought an internal administrative review of this suspension but did not appeal to the Social Security Appeals Tribunal, the Administrative Appeals Tribunal or to the courts. She did lodge a complaint with the Human Rights and Equal Opportunity Commission, which was promptly dismissed.

All but one of the UN Human Rights Committee were untroubled by Ms Faure's failure to exhaust domestic remedies. They observed:[12]

> It would be futile to expect an author to bring judicial proceedings which would merely confirm the undisputed fact that the primary legislation in question, in this case the 1997 Act and the requirement of participation in the Work for the Dole program imposed pursuant to it, does in fact apply to her, when what is being challenged before the Committee is the substantive operation of that law, the content of which is not open to challenge before the domestic courts.

Ms Faure had particularly objected to a work requirement that she do concreting on a training building site. She emphasised the high degree of mental constraint on her resulting from the threat to suspend unemployment benefits, arguing that 'the prospective scenario of starvation cannot be reasonably construed otherwise'.[13] The community work coordinator for her project had advised that 'the concreting was minor, there were other young women involved and nobody was asked to do anything they were incapable of physically performing'.[14]

The committee decided that Ms Faure had not been subjected to forced or compulsory labour, but nonetheless the Australian government was still found to be in breach of article 2 of the covenant that provides:[15]

> Each State Party to the present Covenant undertakes to ensure that any person whose rights or freedoms as herein recognized are violated shall have an effective remedy, notwithstanding that the violation has been committed by persons acting in an official capacity.

Taking out the symbolic feather to slap the wrists of the Australian government, the committee ruled that the publication of its views 'on the merits of the claim constitutes sufficient remedy for the violation found. The State party is under an obligation to ensure that similar violations of the Covenant do not occur in the future.'[16] The committee remained convinced that complainants should be provided with a domestic remedy whereby they could 'challenge the substantive elements of the Work for the Dole program'. The committee was concerned that there was still no domestic remedy 'available to challenge the substantive scheme for those who are by law subject to it'.[17]

We have reached the stage that the UN Human Rights Committee is able to give such an expansive reading of the rights set down in the international covenant that there is no realistic prospect of a domestic remedy complying with the reading. So complainants are free to bypass domestic courts and tribunals where they would be required to adduce evidence and argue propositions of law. Before the Human Rights Committee they can immediately complain about the policy of the impugned domestic law and the committee can find that the nation state has failed to provide an appropriate venue for the hearing of such complaints, even if the committee in the end is not convinced that there has been a breach of any substantive rights contained in the international covenant.

The first optional protocol procedure is no substitute for a domestic law guaranteeing rights and providing domestic procedures in which both parties have the opportunity to be heard, and to have their case determined according to law informed by a coherent jurisprudence consistent with community values in striking the appropriate balance between right and duty, privilege and liability. The one dissenting voice on the Human Rights Committee in the Faure case highlighted the extent to which her fellow members have lost the plot. Ms Ruth Wedgwood observed:[18]

> In a world that is still replete with problems of caste, customary systems of peonage and indentured labour, forced labour in remote areas under conditions that often mimic slavery, and the disgrace of sexual trafficking in persons, it demeans the significance of the International Covenant on Civil and Political Rights to suppose that a reasonable work and training requirement for participation in national unemployment benefits in a modern welfare state could amount to 'forced or compulsory labour' within the meaning of Article 8(3)(a).

There is little that is value added in the contemporary communications of the UN Human Rights Committee. Their findings carry little domestic political or legal clout and that is not just because the government of the day had a heightened suspicion about the findings of UN human rights bodies. Unfortunately an Australian government of either political persuasion wanting to further a human rights agenda would find little assistance from the UN committee. The committee's reports no longer provide any political disincentive for government policies which work a continuing breach of human rights.

A week before Christmas 2004, Justice Michael Kirby was in the national capital receiving an honorary doctorate. Before his university audience, he recited a litany of Australia's shortcomings in human rights. He said:[19]

> In the past year more than half a million British assisted migrants (who enjoyed common nationality when they came to Australia in the 1960s and 1970s) were revealed as vulnerable to ministerial deportation. If

> such laws are valid, the courts must uphold them. Earlier, the High Court unanimously upheld a law providing for detention of children behind razor wire in remote parts of this continent. That law is unchanged although Parliament was thrice told that it is contrary to the international law of human rights.
>
> There were many other decisions of the High Court during the past year in which the Court was divided on matters of deep principle . . . [including] the right under federal law to hold a stateless person in detention indefinitely, despite the lack of any court order to punish him for any offence.
>
> The list goes on. Of course many Australians, perhaps most, do not care. But for me, I confess that it makes depressing reading. Most judges of our tradition – perhaps most lawyers – like to think that in Australia we are always working towards just laws and court decisions that uphold fundamental human rights. Alas, in many things in the law, we seem to fall short. And there is not much that the courts can do about it.

Though there is nothing novel in Kirby's protest against our national shortcomings in the protection of human rights, his note of despair is new. He now sits on a court whose decisions make 'depressing reading' for at least one of its members. What is more disturbing, he has concluded that 'there is not much that the courts can do about it'. Just a few hours before, on the other side of the globe, unknown to those in the Canberra graduation hall, the House of Lords was delivering its opinion in a case which was a damning condemnation of the Blair government's encroachment on civil liberties in the name of national security post-11 September.

Since the *Tampa* incident, Australia's treatment of asylum seekers arriving in Australia without visas has been a contentious political question played out in the courts as well as in Parliament and on the nation's airwaves. There has been little that the Australian courts have been able to do to contain the government's policy of mandatory detention for all those arriving in Australia without a visa. While the Australian courts were powerless to order the release of children from behind the razor wire, the law lords by a majority of eight to one were striking down a law which permitted the UK government to keep suspected international terrorists in detention. While Kirby sees himself as a lone voice on the High Court of Australia, he would have been very much at home amongst the majority of eight in the Lords.

While the majority of Australia's High Court authorised the long-term mandatory detention of a stateless Palestinian asylum seeker who was no security threat to the community, their colleagues on the House of Lords said such detention could not even be imposed on suspected international terrorists. The Lords followed the lead of the US Supreme Court which had already struck down mandatory detention of convicted foreigners who had served their prison terms and who could not be deported.

Their lordships were very unimpressed with the UK government's attempt to exclude the courts from any role by distinguishing between democratic institutions and the courts. The most senior law lord, Lord Bingham of Cornhill said: 'The Attorney General is fully entitled to insist on the proper limits of judicial authority, but he is wrong to stigmatise judicial decision making as in some way undemocratic'.[20] Meanwhile, Australian Attorney-General Philip Ruddock had made an art form of such stigmatisation while minister for Immigration.

Though the UK decision was shaped by a consideration of the interplay between the European Convention on Human Rights and Westminster's legislation, Lord Hoffmann was insistent: 'I would not like anyone to think that we are concerned with some special doctrine of European law. Freedom from arbitrary arrest and detention is a quintessentially British liberty, enjoyed by the inhabitants of this country when most of the population of Europe could be thrown into prison at the whim of their rulers.'[21] He had to concede that the judges would have been powerless to intervene in this case prior to the passage of the UK *Human Rights Act 1998*, which rendered their parliament's attempts to suspend habeas corpus or to introduce mandatory detention for people not convicted of criminal offences subject to judicial review.

A major chasm has opened between the decisions of Australia's High

Court, which has no bill of rights against which to assess national security legislation, and the UK House of Lords and the US Supreme Court, which do have bills of rights against which they can scrutinise parliament's overreach. Post-11 September, Australia's judicial isolation is now a problem. In the past, the shortfall in scrutiny of the excesses of executive government could be corrected in part by a Senate which the government did not control. That corrective disappeared in July 2005.

There was a time when Australian governments could also be reined in by the decisions and observations of international tribunals and UN bodies. But that corrective has also disappeared with the Howard government preferring Bush-style unilateralism. For example, in the case of the Bakhtiyari family who had spent more than two years in detention, the UN Human Rights Committee found: 'Whatever justification there may have been for an initial detention for the purposes of ascertaining identity and other issues, the State party has not, in the Committee's view, demonstrated that their detention was justified for such an extended period.'[22] The committee concluded that the continuation of immigration detention for Mrs Bakhtiyari and her children for such a length of time, without appropriate justification, was arbitrary and contrary to the International Covenant on Civil and Political Rights.

The Australian government simply disregarded the decision as the opinion of a group of foreign do-gooders imbued with human rights rhetoric and no appreciation of the unique problems Australia confronted in the post-11 September world. In so far as the Howard government had provided the Australian public with an explanation for prolonged mandatory detention of asylum seekers, Mr Ruddock, when minister for Immigration, never tired of putting the case in these terms:[23]

> Detention is not punitive nor meant as a deterrent. But it is essential that unauthorised arrivals are not allowed to enter the community until we are able to establish their identity and that they do not constitute a security and health risk.
>
> Detention ensures that they are available for processing any claims

> to remain in Australia and that importantly they are available for quick removal should they have no right to remain.
>
> The situation for people who overstay their visa is fundamentally different. We know who they are and have already assessed that they do not constitute a danger to the Australian community.
>
> Nobody is forced to remain in detention. Detainees can choose to leave detention by leaving Australia. They can go wherever they wish to any country where they have, or can obtain, the right to enter, and we will do our best to facilitate that.

This particular Ruddock rendition came from his 2001 address to the synod of his own Anglican Church. It was his preferred statement which was then packaged as part of a departmental information kit and sent to those sensitive Christians upset at the sight of children behind razor wire. In hindsight, we now know that this political explanation for the detention was dictated in part by constitutional doubts about mandatory detention in light of the High Court's 1992 decision about the detention of Cambodian boat people. The High Court as then constituted wanted to ensure that there were some limits on the power of government mandatorily to detain asylum seekers who had not been convicted of any criminal offence. Ruddock was anxious to clarify that detention was designed and finely tailored to assist with the processing of asylum claims by persons arriving in Australia without a visa, and to assist with the removal of those persons who no longer had claims pending or who no longer had authorisation to remain in Australia. He justified the discrimination of treatment between people with visas and those without visas by arguing that government had already had the opportunity to scrutinise visa holders before they arrived in Australia. But government anxious for the security and wellbeing of the Australian community was entitled to keep people without visas segregated from the community until there was the opportunity to determine that they were no threat to the community.

This explanation was starting to wear thin when families including children were kept in detention for years rather than months while their claims were disputed in the courts. What was the need for ongoing detention in remote places like Woomera, Curtin, Port Hedland and Baxter, once government knew that parents and their children were neither a health nor security risk? What was the need or justification for mandatory detention of failed asylum seekers where there was no immediate prospect of their safe return to Iraq, Iran or Afghanistan?

After the first Gulf war, there had also been a recurring problem with a trickle of Palestinians who were arriving in Australia on boats, with no way of getting back to the Gaza Strip. Especially problematic were those Palestinians who had lived for years in Kuwait. Given Saddam Hussein's support for the Palestinian cause, many of these people had to leave Kuwait and they were technically stateless. No nation on earth was obliged to take them and Israel was not willing to let them go to the Gaza Strip. Some of these Palestinians arrived in Australia without visas, without passports, without nationality and with nowhere to go. Once rejected as refugees, they then applied to the government to be removed from Australia. But there was no country willing to accept them. Were they to spend the rest of their lives in detention? Was there any realistic prospect that they would ever be released? Their situation highlighted the inaccuracy in Ruddock's particularistic explanation for the rationale of the broadly framed mandatory detention rule. These Palestinians were no longer awaiting the process of a claim. They had no real prospect of being removed. Government had more than enough time to assess that they were not health or security risks to the Australian community. So why keep them locked up? One of the Palestinian detainees, Mr Al-Kateb, appealed to the High Court.

In 1992, the High Court had no need to consider the situation of stateless people with nowhere to go when it was ruling on the detention of the Cambodian boat people. With a change in the composition of the High Court and with a change in political environment post-11 September, government was emboldened to submit to the High Court in November 2003 that the law permitting detention until a person was removed from Australia or until they were granted a visa could entail detention without end. The Commonwealth solicitor-general, David Bennett, QC, submitted that the legislative provision required detention 'until' a visa was issued or 'until' they could be removed. He told the court:[24]

> Now of course 'until' can involve a long wait. It can involve something continuing forever. We are all familiar with the expression 'until hell freezes over'. That is a use of the word 'until' meaning, in effect, forever, because it refers to an event which will never occur.

When some commentators expressed shock at this description in the media overnight, the solicitor-general returned to court the next day and explained:[25]

> The point of that example, of course, is merely to illustrate that the word 'until' can be used and is frequently used to describe something which may not have a termination point. There are, of course, many love songs, with which your Honours may or may not be familiar, in which the person singing the song proclaims that his love for a person will continue until a list of events which are obviously never going to occur.

By a slender majority of four to three, the High Court bought the argument. The majority of judges were convinced that the Parliament had power to make a law mandating detention of unauthorised arrivals, without the need for a court order or periodic court review, not only to assist with the processing of claims and with the pending removal of persons but also to keep them segregated from the Australian community. It is only lawmakers and judges from an island nation continent without land borders who could realistically implement a proposal for mandatory detention for all unauthorised arrivals for the entirety of their stay within a community. It is only a country without any bill of rights which could countenance such an outcome.

Justices in the majority were happy to loosen the constitutional constraints on mandatory detention imposed by executive government with approval from Parliament without any need for judicial supervision. Justice Callinan surmised, 'It may be the case that detention for the purpose of preventing aliens from entering the general community, working, or otherwise enjoying the benefits that Australian citizens enjoy is constitutionally acceptable'.[26] He was prepared to give government carte blanche:[27]

> It may be that legislation for detention to deter entry by persons without any valid claims to entry either as a punishment or a deterrent would be permissible, bearing in mind that a penalty imposed as a deterrent or as a disciplinary measure is not always to be regarded as punishment imposable only by a court. Deterrence may be an end in itself unrelated to a criminal sanction or a punishment.

Justice Hayne, who brought Justice Heydon along with him, could accept endless detention of a stateless person who had come without a visa because he viewed the segregation of such a person from the community as a legitimate government objective within the constitutional power of Parliament. Parliament had power to authorise executive government to exclude unauthorised arrivals from the Australian community 'by prevention of entry, by removal from Australia, *and* by segregation from the community by detention in the meantime'.[28] Hayne was adamant that such long-term segregation was not punitive. Having considered that government action to prevent a person reaching Australia would be viewed as punitive 'only in the most general sense', he held that: 'Segregating those who make landfall, without permission to do so, is not readily seen as bearing a substantially different character'. He did concede:[29]

> [As] Immigration Detention Centres are places of confinement having many, if not all, of the physical features and administrative arrangements commonly found in prisons, it is easy to equate confinement in such a place with punishment.

But quoting the Oxford academic H. L. A. Hart, Justice Hayne thought he succeeded in demonstrating that such detention was not really legal punishment. He explained away the risk that an individual would spend the rest of his or her life in prison without ever having been convicted of a criminal offence and with no term of imprisonment having been imposed by a court:[30]

> It is essential to confront the contention that, because the time at which detention will end cannot be predicted, its indefinite duration [even, so it is said, for the life of the detainee] is or will become punitive. The answer to that is simple but must be made. If that is the result, it comes about because the non-citizen came to or remained in this country without permission.

Don't come to Australia without permission. You might end up in prison for life! Chief Justice Gleeson was one of three dissenting judges in the case. The dissenting judges found this outcome an extraordinary proposition. Gleeson saw the case as a straightforward exercise in statutory interpretation: 'The Act does not in terms provide for a person to be kept in administrative detention permanently, or indefinitely'. He drew a simple distinction:[31]

> A scheme of mandatory detention, operating regardless of the personal characteristics of the detainee, when the detention is for a limited purpose, and of finite duration, is one thing. It may take on a different aspect when the detention is indefinite, and possibly for life.

He went on to conclude:[32]

> The Act does not say what is to happen if, through no fault of his own or of the authorities, [a person who arrived without a visa] cannot be removed. It does not, in its terms, deal with that possibility. The possibility that a person, regardless of personal circumstances, regardless of whether he or she is a danger to the community, and regardless of whether he or she might abscond, can be subjected to indefinite, and perhaps permanent, administrative detention is not one to be dealt with by implication.

The chief justice said that there was a choice between treating the detention as suspended or as indefinite. Given the legislative silence, Gleeson thought that he could have resort to a fundamental principle of interpretation that the courts do not impute a legislative intent to abrogate human rights and freedoms unless such an intention is clearly manifested by unambiguous language.

Where the three dissenting judges found ambiguity, Justice McHugh like the other members of the majority could find only clarity of language, tragedy of circumstance and ambiguity of moral propriety being visited upon Parliament and not upon the courts. None of the chief justice's close reasoning helped Justice McHugh, who conceded that the situation of the applicant was 'tragic'.[33] Even if it were impossible to remove a person from Australia, McHugh would permit Parliament to authorise government to keep a person in detention for the term of his or her natural life for the purpose of preventing entry into Australia or 'remaining in the Australian community'.[34] McHugh could find no constitutional restraint on Parliament legislating for the detention of unlawful non-citizens 'even when their deportation is not achievable' because detention even for life would be 'reasonably regarded as effectuating the purpose' of preventing such persons from entering or remaining in the Australian community.

The tragedy of this High Court decision is not just that there is no constitutional constraint on such paranoid and overreached legislation by Parliament. It is also that the court is lax in its interpretation of the meaning and application of such legislation, preferring the view that the legislation covers all cases of unauthorised arrivals, including cases that were unforeseen by the High Court itself in 1992. When mandatory detention was first introduced, neither Parliament nor the High Court envisaged instances in which people would be kept in detention for life. It was always assumed that people who had come without permission could end their detention by simply signing on the bottom line, requesting removal back home. In the 2004 decision, the High Court majority pointed out several times that the High Court judges in 1992 did not even advert to the possibility of lifelong detention. True, back then they did not, and neither did Parliament. By applying tried and tested canons of statutory construction, the High Court could have avoided the deprivation of liberty 'until hell freezes over'. It is one thing to justify short-term detention of someone because it was 'their own fault' that they came without permission. It is another to purport to justify detention for life because, through no fault of their own, there is nowhere else for them to go. Rather than waiting for hell to freeze over, the Howard government decided to release Mr Al-Kateb into the community on a bridging visa.

In Australia, the difference in treatment of asylum seekers entering Australia without visas and those entering with visas counts for nothing in determining the validity of legislation. The asylum seeker who arrives with a tourist visa or business visa is not taken into detention to assist with the processing of their claim. Neither are they taken into detention if their claim is rejected and there is no prospect of removing them to another place. There is no coherent rationale for the difference of treatment once you know the identity of the unauthorised arrival and know that they are neither a health nor a security risk.

The High Court's lack of armoury, given the absence of a bill of rights, and its laxity in the use of its limited armoury, are highlighted by a study of the 2004 House of Lords decision. While the High Court has been powerless to curtail the long-term detention of children who are asylum seekers and the detention for life of stateless asylum seekers, the House of Lords has been able to spike government's attempts to detain suspected international terrorists without charge. In the United Kingdom the difference in treatment between suspected international terrorists who could not be removed to another country and other suspected terrorists who could be removed or who were UK citizens remaining in the community was determinative.

Post-11 September, the UK parliament passed the *Anti-terrorism, Crime and Security Act 2001*. Suspected international terrorists living in the United Kingdom who were not UK citizens could be rounded up and deported. Those who were UK citizens could be taken into long-term detention only if they were charged with, and convicted of, offences. There were some suspected international terrorists who could not be removed to other countries because they faced the risk of torture or cruel and inhuman treatment on their return. Parliament legislated to allow open-ended detention of these people, without charge, in Belmarsh prison. They could apply to the Special Immigration Appeals Commission for bail, appealing against the government's certification of them as suspected international terrorists. Not even the availability of this bail procedure could save the legislation. The House of Lords maintained its traditional approach that detention was permissible 'only for such time as was reasonably necessary for the process of deportation to be carried out'.[35] If there was no reasonable prospect of deportation in the near future, the detention could not be justified.

Unlike the Australian High Court, the House of Lords is now equipped with a strong constitutional armoury in the *Human Rights Act 1998* (UK). This Act gives domestic effect to the European Convention of Human Rights, which extends the fundamental human right to liberty and security of any person not only to citizens, but to all people in the jurisdiction. Article 5 of the European convention specifies the cases in which people can be deprived of their liberty. The state can detain a person 'against whom action is being taken with a view to deportation'. Lord Hope of Craighead said: 'The article 5 right to liberty is a fundamental right which belongs to everyone who happens to be in this country, irrespective of his or her nationality or citizenship'.[36] Lord Bingham promptly put paid to any attempt to extend the power to detain to long-term detention even of a suspected international terrorist, let alone of a peace loving, stateless Palestinian who was not suspected of being a threat to anybody. He said:[37]

> There is no warrant for the long-term or indefinite detention of a non-UK national whom the Home Secretary wishes to remove. Such a person may be detained only during the process of deportation. Otherwise, the Convention is breached and the Convention rights of the detainee are violated.

Under the *Human Rights Act*, the UK government is able to derogate from the rights set out in the European convention when there is a public emergency threatening the life of the nation. The law lords were happy to pay deference to government in the making of such a derogation, noting that the home secretary had referred to secret evidence that the law lords were not invited to examine. The lords were prepared to give the government the benefit of the doubt, trusting their security assessments, despite what Lord Hoffmann described as 'the widespread scepticism which has attached to intelligence assessments since the fiasco over Iraqi weapons of mass destruction'.[38] But the lords were insistent that they still had their role to play as judges. When it came to long-term detention of a person already in the United Kingdom they had little sympathy for the government's reliance 'on the old-established rule that a sovereign state may control the entry of aliens into its territory and their expulsion from it'.[39] The lords reaffirmed that habeas corpus protection is not restricted to British subjects only because 'Every person in the jurisdiction enjoys equal protection of our laws'.[40] The lords insisted that any derogation of rights otherwise guaranteed under the European convention and international instruments such as the Convention on the Elimination of Racial Discrimination must 'go no further than is strictly required by the exigencies of the situation'.[41] Furthermore, the instrument of derogation did not excuse the government from the prohibition of discriminating 'on grounds of nationality or immigration status'.[42] On this basis, the House of Lords quashed the government's derogation order and declared that the law which permitted long-term detention of suspected international terrorists was incompatible with the European convention.

In reaching this conclusion, the lords referred to many parliamentary reports and reports of the UN Commission on Human Rights, as well as the Committee on the International Convention on the Elimination of all Forms of Racial Discrimination (CERD). Though such reports are not legally binding, the lords were still happy to quote them, noting that the findings were 'inimical to the submission that a state may lawfully discriminate against foreign nationals by detaining them but not nationals presenting the same threat in time of public emergency'.[43]

The lords went out of their way to pay due deference to the government, noting 'the heavy burden, resting on the elected government and not the judiciary, to protect the security of this country and all who live here'.[44]

But Parliament has charged the courts with their responsibility as well. According to Lord Nicholls of Birkenhead: 'The duty of the courts is to check that legislation and ministerial decisions do not overlook the human rights of persons adversely affected'.[45]

It was no answer for the government to claim that the foreigners in detention could choose to leave the United Kingdom at any time. The government had submitted that their prison has only three walls. The detainees could leave on request. Lord Nicholls said:[46]

> But this freedom is more theoretical than real. This is demonstrated by the continuing presence in Belmarsh of most of those detained. They prefer to stay in prison rather than face the prospect of ill treatment in any country willing to admit them.

Not even Michael Kirby could match Lord Hoffmann's declaration: 'The real threat to the life of the nation, in the sense of a people living in accordance with its traditional laws and political values, comes not from terrorism but from laws such as these. That is the true measure of what terrorism may achieve.'[47]

Baroness Hale of Richmond proclaimed, 'Belmarsh is not the British Guantanamo Bay'.[48] She made a declaration which is now unthinkable in Australian superior courts:[49]

> It is not for the executive to decide who should be locked up for any length of time, let alone indefinitely. Only the courts can do that and, except as a preliminary step before trial, only after the grounds for detaining someone have been proved. Executive detention is the antithesis of the right to liberty and security of person.

Some Australian lawyers might debate whether we have strayed far from our jurisprudential roots in this age of national isolationism, with our judges and the voters showing such great deference to politicians who tell us how we need to segregate those without visas from the community even if they are not a security risk. No-one can doubt that our judges are now cultivating a barren judicial field which is far removed from the English law lords' garden of guaranteed European rights and freedoms.

The US Supreme Court has also flexed its muscle against government wanting to detain individuals at home and abroad without court supervision. The cases, including the claim by Australia's own David Hicks, have related to very different legal questions from the Australian and UK cases.[50] But the judicial rhetoric of the US Supreme Court is resonant with much of what has been said by the House of Lords and by Michael Kirby. It finds no resonance in the judgments of the majority of Australia's High Court who think they are now bound to defer to government and to Parliament on basic human rights, despite the risks of unchecked executive power at this time of national and international uncertainty. The key swing voter on the US court as it was then constituted, Justice Sandra Day O'Connor, acknowledged that 'history and common sense teach us that an unchecked system of detention carries the potential to become a means for oppression and abuse of others'.[51] Because the US Constitution includes the bill of rights, there is a need for the US court to strike an appropriate constitutional balance between individual rights and national security. The present Australian High Court has been able to excuse itself from any such balancing exercise, interpreting Australian statutes as valid implementation of executive government's will to place national security at such a premium that people (including children) who constitute no security risk could be held in long-term, non-reviewable detention. In the United States, O'Connor observed: 'Striking the proper constitutional balance here is of great importance to the nation during this period of ongoing combat. But it is equally vital that our calculus not give short shrift to the values that this country holds dear . . . It is during our most challenging and uncertain moments that our nation's commitment to due process is most severely tested; and it is in those times that we must preserve our commitment at home to the principles for which we fight abroad.'[52]

When our High Court came to review the lawfulness of indeterminate detention for harmless stateless Palestinians, they distinguished a 2001 US Supreme Court decision in which the judges had placed limits on the indeterminate detention of foreigners who had actually been convicted of serious offences in the United States and who could not be removed from that country on the completion of their prison terms.[53] Justice McHugh acknowledged that the indefinite detention of an alien in the United States would be problematic, but that was because their constitution's due process clause applied to all persons in the United States, including aliens, whether their presence 'is lawful, unlawful, temporary or permanent'.[54] Justice Callinan noted with some relief that the US decision could be disregarded 'because of the absence of the complication of a constitutional provision in Australia such as the Fifth Amendment'.[55] Callinan also preferred the views of the dissenting judges in the US decision because their judgments contained 'more orthodox expressions of constitutional principle and practical reality'.[56] It is troubling that a Palestinian asylum seeker could legally be kept in lifetime detention in Australia without judicial intervention. Offsetting 'practical reality' and 'the complication of a constitutional provision' ought to bear greater fruit for individual liberty. Justice Hayne, who was the only other member of the High Court majority who wrote a substantive judgment, saw no need to refer to the 2001 US decision though he did refer to a dissenting judgment of Judge Learned Hand from 1952:[57]

> Think what one may of a statute . . . when passed by a society which professes to put its faith in freedom, a court has no warrant for refusing to enforce it. If that society chooses to flinch when its principles are put to the test, the courts are not set up to give it derring-do.

For their part, the dissenting judges in the High Court thought the 2001 US decision helpful. Kirby thought it 'highly relevant to the decision in this case', urging 'the approach that we should take is precisely the same'.[58] Justice Gummow thought it useful to follow the approach of the majority in the US decision, who affirmed that there runs through immigration law 'the distinction between an alien who has effected an entry into [the country] and one who has never entered'.[59]

It is only an isolated judiciary with a depleted armoury for the defence of human rights that can resign itself to possible lifetime detention of a stateless person with the observations of Justice Callinan:[60]

> This country has no greater obligation to receive stateless persons who cannot establish their entitlement to the status of refugee, than others who are not stateless . . . Whether statelessness calls for a different treatment, as it may well do for practical and humanitarian reasons, is a matter for the legislature and not for the courts. Nor should the appellant be accorded any special advantages because he has managed illegally to penetrate the borders of this country over those who have sought to, but have been stopped before they could do so.

Perhaps the only cure for Justice Kirby's depression is a bill of rights which would force our judges to take up the slack in a post-11 September world in which the government will control the Senate, while thumbing its nose at international conventions and determinations. But that would require popular support for such a constitutional or legislative initiative, putting Australia once more in touch with other jurisdictions including the United Kingdom, from whom we are now removed by a vast judicial chasm. At this time any informed Canberra observer knows that we will be waiting until hell freezes over. Meanwhile some High Court judges have no qualms about the prospect of a stateless Palestinian spending his life in detention in the Australian desert. After all, he came here without permission and it is not really punishment. In his journey from the bench to the academy, Michael Kirby warned: 'Law alone is not enough. Justice is the precious alchemy of Australian law'.[61] Now that the government parties control the Senate and there is no bill of rights to keep government in check, that alchemy is in even shorter supply in isolated Australia.

Days prior to his retirement from the High Court, Justice McHugh had cause to lament publicly the outcome in the *Al-Kateb* case. He told law students:[62]

> *Al-Kateb* highlights that, without a Bill of Rights, the need for the informed and impassioned to agitate the Parliament for legislative reform

> is heightened. While the power of the judicial arm of government to keep a check on government action that contravenes human rights is limited, the need for those with a legal education, like yourselves, to inform the political debate on issues concerning the legal protection of individual rights is paramount.

Conscientious police implementing the new anti-terrorism laws are sure to have a watchful eye for persons of Middle Eastern appearance, keeping close watch on mosques and other places where Muslims are likely to congregate. The risk of human rights violations against members of religious and ethnic minorities is heightened. The Australian safeguards against abuse are reduced, with concerned citizens being left dependent on political debate rather than judicial supervision of unwarranted target or stereotyped groups. The propensity for many in the Australian media gratuitously to identify persons as Muslim or Middle Eastern makes political debate an even less reliable safeguard, given the majority's comfort with increased police powers that are unlikely to affect them. Politicians seeking the right balance between individual liberty and community security will receive little guidance from the courts. The Australian courts are less relevant in the striking of the right balance than are the courts in the United States, Canada, the United Kingdom and New Zealand. While Justice McHugh puts his hope in the informed and impassioned citizens with legal training, Justice Kirby may be closer to the mark with his observation that perhaps most Australians just do not care. While trusting our politicians and our police, and placing faith in an informed, attentive citizenry, we also need to provide those whose civil liberties are most threatened in a heightened security environment with access to courts that can keep in check even unwitting excesses by the executive government.

CHAPTER SEVEN

KEEPING RELIGION IN PLACE IN THE AUSTRALIAN COURTS

Religious leaders have access to the media and are able to lobby politicians just like any other citizens. Occasionally in their lobbying they may be able to convince the politicians that they speak for a sizeable number of voters. In recent times, the Australian Catholic bishops have experimented with applications to be heard in the courts in litigation between other parties who are raising what the bishops regard as sensitive moral questions. Also, emotions have run high in some community sectors with claims that the religious affiliation of judges might affect the outcome of litigation in very controversial matters. We need to set appropriate limits on the intervention of religious authorities in litigation when those authorities are not themselves parties to the dispute. It would be objectionable if there were evidence that a judge's religious views resulted in a changed outcome to litigation, rendering the decision less just and less a decision made according to law. There could be no objection if judges' religious views fortified them and informed their reasoning in giving a decision which was just according to law. Religion needs to be kept in its place in the courts.

Musing on the relationship between rights and values, Chief Justice Murray Gleeson told his fellow Catholic lawyers in 2004: 'In the past, religion provided many of the common values by reference to which conflicts of rights or interest were resolved. Our law still reflects many Christian values.' He then reflected on the nature of a pluralist society:

> By definition, that means that there is competition, not only when it comes to applying values, but also in identifying values. Everybody is aware that our society is rights-conscious. A rights-conscious society must also be values-conscious. If it is not, then we have no way of identifying those interests that are rights, or of resolving conflicts between them. Rights cannot work without values.

When interviewed about this speech in a broad-ranging profile in 2006, Gleeson told the *Australian Financial Review*:

> I don't think judges should allow idiosyncratic values to influence their reasoning process. I can't think of any examples in which I have self-consciously applied my own values except insofar as they are reflected in . . . legal principles. But self analysis is a risky process. A judge's duty is to administer justice according to law and if you can't perform that task then you shouldn't be a judge.

In the United States, it is commonplace for interest groups, including religious groups, to submit *amicus curiae* (friend of the court) briefs to the Supreme Court in any controversy impinging on their world view. Supreme Court appointments are great political events, with senators and the media trawling the history of any candidate, including their religious affiliations. At the moment a majority of the Supreme Court is Catholic, heightening the concern by some groups that the judges' religious views may have an unwarranted impact on decisions relating to contested moral issues such as abortion and gay rights. In Australia, we have been spared much of this controversy, in part because we do not have a constitutional bill of rights that leaves the last word on moral controversies in the public square to the judges. There does seem to be a heightened suspicion of the High Court's resolution of conflicts relating to political and moral issues like land rights, abortion and gay rights when the majority of judges are classified as Catholic because of their family history and education.

Emulating their US confreres, the Australian Catholic bishops have adopted a strategy of seeking to put their perspective directly to courts when the judges are determining cases which relate to contested moral questions. On three occasions, the bishops have been given standing as *amicus curiae* to put their case in relation to the private litigation between two parties, neither of whom sought the intervention of the bishops. The bishops have argued that the litigation in each case would have an impact not only on the two parties to the dispute, but also on other persons in society including Catholics and Catholic institutions who might be adversely affected were the bishops' perspective of the moral good to be undermined by decision of the court. I will consider all three cases.

In the *Superclinics* case, a woman was claiming damages for the wrongful birth of her child on the basis that the doctor employed by Superclinics failed to detect her pregnancy in time for her to have a safe, legal abortion. Once her pregnancy was detected at nineteen weeks, her general practitioner advised that an abortion would be unsafe. The bishops were concerned that in such a case there would have been no grounds for a legal abortion because, in their opinion, the life and health of the mother were not in danger. In the New South Wales Court of Appeal, one of the judges was Michael Kirby, prior to his appointment to the High Court. Kirby delivered a judgment which gave a very broad reading of the circumstances in which an abortion would be permitted. In New South Wales, the criminal courts had allowed a doctor to plead the defence of necessity to a charge of having performed an unlawful abortion. The social and economic cost to the mother during the course of pregnancy was relevant to this defence of necessity. Justice Kirby thought it relevant to consider the cost and burden that the child would be to the woman throughout all the years of childhood, and not just during the course of the pregnancy. Having noted that earlier court decisions allowed 'a consideration of the economic demands on the pregnant woman and the social circumstances affecting her health when considering the necessity and proportionality of a termination', he went on to say, 'There seems to be no logical basis for limiting the honest and reasonable expectation of such danger to the mother's psychological health to the period of the currency of the pregnancy alone'.[3]

Given that there are many Catholic hospitals in Australia and many Catholic agencies, such as Centrecare, that provide counselling to pregnant women, the bishops were worried that: 'If the law in Australia recognises the existence of a cause of action arising out of the lost opportunity to provide an abortion, the law will imply the existence of a positive duty to advise every pregnant woman about the possibility of an abortion'.[4] The bishops were anxious because neither party to the litigation wanted to challenge the previous court decisions which had conceded the defence of necessity to any charge of performing an unlawful abortion. The matter had never been tested in the High Court. The bishops thought this would be a suitable test case to attempt to reverse these earlier decisions of the courts lower in the hierarchy.

The day after the bishops and the Australian Catholic Health Care Association had been given leave by the High Court to appear as *amicus curiae*, so too had the Abortion Providers' Federation of Australasia, wanting to argue the opposite position from the bishops. All these interveners were given permission only to make written submissions disputing the correctness of earlier, lower court decisions allowing a defence of necessity to the charge of performing an unlawful abortion. Neither of the parties to the litigation wanted to agitate that question. The Women's Electoral Lobby then decided that it would apply for standing, but before their application could be decided, the parties to the litigation announced that they had settled their case. The litigation concluded with Justice Kirby's expanded reading on the defence to abortion now standing as the most authoritative statement of the law in Australia.

No-one knows what would have happened if the bishops had stayed out of the litigation. Presumably the parties would have proceeded to judgment without reaching an earlier settlement. But no-one knows how the High Court would have treated the legal questions in the appeal. The bishops took a gamble. The settlement of the litigation was a worst case scenario for them, with the Kirby judgment left standing.

In the second case, Dr John McBain, a Victorian medical practitioner of IVF, had seen Lisa Meldrum as a patient who was anxious to have Dr

McBain provide IVF services to her by removing an ovum, fertilising it with a donor's sperm, and returning the embryo to her womb. Ms Meldrum was a single woman in her late thirties. She had been in several relationships but had never managed to conceive. The legal problem was that the Victorian *Infertility Treatment Act 1995* (Vic) restricted the availability of IVF to a woman who was either married and living with her husband on a genuine domestic basis or living with a man in a de facto relationship. Dr McBain commenced proceedings in the Federal Court to ascertain whether the Victorian law was contrary to the Commonwealth *Sex Discrimination Act*, which prohibited people from discriminating against others, on the basis of their marital status, in the delivery of services. Other states, including New South Wales, made IVF available to women regardless of their marital status.

In desperation, Ms Meldrum had made trips to Albury seeking IVF treatment, but Dr McBain was concerned that this travel was less than ideal for one in Ms Meldrum's situation. Because the litigation involved the constitutionality of a state law arguably in conflict with a valid Commonwealth law, the judge provided the usual notices to the respective governments, giving them the opportunity to appear in the proceedings. The Commonwealth made no appearance. There had been a change of government in Victoria and the new government had no desire to agitate the lawfulness of the Victorian law restricting single women from accessing IVF. The Catholic bishops considered seeking leave to be joined as a party to the proceedings but in the end sought to be heard only as *amicus curiae*. The judge gave them standing as there was no party to the proceedings wanting to argue the validity of the Victorian law. Justice Sundberg then ruled that the Victorian provision was in conflict with the Commonwealth's *Sex Discrimination Act*. The new Victorian government and Dr McBain were both happy with that decision and had no intention of appealing the matter. The bishops were not a party to the proceedings so they had no right of appeal. They then took the extraordinary and expensive step of applying directly to the High Court, seeking an order that the Federal Court had made an error of law.

The hearing took three days in the High Court, with numerous other intervenors. They included the Australian Family Association, which was anxious that IVF not be made available to lesbian women in Victoria, and the Women's Electoral Lobby and the Human Rights and Equal Opportunity Commission, who wanted IVF available to all women regardless of their marital status or sexual orientation. Meanwhile, the politics of the dispute had become very partisan, with the Howard government introducing legislation at the time of the federal ALP conference seeking to restrict the scope of the Commonwealth *Sex Discrimination Act* so that states could exclude its availability to women who were not married or living in a long-term heterosexual relationship. This time the bishops were going to extraordinary lengths seeking High Court intervention in a dispute which had been long settled between the parties. The bishops could hardly argue that the outcome of the legislation affected the way that Catholic hospitals conducted their facilities, given that Catholic institutions are not supposed to provide IVF to any women regardless of their marital status. The Vatican had issued a declaration in 1987, *Donum Vitae*, stipulating that all IVF was contrary to Catholic teaching. The Vatican declaration purports to rule out IVF, even for a married couple who use their own sperm and ova and who are guaranteed that no surplus embryos will be produced. The Congregation for the Doctrine of the Faith, headed by Cardinal Ratzinger, said:[5]

> Homologous IVF and embryo transfer is brought about outside the bodies of the couple through actions of third parties whose competence and technical activity determine the success of the procedure. Such fertilization entrusts the life and identity of the embryo into the power of doctors and biologists and establishes the domination of technology over the origin and destiny of the human person. Such a relationship of domination is in itself contrary to the dignity and equality that must be common to parents and children.

The bishops may well be opposed to all IVF. But is it right for them to take any opportunity offered to restrict it? They know they cannot ban all IVF throughout Australia. As a default position, they hoped they could ban it for single women in Victoria. There may be some instances of IVF that they find less acceptable than others. For example, they might be more accepting of IVF for married couples than for single persons. It might then be different if Victoria were the first state to contemplate extending IVF to single women. But given that it was available to single women who travelled across the border to Albury, there was no defensible rationale for seeking High Court intervention in a case which the parties had decided not to appeal. The bishops were no longer appearing as *amicus curiae* in continuing legal proceedings. This time they were trying to institute fresh legal proceedings so as to frustrate the outcome of earlier proceedings which related to parties with which they had no relationship. The bishops submitted to the High Court that the decision of the Federal Court permitted services to be provided to unmarried women that 'violate the most basic beliefs of Catholics about the dignity of marriage and family, and the rights of children'.[6]

The High Court unanimously dismissed this extraordinary application by the bishops. Such a course of action is unlikely to be tried again. Neither should it be. The legal dispute between the parties had been resolved. The Infertility Treatment Authority of Victoria, which had been a party to the original proceedings, had been advertising the availability of IVF services to single women once the Federal Court case was complete and there was no appeal by any of the parties. The bishops had tendered evidence to the High Court which suggested that several IVF procedures had now been performed on single women in Victoria. There was even a suggestion that Ms Meldrum had now received IVF services. If the High Court were to intervene in a case in which none of the parties had appealed after some of the parties had ordered their affairs consistent with the judgment of the Federal Court, it would cause massive disruption to the certainty of the legal processes. All doctors who had provided IVF services in good faith to single women would then have been liable for prosecution.

Given that IVF was already available legally to single women in Queensland, Tasmania and New South Wales, the bishops could not argue that the beliefs of Catholics would be further violated by an extension of the service to single women in Victoria. The formal teaching of the Catholic Church, as formulated by Cardinal Ratzinger's Congregation of the Faith, would deny IVF even to a married couple using their own gametes. There are many Australian Catholics who are unpersuaded by this teaching. It is one thing for the bishops to proclaim the formal teaching of the Church. It is another matter for the bishops to declare to a civil court that this practice 'violates the most basic beliefs of Catholics'. Most Australian Catholics probably see some case for the provision of IVF services. If the majority of Australian Catholics held the same strong moral views as the bishops on the issue, it is likely that IVF would be more tightly circumscribed by the laws passed in the Australian parliaments. Given that the bishops have failed to mobilise their church members in sufficient numbers to have their elected representatives restrict (or even ban completely) IVF, it is not proper for the bishops to use court processes claiming a violation of Catholic beliefs. Once such a matter reaches the courts, the bishops can speak only for themselves. They cannot purport to represent all Australians who happen to be Catholic.

The bishops' interest in this case could not be put as high as was their interest in *Superclinics*. In the Victorian case, the bishops were disputing the law relating to a service which is not supposed to be provided by Catholic health facilities and which they have no obligation to provide. In *Superclinics*, the bishops were concerned that they may be required by law to counsel the availability of abortion contrary to their religious beliefs. In this case, there could be no conceivable state interference with religious institutions requiring the delivery of services contrary to the religious beliefs of the owners of the facilities.

In the Victorian case, they had played out their role as *amicus curiae* in the original trial. Given that there was no appeal by the parties, they had no further role to play. Trying to agitate the matter afresh in the High Court, they were strangers who had no business interfering in the final curial resolution of the matter between the parties. The peculiar nature of the proceedings was highlighted by the application in the High Court by a citizen, Ms Purcell, who wanted to be heard. She told the full bench of the High Court:[7]

> Legislation should not be influenced more strongly by any one group or religion. Of course, the Catholic Church makes a fine contribution in all spheres of life, but it should not seek to domineer or hector people into believing things that they do not agree with. IVF practices are not illicit practices. They are gruelling, they are expensive and they have a low success rate, but they also have great potential for joy. They are becoming more widely available. Finally, just one controversial point, which, with respect to the Catholic Church, that they may consider, is that even with the immaculate conception of the Virgin Mary, she was unmarried. Is that an illicit practice?

When the High Court unanimously dismissed the bishops' application, the Chief Justice Murray Gleeson observed:[8]

> People who were not parties to litigation do not have a claim of right to have judicial decisions quashed because they are erroneous. Suppose, for example, a taxpayer became involved in litigation against the revenue authorities, in the Federal Court, and the litigation raised a question as to the interpretation of a certain provision of the Act, under which tax is assessed. That question might affect many other taxpayers as well. Suppose a Federal Court judge answers the question adversely to the taxpayer, who accepts the decision and does not appeal. It does not follow that some other taxpayer, affected by the same issue, could have the decision quashed. The second taxpayer's adverse opinion of the correctness of the judge's reasoning does not give rise to a justiciable issue between the second taxpayer and the judge; and the judge has made no determination of the second taxpayer's rights, even though, in a precedential sense, the decision may affect the assertion of those rights.

The Catholic bishops successfully fought off the belated application of the Women's Electoral Lobby to have the bishops pay their costs of $216,000. Presumably, the bishops' costs were much greater as they had been in the litigation from the beginning and in the High Court they retained one of Australia's most eminent counsel. How do church leaders come to expend so much money on such a lost cause? And on a case that is likely to heighten animosity towards a church which is suspected of having an agenda running against people anxious to bear children outside of regular marriage relationships? It was particularly unfortunate that in this case one of the other intervenors sharing the bishops' perspective on the litigation had mistakenly submitted materials to the full bench of the High Court which were very demeaning of homosexuals. From the bench, Justice McHugh said this material 'seemed to be an irrelevant and gratuitous attack on homosexuals, which had no bearing whatever on the issues'.[9] Counsel for the Australian Family Association, not having read the papers, withdrew them, pointing out that they had been included by mistake.

The third case of intervention by religious leaders, *BWV*, related to a woman who was diagnosed with Pick's Disease in 1994. Five years later, she was confined to a nursing home. After three years in the nursing home, and at the age of sixty-eight, she was in an advanced state of dementia, in the terminal stage of her disease, with no cognitive capacity, unable to communicate. There was no prospect of improvement or recovery. She had been receiving hydration and nutrition through a PEG (percutaneous endoscopic gastrostomy) for at least five years by this time. Her husband and six children were all agreed that they did not want her life prolonged unnecessarily. They thought the time had come to withdraw the PEG, so they consulted the Public Advocate. The husband applied to the Victorian Civil and Administrative Tribunal requesting to be appointed guardian so that he might direct the termination of all medical treatment in accordance with the wishes of his wife. He was confident he could state his wife's wishes, having recalled conversations between them when she was well and able to communicate. The Public Advocate appeared in the proceedings and supported the application. The Right to Life Association appeared and opposed the application.

The Victorian *Medical Treatment Act 1988* distinguished between palliative care and medical treatment. Only medical treatment could be withdrawn at the request of a patient or their guardian. Palliative care was always to be provided. Palliative care was defined to include:

> (a) The provision of reasonable medical procedures for the relief of pain, suffering and discomfort; or
> (b) the reasonable provision of food and water.

Was the provision of hydration and nutrition through a PEG to be classified as palliative care or medical treatment? In 1990, the Supreme Court of the United States had considered the matter in *Cruzan* v *Director, Missouri Department of Health.*[10] Chief Justice Rehnquist decided that feeding by implanted tubes was 'a medical procedure with inherent risks and possible side effects, instituted by skilled healthcare providers to compensate for impaired physical functioning which analytically was equivalent to artificial breathing using a respirator'.[11] Then in 1993, the House of Lords considered the matter in *Airedale National Health Service Trust* v *Bland.*[12] Lord Keith of Kinkel stated:[13]

> I am of the opinion that regard should be had to the whole regime, including the artificial feeding, which at present keeps [the patient] alive. That regime amounts to medical treatment and care, and it is incorrect to direct attention exclusively to the fact that nourishment is being provided. In any event, the administration of nourishment by the means adopted involves the application of a medical technique.

Lord Goff of Chieveley stated:[14]

> There is overwhelming evidence that, in the medical profession, artificial feeding is regarded as a form of medical treatment; and even if it is not strictly medical treatment, it must form part of the medical care of the patient.

Lord Lowry said:[15]

> The overwhelming verdict of informed medical opinion worldwide, with particular reference to the common law jurisdictions, where the relevant

> law generally corresponds closely with our own, that therapy and life-supporting care, including sophisticated methods of artificial feeding, are components of medical treatment . . . In this connection it may also be emphasised that an artificial feeding regime is inevitably associated with the continuous use of catheters and enemas and the sedulous avoidance and combating of potentially deadly infection.

The tribunal decided that there was near unanimity in the medical profession and in the international jurisprudence that the artificial provision of food and water was a medical procedure. It further accepted the submission of the Public Advocate that 'the provision of food and water cannot be said to be reasonable when it is provided to a person who is dying, not for the primary purpose of palliation, but with the aim of deferring or suspending the process of dying'.[16] The tribunal thought the husband would be an appropriate guardian but as an added precaution for the best interests of the patient decided to appoint the Public Advocate as sole guardian with the understanding that he could direct the withdrawal of the PEG consistent with the family's wishes and consistent with what the husband understood to be his wife's wishes.

Out of abundant caution the Public Advocate then sought a declaration from the Victorian Supreme Court that refusal of further nutrition and hydration administered via a PEG would constitute refusal of 'medical treatment', rather than refusal of 'palliative care'. This time the Right to Life Association was joined by the Catholic archbishop of Melbourne, Denis Hart, and Catholic Health Australia Incorporated wanting to be heard as *amici curiae*. Justice Morris concluded:[17]

> Unquestionably in my judgment, the use of a PEG for artificial nutrition and hydration, or for that matter any form of artificial feeding, is a 'medical' procedure. Artificial nutrition and hydration involves protocols, skills and care which draw from, and depend upon, medical knowledge. Artificial nutrition and hydration will inevitably require careful choice of and preparation of materials to be introduced into the body, close

> consideration to dosage rates, measures to prevent infection and regular cleaning of conduits. These are not matters of common knowledge.

Justice Morris thought he did not need to consider whether the provision of food and water in these circumstances was reasonable because Parliament had intended the 'provision of food and water' under the heading of palliative care to be confined to 'the ordinary, non-medical provision of food and water'.[18] The Public Advocate then authorised the withdrawal of the PEG and the woman died within the month.

In March 2004, Pope John Paul II declared to a specially convened Vatican international congress on 'Life-Sustaining Treatments and Vegetative State: Scientific Advances and Ethical Dilemmas':[19]

> I should like particularly to underline how the administration of water and food, even when provided by artificial means, always represents a *natural means* of preserving life, not a *medical act*. Its use, furthermore, should be considered, in principle, *ordinary* and *proportionate*, and as such morally obligatory, insofar as and until it is seen to have attained its proper finality, which in the present case consists in providing nourishment to the patient and alleviation of his suffering.

This declaration of the pope is contrary to the statements by the House of Lords and the US Supreme Court as well as the ruling by the Victorian Supreme Court. Though bishops in future may be expected to seek intervention in court proceedings urging that the artificial provision of hydration and nutrition can never be a medical act, they cannot expect much success. The courts are not going to look to a religious authority in settling questions of statutory construction, especially when the terms used in the legislation are well familiar to the courts and to medical experts, who generally agree that the characterisation of a medical act depends more on the procedures used than on the materials introduced to the body by means of the procedure. Food, water and air may be ordinary daily things. But there are circumstances in which they can be delivered to the body only by means that are anything but natural and in circumstances which might be properly categorised as burdensome or extraordinary.

Some theologians have even argued that the pope was trying to force a new development of Catholic doctrine because in the past, the use of a PEG was viewed by many moral theologians as medical treatment. The ordinariness or proportionality of its use would depend on the circumstances of the patient. It is appropriate for the church authorities to direct their own health facilities to view feeding and hydrating as 'a kind of basic caring which should be given unless there are very strong reasons against it in a particular case'. Bishop Anthony Fisher describes it as a simple case of always providing care even when we cannot cure.[20] But where parliaments have passed laws after protracted inquiries and conscientious voting on clauses distinguishing medical treatment from palliative care, there is little point in the bishops continuing to trouble courts with their distinctive view that the provision of food and water is never a medical act. Even within the hierarchy of the Catholic Church there is no agreement on the late Pope John Paul II's formulation of the issue.

For example, the US Bishops Conference issued their *Ethical and Religious Directives for Catholic Health Care Services* in 1995. These directives provide:[21]

> There should be a presumption in favour of providing nutrition and hydration to all patients, including patients who require medically assisted nutrition and hydration, as long as this is of sufficient benefit to outweigh the burdens involved to the patient.

These directives were painstakingly worked out over a six-year period. The bishops had only one query when they came to vote on this particular directive. They wanted to be assured that it left open the question of hydration and nutrition because there had been a variety of approaches in different dioceses of the United States. Being assured that this directive did leave open the question, the bishops voted unanimously to endorse the document. Relying on this directive, many US bishops and theologians were satisfied with the moral propriety of withdrawing Terri Schiavo from life support in 2005 on the directive of her guardian, regardless of the personal animosity that had developed between her husband as guardian and her parents, who wanted to see her live at any cost.

The Australian bishops and Catholic Health Australia had also issued their own guidelines before John Paul II's statement. After his statement they issued a 'Briefing Note on the Obligation to Provide Nutrition and Hydration'. It notes:[22]

> While the act of feeding a person is not itself a medical act, the insertion of a tube, monitoring of the tube and patient, and prescription of the substances to be provided, do involve a degree of medical and/or nursing expertise. To insert a feeding tube is a medical decision subject to the normal criteria for medical intervention.

No ongoing medical intervention is morally obligatory if it is therapeutically useless or an undue burden on the patient, family or healthcare workers.

In all three of these court cases, the religious authorities have been spectacularly unsuccessful in achieving their objective. There are some lessons to learn. In the Australian tradition, it is usually best to leave litigation to the parties. There are cases in which the court might be helped by the intervention of a citizen or a group who have a distinctive perspective to add to the law in dispute between the parties. Courts can be expected to treat all such intervenors equally regardless of their religious motivations or religious perspectives on the issues in dispute. The submission of *amicus curiae* briefs in the litigation process is no alternative to the parry and thrust of parliamentary debate and public discussion about religious and moral issues. It does not provide a back door through which religious advocates are likely to achieve their policy objectives, having failed in Parliament or in the public forum.

If a religious group does get leave from the court to appear as *amicus curiae* in a controversial matter, other community groups opposed to the religious perspective are likely to be just as well resourced and anxious to intervene, putting the contrary argument. In *Superclinics*, the bishops were anxious to put their interpretation on earlier lower court decisions about abortion. The Abortion Providers and the Women's Electoral Lobby were just as anxious to offer their interpretation. If there had been a need for the High Court to consider these lower court precedents in reaching their decision, they would have considered the differing interpretations of those decisions regardless of what the parties to the dispute submitted. The effect of the bishops' intervention may simply have been a beacon call to the pro-abortion groups with the result that the parties preferred to settle out of court rather than risk a political showdown on the issue of abortion. Justice Kirby's expanded reading of the social and economic factors to be considered when the defence of necessity was raised would have been considered by the High Court had the appeal run its course, because this expanded reading was directly relevant to the disputed question of damages. There was a slight chance that the majority of the High Court would have agreed with Kirby's expanded reading of the defence of necessity. It was more likely that the majority would not have extended the defence beyond the earlier judicial formulations.

While it is proper, acceptable and sometimes useful for religious groups to seek leave to appear as *amicus curiae*, it is neither proper, acceptable nor useful for them to seek, as the bishops did in the McBain litigation, to institute proceedings in the High Court after the parties to the dispute have concluded their litigation and decided not to appeal. It may be regrettable that a newly elected government decides not to pursue compliance with legislation presented to Parliament by an earlier government of another political complexion. It is a dangerous strategy for religious authorities to seek to fill that gap, especially when they want to agitate for a legal restriction which does not apply in other jurisdictions. If IVF had been restricted to married women in all Australian jurisdictions, there may have been a case for the bishops wanting to stop the extension of IVF to single women by government default in one state while that state's laws still maintained the restriction. But that was not the case here.

It is very unhelpful for the courts to be told that the religious authorities are participating in litigation so as to uphold the teaching of their church, when everyone knows that there are many members of that church who have little interest in or commitment to that particular teaching. The Vatican's official ban on IVF is so comprehensive that it is seriously disputed by many moral theologians within the Catholic Church, and there are many Catholic couples who have sought access to IVF despite the declaration of the Congregation for the Doctrine of the Faith.

Courts have to resolve legal disputes usually by interpreting statutes or developing and applying the common law. Neither of these tasks is assisted by religious interpretations of the particular statute or common law rule. In future, courts in jurisdictions other than Victoria may still need to determine if the provision of artificial hydration and nutrition is a medical act or not. No court will be assisted by the late Pope John Paul's declaration that the provision of food and water can never be classified as a medical act. The courts will be guided by the approach of other courts, including the House of Lords and the US Supreme Court, now joined by a single judge decision of the Supreme Court of Victoria.

The Catholic bishops had a credible reason for wanting a ruling in *Superclinics* – a ruling that Catholic hospitals and counselling services would not be required to advise a woman about the availability of abortion in any circumstances when she would face future economic and social pressures during the life of the child prior to adulthood. It would be unbearable for Catholic institutions to risk an award of damages for wrongful birth simply because they failed to advise the availability of abortion as an option. But there was no similar problem confronting them with the conduct of their institutions in the provision of IVF services. Under Vatican teaching they are not supposed to provide such services to any women, whether they are married or single, heterosexual or lesbian. There was also no real problem confronting them with the feeding tube case. If a guardian sought to remove a PEG from a patient in a Catholic institution, contrary to the teaching of the Church, the Catholic institution would be required to release the patient at the request of the guardian to another institution where the PEG could be removed.

It is one thing for religious authorities to want legal clarity about their entitlements to conduct their own institutions in accordance with their religious beliefs. It is quite another for religious authorities to seek to use other people's legal disputes to further the proclamation of their religious insights contrary to popular opinion in the community.

The religious claims of religious authorities are unlikely to assist judges in the resolution of legal disputes, even if those judges are members of the particular religious group. Given that most disputes relate to the interpretation of statutes or the development and application of the common law, judges may take into account the contemporary values of the community in choosing which ambiguous meaning of a statute to adopt or in developing the common law where there is a lacuna. This is what the High Court did in *Mabo*. There has been much misinformed commentary from the Right about the Catholic perspectives which informed the majority in that case. As we shall see, there has been even more misinformed commentary from the Left about the Catholic perspectives informing the court's interpretation of a statute defining the defence of provocation in a murder case involving a homosexual advance by the victim.

In *Mabo*, the High Court of Australia had, for the first time, to address the question of whether Aborigines and Torres Strait Islanders could have had rights to land which survived the assertion of British sovereignty. All seven judges were agreed that they could not question the assertion of sovereignty by the British Crown. They also agreed that Aborigines and Torres Strait Islanders could have had rights to land prior to the assertion of sovereignty. Six of the judges thought that any such rights could survive the assertion of sovereignty by the Crown. It did not matter how you classified the Crown's mode of acquisition of the new territories. Whether the Crown asserted sovereignty by settlement, conquest or cession, native title rights could survive until the Crown extinguished them, either by granting the land to a third party or by dedicating the land to some public use, inconsistent with continued use and occupation by the traditional owners. After 1975, any surviving native title rights would be protected by operation of the Commonwealth's *Racial Discrimination Act*, which ensured that native title holders would be treated in a non-discriminatory way, suffering any government interference with their property rights only on the same terms and conditions that would affect any other property holder. By a bare majority of four to three, the court decided that these rights could have been extinguished by the Crown prior to 1975 without the need for payment of compensation.

For some years commentators Hugh Morgan and Ray Evans had agitated about what they perceived as the Catholic thinking behind the High Court's *Mabo* decision.[23] The suggestion was that the majority of judges, who had been educated at Catholic schools, must have allowed their Catholic perspective or values to influence their decision because it was inconceivable to these good Protestant gentlemen how else the court could have reached such a decision. They were particularly concerned that the lead judgments were written by Justice Brennan, 'regarded as a conservative Catholic', and by Justice Deane, 'a Catholic of some standing'.[24] Their anxiety was heightened by this author's relationship to Justice Brennan. Hugh Morgan offered public advice that I should have been particularly conscious of my father's standing, 'and sensitive to the implications of remarks which could quite incorrectly, give rise to suggestions of influence'.[25] At the commencement of the *Mabo* proceedings in March 1988, my father made a statement from the bench:[26]

> I have informed counsel appearing in this case that my son Fr Frank Brennan SJ is an adviser to the Australian Catholic bishops on matters relating to the land rights of Aboriginal and Islander peoples and that he is actively engaged in a ministry to these peoples. As this matter raises for consideration the question whether Islander people enjoy traditional rights with respect to land, not being rights arising under a statute, it is appropriate that the information I have given counsel should appear on the public record.

Counsel offered no comment and neither did the likes of Evans and Morgan until four years later, when the litigation was well complete. I regarded my father's statement as an excess of judicial scrupulosity. Morgan was convinced that 'in *Mabo*, and all that followed from it, we are engaged in a struggle for the political and territorial future of Australia'.[27] Evans discerned a 'Gnostic heresy which seized the collective minds of the High Court'.[28] By 1999, Evans was publicly lamenting that 'Justice Brennan not only sat on the case but wrote the lead judgment, despite the fact that, in Australia, his son was, and has been for a decade, one of the most active and influential advocates for the revolutionary policies which were embodied in the *Mabo* judgment'.[29]

Then James Franklin in *Corrupting the Youth*, his history of philosophy in Australia, asserted that 'the most dramatic outcome of Catholic philosophy in recent times has been the High Court's *Mabo* decision on Aboriginal land rights'.[30] Keith Windschuttle took up the call with the observation that: 'The majority of those who supported *Mabo* were Catholics':[31]

> One of the critical issues in the debate over native title is the attitude the pre-contact Aborigines had to the land. Most discussion assumes they had clearly defined territories, which were exclusively theirs. This concept was one of the principal assumptions on which the *Mabo* decision was made. Justice Sir Gerard Brennan has made clear that his own judgment had been informed by his son, Father Frank Brennan, the Jesuit barrister and advisor to the Catholic bishops on Aboriginal affairs.

Justice Brennan had made no such thing clear. Windschuttle's claim was false, uninformed speculation. Justices Brennan and Toohey had extensive experience of Aboriginal land rights before they became High Court judges. Toohey was the first Aboriginal Land Commissioner in the Northern Territory, when the Commonwealth Parliament passed the *Aboriginal Land Rights (Northern Territory) Act 1976* implementing the key recommendations of the Woodward Royal Commission. While still a barrister, Brennan had been briefed by the Commonwealth as the senior counsel for the Northern Land Council in the Woodward Commission.[32] Sir Edward Woodward had 'particularly asked' that Brennan 'be briefed for the Northern Land Council'.[33] Woodward acknowledged that Brennan drafted key sections of the land rights bill then presented to government. In his autobiography, Woodward said that Brennan 'did an outstanding job' and 'had some influence on my approach to the report'. Attesting to Brennan's advocacy of the Aboriginal claims, Woodward wrote:[34]

> I have always taken the view, in conducting or advising any Royal Commission or Board of Inquiry, that recommendations should be reasonably capable of implementation after taking into account financial and political realities. I did not depart from that principle in this case, but I bore in mind Brennan's submission to me that 'this is a report which will for all time mark the high-water mark of Aboriginal aspirations. Whatever Your Honour does not recommend in favour of Aborigines, at this stage, will never be granted.'

It was in response to this advocacy that Woodward finally recommended that traditional owners exercise a veto over mining developments on their lands. In his final report, Woodward said, 'Of all the questions I have had to consider, that of mineral rights has probably caused me the most difficulty and concern'.[35] Causing great angst to the mining industry (especially Hugh Morgan), Woodward, though denying Aboriginal ownership of minerals, was sufficiently influenced by Brennan's advocacy that he concluded: 'I believe that to deny Aborigines the right to prevent mining on their land is to deny the reality of their land rights'.[36]

No doubt Brennan's advocacy experiences in the 1970s did directly inform his judicial mind in later years. Like Justices Mason and Deane, he then spent more than ten years on the High Court before the determination of *Mabo*, hearing numerous land rights appeals from the Northern Territory. Professor Tony Coady has observed in his review of Franklin's *Corrupting the Youth* that 'Franklin's idea that Catholic philosophy via natural law theory had a big influence on the *Mabo* decision' is 'unconvincing', 'since resorting to morality to justify legal decisions has foundations other than natural law, as is clear in the work of the Oxford philosopher Ronald

Dworkin and in much of the human rights movement'.[37] No-one could seriously postulate that it is only a Catholic mindset that could result in the High Court finding for Aborigines in their common law claims to land. Most other superior courts in other equivalent countries have done the same, regardless of the religious affiliations of the judges. When it came to the question of compensation for past dispossession, there was a division among the judges and no agreement among the Catholics: Justices Mason, Brennan, Dawson and McHugh holding that no compensation was payable and Justices Deane, Gaudron and Toohey holding that it was payable.

The Brennan judgment was the most conservatively and judicially crafted of the majority judgments. Unlike others, he did not quote historians such as Henry Reynolds. He actually confined himself to the historical record regarding the Torres Strait Islands. Presumably that is why the Brennan judgment commanded the assent of Chief Justice Mason and Justice McHugh, two judges very unlikely to subscribe assent to a judgment 'informed by' a priest who was a son of the judge.

Addressing the Australian Judicial Conference in 2005, Sir Gerard Brennan said:[38]

> Occasionally, but only occasionally, changes in the enduring values of a society may evoke changes in the common law. Perhaps *Mabo [No 2]* is the most dramatic modern example. The recognition of native title flowed from the change in the values of a society which, in earlier times [to adopt the language of Lord Sumner][39] had perceived Aborigines as: 'so low in the scale of social organization that their usages and conceptions of rights and duties are not to be reconciled with the institutions or the legal ideas of civilized society. Such a gulf cannot be bridged. It would be idle to impute to such people some shadow of the rights known to our law and then to transmute it into the substance of transferable rights of property as we know them.' But now we are in a society which regards all people as equal before the law. Thus the enduring value which led to the decision in *Mabo* was the value of equality.

We do not need a particular religious sensibility to espouse the value of equality. From such a value we might derive the principle that the state should not discriminate against people on the basis of their race when the state decides the terms and conditions on which it is appropriate to separate people from the lands on which they and their ancestors have resided for many generations.

When appointed governor-general in 1995, Sir William Deane explained the two key ideas underpinning all his High Court judgments: the source of all authority being the people as a whole, and the intrinsic equality of all people.[40] After his retirement he explained:[41]

> The basis of natural law is the belief that some things are innately right and some innately wrong, flowing from the nature of things, including our nature as human beings. That approach provides a philosophical basis for seeing such things as human rights as going deeper than any particular act of Parliament or what have you. That is not exclusively Catholic. It runs through Christian belief.

Critics like Evans and Morgan think it inconceivable that a judge discharging his judicial oath could find in favour of common law native title rights. They think it could only occur if the judges are infected by a Gnostic or Catholic conspiracy. *Mabo* was the first case in which the full bench of the High Court was asked to consider the common law recognition of land rights. The superior courts of Canada and New Zealand have since approved the decision. It was no surprise that Justice Brennan, in light of his earlier experience as an advocate and judge in land rights cases, would write an authoritative, knowledgeable judgment, gaining the concurrence of two other justices including the chief justice. Equally it was no surprise that Justices Deane and Gaudron would write a strong judgment insisting upon the equality before the law of all people, including Aborigines. Their religious beliefs and upbringing may well have provided a context and underpinning for their convictions about equality. From the value of equality for all, they derived principles of law which, when applied to the facts at hand, rendered a decision which even John Howard has described often as being 'based on a good deal of logic and fairness and proper principle'.[42] Judges of other faiths and none could have reached the same decision and with similar reasoning, quoting similar legal sources.

Even some of the strongest supporters of the *Mabo* decision were convinced that it was based on the religious beliefs of the judges. David Marr asserted that 'Brennan's brand of Catholicism brings with it . . . an instinct for racial justice that gave Australia *Mabo*'.[43] This brings us from the Right to the Left of politics critiquing the religious affiliation of judges. On 23 July 1999, I received David Marr at my office in Kings Cross, next door to the Church of St Canice. After he had expressed misgivings about the conflicts between Archbishop Pell and gay rights supporters wearing rainbow sashes at St Patrick's Cathedral in Melbourne, I proudly told him that St Canice's was the church for the Acceptance group's weekly Friday evening liturgy (Acceptance being a Catholic homosexual group who have prayed and worshipped freely in our church since 1989).

Marr had been upfront in his defence of the High Court in the wake of the Howard government's attacks on the court following the 1996 *Wik* decision. Prior to the second Senate debate on *Wik*, he had spoken on Radio National's *Law Report* a couple of times in September 1997, saying:[44]

> There is a frustrated lashing out and part of that lashing out is being harnessed at the moment against the High Court and I think it's very unfortunate, and it's very dangerous and I was very glad to, I'm very glad to see some statements recently of the Attorney General Daryl Williams where he is calling for greater respect for the Court. That's a pretty good sign. But it's a two way street in Canberra – I think the Government could show a lead here to the rest of the country.

A week later he said:[45]

> And I think a lot of the quite extraordinarily hostile and primitive rhetoric . . . that's been thrown by politicians at the High Court in the last year, is, I hope

> anyway, a process of a new government settling down to the reality that you can rule this country, but you don't necessarily therefore rule the roost.

At the end of our discussion about other matters, Marr told me that he was writing a book, one of the longer chapters of which was taking strong exception to the homophobic views of Catholic High Court judges. Marr gave me his thumbnail sketch of the *Green* case, which was heard by the court a fortnight before the delivery of the *Wik* decision. The court's treatment of this case now features as the chapter 'Ordinary men: The High Court blesses homophobia' in his book *The High Price of Heaven.* Marr's account of the High Court's activity a fortnight before *Wik* makes the Howard government's attacks look almost restrained and reasoned.

According to Marr, this murder case was dominated by three homophobic Catholic judges who 'had an opportunity to establish in law principles that few Parliaments in the Commonwealth would be brave enough to legislate'.[46] He speculated on the inherited and learnt prejudices of the three 'Catholic' judges in these terms:[47]

> Of all the mainstream faiths it's Catholicism that remains most robustly convinced that for a man to make a pass at another man is a sin of the blackest kind. Such bigotry comes in the guise of plain teaching to Catholic children: to Michael McHugh at his mother's knee, to John Toohey at the Jesuits' St Louis School in Perth, and in the schoolboy Gerard Brennan swotting for his life under the direction of the Missionaries of the Sacred Heart at Downlands College, Toowoomba.

There were at least three obstacles to Marr's anti-Catholic thesis: the evidence, the law and the appeal judges' rightly confined perception of their role. Furthermore, it probably came as some news to Justice McHugh to see himself classed as a Catholic judge regardless of what he had imbibed at his mother's knee.

The accused, Malcolm Green, aged twenty-two, was a friend of the victim, Don Gillies, aged thirty-six. On the night of the killing at Mudgee, the two men shared a meal. They had both been drinking. Green accepted an offer to stay at Gillies' house. Green went to bed. After Green had gone to bed, the naked Gillies came into the room and got onto the bed with him. Green tried to rebuff Gillies' advances. Green went berserk and killed Gillies.

At trial, Green claimed that he came from a family where there had been terrible sexual abuse by his father towards his sisters. As a teenager Green had sought out his father in a mining town and reported the father's wrongdoing to anyone in the town prepared to listen. He had never seen his father again. Don Gillies then became something of a father figure for Green. Green claimed that the flashback of his father's abuse caused him to lose self-control when Gillies then made unwelcome advances on him. Green's reaction to Gillies had nothing to do with homophobia. Malcolm Green's defence counsel, Tom Molomby, later explained: 'The man whom Malcolm had come to regard as a substitute father unexpectedly behaved in a way which triggered all the pent-up rage against his real father'.[48] The trial judge directed the jury that this evidence was not relevant to the issue of provocation. Under the relevant New South Wales law, an act is done under provocation if 'the conduct of the deceased was such as could have induced an ordinary person in the position of the accused to have so far lost self-control as to have formed the intent to kill or to inflict grievous bodily harm upon the deceased'. The jury convicted Green of murder.

Green appealed to the New South Wales Court of Criminal Appeal, which thought that the trial judge had made mistakes. But the court decided by two to one that there was no need to upset the murder verdict because there had been no miscarriage of justice. The case was then successfully appealed to a bench of five High Court judges, conveniently classified by Marr as three Catholics (the majority) and two Protestants (the dissentients). The majority ruled that the trial judge was in error in ruling that the accused's family history of sexual abuse and violence was irrelevant to the issue of provocation. It was for the jury to determine whether an ordinary person having suffered in a family where he knew his father to have sexually abused his sisters could have lost self-control in the wake of the victim's actions, given that the victim had become something of a father figure for the accused. Green's personal characteristics and family history would be relevant when the jury came to consider whether the accused could have 'so far lost self-control as to have formed the intent to kill' or do grievous bodily harm.

According to Marr, the judges had to decide 'a question of values. Could Malcolm Green's response to that light touch on his groin be excused in any way as the response of an ordinary Australian?'[49] Marr was adamant that only Catholic homophobic judges would want to leave this question to a jury. He thought any non-homophobic judge would insist that the question not be left for a jury to decide. In answering this question, Marr thought the judicial reasons were to be found in the judges' lives 'as much as their law books'.[50] But there was first the question of the evidence. It suited Marr's theory to class Gillies' action as a light touch, an amorous advance. It also suited his theory to claim that Malcolm Green was sober while Don Gillies was drunk.[51] In academic controversy since the case, Tom Molomby, the counsel for Green at trial and in all appeals, made it clear that the accused and the victim 'drank a lot. Don's blood alcohol at autopsy was 0.235. Malcolm's must have been similar.'[52]

In the High Court appeal, Tim Game, SC, senior counsel for the accused appellant Green, said in his opening submissions:[53]

> So that what took place in the bed – and we do not agree with the description of it as merely an amorous touching but an unwanted and rejected on more than one occasion sexual advance by a naked person who has invited a person to stay at his place, who has a particular relationship with him, and it is that particular relationship which goes to the heart of this case.

For his part, the New South Wales solicitor-general argued in the High Court appeal that this was a case of a gentle, amorous advance. Justice McHugh took issue with this classification, quoting from later extracts of the evidence and concluding, 'So, in its context he may have been gentle to start with but then there is this pulling towards him, he pulled him close to him so that there was no room in between them, and that is when he got aggressive'.

Then later the solicitor-general, Keith Mason, QC, was asked for clarification of his use of the term 'amorous' in this exchange with the bench, there being disagreement between the parties as to how the behaviour could be described:

> MR MASON: I do understand, with respect, what your Honour is putting to me, but it remained in the context of an amorous, not a physically, aggressive approach.
> BRENNAN CJ: When you say 'amorous', you mean sexual?
> MR MASON: I mean sexual.

David Marr read this exchange as a reproach by the chief justice which astonished the other judges and lawyers. Marr heard the chief justice speaking 'with visceral disgust'.[54] Presumably, there was nothing to stop the very experienced solicitor-general saying: 'No, I mean amorous. I don't accept sexual'. The bench was seeking for common ground between counsel for the parties, and the bar was free to put the case for any classification it might choose. Where on the spectrum between gentle, amorous advance and aggressive, physical assault did this physical act come? Justice McHugh then resumed:

> It has been running through my mind throughout this argument the position of a woman in this whole situation, and I do not think you can distinguish between either case either in terms of fear, in terms of sexual assault. It is a sexual assault. If a woman was in bed in these circumstances and a male got in bed with her and she pushed him away, I would not have thought you would talk about it as being amorous.

The approach of McHugh and Brennan in these quotes seems simply to reveal the time-honoured judicial principles applied in an appeal court. The appeal judge seeks out what is common ground in the submissions of counsel (and therefore as close an approximation to truth as the appellate process can reach on the facts) knowing that each counsel is putting the best light possible on their client's case (in this instance, Game arguing for physical assault and Mason for amorous advance). The judge argues by analogy or comparison attempting fairness and non-discrimination in all cases (in this instance, McHugh saying it would be the same whether or not the victim was a man or woman, homosexual or heterosexual, making advances of a sexual nature whether the advances be between man and woman, man and man, woman and woman).

Green's counsel was adamant that the court could not attach the description 'amorous' to the deceased's actions. He described them at the very outset as 'an unwanted and rejected on more than one occasion sexual advance'. Then, under cross-examination from Justice Kirby, counsel for Green reconfirmed that the advance could not be classified as 'amorous'. When invited by Kirby to classify it, he said it 'is an indecent assault, it is both a physical and a sexual assault and it is persistent'. McHugh clarified with Mason that the advance (whatever its character at the outset) had become aggressive. Meanwhile Chief Justice Brennan had asked his question which Marr found so offensive: 'When you say "amorous", you mean sexual?' Marr said this was an 'outburst' that 'hung in the air. Judges and lawyers alike were astonished. Couldn't Don Gillies be amorous?' Yes, presumably he could, but Green's case was that Gillies had been anything but amorous on this occasion. 'Can homosexuals only be sexual?' No, presumably not, but on this occasion, according to Green who was the accused, Gillies was being sexual and physical in a most unwelcome and unloving way.

The case was sent back for retrial before a jury rightly instructed on the law of provocation – with neither the transcript of argument nor the written judgments revealing any animus whatever to homosexuals nor Catholic bigotry. The High Court was wrestling with a transcript of evidence from an accused, trying to determine whether the deceased victim committed what the accused, in light of his personal history, would perceive as an amorous advance or a physical assault. This was a difficult question of fact, not law, which the High Court majority said was peculiarly within the province of a jury.

There is no way one could dispassionately bring the evidence down to Marr's simple question: 'Could Malcolm Green's response to that light touch on his groin be excused in any way as the response of an ordinary Australian?' In the Australian criminal law, the accused is presumed to be innocent until proven guilty beyond a reasonable doubt (whatever the sexual orientation or gender of the victim). In the end, the majority of the High Court thought this was all a matter for the jury. Was it only a light touch? Was Green's response one which could be the response of an ordinary person? Only a jury hearing the evidence could decide. At the appeal, the bench was trying to find a neutral or agreed description of Gillies' act towards Green. It is fanciful for Marr to suggest, 'Brennan seemed to be reproaching the Crown's advocate for linking homosexuality and love'. Responding to Marr's description of the case, Molomby says:[55]

> It is quite inaccurate, and indeed unfair, to say that Green was provoked 'because a naked man climbed into his bed, hugged him and gently touched his groin'. Nor can one correctly say that the case establishes 'that violence will be looked on a little kindly by the courts if it's provoked by one man making a pass at another'. These formulations by Marr omit the crucial elements which make this case so different from the usual.

Justice Gummow in dissent earned no animosity from Marr though he also made it clear that this was not 'a case in which the accused suggested that his response to the overtures of the deceased sprang from a strongly felt aversion to any sexual activity of the nature apparently being urged on him by the deceased'.[56] Gummow agreed with the 'Catholic' majority about the key issue in the case:[57]

> In truth, however, the particular elements said to constitute the position of the accused were his beliefs as to those episodes in his past family history particularly involving the sexual abuse of his sisters but also involving the physical violence inflicted by his father upon his mother and sisters.

Justice Gummow dissented from the majority because in his view the accused's family history was 'insufficiently related to the provocation presented by the conduct of the deceased'.[58] For his part, Justice Kirby in his dissenting judgment wrote: 'Assuming that it was appropriate to leave provocation to the jury in this case (a proposition which I doubt), the jury's verdict in this case was not only proper. It was inevitable. There was therefore no substantial miscarriage of justice.'[59] It just happens that Justice Kirby was wrong. As Marr notes about the retrial: 'This time the jury convicted him only of manslaughter and his sentence was reduced by a third to a little over ten years'.[60]

Green had a defence according to law which should have been put to the jury on the available evidence, no matter what the sexual orientation of his victim. If on the jury, citizens Brennan, Toohey and McHugh, like Marr, might have found the defence unfounded and they might have raised the very questions which he did about the evidence. The concern at the appeal stage is not for the judges to put themselves in place of the jury. Their job is simply to ensure the jury is rightly apprised of the law and the evidence. We must clearly distinguish the role of jury, trial judge and appeal judges.

Marr's interpretation of the transcript in the *Green* case is all the more surprising given the High Court's proactive ruling in *Croome and Toonen* v *Tasmania*, which resulted in the Tasmanian parliament's abandonment of its anti-sodomy law. The case first came before (the Catholic) Chief Justice Brennan in chambers on 6 December 1995. He considered the matter again on 15 March 1996 and then referred it to the full bench which heard argument three months before argument was heard in *Green*. Justice Kirby rightly excused himself from Croome's case on the grounds of connection with the plaintiffs. All members of the bench gave standing to the plaintiffs to bring the action. In the past, standing had not been granted in such circumstances. Two months after the hearing of the appeal in *Green*, the Catholics Brennan and Toohey joined with Justice Dawson in the *Croome* judgment saying:[61]

> The plaintiffs plead that they have engaged in conduct which, if the impugned provisions of the Code were and are operative, renders them liable to prosecution, conviction and punishment. The fact that the

> Director of Public Prosecutions does not propose to prosecute does not remove that liability. Liability to prosecution under the impugned provisions of the Code will be established if the Court were to determine the action against the plaintiffs even if liability to conviction and punishment under those provisions cannot be determined by civil process. Controversy as to the operative effect of the impugned provisions of the Code will be settled and binding on the parties. The plaintiffs have a sufficient interest to support an action for a declaration of s 109 invalidity.

After this win for Croome and Toonen, there was no need for further court proceedings because the Tasmanian parliament then removed the offending statute from the books. Consideration of this case should have given Marr further pause in the formulation of his bizarre anti-Catholic thesis. Any serious social commentator should be capable of weighing the evidence and appreciating the task of an appeal judge when opposing counsel do not agree that the evidence could be interpreted only one way. Like Marr, I mourn Gillies' death. Unlike Marr, I am pleased that Green finally was accorded a fair trial according to law.

Anti-Catholic prejudice in the public forum should be as unacceptable as anti-gay prejudice. Molomby asserts that in this instance Marr's accusations were 'wrong, and damaging not only to his own cause, but to the integrity of intellectual debate in general'.[62] An admirer of Marr's advocacy and writing in other instances, I trust that respectful public dialogue can correct the errors of religious and other prejudice.

On assuming office, all judges swear to 'do right to all manner of people according to law without fear or favour, affection or ill-will'. At his own swearing in as chief justice in 1995, Gerard Brennan reflected on the oath:[63]

> It precludes partisanship for a cause, however worthy to the eyes of a protagonist that cause may be. It forbids any judge to regard himself or herself as a representative of a section of society. It forbids partiality and, most importantly, it commands independence from any influence that

> might improperly tilt the scales of justice. When the case is heard, the judge must decide it in the lonely room of his or her own conscience but in accordance with the law. That is the way in which right is done without fear or favour, affection or ill-will.

A judge's religious beliefs may assist in maintaining the commitment to the oath. Such beliefs should not result in the shaping of the common law, the granting of equitable relief, the interpretation of a statute or the Constitution in a manner inimical to the doing of right to all according to law. The common law of Australia was enhanced in its development by the High Court's decision in *Mabo* because the value of equality and respect for others' property found expression in the principle of non-discrimination, which rendered rules of law precluding distinctions based on classes of occupation (conquest, cession and settlement) or classes of people (those so primitive as to have no notion of private property and those so developed as to entertain British notions of property). The criminal law was rendered more just as the result of a High Court decision permitting a jury to consider the circumstances of an accused when those circumstances could have contributed to and explained the provocation suffered at the hands of a victim regardless of whether the accused or the victim was homosexual or heterosexual. The conscientious judge has no interest in tempering right according to law because a particular message might be sent to a constituency, or because a religious prejudice or belief might be confirmed.

CHAPTER EIGHT

A PRESENT CASE IN POINT – SAME-SEX MARRIAGE

Let us now consider church–state concerns about same-sex marriage and the failure to accord same-sex couples their due. This is a live issue in Australia, the United States, Canada, the United Kingdom and New Zealand. In some jurisdictions, the legislators have passed laws to recognise same-sex civil unions, stopping short of classifying such a relationship as marriage. In other jurisdictions, the courts have said that same-sex couples are entitled to marry if they are not to suffer discrimination. In Australia, we are gradually reducing the discrimination against same-sex couples but to date have usually denied them equal access to adoption of children and creation of children by state authorised and funded artificial reproduction.

In 2003, the Tasmanian parliament passed the *Relationships Act* which allows people to register a significant or caring relationship. Partners to such relationships may seek court orders for maintenance and adjustments to property rights.

On 13 August 2004, the Senate was debating a bill which would amend the Commonwealth *Marriage Act* by specifying that 'marriage' means 'the union of a man and a woman to the exclusion of all others, voluntarily entered into for life'.[1] The bill also provided that a union solemnised in a foreign country between a man and another man, or between a woman and another woman, 'must not be recognised as a marriage in Australia'. The bill was passed overwhelmingly by thirty-eight to six. The Labor Party joined with the government, rejecting all amendments from the Democrats and the Greens, forcefully stating: 'Labor have in fact made clear that we will not support a change to the existing legal status of marriage'.[2]

I was riveted by the debate because I had never heard such sustained emotional intensity in the parliamentary speeches of our elected politicians. Senator Andrew Bartlett, leader of the Democrats, was close to breaking down as he commenced his assault on the bill, claiming that it was an anti-family measure that would degrade marriage. He said:[3]

> It encourages and reinforces a decline in moral standards and decency that will strike at the heart of our society if we do not stand against it. It will obviously pass today, but that will not be the end of the battle. There have been plenty of immoral laws passed in the past. That does not mean you just say, 'Well, we lost that one', and give up; you continue to fight until the immorality that it represents is overturned.

I had long been an admirer of Senator Bartlett for his principled stand in support of asylum seekers, especially the children who were held in remote detention centres for years by the Howard government. He felt acutely the suffering of families who had been separated or detained under the policy. But here was a display of moral outrage which I did not share and did not quite understand. I could readily understand the righteous anger of those non-government members who thought that the issue of same-sex marriage was being brought before the Parliament on its last sitting day before a federal election so as to create a wedge issue in the forthcoming election campaign. But even that anger should have been tempered by the government revelations that there were already court proceedings under way in which parties were seeking court orders recognising same-sex marriages which had been registered overseas.

Government members had a legitimate argument that the elected politicians rather than the unelected judges should determine if and when there would be a substantive change to the institution of marriage which, to date, has been constituted by 'the union of a man and a woman to the exclusion of all others, voluntarily entered into for life'. Presumably there are many citizens and politicians committed to upholding moral standards and decency who remain convinced that the institution of marriage should be maintained as it has been for many generations, without intending harm to homosexuals, lesbians and their children.

Half an hour after Senator Bartlett spoke, Senator Bob Brown, leader of the Greens and one of a handful of openly professed gay members of parliament, commenced his address:[4]

> One of the things that is not talked about in this parliament very much is love. But love is the highest human value and it is in the heart of everybody. It is everybody's right to express it. Any sensible liberal society, besides practising acceptance, will promote love. This legislation is about hate. In any liberal society it is important that we try to minimise this negative human expression – this antithesis to love – corral it where we can and in any way possible remove it. Today the government of this country and the alternative government, the Labor Party, are promoting hate, the most negative of human values, over love, the most positive and wonderful of human values.

Here was I, an Australian citizen, thinking I was not absorbed with hate, presuming that I was committed to upholding basic morality and decency, admittedly a tad cynical about the motives of government introducing such legislation on the last day of sitting before an election, but nonetheless in agreement with the bill. It seemed sensible, prudent and fair to me that marriage be presently confined to a man and a woman, and that any fundamental change to the institution of marriage so as to include a relationship between two men or two women (or between more than two persons) should be made by our elected politicians or even by referendum of all the citizens, rather than by unelected judges. If there were to be a change in the law, I was far from convinced that now was the time. Had there been sufficient consideration of the long-term consequences? Was there sufficient public understanding and endorsement of the need for change?

How could I explain myself to those like Senators Bartlett and Brown? How could I understand them and address their concerns? Could I do this without referring to my religious beliefs? Would it be appropriate to refer to my religious beliefs? Being a Catholic priest, I am a member and representative of a church which not only recognises marriage as the indissoluble union between a man and a woman, but which also defines marriage to be a sacrament, one of the very privileged moments of life when the Church acknowledges that God's grace has been bestowed on the couple. The senior leadership of my church has been very specific in condemning not only same-sex marriage but also any form of civil recognition of homosexual unions. When he chaired the Vatican's Congregation of the Doctrine of the Faith, the present pope issued a document asserting that 'all Catholics are obliged to oppose the legal recognition of homosexual unions' whether or not such civil unions were classified as marriages. The Congregation gave a specific direction to Catholic politicians:[5]

> When legislation in favour of the recognition of homosexual unions is proposed for the first time in a legislative assembly, the Catholic law-maker has a moral duty to express his opposition clearly and publicly and to vote against it. To vote in favour of a law so harmful to the common good is gravely immoral.

We have come a long way from Cardinal Newman being able to assure Prime Minister Gladstone that there would be no church interference in domestic politics. The state has no function to perform in telling churches what marriages or unions should be formally recognised or sacramentalised by the churches. Church leaders and church members who are citizens of the state have the same entitlement as any other citizens to express their preferences for the law and to participate in political debate about the desirable content of the law. Citizens participating in the political processes of a democratic state can make their choices at elections between candidates on whatever basis they choose. They can also contribute to public debate of issues in whatever way they choose. Some citizens will choose to speak from the perspective of a comprehensive world view which is not shared or even comprehensible to many other citizens. That comprehensive world view may be informed by religious belief as well as myth, prejudice, unreflected preference, ignorance or ideology. Church leaders are entitled to articulate the religious view of their churches, commending such a view to their church members but also commending their religious view to other citizens, who of course are free to disregard such religious utterances. Some citizens, hopefully including church leaders and official spokespersons for churches, will decide to couch their arguments and preferences about law and policy in terms which are accessible to a wider range of citizens, and not simply their co-religionists.

Citizens invested with public office whether by election to the Parliament, elevation to the bench, or employment in the public service have an obligation when discussing or implementing law or policy in their public roles to speak or act in a manner consistent with their public office. There will be circumstances in which it will be acceptable for politicians to speak out of their religious convictions when it would be improper for a judge to do so. There will be times when it is more efficacious for the politician not to speak confessionally but to speak with the voice of public reason. Public debate of controversial issues can be assisted by the public intellectual committed to speaking with the voice of public reason, conceding the liberty of all citizens to speak in whatever voice they choose. Same-sex marriage is a very emotional and political issue. Public deliberation about appropriate law or policy can be assisted by a dispassionate consideration of the question.

There may be some purpose in providing state recognition of civil partnerships between two individuals wanting to commit themselves to a long-term relationship in which each of the partners takes primary responsibility for the other and expects to receive nurture, support and assistance from the other in an exclusive and permanent way. It should be no concern of the state whether such partners share a sexual relationship.

Given the utility of such state recognition, it should be available to those who seek it and are eligible in the same way that the state is prepared to recognise the marriage of a man and woman, regardless of whether or not they desire or are able to bear each other's children. Such partners should be guaranteed freedom from discrimination in their enjoyment of access to financial and other benefits, including superannuation, tax concessions and bereavement leave. As well as being eligible for these benefits, they may want to register with the state their committed, exclusive relationship, thereby assisting them with the recognition and protection of their relationship.

If there is such registration of 'civil unions', it is not self-evident why registration should be restricted to two-person partnerships. Some US legal scholars are already arguing, 'We should respect . . . claims made against the hegemony of the two person unit'.[6] Would the logical conclusion be for the state to set up a 'state friendship registry', providing recognition and 'generous public benefits to every emotionally satisfying, long-term relationship'?[7] Could interdependent adult siblings, best friends, or religious celibate communities register? Or should registration be restricted to those 'family units' which are most likely to take primary responsibility for children? Perhaps the state does have an interest in encouraging the stability of two-person relationships simply because most long-term sustaining relationships are exclusively between two people.

Neither law nor policy should discriminate against people only on the basis of their sexual orientation. The law and policy regarding same-sex marriage need to take into account the rights of children in such a marriage, as well as the rights of the partners. The best interests of children are to be the paramount concern of lawmakers when drafting laws or policies which will affect children yet to be born or yet to be brought into the jurisdiction. In the case of adoption, when there is a shortage of children available for adoption and when all other factors are equal, the state is entitled to have a preference for an opposite-sex couple in a stable relationship as the adopting parents of an unrelated child, over a same-sex couple or a single person. In the case of assisted reproduction, the state is entitled to consider limiting access to such technology if the child will be deprived nurture by (and even knowledge of) their genetic father and mother. But then the question will arise whether the state is practically able to impose such a limitation. The result of such a limitation may be that people will legally avail themselves of assisted reproduction but in circumstances where state-imposed safeguards and protocols are not followed. This could further disadvantage children born from such a process.

An expansive change to a fundamental social institution should be made only by the citizens or their elected representatives, and not by judges choosing to recognise foreign same-sex unions. This change would be justified only if the citizens could be assured that the rights and best interests of children of same-sex unions would be protected. The state has an interest in ensuring that, as far as possible, all children are created and given an opportunity to be nurtured by their known natural parents until it is proved that the known natural parents are not able to raise their children appropriately. The state could ensure protection of children and non-discrimination against same-sex couples by extending all non-parenting benefits and responsibilities of marriage to couples entering into civil unions. The provision of full parenting benefits is more problematical.

John Mahoney proposes: 'Any genetic procedure that will turn out to be harmful to the future child or to a future generation, or contrary to their interests, is morally unacceptable'.[8] Children have a natural right to be conceived with a natural biological heritage with an ovum from the genetic material of one woman and a sperm from the genetic material of one man – the woman being, and being known as, the biological mother of the child, and the man being, and being known as, the biological father of the child. Children have a natural right to know their biological origins. It is rational for the state to withhold approval or funding of any procedure for the creation of a child unless the procedure is consistent with the child's right to a natural biological heritage. Even in a pluralist democracy with some citizens committed to investigating the limits of scientific endeavour in the creation of human beings, religious citizens are entitled to maintain that it is *prima facie* harmful to children if they are created without the right to know their biological origins and without a natural biological heritage from one man and one woman.

The rights to a natural biological heritage and to knowledge of biological origins are natural rights of the human person in that they are not dependent for philosophical cogency on the positive or common law of the state. No matter what our jurisprudential disposition, we cannot postulate a just law that denies either of these rights. Each of these rights is constitutive of the human person's self-identity, which precedes citizenship and which cannot be denied by other citizens or the state, even in the interests of other citizens who seek the prerogative to bear children without these rights. The right to bear children does not include the right to bear children denied their natural rights of biological identity and knowledge.

In Australia we still restrict the availability of adoption and, in some jurisdictions, IVF in such a way that they are not available to single people or same-sex couples in the same way that they are made available to married couples and opposite sex, de facto couples. We should review and maintain our adoption and IVF laws and policies consistent with the best interests of the children who are to be adopted or created as the result of such procedures. The interests of the child should always be paramount. For example, the state has good grounds for restricting the availability of adoption and IVF until it is proven that children are not disadvantaged by being brought up by same-sex couples or single people rather than by couples who can provide children with one male parent and one female parent. When adoption and IVF are made available to single people, same-sex couples can rightly claim discrimination if they do not enjoy equal access. Denying lesbian couples access to IVF would stop only a small number from conceiving. Ironically, infertility is now less a problem for a lesbian couple than for a heterosexual couple. 'For lesbians, if one partner is infertile the other may well be able to conceive, and if the chosen donor is infertile, they can choose another donor more easily than a wife can choose another husband.'[9] The only practical outcome of prohibiting lesbians from accessing IVF may be to express public disapproval of their conceiving.

Some same-sex couples will still seek state authorisation and assistance for the parenting of children who are not the children only of such a couple. Authorisation and assistance should be granted only if the parenting arrangement is in the best interests of the child, the state applying the same scrutiny as it would to any other prospective parent. These couples and homosexual people generally will also seek greater community acceptance and endorsement of their life choices and commitments. Endorsement rather than tolerance cannot be imposed on the majority of citizens. Endorsement will not be forthcoming if same-sex unions are equated with marriage while the majority of married citizens continue to distinguish their marriage from a same-sex union. The law can have an educative effect on citizens, having a normative effect on their behaviour even if the law is not strictly enforced. But lawmakers must be cautious in shaping a law or enforcing it if the law is contrary to the will of the people.

At this time in Australia, a same-sex union should not be called marriage. Marriage is a civil institution (and for many a religious vocation) in which the commitment to a person of the opposite sex and the bearing and/or nurture of their own children are usually understood to be key elements. The term 'marriage' has a popular and religious meaning which reflects people's lived experience in families headed by a mother and a father. The legal definition of marriage should continue to follow the contours of that meaning and experience.

Despite the pre-election heat generated in the Senate in August 2004, it is doubtful whether the Commonwealth Parliament or the courts do have power under the Australian Constitution to recognise 'same-sex marriages' as marriages. The Commonwealth Parliament can legislate only in respect to those matters listed in the Constitution. Section 51 (21) of the Constitution provides: 'The Parliament shall, subject to this Constitution, have power to make laws for the peace, order, and good government of the Commonwealth with respect to marriage'.

In 1984 the High Court struck down the Commonwealth Parliament's attempt to expand the jurisdiction of the Family Court by deeming that a child of a marriage would include a child who had been 'treated by the husband and wife as a child of their family if, at the relevant time, the child was ordinarily a member of the household of the husband and wife'.[10]

Chief Justice Gibbs (with Justices Mason, Wilson, Deane and Dawson in agreement) said:[11]

> It would be a fundamental misconception of the operation of the Constitution to suppose that the Parliament itself could effectively declare that particular facts are sufficient to bring about the necessary connexion with a head of legislative power so as to justify an exercise of that power. It is for the courts, and not for the Parliament, to decide on the validity of legislation, and so it is for this Court to decide in the present case whether there is in truth a sufficient connexion between the institution of marriage and a law which treats as a child of the marriage a child who is not in fact the natural or adopted child of either party to the marriage, but who was, at a particular time, treated by the parties to the marriage as a member of their family and was, at that time, ordinarily a member of their household.

On this reasoning, it would be constitutionally very suspect for the Commonwealth Parliament to purport to expand the definition of marriage. Justice Brennan said:[12]

> The scope of the marriage power conferred by s.51 (21) of the Constitution is to be determined by reference to what falls within the conception of marriage in the Constitution, not by reference to what the Parliament deems to be, or to be within, that conception.

Justice Brennan said that the marriage power does not 'support a law regulating what is deemed to be, but what would not otherwise be, an incident of the marriage relationship'.[13] On this reasoning the marriage power would not support a law that deemed a relationship (a same-sex relationship) to be a marriage if it were not a marriage within the meaning of the Australian Constitution.

In 1991, the High Court had cause to consider whether there could be an offence of rape in marriage. Concluding that there could be, Justice Brennan said, 'The legal nature of the institution of marriage is not to be found in the common law'. Having referred to the writings of various legal historians, he observed: 'The doctrines of the law of marriage were developed in the ecclesiastical courts, not in the courts of common law'.[14] Having traced this history, he observed, 'In *Hyde* v. *Hyde and Woodmansee*, Lord Penzance defined marriage as "the voluntary union for life of one man and one woman, to the exclusion of all others" and that definition has been followed in this country and by this Court'.[15]

Justice Dawson observed:[16]

> The power of the Commonwealth Parliament to legislate with respect to marriage (Constitution, s 51 (21)) is predicated upon the existence of marriage as a recognizable (although not immutable) institution. Just how far any attempt to define or redefine, in an abstract way, the rights and obligations of the parties to a marriage may involve a departure from that recognizable institution, and hence travel outside constitutional power, is a question of no small dimension.

On 9 December 2004, the Supreme Court of Canada gave an advisory opinion on the federal government's proposal for an act redefining marriage for civil purposes as the 'lawful union of two persons to the exclusion of all others'. Deciding that the Canadian parliament would have legislative competence to pass such a law pursuant to s 91(26) of Canada's *Constitution Act 1867*, which confers on that parliament competence in respect of 'marriage and divorce', the court unanimously took a different approach to Justice Brennan in their consideration of *Hyde*'s case. They said:[17]

> *Hyde* spoke to a society of shared social values where marriage and religion were thought to be inseparable. This is no longer the case. Canada is a pluralistic society. Marriage, from the perspective of the state, is a civil institution. The 'frozen concepts' reasoning runs contrary to one of the most fundamental principles of Canadian constitutional interpretation:

> that our Constitution is a living tree which, by way of progressive interpretation, accommodates and addresses the realities of modern life.

In a mode of reasoning very different from the Australian High Court, the Canadian Supreme Court said, 'In determining whether legislation falls within a particular head of power, a progressive interpretation of the head of power must be adopted'.[18] Viewing the Constitution as a 'living tree' which is 'capable of growth and expansion within its natural limits', the court was faced with 'competing opinions on what the natural limits of marriage may be'.[19] The court had no problem including same-sex marriage within the natural growth of the concept of marriage. Conceding that: 'Several centuries ago it would have been understood that marriage should be available only to opposite-sex couples', the court boldly stated: 'The recognition of same-sex marriage in several Canadian jurisdictions as well as two European countries belies the assertion that the same is true today'.[20]

It is unlikely that the present High Court of Australia would abandon its standard canons of interpretation of s.51 of the Australian Constitution. Whereas the United States is considering a constitutional amendment to preclude the Supreme Court from recognising same-sex marriage,[21] in Australia we would probably need a constitutional amendment for the Commonwealth Parliament to have legislative power to recognise same-sex relationships as marriages. Meanwhile, state and territory parliaments could legislate to recognise same-sex relationships in much the same way as they recognise opposite sex, de facto relationships. They do not have the constitutional power to define such relationships as marriages.

Those advocating the recognition of same-sex marriage need to consider the constitutional and political difficulties. At this time, there is no chance that a constitutional amendment would be proposed by Parliament or passed by the people. In Australia, there has been little agitation in the gay and lesbian community for the recognition of same-sex marriage. They have worked incrementally, seeking equality of treatment and recognition in relation to all non-parenting rights. Many Australians, including those who are gay or lesbian, are anxious to give highest priority to the best interests of the child when it comes to any issue relating to parenting rights. Understandably, there are many gay and lesbian couples who think they can be just as good parents as heterosexual couples. They concede that some gay and lesbian couples would not make suitable parents. But then again, there are many heterosexual couples who do not make suitable parents. The issue then is whether gay and lesbian couples should be automatically excluded from being able to adopt children or to have them conceived through IVF with state assistance (including Medicare) and approval.

Sexual relations between homosexuals used to be a criminal offence even if the participants were adults acting consensually and in private. The justification for this law was the maintenance of public morality or public order. In most countries, decriminalisation of homosexual activity preceded the extension of the principle of non-discrimination. In the United States, this order was reversed, given the Supreme Court's unwillingness to overrule the 1986 decision, *Bowers* v *Hardwick*[22] when *Romer* v *Evans*[23] was decided in 1996. By 1996, the Supreme Court was ready to strike down provisions that discriminated against homosexuals in the realm of civil law while still upholding criminal sanctions. The criminal sanctions were not rendered unconstitutional until the 2003 decision in *Lawrence* v *Texas*.[24]

Some citizens would still argue for the criminalisation of homosexual relations. But those days have gone. In the public forum, it is now accepted that it is usually not rational to discriminate against a person on the basis of their sexual orientation. Citizens in a free state are entitled to have personal preferences, but the state is entitled to proscribe a citizen's personal choices which would discriminate arbitrarily against citizens in the allocation of public goods, offices and services. Many citizens would now claim that it is morally wrong to discriminate against people on the basis of their sexual orientation, which is not malleable and not theirs by choice. Some religious citizens would even add that sexual orientation (whatever it is) is a gift from God. Others would abhor discrimination by the law, but remain convinced that the law can have an educative and normative effect on those confused teenagers who are working out their sexuality which is malleable, and who do have a choice about lifestyle.

Despite the US Supreme Court's broad-ranging rulings in *Romer* v *Evans* and *Lawrence* v *Texas*, some discriminating laws against homosexuals may still survive judicial scrutiny in the United States. For example, the Supreme Court recently has left stand the decision of the 11th Circuit, which upheld legislation in Florida precluding homosexuals from being able to adopt children.[25] The 11th Circuit has twice considered the issue and decided that the legislature could reasonably believe that the state's prohibition on 'adoption into a homosexual environment would further its interest in placing adoptive children in homes that will provide them with optimal developmental conditions'.[26] Judge Birch for the majority read *Romer* v *Evans* 'to stand for the proposition that when all the proffered rationales for a law are clearly and manifestly implausible, a reviewing court may infer that animus is the only explicable basis'.[27] Animus alone could not constitute a legitimate government interest. Until it can be proved that children adopted into homosexual families are not placed at a disadvantage compared with children adopted into other family units, the state has an ongoing legitimate interest in restricting the availability of adoption to homosexual couples, at least when the child is not related to either homosexual partner. To hold such a view until there is compelling sociological evidence to the contrary is not to act only out of animus towards people who are gay or lesbian.

In countries such as Canada and the United States, it is commonplace for citizens seeking social reform to pursue a twin track strategy. They agitate for law reform in the parliaments, seeking popular support for their proposals. But given the open textured nature of their bills of rights, they also have the opportunity to agitate social and political questions in the courts, claiming that laws are discriminatory.

On 14 January 2001, Reverend Brent Hawkes of the Metropolitan Community Church of Toronto presided at the weddings of two gay couples. He registered the marriages in the church register, issued marriage certificates and then submitted the documentation to the Ontario office of the registrar-general, who refused to accept the documents for registration because there was a federal prohibition on same-sex marriage. The couples and the Metropolitan Church then commenced litigation against the federal and state governments, claiming an infringement of the couples' equality rights under the Canadian *Charter of Rights and Freedoms.* Section 15(1) of the charter provides:

> Every individual is equal before and under the law and has the right to the equal protection and equal benefit of the law without discrimination and, in particular, without discrimination based on race, national or ethnic origin, colour, religion, sex, age or mental or physical disability.

The Metropolitan Church also claimed a breach of its freedom of religion and its right to be free from religious discrimination. This argument failed because the court said it was concerned only with marriage as a legal institution, and not as a religious and social institution: 'We do not view this case as, in any way, dealing or interfering with the religious institution of marriage'.[28]

By the time the case reached the Court of Appeal in Ontario, courts in Quebec and British Columbia had also considered the issue.[29] The Ontario Court of Appeal accepted that 'there is a common law rule that excludes same sex marriages'.[30] But that was not the end of the matter for a nation with a written Constitution which included a charter of rights. Taking a different approach from the Australian High Court, the Ontario court said the term 'marriage' 'does not have a constitutionally fixed meaning'.[31] The attorney-general of Canada submitted that the word 'marriage' was 'a descriptor of a unique opposite sex bond that is common across different times'. Though marriage was a concept in the common law, it was not a concept derived by or from the common law. Rather, 'it is a historical and worldwide institution that pre-dates our legal framework'.[32] The court was not concerned with the source from which the concept of marriage derived. The court was concerned that the concept of marriage put forward by the attorney-general effected a formal distinction between same-sex and opposite-sex couples. It was irrelevant that this formal distinction was rarely adverted to in the past. In determining whether the failure to register the solemnised union of a same-sex couple was discriminatory, the court was not assisted by the circular reasoning of the argument that 'marriage is heterosexual because it "just is"'.[33]

All parties to the litigation conceded that procreation and child rearing were not the only reasons that people want to marry. Couples, including same-sex couples, desire 'intimacy, companionship, societal recognition, economic benefits, the blending of two families', with the result that the restriction of marriage to opposite-sex couples 'does not accord with the needs, capacities and circumstances of same-sex couples'.[34] The court concluded that 'the dignity of persons in same-sex relationships is violated by the exclusion of same-sex couples from the institution of marriage'.[35]

Under the Canadian charter, the court first assesses whether the impugned government action violates one of the enumerated rights or freedoms, including the right not to be discriminated against within the terms of s.15 of the charter. The court must then determine whether the discrimination can be justified, being within such reasonable limits prescribed by law as can be demonstrably justified in a free and democratic society. The attorney-general outlined three specific purposes of marriage: uniting the opposite sexes, companionship, and encouraging the birth and raising of children of the marriage. But any law which gave preference to the uniting of the opposite sexes or to companionship between persons of the opposite sex would continue to demean the dignity of same-sex couples and perpetuate 'the view that persons in same-sex relationships are not equally capable of providing companionship and forming lasting and loving relationships'.[36]

The court affirmed that the state had a legitimate interest in encouraging procreation and childrearing. But then their Honours glibly concluded:[37]

> We fail to see how the encouragement of procreation and childrearing is a pressing and substantial objective of maintaining marriage as an exclusively heterosexual institution. Heterosexual married couples will not

> stop having or raising children because same sex couples are permitted to marry. Moreover, an increasing percentage of children are being born to and raised by same sex couples.

They failed to consider whether the state had a legitimate interest in encouraging the birth of children in a family with their mother and their father or in preferring the adoption of children into families with an adult male and an adult female. The court simply asserted that the recognition of same-sex marriage would not disadvantage the children of heterosexual marriages. Policymakers and legislators concerned about the optimal conditions for the creation and nurturing of future children are entitled to consider not only the wellbeing of children who are presently placed with same-sex couples.

Could not the state have an interest in giving preference to a traditional marriage with a man and a woman as the preferred and privileged locus for the bearing and nurturing of children? If the state were to continue to give such preference, it would need to assess the ongoing harm to those children in families of same-sex unions. Such children would not enjoy the full social recognition of being members of families founded on state-recognised marriage. This disadvantage needs to be weighed against the benefits to future children in a society where a greater majority of its citizens would continue to be born and nurtured by their natural mother and father, continue to be born of only two parents, and continue to be adopted (if need be) into families with an adult male and an adult female.

The moral calculus is difficult given the absence of reliable, longitudinal studies of adults who, as children, were nurtured by gay couples, deliberately deprived the nurture and even the knowledge of both their natural parents.[38] This calculus will be even more difficult when children are born with more than one father or more than one mother as the result of new technology permitting the use of genetic material from more than one ovum or one sperm in the creation of the embryo. The crunch question is whether these are issues simply for determination by the couple or whether the state has an ongoing interest in the wellbeing of children whose creation and nurture could be so novel once the full protection of marriage is extended to same-sex couples wanting to utilise the new assisted reproductive technology (ART) so they can bear their own children without any outside genetic input.[39]

The Ontario Court of Appeal was so bold as to proclaim that '"natural" procreation is not a sufficiently pressing and substantial objective to justify infringing the equality rights of same sex couples'.[40] There are many people who enjoy and cherish the knowledge and nurture of their natural parents. A law which will have the inevitable effect of removing that prospect for an increasing percentage of children in the future needs to be scrutinised, not just for its enhancement of the dignity and choice available to otherwise childless couples but also for its prospective diminishment of the dignity of children of such unions.

The benefit to the same-sex couple and the detriment to the child need to be weighed. The issue is not best resolved by courts rushing ahead of the will of elected legislators or even further ahead of the citizens who have hardly had the time to consider these aspects of the question. There are citizens of goodwill who wish no harm to same-sex couples, who want to enhance the dignity of, and tolerance towards, such couples, but who have reasoned reservations about extending the full rights of marriage, including state assistance with procreation and adoption of children. It is too readily assumed that children of the future will cope and thrive with being members of a society which decided to permit their birth and nurture without access to their father or mother or without the natural heritage of one father and one mother.[41] There may be some children who in future rejoice at having two genetic mothers who nurtured them without a known father, even though that father was known to be still alive and fit to perform the duties of a father. There may also be some who will be troubled by such a heritage when most of their friends have a known mother and father. They may be even more troubled by the realisation that this novel heritage was visited upon them by the choice of a couple who were authorised by the state so to act because natural procreation was judged not to be 'a sufficiently pressing and substantial objective to justify infringing the equality rights of same sex couples'.

The Ontario Court of Appeal was unanimous in ordering a remedy for the infringement of constitutional rights by reformulating the common law definition of marriage as 'the voluntary union for life of two persons to the exclusion of all others',[42] and ordering the clerk of the City of Toronto to issue marriage licences to the couples. Same-sex marriages are now registered in Ontario, British Columbia and Quebec. The Canadian parliament has now legislated the recognition of same-sex marriage after the Supreme Court of Canada gave an advisory opinion that the parliament had exclusive legislative authority to pass a law recognising same-sex marriages throughout Canada and such a law is consistent with the Canadian *Charter of Rights and Freedoms.*[43]

Back in 2001, same-sex couples also commenced a test case for the registration of their marriages in the courts of Massachusetts, in the United States. They challenged the state marriage statute on both equal protection and due process grounds. They claimed that their fundamental rights were breached and that they were a suspect class, thereby requiring the court to apply strict scrutiny of the impugned law. By a narrow majority (four to three), the Massachusetts Supreme Judicial Court decided that the marriage law precluding same-sex marriage did not even survive rational basis review and thus saw no need to decide whether the case involved fundamental rights or a suspect class.[44]

Among the rationales offered by the government for the prohibition on same-sex marriage were the provision of a favourable setting for procreation and ensuring the optimal setting for child rearing, which the government defined as 'a two-parent family with one parent of each sex'. By four to three, the Court of Appeal rejected these rationales on the basis that not all married couples bear children and not all children are born into or adopted into such a family. Chief Justice Marshall asserted: 'It is the exclusive and permanent commitment of the marriage partners to one another, not the begetting of children, that is the *sine qua non* of civil marriage'.[45] While conceding that the welfare of children is a paramount state policy, Chief Justice Margaret Marshall said, 'Restricting marriage to opposite-sex couples, however, cannot plausibly further this policy'.[46] She went on to say:[47]

> The department has offered no evidence that forbidding marriage to people of the same sex will increase the number of couples choosing to enter into opposite-sex marriages in order to have and raise children. There is thus no rational relationship between the marriage statute and the Commonwealth's proffered goal of protecting the 'optimal' child-rearing unit. Moreover, the department readily concedes that people in same sex couples may be 'excellent' parents. These couples (including four of the plaintiff couples) have children for the reasons others do – to love them, to care for them, to nurture them. But the task of child rearing for same sex couples is made infinitely harder by their status as outliers to the marriage laws.

The dissenting judges did not share the chief justice's optimism. Justice Martha Sosman in dissent said:[48]

> The Legislature can rationally view the state of the scientific evidence as unsettled on the critical question it now faces: Are families headed by same sex parents equally successful in rearing children from infancy to adulthood as families headed by parents of opposite sexes? Our belief that children raised by same sex couples *should* fare the same as children raised in traditional families is just that: a passionately held but utterly untested belief. The Legislature is not required to share that belief but may, as the creator of the institution of civil marriage, wish to see the proof before making a fundamental alteration to that institution.

Justice Sosman went on to say:[49]

> Shorn of these emotion-laden invocations, the opinion ultimately opines that the Legislature is acting irrationally when it grants benefits to a proven

> successful family structure while denying the same benefits to a recent, perhaps promising, but essentially untested alternate family structure.

Justice Robert Cordy in his dissent observed:[50]

> [T]he Legislature could rationally conclude that a family environment with married opposite-sex parents remains the optimal social structure in which to bear children, and that the raising of children by same-sex couples, who by definition cannot be the two sole biological parents of a child and cannot provide children with a parental authority figure of each gender, presents an alternative structure for child rearing that has not yet proved itself beyond reasonable scientific dispute to be as optimal as the biologically based marriage norm.

Following the lead of the Ontario court, the Massachusetts court corrected the state's interference with the couples' constitutional rights by construing civil marriage to mean the voluntary union of two people as spouses, to the exclusion of all others. However, the court stayed its judgment for six months 'to permit the Legislature to take such action as it may deem appropriate in light of this opinion'.[51] Marriage licences were issued to gay couples in Massachusetts only after 17 May 2004.

There are many citizens of goodwill who bear no animus to gay couples and who care deeply for the children being brought up by gay couples. Nonetheless they have sufficient concern for the common good and for the future wellbeing of all children (including those who as adults will be gay or lesbian) who will be future members of the society and citizens of the state, that they want to urge caution about a too-ready state endorsement and encouragement of gay marriage as an appropriate institution for the creation and nurturing of an increasing number of children. This is a rational concern not born of animus.

Many opponents of same-sex marriage are not motivated by these specific concerns. Some are motivated by an honestly held belief that sexual activity should be confined to people open to the bearing of each other's children. Some are motivated by religious conviction. Others are motivated by animus or unreflected prejudice. Conceding these mixed motivations, it is surely too soon to recognise same-sex marriage. Over time, there can be a public sorting of these mixed motivations. Such a fundamental change to a social institution should be made by the citizens or their elected legislators rather than by unelected judges. Confidence in the judiciary is not enhanced when a divided bench boldly rules there is no rational basis for citizens or the state to claim that the jury is still out on the suitability of same-sex marriage for the creation and nurturing of children.

Theologian Rosemary Radford Ruether asks:[52]

> If marriage is not allowed for gay people, what is the alternative that conservative Christians are demanding? For some, gay people shouldn't exist at all; they can and should be converted to heterosexuality. But few medical and psychological experts now share this view. Sexual orientation has proved to be deeply embedded and not easily changed. Another alternative is lifelong celibacy. But celibacy has generally been recognized in the Christian tradition to be a special gift, not given to most people. Why should all gay people be assumed to have this gift? If conservative Christians demand that gays remain unmarried, but they are not capable of celibacy, what are we saying? That they should be promiscuous, that they should have uncommitted relations?

Even within conservative Christian circles, there is a growing tolerance and appreciation of those who live and profess a monogamous, faithful, loving, homosexual relationship. Such homosexual couples see themselves living a vocation, not choosing a self-indulgent lifestyle. It would be wise for gay rights advocates to acknowledge that there are many heterosexual people in marriage relationships who, though bearing no animus towards homosexual people, find it difficult to conceive a marriage relationship properly defined without the potentiality and openness to bearing and nurturing each other's children. These are heterosexual people who, from the experience of their own marriages, cannot see that a same-sex partnership can properly be described as a marriage. For them, marriage is an institution which is necessary and sufficient for the bearing and nurture of the children of the marriage. They concede that some married couples cannot or do not wish to conceive their own children. But they do not see that as sufficient reason to extend the definition of marriage to a relationship between people who could not bear each other's children exclusively and together even if each were fertile and willing to conceive. Even if wanting to enhance the commitment of same-sex couples through social recognition, these people in good faith cannot equate such partnerships with marriage as they know it and experience it. For their children and future generations, they want to maintain the distinctiveness of marriage as the socially endorsed and recognised relationship for the creation and nurture of future generations.

Surely the state has a legitimate interest in maintaining a public order based, in part, on a social institution (marriage) which privileges and assists citizens who commit themselves to each other in a way that usually results in the birth and nurture of children, as well as providing the basic social unit for the parents to care for each other and for their children, and later for the children to care for their parents. The paramountcy of this social institution is more questionable now in societies like Australia, given the fact that more marriages are childless, more children are not born into married families, and many marriages are temporary. With a still declining birthrate of 1.7, the state also has an interest in encouraging the birth of more children, whether in or out of wedlock. It is a major social step for the state to legislate that marriage need no longer by design be the privileged means of creating the basic natural communities in which citizens find intimacy and the space to create and nurture their own children, who have the opportunity to know and to live with their own father and mother.

The widening gulf between church leaders and elected lawmakers was highlighted graphically by Mark Latham when debating the Research Involving Embryos and Prohibition of Human Cloning Bill 2002. He told the House of Representatives:[53]

> They talk about the slippery slope and society sliding further down this slope but they have no strategy for crawling back up. They have no strategy or public position for crawling back up the slope that they claim is so slippery. Ultimately, they are engaged in the politics of futility. This is not logic. This is not reason. This is not rationality. The only reason I can see for opposing the bill is religious fundamentalism. The politics of futility is taking a position irrespective of argument, logic, reason, debate or the sort of discussion that we normally have in a debating chamber such as this. In effect, the impotent are pure . . . Unhappily, it reflects the rise of religious fundamentalism on the coalition side of the parliament. It is a politics that dispenses with facts, dispenses with logic, dispenses with argument and puts fundamentalism at the core of this parliament's work.

When it comes to moral issues and the law, church leaders often feel besieged, fearing that they are on this slippery slope. Often there is no way of crawling back up to the halcyon days when the law was presumed to reflect the Church-backed moral consensus. In the search for a strategy or public position on same-sex marriage, it is essential that church leaders be seen to speak only once they have been attentive to the reflections on experience of their homosexual members. It is also essential that there is an unequivocal commitment to non-discrimination and affirmation that the law is not well situated to enforce sexual morality when there is no community consensus about that morality. Though some teenagers ambivalent about their sexuality may be assisted by laws that give preference to heterosexual relationships, others in their quest and in their later relationships will find such laws to be oppressive. In such circumstances the morality of sexual activity must be left to the conscience of the individual, who can be guided and assisted voluntarily by others including their co-religionists. The state will intervene only on proof that there is threatened harm to others who are vulnerable and not yet consulted. In the sphere of same-sex relations, this requires the state to focus on the children who will be born and nurtured in such relationships in the future.

Some church leaders are willing to tolerate same-sex couples in society but they are loath to endorse their relationships because such endorsement would entail a contradiction with their church's teaching on the appropriate means of sexual expression. This is most notably the case with the Roman Catholic Church and some of the more fundamentalist Protestant churches. Church leaders need to accept that their teaching role is primarily with their own church members. They might not be the best of teachers in the public square.

The Canadian Catholic bishops intervened in the proceedings before the Supreme Court of Canada instituted by the governor in council seeking a court ruling on the constitutionality of the proposed bill extending the capacity to marry to persons of the same sex. The court was asked if the freedom of religion guaranteed by the Canadian *Charter of Rights and Freedoms* would protect religious officials from being compelled to perform a marriage between two people of the same sex that is contrary to the officials' religious beliefs. The bishops expressed strong objection to those who compare opponents of same-sex marriage with those who opposed interracial marriage in an earlier century because this 'paints all those in favour of traditional marriage, or who condemn homosexual sexual conduct, as the moral equivalents of racists'. The bishops asserted that 'neither the courts nor the State can force all citizens to publicly approve sexual relationships they find morally offensive'. While conceding the need and desirability of tolerance, the bishops said, 'This does not mean promotion, or approval'. The bishops feared that same-sex marriage legislation 'would require all Canadians to treat same sex unions, and the intimate sexual relationships underlying those unions, with the same public respect and approval as intimate sexual relations underlying heterosexual marriages. Put another way, the state would require all Canadians to treat homosexual sexual conduct as a good.'[54]

The bishops were afraid that state recognition of same-sex marriage would result in a particular ideological opinion being instituted as a universal and binding norm holding 'that intimate sexual relations at the core of same sex unions must be treated as a good'. They told the court of their added fear:[55]

> Once this social and moral orthodoxy is established, it would be a small step to remove charitable status and other public benefits from individuals, religious groups, or affiliated charities who publicly teach or espouse views contrary to this claimed orthodoxy. It would add the legitimacy of the Court and of the law to the false charge, which is also being made, that those who teach or espouse these views are hate-mongers.

The bishops were concerned that the legal recognition of same-sex marriage entails not only tolerance of homosexual sexual activity but also moral approval of it, 'a demand that could only be met by many Canadians through the abrogation of their religious beliefs'.

Even though these views are sincerely held, such arguments are not very helpful in the public forum. The civil law permits many activities by citizens which must then be tolerated by other citizens. This does not mean that all citizens are taken to give their moral approval to such activities. To take a trite example, the law permits the sale of junk food or junk literature to citizens. We must then tolerate such sales and purchases by our fellow citizens. We are not to be taken to give our moral approval to any such sale or purchase. The state cannot order us to participate in any such sale or purchase. Or, to take another complex moral issue – abortion. In most jurisdictions, the law tolerates abortion as a mother's prerogative in the early stages of pregnancy. This does not mean that all citizens morally approve abortion on demand.

Churches such as the Anglican Church, which permits marriage and sexual relations to its clergy and which has a less centralised hierarchy for the defining of doctrine and morals, finds itself in a far more conflicted situation than the Catholic Church in agitating these issues in the public square. It would be imprudent of Catholic bishops to think that they are better positioned than their Anglican colleagues when it comes to offering advice to government and legislators on these issues. The Anglicans are more likely to be facing the broad panoply of concerns of church members who are engaged in a variety of sexual relationships and who do not expect to be given clear moral answers by people in authority.

While the Catholic bishops in Canada restated their commitment not to give moral approval to same-sex unions, the Anglican Church of Canada General Synod of 2004 carried a resolution affirming 'the integrity and sanctity of committed adult same-sex relationships', requesting its Faith Worship and Ministry Committee 'to prepare resources for the church to use in addressing issues relating to human sexuality, including the blessing of same-sex unions and the changing definition of marriage in society'.

There is no purpose to be served by the Catholic bishops claiming in the public square that they are more reliable in expressing the Christian viewpoint on same-sex relationships than the general synod of the Anglican Church. There is every prospect that legislators and citizens who are not active members of either church will presume that the Anglican response is more attentive to the lived experience of all citizens, including those in same-sex relationships.

It is counterproductive in the public square for church leaders in countries such as Canada, the United States and Australia to be simply repeating the claims of the Roman Catholic Church's Congregation of the Faith:[56]

> The homosexual inclination is . . . 'objectively disordered' and homosexual practices are 'sins gravely contrary to chastity'.
>
> Those who would move from tolerance to the legitimization of specific rights for cohabiting homosexual persons need to be reminded that the approval or legalization of evil is something far different from the toleration of evil.

Many non-church members are not assisted by this specialised church language about issues of such complexity. They are not reassured by the authors holding such judgments in tension with the solicitous observation:

> [A]ccording to the teaching of the Church, men and women with homosexual tendencies 'must be accepted with respect, compassion and sensitivity. Every sign of unjust discrimination in their regard should be avoided'.

In the United States, it is more likely that legislators and citizens having no allegiance to a Christian church would be guided by the resolutions of the Episcopal Church than by the statements of the Vatican's Congregation of the Faith. At their 2000 General Convention, the Episcopal Church passed a motion about same-sex relationships:[57]

> We expect such relationships will be characterized by fidelity, monogamy, mutual affection and respect, careful, honest communication, and the holy love which enables those in such relationships to see in each other the image of God.

In 2003, the Episcopal Church acknowledged:[58]

> That, in our understanding of homosexual persons, differences exist among us about how best to care pastorally for those who intend to live in monogamous, non-celibate unions; and what is, or should be, required, permitted, or prohibited by the doctrine, discipline, and worship of the Episcopal Church concerning the blessing of the same.

An honest acknowledgment of disagreement between church members following broad consultation with church members, including those who are gay and lesbian, rather than an internally conflicted document purporting to state the official church position, is more likely to commend itself to citizens and legislators in societies which themselves are in disagreement about the greater good for society through law and policy.

In Massachusetts, there are now thousands of married same-sex couples. In Boston there are fourteen same-sex marriages registered each week. It is estimated that up to twenty-five per cent of these married couples are raising children as members of their family. Marking the first anniversary of the *Goodridge* decision (two weeks after all eleven state referenda opposing same-sex marriage were carried overwhelmingly on the day of the US election[59]), Arlene Isaacson, co-chairwoman of the Massachusetts Gay and Lesbian Political Caucus, said: 'The country wasn't ready. Our community hadn't done enough work on the ground, even though the political allure of this issue would have caused the radical right to glom onto this issue'.[60] During the course of the 2004 US election campaign, gay rights campaigners acknowledged that: 'Our legal strategy is at least ten years ahead of our political and legislative strategy' and that the issue had to be won in the court of public opinion. 'The gay marriage issue is being fought primarily in the culture, not in the courts.'[61]

But for the 2003 decision of the Massachusetts court, it is very unlikely that there would have been eleven state referenda opposing gay marriage, permitting the Republicans to highlight the issue and mobilising voters who otherwise may have stayed away. The presence of the same-sex marriage issue on the electoral radar assisted the Bush campaign and was an obstacle for the Kerry campaign. Meanwhile, the Californian *Domestic Partner Rights and Responsibilities Act 2003* caused hardly an electoral ripple and came into effect on 1 January 2005. The UK *Civil Partnerships Act* received royal assent on 18 November 2004 with little public agitation.[62] Undaunted, the Chief Justice of Massachusetts delivered a speech during the presidential election campaign:[63]

> Judges do become the focus of attack politics. It has been so since our country's founding and is certainly evident in the heated political climate today. It would be foolish, in my judgment, to heed the voices of those who would curtail a judge's independence . . . It would be foolish to tinker with the [John] Adams model of constitutional government that has served us so well for more than two centuries.

We can question the jurisprudence and the wisdom of the courts without threatening their independence. We can even question the political acumen of the judiciary in making such a speech during an election campaign when their own controversial judgment has become an issue in the campaign. Regardless of the views of the Massachusetts judiciary, the jury is still out on whether same-sex couples provide a place as good for the procreation and nurturing of children as do heterosexual couples, most of whom bear and nurture their own naturally conceived children. All citizens have an interest in ensuring that assessment is made before the institution of marriage is redefined. In the meantime, same-sex couples and their children may continue to experience an infringement of their dignity. If marriage is redefined to include same-sex couples before such an assessment is made, the state would still have a rational interest in restricting the availability of technology to these couples wanting to bear their own children with genetic material from both partners as well as from one unknown parent of the opposite sex.[64] The state would also have a rational interest in being able to give preference to heterosexual couples in the adoption of children who are unrelated to the adopting parents. State assertion of these interests would inevitably give rise to claims that same-sex marriage was second-class marriage.

In most jurisdictions marriage is still the social institution, recognised by the state, that maximises the prospect that children will be able to know and be reared within their own biological family by the mother and father. It is rational to offer married couples preference over other people in the adoption of an unrelated child because such preference maximises the prospect that the adopted child will be reared in a family with an adult male and an adult female committed to each other and to them in love. The state has an interest in maintaining the institution of marriage as the privileged institution within which children can be reared.

If all the benefits of marriage were to be extended to same-sex couples the law might have to grant them the same right as other married couples to create and nurture their children, which in their case might include the use of the new reprogenetic technologies whereby an embryo is produced from the sperm of both male partners or from the ova of both female partners.[65] If all the benefits of marriage were to be extended to same-sex couples, the law would also need to grant same-sex partners the same right to adopt as a husband and wife, thereby depriving the adopted child (when all other factors are equal) the opportunity to be reared by an adult male and an adult female. Of course, there are instances in which all other factors are not equal and adoption by a same-sex couple would be appropriate.

For example, a child for adoption may be the natural child of one of the partners.

A law which restricts marriage to heterosexual couples, maximising the potential good for adopted children and children conceived with genetic material from people other than those who will nurture them, can be justified as being rational and non-discriminatory. Such a law can still be espoused by lawmakers who bear no animus against homosexuals, insisting that the state not discriminate in the granting of individual or collective entitlements to couples regardless of whether they are in a heterosexual or homosexual union. Such a law can be justified as being in the best interests of the children of the society, maximising the prospect of their being created and reared by their natural father and natural mother, and also maximising the prospect that, if adopted, these children (all other factors being equal) would be raised by a man and a woman who constitute a family unit.

If our elected politicians decided to recognise same-sex marriage to enhance the dignity and social acceptance of same-sex couples living in committed monogamous relationships, there would still be compelling arguments for placing limits on a same-sex couple's capacity to bear a child with the genetic inheritance of them both or their entitlement to adopt a biologically unrelated child when an equally capable opposite-sex couple are available to adopt. These arguments are less compelling and the outcome more discriminatory once the law and policy make assisted reproductive technology and adoption more readily available to people other than those living in established heterosexual relationships (either marriage or de facto).

Single people can readily adopt in Canada, whereas they can only adopt in very special circumstances in Australia.[66] While the Canadians have now passed the *Assisted Human Reproduction Act 2004* which provides that 'persons who seek to undergo assisted reproduction procedures must not be discriminated against, including on the basis of their sexual orientation or marital status',[67] UK law requires that medical authorities withhold treatment services 'unless account has been taken of the welfare of the child who may be born as a result of the treatment (including the need of that child for a father)'.[68] The UK provision gives effect to the 1984 Warnock

Committee's conclusion that 'we believe, as a general rule, it is better for children to be born into a two-parent family, with both father and mother'.[69] To agree with the Warnock view twenty-two years later is not necessarily an indication of animus towards homosexuals.

Some advocates for same-sex marriage have little interest in the institution of marriage other than its utility as a vehicle for agitating a gay rights agenda at a time when most discriminatory measures regarding financial and other personal benefits have been removed, and when official state tolerance is assured. For some of these advocates, same-sex marriage is the ideal vehicle for shifting some of their opponents from tolerance to acceptance and even endorsement, or for sharing the public space of endorsement with opponents who will experience more public discomfort because of their views. That's politics.

None of these motivations should distract us from a dispassionate consideration of the claims of those homosexual people who genuinely do want to marry so that state recognition of their union might support and encourage them in their commitment and love, encouraging their fellow citizens to acknowledge and respect their commitment to monogamous faithful love of their spouse. Such people deserve a considered response from their government and their fellow citizens, regardless of the views of other citizens about the morality of sexual activity which is not both unitive and procreative between a man and a woman open to the possibility of bearing and nurturing each other's children. The hallmarks of such a considered response in the public forum should include the principle of non-discrimination, respect for individual commitments of love and fidelity between self-determining citizens, and concern for the wellbeing and nurture of children.

No-one's interests will be served by unelected judges racing ahead of the community and the elected politicians, purporting to strike the appropriate balance between the enhanced liberty and dignity of homosexuals wanting their relationships to be recognised and approved by the state, and the wellbeing of children who will be exposed to novel ways of birth, heritage and nurture. The elected politicians should proceed cautiously when the complexity of the issues results in experts advising our law reform commissions:[70]

> It is important to recognize that some children born as a result of ART may be curious or anxious about their biological identity, require access to genetic information, and may wish to form relationships with their biological parents where possible.

The challenge for lesbian parents is to strike a balance between their own need for integrity of their family unit, and the child's need to know their biological father.

Some enhanced liberty and dignity of same-sex couples could be achieved by the registration of civil unions. But there are still good grounds for them not enjoying the same privileged state authorisation as married couples when seeking to adopt children not their own, and when wanting to create children not exclusively theirs.

CONCLUSION

ENACTING VALUES FOR THE GOOD OF ALL

Religious people, like all citizens in a democracy under the rule of law, have the opportunity in the privacy of their own lives and in community with others to live out their comprehensive idea of the good life, which includes the fullest possible compliance with the moral law as they and their own religious community discern and define that moral law to be. The civil law, government policy and administration ought to provide them with protection in the pursuit of this goal. In return, they need to respect the desire of other citizens to live out their notion of the good life, even though it may not comply with theirs, and even if it is in contradiction to theirs.

There will be conflicting world views. These views can be accommodated within a democracy under the rule of law if all citizens and groups of citizens are required to respect the basic rights and freedoms of others, as these rights and freedoms are defined by law. No matter what their comprehensive world views, all citizens in the nation state are required in the public forum to respect the zone of privacy of others and to respect the communal values which in Australia include tolerance, compassion, self-determination and equal dignity of all in the exercise of their conscience.

When agitating for a particular government policy or law, or mode of administration of government policy and law, each needs to take account of the role of government, the role of law, and the practicalities of administration. Seeking a moral good as an end in itself is one thing. Seeking to have others uphold a moral good by coercion of law or government action is another. This requires an appreciation of the limits of law and the restrictions on administration. Though it may be desirable to have all citizens do a good action, the cost of attempted compliance by all may be an undermining of the rule of law or an impugning of the integrity and coherence of government and its administration.

Religious citizens, inspired by their religious authorities, are free to pursue the good amongst themselves and they are at liberty to agitate for a comprehensive law and policy imposing this perspective of the good on all. Public officials, whether they are judges, ministers, public servants or elected members of parliament are free to consider the religious citizens' claims. They should reject or disregard those claims which are in conflict with the public trust that attaches to the position of the public official. They should reject those claims which, if implemented, would undermine the integrity of the law or policy and its mode of implementation. They should reject those claims which would result in an interference with the basic rights and liberties of citizens who do not share the religious viewpoint. They should also reject those claims if their implementation would run counter to the contemporary social values of equality, tolerance, compassion and dignity for all people at all stages of the life cycle.

If there is no violation of public trust, the integrity of the law and administration, basic rights and liberties, and community values, then public officials are at liberty to act in the light of a religious perspective. In such a case, religiously inspired and informed action by a legislator, judge or public servant would be consistent with their public duty, consistent with the basic rights and liberties of all, and consistent with the community values. When this is not possible, the religious citizens, like other citizens, will accept that the nation state with its power to coerce individuals does not exist in order to legislate and impose a particular way of acting on all citizens, even if that way of acting is the overwhelming preference of the majority of citizens. The sanction of the law enforcing public policy justifies coercion on all citizens only to the extent necessary to maintain public security and peace and to uphold the basic rights and liberties of all citizens, including the most vulnerable, against each other and against the state.

A simple thought experiment illustrates the limits of the religious world view informing law and policy. Imagine a homogeneous religious community living on an isolated island. They could voluntarily enter into a social contract agreeing to order their social affairs consistent with their religious beliefs. If they were then incorporated into a nation state with the non-religious people on the adjacent island, they would have no legitimate expectation that the new nation's laws would coerce all citizens to act consistent with their religious beliefs. If the new nation state were a democracy under the rule of law, they would retain the legitimate expectation that they could continue to live their religious life publicly as well as privately, provided they respected the basic rights and liberties of their fellow non-religious citizens and provided they honoured any shared community values. There will always be informed public disagreement about what constitutes basic rights and liberties and shared community values. That is why there will be not only politics but also political morality in a democracy under the rule of law.

The health of the *polis* (the political community in the life of the nation state) is threatened when the members of one group, privately or under their breath, despair that their fellow citizens are incapable of reasoned discourse about contested moral questions because of their world view or because of their irrational prejudice. Appropriate checks and balances on all power exercised in the name of the people, and a commitment to respectful public dialogue acknowledging differing world views preserve the *polis*. The religious person who participates in public life needs to respect the secular humanist who shares a common commitment to politics and political morality. The religious citizen can give such respect while still confessing: 'Secular humanism is not for me'. The religious citizen is entitled to similar respect from the secular humanist who confesses: 'Religion is not for me'. None of us can provide to all our fellow citizens a definitive and appealing explanation of love, suffering, death and the deepest purposes of human life and relationships. The reflective and articulated views of all citizens should be valued when decisions are made about laws and policies affecting same. This is difficult when religion is lampooned as being irrelevant to any serious public deliberation because it is thought to be relevant only to second-rate people.

We Australians are used to political leaders who have little time for religion in their own lives or in the public forum. Mark Latham put such views on public display when he published his diaries detailing his 'first law of the church': 'the greater the degree of fanaticism in so-called faith, the greater the degree of escapism either from addiction (alcohol, drugs, gambling or sex) or from personal tragedy . . . Organised religion: just another form of conservative command and control in our society.'[1]

There is a poignant rendition of the public intellectual's view of religion in Karen Armstrong's recent biography, *The Spiral Staircase.* While a student at Oxford, she was the live-in nanny for Jacob Hart, the epileptic son of Herbert and Jenifer Hart, Herbert being the esteemed professor of jurisprudence who wrote the highly influential *The Concept of Law*. Jenifer Hart asked Karen Armstrong to take Jacob to mass regularly at Blackfriars in Oxford:[2]

> I know it must sound perfectly mad. Herbert and I, of all people! Can't you imagine what our friends are going to say? I know it seems illogical, inconsistent. But I've often thought that Jacob ought to have some kind of religion. All that ritual for example – he'd simply love that. And religion is supposed to give some form of comfort, isn't it?

Armstrong then describes the conversation with Jenifer Hart:[3]

> 'You see, it's all very well for people like Herbert and me to reject religion. But Jacob – he needs something – he needs some kind of support.'
>
> 'What you mean is,' I said caustically, 'that religion is really just for idiots, weaklings and defectives'.
>
> 'Oh dear,' Jenifer grinned rather nervously at me. 'How awful. But yes . . . yes. If I'm honest, I suppose that is what I think.'

There will always be citizens, including some who are healthy and intelligent, who see a need for 'something – some kind of support'. Contemplating life and death, suffering and love, they will be convinced that a religious perspective is essential for human flourishing in community. There will also be citizens who have no need for religious support or belief. Neither perspective is trumps in a democracy under the rule of law. Each perspective provides those citizens of the alternative persuasion with challenges for living and acting respectfully.

Some religious people claim to have a comprehensive world view, confident that their religious tradition provides them with insights and moral clarity about all social questions. These citizens need to be cautious lest they disrespectfully foist their views on other citizens who see the world differently and in good faith. Whereas secular humanists and religious citizens will often be in agreement in questioning the morality of war and in urging greater protection of vulnerable citizens, they will often take contrary positions on laws and policies affecting sexual relationships and the beginning and end of life.

There will be ongoing public disputes in drawing the boundaries of humanity – at either end of the life cycle. Is the embryo to count as the property of the individual, who is free to do with it as she wishes, or is it to count as an entity deserving of respect and protection by the state against the citizen who wants to view this entity merely as a collection of cells to be experimented upon or aborted? Where the embryo or foetus is within the womb of a woman, that woman retains a prerogative because the state is unable to impose its will against the will of the woman before the foetus is viable.

By keeping religion and politics in place, it is possible to approach more dispassionately a public debate such as the one that occurred in the Commonwealth Parliament on the Therapeutic Goods Amendment (Repeal of Ministerial Responsibility for Approval of RU486) Bill in 2006. RU486 is an abortion drug. It kills the foetus. It may also have some adverse health effects on the mother. In a variety of circumstances, abortion is lawful in the states and territories. The Commonwealth Parliament has no power to make laws about the lawfulness or unlawfulness of abortion. However, the Commonwealth Parliament does have power to regulate Medicare payments and the importation of drugs. There is no evidence that the introduction of RU486 has increased the number of abortions performed in other countries. There is no reason to believe that the introduction of the option of drug induced abortion in addition to surgical abortion would reduce the number of abortions.

The abortion rate in Australia is as high as or higher than the rate in other equivalent countries. In 2003, there were an estimated 19.7 induced abortions per 1,000 women aged 15 to 44 years in Australia. When RU486 was introduced in the United Kingdom (in 1991) the abortion rate was 15.5 per 1,000 women aged 15 to 44 years. Many surveys reveal that a majority of Australians are concerned about the high frequency of abortion in Australia. But in most circumstances, they think the decision should be made by the mother in consultation with her doctor.

The Therapeutic Goods Administration (TGA) is not the appropriate body to decide if the options for abortion should be increased to include drug induced abortion. It makes good sense for that decision to be made on a conscience vote by the Parliament. Once Parliament decided by its vote to indicate its agreement with the expansion of abortion options to include drug induced abortion, it then made good sense to entrust to the TGA the task of determining whether RU486 was safe for women.

In deciding how to vote on the conscience vote, every member of parliament was free to express their personal view on the morality of abortion. Each member then needed to consider what was the desirable law or policy. The vote was not about providing women with better and more realistic options to abortion. The vote was about increasing or restricting the range of options for how an abortion would be committed once a woman and her doctor decided on an abortion without any interference from the law.

The members who voted for the bill were voting for a measure which was unlikely to increase the number of abortions, but which will definitely not decrease the number of abortions. Those who voted for the measure might appear to have endorsed the ready availability of abortion in the Australian states and territories. They might have considered in good conscience that the range of options for the performance of abortion should not be expanded until the range of realistic options other than abortion could be increased. They might have considered in good conscience that a vote in favour of the bill would have obligated them to do more in the future to reduce the number of abortions chosen under the law by means of providing women with more realistic choices to proceed with their pregnancy despite the burdens.

Bishop Anthony Fisher told the Senate committee:[4]

> Australians are deeply concerned that the abortion rate is already too high, and clearly this new direction will not help decrease abortion. The public clearly would like to see rates decreased and therefore looks to our leaders for ways to bring that about. Above all, they should be looking to ensure the women are offered real alternatives to abortion rather than alternative methods of abortion.

All members of parliament ought be able to reply, 'Hear, hear!' to that, regardless of how they voted on the RU486 bill.

There will be conscience votes again in our parliament relating to bioethical questions, same-sex marriage and euthanasia. The person who has been described as being in a persistent vegetative state is still entitled to recognition as a human person deserving their full human dignity. In recognition of their full human dignity, we can apply the golden rule and ask: 'What would I want done in recognition of my own dignity in similar circumstances?' I would want my self-determination recognised. If I had no prospect of recovery, no prospect of regaining consciousness, and if I were subject to ongoing burdensome medical treatment, I would want my relatives or the state to be in a position to say that it was time for nature to take its course. I should enjoy palliative care as I died without the compulsory, ongoing provision of artificial nutrition, hydration or respiration.

The state has no interest in inquiring into the sexual habits of citizens except in so far as those habits impact on minors or on other adults without their informed consent. Between consenting adults, the state has no interest able to be upheld without violating community values of self-determination and tolerance, as well as undermining the integrity of the law and its mode of administration. The state has an interest in preserving and sustaining relationships between adults which are monogamous, sustaining, nurturing, faithful and able to provide the basis for a home environment where individuals, including children, are cared for and nurtured. Once again the state has no interest in the sexual relations between such people and definitely has no interest in whether some religious people would categorise such sexual relations as intrinsically disordered. However, the state does have an interest in providing appropriate conditions for the nurture of the limited number of children available for adoption and of the children deliberately created with assisted reproductive technology approved by the state.

There are many heterosexuals who, regardless of whether or not they hold religious views, would see it as intrinsically disordered for them to have sexual relations with people of the same sex. There are homosexuals who would see it as intrinsically disordered for them to have sexual relations with someone of the opposite sex. Homosexuals seeking loving, faithful, monogamous, permanent and supportive relationships are entitled to seek such relationships without state interference and, once they have found them, they should have the same entitlement as other people to have the state support them. The fact they will not bear each other's children is no more relevant than the state's failure to distinguish in marriage between those couples (man and woman) who are able and anxious to conceive and bear children and those who are not. But the state is entitled to restrict adoption and ART of children to opposite-sex couples who can provide the children with a mother and a father.

Religious people are as entitled as anyone else to engage in the legal and political processes agitating their policy preferences in light of their comprehensive world view. As Tony Abbott said during the RU486 debate, 'Religious faith is not some kind of contaminant to be driven out of our public life'.[5] Religious authorities are free to press their viewpoint with their co-religionists, even threatening them with exclusion from the religious group. That is their prerogative. Such a threat could even include a demand that the individual forego the following of their conscience and comply with the dictate of the religious authority. That would be an internal matter for the religious community. But even in the Catholic community, there are good grounds for rejecting such a claim. The formed and informed individual conscience is the primary means for the believing community arriving at the truth in novel and uncertain circumstances. History is replete with religious authorities mistaking the moral good in times of change and uncertainty. A living tradition is the fruit of inter-generational affirmation of the primacy of conscience.

Even if a religious community permitted coercion of conscience within its own religious domain, religious leaders in the democratic nation state who demand such wooden compliance in the public forum are, at the least, guilty of violating the community value of equal respect for the dignity of all citizens. It is not just an issue of political efficacy but also of political morality. It is wrong in the democratic nation state with a plurality of citizens constituting a multicultural and multi-religious *polis* to demand compliance with religious authority rather than personal conscience on matters of civil law and government policy. Insistence on the primacy of church authority in the public forum has a chilling effect on any humble and open inquiry into truth when the majority of interlocutors are not subject to that church authority.

In his recent book, *A Church that Can and Cannot Change*, Judge John T. Noonan surveys the history of the changing church teaching on slavery, usury and religious freedom through the centuries and concludes:[6]

> As the history of usury demonstrates, much of the teaching of morals has been by papal pronouncements of law; and, as that history also demonstrates, the reception of a law by the Christian people is essential to its vitality. The process is not one of ratification but of giving reality to the law in the consciences of the faithful. If the faithful do not comprehend

> the reason of the law and how it comports with their obligation in conscience to God, the law will lapse as it did in the case of the sixteenth century commands on usury. *Cessante ratione, cessat ipsa lex*, 'When the reason for the law ceases, the law itself ceases'. The old canonical maxim applies when consciences, bound to obey God, cannot grasp the law's rationale. Capacity to receive does not extend to receiving what is contrary to conscience.

Coercion of conscience even within the confines of the religious community is no longer defensible. Benedict XVI put the position well for Catholics when he said prior to his becoming pope: 'The true law of God is not an external matter. It dwells within us. It is the inner direction of our lives, which is brought into being and established by the will of God. It speaks to us in our conscience.'[7]

Religious leaders were seriously wrong to suggest during the 2004 US election that the choice was between the politician who had committed intrinsically evil acts and the one who had not. At most, John Kerry was stating that the law is not the appropriate instrument for trying to restrain others from committing intrinsically immoral acts. George W. Bush was saying that he would do what he could to appoint people to the bench who may be able to have the matter referred back to the states, where they may or may not decide that the criminal law could be used to restrain some people from committing intrinsically immoral acts. He would have been content to see Harriet Miers appointed to discharge that commitment to the religious Right. Kerry had indicated that he was not so willing to engage in war or to apply the death penalty as was Bush. In good conscience, every citizen had to choose between a rock and a hard place. They were not helped by religious leaders arguing that the choice was between a rock and a soft place. There are no soft places for religious citizens looking for selectable and electable candidates in a modern democracy.

If we are to forestall the claims by fundamentalist Muslims to implement Sharia law in a democratic nation state where they are in the majority, or at least an influential minority, we need to set right the terms on which

Christians and their churches bring their religious perspective to bear on questions of law, policy and political agitation. Our contemporary need to be more attentive to the religious aspirations and thinking of Australian Muslims has provided the opportunity to reflect publicly on the place of religion in our law and politics. The enactment of broad, sweeping anti-terrorism laws likely to target those of Middle Eastern background, especially Muslims, has highlighted the continuing shortfall in Australia of checks and balances requiring popular governments to justify the infringement of civil liberties, despite the popular appeal of such measures in a climate of fear.

Muslims and other members of minority faiths in Australia should have the same opportunity and be subject to the same constraints as Christians from the major denominations when contributing to public debate, occupying positions of public trust and living a communal life in accordance with their comprehensive world view. It should be no insult to Muslims to insist that they follow the same rules and enjoy the same rights as other Australians. It should be no disrespect to Muslims to insist that Australians exercise their rights, including free speech, without legal restraint but with due regard for the sensitivity of others.

There is a need to set right the parameters for religious participation in public life. Religious leaders who insist that conscience can err and therefore should be subject to church edict risk creating a situation in which their candidates are unelectable. John Henry Newman still needs to be able to refute Gladstone's concern that Catholics are trouble for democracy. The Vatican has expanded the scope and particularity of church teaching. The state legislates about more moral issues. They are no longer independent realms. Thus the need for a stronger insistence on the primacy of the individual conscience in the performance of civic duties. Religious authorities can assist the citizen or public official seeking to form and inform conscience. But they can provide little assistance to those wanting to know what is the most desirable law or policy, let alone how it should be administered. They cannot determine what priority should be given to the resolution of one particular moral issue over all the other moral questions confronting the government, courts and administration of the nation state.

Any religious person is entitled to express his or her comprehensive religious world view and to espouse it for acceptance by the citizens generally. Religious authorities cannot impose their moral and religious views on their co-religionists for the purposes of their co-religionists' participation in the life of the nation state – whether they are governors, judges, ministers of the crown, members of parliament, public servants or voters.

Religious authorities must respect the primacy of the conscience of every citizen and the primacy of their civic duty in the public forum. They may instruct their co-religionists on the content of the moral law. They not only may, but should, state their religious ideals including those moral teachings which are normative for their religious adherents. But they may not enforce a particular means of the moral law being achieved through civil law, policy, or administration of the law which applies to all citizens regardless of their commitment to the moral law. They may not set a hierarchy within the moral law as to which matters are more or less important in the political disputes of the day (abortion versus Iraq war; stem cell research versus death penalty; same-sex marriage versus equitable health and education policy). Christian leaders in the United States would fulfil their tasks as religious leaders and as faithful citizens if they were to urge the election of a candidate who, unlike their opponent, was of proven good character, was committed to reducing the number of abortions, was opposed to a defence policy based on pre-emptive strikes, was opposed to the creation of human embryos only for experimentation and destruction, was committed to non-discrimination against gays and lesbians while being committed to laws and policies which ensured adopted children and children created through ART had access to a mother and a father, and who espoused greater equity in the provision of health and education services. The problem is that there is never such an ideal candidate, nor such an intolerable opponent. Thus the need for religious leaders to avoid the endorsement or scratching of any candidate in a two-horse race.

The religious person can say: 'This is my religious view. This is the moral law. In fulfilment of my civic duties, I can in good conscience do this in order to achieve more fully the purposes of the moral law.' Or alternatively, such a person might say, 'In accordance with my civic duties, I am not in a position to do this in order to achieve this aspect of the moral law. I cannot do this in good conscience because it would be a breach of my civic duty.' The moral law enacted into law or policy should be consistent with the community values of respect for the individual, self-determination, tolerance, equality and compassion, and with the community sense of the breadth of the circle of humanity. The religious person may espouse a widening of the circle of humanity so as to extend the primary civic values to all, but this may not be done by denying the civic values to the individual in the exercise of their self-determination.

No matter which way the next case goes on partial-birth abortion, there will be no fewer abortions performed in the United States. If we are to criminalise some abortions, we have to be prepared to implement such a law without bringing the law and its agents into a cul de sac of non-compliance, corruption and unnecessary politicisation.

If we are to debate better the morality of military pre-emption next time the Bush White House decides to engage in military action, not just to counter terrorism but also to counter tyranny, we need to concede the gap between the principles of just war and the application of the principles. This requires access to confidential, accurate intelligence information before there can be a prudent assessment made of the justification for action, when those governments providing the military pressure for international compliance have a prerogative to proclaim that war is now the last resort.

Debating same-sex marriage, we need to respect the hopes and desires of all people in the privacy of their affairs while giving highest priority to the wellbeing of children and also being attentive to the self-perception of those citizens who have always regarded their own marriages as deserving state protection and recognition for the wellbeing of the children created from such a union. If the issues of non-discrimination in access to benefits are rectified, the further demand for recognition of same-sex marriage is an issue of tolerance and endorsement best handled by elected legislators rather than unelected judges forcing the pace of social change, risking further politicisation of the issue and of the courts.

Preaching to the Knights of Malta a week before the 2004 US election, Archbishop John Quinn of San Francisco concluded: 'The voting booth, like the confessional, admits only one person at a time. There each of us stands before our conscience. But not alone. We hope that the charioteer of the virtues, prudence, stands with us.'[8] Religion once again has a place at the table of public discussion on law and policy. That place is subject to constitutional constraints. Members of parliament, judges, ministers and public servants have discrete functions to perform. Each of them, like every voter, has a conscience which must be accorded primacy. As the now Pope Benedict XVI said in his 1969 commentary on the Second Vatican Council's Pastoral Constitution on the Church in the Modern World, *Gaudium et Spes*:[9]

> [C]onscience is presented as the meeting-point and common ground of Christians and non-Christians and consequently as the real hinge on which dialogue turns. Fidelity to conscience unites Christians and non-Christians and permits them to work together to solve the moral tasks of mankind, just as it compels them both to humble and open inquiry into truth.

Religious citizens can still answer directly Gladstone's concern as did Newman. Maybe Newman was too sanguine about the issues which in time could be under the purview of the state and which at the same time could be declared acceptable or not by the teaching authority of the bishops. More than ever, it is necessary that all citizens be assured that they retain their moral and mental freedom, and that they do not have to place their civil loyalty and duty at the mercy of another who is not a citizen of the state.

You can be a religious person without renouncing your moral and mental freedom, and without having to place your civil loyalty and duty at the mercy of another. You may well be ably assisted in the discharge of your civil loyalty and duty by the wise guidance and teaching of another who happens to be a religious authority. In the public forum, all religious authorities need to acknowledge the primacy of the citizen's conscience over the teaching authority of the citizen's church when it comes to the Church's and the citizen's participation in the law and policy making of the state.

The wise religious authority will acknowledge that 'experience, especially experience enlarged by empathy, adds to the force of a teaching'.[10]

Citizens who are appointed to positions of public trust in the state are obliged to fulfil that trust in good conscience without renouncing their moral and mental freedom to any church authority, and without placing their civil loyalty and duty at the mercy of any church authority. In the exercise of their moral and mental freedom as state officials, they may be assisted by the teachings of their church but those teachings, like all utterances, would need to be scrutinised and freely adopted by those state officials as being consistent with the proper discharge of their public trust. For example, it would have been wrong for a judge (even if she were a good Catholic) to change her interpretation of a statute about what constituted medical treatment so as to reach the conclusion espoused by the pope. She would need faithfully to interpret the statute according to the canons of construction regardless of the preferred policy outcome of any person, including herself and the pope. If the judge applying the canons of construction decided that the statute was so ambiguous as to be equally open to a number of interpretations, she would be right to adopt that interpretation consistent with her personal policy preference. That may happen to coincide with the personal policy preference of the pope. She would be wrong to adopt an interpretation consistent with the policy preference of the pope if it were not her own personal policy preference. It would be improper for a judge to say, 'I will interpret any ambiguous statute so as to maximise the possibility of achieving an outcome consistent with the teaching of the pope'. Mind you, she may well find that her own interpretation of ambiguous statutes is consistent with the teaching of the pope. Her reasoning would not be: 'The Pope says X and therefore I will adopt X'. Rather it would be: 'I will adopt X because it is consistent with values often found in the law including the protection of the weak and vulnerable, and the maintenance of public institutions, and the acknowledgment of the individual's unique dignity and entitlement to self determination and a dignified death'.

The late US Chief Justice Rehnquist delivered his last judgment in June 2005 joining the Supreme Court majority who upheld the right of the State of Texas to maintain a monument of the ten commandments as one of a series of monuments surrounding the Texas State Capitol and commemorating the ideals of the Texan settlers and residents. Rehnquist did not think the monument violated the clause of the US Constitution prohibiting the establishment of religion. He described the Supreme Court's cases on the establishment clause as being Janus-like, with one face looking towards the strong role played by religion and religious traditions in US history and the other face looking towards the principle that 'governmental intervention in religious matters can itself endanger religious freedom'. He boldly asserted, 'Our institutions presuppose a Supreme Being, yet these institutions must not press religious observance upon their citizens'.[11] Turning his eye from the Texas State Capitol, he surveyed the architecture around Washington DC: 'We need only look within our own Courtroom' which features a couple of statues of Moses and representations of the ten commandments. Rehnquist was untroubled about these features as 'Moses was a lawgiver as well as a religious leader'.[12]

Manning Clark once described Australia as 'a society unique in the history of mankind, a society of men holding no firm beliefs on the existence of God or survival after death'.[13] Moses and the ten commandments do not feature in Australian courtrooms. In the public forum, our leaders do not often speak religious thoughts or admit to religious impulses. Thus my surprise when I attended the mass celebrated by Bishop Carlos Belo in the Dili Cathedral in 2001 giving thanks for Australia's contribution to the liberation of East Timor. At the end of the mass, Major-General Peter Cosgrove spoke. This big Australian army officer in military dress was accompanied by a translator who was a petite Timorese religious sister in her pure white habit, replete with veil. He recalled his first visit to the cathedral three months earlier when he was so moved by the singing that he realised two things: first, the people of East Timor had not abandoned their God despite everything that had happened; second, God had not abandoned the people of East Timor. As he spoke, I was certain that despite the presence of the usual media scrum, not one word of this speech would be reported back in Australia. It was unimaginable that an Australian solider would give such a speech in Australia. If he were a US general, we would expect it. Here in Australia, the public silence about things religious does not mean that religion does not animate and inspire many of us. It just has a less acknowledged place in the public forum. It marks its presence by the reverence of the silence. That is why we Australians need to be so attentive to keeping politics and religion in place. Each has its place and each must be kept in place for the good of us all, and for the good of our Commonwealth.

ENDNOTES

Abbreviations used in the following citations:

AC	Appeal Cases
CCPR/C	Views of the Human Rights Committee under the Optional Protocol to the International Covenant on Civil and Political Rights
CLR	Commonwealth Law Reports
CPD (HofR)	Commonwealth Parliamentary Debates (House of Representatives)
CPD (S)	Commonwealth Parliamentary Debates (Senate)
DLR	Dominion Law Reports
SCC	Supreme Court of Canada
US	United States Reports
VCAT	Victorian Civil and Administrative Appeals Tribunal
VR	Victorian reports

Introduction

1. ABC TV, *7.30 Report*, Interview with Kerry O'Brien, 9 February 2006.
2. *Sydney Morning Herald*, 6 July 1998.
3. CPD (S), p. 142, 21 June 2005.
4. *Daily Telegraph*, 7 July 1998.
5. ibid.

6. It also proposes:
   - a parliamentary joint standing committee on human rights which will receive submissions, hold hearings and scrutinise the attorney-general's compatibility statements
   - power vested in the courts to read down subordinate legislation so that it is applied in a manner consistent with the Human Rights Act
   - power vested in the courts even to strike down some subordinate legislation which cannot be interpreted and applied in a manner compatible with the Human Rights Act
   - power vested in the courts to declare primary legislation incompatible with the Human Rights Act. Such legislation would still be valid and applicable but the attorney-general would be required to report to the House of Representatives once he or she considered the court's reasons
   - public authorities, including courts and tribunals, to be required to act consistently with the Human Rights Act.
7. ABC TV, *Insiders*, 4 December 2005.

Chapter 1

1. CPD (HofR), p. 2, 11 October 2005.
2. ibid., p. 3.
3. Anthony Howard, *Basil Hume: The Monk Cardinal* (London: Headline, 2005), p. 327.
4. ibid., p. 324.
5. ibid., p. 325.
6. *The Australian*, 11 January 2006.
7. ibid.
8. 36.5 per cent of Australia's Muslims (102,566) are Australian-born. Those born overseas come mainly from Lebanon (29,321) and Turkey (23,479).
9. Abdullah Saeed, *Islam in Australia* (Melbourne: Allen & Unwin, 2003), pp. 206–7. He is head of the Arabic and Islamic Studies program at the University of Melbourne.

10. ibid., p. 205.
11. In recent years in the Catholic tradition, the popes have given public addresses to the UN as well as an annual address to diplomats. They have also given an annual peace message addressed to all people of goodwill. These addresses make more accessible the Catholic religious tradition. The advent of the UN Special Rapporteur on Religious Intolerance has provided a comprehensive UN reporting agency which is able to monitor religious freedom in nation states. In response to the political strength of the religious Right, the United States Congress has established an Office of International Religious Freedom which reports on other countries, and an Advisory Commission on Religious Freedom Abroad.
12. Most countries are now signatories to the 1981 Declaration on the Elimination of All Forms of Intolerance and of Discrimination Based on Religion or Belief.
13. By 'simple majoritarianism' I mean the political claim that the view of 50 per cent plus one of the voters is correct, regardless of the decision's impact on the rights of an individual or minority.

Chapter 2

1. W. E. Gladstone, *The Vatican Decrees in Their Bearing on Civil Allegiance* (London: John Murray, 1874), p. 12.
2. J. H. Newman, 'A Letter Addressed to His Grace The Duke of Norfolk on Occasion of Mr Gladstone's Recent Expostulation' (1875), in *Certain Difficulties Felt By Anglicans in Catholic Teaching Considered*, vol. 2 (Westminster: Christian Classics, 1969), p. 246.
3. ibid., p. 257.
4. ibid., p. 261.
5. Theologians such as Germain Grisez and John Ford, who advised Pope Paul VI in his preparation of *Humanae Vitae,* were of the view that this teaching was infallible, declaring authoritatively the earlier irreformable papal teaching on the issue in 1930. This is no longer a widely held view, especially given the definitive wording that Pope

John Paul II used in *Evangelium Vitae* declaring abortion, euthanasia and the direct, voluntary killing of an innocent human being to be grave moral disorders. No such wording was used by Paul VI in *Humanae Vitae*. In relation to abortion, John Paul II said:

> By the authority which Christ conferred upon Peter and his Successors, in communion with the Bishops – who on various occasions have condemned abortion and who in the aforementioned consultation, albeit dispersed throughout the world, have shown unanimous agreement concerning this doctrine – I declare that direct abortion, that is, abortion willed as an end or as a means, always constitutes a grave moral disorder, since it is the deliberate killing of an innocent human being. This doctrine is based upon the natural law and upon the written Word of God, is transmitted by the Church's Tradition and taught by the ordinary and universal Magisterium.

At the time Cardinal Ratzinger cautioned that even these declarations were not infallible. There is no way that the bishops throughout the world would show unanimous agreement concerning Paul VI's teaching on contraception. Many would prefer a teaching consistent with the recommendations of the majority of the commission established by Paul VI.

6. Cardinal Pell, 'From Vatican II to Today', Address to Catalyst for Renewal's Bishops Forum, 30 May 2003.
7. Cardinal Pell, Address to the National Press Club, 21 September 2005.
8. Pius XII, 'De Conscientia Christiana in Iuvenibus Recte Efformanda', Radio address for Family Day (23 March 1952), in *Acta Apostolica Sedis*, 44 (12–28 April 1952): p. 271; translated in *The Pope Speaks: The Teachings of Pope Pius XII* (New York: Pantheon, 1957), p. 93.
9. J. H. Newman, 'A Letter Addressed to His Grace The Duke of Norfolk', p. 255.
10. *Dignitatis Humanae*, para. 14.
11. J. Ratzinger, 'Conscience and Truth' (1991), in *Crisis of Conscience*, ed. J. M. Haas (New York: Crossroad Herder, 1996), p. 9.

12. Quoted in J. Mahoney, *The Making of Moral Theology* (Oxford: Clarendon, 1987), p. 187.
13. ibid., p. 192.
14. *Dignitatis Humanae*, para. 3.
15. Cardinal Pell, 'Cardinal Newman on Conscience', Thomas More Forum, Canberra, 20 September 2005.
16. John Courtney Murray, 'Religious Freedom', in *The Documents of Vatican II*, ed. Walter Abbott (London: Geoffrey Chapman, 1966), p. 674.
17. 'The Inconvenient Conscience', *First Things* (May 2005): p. 24.
18. Archbishop Javier Lozano Barragan, 'Our Vision of Health Must be Holistic', Address by President of the Pontifical Council for Pastoral Assistance of Health Care Workers, Head of the Holy See Delegation to the 26th Special Session of the UN General Assembly, 27 June 2001.
19. Quoted in Delia Gallagher, 'Vatican Looking at Collaboration with the Global Fund', *Zenit News*, 6 November 2003.
20. *Zenit News*, 5 February 2005.
21. J. H. Newman, 'A Letter Addressed to His Grace The Duke of Norfolk', p. 256.
22. *Gaudium et Spes*, para. 16. Here the Vatican Council was taking up the idea expressed by Pius XII in his 1952 radio address (see note 9): 'Conscience is, so to speak, the innermost and most secret nucleus in man. It is there that he takes refuge with his spiritual faculties in absolute solitude: alone with himself or, rather, alone with God – Whose voice sounds in conscience – and with himself. There it is that he decides for good or evil; there it is that he chooses between the way of victory and that of defeat. Even if he should wish to do so, a man could never shake off conscience; with it, whether it approves or condemns, he will travel along the whole way of his life, and likewise with it, a truthful and incorruptible witness, he will come up for God's judgment.'
23. *Gaudium et Spes*, para. 43. This is a development on the earlier

teaching of the Second Vatican Council in its 1964 Dogmatic Constitution on the Church (*Lumen Gentium*) in which the church fathers declared: 'The laity should, as all Christians, promptly accept in Christian obedience decisions of their spiritual shepherds, since they are representatives of Christ as well as teachers and rulers in the Church. Let them follow the example of Christ, who by His obedience even unto death, opened to all men the blessed way of the liberty of the children of God' (para. 37).

24. *Humanae Vitae* (1968), para. 11.
25. 'Schema Documenti de Responsabili Paternitate' (Papal Commission final report, 1966), in R. B. Kaiser, *The Politics of Sex and Religion* (Kansas City: Leaven Press, 1985), appendix B, p. 252.
26. J. Ford, Address on the Occasion of the Cardinal Patrick O'Boyle Award, Washington DC, 1978, personal papers, John J. Burns Library, Boston College.
27. Box 27, folio 7, p. 8, New England Jesuit Archives.
28. *Veritatis Splendor*, para. 60.
29. J. Ratzinger, *Church, Ecumenism and Politics* (New York: Crossroad, 1988), p. 165.
30. J. Ratzinger, 'Conscience and Truth', p. 2.
31. ibid., p. 5.
32. ibid., p. 7.
33. ibid., p. 8.
34. ibid., p. 15.
35. Pope Benedict XVI, *Deus Caritas Est*, para. 28, 25 December 2005.
36. Congregation for the Doctrine of the Faith, *Donum Vitae*: Instruction On Respect For Human Life In Its Origin And On The Dignity Of Procreation – Replies To Certain Questions Of The Day, 22 February 1987, para. 4.
37. ibid., para. 1.
38. Professor Michael J. Sandel, *New England Journal of Medicine* 351(3) (2004): p. 208.
39. Catholic ethicists like Fr Norman Ford say 'it is philosophically

credible to hold that an embryonic human individual with a rational human nature is a natural person' in N. Ford and M. Herbert, *Stem Cells* (Strathfield: St Pauls Publications, 2003), p. 73. Even if it is credible, this does not provide any imperative for the legislators in a pluralist democracy to legislate as if every human embryo were a natural person with a rational human nature.

40. Catholic Health Australia, *Code of Ethical Standards for Catholic Health and Aged Care Services in Australia* (2001), p. 22.
41. Benedict XVI, *Deus Caritas Est*, para. 28.

Chapter 3

1. Congregation for the Doctrine of the Faith, *Doctrinal Note on Some Questions Regarding the Participation of Catholics in Political Life*, 24 November 2002, para. 1. The note was directed 'to the Bishops of the Catholic Church and, in a particular way, to Catholic politicians and all lay members of the faithful called to participate in the political life of democratic societies'.
2. ibid., para. 3.
3. ibid., para. 6.
4. ibid., para. 2.
5. ibid., para. 3.
6. ibid., para. 4.
7. The document was approved by the Administrative Committee of the US Catholic Bishops Conference in September 2003 and issued with this prefatory note: 'Every four years since 1976, the Administrative Committee of the US Conference of Catholic Bishops has issued a statement on the responsibilities of Catholics to society. The purpose of the statement is to communicate the Church's teaching that every Catholic is called to an active and faith-filled citizenship, based upon a properly informed conscience, in which each disciple of Christ publicly witnesses to the Church's commitment to human life and dignity with special preference for the poor and the vulnerable.'

8. R. Burke, Canonical Notification in Accordance with Canon 915, 8 January 2004.
9 R. Chaput, 'How to tell a Duck from a Fox: Thinking with the Church as We Look Towards November', *Archdiocese of Denver Newsletter*, 14 April 2004.
10. G. Weigel, 'A Catholic Votes for George W Bush', *America* 191(8) (2004): p. 15.
11. T. McCarrick, 'The Call to Serve in a Divided Society', Canisius Lecture, Boston College, 3 March 2005, p. 6.
12. See *Origins* 34(12) (2004): pp. 188–9.
13. T. McCarrick, Opening Comments, Task Force on Catholic Bishops and Catholic Politicians, US Catholic Bishops' Spring Meeting, Denver, 15 June 2004.
14. *Catholics in Political Life* was developed by the US Conference of Catholic Bishops (USCCB) Task Force on Catholic Bishops and Catholic Politicians in collaboration with Cardinal Francis George, Archbishop Charles Chaput and Bishop Donald W. Wuerl. It was approved for publication by the full body of bishops at their June 2004 general meeting.
15. This letter was sent to McCarrick in early June 2004 and was leaked in the Italian press on 3 July 2004.
16. See H. Prejean, 'Death in Texas', *New York Review of Books* 52(1) (2005): p. 4. Sister Prejean writes: 'When Bush left the governor's office, he had denied clemency in all cases and refused to commute from death to life imprisonment a single death sentence but one – that of Henry Lee Lucas – and that because knowledge of Lucas's innocence of the murder for which he was about to be killed had become the subject of such national scrutiny that Bush could not afford politically to ignore it. Besides, the Lucas case became public during the 2000 presidential campaign, when Bush had begun to portray himself as a "compassionate conservative".'
17. Letter of J. Ratzinger to T. McCarrick, 9 July 2004.
18. Quoted in *Origins* 34(12) (2004): pp. 187–8.

19. G. Weigel, 'A Catholic Votes for George W. Bush', p. 15.
20. 'On our Civic Responsibility for the Common Good', Pastoral Letter to the Church of St Louis, 1 October 2004, para. 30.
21. R. Neuhaus, 'The Public Square', *First Things* 149 (January 2005): p. 64.
22. 410 US 113.
23. 505 US 833.
24. 505 US 833 at 954.
25. 505 US 833 at 867.
26. This was the description used by Senate minority leader, Senator Tom Daschle. See William McGurn, 'Bob Casey's Revenge', *First Things* 149 (January 2005): p. 7.
27. 410 US 113 at 116.
28. 505 US 833 at 943. I provide a more detailed treatment of the *Roe* and *Casey* decisions in *Legislating Liberty* (St Lucia: University of Queensland Press, 1998).
29. 530 US 914 at 956.
30. 530 US 914 at 958.
31. *Partial-Birth Abortion Ban Act of 2003*, s.2 Findings (5).
32. ibid., Findings (2).
33. ibid., Findings (14)B.
34. ibid., Findings (14)G.
35. *National Abortion Federation* v *Ashcroft*, US District Court, Southern District of New York, 03 Civ 8695 (RCC) at p. 88.
36. AMA Policy Finder, H-5.982, Late-Term Pregnancy Termination Techniques.
37. Remarks of President Bush at signing of the *Partial-Birth Abortion Ban Act of 2003*, 5 November 2003.
38. 539 US 558 (2003) at 591–2.
39. President's interview with Elisabeth Bumiller, David E. Sanger and Richard W. Stevenson, *New York Times*, 28 January 2005.
40. Letter to US Senators, 6 January 2005.
41. Address to the Acton Institute Annual Dinner, Grand Rapids, Michigan, October 2004, quoting from Australian Bureau of

Statistics, *Australian Demographic Statistics, March Quarter, 2004* (Canberra: ABS, 2004).

42. Australian Institute of Health and Welfare, *Use of Routinely Collected National Data Sets for Reporting on Induced Abortion in Australia, December 2005* (Canberra: AIHW, 2005).
43. *The Australian*, 6 February 2006.
44. John C. Green, 'The American Religious Landscape and Political Attitudes: A Baseline for 2004', *The Pew Forum on Religion and Public Life*, Washington DC (2004), pp. 40–1.
45. John Paul II, *Evangelium Vitae*, 25 March 1995, para. 62.
46. *New York Times*, 10 October 2004.
47. *New York Times*, 12 October 2004.
48. 'Voting our Conscience, Not our Religion', *New York Times*, 11 October 2004. Roche adds: 'The overall abortion rate (calculated as the number of abortions per 1,000 women between the ages of 15 and 44) was more or less stable during the Reagan years, but during the Clinton presidency it dropped by 11 percent'.
49. *New York Times*, 20 October 2004.
50. Canisius Lecture, Boston College, 3 March 2005, reported in 'Cardinal McCarrick Inaugurates BC Lecture Series', *The Pilot* (Boston), 11 March 2005.
51. Benedict XVI, *Deus Caritas Est*, para. 28.
52. R. Burke, 'On our Civic Responsibility for the Common Good', Pastoral Letter to the Church of St Louis, 1 October 2004, para. 42.
53. Senator John F. Kennedy, Address to the Greater Houston Ministerial Association, Houston, Texas, 12 September 1960.
54. Senate Judiciary Committee, Transcript of Hearing, 13 September 2005.
55. H. Miers, Speech to the Executive Women of Dallas, Spring 1993, p. WH3-05192.
56. Senate Judiciary Committee, Transcript of Hearing, 10 January 2005. The legal doctrine of *stare decisis* requires courts to stand by their earlier decisions unless there are compelling reasons for overruling the earlier precedents.

Chapter 4

1. M. Latham, *The Latham Diaries* (Melbourne: Melbourne University Press, 2005), p. 347.
2. ABC TV, *Insiders*, Interview with Barry Cassidy, 7 August 2005.
3. ABC Radio, *AM*, 29 September 2004.
4. ABC TV, *Insiders*, 7 August 2005.
5. A statement from Archbishop Peter Jensen on industrial relations reform, 8 August 2005.
6. *Sydney Morning Herald*, 6 August 2005.
7. ABC TV, *Lateline*, 19 August 2005. Archbishop Jensen took up this statement by Turnbull in his ABC Boyer lectures, saying: 'The real issue is, can we trust each other to use our freedom well? Will my freedom to bargain be at the expense of your ability to look after your family? Will my freedom to open my shopping mall on weekends, be at the expense of your freedom to have a weekend off from work, at the same time as the rest of your family? The classic liberal account of this – that I should not harm others in the exercise of my liberty – is far too shallow to help in real life.' (Lecture 6: 'Jesus, Freedom and the Choices We Make', 18 December 2005.)
8. Letter to P. Ruddock, 2 April 2002.
9. *The Weekend Australian Magazine*, 10–11 September 2005.
10. A. Bolt, 'Honesty and the Issues', *The Sydney Papers* 16(1) (Summer 2004): p. 117.
11. CPD (HofR), p. 91, 21 June 2005.
12. Benedict XVI, *Deus Caritas Est*, para. 28.
13. CPD (HofR), p. 5247, 20 August 2002.
14. CPD (HofR), p. 10113, 11 December 2002.
15. ibid., p. 10114.
16. *The Australian*, 20 December 2005.
17. Legislation Review of Australia's *Prohibition of Human Cloning Act 2002* and *Research Involving Human Embryos Act 2002*, *Issues Paper*, August 2005, p. iv.
18. ibid., p. 3.

19. Legislation Review of Australia's *Prohibition of Human Cloning Act 2002* and *Research Involving Human Embryos Act 2002*, *Reports*, December 2005, p. 80.
20. ibid., p. 53.
21. *The Australian*, 20 December 2005.
22. Legislation Review, *Reports*, December 2005, p. xvii. ART embryos are those created with assisted reproductive technology.
23. N. Minchin, 'Facts Don't Match Rhetoric in Embronic Research Debate', http://www.conservative.com.au/articles/nick_minchin_Dec_05.htm.
24. Legislation Review, *Reports*, December 2005, p. 74.
25. Quoted in ibid., p. 74.
26. ibid.
27. W. Kasper, Address to the international ecumenical conference at Ushaw College, Durham, 13 January 2006. The latter comment was made at the follow-up press conference, reported by Catholic News Service, 13 January 2006.

Chapter 5

1. *The National Security Strategy of the United States of America* (Washington: United States National Security Council, 2002), p. 15.
2. DIO transcript, 16 October 2003, p. 3, quoted in Parliamentary Joint Committee on ASIO, ASIS and DSD, *Intelligence on Iraq's Weapons of Mass Destruction* (Canberra, December 2003), p. 81.
3. CPD (HofR), P. Jull speaker, p. 25367, 1 March 2004.
4. CPD (HofR), J. Howard speaker, p. 10651, 4 February 2003.
5. ibid., p. 10642.
6. DIO transcript, 16 October 2003, p. 4, quoted in *Intelligence on Iraq's Weapons of Mass Destruction*, p. 95.
7. H. Blix, *Disarming Iraq* (New York: Pantheon Books, 2004), p. 167.
8. Wilton D. Gregory (President, US Conference of Catholic Bishops), Statement on Iraq, 26 February 2003.
9. Letter of Bishop Wilton D. Gregory to President George W. Bush, 13 September 2002.

10. G. Weigel, 'A Catholic Votes for George W. Bush', *America* 191(8) (2004): p. 15.
11. H. Blix, *Disarming Iraq*, p. 270.
12. ibid., p. 271.
13. On 30 May 2003, *USA Today* carried this report. '"The truth is that for reasons that have a lot to do with the U.S. government bureaucracy, we settled on the one issue that everyone could agree on which was weapons of mass destruction as the core reason", Wolfowitz was quoted as saying in a Pentagon transcript of an interview with *Vanity Fair*. The magazine's reporter did not tape the telephone interview and provided a slightly different version of the quote in the article: '"For bureaucratic reasons we settled on one issue, weapons of mass destruction, because it was the one reason everyone could agree on"'.
14. H. Blix, *Disarming Iraq*, p. 274.
15. J. Howard, Address to the National Press Club, Great Hall, Parliament House, 14 March 2003.
16. Pastoral letter from Archbishop Peter Jensen concerning the war in Iraq, 21 March 2003.
17. *The Australian*, 11 February 2003.
18. *The Australian*, 11 June 2003.
19. Bishop Tom Frame, Address to the Western Australian Council of Churches, 4 April 2004.
20. *The Australian*, 4 February 2003.
21. Statement of Australian Catholic Bishops Conference on the Iraq war, 5 March 2003.
22. Pope John Paul II, Address to President George W. Bush, 4 June 2004.
23. CPD (HofR), p. 12551, 18 March 2003.
24. Radio 2UE, Interview with Steve Price, 19 March 2003.
25. CPD (S), p. 11685, 17 June 2003.
26. Lecture published in F. Sullivan and S. Leppert, eds, *Church and Civil Society* (Adelaide: Australian Theological Forum Press, 2004).
27. Channel 9 TV, *Sunday*, 14 March 2004.

28. Archbishop Peter Carnley, Graduation Address, Melbourne College of Divinity, 15 April 2005.
29. Letter of Bishop W. Gregory (President, US Catholic Conference of Bishops), 13 September 2002.

Chapter 6

1. J. Howard, Address to National Press Club, 25 January 2006.
2. F. Brennan, *Legislating Liberty* (St Lucia: University of Queensland Press, 1998), p. 178.
3. ibid., p. 185.
4. See, for example, Communication no. 1153/2003, *Llantoy* v *Peru*; Views adopted on 24 October 2005, CCPR/C/85/D/1153/2003, para. 5.2.
5. ibid., para. 2.8.
6. ibid., Appendix: Dissenting Opinion by Hipolito Solari-Yrigoyen.
7. Communication no. 941/2000, *Young* v *Australia*, Views adopted on 6 August 2003, CCPR/C/78/D/941/2000, para. 12.
8. ibid., para. 9.4.
9. CPD (HofR), p. 22660, 24 November 2003.
10. CPD (HofR), pp. 29383–4, 27 May 2004.
11. Communication no. 1036/2001, *Faure* v *Australia*, Views adopted on 31 October 2005, CCPR/C/85/D/1036/2001, para. 2.1.
12. ibid., para. 6.2.
13. ibid., para. 5.2.
14. ibid., para. 4.17.
15. Article 2, para. 3(a).
16. Communication no. 1036/2001, *Faure* v *Australia*, Views adopted on 31 October 2005, CCPR/C/85/D/1036/2001, para. 9.
17. ibid., para. 7.3.
18. ibid., appendix.
19. M. D. Kirby, 'The Long Journey to Justice for All', Graduation Address, Australian National University, 17 December 2004.
20. *A & Others* v *Secretary of State for the Home Department*, [2005] 2 AC 68 at p. 110.

21. ibid., p. 190.
22. Communication no. 1069/2002, *Bakhtiyari* v *Australia*, CCPR/C/79/D/1069/2002 (6 November 2003), para. 9.3.
23. P. Ruddock, 'Ensuring A Fair Go For Those Most In Need: Australia and Refugees', Address to the 12th Australian Anglican Synod, 27 July 2001.
24. *Behrooz & Others* v *Secretary DIMIA*, *SHDB* v *Godwin & Others*, [2003] High Court of Australia Transcript 456 (12 November 2003).
25. [2003] High Court of Australia Transcript 458 (13 November 2003).
26. *Al Kateb* v *Godwin*, (2004) 219 CLR 562 at p. 658.
27. ibid., p. 659.
28. ibid., p. 648.
29. ibid., p. 650.
30. ibid., p. 651.
31. ibid., p. 575.
32. ibid., pp. 577–8.
33. ibid., p. 581.
34. ibid., p. 585.
35. *A & Others* v *Secretary of State for the Home Department*, [2005] 2 AC 68 at p. 92.
36. ibid., p. 134.
37. ibid., p. 92.
38. ibid., p. 131.
39. ibid., p. 116.
40. ibid., p. 113, quoting *R* v *Secretary for the Home Department, Ex parte Khawaja*, [1984] AC 74 at pp. 111–2.
41. ibid., p. 124.
42. ibid., p. 115.
43. ibid., p. 121.
44. ibid., p. 128.
45. ibid.
46. ibid.
47. ibid., p. 132.

48. ibid., p. 171.
49. ibid., pp. 170-1.
50. See *Hamdi* v *Rumsfeld, Rasul* v *Bush, Rumsfeld* v *Padilla*, 542 US __ (2004).
51. *Hamdi* v *Rumsfeld*, 542 US __ (2004), 28 June 2004, p. 23.
52. ibid., p. 25.
53. *Zadvydas* v *Davis*, 533 US 678 (2001).
54. *Al-Kateb* v *Godwin*, (2004) 219 CLR 562 at p. 587.
55. ibid., p. 654.
56. ibid.
57. ibid., p. 652, quoting *US* v *Shaughnessy* (1952), 195 Federal Reporter (2nd Series) 964 at 971 (2nd Cir).
58. ibid., p. 620.
59. ibid., p. 601, quoting *Zadvydas* v *Davis* at p. 693.
60. ibid., p. 662.
61. M. D. Kirby, 'The Long Journey of Justice for All', Graduation Address, Australian National University, 17 December 2004.
62. M. McHugh, 'The Need for Agitators – the Risk of Stagnation', (2007), 9 Constitutional Law and Policy Review 46 at p. 49.

Chapter 7

1. Murray Gleeson, 'Rights and Values', Melbourne Catholic Lawyers Association, 18 June 2004.
2. Marcus Priest, 'The Smiler', *Australian Financial Review Magazine* (May 2006): pp. 68–73 at 70.
3. *CES* v *Superclinics (Australia) Pty Ltd*, (1995) 38 NSWLR 47 at p. 60.
4. Australian Catholic Bishops Conference, 'Aide-memoire to the High Court Superclinics Litigation', 20 September 1996.
5. Congregation For The Doctrine Of The Faith, *Donum Vitae*: 'Instruction On Respect For Human Life In Its Origin And On The Dignity Of Procreation – Replies To Certain Questions Of The Day', 22 February 1987, para. 5.

6. Quoted by Justice McHugh in *Re McBain; Ex parte Australian Catholic Bishops Conference*, (2002) 209 CLR 372 at p. 423.
7. *Australian Catholic Bishops Conference & Another, Ex parte— Re Justice Sundberg*, High Court Transcript C22/2000 (4 September 2001).
8. *Re McBain; Ex parte Australian Catholic Bishops Conference*, (2002) 209 CLR 372 at p. 395.
9. Transcript, *Australian Catholic Bishops Conference & Anor, Ex parte — Re Sundberg & Anor*, C22/2000, 5 September 2001.
10. (1990) 497 US 261.
11. ibid., per Chief Justice Rehnquist at p. 274.
12. [1993] AC 789.
13. ibid., p. 858.
14. ibid., p. 870.
15. ibid., p. 876.
16. *BWV*, [2003] VCAT 121 (28 February 2003) at para. 12.
17. *Re BWV; Ex parte Gardner*, (2003) 7 VR 487 at p. 504.
18. ibid., p. 507.
19. Pope John Paul II, 'Address to the Participants in the International Congress on Life-Sustaining Treatments And Vegetative State: Scientific Advances And Ethical Dilemmas', 20 March 2004.
20. Address to Catholic Health Australia Conference, September 2004.
21. Directive 58.
22. The note was issued on 3 September 2004.
23. See R. Evans, 'Gnosticism and the High Court', *Quadrant*, June 1999, pp. 20–6; and my response, 'Justice Brennan and Mabo', *Quadrant*, September 1999, Letters, pp. 5–6.
24. R. Evans, 'Gnosticism and the High Court', pp. 24, 25.
25. H. Morgan, 'The Dangers of Aboriginal Sovereignty', *News Weekly*, 29 August 1992, p. 12.
26. The statement appears in the court transcript of 15 March 1988.
27. Letter to author, 19 September 1994.
28. R. Evans, 'Gnosticism and the High Court', p. 26.
29. ibid., p. 24.

30. J. Franklin, *Corrupting the Youth* (Sydney: Macleay Press, 2003), p. 388.
31. K. Windschuttle, 'Mabo and the Fabrication of Aboriginal History', in *Upholding the Australian Constitution*, ed. John Stone, vol. 15, Proceedings of the Samuel Griffith Society (Melbourne, 2003), p. 283 at pp. 284, 294–5.
32. At Brennan's swearing in as a High Court judge in February 1981, Attorney-General Peter Durack, QC, informed the court, 'There are two events during your time at the Bar which I think deserve special mention. The first was the case in which you appeared for the small landholders in Fiji and the result of the case was a victory for the Fijians which was of great significance. The second concerned the work you did for the Northern Land Council and the Aboriginal Land Rights Royal Commission conducted by Mr Justice Woodward. That report by Mr Justice Woodward formed the basis of legislation adopted by successive Federal Governments for Aboriginal land rights. Many of Mr Justice Woodward's recommendations followed submissions you made on behalf of the Northern Land Council and, of course, it was an investigation which had tremendous significance for Australia's Aboriginal people.'
33. A. E. Woodward, *One Brief Interval* (Melbourne: The Miegunyah Press, 2005), p. 135.
34. ibid., p. 141.
35. A. E. Woodward, *Aboriginal Land Rights Commission, Second Report* (Canberra: AGPS, 1974), p. 103.
36. ibid., p. 108.
37. The *Age*, 14 February 2004.
38. F. G. Brennan, 'The Common Law: Law for a Time, Law for a Place', Judicial Conference of Australia, 2005 Colloquium Papers, 3 September 2005, p. 8.
39. *In re Southern Rhodesia* (1919) AC 211, at pp. 233–4.
40. T. Stephens, *Sir William Deane: The Things that Matter* (Sydney: Hodder Headline, 2002), p. 96.

41. ibid., p. 100.
42. CPD (HofR), p. 345, 6 May 1996. Again, on 26 June 1996, John Howard told Parliament: 'I have always regarded the Mabo decision itself as being a justified, correct decision. I have stated that on a number of occasions.' (CPD [HofR], p. 2791, 1996).
43. D. Marr, *The High Price of Heaven* (Sydney: Allen & Unwin, 1999), p. 53.
44. ABC Radio National, *Law Report*, 9 September 1997.
45. ABC Radio National, *Law Report*, 16 September 1997.
46. D. Marr, *The High Price of Heaven*, p. 71.
47. ibid., p. 62.
48. T. Molomby, 'Cases and Causes: The High Price of Propaganda', *Quadrant* 47 (April 2003): p. 16.
49. D. Marr, *The High Price of Heaven*, p. 61.
50. ibid.
51. Marr asks rhetorically at p. 55, 'And why was Green so sober and Gillies so drunk?'
52. T. Molomby, 'Cases and Causes: The High Price of Propaganda', p. 16. Marr expresses his gratitude to Tom Molomby 'for help with the law', though not with the facts, in writing his chapter (see D. Marr, *The High Price of Heaven*, p. 293).
53. *Green* v *The Queen*, High Court of Australia Transcripts, S172/1996 (10 December 1996).
54. ibid., pp. 68, 70.
55. T. Molomby, 'Cases and Causes: The High Price of Propaganda', p. 16.
56. *Green* v *The Queen*, (1996–97) 191 CLR 334 at 384.
57. ibid., p. 385.
58. ibid., p. 386.
59. ibid., p. 416.
60. D. Marr, *The High Price of Heaven*, p. 70.
61. *Croome & Another* v *The State of Tasmania* (1996–97) 191 CLR 119 at pp. 127–8.
62. T. Molomby, 'Cases and Causes: The High Price of Propaganda', p. 15.
63. (1995) 183 CLR ix at p. x.

Chapter 8

1. The same wording has appeared, uncontroversially and perhaps unnoticed, in the *Family Law Act* since 1975. Section 43(a) provides that courts are to have regard to 'the need to preserve and protect the institution of marriage as the union of a man and woman to the exclusion of all others voluntarily entered into for life'.
2. CPD (S), Senator Ludwig speaker, p. 26560, 12 August 2004. (The *Hansard* for 12 August 2004 includes the debate of 13 August 2004.)
3. ibid., p. 26533.
4. ibid., p. 26544.
5. Congregation for the Doctrine of the Faith, 'Considerations Regarding Proposals to Give Legal Recognition to Unions Between Homosexual Persons', 3 June 2003, para. 10.
6. David L. Chambers, 'What If? The Legal Consequences of Marriage and the Legal Needs of Lesbian and Gay Couples', *Michigan Law Review* 95 (1996): p. 490.
7. Richard Stith, 'Keep Friendship Unregulated', *Notre Dame Journal of Law, Ethics and Public Policy* 18 (2004): p. 271.
8. J. Mahoney, 'Christian Doctrines, Ethical Issues and Human Genetics', *Theological Studies* 64 (2003): p. 737.
9. Personal communication, Bruce Meagher to author, 18 October 2005.
10. s. 5(1)(f) *Family Law Act 1975*.
11. *In the Marriage of Cormick*, (1984) 156 CLR 170 at p. 177.
12. ibid., p. 182.
13. ibid.
14. *The Queen* v *L*, (1992) 174 CLR 379 at p. 391.
15. ibid., p. 392.
16. ibid., p. 404.
17. *Reference re Same-Sex Marriage, Supreme Court of Canada*, 2004 SCC 79, para. 22, 9 December 2004.
18. ibid., para. 29.
19. ibid., para. 27.

20. ibid., para. 25.
21. In his dissent in *Lawrence* v *Texas* in which the majority struck down a state law criminalising homosexual sodomy, Justice Scalia observed: 'One of the benefits of leaving regulation of this matter to the people rather than to the courts is that the people, unlike judges, need not carry things to their logical conclusion. The people may feel that their disapprobation of homosexual conduct is strong enough to disallow homosexual marriage, but not strong enough to criminalize private homosexual acts – and may legislate accordingly. The Court today pretends that it possesses a similar freedom of action, so that we need not fear judicial imposition of homosexual marriage, as has recently occurred in Canada (in a decision that the Canadian Government has chosen not to appeal) . . . At the end of its opinion – after having laid waste the foundations of our rational-basis jurisprudence – the Court says that the present case "does not involve whether the government must give formal recognition to any relationship that homosexual persons seek to enter." Do not believe it. More illuminating than this bald, unreasoned disclaimer is the progression of thought displayed by an earlier passage in the Court's opinion, which notes the constitutional protections afforded to "personal decisions relating to marriage, procreation, contraception, family relationships, child rearing, and education," and then declares that "[p]ersons in a homosexual relationship may seek autonomy for these purposes, just as heterosexual persons do." Today's opinion dismantles the structure of constitutional law that has permitted a distinction to be made between heterosexual and homosexual unions, insofar as formal recognition in marriage is concerned. If moral disapprobation of homosexual conduct is "no legitimate state interest" for purposes of proscribing that conduct, as the Court coos (casting aside all pretense of neutrality), "[w]hen sexuality finds overt expression in intimate conduct with another person, the conduct can be but one element in a personal bond that is more enduring," what justification could there possibly be for denying the

benefits of marriage to homosexual couples exercising "[t]he liberty protected by the Constitution"? Surely not the encouragement of procreation, since the sterile and the elderly are allowed to marry. This case "does not involve" the issue of homosexual marriage only if one entertains the belief that principle and logic have nothing to do with the decisions of this Court. Many will hope that, as the Court comfortingly assures us, this is so.' 539 US 558 (2003) at pp. 604–5.

22. 478 US 186 (1986).
23. 517 US 620 (1996).
24. 539 US 558 (2003).
25. Florida Statute no. 63.042 provides that 'no person eligible to adopt . . . may adopt if that person is a homosexual'. According to the Victorian Law Reform Commission's paper, *A.R.T., Surrogacy and Legal Parentage: A Comparative Legislative Review* (Melbourne: VLRC, 2004), there are only eight states and the District of Columbia in the United States that allow second-parent adoption by a member of a same-sex couple statewide. There are counties in some 22 US states that permit gay and lesbian couples and same-sex couples to adopt (see footnote 242 at p. 56).
26. *Lofton* v *Secretary of the Department of Children and Family Services*, 377 Federal Reporter (3rd Series) 1275 (11th Cir. 2004) at p. 1276. The court en banc had been petitioned to review the earlier decision of a three member bench reported at 358 F.3d 804 (11th Cir. 2004).
27. ibid., p. 1280.
28. *Halpern* v *Attorney General of Canada*, 225 DLR (4th) 529 at p. 549 (2003).
29. By September 2004, the courts of six provinces and territories had affirmed that to exclude same-sex couples from marriage was constitutionally prohibited discrimination.
30. *Halpern* v *Attorney General of Canada*, 225 DLR (4th) 529 at p. 544 (2003).
31. ibid., p. 547. The Ontario court thought that 'the term "marriage" as used in s.91(26) of the *Constitution Act 1867* has the constitutional

flexibility necessary to meet the changing realities of Canadian society without the need for recourse to constitutional amendment procedures'.

32. ibid., p. 552.
33. ibid., p. 553.
34. ibid., p. 559.
35. ibid., p. 562.
36. ibid., p. 565.
37. ibid.
38. In September 2004, the Victorian Law Reform Commission released a paper by Dr Ruth McNair, 'Outcomes for Children Born of A.R.T. in a Diverse Range of Families'. McNair is obviously very sympathetic to providing ART services to same-sex couples anxious to nurture their own children. But the state's rational concern to move cautiously or not at all is justified in light of observations such as:

    > By contrast, two systematic reviews of outcomes for children in lesbian and gay families have been conducted that used similar standardised and validated criteria to evaluate the methodological strength (still restricted to quantitative, comparative studies) and identified 23 and 8 studies respectively (Anderssen, Amilie & Ytteroy 2002; Hunfeld, Fauser & Passchier 2002). All studies reviewed were found to be methodologically rigorous, and both reviews found that the children in lesbian families fared at least as well as those in heterosexual families on all measures. Both found that there were insufficient studies involving gay men and single parents to be conclusive. (pp. 51–2)
    >
    > The consistency of findings of positive outcomes for children across so many of the lesbian parent studies could be partly because samples are drawn from volunteer groups of lesbian mothers, who may not be representative of all lesbian mothers. Many of the studies have recruited predominantly Anglo-Saxon, middle class parents, and it is clear that studies are needed to sample a wider range of people (Demo & Allen 1996). It has been highlighted that volunteer mothers

whose children are experiencing problems are less likely to take part (Golombok et al. 1997). (p. 52)

It is possible that participants in lesbian and gay family studies tend to focus on positives and do not report negative consequences for their children. (p. 53)

There are few longitudinal studies that follow children's progress through adolescence to adulthood. (p. 54)

Older children and adults who have grown up in lesbian and gay families from conception have rarely been studied to date. (p. 54)

39. See Maggie Gallagher and Joshua K. Baker, 'Do Moms and Dads Matter? Evidence from the Social Sciences on Family Structure and the Best Interests of the Child', *Margins Law Journal* 4 (2004): p. 161. Gallagher and Baker pose two separate questions (p. 176): 'The first question is: Are gays and lesbians, on average, just as likely to be good parents as heterosexual parents? The second question is: Do children raised by unisex couples do just as well as children raised by married mothers and fathers? While this first question may be relevant to certain policy questions regarding the parental fitness of specific individuals (e.g., in a child custody dispute), it does not speak to the issue of family structure. Our primary interest is in the social science evidence on the latter question, which goes to the core of the family structure debate.' Having surveyed the various studies, and their deficiencies, including the fact that the vast majority of studies related to the family structure debate simply compare single lesbian mothers to single heterosexual mothers, they conclude: 'A substantial body of evidence suggests that family structure matters and that children do better, on average, when they are raised by the household of their own married mother and father' (p. 180).
40. *Halpern* v *Attorney-General of Canada*, 225 DLR (4th) 529 at p. 565.
41. There may be a strong case for adoption by a same-sex couple when a child is the biological child of one of the partners.
42. *Halpern* v *Attorney-General of Canada*, p. 570.
43. Supreme Court of Canada, *Reference re Same-Sex Marriage*, 2004 SCC 79 (9 December 2004).

44. *Hilary Goodridge & Others* v *Department of Public Health & Another*, 798 N.E. 2d 941 (Mass. 2003). Marshall CJ explained rational basis review at p. 960: 'For due process claims, rational basis analysis requires that statutes "bear[ ] a real and substantial relation to the public health, safety, morals, or some other phase of the general welfare." *Coffee-Rich, Inc.* v. *Commissioner of Pub. Health*, quoting *Sperry & Hutchinson Co.* v. *Director of the Div. on the Necessaries of Life*, 307 Mass. 408, 418 (1940). For equal protection challenges, the rational basis test requires that "an impartial lawmaker could logically believe that the classification would serve a legitimate public purpose that transcends the harm to the members of the disadvantaged class." *English* v. *New England Med. Ctr*, supra at 429, quoting *Cleburne* v. *Cleburne Living Ctr, Inc*, 473 U.S. 432, 452 (1985) (Stevens, J, concurring).'
45. ibid., p. 961.
46. ibid., p. 962.
47. ibid., p. 963.
48. ibid., p. 980.
49. ibid., p. 981.
50. ibid., pp. 999–1000.
51. ibid., p. 970.
52. R. Reuther, 'Marriage Between Homosexuals is Good for Marriage', *National Catholic Reporter*, 18 November 2005.
53. CPD (HofR), p. 5343, 21 August 2002.
54. Canadian Conference of Catholic Bishops, Factum of the Intervener, *In the Matter of a Reference by the Governor in Council*, court file no. 29866.
55. ibid., para. 58.
56. Congregation for The Doctrine of The Faith, *Considerations Regarding Proposals to Give Legal Recognition to Unions Between Homosexual Persons*, 3 June 2003.
57. Resolution D039, Episcopal Church (USA) General Convention 2000, quoted in *The Windsor Report 2004*, The Lambeth Commission

on Communion (London: The Anglican Communion Office, 2004), p. 80.

58. Resolution C051, Episcopal Church (USA) General Convention 2003, quoted in *The Windsor Report 2004*, The Lambeth Commission on Communion, p. 79.
59. The margin of approval for state constitutional amendments opposing same-sex marriage ranged from 56 per cent approval in Oregon to 86 per cent approval in Mississippi. The approval rate in other states was: Arkansas (75 per cent), Georgia (77 per cent), Kentucky (75 per cent), Montana (66 per cent), North Dakota (73 per cent), Ohio (62 per cent) and Oklahoma (76 per cent).
60. *Boston Globe*, 18 November 2004.
61. *New York Times*, 12 November 2004.
62. Since then, the New Zealand Parliament has passed its Civil Unions Bill by a vote of 65 to 55.
63. *Boston Globe*, 19 October 2004, p. B6.
64. I am thinking of the case when two ova are used, with the nucleus being taken from one and the mitochondrial DNA from the other, and sperm from an anonymous donor.
65. See M. Somerville, 'What About the Children?', in *Divorcing Marriage*, (Montreal: McGill–Queen's University Press, 2004), p. 67.
66. In the United Kingdom, adoption since 2002 has been available to couples 'whether of different sexes or the same sex, living as partners in an enduring family relationship'.
67. Section 2(e), *Assisted Reproduction Act 2004.*
68. Section 13(5), *Human Fertilisation and Embryology Act 1990* (UK).
69. Mary Warnock, *Report of the Committee of Inquiry into Human Fertilisation and Embryology* (London: Department of Health and Social Security, 1984), para. 2.11.
70. John Seymour and Sonia Magri, *A.R.T. Surrogacy and Legal Parentage: A Comparative Legislative Review* (Melbourne: Victorian Law Reform Commission, 2004), p. 68.
71. Ruth McNair, *Outcomes for Children Born of A.R.T. in a Diverse*

Range of Families (Melbourne: Victorian Law Reform Commission, 2004), p. 61.

Conclusion

1. M. Latham, *The Latham Diaries* (Melbourne: Melbourne University Press, 2005), p. 114.
2. Karen Armstrong, *The Spiral Staircase: A Memoir* (London: Harper Perennial, 2005), pp. 135–6.
3. ibid., p. 137.
4. Senate Community Affairs Committee, Transcript, 6 February 2006, p. CA13.
5. CPD (HofR), p. 75, 15 February 2006.
6. John T. Noonan, *A Church that Can and Cannot Change* (Notre Dame, Indiana: University of Notre Dame Press, 2005), pp. 203–4.
7. J. Ratzinger, *God is Near Us* (San Francisco: Ignatius Press, 2003), p. 105.
8. Quoted in *Origins* 34(21) (2004): p. 335.
9. J. Ratzinger, 'The Dignity of the Human Person', in Burns and Oates, eds, *Commentary on the Documents of Vatican II*, vol. 5 (1969), p. 136.
10. John T. Noonan, *A Church that Can and Cannot Change*, p. 204.
11. *Van Orden* v *Perry*, 545 US __ (2005); 27 June 2005, Slip Opinion, p. 4.
12. ibid., p. 10.
13. C. M. H. Clark, *Selected Documents in Australian History*, vol. 2 (Sydney: Angus & Robertson, 1955), p. 109.

INDEX

Also by Frank Brennan
TAMPERING WITH ASYLUM
Revised Edition

In August 2001 a Norwegian vessel picked up 433 asylum seekers from a boat sinking in international waters between Australia and Indonesia. What the Howard government did in response created waves internationally.

By denying the *Tampa* and its cargo of asylum seekers permission to dock at Christmas Island, Australia signalled that it was dramatically closing its national borders. Trading on fear, and rushing in legislation to give their move legal backing, the Howard government effectively excluded asylum seekers from the Australian courts.

Frank Brennan argues that the government's response was a massive overreaction, possible only in a remote country such as Australia with few asylum seekers and no land borders. He compares Australia's policy with that of the United States and Europe and provides a practical blueprint for countries wanting to humanely protect asylum seekers.

This revised edition includes an epilogue bringing the book up to date with the latest developments. The epilogue covers the Cornelia Rau and Vivian Alvarez Solon cases, Liberal backbencher Petro Georgiou's successful campaign to get children out of detention centres, and the Senate's thwarting of the government's 2006 attempt to extend the Pacific Solution.

'A timely, topical book . . . penetrating.'

Canberra Times

'A powerful book.'

Australian Financial Review

'A valuable contribution to the assessment of our treatment of asylum seekers.'

Journal of Australian Studies Review of Books

'Necessary reading.'

Australian Book Review

ISBN 978 0 7022 3581 8

UQP

Other UQP Non-fiction

TRANSLATING LIVES
Edited by
Mary Besemeres and Anna Wierzbicka

I can't find English words suitable for talking about my tiny granddaughter . . . in Polish I could say that she has dear-little-curls or dear-little-teeth, or for her age she is dear-little-small. In English, I would have to use 'loveless' words like 'curls', 'teeth' or 'small', and I couldn't do that . . .

Although Australia prides itself on being multicultural, many Australians have little awareness of what it means to live in two cultures at once, and of how much there is to learn about other cultural perspectives.

Translating Lives is an immensely moving collection of personal stories tracing the experiences of twelve people living in Australia who speak more than one language. Contributors including Kim Scott and Eva Sallis show how their experiences of language colour the way they relate to people and the way they see the world. Through their eyes, we learn how language, culture and identity are intrinsically linked.

Illuminating and insightful, *Translating Lives* is an engrossing read for every Australian wanting to understand the complex culture we live in today.

> '*Translating Lives* is a book of revelations. It is a journey through an Australia composed of a multiplicity of languages and, therefore, many inner worlds.'
>
> Arnold Zable

ISBN 978 0 7022 3603 7

UQP

DOWN TO THIS
Shaughnessy Bishop-Stall

The rules I've set out for myself are simple: no money or friends, except those I might find from here on in. I'll do what the others do to get by, be whatever bum I choose: vagrant, beggar, wino, criminal, busker, con man or tramp, on any given day.

In November 2001, 27-year-old Shaughnessy Bishop-Stall packed his life in a bag – complete with tent, notebooks, pen and a broken heart – and set out to spend a year in Tent City, the largest homeless settlement in North America.

When he arrives, he finds an anarchic community of fugitives, drug addicts, prostitutes, dealers and ex-cons, a society where the rules are made up nightly and your life depends on knowing them. Not only does Bishop-Stall manage to survive, but against all odds his own heart and spirit slowly mend. An astonishing account of birth, suicide, brawls, binges, good and bad intentions, fiendish charity and the sudden eloquence and generosity of broken souls, *Down to This* is not just a memoir but also a fascinating look at the lives of those on the fringes of society.

'Impossible not to be transfixed.'

The Vancouver Sun

'After a gonzo plunge into homelessness and booze, Bishop-Stall surfaces with a terrific book, evocative of the writing of Hunter S Thompson. A surprising new talent who writes with verve, wit and insight about life on the urban margins.'

Maclean's

'Brilliant writing, verging on the poetic.'

The Globe and Mail

ISBN 978 0 7022 3593 1

UQP

EUROPEAN COM

Revision WorkBook

Robert M. MacLean LLB, Dip LP, LLM

HLT Publications

HLT PUBLICATIONS
200 Greyhound Road, London W14 9RY

ISBN 1 85352 787 4

British Library Cataloguing-in-Publication.

A CIP Catalogue record for this book is available from the British Library.

Printed and bound in Great Britain.

CONTENTS

ACKNOWLEDGMENTS

The Author and the Publisher wish to thank the University of London LLB (External) and the University of Glasgow for their kind permission to reproduce and publish problems from past examination papers.

Caveat

The answers given are not approved or sanctioned by either the University of London or the University of Glasgow and are entirely our responsibility. They are not intended to be 'model answers', but rather suggested solutions.

These solutions are designed to perform two fundamental purposes, namely:

a) to provide a detailed example of a suggested solution to an examination question; and

b) to assist students with research into the subject of European Community law and to further their understanding and appreciation of the nature of Community law.

Note

Please note that the solutions to this WorkBook incorporate the law as it stood in February 1991. It has not been able to include Community legislation or cases reported after this date.

INTRODUCTION

This Revision WorkBook has been designed specifically for those students studying European Community law at the undergraduate level. Each individual chapter of the text deals with a particular subject matter found in the curricula of most courses dealing with Community law. At the same time, coverage has not been restricted to any one particular syllabus but has been designed to embrace all the principal topics which are found in university and polytechnic examinations on this subject. The text is best used as a supplement to the recommended reading suggested by course organisers of individual programmes.

Each chapter contains an introduction which explains the scope and general contents of the topic covered. This is followed by detailed 'key points' which advise students on the minimum content of materials with which they must be familiar in order to properly understand the subject. Recent cases and relevant materials are included where appropriate.

The most valuable feature of the Revision WorkBook remains the examination questions themselves which direct the attention of the student to the issues most frequently raised in examination papers. Questions have been selected in order to cover the most popular issues raised in examinations. Each question has a skeleton solution followed by a suggested solution. Although students are not expected to produce a skeleton solution in examinations, it is a useful examination technique which assists to ensure a well structured, balanced and logical answer.

This Revision WorkBook has been prepared by university lecturers experienced in teaching this specific syllabus and the solutions are intended to be illustrations of full answers to problems commonly posed by examiners. They are not 'model answers', for at this level there is almost certainly more than one solution to each problem. Nor are the answers written to the exacting time limits of examinations. They are designed to bring the most salient and important points of law to the attention of the student and to illustrate an appropriate methodology in each case.

The opportunity has been taken, where appropriate, to develop themes, suggest alternatives and to set out additional material to an extent not possible by the student in the examination room. This has been done to provide the student with a full answer from which he or she might select the most relevant points while at the same time benefiting from the variety of the questions.

We believe that, in writing full opinions to each question, we can assist you with your study of Community law and can further your understanding and appreciation of the law of the European Community.

HOW TO STUDY EUROPEAN COMMUNITY LAW

Despite nearly two decades of British membership of the European Community, the importance of Community law seems to have only recently been recognised. European Community law has become an increasing part of the curricula of degree courses at both universities and polytechnics throughout the United Kingdom. It is also only a matter of time before European Community law becomes a mandatory requirement for those intending to enter the legal profession.

The recent recognition of the importance of Community law in many respects reflects the dramatic transformation which the European Community has undergone throughout the course of the last decade. The institutional changes in the structure of the Community, together with the legislative programme designed to complete the internal market programme by 1992, both serve to reiterate the determination of the Member States to ensure that the Community becomes an effective force in European integration. Further, the growing volume of legislation emanating from the Community is itself evidence of the increasingly important role of the European Community as a source of legal principles.

European Community law is a sui generis species of law. It has been created by drawing upon the reservoir of legal principles contained in the legal systems of the Member States. For various reasons, the English legal system has not played a significant role in this evolution. Community law has been fashioned under the influence of the civilian legal systems of continental Europe. For that reason, students with common law backgrounds may not readily identify with some of the concepts and institutions of Community law. Students must therefore exercise patience when studying Community law in order to appreciate the unique nature of Community law.

To understand Community law, a basic comprehensive of the fundamental elements of this system must be achieved. This requires intensive consideration of subjects such as the relationship between the Community legal order and the legal systems of the Member States, the different forms of Community legislation and the hierarchy which exists between them, the judicial techniques of the European Court and the fundamental principles of Community law which have been developed in order to allow the Community to function on the basis of the rule of law. These matters form the essential core of the Community legal system, and the edifice of Community law has been erected upon them.

Further, it is also important to acquire a comprehensive and overall perception of the subject and to understand how particular topics interrelate. European Community law is characterised by an extensive overlapping of topics. Points which are brought up in one particular section of the syllabus continuously recur in other areas of the subject. An overall general knowledge of each individual topic will ultimately facilitate the acquisition of an extensive and detailed knowledge of the complete subject.

Students should also adopt an appropriate methodology towards answering questions of Community law. Legal authority in Community law is derived primarily through the Community Treaties and secondarily through Community legislation, particularly Regulations and Directives, and the decisions of the European Court. The European Court has been responsible for a considerable number of the fundamental principles of the Community, and cases of important legal significance have been cited throughout the text. Familiarity with these precedents is absolutely essential to the study of Community law.

Once the basic skills and methodology have been acquired in approaching problems involving questions of Community law, the task of identifying and applying the relevant legal principles to the issue becomes increasingly simplified. These skills may best be acquired through a study and appreciation of the techniques involved in answering examination questions. The objective of this text is therefore not primarily to provide students with pro forma answers to questions, but to teach them the skills involved in approaching questions which have European legal implications.

REVISION AND EXAMINATION TECHNIQUE

It is not the purpose of this Revision WorkBook to serve as a substitute for attending lectures, studying the recommended readings or attempting take home essay questions. Engaging in such practices would not only be dangerous because individual lecturers stress different areas of the syllabus, but also because they can never lead to a proper appreciation of the subject. A failure to spend time learning the law will inevitably be exposed. Acquiring legal qualifications is only the beginning of a legal career. In a competitive legal environment, those not thoroughly familiar with the law will be less likely to succeed.

Engaging in such practices also has other limitations. They deprive the student of opportunities to clarify points of difficulty and to expand upon difficult matters during the course of the programme. An exchange of ideas is essential for a complete appreciation of the complexities involved in the application of European Community law, and may provide insight into difficulties which might arise in final examinations. This WorkBook is therefore designed to supplement diligence and effort, the combination which most often leads to success.

An individual syllabus should therefore be supplemented by reference to the various relevant chapters in this WorkBook. Familiarity with the principal issues and the types of question which might arise allows students an opportunity to formulate appropriate responses to possible questions arising during the term. In turn, this should encourage the expansion of ideas and alternative proposals for answering questions at the end of the course.

A number of points are relevant to the study and revision of Community law. A proportional relationship may be established between relevancy and final score. Students should therefore avoid commentary and deviation from the terms of the question. As many relevant points as possible should be included in an answer. Vagueness can be avoided by becoming acquainted with the principal concepts and principles in each individual area of the syllabus. For this purpose, the WorkBook emphasises the most important basic issues in the key point sections of the book.

Further, in law relevancy is almost invariably related to authority. The sounder the legal authority adduced in support of a proposition, the greater the cogency of the argument. Frequently, although a student has correctly answered the problem, the answer will not score highly. This may often be attributed to the lack of authority cited to support the argument. Problems are posed not only for the purpose of testing common sense, but also in order to ascertain a candidate's knowledge of the law.

At the same time, methodology is important. This is the style adopted by a candidate for reaching a particular conclusion to a question. Although methodology is often related to organisation, it is best acquired through practice. While this WorkBook is designed to facilitate the acquisition of an appropriate methodology by proposing suggested solutions, there is no substitute for trial and error prior to the examination.

In European Community law, questions fall into two main categories. On the one hand an examiner may pose an 'essay type' question which will specify a particular topic for discussion. Although at first it might appear that such questions allow an almost infinite discretion for answering, in fact the examiner will undoubtedly have a number of basic points in mind which must be covered in a successful answer. Consequently, essay type questions are best attempted on subjects in which the student has acquired a familiarity with the basic concepts.

On the other hand, an examiner may set a 'problem type' question. In such cases, the student is presented with a set of hypothetical facts and instructed to apply the law. Unless suggested to the contrary, the stated facts require no proof and the student should proceed on the basis that these facts are supported by sufficient evidence. The student should refrain from deducing the existence of facts to the contrary unless such an inference is unavoidable.

Obviously, in order to remain relevant, the student must be able to distinguish between relevant and irrelevant facts, and must be able to apply the law to the relevant facts. Again an examiner will require that a number of basic points are covered to score a reasonable mark. In order to attempt such questions, read the facts carefully, ascertain the most important matters, and sketch out the applicable law prior to attempting the problem itself. Organisation will also ultimately result in a higher score and more often than not less time will be spent answering the question.

Where the law on a certain matter is unsettled, the examiner will be attempting to solicit comment on the nature of the controversies which have created this state of affairs. In addition, the examiner may also be looking for an outline of the opposing view. The candidate need not support one or other opinion, but should refer to which side of the argument is legally most plausible.

Questions may also be divided into a number of parts. Most frequently, all the sections will relate to the same topic, if not the same principles behind a specific area of Community law. The problem may be phrased in such a way that the only plausible answer to another part of the question is to answer the first in a certain manner. If a discrepancy does arise between the answer to the first part, and the answer suggested by the language of the later part, most often this will not be fatal if a cogent, reasoned legal argument has been advanced in the answer to the first part. A student may propose alternative solutions to the later part of the question, although most likely this process will be time consuming.

Finally, there is no substitute for proper preparation before entering the examination room. If a student has to ascertain distinctions and differentiations under examination conditions, not only will the answer be confused, but it will also most likely be insufficient. An appreciation of the major concepts, principles and rules of Community law is best acquired before endeavours are made in the examination room.

TABLE OF CASES

TABLE OF COMMUNITY LEGISLATION

Community Regulations

Community Directives

Community Decisions

TABLE OF UNITED KINGDOM LEGISLATION

1 THE ORIGINS AND NATURE OF THE EUROPEAN COMMUNITY

1.1 Introduction

The European Community consists of three separate, yet closely related, economic organisations each established by independent international agreements. The first European Community was the European Coal and Steel Community (ECSC) formed in 1951 by six states - Belgium, France, Germany, Italy, Luxembourg and the Netherlands. Its success encouraged the expansion of the concept of the common market to all aspects of economic production. This was achieved by the negotiation of two more agreements, the European Economic Community (EEC) Treaty and the European Atomic Energy (Euratom) Treaty. Membership of the European Community was increased by the admission of the United Kingdom, Ireland and Denmark in 1973, followed by Greece in 1981, and Spain and Portugal in 1986.

1.2 Key points

a) *The treaties founding the European Community*

i) The European Coal and Steel Community (ECSC) Treaty

The ECSC Treaty was signed in Paris on 18 April 1951 and consists of 100 Articles, three annexes and three protocols, together with a convention relating to transitory provisions. This Treaty established the world's first genuine supranational organisation. The purpose of the ECSC Treaty was to establish a common market for coal and steel products.

The ECSC Treaty required the Member States to abolish import and export duties and charges having equivalent effect, as well as quantitative restrictions, on the movement of coal and steel products. In addition, measures or practices which discriminated between producers, purchasers or consumers on the basis of nationality were prohibited. Restrictions were also placed on the rights of Member States to grant subsidies or aid in order to promote domestic production.

The Treaty rationalised coal and steel production throughout the six participating states and reduced levels of protectionism in these industrial sectors. The result was a more efficient industry and a significant increase in the gross national products (GNP) of the participating states.

Since the negotiation of the EEC Treaty, the significance of the ECSC Treaty has declined. Indeed, the European Court has held that Community legislation made under the EEC Treaty will automatically apply to steel products in the absence of ECSC Treaty provisions to the contrary: see *Deutsche Babcock Handel* v *Hauptzollamt Lubeck-Ost* Case 328/85, not yet reported.

ii) The European Economic Community (EEC) Treaty

The EEC Treaty was signed in Rome on 25 March 1957 and consists of 248 Articles, four annexes, three protocols and an implementing convention on the association of overseas countries and territories with the Community. Article 2 of the Treaty identifies four objectives for the common market: (1) the promotion of harmonious economic development throughout the Community; (2) continuous and balanced economic expansion among the Member States; (3) the raising of standards of living among the population of the Community; and (4) the development of closer relations among the Member States.

In order to construct the common market, Article 3 of the EEC Treaty instructs the Member States to pursue the following policy goals:

- the elimination, as between Member States, of customs duties and of quantitative restrictions on the import and export of goods, and of all other measures having equivalent effect;
- the establishment of a common customs tariff and a common commercial policy towards third countries;
- the abolition, as between Member States, of obstacles to the free movement of persons, services and capital;
- the adoption of a common agricultural policy;
- the adoption of a common transport policy;
- the creation of a Community competition policy;
- the approximation of the laws of the Member States to the extent required for the proper functioning of the common market;
- the creation of a European Social Fund to improve employment opportunity for workers;

- the establishment of a European Investment Bank to facilitate the economic expansion of the Community; and
- the association of overseas countries and territories in order to increase trade and promote economic development.

The states participating in the EEC Treaty agree to consolidate their individual economies into one single, enlarged internal market and to simultaneously form one single entity for the purpose of conducting economic relationships with non-participating states. Authority to administer the economic development of the organisation has been delegated to a centralised body with an institutional structure which functions independently from the influence of one or more Member States. The formation of the European Economic Community involves the transfer of a considerable degree of national sovereignty to create a supranational body capable of regulating its economic affairs.

iii) The European Atomic Energy (Euratom) Treaty

The Euratom Treaty was also signed in Rome on 25 March 1957, and contains 225 Articles. The purpose of this agreement is to create a specialist market for atomic energy. Euratom is designed to develop nuclear energy, distribute it within the Community and sell the surplus to non-Community states.

Since the objectives of Euratom differ from those of the ECSC Treaty and the EEC Treaty, it is no surprise that the goals of Euratom are also different. Among the main goals of Euratom are the following:

- to promote research and to ensure the dissemination of technical information throughout the Community;
- to establish uniform safety standards to protect workers and the general public from atomic hazards;
- to promote investment in the nuclear energy industry;
- to maintain regular and reliable supplies of ores and nuclear fuels; and
- to make certain that nuclear materials are not diverted for aims other than peaceful purposes.

b) *The structure of the European Economic Community*

The EEC Treaty seeks to achieve the creation of the common market by pursuing four fundamental principles:

i) The free movement of the factors of production - goods, labour, services and capital - within the territory of the Community.

ii) The progressive approximation of economic policies among Member States, including the creation of common Community policies in key economic sectors such as agriculture, competition and transport.

iii) The creation of a Common Customs Tariff (CCT) for the regulation and administration of trade between Community and non-Community countries.

iv) The establishment of a Common Commercial Policy (CCP) for the conduct of economic relations between the Community and the rest of the world.

The first two of these principles are matters which fall within the internal competence of the Community, while the second two concern the external competence of the Community.

c) *The Single European Act*

Progress towards the creation of a common market under the EEC Treaty has been painfully slow. While the Community was reasonably successful in erecting a Common Customs Tariff and in implementing the Common Commercial Policy, by the early 1980s the Community had failed to achieve the transition toward the free movement of factors of production: see the *Commission Report on Completing the Internal Market* COM (85) 310 Final (1985). This failure led to a re-evaluation of the organisational structure and general goals of the Community, culminating in the adoption of the Single European Act in 1986.

The Single European Act is an international agreement among the Member States of the Community and not a statute of the British Parliament. This agreement made a number of significant changes to the Community Treaties including:

i) The inauguration of the internal market programme designated for completion by 1992: Article 8A EEC Treaty.

ii) The introduction of majority voting in the Council of Ministers for the enactment of certain measures: Article 100A EEC Treaty.

iii) The creation of the cooperation procedure for the participation of the European Parliament in the Community legislative process: Articles 7(2), 49, 100A(1) EEC Treaty.

iv) Recognition of the European Council as a formal organ of the European Community: Article 2 Single European Act.

v) The grant of authority to the Council of Ministers to create a Court of First Instance: Article 168A EEC Treaty.

In addition to these changes, the Single European Act also reaffirms the political objectives of the Community. It reiterates the commitment expressed in the preamble to the EEC Treaty to 'lay the foundations of an ever closer union among the peoples of Europe', by stressing the need to strive for 'concrete progress towards European unity'. Cooperation in both economic and monetary policy is added as an express aim of the Community, as is the preservation, protection and improvement of the environment.

d) *The nature of European Community law*

European Community law is a supranational species of law which prevails over the laws of all Member States, including the law of England. As the European

Court has explicitly observed, the Community Treaties have created a new legal order which now interacts to form part of the legal systems of all Member States and constitutes a body of principles which their courts and tribunals are bound to apply: *Costa* v *ENEL* [1964] ECR 585.

This new legal order has a number of characteristics features:

i) Community law is a sui generis form of law which evades the traditional classifications made within English law. It transcends the distinction often drawn between public law and private law and also the distinction between civil and criminal law.

ii) Community law not only provides a defence to legal proceedings, but may also furnish grounds for legal action or for interim injunction.

iii) Principles of Community law cannot be categorised into a distinct group of principles in the same way as the law of tort or contract may be in English law. Community law is capable of pervading any branch of national law, public or private.

iv) Community law - whether in the form of Treaty provisions, Community regulations or unimplemented Community directives - prevails over prior and subsequent inconsistent provisions of national law.

1.3 Relevant cases

Costa v *ENEL* [1964] ECR 585: The Community Treaties have established a new legal order stemming from the limitation of sovereignty or a transfer of powers from the Member States to the European Community and have thus created a body of law which binds both their nationals and themselves.

Donckerwolke v *Procureur de la Republique* [1975] ECR 1921: Member States are prohibited from enacting measures of national legislation on matters which fall within the competence of the Community by virtue of the Community Treaties unless express authority to do so has been delegated.

EC Commission v *EC Council* [1971] ECR 263: The Member States no longer have the right, acting individually or even collectively, to enter into international obligations with third states if the subject-matter of such agreements falls within the scope of the Community Treaties.

R v *Secretary of State, ex parte Factortame* Case 213/89, Judgment of 19 June 1990, not yet reported: Decision of the European Court upholding the validity of Community law over a statute of the British Parliament enacted in 1988.

1.4 Relevant materials

J Weiler, 'The Community System: The Dual Character of Supranationalism' (1981) 1 Yb Eur Law 276.

Delors Report on Economic and Monetary Union in the European Community (June 1989).

G F Mancini, 'The Making of a Constitution for Europe' (1989) 26 CML Rev 595.

A Campbell, 'The Single European Act and Its Implications' (1986) 35 ICLQ 932.

1.5 Analysis of questions

Questions relating to the origins and nature of the European Community present complex problems since it is often difficult to ascertain the legal principles that the examiner is trying to elicit. Students attempting questions in this field may be penalised if their answer is vague, even although this particular part of the syllabus is relatively undefined.

1.6 Questions

Question 1

'The Community constitutes a new legal order in international law, for whose benefit the States have limited their sovereign rights, albeit within limited fields, and the subjects of which comprise not only the Member States but also their nationals.' Case 26/62 *Van Gend en Loos* v *Netherlands.* Discuss.

University of London LLB Examination
(for External Students) European Community Law 1989 Q1

General comment

A basic question requiring the student to discuss the unique nature of the European Community in the international society.

Skeleton solution

- Nature of sovereignty; power to legislate.
- Limits on state sovereignty.
- Scope of Community law.
- Rights of individuals under Community law.

Suggested solution

The European Community is a supranational organisation. It is neither an international organisation nor a federal state. By merging certain aspects of their sovereignty, the Member States have created a unique legal structure. Further, the law which emanates from this structure also has a supranational character. By creating a Community of unlimited duration which has its own institutions, its own personality, its own legal capacity, a capacity to conduct international relations and real legislative powers stemming from the transfer of sovereignty from the Member States to the Community, the Member States have established a sui generis form of law - European Community law.

Membership of the European Community entails a significant transfer of sovereignty from the Member States to the Community. For example, Member States no longer possess sufficient sovereignty to enact legislation on matters which fall within the competence of the Community: *Donckerwolke* v *Procureur de la Republique* (1975).

Equally, Member States can no longer enter international agreements with non-Community states if the subject-matter of such agreements relates to issues within the domain of the Community: *EC Commission* v *EC Council (ERTA)* (1971). However, perhaps the greatest limitation on the sovereignty of Member States is that Community law prevails over inconsistent prior or subsequent national legislation: *R* v *Secretary of State, ex parte Factortame* Case 213/89 (1990).

The European Community legal system is unlike the international legal system. While the jurisdiction of the International Court of Justice is confined to disputes among sovereign states, the EEC Treaty expressly recognises the rights of individuals to challenge acts of the Community institutions in the European Court, and national courts are able to refer disputes involving individuals for consideration by the European Court under the preliminary reference procedure established by Article 177 of the EEC Treaty. The European Court has also expanded the application of Community law to individuals by recognising the right of individuals to rely upon Community Treaty provisions, regulations and directives. National courts have greatly assisted in this process by acknowledging that the jurisprudence of the European Court requires that Community rights can be vindicated in national courts and tribunals by individuals.

While the force of Community law resides in the transfer of sovereignty by Member States, at the same time the European Court has recognised that the legal systems of the individual Member States form an integral part of the Community legal system: *Costa* v *ENEL* (1964). Both the European Court and the House of Lords have recognised that rights of individuals under the Community Treaties must be protected by national courts: per Lord Bridge of Harwich in *R* v *Secretary of State, ex parte Factortame* (1989). Directly enforceable Community rights are part of the legal heritage of every citizen of the Member States of the Community. Such rights are automatically available and must be given unrestricted retroactive effect. The persons entitled to the enjoyment of such rights are also entitled to direct and immediate protection against possible infringement of them. The duty to provide such protection rests with the national courts.

Recognition by national courts of the rights of individuals under Community law allows individuals to rely on such rights in national courts and tribunals. Therefore, Community law can be used as a defence to a civil action or as a ground for initiating a civil action. Thus, in *Brown* v *Secretary of State for Scotland* (1988), the plaintiff founded upon Community law to establish rights in a civil action concerning the right of foreign nationals to seek state support for further education. Conversely, in *Société Technique Minière* v *Maschinenbau Ulm GmbH* (1966), the defendants relied on Article 85(2) of the EEC Treaty as a defence to an action for breach of a contract dealing with exclusive sales rights. Equally, Community law can constitute a ground for a criminal prosecution or may be a defence to such an action. For example, in *Anklagemyndigheden* v *Hausen and Son I/S* Case 326/88 (1990), the defendant was charged with violations of Community regulations concerning maximum permitted daily driving periods and compulsory rest periods and fined accordingly. Similarly, in *Pubblico Ministero* v *Ratti* (1979), an accused charged with failure to comply with minimum manufacturing standards relied on an unimplemented Council directive to avoid liability.

A number of corollaries stem from the principle that Community law confers rights on individuals which national courts and tribunals must recognise. First, the European Court will not permit the efficacy of Community rights to vary from one Member State to another. Community rights must be consistent throughout the Community. Second, Member States cannot maintain national measures which would deny access to such rights: *Factortame case* above. Third, Member States cannot remove the power to enforce Community rights from national courts. Finally, where the legislation of a Member State is declared incompatible with Community law, the legislative bodies of the state are under an obligation to amend or repeal the offending legislation.

Question 2

'The structure of the EEC Treaty suggests that the architects of the Community believed that economic integration was the road to political harmony.'

Discuss.

Question prepared by the Author
February 1991

General comment

A question requiring a simple narrative answer based on the functions of the European Community.

Skeleton solution

- The four fundamental principles of the economic integration within the EEC.
- The four freedoms; coordination of economic policy; the CCT and the CCP.
- The failure of the Community to achieve these objectives.
- The amendments made by the Single European Act.

Suggested solution

As expressed in the EEC Treaty, economic integration between the Member States is to be achieved through adherence to four fundamental principles: (a) the free movement of the factors of production - goods, labour, services and capital - within the territory of the common market; (b) the progressive approximation of economic polices among Member States, including the creation of common Community policies in key economic sectors such as agriculture, fisheries and transport; (c) the creation of a common customs tariff (CCT) for the regulation and administration of trade between the Community and non-Community countries; and (d) the establishment of a common commercial policy (CCP) for the conduct of economic relations between the Community and the rest of the world.

The free movement of factors of production is pursued through the elimination and progressive reduction of four forms of discrimination: (1) between domestic products and products originating from other Member countries as regards commercial transactions; (2) between nationals and other Community citizens in the field of employment; (3) between domestic suppliers of services and Community suppliers of similar services; and (4) between domestic capital and similar forms of investment from Member countries. In particular, the elimination of discrimination requires the abolition of customs duties and quantitative restrictions on intra-Community trade. As a consequence of Community membership, Member States may no longer unilaterally impose tariffs or quotas on goods originating within the Community. Equally, laws and administrative practices which discriminate against workers from Community countries seeking employment in other Member States are contrary to Community law, as are national laws and practices which limit the supply of services or investment from Community countries.

Coordination of economic policy in fields such as agriculture, fishing, transport, competition, regional development and social policy is essential to ensure that these freedoms are promoted, and not gradually eroded or undermined by inconsistent national economic policies. The most successful, and also the most controversial, Community economic policy is the Common Agricultural Policy (CAP) which is designed to increase agricultural productivity, to ensure a fair standard of living among the agricultural community and to stabilise agricultural markets within the Community. Although most of the Community policies were originally specified under the Community Treaties, a number of other policies, including the environment protection policy, the regional assistance policy and the energy policy, have been derived as a consequence of the functions of the Community.

The flow of commodities and products into the Community from foreign states is regulated by the common customs tariff which creates a single customs union from the individual customs territories of the Member States. In essence, the common customs tariff is a comprehensive tariff schedule which applies to goods entering the Community from destinations outside the Community. This system ensures that products entering the Community are liable to the same uniform rates of customs duties regardless of the port of entry in the Community. In addition to specifying applicable rates of duty on non-Community goods, the common customs tariff also regulates reliefs from duty, customs valuation and customs classification.

Functioning in conjunction with the common customs tariff, the common commercial policy serves to regulate the external economic policy of the Community towards non-Community states. In discharging its responsibilities under the common commercial policy, the Community enters into international economic agreements to regulate trading relationships between the Community and third states. The Community, through the agency of the European Commission, undertakes multilateral negotiations within the General Agreement on Trade and Tariffs (GATT) and pursues bilateral economic negotiations with individual states. An extensive network of agreements now exists between the Community and third states regulating economic matters. These agreements may be classified according to form and content into four groups: (a) multilateral trade agreements negotiated within the context of the GATT; (b) bilateral free-trade agreements; (c) association agreements, which are usually concluded with states about to become members of the Community; and (d) development and assistance agreements with developing states.

The original draftsmen of the Community Treaties clearly believed that the pursuit of these four fundamental objectives would ultimately achieve the creation of a comprehensive common market among the Member States of the Community. In reality, progress towards this goal has been painfully slow. This lack of progress was generally attributed to the cumbersome decision-making processes within the Community which obstructed the adoption of measures to eradicate barriers and impediments to the free movement of goods, labour, services and capital. These failures led to a re-evaluation of the organisational structure and general goals of the Community, culminating in the adoption of the Single European Act in 1986.

The Single European Act revives the idea of closer unity through integration by inaugurating the internal market programme and by making certain changes to the constitutional structure of the Community. The principal goal of the Single European Act is the creation of the 'internal market' which is defined as 'an area without frontiers in which the free movement of goods, persons, services and capital is ensured in accordance with the provisions of [the EEC Treaty]': Article 8A EEC Treaty. The concept of the internal market is therefore considerably more refined than that of a common market. The internal market programme concentrates on achieving the basic goal of the free movement of goods, labour, services and capital. This reflects a desire on the part of the member States of the Community to achieve at least the bare minimum level of economic integration in order to sustain the momentum towards true political, economic and monetary union among the Member States.

In common with the EEC Treaty, the Single European Act itself is based on the idea that economic integration will act as a catalyst to political union. It expressly recognises the need for closer political cooperation within the Community and the recognition of the European Council as an organ for the co-ordination of foreign policy within the Community is symptomatic of this desire. By stressing the importance of achieving a true internal market within the Community, the Single European Act has reaffirmed the determination of the Community to pursue the policy of unity through economic integration.

Question 3

Discuss and evaluate the system established by the EEC Treaty for enforcing the fulfilment by Member States of their Treaty obligations.

University of London LLB Examination
(for External Students) European Community Law 1989 Q4

General comment

A problem requiring a narrative description of the techniques used for the enforcement of obligations among the Member States of the Community.

Skeleton solution

- The rule of law in the European Community.
- Actions between states and actions brought by the Commission.
- Effect of decisions of the Court.
- Enforcement mechanisms.

Suggested solution

The European Community is based on the rule of law. Disputes between Member States and disputes between Community institutions and Member States must be settled through the proper procedures, with final recourse to the European Court for adjudication on the merits of the dispute. In order to enforce Community obligations, the EEC Treaty provides that actions for infringement of Community law against Member States may be raised by either another Member State or the European Commission acting on behalf of the Community.

One Member State may bring a direct action against another if it considers that the other state has failed to fulfil its obligations under the Community Treaties: Article 170 EEC Treaty. The Court exercises exclusive jurisdiction over all disputes between Member States arising out of the subject matter of the Community agreements. Member States are expressly forbidden to resolve such disputes by any other means: Article 219 EEC Treaty.

However, the right of a Member State to initiate a direct action against another Member State is subject to certain preconditions. A Member State alleging a violation of Community law must first bring the matter to the attention of the European Commission. The Commission is required to deliver a reasoned opinion on the matter after allowing the parties in dispute to submit arguments. Only after the Commission has delivered this opinion, or has failed to do so within the prescribed period, may the Member State continue. If the Commission indicates that it has no intention of pursuing the action, or if the Commission fails to deliver an opinion within three months of the matter being raised, the complaining state may bring the action itself.

Direct diplomatic confrontation between Member States is avoided if the European Commission pursues the matter in the name and interests of the European Community. A large majority of complaints are settled after the Commission delivers its reasoned opinion on the merits of the case. The remaining cases are often continued by the Commission on behalf of the complaining Member State.

Only one case by one Member State against another has actually proceeded to judgment and this involved proceedings brought by France against the United Kingdom: *France* v *United Kingdom (Re Fishing Mesh)* (1979). The United Kingdom enacted an Order in Council which regulated the size of the mesh of fishing nets in an attempt to conserve fishing stocks. Fishing policy is a matter within the competence of the Community and the Council of Ministers had earlier passed a resolution allowing Member States to introduce conservation measures, but only on the condition that prior consultations were held with the Commission. The United Kingdom had failed to enter into such consultations prior to enactment of the Order. The master of a French trawler was arrested by British fishery protection officers and convicted of using nets with a smaller mesh than the minimum authorised by the Order in Council.

France complained to the Commission that the Order had been adopted without the prior approval of the Commission and was therefore contrary to Community law. The Commission furnished a reasoned opinion which supported the contentions of the French government, but did not assume responsibility for continuing the action. The French government therefore brought the matter before the European Court in the form of a direct action against the United Kingdom. The European Court held that the British Order in Council had indeed been enacted without the necessary requirements being observed and consequently the United Kingdom was held in breach of Community law.

Although actual inter-state proceedings before the Court have been extremely rare, Member States frequently threaten to take such measures. For example, in 1990, the United Kingdom warned France that a direct action would be raised under the inter-state procedure after the French government threatened to restrict exports of cars to France manufactured in the United Kingdom by Japanese corporations. France claimed that the cars in question failed to satisfy the Community rules of origin and were therefore not Community goods entitled to unrestricted entry into the French market. The French government also averred that Japanese investment in car manufacturing within the United Kingdom was in reality an indirect means of circumventing French quotas on the importation of Japanese cars. In reply, the British government argued that at least 80 per cent of the costs of the cars in question had been incurred in the United Kingdom, a percentage which clearly satisfied the rules of origin adopted under the EEC Treaty. As an immediate consequence of the threatened action, the French government eventually agreed to allow the vehicles into France as Community goods.

In contrast to actions between Member States, enforcement actions by the European Commission against Member States are a common occurrence. Under Article 155 of the EEC Treaty, the Commission has primary responsibility for ensuring that the Member States uphold their Community obligations. Article 169 of the EEC Treaty authorises the Commission to commence proceedings against any Member State suspected of violating its Community obligations. The same provision also specifies a formal pre-litigation procedure which must be exhausted before commencing actual proceedings in the Court.

In practice, even before engaging in this formal procedure, the Commission informally notifies the Member State alleged to have violated its Community obligations and invites comments on the behaviour under investigation. While such communications are often successful, a failure on the part of a Member State to justify its conduct, or a refusal to remedy the behaviour in question, will set the formal pre-litigation procedure in motion.

If informal communications have proved unsuccessful the Commission delivers a reasoned opinion on the matter after giving the Member State concerned an opportunity to submit its observations. Should the Member State fail to comply with the terms of the Commission opinion within the period prescribed, the next stage is to bring the matter to the attention of the Court. Since the purpose of delivering a reasoned opinion is to give the defendant state an opportunity to respect its Community obligations, the Commission must allow a reasonable period for the Member State to comply. A reasonable period is determined in the light of the facts surrounding the case. If the Commission imposes excessively short time limits, the action may be dismissed by the Court: *EC Commission* v *Belgium (University Fees Case)* (1989). In the event that the formal pre-litigation process fails to procure a satisfactory resolution of the issue, the Commission can initiate proceedings before the European Court.

If the Court decides that a Member State has contravened its Community obligations it will only rule that a violation of the obligation has occurred. Thereafter the government of the offending Member State is obliged to 'take the necessary measures' to amend or repeal its laws or practices to conform to the decision of the Court. No specific period is specified within which a state must act to comply with the judgment, but prima facie the period for compliance 'should be no longer than the minimum period needed for adopting the remedial measures required': *EC Commission* v *France (Re Tobacco Prices)* (1990).

While the record for conforming with decisions of the European Court was originally respectable, the enlargement of the Community has also brought an increasing tendency for states to fail to implement the decisions of the Court. As the Commission has observed, in 1989 there were approximately 50 judgments given prior to July 1988 which had not been implemented by Member States: *EC Commission Sixth Annual Report to the European Parliament* (1990).

There are a number of notorious cases where Member States have persistently refused to adhere to the decisions of the European Court. In such cases, the European Court has adopted a policy of repeatedly bringing actions for non-compliance in the European Court. One example of this practice was the proceedings brought against Italy in connection with its export taxes on art treasures. The European Court held that the tax contravened the provisions of the EEC Treaty regarding the free movement of goods: *EC Commission* v *Italy (Re Tax on Art Treasures)* (1969). Italy failed to remove the tax and another action was brought by the Commission. In this case, the Court held that Italy had failed to comply with the terms of the first judgment and had accordingly again failed to observe its obligations under Article 171: *EC Commission* v *Italy (Re Failure to Implement Community Obligations)* (1972).

Another illustration of a Member State failing to comply with a decision of the Court occurred after the Court condemned France for its ban on imports of mutton and lamb from the United Kingdom: *EC Commission* v *France (Re Imports of Mutton and Lamb)* (1979). However, in this case, when the Commission brought an action for a declaration of non-compliance under Article 171, the Court refused to grant interim measures requiring France to implement the earlier decision since France was already under such an obligation as a consequence of Article 171.

Question 4

'Community law is not like national law: it is not like international law; it is a special category of law.' Discuss.

University of Glasgow LLB Examination
1989 Q3

General comment

A problem which focuses on the nature of European Community law itself and requires a contrast to be drawn with other forms of law.

Skeleton solution

- Differences between Community law and national law.
- Differences between Community law and international law.
- Characteristics illustrating the unique nature of Community law.

Suggested solution

Community law is unlike national law for a number of reasons. First, national law is incapable of regulating relationships between sovereign states. Secondly, national laws do not possess the special characteristics of Community law. Principles of Community law may be given direct effect in a number of different legal systems; and these principles prevail over inconsistent provisions of national law. However, unlike national law, Community law does not regulate the whole spectrum of relationships between individuals in a domestic society. Community law is confined to the parameters set by the Community Treaties, although the judicial activism of the European Court has stretched the application of Community law to its fullest.

Nor does Community law have many features in common with international law. International law is the law which regulates the relations between states. The sources of international law are international agreements and international custom, supplemented by general principles recognised by civilised states and the writings of respected jurists: Article 38(1) Statute of the International Court of Justice. While limited mechanisms have been established to confer international rights upon individuals, such as the international human rights agreements, on the whole international law is confined to inter-state relations. In addition, the international law of economic relations is primitive, centring around the General Agreement on Tariffs and Trade (GATT).

Although the Community itself is founded upon three international treaties, as amended, Community law is applicable to both Member States and individuals. Further, Community law has its own independent sources of law. The European Court generally avoids referring to international law as a reservoir of legal principles, mainly because international norms regulating economic relations are underdeveloped.

Nor is the international community as institutionally organised as the Community. While the Community has organs to perform legislative, executive and judicial functions, the counterpart institutions at the international level cannot claim to be as effective in the promulgation of legal measures, the adjudication of disputes or the enforcement of judgments.

European Community law is a supranational species of law which prevails over the laws of all Member States, including the laws of the British Parliament. It transcends the public and private distinction which is frequently draw in English law. Community law may be invoked in an extensive range of actions, both civil and criminal. Not only does it provide a defence to legal proceedings, but it may also furnish grounds for legal action or for interim injunction: *Argyll Group plc* v *Distillers plc* (1986); and *Holleran* v *Daniel Thwaites plc* (1989). Principles of Community law cannot be categorised into a distinct group of principles in the same way as the law of tort or contract may be. Consequently, it cannot be stated with certainty that a particular area of British law will remain unaffected, or unlikely to be affected, by Community law.

Matters concerning issues of Community law most frequently arise where there is a cross border element involving another Member State, or where a subject has been regulated by Community measures of harmonisation, or where Community measures are necessary to implement Community policies in sectors such as fishing, agriculture or commerce. Community law now extends into areas inconceivable even a decade ago. It regulates almost all commercial activities including the export and import of goods to and from the United Kingdom to other Member States, manufacturing, commerce, the supply of services, investment, fishing, and farming. Community law also now functions in a number of related areas of law including employment law, social security law, company law, competition law, tax law, consumer protection law, banking law, insurance law and intellectual property law.

Further, the competence of the Community to enact legislation has been considerably expanded as an immediate consequence of the Single European Act which initiated an extensive Community legislative programme designed to create an internal market within the Community, defined as '[a]n area without internal frontiers in which the free movement of goods, persons, services and capital is ensured in accordance with the provisions of the [EEC Treaty]'. The deadline for the completion of this goal has been set as 31 December 1992. The creation of the internal market requires the elimination of barriers and factors which inhibit the free movement of goods, labour, services and capital. In turn, this involves the removal of physical barriers to the free movement of the economic factors of production, such as customs formalities, the removal of technical barriers, such as laws discriminating between nationals and non-nationals, and the removal of fiscal barriers, such as disparities in VAT rates among Member States.

However, political initiatives have not been the only source of impetus for the growth of Community law within national legal systems. The European Court of Justice itself has been a catalyst towards extending the scope of Community law far beyond the terms of the Treaty of Rome. In a number of judgments, the European Court has created fundamental principles of Community law through the process of interpretation. Both the principles of the supremacy of Community law over national law and the direct effect of provisions of Community Treaties and unimplemented Community directives owe their origins to the jurisprudence of the European Court.

The unique nature of Community law also requires the legal systems of each Member States to adapt to its characteristics. Within the United Kingdom, even accepted constitutional doctrines and precepts require modification to facilitate the reception of Community law. For example, the constitutional principle that Acts of Parliament cannot be reviewed in the event of inconsistency with international obligations entered into by the United Kingdom requires modification in light of the three Community Treaties, in particular the Treaty of Rome establishing the European Economic Community. Indeed, even the House of Lords has been prepared to concede that inroads have been made into the principle of parliamentary sovereignty by accession to the European Community: *R* v *Secretary of State, ex parte Factortame* (1989).

2 THE INSTITUTIONS OF THE EUROPEAN COMMUNITY

2.1 Introduction

As originally conceived, each of the three separate European Communities (the European Coal and Steel Community, the European Economic Community and Euratom) possessed a separate Commission (a High Authority in the case of the ECSC) and Council of Ministers but shared a single Parliamentary Assembly and Court of Justice. An agreement was negotiated in 1965 to merge these separate institutions with effect from July 1967. This process resulted in the creation of four principal organs: the Council of Ministers, the European Commission, the Parliamentary Assembly (now known as the European Parliament), and the European Court of Justice. The Single European Act altered this structure by recognising the European Council, until then an informal gathering of the Heads of States, as a Community organ and by empowering the Council of Ministers to create a second division within the European Court of Justice, to be known as the Court of First Instance.

2.2 Key points

a) *The European Council*

i) Composition and structure

The European Council consists of all the Heads of Government of the Member States and their respective Foreign Ministers, together with the President of the European Commission who is assisted by another Commissioner. The Single European Act specifies that the European Council shall convene twice each year.

ii) Competence and powers

The European Council is designed to facilitate the coordination of European Foreign policy. Responsibility for the agenda lies with the Member State which has the Presidency of a separate Community institution - the Council of Ministers.

The Council possesses no formal powers. Rather, it is a forum for discussions, on an informal basis, relating to issues of common Community concern. However, the Single European Act places an obligation on Member States to 'endeavour jointly to formulate and implement a European foreign policy' within the Council. Through consultations at this level, Member States agree to maximise their combined influence on global affairs through coordination, convergence, joint action, and the development of common principles and objectives.

b) *The Council of Ministers*

i) Composition and structure

The Council of Ministers consists of one national representative from each Member State, the exact composition varying according to the subject of discussions. A distinction is drawn between two types of Council meetings:

- General Council meetings: these are attended by the Foreign Ministers of the Member States.
- Specialised Council meetings: these meetings are attended by the various national Ministers with responsibility for the subjects on the agenda for discussion.

The office of the President of the Council rotates in alphabetical sequence among the Member States in six month periods. The Presidency of the Council of Ministers has been synchronised with the Presidency of the European Council. This ensures that a single Member State is responsible for the general progress of the Community as a whole during its period of tenure.

Since the government Ministers who participate in the Council of Ministers also have national responsibilities and therefore cannot be permanently present in Brussels, a subsidiary organ has been established in order to maintain consistency and continuity in the work of the Council. This organ, called the Committee of Permanent Representatives (known by the French acronym COREPER), has been formed to perform two main functions:

- to provide liaison between national governments and Community institutions for the exchange of informations; and
- to prepare draft Community legislation with the Commission for final submission to the Council itself.

COREPER is composed of the ambassadors of the Member States accredited to the Community, often assisted by national officials from the civil services of their respective Member States. The individual members of

COREPER represent the interests of their respective countries and not those of the Community.

ii) Competence and powers

The Council of Ministers is the principal decision-making organ of the Community and has competence to deal with the following matters:

- the adoption of Community legislation;
- the formulation of Community policies;
- the finalisation of international agreements with foreign states on matters which fall within the competence of the Community;
- drafting the Community budget in conjunction with the European Parliament;
- taking those decisions required to ensure that the objectives specified in the EEC Treaty are achieved.

Article 145 of the EEC Treaty allows the Council to delegate authority to the European Commission for the implementation of policies and rules established by the Council.

The most important power of the Council of Ministers is the capacity to enact Community legislation. The Community legislative process is exceedingly complex, particularly after the amendments made by the Single European Act. As a result of these amendments, two legislative procedures now exist:

- the original legislative procedure; and
- the 'cooperative procedure';

The European Parliament is more closely involved in the law-making process when the cooperation procedure is required. Cooperation procedure extends to Community legislation regulating the following subjects:

- the elimination of discrimination on the ground of nationality (Article 7(2) EEC Treaty);
- the freedom of movement of workers and the freedoms of providing services and establishment (Article 49 EEC Treaty); and
- harmonisation measures relating to the establishment and functioning of the internal market (Article 100A(1) EEC Treaty).

If a proposed measure is not concerned with these subjects, the original legislative procedures are applicable.

iii) Voting

Article 148 of the EEC Treaty stipulates that 'save as otherwise provided, the Council shall act by a majority of its Members'. In reality, most treaty provisions require qualified majorities or unanimity. A common requirement is for the use of a qualified majority. A system of weighted voting has been created for the purpose of determining a qualified majority under Article 148 EEC Treaty. According to this scheme, votes are allocated on the following basis:

10 votes - France, Germany, Italy and the United Kingdom

8 votes - Spain

5 votes - Belgium, Greece, the Netherlands and Portugal

3 votes - Denmark and Ireland

2 votes - Luxembourg

Seventy-six votes have been created and a qualified majority is 54 votes.

In 1965 an informal amendment was made to the application of the principle of majority voting in the Community treaties. This understanding was embodied in the 'Luxembourg Accords' which declared that where 'very important interests' of a Member State are at stake, the Council will endeavour, within a reasonable time, to reach a solution acceptable to all Member States. Failing such a settlement, a decision may not be adopted in the absence of unanimity despite explicit provisions to the contrary specifying majority voting. This understanding made no formal amendment to the EEC Treaty, but is widely accepted as embodying the political reality behind the Community itself.

c) *The European Commission*

i) Composition and structure

The European Commission is composed of 17 Commissioners - two from each of the five largest Member States together with one from each of the smaller Member States (Article 10 Merger Treaty, as amended). Commissioners are appointed by agreement between the various Member States and hold office for renewable periods of four years. The President of the Commission is appointed for a renewable term of two years through similar procedures.

The Commission functions as a collegiate body and recognises the principle of collective responsibility. Voting within the Commission is by simple majority and deliberations are private and confidential. In order to ensure efficiency within the Commission, special responsibilities are distributed to each individual Commissioner.

The Commissioners are also assisted by a considerable body of Community civil servants. This Secretariat is organised into 20 departments known as Directorates-General. Each department is presided over by a Director-General who is responsible to the Commissioners whose portfolio includes that particular department. As a matter of policy, the Directors-General are invariably of a different nationality from the Commissioners to whom they are responsible.

ii) Competence and powers

The Commission performs four separate functions which are set out in Article 155 of the EEC Treaty:

- to ensure respect for the rights and obligations imposed on Member States and Community institutions by both the Community Treaties and measures made under the authority of these agreements;
- to formulate, participate and initiate policy decisions authorised under the Community Treaties;
- to promote the interests of the Community both internally and externally; and
- to exercise the powers delegated to it by the Council for the implementation and administration of Community policy.

The Commission has ultimate responsibility to ensure that the interests of the Community are protected.

The most important power of the Commission is the ability to institute proceedings before the European Court against:

- any Member State suspected of violating its Community obligations (Article 169 EEC Treaty); and
- any Community institution considered to have acted outside its power: (Article 173 EEC Treaty).

The Commission has also been delegated a considerable range of executive and legislative powers by the Council of Ministers. For example, Article 87(1) EEC Treaty authorises the Council to delegate responsibility for the administration of competition policy to the Commission. In the discharge of this function, the Commission has authority, in certain circumstances, to investigate complaints, to impose fines, and to require Member States to take appropriate action to prevent or terminate infringements of competition policy. Often delegated authority also vests power to legislate in the Commission.

d) *The European Parliament*

i) Composition and structure

Members of the European Parliament were originally appointed by their respective national parliaments according to internal parliamentary procedures. In 1976 the Member States agreed the Act Concerning the Election by Direct Universal Suffrage of Members to the European Parliament which facilitated direct elections to the European Parliament.

A total of 518 members of the European Parliament (MEPs) are elected for terms of five years. Seats are allocated to Member States in approximate proportion to their populations. On this basis, the following distribution has been made:

81 representatives - Germany, France, Italy and the United Kingdom

60 representatives - Spain

25 representatives - The Netherlands

24 representatives - Belgium, Greece and Portugal

16 representatives - Denmark

15 representatives - Ireland

6 representatives - Luxembourg

The distribution of seats within the United Kingdom is regulated by the European Parliamentary Elections Act 1978. Constituencies were drawn up by the Boundary Commissioners and 66 seats were allocated to England, 8 to Scotland, 4 to Wales, and 3 to Northern Ireland.

Members of the European Parliament are seated according to their political affiliations and views and not their nationalities. The majority of parties in the European Parliament are coalitions between national parties. In February 1991, the Socialist party was the largest single party, followed by the European Peoples' Party, and then the European Democrat Party (which is essentially composed of British Conservative MEPs).

ii) Competence and powers

The European Parliament represents the interests of the peoples of Europe. As originally conceived, the European Parliament lacked all real powers other than an advisory competence. The Parliament has, however, gradually acquired a significantly more important role in the functioning of the Community although this role still remains disproportionate to the democratic legitimacy of the Parliament. The Single European Act recognised that the Parliament should enjoy a greater degree of participation in the Community decision-making processes but, despite the amendments made by the Single European Act, the powers of the Parliament remain more advisory and supervisory that legislative.

The most important powers of the European Parliament are the following:

- The consent of the Parliament is required for the admission of new Members into the Community and for the conclusion of association agreements between the Community and third countries (Articles 237-238 EEC).

- The European Commission is obliged to answer questions submitted by

Members of the European Parliament (Article 140 EEC). Both written and oral questions may be submitted.

- The Commission is required to submit an annual general report to the Parliament on the affairs of the Community which is the subject of an annual parliamentary debate (Article 143 EEC).
- The Commission may be collectively dismissed by a motion of censure carried by a two-thirds majority in Parliament (Article 144 EEC).
- The Community budget is prepared by the Commission and submitted to the Council of Ministers, but the Parliament may approve or modify the budget depending on the expenditure involved (Article 203 EEC, as amended).
- The opinion of the Parliament must be sought during the decision-making processes before the adoption of certain measures (Articles 43, 54, 56 and 87 EEC).

While the European Parliament exercises considerable supervisory control over the Commission, the same cannot be said of its relationship with the Council of Ministers.

e) *The European Court of Justice*

i) Composition and structure

The European Court of Justice itself consists of 13 judges assisted by six Advocates-General. Each Member State appoints a judge of its own nationality while the office of the thirteenth judge rotates among the five largest states. A thirteenth judge is required to allow decisions on a majority basis when the full Court convenes to hear a case.

The six Advocates-General are appointees from the five largest states with the sixth position rotating among the smaller states. Advocates-General are creatures from the civilian legal tradition with no counterpart in common law legal systems. In each case before the Court, an Advocate-General is appointed to deliver an impartial and legally reasoned opinion after the close of the pleadings by the parties, but before the judges sitting on the case render their decision. This opinion is a preliminary to a decision by the Court and the Advocate-General is not given a vote in the actual voting among the judges.

The structure and organisation of the Court is regulated by a separate Protocol to the EEC Treaty - Protocol on the Statute of the Court of Justice of the European Economic Community. Matters of procedure are regulated by this Protocol, including the content of oral and written pleadings, rights of production, citation of witnesses, costs and expenses, and periods of limitation. These rules are supplemented by others contained in the Rules of Procedure of the European Court of Justice.

ii) Jurisdiction

The jurisdiction of the European Court of Justice may be classified into three distinct categories:

- Contentious jurisdiction: this refers to the right of the Court to hear direct actions between Member States and Community institutions, as well as actions by individuals against the acts of Community institutions.
- Plenary jurisdiction: this refers to the right of the Court to award damages for unlawful acts committed by Community institutions.
- Preliminary Ruling jurisdiction: the European Court has jurisdiction to hear cases referred by the national courts of Member States on matters relating to the interpretation and application of Community law.

The nature of the jurisdiction of the European Court forms the next two chapters of this book.

f) *The Court of First Instance*

i) Composition and structure

The Single European Act authorised the Council of Ministers to create a Court of First Instance to alleviate the volume of work before the European Court of Justice. The Court of First Instance was established by Council Decision 88/591 and consists of 12 judges who were first appointed in July 1989. Members of the Court are appointed by agreement between the Member States for periods of six years. The members of the Court of First Instance elect a President from among their own number.

No provision has been made in the Council Decision for the appointment of Advocates-General to the Court of First Instance. However, judges of the Court may be called upon to perform the task of an Advocate-General. The actual organisation of the Court is specified in the Rules of Procedure for the Court of First Instance.

ii) Jurisdiction

The jurisdiction and powers of the Court of First Instance have been carved from those of the European Court of Justice itself. The Court of First Instance does not extend the jurisdiction of the European Court, but rather, it exercises certain aspects of the Court's functions. In particular, the creation of the new Court does not alter the jurisdictional relationships between the European Court system and the individual national courts and tribunals of the Member States.

The jurisdiction of the Court of First Instance is strictly defined in Council Decision 88/591. This jurisdiction extends to the following classes of actions:

- Actions or proceedings by the staff of Community institutions.

- Actions for annulment and actions for failure to act brought against the Commission by natural or legal persons and concerning the application of Articles 50 and 57-66 of the ECSC Treaty. Such actions relate to Commission decisions concerning levies, production controls, pricing practices, agreements and concentrations.
- Actions for annulment or actions for failure to act brought by natural or legal persons against an institution of the Community relating to the implementation of competition policy.

Where these actions are accompanied by claims for damages, the Court of First Instance has jurisdiction to decide the related claim.

The Court of First Instance cannot hear cases brought by either Member States or Community institutions. Nor may the Court answer questions submitted by national courts through the preliminary ruling procedure which is reserved to the European Court of Justice.

Appeal from the Court of First Instance to the European Court is competent but only on point of law and subject to the appellant demonstrating the existence of one of the grounds of appeal specified in Article 51 of the amended European Court of Justice Statute. Three grounds of appeal have been established:

- Lack of competence on the part of the Court of First Instance, such as an excess of its jurisdiction.
- A breach of procedure before the Court which has had an adverse effect on the interests of the appellant.
- An infringement of Community law by the Court of First Instance, such as an error in the interpretation or application of Community legal principles.

2.3 Relevant cases

EC Commission v *EC Council (Re Generalised Tariff Preferences)* [1987] ECR 1493: Decision relating to the legal basis and voting requirements for the adoption of measures by the Council of Ministers.

United Kingdom v *EC Council (Re Hormones)* [1988] 2 CMLR 453: A challenge by the United Kingdom to the authority of the Council for the adoption of Community legislation regulating the use of certain hormones in livestock farming.

EC Commission v *EC Council (Re Harmonised Commodity Description)* [1990] 1 CMLR 457: A failure by the Council of Ministers to consult the European Parliament on the adoption of a measure when specified in the Community Treaties renders the putative measure void.

European Parliament v *EC Council (Re Chernobyl)* Case 70/88, 22 May 1990, not yet reported: The European Parliament has locus standi to challenge acts of the

Council of Ministers which do not conform to the provisions of the Community Treaties.

2.4 Relevant materials

D Lasok & JW Bridge, *Law and Institutions of the European Communities* (fourth edition, 1987).

R Bieber, 'Implications of the Single European Act for the European Parliament' (1986) 23 CML Rev 767.

K Borgsmidt, 'The Advocate-General at the European Court of Justice' (1988) 13 EL Rev 106.

D Edward, 'The Impact of the Single European Act on the Institutions of the Community' (1987) 24 CML Rev 9.

C-D Ehlermann, 'The Internal Market Following the Single European Act' (1987) 24 CML Rev 361.

2.5 Analysis of questions

Questions dealing with this particular subject-matter most often take the form of narrative essays rather than factual problems. Most often, the student is asked to analyse or examine the relationships between institutions rather than provide a description of the nature of one particular institution. An understanding of the roles and powers of each Community organ is therefore essential, as is a basic comprehension of their interaction.

2.6 Questions

Question 1

Write notes on two of the following:

a) The European Council;

b) The Council of Ministers;

c) The European Commission;

d) The European Court of Justice.

University of Glasgow LLB Examination
1989 Q1

General comment

A general narrative question requiring the student to demonstrate a basic familiarity with the institutions of the Community.

Skeleton solution

- The European Council: structure, function, powers.
- The Council of Ministers: structure, function, powers.
- The European Commission: structure, function, powers.

- The ECJ: structure, functions, powers.

Suggested solution

a) *The European Council*

The European Council is not an original institution of the Community, but rather an example of the Community adapting to an evolving role. In the early 1970s, the Heads of State or Government of the various Member States habitually convened on an ad hoc basis to discuss matters involving political cooperation. At one such meeting in Paris in 1974, an informal agreement was made to convene this group, together with the respective Foreign Ministers of the Member States, regularly three times each year to discuss matters of political cooperation and foreign policy which related to the progressive development of the Community. These institutionalised meetings became known as the European Council and were born as a consequence of the need to coordinate and harmonise certain aspects of foreign policy in order to prevent erosion of the objectives specified in the Community Treaties.

The Single European Act (SEA) formally recognised the status of the European Council within the Community and provided an institutional basis for the functioning of the organ (Article 2 SEA). The European Council now consists of all the Heads of Government of the Member States and their respective Foreign Ministers, together with the President of the European Commission who is assisted by another Commissioner. The SEA specifies that the European Council shall convene twice each year to coordinate European foreign policy. Responsibility for the agenda lies with the Presidency of a separate Community institution, the Council of Ministers.

The Single European Act also places an obligation on Member States to 'endeavour jointly to formulate and implement a European foreign policy' within this forum (Article 30(1) SEA). Through consultations at this level, Members agree to maximise their combined influence on global affairs through coordination, convergence, joint action, and the development of common principles and objectives. The European Commission and the European Parliament are closely associated with the formulation of policy at this level. The Commission is directly involved in the deliberations of the European Council through the participation of the President and his assistant. The views and opinions of the European Parliament are periodical requested on specific matters and the Parliament is regularly informed of the outcome of discussions within the European Council. This exchange of views within the Community facilitates the harmonious development of Community policy.

The European Council is a forum for an informal exchange of views between the Heads of Government of the Member States and has no legislative capacity itself. The advantage of the European Council is that both Community and non-Community concerns may be discussed. In recent years, the European Council has discussed subjects ranging from German reunification, the recent political developments in Eastern Europe, political and monetary union in Europe, to terrorism and sanctions against South Africa. In accordance with Parliamentary convention, the British Prime Minister reports to the House of Commons on the discussions held in the European Council (See Hansard, HC, 1 May 1990, Cols 902-921; Hansard, HC, 12 December 1989, Cols 845-856; Hansard, HC, 29 June 1989, Cols 1109-24; Hansard, HC, 6 December 1988, Cols 173-186).

b) *The Council of Ministers*

The Council of Ministers consists of one national representative from each Member State, the exact composition varying according to the subject of discussions. A distinction can be drawn between two types of Council meetings:

i) General Council meetings: these are attended by the Foreign Ministers of the Member States. At these discussions the agenda deals with topics concerning external relations as well as matters of general concern to the Community.

ii) Specialised Council meetings: these meetings are attended by the various national Ministers with responsibility for the subjects on the agenda for discussion. For example, when agriculture is the subject of the negotiations, the British Minister for Agriculture convenes with his counterparts from other Member States. Subjects dealt with during Specialised Council meetings include transport, industry, fishing and commerce.

The Council is assisted by a small, permanent General Secretariat located in Brussels. This body acts as a civil service to the Council and is organised into six Directorates-General, each dealing with specific areas of Community concern. However, both the role and personnel of the Secretariat are restricted as a consequence of the reliance placed by the Council on civil servants from national administrations.

The Council of Ministers is the principal decision-making organ of the Community. It adopts Community legislation, formulates Community policies and finalises international agreements with foreign states on matters which fall within the competence of the Community. The Council also drafts the Community budget in conjunction with the European Parliament. Further, under Article 145 of the EEC Treaty, the Council is empowered to take all decisions necessary to ensure that the objectives specified in the Community Treaty are achieved. The same provision allows the Council to delegate authority to the European Commission for the implementation of the rules laid down by the Council.

No single, unified decision-making procedure is specified in the EEC Treaty and this often leads to friction between the Commission and the Council on the one hand and individual Member States and the Council on the other hand. Authority to adopt particular measures is dispersed throughout the Treaty and is subject to different voting majorities depending on the specific power being exercised. Naturally, the final content of a Community measure will depend on whether a measure was adopted by a majority or required unanimity. Where the adoption of a measure requires unanimity, Member States tend to limit the authority of the Community to act. A measure will be void if adopted on the wrong legal basis by the Council.

The problems created by the lack of a single decision-making process are illustrated by a recent case involving a challenge by the Commission to regulations adopted by the Council dealing with generalised tariff preferences for third world states. The Council adopted regulations, acting on authority vested by two separate provisions of the EEC Treaty, one specifying unanimity and the other requiring a qualified majority. The measures were adopted on the basis of unanimity, this being the minimum requirement for the exercise of both of these powers. The Commission argued that the measures could have been adopted by the Council under the provision requiring a qualified majority. The European Court held in favour of the Commission by deciding that the Council should not have adopted the measure on the basis of unanimity when a qualified majority would have sufficed: *EC Commission* v *EC Council (Re Generalised Tariff Preferences)* (1987). Members of the Council had made the adoption of the measure unduly difficult. Since the regulations were not adopted on the correct legal basis they were declared void.

In a similar case, the United Kingdom challenged the adoption of a Council directive prohibiting the use of certain hormones in livestock farming: *United Kingdom* v *EC Council (Re Hormones)* (1988). The Council adopted the measure on the basis of Article 43 of the EEC Treaty which allows the use of a qualified majority. The United Kingdom maintained that the necessary legal basis was Article 100 of the EEC Treaty. The Court held that Article 43 provided a sufficient legal basis for the adoption of the measure. This case illustrates the confusion which often surrounds the exercise of authority by the Council.

Cases challenging the legal authority for measures adopted by the Council are likely to become more frequent following upon the amendments made to the EEC Treaty by the Single European Act. Article 100A allows the adoption of harmonisation measures for the internal market programme on the basis of a qualified majority, while Article 100 requires unanimity for the adoption of similar measures not relating to the internal market programme. The Commission has proposed the adoption of a number of measures under Article 100A which were previously considered to require unanimity under Article 100. Many Member States view this development as an attempt to circumvent the requirements of unanimity. However, the European Court has demonstrated a propensity to permit the adoption of measures by qualified majority where this is feasible.

The general rule regarding voting in the Council is stipulated in Article 148(1) of the EEC Treaty which states that 'save as otherwise provided, the Council shall act by a majority of its Members'. In reality, most Treaty provisions concerning issues other than those of minor significance require qualified majority or unanimity. A significant number of provisions require unanimity including Article 235 of the EEC Treaty which allows the Council to take appropriate measures to achieve the objectives of the EEC Treaty where the Treaty itself does not expressly confer the power to do so. A more common requirement, however, is that of a qualified majority. A system of weighted voting has been created for the purposes of determining a qualified majority by Article 148 of the EEC Treaty.

In 1965 an informal amendment was made to the application of the principle of majority voting in the Community Treaties. The settlement reached was embodied in the 'Luxembourg Accords' which declared that where the 'very important interests' of a Member State are at stake, the Council will endeavour, within a reasonable time, to reach a solution acceptable to all Member States. Failing such a settlement, a decision may not be adopted in the absence of unanimity despite provisions to the contrary specifying majority voting. The requirement of unanimity vests a right of veto in the Council in favour of any Member State opposing the adoption of a measure alleged to affect its important interests.

Even prior to the Single European Act, the importance of the formula embodied in the Luxembourg Accords appeared to have significantly declined. Member States had gradually adopted a policy of abstaining from voting to demonstrate displeasure as opposed to attempting to exercise a veto. But, in 1982, the British government relied upon the undertaking made in the Luxembourg Accords to prevent the adoption of agricultural price increases which allegedly threatened the interests of the United Kingdom. The British Foreign Secretary, Francis Pym, argued in favour of the continued existence of the right of veto, but this argument was rejected by other Member States who adopted the price increases despite British opposition.

The Single European Act also introduced changes in voting and procedure which directly challenge the application of the Luxembourg Accord formula in areas concerning the internal market programme. This agreement facilitates the use of majority voting for legislation designed to implement measures required for the creation of the internal market. Despite these changes the British government adhere to the view that the Luxembourg formula remains unaffected. In the House of Lords, in 1986, Baroness Young claimed on behalf of the government that:

'[N]othing in the Single European Act affects the ability of a Member State to invoke the Luxembourg compromise: in other words to state that, because a very important national interest is at stake, discussions must be continued until unanimous agreement is reached' (Hansard, HL, 1986, Vol 479, Col 1007).

While an argument may be made to support the proposition that the Luxembourg Accord formula continues to apply to areas not affected by the Single European Act, express amendments made to the EEC Treaty rule out this possibility in relation to changes in voting majorities brought by the Single European Act. Since the European Court would not support an argument based on the Luxembourg Accords, the onus is on those asserting the existence of the veto to prove its continued vitality.

c) *The European Commission*

The European Commission has been conceived as an autonomous Community institution, free from national allegiance and the influence of Member States. It embodies the Community spirit and generates the momentum for European integration. It is composed of 17 Commissioners - two from each of the five largest Member States and one from each of the smaller States. Each Commissioner takes an oath to uphold the interests of the Community prior to entry into the Commission. It is improper for a Commissioner to act in a manner incompatible with the interests of the Community or for a Member State to attempt to influence the behaviour of a Commissioner.

To assist in the discharge of their responsibilities, each Commissioner has a private office and a departmental staff. A principal private secretary to the Commissioner is in charge of this office, and occasionally the private secretary may act as a substitute for the relevant Commissioner at Commission meetings. In essence, the role of the Commissioners is to provide impetus and direction to policy formulation within the Community.

Special responsibilities are delegated to each Commissioner. Individual authority to perform certain tasks is often agreed in advance among the Commissioners. Under the internal regulations which govern internal procedure, draft policy decisions are formulated and then circulated among the Commissioners. If no amendments are proposed within a fixed period, the draft is adopted by the Commission. Where objections have been raised to the content of the proposal, a full meeting of the Commission is convened for the purposes of discussion. To prevent excessive bureaucracy, written procedures have been adopted as a substitute for continuous meetings.

The Commission performs four separate functions which are set out in Article 155 of the EEC Treaty. First, it must ensure respect for the rights and obligations imposed on Member States and Community institutions by both the Community treaties and measures made under the authority of the Treaties. Second, it must formulate, participate and initiate policy decisions authorised under the Community Treaties. Third, it must promote the interests of the Community both internally and externally. Fourth, it must exercise the powers delegated to it by the Council for the implementation and administration of Community policy. Each of these responsibilities ensure that the Commission is able to protect the interests of the Community.

The Commission may institute proceedings before the European Court of Justice against any Member State suspected of violating its Community obligations or any Community institution considered to have acted outside its powers. Actions are frequently brought by the Commission against Member States for failure to implement Community legislation and for violations of Community law. Actions against Community institutions are also frequently brought against the Council, generally for infringements of the procedural or substantive provisions of the Community Treaties.

In addition to ensuring respect for Community law, the Commission is responsible for the formulation of proposals for Community measures. In general, draft proposals are formulated by the Commission in the following stages. First, the Commission enters discussions with various interested parties at the political levels, in trade unions and in the civil service in order to draft the essential elements of a proposal. Second, with the assistance of its own specialist departments and its legal service, the Commission considers its policy options and drafts proposals to implement policy. Third, this draft is submitted to both the Council, generally through the medium of COREPER, and the European Parliament for consultations. Fourth, the Council and Commission agree on the broad policy aspects and thereafter the Directorate-General concerned with the matter enters into discussions with experts to evaluate the practical implications of the proposal. Finally, these procedures must be exhausted before the Commission submits its final draft proposal to the Council at which point the proposal enters into the formal Community decision-making procedures. In discharging this responsibility the Commission acts as a coordinator, as well as an initiator of policy.

The Commission promotes the interests of the Community internally by establishing offices in the capitals of the Member States. The Commission also dispatches representatives to the capitals of major trading partners and participates in international organisations and conferences concerned with matters within the scope of the Community.

Finally, the Commission has been delegated a considerable range of executive and legislative powers by the Council. Since the day-to-day administration of Community policy would effectively stultify the Council of Ministers, authority to administer policy is frequently conferred upon the Commission. For example, Article 87(2) of the EEC Treaty authorises the Council to delegate responsibility for the administration of competition policy to the Commission, subject to the drafting of appropriate regulations as guidelines. In the discharge of this function, the Commission has authority, in certain circumstances, to investigate complaints, to impose fines on undertakings considered to have violated competition rules, and to require Member States to take appropriate action to prevent or terminate infringements of competition policy by nationals.

d) *The European Court of Justice*

As a court of law, the European Court of Justice consists of two divisions: the European Court of Justice itself and the new Court of First Instance. Both divisions together form the judicial organ of the European Community.

The original European Court consists of 13 judges assisted by six Advocates-General. Each Member State appoints a judge of its nationality while the office of the thirteenth judge rotates among the five largest states. The six Advocates-General are appointees from the five largest states with the sixth position rotating among the smaller states. The structure and organisation of the European Court is regulated by a separate Protocol to the EEC Treaty. This Protocol specifies the rights and duties of judges and Advocates-General, including the right to immunity from legal proceedings and the duty to remain impartial. Matters of procedure are also regulated by this Protocol including the content of oral and written pleadings, rights of production, citation of witnesses, costs and expenses, and periods of limitation. The rules created under the Protocol for the regulation of procedure have been supplemented by rules of procedure enacted by the Court itself.

The jurisdiction of the European Court may be divided into three categories. The contentious jurisdiction of the Court refers to the right of the Court to hear direct actions between Member States and Community institutions, as well as actions by individuals against the acts of Community institutions, on the grounds of violations of Community law. The plenary jurisdiction of the Court refers to the powers of the Court to award damages for unlawful acts committed by Community institutions. Finally, the Court has jurisdiction to hear cases referred by the national courts of Member States on matters relating to the interpretation and application of Community law.

The European Court has created a number of chambers in an attempt to alleviate the work of the Court. Four chambers of three judges and two chambers of six judges have been established. The distribution of cases to the chambers depends on the complexities of the case and the rights of the parties to the action. Under Article 95 of the Rules of Procedure, the Court may assign any direct action or reference for a preliminary ruling to a chamber. The test for assignment of a case to a chamber is whether or not the difficulties or importance of a case require consideration by the full Court. Under the Rules of Procedure, the full Court must be convened if a Member State or a Community institution is a party to the action and has insisted on the case being heard by a full Court. The actual decision to assign a case to a chamber is made at the end of the written stage of the procedure and after consideration of the preliminary report of the case.

As a direct result of the long delays in cases being heard before the European Court, the Single European Act amended the Community Treaties to allow the creation of a Court of First Instance as an additional division of the European Court. The Court of First Instance is not a separate institution of the Community, but an integral part of the European Court itself. The jurisdiction and powers of the Court of First Instance are derived from those of the European Court of Justice itself. It consists of 12 members who are appointed by agreement between the Member States for periods of six years. This requirement will ensure that each Member State has a national on the Court. The members of the Court of First Instance elect a President from among their number. No provision has been made in the Council Decision for the appointment of Advocates-General.

The jurisdiction of the Court of First Instance is strictly circumscribed by the Council Decision establishing the Court and extends to the following classes of action: (1) staff cases; (2) actions for review of penalties imposed, or decisions made, by the Commission under the authority of the ECSC Treaty; and (3) competition cases. Where these cases involve damages, the Court of First Instance has jurisdiction to decide the related claim.

The most significant jurisdiction of the new Court is possibly over competition cases under the EEC Treaty. The majority of cases brought on this basis will relate to challenges by undertakings against Commission decisions affecting them. For example, cases contesting levels of fines for violations of Community competition policy fall within the jurisdiction of the new Court and are likely to arise quite frequently.

Appeal from the Court of First Instance to the European Court of Justice is possible but only on a point of law and subject to the appellant demonstrating the existence of one of the grounds of appeal specifically provided in the Article 51 of the amended Court of Justice Statute. Three grounds of appeal are established: (1) lack of competence on the part of the Court of Instance, such as lack of jurisdiction; (2) a breach of procedure before the Court which has had an adverse effect on the interests of the appellant; or (3) an infringement of Community law by the Court of First Instance, such as an error in interpretation or application of Community principles.

Appeals must be brought within a period of two months from the notification of the decision which is the subject of the appeal. Articles 49 to 54 of the Statute of the European Court, together with Articles 110 to 123 of the Rules of Procedure of the European Court, have been inserted to regulate the matter of appeal between the two courts. An appeal does not suspend the decision of the Court of First Instance unless the Court of Justice makes out an order to that effect. However, a judgment from the Court of First Instance which annuls a regulation does not take effect until after the expiry of the two month period for lodging an appeal.

Question 2

'The legislative process in the EEC depends on cooperation between the relevant institutions.' Discuss.

University of Glasgow LLB Examination
1987 Q2

General comment

A question requiring comment on the relationship between two or more institutions of the European Community.

Skeleton solution

- Sketch of the participants in the legislative process.
- Outline of the legislative processes.
- The nature of the amendments made by the SEA.
- The desirability for cooperation in these processes.

Suggested solution

The promulgation of Community legislation requires the participation of three main Community institutions - the Council of Ministers, the European Commission and the European Parliament. Throughout the evolution of the European Community, the relationships between each of these organs has gradually altered, particularly in relation to the Community legislative mechanism. Significant amendments have been made to the original constitutional structure of the Community legislative process, both by the Member States themselves and by decisions of the European Court. Cooperation between these organs has become an essential element in the Community legislative process as influence in this process has become more widely dispersed among the participants.

Due to the amendments made by the Single European Act, two separate legislative procedures have been created: the original legislative procedure; and the 'cooperation procedure'. The primary difference between these procedures is the participation of the European Parliament in the legislative process.

The European Commission has responsibility for drafting proposed Community legislation regardless of which of these two procedures is adopted. The Commission consults numerous interested parties and frames the proposed legislation in the light of these consultations. Thereafter draft proposals are sent to the European Parliament for consideration. The European Parliament is divided into a number of committees each specialising in a separate aspect of the Community affairs. A proposal is considered by the appropriate Parliamentary committee which prepares a report. This report may be debated by the full Parliament before a final opinion is sent along with the proposal back to the Commission. Technically, the European Parliament need not be consulted in relation to legislative proposals unless the proposals concern subject matters which require the European Parliament's attention. However, the European Commission has adopted a convention of submitting all proposed legislation to the Parliament for its comments even when this procedure is not strictly required.

Even when the participation of the Parliament is required at this stage of the proceedings, its role in the legislative process is primarily advisory. The Parliament possesses no original authority to amend the content of a proposed legislative measure. Nevertheless, where the Community Treaties specify consultations with the Parliament prior to the adoption of a measure, failure to do so renders a putative measure void: *EC Commission* v *EC Council (Re Harmonised Commodity Descriptions)* (1990).

The proposal is then returned to the Commission which sends it to the Committee of Permanent Representatives (COREPER) after revision or amendment in the light of comments made by the European Parliament. A working group composed of national officials has been established within COREPER which prepares a report on the proposal for the Council of Ministers. Amendments to the proposal may be suggested by the national representatives and the Commission has discretion whether or not to accept these suggestions.

The proposal, together with the report from COREPER, is then sent to the Council of Ministers for full consideration. The Council must adopt the proposal in accordance with the voting majority specified in the appropriate treaty provision. For example, if the Council acts under Article 100 of the EEC Treaty, and adopts measures harmonising national laws, unanimity is required. Where a qualified majority is required for the adoption of a proposal, the formula elaborated in Article 148 of the EEC Treaty is applicable.

The Council may amend a Commission proposal, but this requires unanimity on the part of the Council under Article 148 of the EEC Treaty. Failing unanimity, the Council must either accept the proposal on the basis of the specified voting majority or reject it. Alternatively, the Council may refer the proposal back to the Commission for reappraisal and resubmission. In practice, Commission proposals are continuously passing between the Council and the Commission prior to the adoption of a final text. Any absence of goodwill on the part of either institution tends to undermine this process and prevent the adoption of proposed measures. Naturally, cooperation between the Council of Ministers and the Commission is desirable for the promotion of the objectives of the Community.

Under the cooperation procedure, an even greater degree of collaboration is required between the Council of Ministers and the European Parliament. The cooperation procedure adds a second reading stage for certain types of Community legislation, at which point the European Parliament can exercise a greater influence on the content of proposed legislation. Under the cooperation procedure, responsibility for the initiation of proposals continues to reside in the European Commission which formulates proposals which are sent to the European Parliament in the normal manner before being resubmitted to the Council. The Council of Ministers is then required to reach a 'common position' on the proposed measure acting by qualified majority. A common position is simply a consensus on the basic elements of the proposal. However, no time limit is imposed on the Council to reach a common position.

This common position is referred to the European Parliament which has a three month period to consider its position and arrive at one of the following decisions: (1) approve the Council position; (2) make no decision on the Council position; (3) amend the Council position, which requires an absolute majority; or (4) reject the Council position by an absolute majority. If the Parliament approves the Council position, or makes no decision, the Council may proceed to act on the common position. If the position is amended, the Commission has one month to consider the amendments proposed by the Parliament with a view to amending its original proposal. When the Commission resubmits the amended proposals to the Council, the Council may adopt the revised proposals (by a qualified majority), adopt the amendments not approved by the Commission (by unanimity), amend the Commission proposal itself by unanimity, or refrain from acting at all on the measure. Proposals resubmitted from the Commission lapse if the Council has not acted within the prescribed period.

This description of the Community legislative processes makes it clear that cooperation among the various organs is essential because power to legislate is not vested in any single Community institution. While the Council of Ministers retains almost absolute control over the final content of a particular Community measure, its legislative authority is effectively circumscribed by the requirement that, in the majority of cases, this power may only be exercised on the basis of a proposal from the European Commission. The Council is unable to initiate a legislative proposal itself. The actual content of Community legislation is therefore largely dictated not by the Council but by the Commission, although the final decision on the adoption of a measure resides with the Council.

Cooperation between the Commission and the European Parliament and between the Council and the European Parliament under the so-called 'cooperation procedure' is essential to the smooth passage of Community legislation. But cooperation between each organ involved in the legislative process cannot be automatically assumed since each particular organ represents the interests of a particular group. The interests of the Member States are vested in the Council of Ministers, those of the Community itself in the Commission, and those of the people of Europe in a constitutionally disadvantaged European Parliament. Inevitably these interests will conflict. In the event of such a conflict, the interests of the Member States will tend to prevail since substantial executive and legislative powers have been merged in the Council of Ministers. Consequently, promotion of cooperation among the various organs of the Community is most in the strategic interests of the Community itself.

Question 3

Discuss the effect of the Single European Act on the influence of the European Parliament on law-making in the Communities.

University of London LLB Examination
(for External Students) European Community Law 1990 Q1

General comment

A problem requiring analysis of recent constitutional developments within the Community.

Skeleton answer

- The nature of the changes made by the SEA.
- The previous powers of the European Parliament.
- The new powers given to the Parliament.
- The effects of these powers on participation in the legislation process.

Suggested solution

The original legislative procedure for the creation of Community law has been significantly modified by the amendments made to the Community Treaties by the Single European Act. These changes introduced the 'cooperation procedure' designed to facilitate the passage of Community legislation dealing with specific subjects.

The Single European Act also introduced changes to the voting majorities required for the adoption of proposals. Article 100A of the EEC Treaty specifies adoption by a qualified majority for measures intended to implement the internal market. However, fiscal provisions and proposals relating to the free movement of persons or the rights and interests of employed persons are specifically excluded. Adoption of measures relating to these subjects will continue to require unanimity under Article 100 of the EEC Treaty. Further, Article 100A(4) of the Treaty allows a Member State to derogate from the obligations of a measure adopted on the basis of a qualified majority if the measure is alleged to adversely affect the security or welfare of a Member. The existence of the qualified majority voting requirements implies that proposals by the European Parliament have a greater chance of becoming law than had previously been the case in the original procedure.

The amendments made by the Single European Act allow the European Parliament to exercise grater influence over the legislative process. However, this influence is limited by a number of factors. First, the cooperation procedure only extends to Community legislation regulating the following subjects:

a) the elimination of discrimination on the grounds of nationality (Article 7(2) EEC Treaty);

b) the freedom of movement of workers and the freedoms of providing services and establishment (Article 49 EEC Treaty);

c) harmonisation measures relating to the establishment and functioning of the internal market (Article 100A(1) EEC Treaty).

If a proposed measure is not concerned with these issues, the original legislative procedures are applicable. The impact of the participation of the European Parliament in the legislative process is confined to these subjects and is therefore significantly circumscribed. Even although the single internal market programme itself involves 282 proposed measures of Community law, important subjects fall outside the cooperation process, including agriculture, transport and competition policy.

Second, despite the changes brought by the Single European Act, the constitutional position of the Council has not been usurped or undermined since it continues to exercise ultimate authority to adopt measures. The final decision on the nature and content of a particular legislative measure remains at the discretion of the Council of Ministers. This fact is underlined by the provisions of the Single European Act itself which provides that, if the Council fails to act within three months of receiving a resubmitted proposal, that proposal shall be deemed not to have been adopted. This time limitation places pressure on the other institutions. Where unanimity is required, neither the Parliament nor the Commission can afford to insist on a proposal which will not be adopted by the Council within this time frame.

Ironically, the influence of the European Parliament over the Council of Ministers has however been most significantly consolidated by a recent decision of the European Court unrelated to the Single European Act. Prior to 1990, the European Court had consistently ruled that the European Parliament lacked standing to bring actions for judicial review to challenge acts of the Council under Article 173 of the EEC Treaty: *European Parliament* v *EC Council (Re Comitology)* Case 302/87 (1988); *European Parliament* v *EC Council (Re Transport Policy)* (1985). However, in a case concerning the adoption of Community regulations to deal with the problems caused by the Chernobyl disaster, the European Court reversed its original line of reasoning and declared that the Parliament should not have to rely on the Commission to ensure that Community obligations are maintained in its interest: *European Parliament* v *EC Council (Re Chernobyl)* Case 70/88 (1990). According to the decision of the Court, the European Parliament is allowed to bring actions to annul the acts of other Community institutions in order to safeguard its rights and prerogatives.

This development will significantly alter the constitutional balance in the Community legislative processes and represents an endorsement by the European Court of the right of the Parliament to have a greater participation in the decision-making processes within the Community.

Question 4

'Although the European Parliament has only limited legislative powers but more extensive advisory and supervisory powers, one cannot claim that the Community legislative process is devoid of democratic participation.' Discuss.

University of Glasgow LLB Examination
1987 Q6

General comment

A question focussing on the role of one particular organ within the constitutional framework of the Community.

Skeleton solution

- Powers of the European Parliament.
- Influence of the Parliament in the legislative process.
- Democracy: debate, legislative influence, limitations.

Suggested solution

Three Community institutions are involved in the Community legislative process - the Council of Ministers, the European Commission and the European Parliament. Each of these organs performs a distinct role within this process and, while much of the power to legislate resides with the Council of Ministers, the Council would be unable to function without the participation of the other two organs. However, the European Parliament is the only Community institution that can claim to be a body directly elected by the peoples of Europe. Neither the Council of Ministers nor the European Commission is constituted through democratic processes. The Council of Ministers is composed of representatives from the various national governments of the Member States. While the governments of the Member States of the Community are elected through democratic procedures, the officials which together constitute the Council of Ministers can scarcely claim to represent the interests of the peoples of Europe.

Equally, the European Commission is composed of officials nominated by the governments of the Member States. No elections are held throughout Europe to fill the positions of European Commissioners. Despite the fact that the European

Commission is intended to embody the Community spirit and exercises considerable power in Community affairs, Commissioners continue to be appointed by agreement among the various Member States without consultations with the general population.

Only the European Parliament possesses democratic credentials. It is composed of 518 Members of the European Parliament (MEPs) who are elected on the basis of direct national suffrage: see the Act Concerning the Election of Members to the European Parliament 1976. However, even the European Parliament is not a truly democratic institution. Seats on the Parliament are allocated to Member States in a rough proportion to their relative populations. Germany, France, Italy and the United Kingdom all have 81 representatives each; Spain has 60; the Netherlands has 25; Belgium, Greece and Portugal have 25; Denmark has 16; Ireland has 15; and Luxembourg has 6 representatives. But in the United Kingdom, one MEP represents approximately 650,000 constituents, and in Ireland, one MEP represents approximately 225,000 constituents, while in Luxembourg, one MEP represents approximately 60,000 constituents. Thus, even in the constitution of a body purporting to represent the interests of the peoples of Europe, state sovereignty continues to play a significant role in the allocation of democratic representation.

The democratic qualifications of the European Parliament are further tarnished by the system employed for the conduct of elections to the Parliament. The Act Concerning Elections to the European Parliament permits elections to the Parliament in accordance with the procedures for national elections. Within the United Kingdom, the European Parliamentary Elections Act 1978 provides that elections to the Parliament shall be made under the traditional simple majority voting system. This provision was challenged by constituents in the Scottish Lothians constituency who sought an interim interdict (injunction) against the holding of the first European parliamentary elections on the grounds that the 1978 Act was inconsistent with Article 138 of the EEC Treaty which specifies that the Council should draw up measures to allow elections on the basis of 'direct universal suffrage in accordance with a uniform procedure in all Member States': *Price* v *Younger* (1984). All Member States of the Community, except the United Kingdom, use proportional representation to elect national officials. This argument was rejected by the Court on the basis that Article 138 of the EEC Treaty could not be given direct effect. Despite Community declarations specifying proportional representation as the appropriate means of electing MEPs, the United Kingdom persists in electing MEPs on the basis of the first-past-the-post system.

But, the 'democracy deficit' within the Community is most evident when the role of the European Parliament within the legislative process is examined. Under the original legislative procedure the European Parliament is given a number of rights. The opinion of the Parliament must be sought during the legislative procedure prior to the adoption of certain measures, and in particular under Articles 43, 54, 56 and 87 of the EEC Treaty. If the Community Treaties specify consultations with the Parliament before the adoption of a measure, failure to do so renders the putative measure void: *EC Commission* v *EC Council (Re Harmonised Commodity Descriptions)* (1990). However, this right is primarily a right to be consulted; it is not a right to make amendments to the content of the legislation. Suggested amendments from the European Parliament can be rejected by either the European Commission or the Council of Ministers.

It is true that this right of consultation is fortified by a number of ancillary powers granted to the European Parliament against the Commission. The Commission is obliged to answer questions submitted by MEPs - both written and oral - and the Parliament can collectively dismiss the Commission by a motion of censure carried by a two-thirds majority: Article 144 EEC Treaty. However, similar powers are not granted to the Parliament in respect of the activities of the Council of Ministers.

The original constitutional position of the Parliament has been significantly modified by two developments: the amendments made by the Single European Act; and the decision of the European Court in *European Parliament* v *EC Council (Re Chernobyl)* Case 70/88 (1990). The Single European Act introduced the new 'cooperation procedure' for legislation implementing the internal market programme and related subjects. This procedure gives a greater degree of participation to the Parliament in the Community legislative procedures. The decision of the European Court in the *Chernobyl case* recognised the right of the European Parliament to challenge acts of the Council of Ministers in order to uphold the interests of the Parliament. This decision alters the constitutional balance of the European Community and represents an endorsement by the European Court of the right of Parliament to have a greater participation in the decision-making processes within the Community.

Despite these changes, the law-making procedures within the Community continue to lack the minimum degree of democratic participation. Neither the Council nor the Commission are democratic institutions and the European Parliament lacks sufficient influence in the Community decision-making processes. This democracy deficit is particularly disconcerting when one remembers that the institutional balance among the Community organs is not strictly based on the doctrine of the separation of powers. Although a number of institutional checks and balances ensure that each individual organ acts within its own competence, and ultimately subject to judicial review by the European Court, substantial executive and legislative powers have been merged in the Council of Ministers. While the European Parliament is now elected on the basis of universal and direct suffrage throughout the Community, it has little effective influence in these important processes. If the Community is to be constituted on a democratic foundation, a substantial shift of powers must flow from the Council of Ministers to the European Parliament.

Question 5

Can the European Court of Justice be usefully compared with the United States Supreme Court?

University of Glasgow LLB Examination
1989 Q10

General comment

A problem requiring the student to compare the function of one particular organ in the Community with comparable institutions in another country.

Skeleton solution

- The structure of the ECJ and the Supreme Court.
- Constitutional positions.
- Scope and nature of powers.
- Jurisprudence and degree of judicial activism.

Suggested solution

Comparisons between the European Court of Justice and the US Supreme Court have a limited value because of the different constitutional position of the two judicial bodies and their historical development and evolution. While the US Supreme Court is the highest judicial body within the United States, which is a federal state, the European Court exercises a considerably more restrictive jurisdiction as regards subject-matter. It is a supranational court which functions over an organisation of states which could not be described as even a loose confederation. Other significant differences exist between these bodies. However, from the jurisprudence of the European Court, it is clear that the Court perceives itself as a tribunal which presides over an embryonic federation of states.

Under the American Constitution, the jurisdiction of the US Supreme Court is virtually absolute. This jurisdiction is hierarchical and the Supreme Court is the court of final instance. Disputes concerning individuals and governmental authorities may be adjudicated before the Supreme Court. In contrast, the European Court decides disputes between sovereign states concerning the subject-matter of the Community treaties. Individuals have access to the European Court through both the contentious jurisdiction of the Court and by way of a preliminary reference from national courts. However, disputes concerning matters unrelated to the Community treaties are excluded from the jurisdiction of the European Court. Thus, a dispute between an individual and the national authorities of his Member State will not be heard before the European Court unless the matter relates to an issue of Community concern. This is a significant limitation on the ambit of the Court's jurisdiction.

Both the US Supreme Court and the European Court are courts of final instance, where the matter is an issue of Community concern in the case of the ECJ. After the decision in *Marbury* v *Madison*, the Supreme Court has unquestioned authority to declare a legislative measure - from either a state or the federal government - void when it conflicts with the terms of the American constitution. The European Court has assumed the same power after its decision in *Costa* v *ENEL* (1964). In this case, the European Court held that an Italian statute which was inconsistent with Community law could not prevail in the event of a conflict. Through consistent jurisprudence, the European Court has developed the doctrine of the supremacy of Community law which proclaims that Community law prevails over inconsistent provisions of national law, whether passed before or after the Community treaties (or Treaties of Accession) entered into force. Neither the American Constitution nor the Treaty of Rome expressly confers upon the Supreme Court or the European Court the power to declare acts of legislation invalid. However, both courts have assumed this power by pursuing a deliberate policy of judicial activism.

Further, the constitutional sources of authority of both courts are radically different. The American constitution is an instrument which establishes the foundation for the administration of justice within a particular state. The Community Treaties - and in particular the Treaty of Rome - are international agreements among sovereign states. The Community Treaties do not establish a framework for the creation of a single state nor do they safeguard the fundamental rights of individuals. The European Community cannot grant citizenship to individuals, this being a prerogative reserved to individual Member States. In the absence of a constitutional right of European citizenship, the European Court will continue to remain a forum in which disputes between states concerning principles of law established by treaties are adjudicated. Even the most radical decisions of the Court, such as *Cowan* v *Tresor Public* (1990), which extended the protection of fundamental rights established under the constitutions of the Member States to all Community nationals, do not suggest that the Court believes that the Community has become an entity capable of conferring citizenship.

While the European Court has attempted to address the issue of fundamental human rights by asserting that such principles 'form an integral part of the Community system' (*Nold* v *EC Commission* (1974)), in general the Court perceives the rights of individuals in terms of factors of production. In other words, the vast corpus of Community law relating to the individual deals with individuals as workers and concerns their rights under employment law, social security law and the right to further education. On occasion, the European Court has concerned itself with issues such as the right to privacy, the freedom to practice a religion, the right to possess property, the right to lawyer-client privacy, issues of substantive and procedural due process of law, the non-retroactivity of criminal legislation, and the right to refrain from self-incrimination. But, the Court has no explicit mandate to deal with these issues. These matters remain within the scope of the European Convention on Human Rights 1950 and the system of protection established under that agreement. In contrast, these subjects form a considerable part of the volume of cases heard before the US Supreme Court.

It would be a dangerous policy on the part of the European Court if it was to imitate the jurisprudence of the US Supreme Court. While both courts have demonstrated a similar degree of judicial activism, the subject matters dealt with by each court remain undoubtedly distinct. Further, the constitutional position of each court is radically different from the other. It would therefore be a more advisable policy for the European Court to fashion principles itself and to continually refer to treaty sources of authority to support its policy of activism.

3 THE CONTENTIOUS JURISDICTION OF THE EUROPEAN COURT OF JUSTICE

3.1 Introduction

The contentious jurisdiction of the European Court of Justice is the power of the Court to hear direct actions brought against Member States and Community institutions. Actions against Member States and Community institutions may be initiated by other Member States or Community institutions. Individuals and legal persons cannot bring a direct action against a Member State under the contentious jurisdiction of the European Court. However, they may institute an action under the contentious jurisdiction of the Court against a Community institution if they can successfully demonstrate that certain conditions have been satisfied.

3.2 Key points

a) *Actions against Member States*

An action relating to an infringement of Community law by a Member State may be raised by either another Member State or the European Commission acting on behalf of the Community.

Under Article 170 of the EEC Treaty, one Member State may bring a direct action against another if it considers that the Member State concerned has failed to fulfil its obligations under the Community Treaties. The Court exercises exclusive jurisdiction over all disputes between Member States arising out of the subject matter of the Community Treaties. Member States are expressly forbidden from resolving such disputes by any other means: Article 219 EEC Treaty.

A number of procedural preconditions must be satisfied before a Member State can initiate a direct action against another. These are:

i) The Member State alleging the violation must bring the matter to the attention of the European Commission.

ii) The Commission must deliver a reasoned opinion on the matter after allowing the parties in dispute to submit arguments.

iii) Only after the Commission has delivered this opinion, or has failed to do so within the prescribed period of three months from notification of the matter, can the Member State continue its action.

iv) If the Commission indicates that it has no intention of pursuing the action, the complaining state may bring the action itself.

Under Article 169 of the EEC Treaty, the European Commission is authorised to commence proceedings against any Member State suspected of violating its Community obligations. The same provision also specifies a formal pre-litigation procedure which must be exhausted before commencing actual proceedings in the Court:

i) While not strictly required under Article 169, the Commission informally notifies the Member State accused of violating its obligations of the allegations and invites comments on the behaviour under investigation. A failure by a Member State to justify its conduct will set the formal pre-litigation procedure in motion.

ii) The Commission conducts an investigation into the matter and delivers a reasoned opinion on the subject after giving the Member State concerned an opportunity to submit its observations.

iii) If the Member State fails to comply with the terms of this opinion within the prescribed period, the Commission will bring the matter to the attention of the Court. However, the Commission must give the Member State a reasonable time to comply with the reasoned opinion: *EC Commission* v *Belgium (Re University Fees)* [1989] 2 CMLR 527.

Violations of Community law may result from both acts and omissions by Member States. Article 5 of the EEC Treaty requires Member States to take all appropriate measures to ensure respect for Community obligations and to 'abstain from any measure which could jeopardise the attainment of the objectives of this Treaty'. Common causes of action against Member States include the existence of incompatible legislation or the introduction of administrative practices which are inconsistent with Community law.

b) *Actions against Community institutions*

A direct action may also be brought in the European Court to review the acts of Community institutions. The European Court has exclusive jurisdiction to review the legality of acts of Community institutions and has sole competence to declare an act of a Community institution invalid: *Foto-Frost* v *Hauptzollamt Lubeck-Ost* [1988] 3 CMLR 57. The legal consequence of a successful challenge is that the Court will declare the measure null and void.

Community acts and measures which may be challenged include regulations, directives, decisions and all other acts capable of creating legal effects. Measures which have been held not to have such an effect include statements of objection, guidelines and internal procedural matters. See *Les Verts* v *European Parliament* [1989] 2 CMLR 880.

Member States, the European Commission and the Council of Ministers are privileged applicants for the purposes of initiating an action for judicial review of Community acts: *Italy* v *EC Council* [1979] ECR 2575. The standing of these parties in such actions is presumed. The fact that a Member State challenges an act of an institution addressed to another Member State is not a bar to judicial review. See *Italy* v *EC Commission (Re British Telecom)* [1985] ECR 873.

While Article 173(2) of the EEC Treaty explicitly recognises the standing of natural and legal persons to bring an action for judicial review directly to the European Court, such individuals must demonstrate that the act being challenged constitutes 'a decision which is of direct and individual concern' to the applicant. Decisions of the Council or the Commission addressed to a particular individual cause few problems in establishing direct and individual concern: see *Tokyo Electric Company plc* v *EC Council* [1989] 1 CMLR 169.

The fact that the act challenged by the individual is in the form of a Community regulation or a decision addressed to another person does not ipso facto exclude the possibility of establishing that the measure is a decision of direct and individual concern to an unrelated individual. In order to succeed, an individual must demonstrate that the regulation or decision addressed to another person is, despite its form or substance, a decision of direct and individual concern. See *ARPOSOL* v *EC Council* [1989] 2 CMLR 508; and *Sociedade Agro-Pecuaria Vincente Nobre Lda* v *EC Council* [1990] 1 CMLR 105.

Three separate grounds have been established by the Community treaties as a basis for judicial review of the acts of Community institutions. These are:

i) Actions to annul an act of a Community institution.

ii) Actions against a Community institution for failure to act.

iii) The plea of illegality.

i) Actions of annulment

Article 173 of the EEC Treaty expressly confers on the European Court jurisdiction to review the legality of acts of both the Council of Ministers and the European Commission. Although the provision makes no reference to the acts of the European Parliament, the Court has reviewed such acts on a number of occasions. See for example *EC Council* v *European Parliament* [1986] ECR 1339. The Court is empowered to review all acts of the Community institutions other than recommendations and opinions: Article 173(1) EEC Treaty.

An act of a Community institution may be annulled on the basis of one of four separate causes:

- Lack of competence on the part of an institution to adopt a particular measure.
- Infringement of an essential procedural requirement.
- Infringement of a provision of a Community treaty or a rule relating to the application of such provisions.
- Misuse of power by a Community institution.

In practice, these substantive grounds for annulment merge into each other and the jurisprudence of the European Court does not clearly distinguish the application of each cause in particular cases.

According to Article 176 of the EEC Treaty, where an act has been declared void by the Court, the institution which is responsible for the adoption of the putative measure is obliged to take the 'necessary measures' to comply with the judgment of the Court.

The limitation period for actions of annulment is two months from either the publication of the measure which is being challenged or from the date of the notification to the applicant: Article 173(3) EEC Treaty. This period applies regardless of whether the action is brought by a Member State, another Community institution or an individual. While these time limits are onerous, the Court has been prepared to extend the limitation period in cases where the measure being challenged lacks 'all legal basis in the Community legal system': *EC Commission* v *France* [1969] ECR 523.

ii) Actions for failure to act

If a provision of the Community treaties imposes a duty to act on either the Council of Ministers or the European Commission, and one or other of these organs fails to take the appropriate course of conduct, proceedings may be instituted under Article 175 of the EEC Treaty (or the counterpart ECSC Treaty and Euratom Treaty provisions) for failure to act.

As a preliminary requirement to the initiation of an action for failure to act, the alleged omission must be brought to the attention of the institution concerned. Thereafter, the particular organ has two months to define its position. An organ may define its position without adopting a particular measure. For example, where the Commission has explained its position and justified its non-activity in terms which are consistent with its obligations under the Community Treaties, the Court has held an action for failure to act inadmissible: *Alfons Lutticke GmbH* v *EC Commission* [1966] ECR 19. This has created a distinction between a failure to act and a refusal to act. The former constitutes a prima facie grounds for review while the latter amounts to a negative determination which must be challenged on grounds other than an action for failure to act.

iii) Plea of illegality

Under Article 184 of the EEC Treaty, notwithstanding the expiry of the limitation period established for actions of annulment, any party may, in any proceedings which involve a Council or Commission regulation, invoke a plea of illegality in order to have the regulation declared inapplicable. This plea differs from the other grounds for judicial review in that it does not itself constitute a separate or independent cause of action, but allows a party to plead that a regulation is inapplicable in actions initiated on some other jurisdictional basis. The main purpose of this device is to allow challenges to be made to regulations outside the limitation period specified for actions of annulment: see *Simmenthal SpA* v *EC Commission* [1979] ECR 777.

The fact that Article 184 does not constitute a distinct ground for judicial review was made clear in *Worhrmann* v *EC Commission* [1962] ECR 501 where the Court stated:

'It is clear from the wording and the general scheme of this Article that a declaration of the inapplicability of a regulation is only contemplated in proceedings brought before the Court of Justice itself under some other provision of the Treaty, and then only incidentally and with limited effect.'

In order for a plea of illegality to be successful, the regulation upon which the plea is based must be applicable - directly or indirectly - to the principal issue with which the particular application to the Court is concerned: see *Simmenthal SpA* v *EC Commission* [1979] ECR 777.

c) *Plenary jurisdiction*

The term 'plenary jurisdiction' is one more familiar to continental civilian lawyers than their common law counterparts. It refers to the ability of a Court to hear actions which require the Court to exercise its full powers. The plenary jurisdiction of the European Court extends to two principal forms of actions:

i) Actions for damages based on the non-contractual liability of the Community.

ii) Actions to review penalties imposed by Community institutions.

A third ground of plenary jurisdiction related to cases involving disputes between the Community and its staff (staff cases) under Article 179. The jurisdiction to hear such cases was transferred to the Court of First Instance.

Actions based on the contractual liability of the Community do not fall within the plenary jurisdiction of the European Court because jurisdiction to interpret and enforce contractual obligations is governed by the choice of jurisdiction chosen by the parties to the contract: Article 215(1) EEC Treaty. Contractual disputes involving the European Community may therefore be brought before the appropriate national courts. The European Court only exercises jurisdiction over contracts involving the Community if a particular clause in the contract refers disputes to arbitration before the European Court. See *EC Commission* v *Zoubek* [1986] ECR 4057.

i) Actions based on the non-contractual liability of the Community

The European Court has jurisdiction over non-contractual claims against the Community by virtue of Article 178 of the EEC Treaty. Non-contractual liability is a residual category which comprises all the liabilities of the Community other than contractual liability. The Court is instructed by Article 215 of the EEC Treaty to develop the Community law of non-contractual liability from 'the general principles common to the laws of the Member States' in order to 'make good any damage caused by its institutions or by its servants in the performance of their duties'.

One recent case illustrates the elements required for a successful action based on the [non-contractual] liability of the Community. In *Sociedade Agro-Pecuaria Vincente* v *EC Council* [1990] 1 CMLR 105, the European Court observed that:

'[T]he Court has held in previous decisions that by virtue of Article 215(2) of the [EEC] Treaty, the [non-contractual] liability of the Community presupposes the existence of a set of circumstances comprising the unlawfulness of the conduct alleged against the institution, actual damage and the existence of a causal link between the conduct and the alleged damage.'

Three elements are therefore necessary to establish the non-contractual liability of the Community: an unlawful act (or omission) which can be attributed to the Community; injury on the part of the applicant; and a causal connection between the act itself and the commission of the injury.

In certain circumstances, non-contractual liability may be imputed to the Community even although the national authorities of a Member State were actually responsible for the commission of the act which is alleged to give rise to the liability. In *Krohn Import-Export Co* v *EC Commission* [1986] ECR 753, the European Court established the principle that, where a national authority or body is obliged under Community law to comply with the instructions of the European Commission, any claim for compensation based on non-contractual liability should be directed against the Commission and not the national authorities.

ii) Actions to review penalties

The European Court has jurisdiction to review penalties imposed by Community institutions. Article 172 of the EEC Treaty authorises the Council of Ministers to enact regulations to regulate this aspect of jurisdiction. However, in the past, the Council of Ministers has tended to grant this authority in specific regulations dealing with particular subjects, rather than to adopt a comprehensive regulation to govern this aspect of the Court's jurisdiction.

A typical illustration of the Council granting such a power of review is contained in Council Regulation 17/62 which concerns the administration of Community competition policy. As regards competition policy, the jurisdiction of the Court is defined in the following terms:

'The Court shall have unlimited jurisdiction within the meaning of Article 172 of the [EEC] Treaty to review decisions whereby the Commission has fixed a fine or periodic payment; it may cancel, reduce or increase the fine or periodic payment imposed.'

Unlimited jurisdiction permits the Court to cancel, reduce or increase a penalty imposed on a commercial enterprise by the Commission.

3.3 Relevant cases

France v *United Kingdom (Re Fishing Mesh)* [1979] ECR 2923: The sole illustration of a complaint by one Member State against another proceeding to judgment by the Court.

Star Fruit Co SA v *EC Commission* [1990] 1 CMLR 733: A private individual does not have the right to compel the Commission to institute proceedings against a Member State suspected of violating Community law.

EC Commission v *Belgium (Re the Privileges and Immunities of European Community Officials)* [1989] 2 CMLR 797: Neither the constitutional structure of a Member State nor pre-existing provisions of national law constitute a valid defence to an enforcement action.

EC Commission v *France (Re Tobacco Prices)* [1990] 1 CMLR 49: Prima facie, the period for complying with an adverse judgment against a Member State should be no longer than the minimum period needed for adopting the required remedial measures.

Foto-Frost v *Hauptzollamt Lubeck-Ost* [1988] 3 CMLR 57: The European Court has exclusive competence to declare an act of a Community institution null and void and this power cannot be exercised by a national court.

Sofrimport Sarl v *EC Commission* Case 152/88, Judgment of 26 June 1990, not yet reported: A decision outlining the necessary requirements for an individual to establish standing in an action to review an act of a Community organ.

3.4 Relevant materials

LN Brown, *The Court of Justice of the European Communities* (third edition, 1989).

A Dashwood & R White, 'Enforcement Actions under Articles 169 and 170 EEC' (1989) 14 EL Rev 388.

MCEJ Bronckers 'Private Enforcement of 1992' (1989) 26 CMLR 513.

RM Greaves 'Locus Standi under Article 173 when Seeking Annulment of a Regulation' (1986) 11 EL Rev 119.

3.5 Analysis of questions

Questions relating to the contentious jurisdiction of the European Court are particularly popular among examiners. Students must be familiar with the different grounds for the exercise of the contentious jurisdiction of the Court, together with the various causes of action. While this aspect of Community law is particularly complex, it should be pointed out that this subject is a reliable one for preparation for examination purposes.

3.6 Questions

Question 1

Experiencing budgetary and financial difficulties, a Member State unilaterally decides to withhold payments it owes to the Community. The Community wants to take action against the Member State. Advise.

University of Glasgow LLB Examination
1987 Q9

General comment

An essay question requiring analysis of the rights of the Community against Member States.

Skeleton solution

- The role of the European Commission in enforcing treaty obligations.
- Rights of the Commission to take action.
- Relevant procedure.
- Enforcement of judgments.

Suggested solution

Articles 199 to 209 of the EEC Treaty require Member States to contribute to the budget of the European Community and failure to do so would constitute a violation of Article 5 of the EEC Treaty which requires Member States to take all appropriate measures to ensure fulfilment of the obligations arising out of the Treaty.

Article 169 of the EEC Treaty authorises the Commission to commence proceedings against any Member State suspected of violating its Community obligations. Indeed, according to Article 155 of the EEC Treaty, the Commission has primary responsibility for ensuring that the Member States uphold their Community obligations. However, prior to initiating an action in the European Court for enforcement of Community obligations against a Member State, Article 169 specifies a formal pre-litigation procedure which must be exhausted before commencing actual proceedings in the Court. In practice, even before engaging in this formal procedure, the Commission informally notifies the Member State alleged to have violated its Community obligations and invites comments on the behaviour under investigation.

If informal communications have proved unsuccessful the Commission delivers a reasoned opinion on the matter after giving the Member State concerned an opportunity to submit its observations. Failure to follow this procedure is infringement of an essential procedural requirement: *EC Commission* v *Italy* (1970). Should the Member State fail to comply with the terms of the Commission opinion within the period prescribed, the next stage is to bring the matter to the attention of the Court. But, since the purpose of delivering a reasoned opinion is to give the defendant State an opportunity to respect its Community obligations, the Commission must allow a reasonable period for the Member State to comply. A reasonable period is determined in the light of the facts surrounding the case. If the Commission imposes excessively short time limits, the action may be dismissed by the Court: see for example, *EC Commission* v *Belgium (University Fees Case)* (1989).

Neither the constitutional structure of a Member State nor pre-existing provisions of national law constitute a defence against an enforcement action, even where a constituent part of a Member State exercises exclusive authority over a matter, independent from the control of the central government: see *EC Commission* v *Belgium* (1989). As the Court has pointed out, responsibility for the performance of Community obligations rests with Member States and consequently:

'the liability of a Member State under Article 169 arises whatever the agency of the State whose action or inaction is the cause of the failure to fulfil its obligations, even in the case of a constitutionally independent institution': *EC Commission* v *Belgium* (1970).

A Member State may even be liable for the acts of judicial bodies or administrative tribunals for decisions contrary to Community law, despite the doctrine of the separation of powers upon which many of the legal systems of the Member States rest.

If the European Court decides that the Member State in question is in violation of its obligations under Community law, it will render a decision to that effect. But where the European Court decides that the acts or omissions of a Member State are incompatible with Community obligations, the judgment of the Court does not automatically annul the offending measure. The Court will only rule that a violation of the obligation has occurred. The government of the offending Member State is obliged to amend its law or practices to conform to the decision of the European Court under Article 171 of the EEC Treaty. No period is specified within which a state must act to comply with judgments, but remedial action must be initiated immediately and completed as soon as possible: *EC Commission* v *Belgium* (1989). Prima facie, the period for complying with an adverse judgment 'should be no longer than the minimum period needed for adopting the remedial measures required': *EC Commission* v *France (Tobacco Prices Case)* (1990). Since, at least in theory, actions under Articles 169 and 170 are declaratory actions, the Court has no specific power to award damages in favour of those injured or prejudiced by infringing behaviour on the part of a Member State.

No sanction is expressly specified in the EEC Treaty for non-compliance with decisions of the Court. For example, the Community has no authority to withhold payments due to the particular Member State on the basis that the Member State has failed to observe its Community obligations. This position contrasts with the express provisions of the ECSC Treaty which allow the High Authority (the equivalent of the European Commission), with the assent of the Council of Ministers acting by a two-thirds majority, to take two forms of action in the event of the non-observation of an adverse decision by a Member State. First, the High Authority may suspend the payment of any sums which may be due to the Member State under the ECSC Treaty. Second, the High Authority may take measures, or authorise another Member State to take measures, which derogate from the strict terms and purposes of the ECSC Treaty in order to correct the effects of the infringement. However, these provisions were not carried over to the EEC Treaty.

While the record for conforming with Court decisions is respectable, there have been a number of instances where states have demonstrated a reluctance to comply. For example, the French government took almost four years to amend advertising legislation which discriminated against foreign alcohol products: *EC Commission* v *France* (1980).

Where a Member State persistently refuses to comply with adverse judgments, the European Commission has adopted a policy of repeatedly bringing the state before the Court for a declaration by the Court that the state is failing to meet its Community obligations. For example, see: *EC Commission* v *Italy* (1968); *EC Commission* v *Italy* (1972). The purpose of this practice is to coerce the Member State into observing its obligations by embarrassing it in front of the other Member States.

The European Commission should therefore be advised to engage in the pre-litigation stages which must be exhausted prior to the initiation of proceedings against a Member State. In the event that this correspondence is unsuccessful, a formal action should be commenced. An adverse decision by the Court would most likely result in the recalcitrant Member State succumbing to its Community obligations.

Question 2

Liquidgold plc is one of only four manufacturers in the European Community of a new type of liquid sweetener manufactured from barley. Drinkitdown Ltd, a manufacturer of soft drinks, was so attracted by the economics of using this type of sweetener that it has installed new machinery in its factory suitable for use with the barley sweetener. In January it entered into a contract with Liquidgold to purchase 10,000 tonnes of the sweetener each year for the next five years, this quantity being the amount needed to meet its current production requirements.

Last month, fearing adverse effects on the Community sugar industry, the Council adopted a Regulation imposing production quotas on the barley sweetener. An annex to that Regulation, which expressly refers to the four manufacturers by name, fixed Liquidgold's annual quota at 7,500 tonnes.

Having discovered that the other three manufacturers are already bound by contracts covering the whole of their permitted production, Drinkitdown is faced with a choice between cutting back its production or converting its factory to use sugar at a cost of £500,000.

Advise Drinkitdown as to the remedies available to it with regard to the Council Regulation.

University of London LLB Examination
(for External Students) European Community Law 1990 Q4

General comment

A typical problem-type question which requires the application of the relevant law to the facts of the question.

Skeleton solution

- The applicable substantive principles of Community law.
- Standing to challenge a regulation.
- Problem of time bar; plea of illegality.
- Possibility of an indirect challenge through the Article 177 procedure.

Suggested solution

In order to mount a successful challenge against the Council Regulation which imposes production quotas on the barley sweetener, Drinkitdown must establish the existence of one of four separate causes of action: lack of competence; infringement of an essential procedural requirement; infringement of a provision of a Community Treaty or a rule relating to the application of such provisions; or the misuse of power by a Community institution. From the facts of the case, the only possible cause of action would be on the basis of an infringement of the terms of the Community Treaties or the principles of Community law which have been derived from these treaties.

The Regulation was adopted as a measure to protect the Community sugar industry and would therefore be subject to the Common Agricultural Policy (CAP), the objectives of which are set out in Article 39 of the EEC Treaty. This article recognises the general principle of proportionality. This principle requires that measures introduced to regulate a particular activity must be not be disproportionately onerous in relation to their derived benefit. In other words, if the harm caused by the introduction of a regulation outweighs any possible benefit, the measure may be challenged as being contrary to the principle of proportionality which is a recognised rule of Community law: *EC Commission* v *France (Re Imports Restrictions on Milk Substitutes)* (1989). If Drinkitdown could establish that the Council Regulation limiting the production of the sweetener caused more injury than assistance, the Regulation could be challenged on this basis.

Alternatively, Drinkitdown could attempt to demonstrate that the enactment of the Regulation contravenes the principle of legitimate expectation. For example, in

Mulder v *Minister van Landbow* (1989), the European Court held that a farmer who had suspended milk production pursuant to a Community scheme could not be subsequently excluded from the allocation of milk quotas after the scheme had been discontinued. The Court held that the farmer had a legitimate expectation that at the end of the programme he would be in a position no less favourable than that which he would have enjoyed had he not acceded to the scheme. Clearly, Drinkitdown could argue that it had a legitimate expectation that its expenditure on plant conversion would not be misspent as a result of a Community measure.

While Drinkitdown may have a legitimate cause of action to challenge the Council Regulation, in order to show standing Article 173(2) requires individuals and legal persons to demonstrate that the act being challenged constitutes a decision which is of 'direct and individual concern' to the applicant. The fact that the act challenged by the individual is in the form of a regulation or a decision addressed to another person does not ipso facto exclude the possibility of establishing the measure is a decision of direct and individual concern. However, an action for judicial review of a regulation or a decision addressed to another person is considerably more onerous than review of a decision explicitly addressed to an individual.

The Council Regulation imposing the production quotas refers to four manufacturers by name, including Liquidgold, but does not refer to Drinkitdown. Drinkitdown must therefore establish that the Regulation is in fact a 'decision' under Article 173(2), in which it has a direct and individual concern. In order to show that the Regulation is a decision, Drinkitdown must prove that, while the measure takes the form of a regulation, it is in fact a series of individual decisions in the form of a regulation. An example of applicants successfully proving that a regulation made by the Commission constituted a decision is *International Fruit Company* v *E C Commission* (1971). In this case, the particular Community regulation challenged established a system of import licences to limit the importation of dessert apples into the Community according to supply and demand in the market. Importers could only receive an import licence if the volume of their proposed imports did not exceed a certain level. The Court held that this regulation was not a generally applicable measure, but a 'conglomeration of individual decisions taken by the Commission under the guise of a regulation'. This determination was made on the basis that applications over a certain quantity were automatically disqualified from the competition for import licences. In the present case, it would be relatively simple to establish that the Regulation is in fact a conglomeration of individual decisions since the Regulation itself is expressly confined to the activities of four businesses.

If Drinkitdown can establish that the Regulation is in fact a decision, it must then be shown that the decision is of direct and individual concern. In order to have direct concern, the effects of the decision must immediately affect the applicant without depending on the exercise of discretion by another body. Thus, in *ARPOSOL* v *EC Council* (1989), the European Court held that the applicants could not establish direct concern because the implementation of the Community measure depended on the intervention of the national authorities of Member States. In another case, the applicant was refused standing because the administration of a Community measure allocating quotas actually depended on distribution by Member States to individuals: *Bock* v *EC Commission* (1971). However, where the national authorities have no discretion in implementing a Community measure, direct concern may be established: see *Sofrimport Sarl* v *EC Commission* Case 152/88 (1990). The criterion of direct concern may therefore be presumed.

In addition to having a direct concern in the decision being challenged, Drinkitdown must also establish an individual concern. When a decision is not expressly addressed to an individual, in order for the measure to be of individual concern, it must be demonstrated that it affects 'their legal position because of a factual situation which differentiates them individually in the same way as to the person to whom it is addressed': *Sociedade Agro-Pecuaria Vincente Nobre Lda* v *EC Commission* (1990). See also *Dentz und Geldermann* v *EC Council* (1988). The contested measure must affect the applicant by reason of certain peculiar attributes or factual circumstances which differentiate the applicant from all other persons: see *Sofrimport Sarl Case*, above. The mere ability to ascertain more or less precisely, or even to establish the identity of the persons to whom a measure applies, does not immediately imply that the measure is of individual concern to them: *Cargill and Ors* v *EC Commission* Case 229/88 (1990). Individual concern has been established where a regulation named specific undertakings and applied specific measures to them, where the regulation had as its subject-matter the individual circumstances of three named importers, and where a decision was issued by the Commission in response to the requests of a particular group, even although the final decision was addressed to another person. Conversely, if an act applies to objectively determined situations and entails legal effects for categories of persons generally and in the abstract, it has general application and is incapable of having individual effect: *Cooperativa Veneta Allevatori Equini* v *EC Commission* (1989). Drinkitdown might therefore have difficulty establishing that the Regulation is of individual concern.

If Drinkitdown was successful in challenging the validity of the Regulation, it could also be successful in obtaining compensation from the Community for injury sustained as a result of the unlawful measure. Article 215(2) of the EEC Treaty states that, in the case of non-contractual liability, the Community shall, in accordance with the general principles common to the laws of the Member States, make good any damage caused by the institution responsible for the unlawful measure. Article 178 of the EEC Treaty confers jurisdiction on the European Court to decide disputes relating to damages on the basis of the non-contractual liability of the Community.

Alternatively, Drinkitdown may indirectly challenge the validity of the Regulation on any legal grounds by means of reference for a preliminary ruling by a national court to the European Court under Article 177 of the EEC Treaty. Such a reference may be made where it is relevant to the outcome of pending legislation. Indeed, in *Foto-Frost* v *Hauptzollamt Lubeck-Ost* (1988), the European Court held that such a reference was necessary in a case involving a challenge to a Community measure because only the European Court had the power to render such an act invalid. An Article 177 reference may be made regardless of the locus standi of the applicant and any time limits: see *International Fruit Company* v *Produktschap*, above.

If the European Court was prepared to declare the Regulation invalid, it would not be applicable to Liquidgold and therefore Drinkitdown could rely on the sales contract negotiated between itself and Liquidgold.

Question 3

On 1 December 1988 the Commission of the European Communities took a decision instructing the British Customs authorities to stop issuing import licences for textile imports from Guatemala until 31 December 1989. The Commission's decision was taken in accordance with a Council Regulation, approved in July 1985, which established a quota for each of the Member States on such imports and entrusting the Commission with the enforcement of the Regulation.

According to the Commission, the quota assigned to the United Kingdom was reached on 27 November 1977.

On 29 November 1988 Wooltex, a British company, applied to the British Customs authorities for a licence to import 40,000 T-shirts from Guatemala. Wooltex's application was refused on the grounds that it would violate the Commission's decision.

Advise Wooltex as to any remedies which it may have under EEC law.

University of London LLB Examination
(for External Students) European Community Law 1989 Q5

General comment

A problem primarily involving the issue of challenges to measures of Community institutions, but with additional complexities.

Skeleton solution

- Possible proceedings under Article 173.
- Problem of limitation.
- Claim for compensation based on the non-contractual liability of the Community.

Suggested solution

An act of a Community institution may be challenged under Article 173 of the EEC Treaty on the basis of any one of four separate grounds: lack of competence; infringement of an essential procedural requirement; infringement of a Community Treaty or a rule relating to its application; and misuse of powers. The factual circumstances of this problem indicate that a number of these grounds may have relevance in providing Wooltex advice as regards possible remedies against the Commission's action.

An act of a Community institution may be annulled on the basis of a lack of competence if the organ acted without appropriate power. If the wrong institution has acted or, alternatively, if the right body has acted but without the appropriate authority, the act in question may be reduced on the grounds of a lack of competence: see *Meroni and Co* v *ECSC High Authority* (1957-58). If Wooltex can prove that the

Council Regulation delegating authority upon the Commission to issue such decisions is ultra vires the decision can be successfully challenged. If the Council has no competence to delegate authority to the Commission under the terms of the EEC Treaty, the measure itself is null and void. Wooltex may also be able to establish that, by imposing an absolute ban on the importation of textiles, the Commission has exceeded its authority.

Annulment of an act of a Community institution is also possible if, in adopting the measure, the institution was guilty of infringing an essential procedural requirement. The act will only be annulled if the procedural error is substantial or involves an important step in the decision making processes: see *Roquette Freres SA* v *EC Council* (1980). In order to constitute a breach of an essential procedural requirement, the error must significantly compromise the position of the applicant. For example, if a Community measure requires the convening of a hearing to investigate a matter, and no such meeting is held, the omission will normally vitiate any final decision on the matter: *ACF Chemiefarma* v *EC Commission* (1970). Alternatively, where an organ is obliged to set out the reasons for its decision, failure to do so will amount to infringement of an essential procedural requirement: *Control Data Belgium NV* v *EC Commission* (1983). Unfortunately the facts of this case do not suggest these are possible grounds for a valid challenge.

A further complication could be added by the fact that the prescription period for actions of annulment is two months from either the publication of the measure which is being challenged or from the date of notification to the applicant: Article 173(3) EEC Treaty. Where the measure has not been published or notified to the applicant, the two months prescription period runs from the date on which knowledge of the measure may be imputed to the applicant. While these time limits are onerous, the Court has been prepared to extend the limitation period in cases where the measure being challenged lacks 'all legal basis in the Community legal system': *EC Commission* v *France* (1969).

In the event that Wooltex is successful in establishing that the Commission decision is null and void, the question of compensation arises. The European Court has jurisdiction over non-contractual claims against the Community by virtue of Article 178 of the EEC Treaty. The Court has been instructed by Article 215 of the EEC Treaty to develop the law of non-contractual liability of the Community from 'the general principles common to the laws of the Member States' in order to 'make good any damage caused by its institutions or by its servants in the performance of their duties'. A number of principles have been fashioned by the European Court into a rudimentary framework to regulate this matter. In *Sociedade Agro-Pecuaria Vincente* v *EC Council* (1990), the European Court observed that:

'[T]he Court has held in previous decisions that by virtue of Article 215(2) of the [EEC] Treaty, the liability of the Community presupposes the existence of a set of circumstances comprising the unlawfulness of the conduct alleged against the institutions, actual damage and the existence of a causal link between the conduct and the alleged damage.'

Article 215 makes no reference to the element of fault in the commission of the act or omission, merely requiring that the Community shall 'make good any damages caused by its institutions or by its servants'. However, the Court has often referred to the requirement of fault in determining the non-contractual liability of the Community: *Toepfer* v *EC Commission* (1965). At the same time, the Court has not invariably required proof of fault and the jurisprudence of the Court has become a little incoherent: *Adams* v *EC Commission* (1985). The necessity of demonstrating fault appears to vary according to the nature of the act upon which liability is alleged.

Where the liability of the Community is being established on the basis of a measure adopted by a Community institution, no liability will fall on the Community unless adoption of the measure constitutes a flagrant violation of a fundamental rule for the protection of the individual. The Court has stressed that, where a legislative measure is concerned, the unlawfulness of the conduct must constitute a 'sufficiently serious breach of a superior rule for the protection of the individual': *Zuckerfabrik Bedburg & Ors* v *EC Council and EC Commission* (1987).

Even although the British customs authorities refused to grant Wooltex application for a licence, the Community will still remain liable even although national authorities were directly responsible for the commission of the tortious act. In *Krohn Import-Export Co* v *European Commission* (1986), the Court established the principle that, where a national authority or body is bound to comply with the instructions of the Commission, a claim for compensation should be addressed to the Commission and not the national authority.

The second requirement for a claim for non-contractual compensation is the existence of injury sustained by the applicant. The degree of injury is also relevant to the calculation of damages. However, the Court has avoided identifying heads of damages and has been content to assess both injury and damages on an ad hoc basis. Where injuries sustained cannot be attributed to the act of a Community institution, no damages may be awarded: *Comptoir National Technique Agricole SA* v *EC Commission* (1975). The Court has also developed a number of rules to govern the issue of the remoteness of damages.

Question 4

Recent research by British scientists has revealed that certain types of cling-film may constitute a health hazard when used in a particular fashion. Concerned by this revelation, the British Government decide to prevent imports of cling-film from Germany and Sweden. German and Swedish firms affected by this decision want to seek a remedy. Advise these firms as to their rights and remedies.

Question prepared by the Author
February 1991

General comment

A question dealing with a particularly contentious area of Community law.

Skeleton answer

- Nature of the alleged violation.
- Inability of individuals to sue Member States in the ECJ.
- Complaints to the European Commission.
- Remedy before national courts and tribunals.

Suggested solution

The EEC Treaty requires, in addition to the abolition of customs duties, the removal of all quantitative restrictions and measures having an equivalent effect on imports and exports within the Community: Article 30 EEC Treaty. In *Procureur du Roi* v *Dassonville* (1974), the European Court pointed out that 'all trading rules enacted by Member States which are capable of hindering, directly or indirectly, actually or potentially intra-Community trade are to be considered as measures having equivalent effect to quantitative restrictions'. Measures introduced to protect public health are permitted under Article 36, but Member States introducing such measures must show that the purpose of the legislation is in the general interest and is such as to take precedence over the requirement of the free movement of goods which constitutes one of the fundamental rules of the Community: *Cassis de Dijon Case* (1979).

However, individuals and legal persons cannot bring a direct action in the European Court of Justice for judicial review of the actions of a Member State. While individuals and legal persons can raise a direct action against a Community institution under Article 173 of the EEC Treaty, a similar right is not created in respect of actions against Member States. The German and Swedish companies could opt for two alternate courses of action. First, they could complain to the European Commission about the measures adopted by the United Kingdom. Second, they could sue the governmental department responsible for the measure on the ground that the department has been responsible for a violation of Community law.

The European Commission may start an investigation into a violation of a Community obligation by a Member State after a complaint has been received from a private individual or a legal person. A complaint from an aggrieved individual to the Commission has a number of advantages over litigation against the government of a Member State in the courts of that Member State. First, the complainer incurs nominal legal costs since the Commission assumes the responsibility for the prosecution of the case. Second, the weight of the Commission behind a complaint is more likely to expedite an out-of-court settlement of the dispute. In addition, the complainer may remain anonymous in the event of the Commission proceeding with the complaint.

At the same time, if the Commission initiates an action on the basis of a complaint from an individual, the success of the Commission in the subsequent litigation will not give the complainer an automatic right to seek damages or compensation for injuries sustained. Further, the Commission retains absolute discretion to decide whether litigation is the appropriate course of action. A private party alleging injury as a consequence of a violation of Community law by a Member State cannot compel the Commission to institute proceedings against that state: *Star Fruit Co SA* v *EC Commission* (1990).

In the event that the Commission refuses to prosecute the case against the United Kingdom after a complaint by the German and Swedish producers of cling-film, these companies would be obliged to raise an action in the British courts against the responsible governmental department. In such a case, a plaintiff would have to establish that either a remedy for such a breach existed in English law and could be enforced in the English courts or that Community law established such a remedy which the English courts would have to recognise: *Rewe* v *Landwirtschaftskammer Saarland* (1976).

The European Court has already pointed out that 'it must be possible for every type of action provided for by national law to be available for the purposes of ensuring observance of Community provisions having direct effect, on the same conditions as would apply if it were a question of observing national law': *Rewe* v *Hauptzollamt Kiel* (1981). Consequently, in order to be successful, the foreign manufacturers of cling-film must establish that English law provides a remedy for a violation of a duty imposed on the government.

The leading case in English law dealing with the remedies available to a party aggrieved by a violation of Community law is *Bourgoin* v *Ministry of Agriculture, Fisheries and Food* (1986). This case involved an action brought by a French producer of turkeys whose imports into the United Kingdom had been unlawfully restricted by an embargo imposed by the British government. The United Kingdom was held to have violated Community law by the European Court as a consequence of imposing restrictions on imports of turkeys contrary to Article 30 of the EEC Treaty: *EC Commission* v *United Kingdom* (1982). The plaintiffs brought an action against the Minister of Agriculture, claiming injury as a result of lost sales caused by the embargo. The action was brought on the grounds of breach of statutory duty or, in the alternative, that the Ministry was liable under the English tort of misfeasance by knowingly imposing the restrictions in violation of Community obligations. The judge at first instance held that a case for misfeasance could be sustained and this decision was upheld in the Court of Appeal. However, the Court of Appeal rejected the contention that an action could be brought on the basis of a breach of statutory duty. Unfortunately an out of court settlement was reached before an appeal by the House of Lords was heard and consequently the matter remains unresolved in English law. However, the courts of a number of other Member States have recognised the right of an individual to seek redress against a government for injury sustained as a consequence of a breach of Community law, and the foreign manufacturers should not be deterred from seeking a remedy in the English courts.

In the past, the European Court has been reluctant to establish principles to regulate actions brought in national courts for violations of Community law by Member States. Community law does not demand that damages should be available to compensate victims of a breach by a Member State of an obligation arising under the Community Treaties, even if the Article in question gives rise to an obligation which produces direct effects. However, the European Court has recently suggested that the existence of such a right might be established in the future: *Asteris & Ors* v *Hellenic Republic* Cases 106-127/87 (1990).

4 THE PRELIMINARY RULING JURISDICTION OF THE EUROPEAN COURT OF JUSTICE

4.1 Introduction

To ensure the uniform, consistent and harmonious application of Community law throughout the national legal systems of the Member States, the Community Treaties establish a procedure to allow national courts to refer questions of Community law to the European Court for consideration. These references from national courts fall within the preliminary ruling jurisdiction of the Court. Article 177 of the EEC Treaty establishes the essential principles and procedures which govern this aspect of the jurisdiction of the European Court.

4.2 Key points

a) *Scope of the preliminary ruling jurisdiction*

Article 177 of the EEC Treaty confers jurisdiction on the European Court to render preliminary ruling decisions which relate to:

i) The interpretation of the Community Treaties.

ii) The validity and interpretation of acts of the Community institutions.

iii) The interpretation of statutes of bodies established by the Council of Ministers where the relevant statutes so provide.

In addition, a number of Conventions among the Member States of the Community provide for preliminary references from national courts to the European Court for the interpretation of intra-Community agreements. See *Six Construction Ltd* v *Humbert* Case 32/88, Judgment of 15 February 1989, not yet reported, a preliminary reference for an interpretation of the Convention on Jurisdiction and the Enforcement of Judgments 1968.

b) *The obligation to request a preliminary ruling - lower courts*

All national courts and tribunals, other than those against which there is no appeal, have discretion whether or not to refer a case involving a question of Community law to the European Court. If the issue arises before a court against whose decision there is no judicial remedy under national law, technically that court is obliged to refer the matter to the European Court: Article 177(3) EEC Treaty.

Courts and tribunals which exercise a discretion to refer a question should be satisfied that two preconditions exist before making a reference, namely:

i) the court or tribunal must believe that the case involves an issue of Community law; and

ii) the court or tribunal must be satisfied that a decision on the question is necessary to decide the merits of the case.

A prima facie question of Community law will arise where a party relies on a provision of a Community Treaty, or a measure of Community law such as a regulation, a directive or a decision, or a precedent of the European Court (and now also the Court of First Instance).

c) *The obligation to request a preliminary ruling - courts of final instance*

National courts and tribunals of final instance (or last resort) are subject to a different set of obligations as regards seeking preliminary references from the European Court. Article 177(3) of the EEC Treaty declares that these courts are bound to refer a question of Community law to the European Court for a preliminary reference.

This absolute duty has been qualified by the European Court itself, particularly in *CILFIT* v *Ministry of Health* [1982] ECR 3415. Where a question of Community law arises before a national court of final appeal, such a court need not refer the matter for a preliminary ruling if the question has already been settled by the European Court. This discretion applies only 'where previous decisions of the [European] Court have already dealt with the point of law in question, irrespective of the nature of the proceedings which led to those decisions, even although the questions at issue are not strictly identical': *CILFIT*, above.

The European Court has also established a number of guidelines to ensure that this privilege is not abused. A court of final instance which decides not to refer a question to the European Court because of an earlier precedent must give special consideration to the 'characteristic features of Community law and the particular difficulties to which its interpretation gives rise'. Special consideration must be given to the following matters:

i) Community legislation is drafted in several different languages all of which are equally authentic and proper interpretation often involves comparisons with different language versions.

ii) Community law has acquired its own terminology and legal concepts do not necessarily have the same meaning in Community law as in national law.

iii) Every provision of Community law has to be placed in its proper context and interpreted in light of the system established by the Community Treaties, having regard both to its objectives and to the state of the law at that particular point. See *Litster* v *Forth Dry Dock and Engineering Co* [1989] 1 All ER 1134.

In many respects the decision of the European Court in the *CILFIT case* reduces the discretion of courts of last instance to decide questions of Community law themselves because it establishes rigourous criteria for deciding whether or not to refer a question to the European Court.

d) *The nature of the question submitted for a preliminary ruling*

There are no formal requirements regulating the content of a question submitted for a preliminary reference, although obviously the greater the degree of precision, the more accurate the response of the European Court.

The main problem in framing a question for a preliminary reference is that the national court may refer a question which exceeds the jurisdiction of the Court such as, for example, requiring the Court to address issues of national law. Where national courts have inadvertently included questions of national law in a reference, the European Court has generally extracted the pertinent issues of Community law from the reference, bearing in mind the subject-matter of the case.

e) *The authority of a preliminary reference*

The term 'preliminary reference' is somewhat misleading. A preliminary ruling is not an advisory opinion but rather a decision which the referring national court is obliged to apply to the facts of the case: see *Brown* v *Secretary of State for Scotland* (1989) SLT 402. A preliminary reference is binding upon the court which referred the question for consideration in the sense that it represents an authoritative determination of Community law.

Not only are decisions rendered through the preliminary reference procedure binding on the court which referred the question, but they may also be cited as precedents in those Member States which adhere to the principle of stare decisis. Decisions of the European Court are therefore binding as precedents on British courts when they relate to identical points of Community law: *WH Smith Do-It-All & Payless DIY Ltd* v *Peterborough City Council* [1990] 2 CMLR 577.

f) *The functions and responsibilities of the European Court*

The primary responsibility of the European Court in a preliminary reference is to decide the legal merits of the case in terms of Community law. Therefore, the European Court cannot expressly declare that provisions of national law are inconsistent with Community law; this is a matter for the national court. As the Court has expressly observed:

'[T]he Court is not empowered under Article 177 of the [EEC] Treaty to rule on the compatibility with the Treaty of provisions of national law. However, it has jurisdiction to provide the national court with all such matters relating to the interpretation of Community law as may enable it to decide the issue of compatibility in the case before it': *Schumacher* v *Hauptzollamt Frankfurt Am Main* [1990] 2 CMLR 465.

The European Court also cannot take notice of the facts of a particular case. Ascertaining the relevant facts is the concern of the referring court: *Simmenthal SpA* v *Amministrazione delle Finanze dello Stato* [1978] ECR 1453.

Equally, the Court refrains from criticising the reasons behind a particular reference although on occasion the Court has rejected references which have been contrived between the litigating parties for the purpose of obtaining a particular ruling. Thus, in *Foglia* v *Novello* [1980] ECR 745, the Court held that it had no jurisprudence to pronounce on the merits of a case where the parties to the principal action had initiated the proceedings for the sole purpose of obtaining a ruling that a particular law of another Member State was inconsistent with Community law. The Court has expressed its concern at the use of the preliminary ruling procedure in cases where there is no genuine dispute.

g) *The relevance of precedents in the jurisprudence of the European Court*

The European Court, in common with other systems of law based on the civilian model of law, does not adhere to the doctrine of precedent. The Court has, however, adopted a policy of referring to earlier decisions in the course of judgments and repeating, occasionally with slight modifications, parts of decisions from earlier relevant cases. This technique ensures consistency throughout the jurisprudence of the Court.

But, in legal theory at least, the previous decisions of the Court do not constitute binding precedents and on occasion the Court has radically departed from its previous course of decisions. Compare *European Parliament* v *EC Council (Re Comitology)* Case 302/87, Judgment of 27 September 1988, not yet reported, with *European Parliament* v *EC Council (Re Chernobyl)* Case 70/88, 22 May 1990, not yet reported.

4.3 Relevant cases

CILFIT v *Ministry of Health* [1982] ECR 3415: Elaboration of the criteria required in order to allow a court of final instance to refuse a preliminary reference to the ECJ.

SA Magnavision NV v *General Optical Council (No 2)* [1987] 2 CMLR 262: Decision relating to the proper timing of an application for a preliminary ruling in the English courts.

Litster v *Forth Dry Dock and Engineering Co* [1989] 1 All ER 1134: An example of the House of Lords applying the proper methodology to a case involving a question of Community law without reference to the European Court.

WH Smith Do-It-All & Payless DIY Ltd v *Peterborough City Council* [1990] 2 CMLR 577: Description of the function of decisions of the European Court as precedents before English courts and tribunals.

4.4 Relevant materials

H G Schermers & CWA Timmermans (eds), *Article 177 EEC: Experiences and Problems* (1987).

A Arnull, 'The Use and Abuse of Article 177 EEC' (1989) 52 MLR 622.

H Rasmussen, 'The European Court's Acte Clair Strategy in CILFIT' (1984) 9 EL Review 242.

D O'Keefe, 'Appeals Against an Order to Refer under Article 177' (1984) ECR 87.

L N Brown, *The Court of Justice of the European Communities* (third edition, 1989) 169-202.

4.5 Analysis of questions

Many of the questions relating to the subject of preliminary ruling jurisprudence focus on the nature of the relationship between the national courts and the European Court. Thus, issues such as discretion to refer, the form of the question and the role of the Court in this process are particularly popular.

4.6 Questions

Question 1

Should the European Court ever refuse a national court's request for a preliminary ruling?

University of London LLB Examination
(for External Students) European Community Law 1990 Q3

General comment

A difficult essay-type question which, although requiring a narrative answer, refers to a particular topic on which there is little legal authority.

Skeleton solution

- The provisions of the EEC Treaty.
- The policy of the European Court.
- Case law.
- Conclusions.

Suggested solution

Initially, the European Court adopted an extremely liberal policy regarding the admission of references from national courts and tribunals. No formal examination was undertaken into the admissibility of such cases; see for example, *Simmenthal SpA* v *Ministry of Finance* (1976). This was due not only to the relatively light case load of the Court during the early years of the Community but also to a desire, on the part of the Court, to influence the evolution of the Community by forging fundamental principles of Community law. The European Court has always maintained a policy of overt judicial activism.

In the pursuit of this policy, the European Court has been anxious to admit references in order to have an opportunity to fashion principles of Community law through interpretation. Equally, encouraging national courts to refer cases to the Court served the dual purpose of both ensuring uniform interpretation of Community law and acquainting the national courts with the existence of Community law.

The success or otherwise of this process has depended on the cooperation of the national courts. In order to assist national courts to accept the principle of the supremacy of Community law over national law, the European Court has emphasised the importance of cooperation rather than insisting on the development of a hierarchical structure which placed the European Court above national courts and tribunals. Instead the Court has evolved a careful delimitation of responsibilities between the Community system and the legal systems of the Member States, with the European Court interpreting Community law and the national courts applying this interpretation to the facts of the case before them.

A careful balance has been struck by the European Court between furthering the aims of the Community by ensuring the successful development of the Community legal order and consideration for the sentiments within the national legal systems of the Member States.

The practical utility of this policy, together with a growing awareness within the national courts about the existence of Community law, has meant that the European Court has become a victim of its own success. The sheer volume of references from the national courts has meant that a reference can take up to two years before a decision is rendered. Such a heavy workload also implies that the quality of individual judgments may decrease. Further, the quantity of judgments risks diluting their importance.

Yet in the leading case where the Court declined jurisdiction - *Foglia* v *Novello (No 1)* (1980) - the European Court did not specifically address this issue. The case itself turned on its particular facts.

In *Foglia* v *Novello*, a reference was made by an Italian court in an action between two Italians who had entered into a sales contract requiring delivery of the goods in France. The contract provided that the buyer would not be responsible for the payment of any taxes imposed in contravention of Community law. The goods were duly delivered. The seller was required to pay a consumption tax in France and claimed reimbursement from the buyer who refused to pay on the ground that the tax was contrary to Community law. Thus, the Italian courts were required to decide whether the French tax was in accordance with Community law.

The Italian court referred the question to the European Court. The Court took exception to this question because it involved a challenge to the sovereign rights of one Member State in a legal forum where the state was not in a position to defend itself.

More importantly, there were a number of grounds for believing that the whole transaction had been contrived in order to present a test case to the European Court. For these reasons, the European Court refused to accept the reference on the basis that there was no genuine dispute between the parties. The Italian court declined to accept this decision and made a second reference to the Court: *Foglia* v *Novello (No 2)* (1981). However the European Court again rejected the reference on the same grounds.

This ruling was subject to a considerable amount of criticism, not least because it interfered with the delicate relationship between the national courts and the European Court. By substituting the criteria of 'a real dispute between the parties' for 'a question on matters of Community law' (as specified by the EEC Treaty), the European Court created a ground for reviewing decisions of national courts to refer a case for a preliminary reference. The Court could therefore investigate the reasons for the reference and the relevance of the question referred.

This development broke down the cooperative framework which the European Court had patiently developed throughout the course of its jurisprudence and substituted a more hierarchical structure. In addition, the Court conferred upon itself power to investigate the facts of a case in order to ascertain the intention of the parties. This power trespassed on the role of the national court as the finder of facts.

Logic would suggest, however, that there are circumstances in which the Court should, and indeed has, declined a reference. The first ground relates to instances in which the Court determines that the matter at issue has no connection with Community law. The second ground is where the requirements of Article 177 of the EEC Treaty are not satisfied - the reference was not made by a court or tribunal or, alternatively, the question referred does not concern the interpretation of Community law or the validity of a Community measure. The third possibility is when the reference is an abuse of the procedure - an amorphous heading. In *Matthews* (1978), the Court declined jurisdiction when it decided that the questions referred were purely hypothetical and that the parties had attempted to compel the national court to make a reference, thus depriving it of its discretion under Article 177(2). In *Foglia* v *Novello*, it could be argued that jurisdiction had been declined because the Article 177 procedure was being abused because it was being employed to indirectly challenged a French tax when proceedings under Article 169 of the EEC Treaty would have been more appropriate.

It could also be argued that fictitious litigation is an abuse of procedure, since mere academic consultation on a hypothetical issue is not the purpose of Article 177 of the EEC Treaty. It is, however, difficult to develop reliable criteria for determining the existence of fictitious litigation.

In between the two rulings in the *Foglia* affair, two other references were made to the European Court by courts in Italy: *Chemical Farmaceuticic* v *DAF* (1981); and *Vinal* v *Orbat* (1981). Both cases involved facts similar to those in *Foglia* except that the disputed tax was Italian and not French and the disputes were considered 'not to be manifestly bogus'. In both cases, the European Court accepted the reference. It seems likely that the European Court's real reason for its decision in the *Foglia* cases was comity - a desire not to offend France.

The hostile reception received by the decision of the Court in *Foglia* and the potentially devastating consequences of the ruling on the intra-judicial relationship previously built up by the Court may mean that the European Court will adopt a policy of only reluctantly interfering in matters which fall within the competence of national courts. The Court has, however, attempted to alleviate the workload before it by following another tactic - the development of the acte clair doctrine after the *CILFIT case* (1982). By establishing criteria which allow national courts of final instance to decide cases without reference to the European Court, the Court itself has developed a doctrine which builds on European-national judicial cooperation rather than encroaches on the role of national courts and tribunals in the preliminary reference procedure.

Question 2

'Preliminary rulings are essential for the uniform interpretation and application of Community law by national courts.' Discuss.

University of Glasgow LLB Examination
1987 Q4

General comment

A question relating to the function of this procedure within the framework of European integration.

Skeleton solution

- Purpose of Article 177 of the EEC Treaty.
- Jurisprudence of the European Court.
- Exceptions to the general rule: *CILFIT*.

Suggested solution

Article 177 of the EEC Treaty does not establish a hierarchy between the European Court and the national courts of the Member States. Instead, it forms a framework for cooperation to ensure that Community law is interpreted and applied in a uniform manner throughout the Community: see *Rheinmuhlen* (1974). The preliminary reference procedure is designed to allow national courts to refer questions of Community law to the European Court in order to interpret the Community Treaties and the acts of the institutions of the Community. In strict legal terms, the preliminary reference procedure does not create a further forum for appeal on a matter of Community law.

The structure of this relationship clearly suggests that the architects of the Community did not have in mind the creation of a court of appeal on Community matters when they designed the preliminary reference procedure. Rather, they sought to establish a mechanism whereby national courts could seek the guidance and advice of the European Court during their deliberations. The purpose of this procedure was therefore to ensure that Community law was consistently and uniformly applied throughout the Community by national courts and tribunals.

The preliminary reference procedure has, in fact, been instrumental in developing a consistent body of fundamental principles of Community law. For example, the principle of the direct effect of Community treaty provisions was derived by the European Court after a preliminary reference from a Dutch court: *Van Gend en Loos* v *Netherlands* (1963). Similarly, the principle of the supremacy of Community law was originally elaborated by the European Court on the basis of a preliminary reference: *Costa* v *ENEL* (1964).

The Court has also been able to impose a degree of compunction on national courts by means of the preliminary reference device. Thus, reluctant national courts have been brought into line by decisions rendered by way of preliminary references. For example, the House of Lords was extremely reluctant to embrace the principle of the supremacy of Community law in light of the doctrine of parliamentary sovereignty in British constitutional law. In *R* v *Secretary of State, ex parte Factortame* (1990), the European Court expressly upheld the principle of the supremacy of Community law over the Merchant Shipping Act 1988. The Court was able to render this ruling because the House of Lords had referred the question for a preliminary ruling.

However, the preliminary ruling procedure also allows the European Court to maintain consistency on a geographical level as opposed to a jurisprudential level. If the courts and tribunals of Member States were allowed to deviate from the jurisprudence of the European Court when they applied Community law, the result would be chaos.

To prevent this possibility, the European Court has developed a number of rules of interpretation for national courts engaged in the application of Community law: see *CILFIT* v *Ministry of Health* (1982). First, since Community legislation is drafted in several different languages, all of which are equally authentic, the proper interpretation of Community law requires a court to compare different language texts in order to reach the proper decision. Second, Community law has acquired its own terminology and legal concepts do not necessarily have the same meaning as in national law. Finally, every provision of Community law has to be placed in its proper context and interpreted in light of the system established by the Community treaties. In this regard, particular attention must be paid to the objectives of a Community measure and the state of the law at that particular point: see *Litster* v *Forth Dry Dock and Engineering Co* (1989).

The European Court has consistently required that these methods of interpretation be applied by national courts engaged in the application of Community law. Further, these rules have been developed by the Court on the basis of cases referred to it by national courts.

This policy is also evident in the strict criteria laid down by the Court to qualify the absolute duty of national courts of final instance to refer matters of Community law to the European Court under Article 177(3) of the EEC Treaty. According to Article 177(3), national courts of final instance are required to refer questions of Community law to the Court. However, it is clear that, as the European Court develops its jurisprudence, the rigorous application of this provision would result in wasteful repetition. National courts would have to refer questions even if the applicable law had been clearly developed by the Court.

In order to prevent this occurrence, the European Court developed its own principle of acte clair. Where a question of Community law arises before a national court of final appeal, such a court need not refer the question 'where previous decisions of the [European] Court have already dealt with the point of law in question, irrespective of the nature of the proceedings which led to those decisions, even although the questions at issue are not strictly identical': *CILFIT*, above. However, if a national court was to assume responsibility for the application of Community law without reference to the European Court, it would be obliged to uphold the three tenets of construction created to interpret Community law.

Even although the European Court has drawn strict parameters for the application of the acte clair doctrine in Community law, the *CILFIT* decision has considerably lessened the ability of the European Court to regulate the consistent and uniform application of Community law through the preliminary reference procedure. One particular example of the dangers created by the acte clair doctrine is *SA Magnavision NV* v *General Optical Council (No 2)* (1987). This case concerned the right of a Belgian company to provide optical services throughout the United Kingdom by virtue of the freedom to provide services. The exercise of this freedom contravened the Opticians Act 1958 which required supervision by a registered medical practitioner when spectacles were being sold.

The High Court refused to refer the matter to the European Court by way of a preliminary reference, despite being the court of final instance for the particular matter. Watkins LJ, in refusing to make the reference decided that a preliminary reference could not be made to the ECJ because the matter had been resolved and final judgment rendered. In this context, the Court assumed that a 'preliminary reference' is a procedure which must be initiated before the case is heard. However, the preliminary reference procedure can be initiated at any stage of domestic legal proceedings. As a result, no reference was made by the High Court and the court rendered a highly dubious judgment on the basis of a flawed understanding of the scope of Article 30 of the EEC Treaty.

The whole episode of the acte clair doctrine as developed in the *CILFIT case* illustrates how important the preliminary ruling procedure is for maintaining the uniform application of Community law. In the absence of direction from the European Court, Community law would be an incoherent body of principles subject to different interpretations in different Member States. Since the object of the Community Treaties is to create a new legal order among the Member States of the Community, the continuation of uniform interpretation by way of preliminary references is essential.

Question 3

'If in a case before a national court a point of EEC law is sufficiently clear and even if the judge is very knowledgeable about Community law, a ruling by the European Court of Justice could still be sought.' Discuss.

University of Glasgow LLB Examination
1987 Q5

General comment

A complex question involving an opinion-answer on the part of the student.

Skeleton solution

- Obligation of national courts to refer to the ECJ.
- Doctrine of acte clair: *CILFIT*.
- Relevant factors in determining whether a reference should be made by a court.

Suggested solution

Not all national courts are required to submit questions of Community law to the European Court under the preliminary reference procedure established under Article 177 of the EEC Treaty. If all courts and tribunals confronted with issues of Community law made such references, the European Court would be unable to function as its case-load would far exceed its capacity. To ensure this does not happen, Article 177 is selective in specifying which courts are obliged to make such a reference and which are not.

Article 177 makes a clear distinction between the obligations of lower courts and the obligations of courts of final instance. Where a question of Community law is raised before a lower court or tribunal, it may, if it considers that a decision on the question is necessary to enable the court to give judgment, request the European Court to render a preliminary judgment on the question. In contrast, where a question of Community law is raised before a court against whose decision there is no judicial remedy under national law, that court is obliged to bring the matter to the attention of the European Court by way of a preliminary reference.

Where a court has discretion whether or not to make a reference, two factors are relevant. First, the court should be satisfied that the case before it involves a question of Community law. Second, the court must believe that a decision from the ECJ is necessary in order to decide the merits of the case.

A number of decisions of the English courts have attempted to modify these two requirements. Thus, in *Bulmer* v *Bollinger* (1974), Lord Denning MR claimed that the discretion of lower courts to refer decisions to the ECJ could be subject to practical considerations. A number of 'guidelines' were developed in this case. First, the point must be conclusive of the case. Second, the point must not have been decided by the European Court in a previous decision. Third, if the point of law is reasonably clear and free from doubt, the court need not exercise its discretion to refer the case. Finally, the national court should ascertain the facts of the case before it prior to making a reference to the European Court. These criteria have been applied by the English courts in a number of cases: see Bingham J in *Customs and Excise Commissioners* v *ApS Samex* (1983).

The European Court has, however, held that the discretion of inferior courts to refer a question of Community law to the European Court cannot be fettered by the decisions of superior courts: *Rheinmuhlen* (1974). This principle is applicable regardless of whether inferior courts or tribunals adhere to the doctrine of precedent. Consequently, in light of the criticism drawn by the guidelines laid down by Lord Denning, it is doubtful whether inferior English courts are required to apply the criteria specified in *Bulmer* v *Bollinger* before deciding to refer a case for a preliminary reference.

Whether or not a question should be referred to the European Court by a national court which has discretion in the matter must be decided by the court itself. Doubtless, in practice, a number of factors are taken into consideration. Perhaps the paramount consideration is the expertise of the European Court and the inexperience of the national court. At least one judge has been prepared to concede that '[s]peaking entirely for myself, I realise that I am not well qualified to place in its context every provision of Community law nor to interpret it in the light of Community law as a whole': per Hodgson J in *R* v *Secretary of State, ex parte Factortame* (1989).

A similar sentiment was expressed by Bingham J when he expressed the view that 'sitting as a judge in a national court, asked to decide questions of Community law, I am very conscious of the advantages enjoyed by the Court of Justice. It has a panoramic view of the Community and its institutions, a detailed knowledge of the treaties and of much subordinate legislation made under them, and an intimate familiarity with the functioning of the Community which no national judge denied the collective experience of the Court of Justice could hope to achieve': *Customs and Excise Commissioners* v *ApS Samex*, above.

Even if a national judge is sufficiently knowledgeable regarding the applicable Community law, and even if the relevant principles of Community law are apparent, a cogent argument may still be sustained in favour of a preliminary reference. Few British judges possess sufficient knowledge of Community law in order to decide a case concerning the application of Community law, and even fewer would be able to keep abreast of contemporary developments within Community law. Both of these are reasons for remitting a case for a preliminary ruling.

Courts of final instance are subject to a different series of obligations. While Article 177 expressly requires that courts of last resort submit questions of Community law for a preliminary ruling, even these courts exercise a degree of discretion in deciding whether or not to make such a reference. This discretion arises from the decision of the European Court in *CILFIT* v *Ministry of Health* (1982) which established the Community doctrine of acte clair. Courts of final instance are not obliged to submit questions to the ECJ for a preliminary reference if previous decisions of the European Court have dealt with the point in contention. However, even if the national court could exercise an option not to refer under the doctrine of acte clair, naturally it could, of course, continue to make such references if it wished.

Even a court of final instance exercises a degree of discretion whether or not to refer a question to the European Court when the criteria established in the *CILFIT CASE* are applicable. In such circumstances, even these courts would be wise to take into consideration the factors which lower courts have taken into consideration prior to exercising their discretion to refer.

Question 4

'The European Court has on several occasions stated that Article 177 presupposes distinct and separate functions for the national and European courts'; R Plender, *Cases and Materials on the Law of the European Communities* (1989), 178.

Discuss.

Question prepared by the Author
February 1991

General comment

A question discussing the relationship between national courts and the European Court vis-a-vis preliminary references.

Skeleton solution

- Functions and responsibilities of the national courts.
- Functions and responsibilities of the ECJ.
- Relationship between these organs.
- Conclusions.

Suggested solution

In essence, the national courts and tribunals of the Member States are required to perform three principal functions in references for preliminary rulings from the European Court: to determine issues of fact; to ascertain whether a reference should be made; and to apply the decision of the European Court to the facts of the case. In contrast, the European Court is required to decide the question of European law submitted for reference by the national court.

Only national courts and tribunals exercising a judicial function are entitled to refer a question of Community law to the European Court through the preliminary reference procedure. The European Court decides whether or not a particular body constitutes a court or tribunal for the purposes of Article 177 and the status of the body in national law is irrelevant in this determination. A number of factors are taken into consideration by the Court in this determination, including appointment procedure, rules of procedure, the authority upon which the body has been established, compulsory jurisdiction and whether or not the body applies legal principles. Courts of law clearly qualify under these criteria, as do many administrative tribunals such as the Employment tribunal and the VAT tribunal.

Disciplinary bodies for professional groups may or may not constitute tribunals depending on their authority to render binding decisions of a judicial character and whether the body has been created on the basis of statutory authority: contrast *Borker* (1981) with *Broekmeulen* v *Huisarts Registratie Commissie* (1981).

The majority of national courts retain discretion whether or not to refer a question of Community law to the European Court. Where an appeal may be lodged against the decision of the court or tribunal, a discretion to refer may be exercised. In contrast, tribunals and courts against which no appeal may be lodged are obliged to refer the matter to the attention to the European Court by way of preliminary references, although this absolute duty has been modified by the jurisprudence of the European Court itself: Article 177(3) EEC Treaty.

Courts and tribunals which exercise a discretion to refer a question for a preliminary reference should be satisfied that two preconditions exist: Article 177(2) EEC Treaty. First, the court must believe that the case involves an issue of Community law. A prima facie question of Community law will arise where a party relies on a provision of a Community treaty, a measure of Community law such as a regulation, a directive, or a decision, or a precedent of the European Court (and now also the Court of First Instance). Second, the court must be satisfied that a decision on the question is necessary to decide the merits of the case. The decision of an inferior court or tribunal to refer, or not to refer, a case to the European Court may itself be the subject of an appeal.

Courts of final resort are, however, subject to a different series of obligations. The EEC Treaty declares that such courts are bound to refer a question of Community law to the European Court for a preliminary reference. However, the absolute duty has been qualified for cases involving questions of European law already settled by the European Court. In such circumstances, it would be an unnecessary repetition to submit a case to the Court for an identical decision. In *CILFIT* v *Ministry of Health* (1982), the Italian Supreme Court asked the European Court to specify the conditions which must prevail before a court of final instance could avoid referring a question of Community law to the European Court. In other words, the Italian court wanted to know whether a preliminary reference had to be made by a court of final instance when the applicable Community law was unambiguous and not subject to a reasonable interpretive doubt.

The European Court held that where a question of Community law had already been settled, national courts of last resort were not obliged to refer the question to the Court. The Court acknowledged that the correct application of Community law may often be so obvious as to leave no scope for any reasonable doubt as to the manner in which the question raised is to be resolved. Where this was the case, the national court was free to decide the point without seeking guidance from the European Court.

The stage of the proceedings at which an application for a preliminary ruling should be made is another issue for the national court to decide. In making a preliminary reference, particular regard should be made to the national system of pleading. The necessity of referring a question under the preliminary ruling procedure would not normally arise until the pleadings have been adjusted and the real questions focussed in the pleadings.

Also, the facts should be clear and the arguments on the merits of the case fully developed. A reference to the European Court would be inappropriate in the event that preliminary issues of title, competency and relevancy remain unresolved. Similar comments have been made by way of obiter, to the effect that a reference to the European Court is desirable only after the pursuers have established a prima facie case.

No formal requirements regulate the contents of the questions submitted for a preliminary reference, although obviously the greater the degree of precision, the more accurate the response of the European Court. The main problem in framing a preliminary reference is that the national court might refer a question, the response to which exceeds the jurisprudence of the European Court under Article 177. The European Court has no authority to decide matters of national law, which are issues to be decided solely by the national courts.

Where national courts have inadvertently included questions of national law in a reference, the European Court has generally extracted the pertinent issues of Community law from the reference, bearing in mind the subject-matter of the case. The Court will then apply the relevant principles of Community law and return the case to the national courts to apply the preliminary judgment to the facts of the case.

A preliminary reference is binding upon the court which referred the question for consideration in the sense that it is an authoritative determination of Community law. A preliminary ruling is not merely an advisory opinion and the English courts are obliged to apply the relevant Community law to the facts of the case. Further, decisions of the European Court are binding as precedents on the English courts where they relate to identical points of Community law: *WH Smith Do-It-All & Payless DIY Ltd* v *Peterborough City Council* (1990).

The primary responsibility of the European Court in a preliminary reference is to decide the legal merits of the case in terms of Community law. The Court has express jurisdiction in preliminary references to interpret the Community Treaties, to rule on the validity and interpretation of acts of Community institutions, and to interpret the statutes of bodies established by an act of the Community.

As the Court has expressly observed 'the Court is not empowered under Article 177 of the [EEC] Treaty to rule on the compatibility with the Treaty of provisions of national law. However, it has jurisdiction to provide the national court with all such matters relating to the interpretation of Community law as may enable it to decide the issue of compatibility in the case before it': *Schumacher* v *Hauptzollamt Frankfurt Am Main* (1990).

In the event of a conflict, the Court may only conclude that the provision of national law is 'incompatible' with the relevant Community law. The national court has responsibility to apply the relevant law and to determine whether a plaintiff should prevail or a prosecution should be continued.

Nor does the European Court have jurisdiction to take cognizance of the facts of the case. Ascertaining the relevant facts is the concern of the referring court: *Simmenthal SpA* v *Amministrazione delle Finanze dello Stato* (1978). Equally, the Court is unable to criticise the reasons behind a reference although the Court has adopted a policy of rejecting references which have been contrived for the purposes of obtaining a ruling. Thus, in *Foglia* v *Novello* (1980), the Court held that it had no jurisdiction to pronounce on the merits of a case where the parties to the main action had initiated proceedings for the sole purpose of obtaining a ruling that a particular national law of a Member State was inconsistent with Community law: see also *Foglia* v *Novello (No 2)* (1981). The Court expressed its concern at the use of the preliminary ruling procedure in cases where there was no genuine dispute and where the applicants sought to obtain a judgment on the compatibility of the laws of one Member State in the courts of another Member.

While the European Court and national courts have different competences and responsibilities under the preliminary reference procedure, these frequently overlap. In such circumstances, a clear cut distinction in functions is impossible to identify. Moreover, the European Court has demonstrated a tangible propensity to extend its competence further into the affairs of national courts. The fact that the responsibilities of each set of courts is not explicitly defined in Article 177 made this eventually inevitable. Whether this is a development which will serve the long-term strategic interests of the European Court is entirely another matter.

5 EUROPEAN COMMUNITY LEGISLATION

5.1 Introduction

A critical distinction is made between primary and secondary sources of Community law. Primary sources consist of the international agreements entered into by the Member States for the purpose of establishing the constitution of the Community. Secondary sources are measures enacted by Community institutions exercising the authority vested in them by the Community treaties. Naturally, primary sources of Community law prevail over secondary sources in the event of a conflict.

5.2 Key points

a) *Primary sources of Community law*

The three Community Treaties, together with a number of international agreements formally amending these Treaties, form the constitution of the Community and are the ultimate source of legal authority within the Community system. These Treaties function as primary sources of law in two ways:

i) The Community Treaties prescribe the powers of Community institutions to promulgate secondary legislation. Failure on the part of an institution to respect the limits of authority prescribed in the Treaties will render a putative measure null and void: *EC Commission* v *EC Council (Re Generalised Tariff Preferences)* [1987] ECR 1493.

ii) The Community Treaties, in certain circumstances, establish fundamental principles of Community law which have direct effect and may be relied upon by individuals before national courts and tribunals.

b) *Community agreements with third states*

Each of the three Community Treaties confer authority on the Community to enter into international agreements with third states dealing with matters which fall within the competence of the Community. These agreements are also capable of providing a source of directly applicable principles of Community law: see *Demirel* v *Stadt Schwabisch GmbH* [1989] 1 CMLR 412. The Court has also held that such agreements prevail over inconsistent provisions of national law: *Hauptzollamt Mainz* v *Kupferberg & Cie KG* [1982] ECR 3641.

No decision has yet been rendered on the issue of whether the terms of such agreements would prevail over inconsistent secondary legislation. However, under no circumstances would the European Court support the principle that the terms of such agreements are capable of prevailing over conflicting provisions of the Community Treaties.

c) *Intra-Community agreements*

Article 200 of the EEC Treaty requires Member States to negotiate intra-Community agreements to regulate particular subjects including the protection of persons and the protection of individual rights against discrimination, the abolition of double taxation within the Community, mutual recognition of corporations having their seat of incorporation in another Member State, and a system for the reciprocal recognition and enforcement of judgments among Member States.

Four Conventions have been negotiated among the Member States to achieve certain of these objectives:

i) The Convention on Jurisdiction and Enforcement of Judgments in Civil and Commercial Matters 1968.

ii) The Convention on the Law Applicable to Contractual Obligations 1980.

iii) The Convention on the Mutual Recognition of Companies and Bodies Corporate 1968.

iv) The Convention for a European Patent for the Common Market 1975.

In addition, the Lugano Convention on Jurisdiction and the Enforcement of Judgments in Civil and Commercial Matters 1988 extends the terms of the 1968 Jurisdiction and Judgments Convention to the European Free Trade Association (EFTA) countries on the basis of reciprocity with Community Member States. As of February 1991, only two of these agreements have entered into force.

In the past, these Conventions have been given effect through the traditional national procedures for the incorporation of international agreements. Within the United Kingdom, this procedure involves the enactment of enabling legalisation. For example, the 1968 Jurisdiction and Judgments Convention has force of law within the United Kingdom by virtue of the Civil Jurisdiction and Judgments Act 1982.

d) *Secondary sources of Community law*

Both the Council of Ministers and the European Commission have authority to enact secondary legislation although in order to do so they must have authority over the particular subject-matter by virtue of the terms of the Community

Treaties. Article 189 of the EEC Treaty specifies three separate forms of Community secondary legislation:

i) Regulations

A regulation is a general legislative instrument which is binding in its entirety throughout the Community and which is directly applicable within the legal orders of the Member States without the need of intervention on the part of national legislative bodies.

ii) Directives

A directive also has binding effect, but only against the Member State to whom it is addressed and only in relation to the result to be achieved. Directives are not automatically applicable within Member States since Member States exercise a discretion to select the appropriate form of domestic law to incorporate the obligations arising from the directive into national law.

iii) Decisions

A decision is binding in its entirety, but only upon those to whom it is addressed. Decisions may be addressed to both Member States and individuals.

Authority is also conferred upon the Council of Ministers and the Commission to make recommendations and to deliver opinions. Neither of these acts involves the creation of measures which have legal effect.

e) *The distinction between the direct applicability and the direct effect of Community law*

The concept of direct applicability only applies to Community regulations and is derived from Article 189 of the EEC Treaty which provides that regulations shall be 'directly applicable in all Member States'. The quality of direct applicability means that regulations are automatically incorporated into the domestic laws of the Member States immediately upon enactment by the appropriate Community institution. Individual and legal persons may therefore rely on rights and duties created by Community regulations before national courts and tribunals.

The quality of direct applicability was only expressly conferred upon Community regulations. Neither individual Treaty provisions nor Community directives were intended to be directly applicable. In fact the EEC Treaty expressly provides that the national authorities of the Member States retain discretion in selecting the appropriate instrument of national law to implement Community directives. However, the European Court has significantly modified this provision by establishing the principle of direct effect which applies to Treaty provisions and also directives which have not been implemented by Member States within the prescribed period.

While the principles of direct applicability and direct effect perform the same function - to create enforceable rights on behalf of individuals - each principle applies to different forms of Community legislation.

f) *The direct applicability of Community regulations*

The essence of the principle of direct applicability is that a Community regulation which has entered force may be enforced by or against the subjects of the regulation and that the application of such a measure is independent of any measure of national law: *Bussone* v *Ministry of Agriculture and Forestry* [1978] ECR 2429.

Not all regulations create individual enforceable rights. Frequently regulations are not addressed to individuals but to Member States. In such cases, obligations created under regulations are imposed on Member States and function in the field of public - as opposed to private - law: *Gibson* v *Lord Advocate* (1975) SLT 133. Whether or not a particular regulation creates directly enforceable rights for individuals depends on two factors - the subject-matter of the regulation and the nature of the group to whom it is addressed: *Becker* v *Finanzant Munster-Innenstadt* [1982] ECR 53.

g) *Direct effect and Community Treaty provisions*

No provision of any Community Treaty expressly authorises the use of individual Treaty provisions as a reservoir of legal principles, but from the very formation of the Community the European Court has sought to achieve this object. In *Costa* v *ENEL* [1964] ECR 585, the European Court held that where a Treaty article imposes a clear and unconditional obligation upon a Member State, unqualified by any reservation reserving the right of legislative intervention, such a provision could be capable of direct effect and individual rights could be created which were enforceable in municipal courts.

Three specific conditions are therefore required for a provision of a Community treaty to have direct effect:

i) The provision being relied upon must be clear and precise: see *Gimenez Zaera* v *Instituto Nacional de la Seguridad Social* [1987] ECR 3697.

ii) The term must be unqualified and not subject to a right of legislative intervention: *Diamantarbeiders* v *Brachfeld* [1969] ECR 211.

iii) The obligation must not confer a discretion on either Member States or Community institutions to act: *Salgoil* v *Italian Ministry for Foreign Trade* [1968] ECR 453.

The principle of direct effect has been expressly acknowledged in a number of cases involving the courts of the United Kingdom. See *R* v *Goldstein* [1983] 1 All ER 434; *Garden Cottage Foods Ltd* v *Milk Marketing Board* [1984] AC 130; and *Argyll Group* v *Distillers Co plc* [1986] 1 CMLR 764.

h) *Direct effect and Community directives*

Since Community directives are given legal force through national measures, rights and duties are conferred on individuals only after incorporation into national law. Individuals and legal persons may, of course, rely on rights established by directives after the enabling legislation has been enacted. Further, frequently time limits are placed on implementation in order to ensure that Member States do not postpone incorporation indefinitely.

Where a Member State has failed to adopt a directive within the prescribed time period the European Court has, on certain occasions, been prepared to give direct effect to the contents of unimplemented directives notwithstanding the fact that the Member State has not incorporated the measure into internal law. The rationale for the development of this principle has been expressed by the Court in the following terms:

'It would be incompatible with the binding effect given by Article 189 [of the EEC Treaty] to Directives to refuse in principle to allow persons concerned to invoke the obligation imposed by the Directive ... Especially in cases where the Community authorities, by means of a directive, oblige Member States to take a specific course of action, the practical effectiveness of such a measure is weakened if individuals cannot take account of it as part of Community law': *Grad* v *Finanzamt Trunstein* [1970] ECR 825.

Strictly speaking, the provision of an unimplemented directive is not actually given direct effect in the same sense as the application of this concept to Community Treaty provisions. Rather, a Member State is prevented from invoking its own omission or deficiency as a defence to an otherwise competent action.

A number of conditions must be satisfied before direct effect can be given to a term of a Community directive:

i) The term must be sufficiently precise;

ii) The provision in question must specify an obligation which is not subject to any qualification, exception or condition;

iii) The provision must not require intervention on the part of a Community institution or a Member State: see *Van Duyn* v *Home Office* [1974] ECR 1337.

The difference between this test and the analogous test for the direct effect of Treaty provision is that the condition requiring the non-discretionary implementation of the provision is easier to satisfy in the case of directives than for Treaty provisions: see Advocate-General Warner in *R* v *Secretary of State for Home Affairs, ex parte Santillo* [1980] ECR 1585.

Two important limitations are placed on the application of this principle:

i) The principle only applies to directives which are unimplemented after the date set for implementation. The application of directives which have been adopted, but which have not yet entered into force, cannot be anticipated or pre-empted.

ii) The Court has only been prepared to apply this doctrine to the relationship between individuals and the state as opposed to the relationships among individuals themselves. The former is known as 'vertical direct effect' while the latter is known as 'horizontal direct effect'.

In the case, *Marshall* v *Southampton and South West Hampshire Area Health Authority* [1986] ECR 723, the Court confirmed that while a directive might be upheld against defaulting Member States, it cannot be involved directly against other individuals. The rationale for this principle stems from the fact that the concept of the direct effect of directives originates from the doctrine of personal bar.

Although the Court has been unwilling to extend the application of the concept of direct effect of directives to relationships between individuals, it has given a broad interpretation to the national authorities and agencies against whom the concept applies. Unimplemented directives have been applied as a defence to a prosecution by public authorities, against tax authorities, against governmental departments, and against local and regional authorities. In addition, this concept applies against all bodies or organisations which are subject to the control of the state or which possess special powers beyond those which result from the normal rules applicable to relations between individuals: *Foster & Ors* v *British Gas plc* Case 188/89 (1990).

Since the rationale behind this concept is derived from a form of personal bar, it would be inequitable to allow a national authority to rely, as against individuals or legal persons, upon a provision of a directive which has not yet been incorporated into national law even although it should have been: *Officier van Justitie* v *Kolpinghuis Nijmegen BV* [1989] 2 CMLR 18.

5.3 Relevant cases

Hauptzollamt Mainz v *Kupferberg* [1982] ECR 3641: The terms of Community agreements with third states may be given direct effect if the condition being relied upon is unconditional and precise, and also capable of conferring individual rights.

EC Commission v *United Kingdom (Re Tachographs)* [1979] ECR 419: If a Community Regulation is re-enacted into national legislation in order to provide a greater degree of specification, the legislation must satisfy all the obligations incumbent on the Member State.

Anklagemyndigheden v *Hausen and Son I/S* Case 326/88, Judgment of 14 August 1990, not yet reported: If a Community regulation is implemented by a provision of national law, the fact that penalties for violations vary from one state to another does not deprive that legislation of its force.

Van Gend en Loos v *Netherlands* [1963] ECR 1: Where a provision of a Community Treaty imposes a clear and unconditional obligation on a Member State, unqualified by any reservation, such an article is capable of creating enforceable individual rights.

Marshall v *Southampton and South West Hampshire Area Health Authority* [1986] ECR 723: While vertical direct effect may be given to unimplemented directives, the European Court was unwilling to accept a similar application of the concept of horizontal direct effect.

5.4 Relevant materials

L Collins, *European Community Law in the United Kingdom* (fourth edition, 1990) 46-112.

J Steiner, 'Coming to terms with EEC Directives' (1990) 106 LQR 144.

PE Morris 'The Direct Effect of Directives: Recent Developments' (1989) Jour Bus Law, 223-45 and 309-20.

D Curtin, 'The Province of Government: Delimiting the Direct Effect of Directives' (1990) 15 EL Rev 195-223.

O Lando, 'The EEC Convention on the Law Applicable to Contractual Obligations' (1987) 24 CML Rev 159.

PA Stone, 'The Lugano Convention on Civil Jurisdiction and Judgments 1988' (1988) 8 Yb Eur Law 105.

5.5 Analysis of questions

Within this topic, the direct effect of treaty provisions and unimplemented Community directives is the issue which most frequently arises in examinations. In part this is due to the controversial nature of this doctrine. However, frequently issues which form part of this topic also arise as subsidiary points in questions concerning other matters of Community law. Due to the important nature of this particular part of the syllabus, a student would be well advised to acquire an extensive familiarity with both the fundamental principles of this subject as well as the recent jurisprudence of the European Court.

5.6 Questions

Question 1

What is the difference between EEC primary law and secondary legislation?

University of Glasgow LLB Examination
1989 Q2

General comment

A general question requiring a narrative answer.

Skeleton solution

- Distinction between primary and secondary legislation.
- Forms of primary and secondary legislation.

- Supremacy between the two sources.

Suggested solution

Within most legal systems, a distinction is made among sources of legal principles. In terms of Community law, the main distinction is drawn between primary sources and secondary sources. Primary sources of Community law consist of the international agreements negotiated between the Member States to create the European Community. Secondary sources of law are legal measures promulgated by Community institutions under the authority vested in them by the Community treaties.

The primary sources of Community law consist of the three Community Treaties - the ECSC Treaty, the EEC Treaty and the Euratom Treaty - together with those agreements amending these Treaties. Amending agreements of significant constitutional importance include the Convention on Certain Institutions Common to the European Communities 1957, the Merger Treaty 1965, the three Treaties of Accession and their Annexes (1972, 1979 and 1985), the three Budgetary Treaties (1970, 1975 and 1988) and the Single European Act 1986. Although all of these agreements remain constitutionally important, in practice the EEC Treaty has paramount significance because it regulates all forms of economic activity within the Community other than those relating to coal, steel and atomic power.

The three Community Treaties, as amended, form the constitution of the European Community and are the ultimate legal source in the hierarchy of Community legal norms. These Treaties define the powers of the Community institutions. A failure on the part of a Community institution to respect the limits of authority prescribed by the treaties will render a putative measure null and void: see *United Kingdom* v *EC Council [Re Hormones]* (1988); and *EC Commission* v *EC Council (Re Generalised Tariff Preferences)* (1987). The validity of a Community measure is a matter for the exclusive jurisdiction of the European Court and national courts and tribunals are not authorised to rule on such issues: *Firma Foto-Frost* v *Hauptzollamt Lubeck-Ost* (1988).

In addition, these Treaties define the objects and purpose of the European Community, and also establish certain fundamental principles of Community law. Consequently, in certain circumstances, individual provisions of the Treaties may be given direct effect and may be relied upon by individuals before national courts and tribunals. Further, the view that the Community Treaties form the constitution of the Community has been substantially fortified by the fact that the European Court has developed principles from the Community Treaties rather than from sources of international law.

The EEC Treaty also requires Member States to enter into international agreements to regulate particular issues which are not dealt with in detail in the Community Treaties. According to Article 200 of the EEC Treaty, Member States should negotiate conventions to secure for the benefit of their nationals the protection of certain rights, the abolition of double taxation, the mutual recognition of companies and reciprocal recognition and enforcement of judgments and arbitration awards. The status of such agreements has been the subject of some controversy. The European Court has held that Conventions between Member States subsequent to the foundation of the Community are unable to modify the terms of the Community treaties: *Koster Case* (1965). However, if the terms of such agreements fall within the scope of the Community Treaties, the Court has been prepared regard them as sources of Community law.

Secondary sources of Community law are the legislative measures enacted by the organs of the Community under the authority conferred by the Community Treaties. These sources are secondary sources because they derive their authority from the provisions of the founding treaties. Their scope is limited by the Community Treaties and such acts can be challenged against the standards set by the Treaties. Article 189 of the EEC Treaty specifies three separate forms of Community secondary legislation: regulations, directives and decisions. Both the Council of Ministers and the Commission are competent to enact such measures.

A Community regulation is a general legislative instrument which is binding in its entirety throughout the Community and which is directly applicable within the legal systems of the Member States. Thus an individual may rely on the authority of a Community regulation in an English court even although the measure involves no enabling legislation on the part of the British Parliament. National courts are obliged to recognise the force of Community law and to protect rights vested by Community regulations: *R* v *Secretary of State, ex parte Factortame* (1989). Further, while Community regulations are secondary sources of Community law, they still prevail over inconsistent provisions of national law.

Community directives are also binding, but only against the Member State to whom it is addressed and only in relation to the result to be achieved. Directives cannot be addressed to individuals. Also, directives are not automatically applicable within all Member States since Members States are at liberty to select the appropriate form of domestic law to implement the obligations arising from the directive. Within the United Kingdom, Community directives may be implemented either through Acts of Parliament (such as the Companies Act 1989 which implements the Seventh Directive on Company Law) or through statutory instruments. Authority to implement directives in the form of statutory instruments is conferred upon government Ministers by virtue of the European Communities Act 1972 s2(2).

As a source of Community law, directives are less prominent than regulations, although directives have been frequently employed to harmonise the laws of the various Member States. However, the European Court has developed the doctrine of vertical direct effect in cases where Member States have failed to incorporate the obligations imposed under directives into national law. In such cases, individuals may rely on the terms of a directive which has passed its date of implementation. Further, such directives prevail over inconsistent provisions of national law and may be used either as a defence to an action or as a ground of action.

Both the Council and the Commission may also adopt decisions. Decisions are binding in their entirety, but only upon the entity to whom they are addressed.

Decisions may be addressed to Member States, but most frequently decisions are applied to individuals and legal persons. Decisions are commonly used by the Council and the Commission to impose fines for infringements of competition policy and to levy anti-dumping duties on foreign corporations found guilty of dumping. Decisions which impose a pecuniary obligation, such as a fine, are enforced through the relevant procedures in the Member States in which the individual or legal person is situated. Further, Commission decisions, such as those relating to competition, are often treated as precedents insofar as they show the principles upon which Community competition policy is based. In this respect such decisions may also be regarded as a subsidiary source of law in their own right.

The Council and Commission are also authorised to adopt recommendations and opinions. Neither of these acts have legal significance, being merely of political significance. They do not therefore constitute secondary source of law.

While Article 189 of the EEC Treaty purposes to exhaust all the secondary sources of Community law, in practice the decisions of the European Court of Justice cannot be discounted as a source of Community law. The role of the Court in formulating principles of fundamental importance has been significant. However, according to the jurisprudence of the Court, Community law adheres to no doctrine of binding precedent. In practice, the decisions of the Court are often cited as authority for specific propositions, not only by the Court itself, but also by the courts and tribunals of Member States.

Question 2

'To give what is called "horizontal effect" to directives would totally blur the distinction between regulations and directives which the Treaty establishes in Articles 189 and 191.' Advocate-General Slynn in Case 152/84 *Marshall* v *Southampton and South-West Hampshire Area Health Authority*.

Discuss.

University of London LLB Examination
(for External Students) European Community Law 1989 Q3

General comment

A problem concerning the application of the doctrine of direct effect of unimplemented directives which also requires consideration of the relationship between the various secondary sources of Community law.

Skeleton solution

- The legal effect of Community regulations.
- The legal effect of Community directives.
- The concept of horizontal effect and its consequences.
- Contrast between the effects of regulations and unimplemented directives.

Suggested solution

Article 189 of the EEC Treaty provides that regulations 'shall be binding in their entirety and directly applicable in all Member States'. The quality of direct applicability means that regulations are immediately and automatically incorporated into the legal systems of the Member States without the need for intervention on the part of a legislative body such as the British Parliament. Individuals and legal persons may therefore vindicate rights and duties created by Community regulations before national courts and tribunals. An institution of the Community would pass a regulation when it was deemed undesirable that the national authorities of a Member State should be allowed to intervene in its promulgation.

Community directives do not possess the same quality. In fact, the EEC Treaty expressly provides that the national authorities of the Member States retain discretion in selecting the appropriate instrument of national law to implement Community directives. Directives are employed where an institution of the Community intends to create standards which need not be identical throughout the Community.

The essence of the principle of direct applicability is that a Community regulation which has entered force may be enforced by or against the subjects of the regulation and the application of such measures is independent of any measure of national law: *Bussone* v *Ministry of Agriculture and Forestry* (1978). This latter quality is expressly acknowledged in the European Communities Act 1972 s2(1), which requires that all rights and obligations created in accordance with the Community Treaties are 'without further enactment to be given legal effect' within the United Kingdom.

On occasion, Community regulations are, however, re-enacted into national law to provide a greater degree of specification, for example to provide penalties to enforce the contents of the measure. In such cases, the force of law resides in the regulation itself not the national provision: *Variola* v *Amministrazione Italiana delle Finanze* (1973). Further, if a regulation is re-enacted, the legislation must satisfy all the obligations incumbent upon the Member State, partial implementation being insufficient. In *EC Commission* v *United Kingdom (Tachograph Case)* (1979), the British government was held to have violated Community law by not passing legislation making non-compliance with a Community regulation requiring the fitting of tachographs a criminal offence. The European Court held the United Kingdom liable for breach of the Treaty of Rome and declared inconceivable the implementation of a regulation by a Member State 'in an incomplete or selective manner ... so as to render abortive certain aspects of Community legislation which it opposed or which it considered contrary to its national interests'.

Actual penalties prescribed by national law for the enforcement of regulations may vary from one Member State to another. In one case involving the enforcement of Community regulations relating to road transportation, and in particular maximum permitted daily driving periods and compulsory rest periods, the European Court held that no violations of Community law occurred because some Member States adopted a system of strict criminal liability while others had not: *Anklagemyndigheden* v *Hausen and Son I/S* Case 326/88 (1990). This conclusion was reached because the regulation in question left significant discretion to the Member States for the implementation of its rules. Naturally where a regulation specifies criminal penalties, such provisions must be strictly observed.

Directives are given force of law through national measures and rights and duties are conferred on individuals only upon incorporation into national law. Individuals and legal persons may rely on the rights and duties contained in directives but merely by virtue of the terms of the incorporating legislation. Frequently, time limits are placed on implementation in order to ensure that Member States do not postpone incorporation indefinitely.

Where a Member State fails to adopt a directive within the specified time period, the European Court has, on certain occasions, given direct effect to the contents of the unimplemented directive notwithstanding the fact that the Member State has not adopted the measure into internal law. This concept has become known as 'vertical direct effect'. Its purpose is to prevent Member States avoiding their Community obligations: *Grad* v *Finanzamt Traunstein* (1970). The concept of direct effect prevents Member States from invoking their own omissions or deficiencies as a defence to an otherwise competent action.

Substantial limitations are, however, placed on the application of the concept of vertical direct effect by the European Court. In the first place, it only applies to directives which remain unimplemented after the date specified for implementation. The application of directives which have been adopted by the Council but which have not yet passed the expiry date for implementation cannot be anticipated or pre-empted. Second, where a plaintiff is attempting to invoke an unincorporated directive against a defaulting state, the directive in question must create an 'unconditional and sufficiently precise' obligation: *Pubblico Ministero* v *Ratti* (1979). Whether an obligation is sufficiently precise depends on the facts of each case: *Marshall* v *Southampton and South West Hampshire Area Health Authority (Teaching) No 2* (1990) House of Lords.

However, the European Court has consistently refused to extend the concept to direct effect of unimplemented directives to the relationships between individuals. 'Vertical direct effect' is the term which describes the application of unimplemented directives by individuals against governmental bodies and agencies: *Browne* v *An Bord Pleanala* (1990). 'Horizontal direct effect' applies to the relationship between individuals within a society and the application of unimplemented directives. Since many directives affect areas such as company law, employment law, or consumer protection law, this is a considerable restriction.

In the case *Marshall* v *Southampton and South West Hampshire Area Health Authority* (1986) the European Court confirmed that while a directive might be upheld against defaulting Member States, it could not be invoked directly against other individuals. The Court reasoned that since Article 189 defined the binding nature of directives as against Member States to whom they are addressed, the possibility of relying on a directive before a national court is limited to these subjects. Consequently '[i]t follows that a directive may not of itself impose obligations on an individual and that a provision of a directive may not be relied upon as against such a person'. Thus, while Advocate-General Slynn believed that granting horizontal direct effect to unimplemented directives would blur the distinction between the legal effects of regulation and directives, in fact the Court refused to extend the concept because of a self-limiting clause within Article 189 itself.

Although the Court has been unwilling to extend the principle of direct effect to the relationships between individuals, it has given a broad interpretation to the national authorities against whom such unimplemented directives might be enforced. Unimplemented directives have been applied as a defence to a prosecution by public authorities (*Pubblico Ministero* v *Ratti* (1979), against tax authorities (*Becker* v *Finanzamt Munster-Innenstadt* (1982), against governmental departments (*Van Duyn* v *Home Office* (1974), and against local or regional authorities (*R* v *London Boroughs Transport Committee* (1990).

In addition, the principle applies to all bodies or organisations which are subject to the control of the state or which possess special powers beyond those which result from the normal rules applicable to relations between individuals: *Foster & Ors* v *British Gas plc* Case 188/89 (1990). Crown bodies, authorities responsible for the maintenance of public order and safety, and public corporations are all emanations of the state for the purpose of applying the principle of direct effect to unimplemented directives: *Marshall* v *Southampton and South West Hampshire Area Health Authority* (1986); *Johnston* v *Chief Constable of the Royal Ulster Constabulary* (1986).

Question 3

Okeefenokee plc, a subsidiary of a Dutch food company, distributes mineral water and other non-alcoholic drinks in the United Kingdom. Its current stock of products for sale and delivery includes a new drink called Swamp, which is described on the label as 'mineral water' but which consists in fact of carbonated tap water. When visiting her local hypermarket a local authority officer notices the new product. On reading the label, she forms the view that the product contravenes a prohibition contained in a ministerial order on the stocking for sale and human consumption of products which are 'of defective composition'. This expression is not defined in the order.

The officer considers, however, that in taking legal action against Okeefenokee she can rely on EC Council Directive 80/777. This Directive concerns the approximation of the laws of the Member States regarding the exploitation and marketing of natural mineral waters. It obliges Member States to ensure that only waters which meet certain requirements are marketed as natural mineral waters. Swamp does not satisfy these requirements. The deadline for giving effect to the Directive has not expired, and the United Kingdom has still not introduced implementing legislation. Learning of the possibility of legal action against it, Okeefenokee consults you regarding its position under European Community law.
Advise Okeefenokee.

University of London LLB Examination
(for External Students) European Community Law 1990 Q2

General comment

A problem question which requires the application of the principles behind the doctrine of direct effect to particular facts.

Skeleton solution

- Legal force of a ministerial order.
- Legal force of directives which have not entered into force.
- Legal force of unimplemented directives.

Suggested solution

Okeefenokee's liability for the misleading advertising is confined to two separate grounds: under the Ministerial order; and under Directive 80/777.

The Ministerial order is a measure of national law, analogous to an Order in Council. It therefore has force of law within the United Kingdom legal system. However, its provisions are vague. It merely prohibits the stocking for sale and human consumption of products which are 'of defective composition', a term undefined in the Ministerial order. Further, no mention is made of penalties or fines for infringements of the terms of the order. Clearly, Okeefenokee can claim that the Ministerial order is inapplicable to its ventures since it is not engaged in the stocking for sale of products but merely the distribution of particular products throughout the United Kingdom.

The liability of Okeefenokee is therefore limited to possible action under EC Council Directive 80/777. The substance of this directive relates the harmonisation of national laws throughout the Community regarding the exploitation and marketing of natural mineral waters. Under the Directive, Member States must ensure that only waters which meet certain standards may be marketed as natural mineral waters. Swamp fails to satisfy these standards. Is Okeefenokee liable under the directive for misleading product advertising?

Council Directive 80/777 has not been implemented in the United Kingdom. Therefore, the local authority officer would have to rely on the doctrine of the direct effect of unimplemented directives in order to institute the legal proceedings against Okeefenokee.

In the particular circumstances of this case, Council Directive 80/777 could not be given direct effect. First, the doctrine of direct effect only applies to directives which remain unimplemented after the date specified for implementation. The application of directives which have been adopted by the Council of Ministers but which have not yet passed the expiry date for implementation cannot be anticipated or pre-empted. Since the deadline for giving effect to Directive 80/777 has not passed, the United Kingdom is not in breach of its obligations under Community law. It is only once a state has failed to fulfil its obligation to implement a Community Directive that the doctrine of direct effect comes into operation.

Even after the deadline for the implementation of the Directive, the local authority officer could only rely on the Council Directive if the United Kingdom passes enabling legislation to incorporate the obligations contained in Directive 80/777. If the deadline passes for the implementation of the Directive, and if the United Kingdom has failed to implement the Directive, the local authority officer still could not initiate proceedings since she would be unable to rely on the doctrine of the direct effect of unimplemented directives.

The rationale behind the doctrine of direct effect is a doctrine of personal bar (see *Grad* v *Finanzamt Traunstein* (1970). It would therefore be inequitable to allow the national authorities of a state to rely on their omission in order to initiate proceedings. Consequently, national authorities may not rely, as against individuals or legal persons, upon a provision of a directive which has not yet been implemented in national law even although it should have been: see *Officier van Justitie* v *Kolpinghuis Nijmegen BV* (1989). Therefore, in the absence of legislation enacting the directive into English law, no proceedings can be instituted by the local authority officer.

Question 4

Craig, Steven and Andrew are qualified surveyors working part-time for their respective employers. Craig is employed by the Department of Health, Steven is employed by British Rail and Andrew is employed by Smith and Western, a private chartered surveyors firm. All three are dismissed by their employers without notice or compensation. Council Directive 90/888 has been adopted by the Council as part of the Community's European Social Charter, and protects the rights of part-time workers. In particular, the Directive provides for periods of notice and effective compensation when part-time employees are dismissed. Although the deadline date for the implementation of this directive has passed, the United Kingdom has not enacted legislation to implement the obligations of the Directive.

Advise Craig, Steven and Andrew of their respective rights under Community law.

Question prepared by the Author
February 1991

General comment

A simple problem requiring the student to recognise the essential elements of the doctrine of direct effect as it applies to unimplemented directives.

Skeleton solution

- Failure of the UK to implement the Directive.
- Doctrine of the direct effect of unimplemented directives.
- Limitations of its application.
- Rights and duties of the respective employees.

Suggested solution

The United Kingdom is in breach of its obligation under Directive 90/888 for failure to implement the directive in the specified time period. Although a Member State has discretion as to the form and method of implementation of a directive, by failing to implement the directive the United Kingdom has not achieved the desired object of the directive. Consequently, the United Kingdom is in breach of its obligations as defined by Article 5 of the Treaty of Rome.

The deadline for implementation of the Directive 90/888 has passed and so the directive is directly effective vis-a-vis the United Kingdom authorities (*Pubblico Ministero* v *Ratti* (1979). Craig will be able to rely on the terms of the Directive against the Department of Health since it is a governmental organ and therefore estopped from relying on contrary provisions of national law: see *Van Duyn* v *Home Office* (1974).

Equally, Steven will be able to enforce the Directive against British Rail because it is a Crown corporation and therefore an emanation of the state: see *Johnston* v *Chief Constable of the Royal Ulster Constabulary* (1986). All bodies and organisations which are subject to the control of the state or which possess special powers beyond those which result from the normal rules applicable to the relations between individuals are emanations of the state for the purposes of the doctrine of the direct effect of unimplemented directives. Accordingly British Rail would not be justified in dismissing Steven and would also be prevented from relying on contrary national law against him.

However, Andrew would not have a similar recourse against Smith and Western. Obviously, Smith and Western, as a private surveyors firm, cannot be considered an emanation of the state and therefore cannot be caught by the principle of the 'vertical direct effect' of unimplemented directives. Application of the terms of Directive 90/888 to the contractual relationship between Andrew and Smith and Western would require recognition of the 'horizontal direct effect' of directives. In *Marshall* v *Southampton and South West Hampshire Area Health Authority* (1986), the European Court confirmed that while an unimplemented directive could be applied against the authorities of a Member State, it could not be invoked against individuals. Therefore, directives are not horizontally effective and one individual may not rely on a directive as against another individual.

In order for Andrew to obtain enforcement of the directive in the United Kingdom, he may try to obtain an Article 177 preliminary ruling from the ECJ as to the interpretation of the Directive. However, the mandate of the European Court is limited to interpretation of the terms of directives. It may not directly declare the United Kingdom in breach of its Community obligations. This is a matter for the national court, but national courts are under a duty under Article 5 to ensure that Community obligations are respected.

In light of *Foglia* v *Novello* (1981), Andrew must also ensure that the litigation from which the question arises is genuine otherwise the ECJ will decline jurisdiction.

Alternatively, Andrew may complain to the European Commission in the hope that it will bring an Article 169 action against the United Kingdom. An enforcement action is brought when the Commission considers that a Member State is in breach of a Community obligation. However, whether or not such an action should be brought is essentially a matter for the Commission's consideration. Andrew cannot compel the Commission to initiate an investigation into his allegations: see *Star Fruit Co SA* v *EC Commission* (1990). Nor can Andrew bring a direct action against the United Kingdom.

Andrew can only challenge the negative ruling of the Commission if it issues a formal decision stating that the Commission sees no reason to bring such an action. In the event of such a decision, Andrew could bring a direct action requesting annulment of the refusal to act under Article 169 of the EEC Treaty. Naturally, Andrew would have to establish a direct and individual concern in order to acquire standing to bring an action under Article 169.

Question 5

The extension of the doctrine of the direct effect of Treaty provisions to international agreements negotiated by the Community itself represents a dangerous development in the jurisprudence of the Court.

Discuss.

Question prepared by the Author
February 1991

General comment

A question requiring the student to analyse the recent jurisprudence of the European Court with a view to criticising the direction of the Court in a particular issue.

Skeleton solution

- The doctrine of direct effect as it applies to the Community treaties.
- Direct effect and Community agreements.
- The implications of this development.

Suggested solution

No specific provision of any Community Treaty expressly authorises the use of individual Treaty provisions as a reservoir of Community principles, but from the beginnings of the Community, the European Court has sought to achieve this object by developing the principle of the direct effect of Treaty articles. In an early case heard by the Court, the issue was raised whether customs duties introduced after the entry into force of the EEC Treaty could be imposed if contrary to the prohibitions on such duties imposed by Article 12 of that Treaty: *Van Gend en Loos* v *Netherlands* (1963). The critical question was whether the applicant, being an individual, could rely on the treaty provision as a principle of Community law enforceable within a national court. The European Court held that, where a Treaty article imposed a clear and unconditional obligation upon a Member State, unqualified by any reservation requiring legislative intervention, such an article was capable of direct effect and individual rights could be created which were enforceable in municipal courts.

Three specific conditions are required for a provision of a Community Treaty to have direct effect: (a) the provision being relied upon must be both clear and precise (see *Gimenez Zaera* v *Instituto Nacional de la Seguridad Social* (1987); (b) the term must be unqualified and not subject to the requirement of legislative intervention (*Diamantarbeiders* v *Brachfeld* (1969); (c) the obligation must not create a substantial discretion on either Member States or the Community institutions to act (*Salgoil* v *Italian Ministry for Foreign Trade* (1968). The existence of alternative remedies for breach of a Treaty provision which has direct effect does not negate or prevent a right of action under Community law based on another principle capable of direct effect. Eliminating those provisions of the Community Treaties which relate to institutional procedures, transition and accession, and the general provisions, a significant number of treaty provisions are capable of having direct effect.

However, the European Court has extended the application of the principle of direct effect, not only to provisions of the three constitutional Community Treaties, but also to the terms of international agreements negotiated between the Community and third states under the authority vested by the common commercial policy. The case *Hauptzollamt Mainz* v *Kupferberg* (1982), provides an illustration of the application of the principle of direct effect to agreements entered into by the Community. Kupferberg, a German importer, was charged duties on imports of Portuguese port which were later reduced by the German Finance Court applying Article 21 of an Agreement between the European Community and Portugal which prohibited, on a reciprocal basis, discriminatory internal taxation between imported and domestic products. The German tax authorities appealed against the decision of the Finance Court and a preliminary reference was made to the European Court.

The European Court held that, since international responsibility for breach of such agreements rested with the Community, the Court must recognise the need to ensure uniform application of these obligations within the Community. The terms of such agreements could have direct effect if the provision being relied upon is unconditional and precise, and also capable of conferring individual rights which could be enforced in national courts or tribunals: see also *Demirel* v *Stadt Schwabisch Gmund* (1989).

The extension of the doctrine of direct effect to treaty provisions other than those contained in the Community Treaties is a disconcerting development for a number of reasons. First, the Court has not indicated the precise status of the principles of law derived from such treaties in the hierarchy of norms in the Community legal order. It is not clear whether such principles prevail over inconsistent Community secondary legislation, although it is clear that such principles prevail over inconsistent provisions of national law. However, it is unlikely that the Court would hold that principles derived from Community agreements prevail over the constitutional Community Treaties.

Second, the potential scope for the creation of new norms of Community law from this particular source is disturbing. While the European Court has been reluctant to deduce directly enforceable rights from international agreements entered into by the Member States prior to the Treaty of Rome (see *International Fruit Company* v *Produktschap voor Groenten en Fruit* (1972), the same reluctance has not been manifested towards free trade agreements and association agreements concluded by the Community. The Community maintains more than fifty economic agreements with third states.

Third, recognition of Community agreements as a source of Community law creates an additional degree of difficulty in the process of identifying applicable principles of Community law.

The rationale asserted by the European Court for the expansion of the doctrine of direct effect to Community treaties with third states was the need to protect the European Community from international responsibility for a failure to observe international obligations, where the fault or omission was caused by a particular Member State. Whether or not this is a sufficient pretext for causing such a radical upheaval within the Community legal system is an unanswered question.

6 FUNDAMENTAL PRINCIPLES OF EUROPEAN COMMUNITY LAW

6.1 Introduction

The Community Treaties create a new legal order which interacts with the legal systems of all the Member States. This unique form of law required the development of fundamental principles to provide a basis for its proper functioning. Many of these essential principles were not originally stated in the Community Treaties, but have been developed in the jurisprudence of the European Court. The principle of the supremacy of Community law, the protection of human rights within the Community and the standards developed to interpret Community law are all examples of this phenomenon. In contrast, the principles of non-discrimination on the basis of nationality and non-discrimination on the basis of gender were elaborated in the Community Treaties, but have also been substantially developed by the European Court.

6.2 Key points

a) *The supremacy of European Community law*

Neither the Community Treaties or the European Community Act 1972, which gives force to Community law within the United Kingdom, contains express provisions referring to the question of the supremacy between Community law and national law. Notwithstanding this omission, in *Costa* v *ENEL* [1964] ECR 585, the European Court resolved the issue of supremacy between these legal orders in the following terms:

'[T]he law stemming from the Treaty, an independent source of law, [cannot], because of its special and original nature, be overridden by domestic legal provisions, however framed, without being deprived of its character as Community law and without the legal basis of the Community itself being called into question.'

Community law therefore prevails over inconsistent provisions of national law, whether passed before or after the Community Treaties entered into force. Further, as formulated by the Court, the principle of supremacy must be given effect even within the national legal systems of the Member States.

A number of subsequent decisions of the European Court have elaborated on the implications of this doctrine:

i) The principle applies irrespective of whether the inconsistent provision of national law has a civil or criminal character: *Procureur du Roi* v *Dassonville* [1974] ECR 837.

ii) Community law prevails even over inconsistent provisions of the constitutional law of Member States: *Internationale Handelsgesellschaft* [1970] ECR 1125.

iii) The formal source of national law is irrelevant to a determination of supremacy. Both inconsistent statutes and judicial precedents have been declared inapplicable. Even rules of professional bodies may, in certain circumstances, be held inconsistent and thereby inapplicable: *R* v *Royal Pharmaceutical Society of Great Britain* [1989] 2 CMLR 751.

iv) The European Court has extended the principle of supremacy not only to provisions of Community Treaties, but also to Community regulations and, in certain instances, Community directives.

v) Member States are obliged to repeal national legislation found to be inconsistent with Community law: *EC Commission* v *United Kingdom (Re Origin Marking Requirements)* [1985] 2 CMLR 259.

While the European Court has vigorously asserted the supremacy of Community law over national law within the Community legal system, a number of national courts, including those of the United Kingdom, have expressed reservations in relation to this doctrine.

Principles of Community law will prevail over inconsistent provisions of English law enacted prior to 1972 by virtue of the European Communities Act 1972. The fundamental question is whether British courts will give effect to inconsistent statutes enacted after the entry into force of the 1972 Act. English courts have been cautious in their approach to this problem. In order to avoid potential conflicts, a number of principles have been developed:

i) Statutes of Parliament are to be interpreted in order not to conflict with Community law: *Garland* v *British Rail Engineering Ltd* [1982] 2 All ER 402.

ii) In the event of an inconsistency, such a defect should be attributed to an oversight on the part of the parliamentary draftsmen: *Shields* v *E Coomes (Holdings) Ltd* [1979] 1 All ER 456.

iii) Pre-1972 statutes which are inconsistent with Community law are inapplicable, but the legal basis of this proposition is the 1972 Act: *WH*

Smith Do-It-All & Payless DIY Ltd v *Peterborough City Council* [1990] 2 CMLR 577.

The House of Lords has only recently had to address the question of the supremacy between a post-1972 statute of the British Parliament and inconsistent provisions of Community law in *R* v *Secretary of State, ex parte Factortame* [1989] 2 WLR 997. In deciding that the matter should be referred to the European Court for a preliminary reference, Lord Bridge of Harwich, commenting on the nature of Community law explicitly concluded:

'The rules of national law which render the exercise of directly enforceable Community rights excessively difficult or virtually impossible must be overridden.'

In its decision on the merits of this case, the European Court upheld this view and decided that Community law precludes the application of a rule of national law which would constitute an obstacle to the enforcement of Community law: *R* v *Secretary of State, ex parte Factortame* Case 213/89, Judgment of 19 June 1990, not yet reported.

b) *The interpretation of Community law*

Since the European Court is engaged in the interpretation of treaty law and legislation enacted thereunder, the Court has consistently prescribed the 'teleological' or 'purposive' method for the interpretation or construction of Community law. This is the method used to ascertain the content of international obligations and contrasts with the 'literal meaning' approach preferred by the English courts.

The teleological approach is intended to allow flexibility in the interpretation process by emphasising the purpose of a measure and not its strict terminology. The first step in this process is to ascertain the purpose of the particular legislative measure. Article 190 of the EEC Treaty requires that measures of secondary legislation 'shall state the reasons on which they are based'. The purpose of a Community measure therefore can be determined by reference to the preamble or recital which precedes the actual provisions of any Community measure. Once the purpose of the legislation has been identified, its provisions can be interpreted with this purpose in mind.

Section 3(1) of the European Communities Act 1972 specifically requires that any question relating to the meaning or effect of a provision of Community law before a court or tribunal in the United Kingdom is to be treated as a question of law and interpreted in accordance with the provisions laid down by the relevant decisions of the European Court.

The teleological approach to interpretation also means that measures of Community law incorporated into English law must be construed to give effect to the Community measure: see *Elefanten Schuh GmbH* v *Jacqmain* [1982] 3 CMLR 1. For example, legislation implementing Community directives must be interpreted in light of the purpose of the original measure: *Litster* v *Forth Estuary Engineering Ltd* [1989] 1 All ER 1134.

c) *Non-discrimination on the basis of nationality*

Article 7 of the EEC Treaty establishes the fundamental principle that 'any discrimination on the grounds of nationality shall be prohibited'. This obligation extends to all activities within the scope of the Treaty and, in particular, to the exercise of the rights of the free movement of goods, persons, services and capital. The same obligation is repeated in a number of subsequent provisions of the EEC Treaty which stress the importance of this principle as a fundamental rule of Community law.

The obligation of non-discrimination on the basis of nationality has a number of important effects:

i) This obligation precludes Member States from levying tariffs or charges having an equivalent effect.

ii) No Member States can impose, either directly or indirectly, any form of internal taxation on the products of other Member States in excess of that imposed on identical or similar domestic products.

iii) Member States cannot discriminate between domestic and Community suppliers of services nor between domestic investors and Community investors.

iv) The European Court has extended to the principle of non-discrimination not only to the freedom to supply services, but also the freedom to receive services: *Cowan* v *Tresor Public* [1990] 2 CMLR 613.

The principle of non-discrimination also applies to workers but merely as factors of production and not as individuals per se. Thus, nationals of Member States are entitled to the same kind of employment protection as nationals of the host state, the same conditions of employment as well as the same social security and tax advantages. Nationals of Community states are also entitled to the benefit of further education on a non-discriminatory basis. Notwithstanding the scope of these rights, migrant workers are not entitled to the benefits of nationality, such as voting rights in governmental elections or to stand for such elections. The fact that Member States have opened their national territory to the migration of workers within the Community does not exclude the power of the individual Member States to regulate the movement of foreign nationals: *Watson* v *Belmann* [1976] ECR 1185.

d) *Non-discrimination on the basis of gender*

Another fundamental objective of the EEC Treaty, stated in Article 119, is recognition of the basic principle that men and women should be entitled to receive equal pay for equal work. The European Court has ruled on a number of occasions that Article 119 is capable of having limited direct effect. In particular, in *Defrenne* v *Sabena (No 2)* [1976] ECR 455, the Court held that Article 119 prohibited direct and overt discrimination, a concept which was identified by reference to the twin criteria of equal work and equal pay which are specified in the article itself. Unfortunately, the effect of the Court's decision in this case was limited because, according to the Court, the provision could only support claims relating to pay periods after the date of judgment.

'Equal pay' is defined in Article 119 as 'the ordinary basic or minimum wage or salary and any other consideration, whether in cash or kind, which the worker receives, directly or indirectly, in respect of his [or her] employment from his [or her] employer'.

The European Court has defined 'pay' in broad terms. Thus, special travelling allowances, discriminatory retirement dates, discriminatory pension allowances, and discriminatory redundancy payments, have all constituted pay within the meaning of the article.

A number of Community directives have also been adopted by the Community to add substance to the general obligation of non-discrimination in the workplace: see Council Directive 76/207, Council Directive 79/7 and Council Directive 86/613.

e) *The protection of human rights in Community law*

Although each Member of the European Community is also a party to the European Convention on Human Rights 1950, this Convention is not part of Community law. But issues of human rights frequently arise before the European Court of Justice. Indeed, the European Court has acknowledged that 'the fundamental rights generally recognised by the Member States form an integral part of [the] Community system': *Nold* v *EC Commission* [1974] ECR 491. In the past, the European Court has considered issues of human rights relating to the following matters:

i) the right to privacy: *National Panasonic (UK) Ltd* v *EC Commission* [1980] ECR 2033;

ii) freedom to practise a religion: *Prais* v *EC Council* [1976] ECR 1589;

iii) the right to possess property: *Hauer* v *Land Rheinland-Pfalz* [1979] ECR 3727;

iv) the right of lawyer-client confidentiality: *AM&S Europe* v *EC Commission* [1982] ECR 1575;

v) issues of substantive and procedural due process of law: *Musique Diffusion Francaise SA* v *EC Commission* [1985] ECR 1825;

vi) the right to refrain from self-incrimination: *Heylens* [1987] ECR 4097.

However, notwithstanding the Court's extensive jurisprudence on human rights issues, no allegation that a Community measure is void on the ground that it infringes fundamental human rights has yet been accepted by the European Court as a sufficient ground for declaring a rule of Community law null and void.

6.3 Relevant cases

Costa v *ENEL* [1964] ECR 585: The original decision asserting the supremacy of Community law over inconsistent provisions of national legislation.

R v *Secretary of State for Transport, ex parte Factortame* Case 213/89, Judgment of 19 June 1990, not yet reported: Decision of the European Court asserting the supremacy of Community over an inconsistent Act of Parliament enacted after the 1972 Act.

Litster v *Forth Estuary Engineering Ltd* [1989] 1 All ER 1134: Application by the House of Lords of the Community principles of interpretation.

Blaizot v *University of Liege* [1989] 1 CMLR 57: Nationals of Community states are entitled to access to further education facilities on a non-discriminatory basis.

Cowan v *Tresor Public* [1990] 2 CMLR 613: The freedom to supply services also implies the freedom to receive services.

Barber v *Guardian Royal Exchange Assurance Group* [1990] 2 CMLR 513: Pensions which are administered on a discriminatory basis may be contrary to Community law.

6.4 Relevant materials

Lord Mackenzie Stuart, *The European Communities and the Rule of Law* (1977).

S Prechal & N Burrows, *Gender Discrimination Law of the European Community* (1990).

6.5 Analysis of questions

Questions dealing with the issue of fundamental principles of Community law take many different shapes and forms. However, most frequently such questions take the form of problem-type questions requiring the application of Community law to factual circumstances. Students should be particularly aware of the recent developments surrounding the principle of the supremacy of Community law and the controversy surrounding discrimination on the basis of gender.

6.6 Questions

Question 1

'The rules of national law which render the exercise of directly enforceable Community rights excessively difficult must be overridden': per Lord Bridge of Harwich in *R* v *Secretary of State, ex parte Factortame* [1989] WLR 997.

Discuss the principle of the supremacy of Community law in the light of the decision by the House of Lords in the *Factortame* case.

Question prepared by the Author
February 1991

General comment

A question dealing with the issue of the supremacy of Community law and requiring a descriptive answer.

Skeleton solution

- The origins of the principle of supremacy: *Costa* case.
- The scope of the principle of supremacy.
- Pre-*Factortame* decisions of the English courts.
- The decision of the House of Lords.
- The implications of the decision.

Suggested solution

In order to create a supranational organisation with legislative capacity, the Member States of the Community have been required to delegate certain aspects of sovereignty to the European Community. The Community has power to enact laws on those subjects which expressly fall within its competence under the Community Treaties, while Member States continue to retain authority to legislate on all residual matters. However, inevitably, when separate bodies legislate on behalf of the same population, conflicting principles will emerge even although the competence of each body has been strictly defined. In the event of such a conflict, the question of the supremacy of one legal order over the other becomes critical.

No Community Treaty contains express provisions regulating the issue of supremacy between Community law and national law. The only implied reference to the issue of supremacy in the Community treaties is Article 5 of the EEC Treaty which imposes an obligation on all Member States to adopt all appropriate measures to ensure that the obligations of the treaty are observed, together with an additional duty to abstain from all acts which might jeopardise achievement of the objectives of the Treaty. The absence of an express supremacy clause suggests that the draftsmen of the Community Treaties did not intend principles of Community law to prevail over national law.

Despite these omissions, the European Court of Justice has adopted an unequivocal position on the question of supremacy between Community law and national law. In *Costa* v *ENEL* (1964), the Court was asked to decide whether an Italian statute enacted after the creation of the Community could prevail over provisions of the EEC Treaty relating to the regulation of state monopolies. At the outset of the case, the Court reaffirmed its decision in an earlier case that the Community Treaties had created a new legal order in the form of the Community, for the benefit of which the Member States had limited their sovereign rights: *Van Gend en Loos* v *Netherlands* (1963). The Court then continued to resolve the issue of supremacy in favour of Community law on the ground that the objects and purposes of the Community would be frustrated if national law was allowed to deviate from Community law. Community law therefore prevailed over inconsistent provisions of national law, whether passed before or after the Community Treaties entered into force. The principle of supremacy has subsequently become a fundamental principle of Community law, and must be given effect even in the courts and tribunals of the Member States.

The principle of the supremacy prevails over inconsistent provisions of national law regardless of form or content. In particular, Community law prevails regardless of whether the inconsistent provision of national law has a civil or criminal character. An illustration of the application of the principle to criminal proceedings was the *Scotch Whisky case: Procureur du Roi* v *Dassonville* (1974). Criminal charges were instituted against a Belgian importer who had imported Scotch whisky from France without a certificate of origin from the British customs authorities. The Belgian Criminal Code prohibited imports into Belgium in the absence of a certificate or origin. However, the importer had acquired the consignment of whisky from agents in France and not directly from the United Kingdom. Obtaining a certificate of origin in these circumstances was both difficult and expensive.

The importer was prosecuted and a Belgian criminal court asked the European Court for a ruling on whether provisions of the EEC Treaty provided a defence to these charges. The Court held that this requirement was unduly onerous and contravened Article 30 of the EEC Treaty. Since the provision of the Belgian criminal code conflicted with Community law, no charges could be brought on this ground against the importer without contravening Community law.

A more complex problem arises when provisions of Community law are alleged to be inconsistent with guarantees of human rights enshrined in the constitutions of Member States. In *Internationale Handelsgesellschaft* (1970), the European Court had to decide whether Community law prevailed over provisions of German constitutional law embodying fundamental principles of human rights. The European Court upheld the supremacy of Community law, but qualified this decision by asserting that fundamental principles of human rights were also part of Community law.

The principle of supremacy applies to a number of different forms of Community law. Clearly the most obvious application of the principle is inconsistency between national law and a provision of a Community Treaty. However the Court has also extended the doctrine to conflicts between provisions of national law and Community regulations: *Neumann* v *Hauptzollamt Hof* (1967). In addition, the Court has even upheld the supremacy of unimplemented directives which are capable of direct effect over inconsistent provisions of national law: *Marshall* v *Southampton and South-West Hampshire Area Health Authority* (1986).

As a corollary to the principle of supremacy, Member States are obliged to repeal national legislation found to be inconsistent with Community law: *EC Commission* v *United Kingdom [Re Origin Marking Requirements]* (1985). The European Commission bears primary responsibility for ensuring that Member States are brought before the European Court to resolve allegations of inconsistencies. Member States are obliged under Article 5 of the EEC Treaty to adhere to the rulings of the European Court and amend or repeal offending provisions of national law. Where individuals or legal persons wish to challenge the consistency of national law with measures of Community law, the appropriate course is to raise an action in the national court of the offending Member State against the responsible national authority. Although national courts are obliged to ensure that the principle of supremacy of Community law is respected, an application to the European Court for a preliminary reference on the question may be a more appropriate course of action.

The doctrine of the supremacy of Community law has not been embraced with equal enthusiasm by the national courts and tribunals of a number of Member States, particularly those of the United Kingdom and France. In part this may be attributed to the difficulties these courts must face in reconciling the principle of supremacy with accepted tenets of constitutional law. Where the constitution of a Member State provides for the supremacy of international agreements over provisions of internal law, membership of the European Community poses few constitutional problems since the Community Treaties will automatically prevail over inconsistent domestic provisions.

However, the legal systems of a number of Member States, including the United Kingdom, require domestic legislation to give effect to international obligations. According to constitutional principles, treaties entered into by the United Kingdom government have no automatic effect unless given force by a statute or measure of subordinate legislation. Further, Acts of Parliament incorporating international obligations have no greater force than other statutes and may therefore be superseded by subsequent legislation.

The Community Treaties therefore have effect in English law only by virtue of the European Communities Act 1972. Since the 1972 Act is merely a statute of Parliament and because all statutes are subject to the principle that subsequent statutes prevail over prior statues, from a constitutional perspective, the reception of the principle of the supremacy of Community law creates particularly acute problems.

According to the decisions of the English courts before the *Factortame Case*, principles of Community law will prevail over inconsistent provisions of English law enacted prior to 1972 by virtue of the 1972 Act itself: *WH Smith Do-It-All & Payless DIY Ltd* v *Peterborough City Council* (1990). However, the jurisprudence of the English courts became contorted when efforts were made to reconcile the principle of the supremacy of Community law with inconsistent statutes enacted after the 1972 Act. Clearly such statutes should override the 1972 Act by virtue of the constitutional principle that subsequent parliamentary statutes prevail over inconsistent prior statutes.

In order to avoid potential conflicts between Acts of Parliament and Community law, a series of principles of interpretation were derived to assist in the application and construction of inconsistent provisions. Thus, statutes of Parliament are to be interpreted in such a manner as not to conflict with Community law: *Garland* v *British Rail Engineering Ltd* (1982). In the event of an inconsistency, such a defect should be attributed to the oversight of the parliamentary draftsmen. On this basis, even Lord Denning was prepared to embrace the principle of Community supremacy in *Shields* v *E Coomes (Holdings) Ltd* (1979) where, after referring to the *Costa Case* and the *Simmenthal Case*, he declared that '[i]f ... a tribunal should find any ambiguity in the statutes or any inconsistency with Community law, then it should resolve it by giving primacy to Community law'. However, in a rejoinder to this dictum the qualification was made that this principle only applies in the event of accidental oversight and not when Parliament has expressed a deliberate intention to repudiate Community law. A clear intention on the part of Parliament to violate Community law would be given effect by the courts.

Until recently, the courts had managed to avoid a direct confrontation between Community law and an inconsistent Act of Parliament. However, in *R* v *Secretary of State, ex parte Factortame* (1989), the courts were confronted with the question whether the Merchant Shipping Act 1988 conflicted with Community law. The plaintiffs in this case were Spanish nationals who owned a number of fishing vessels registered as British under the previous Merchant Shipping Act. The Merchant Shipping Act 1988 radically altered the conditions under which non-British nationals could register vessels in the United Kingdom. Vessels registered under the previous legislation were required to re-register under the 1988 Act. The vessels owned by the plaintiffs failed to satisfy one or more of the conditions for registration introduced by the 1988 statute, including the requirement that the vessels should be owned, managed or controlled by British nationals.

The plaintiffs brought an action on the basis that the 1988 Act violated Community law by depriving them of enforceable Community rights. The Queen's Bench Division referred the substantive issue to the European Court for a preliminary ruling and ordered that, pending final judgment, the application of the statute should be suspended. The Secretary of State appealed this decision to the Court of Appeal which set aside the order by the earlier court suspending the Act. The plaintiffs appealed to the House of Lords against the decision of the Court of Appeal.

The House of Lords dismissed the appeal on the grounds that no English court had power to make an order declaring an Act of Parliament not to be the law until some uncertain future date. However, the question whether Community law empowered or obliged an English court, irrespective of the position under national law, to provide effective interim protection of putative rights under Community law was referred to the European Court for a preliminary ruling. Further, in deciding that the matter should be considered by the European Court of Justice, Lord Bridge of Harwich, commenting on the nature of Community law stated that rules of national law which render the exercise of directly enforceable Community rights excessively difficult or virtually impossible must be overridden. The question was thereafter submitted by way of a preliminary reference to the European Court for consideration.

In its decision on the merits of the case, the European Court concluded that Community law precludes the application of a rule of national law which would constitute an obstacle to the adoption of Community law: *R* v *Secretary of State, ex parte Factortame* Case 213/89 (1990). Community law must be interpreted as meaning that if a national court considers that the sole obstacle precluding it from granting interim relief is a rule of national law, it must set aside the national rule. This was a resounding endorsement of the principle that Community law prevails over English law regardless of the constitutional obstacles to the implementation of this policy. Further, in common with courts throughout the Community, English courts are obliged to give effect to the decisions of the European Court obtained through the preliminary reference procedure.

Question 2

Fastbuck are in the business of importing leather goods into the United Kingdom from Turkey. The United Kingdom has decided to unilaterally impose a customs surcharge on the importation of leather goods from Turkey. This was achieved by the enactment of the Protection of Domestic Leather Producers Act 1991. Fastbuck are convinced that this statute contravenes the EEC-Turkey Free Trade Agreement. Advise Fastbuck of possible action under Community law to have the 1991 Act declared invalid.

Question prepared by the Author
February 1991

General comment

A problem concerning the application of the principle of direct effect of Community Treaties to a factual situation.

Skeleton solution

- Proper forum for a challenge to the statute.
- Direct effect of Community Free Trade Agreements.
- Application of the principle of supremacy.
- Procedure under Community law to repeal the 1991 Act.

Suggested solution

The first issue for consideration in this question is, whether Fastbuck can, in an action brought in an English court, raise Community law in support of a claim that the terms of the Act are contrary to Community law even although they are consistent with UK internal law. According to the jurisprudence of the European Court, and the House of Lords in the *Factortame Case* (1989), directly enforceable Community rights are part of the heritage of every citizen of the Community. Persons entitled to the enjoyment of such rights are entitled to direct and immediate protection against possible infringement of them. Further, the duty to provide such protection also lies with the national courts of the Member States. Consequently, Fastbuck are entitled to raise an action in the English courts for judicial review of the Protection of Leather Producers Act in the light of Community law.

For the purposes of the problem, it will be assumed that the Free Trade Agreement between the Community and Turkey (a non-Member State), has been validly concluded under Article 113 of the EEC Treaty. A number of provisions of the EEC-Turkey Free Trade Agreement prohibit the introduction of customs duties, charges having equivalent effects to customs duties, and quantitative restrictions on imports and exports between the Community and Turkey. Under Community law, these provisions may be given direct effect and thereby confer directly enforceable rights on individuals which can be vindicated in national courts.

In order to have direct effect in Community law, a provision of an international agreement negotiated between the Community and a third state must satisfy three conditions. First, the provision being relied upon must be clear and precise. Second, the term must be unqualified and not subject to a rights of legislative intervention. Third, the provision must not confer discretion on either Member States or the Community to act: see *Demirel* v *Stadt Schwabisch GmbH* (1989). If these conditions are satisfied, the relevant provision of the EEC-Turkey Free Trade Agreement has direct effect.

The European Court has held that national legislation which is inconsistent with provisions of Community agreements with third states, cannot prevail if the specific terms of the agreement are capable of direct effect: *Hauptzollamt Mainz* v *Kupferberg & Cie KG* (1982). Therefore if Fastbuck can show that the relevant provisions of the EEC-Turkey Agreement have direct effect, these terms will prevail over the 1991 statute.

In a problem of this nature (ie question of supremacy of EEC law over national law), Fastbuck may well wish to ask the Court to apply to the European Court of Justice for a preliminary ruling under Article 177 of the EEC Treaty. Whether such a reference is made, even assuming it considers a decision on the point necessary for it to give judgment, would be a matter for the discretion of the Court, unless it is a court of final appeal.

The European Court has consistently upheld the rule that national law must submit to Community law and that, as well as the Member State being obliged to cancel the provision in question, it might also have to compensate anyone who has suffered loss as a result of the infringement: *Van Gend en Loos* v *Netherlands* [1963] ECR 1. Further, in *Costa* v *ENEL* (1964), the European Court declared that the terms and the spirit of the Community Treaties make it impossible for a Member State to accord precedence to a unilateral inconsistent national measure over the Community legal system since the Member State has accepted the obligations of Community membership on the basis of reciprocity. Similarly, in *Simmenthal* (1978), the Court confirmed that directly applicable measures of Community law preclude Member States from enacting incompatible measures of national law. National courts are therefore under a duty not to apply legislative measures which are incompatible with Community law: *Factortame* above.

Consequently, Fastbuck should challenge the validity of the 1991 Act in the English courts on the ground that the statute contravenes the terms of the EEC–Turkey Free Trade Agreement which contains provisions which have direct effect. A reference to the European Court for a ruling to this effect would overcome any reluctance on the part of the national court of first instance to adopt such a course of action. Once the European Court has declared the 1991 statute incompatible with Community law, the English court would be obliged to give effect to that decision. Any deviation from the opinion would result in a violation of the obligations of Article 5 of the EEC Treaty by the United Kingdom.

Question 3

Explain and assess, using examples drawn from at least two different areas of EEC law, the European Court's approach to the interpretation of the EEC Treaty.

University of London LLB Examination
(for External Students) European Community Law 1989 Q2

General comment

A question requiring a student to demonstrate the application of a fundamental principle of Community law by reference to the jurisprudence of the European Court.

Skeleton solution

- The approach of the ECJ to interpretation.
- Examples from the jurisprudence of the Court.
- Effect of this jurisprudence on the UK courts.

Suggested solution

Since the European Court is engaged in the interpretation of treaty law and legislation enacted thereunder, the Court has consistently prescribed the 'purposive' or 'teleological' method for the interpretation or construction of Community law. This contrasts with the 'literal meaning' approach adopted by the English courts towards the interpretation of statutes.

The teleological approach is intended to allow flexibility in the interpretation process by referring to the purpose of a measure and not the strict terminology. The first step in this process is to ascertain the context of the legislation by reference to its purpose. Thereafter the meaning ascribed to terms is derived by reference to the objects sought to be achieved by the particular legislation. Article 190 of the EEC Treaty requires that measures of secondary legislation 'shall state the reasons on which they are based'. The object of a Community measure may therefore be ascertained by reference to the preamble or recitals which precede the actual terms of any Community measure. The object is borne in mind when considering particular terms of the measure.

The European Court has used this teleological approach of interpreting provisions of law in order to pursue a policy of deliberate judicial activism. Many principles of Community law have been derived in this manner. Equally, the European Court has been frequently criticised for expanding the competence of the Community without specific textual authority: see H Rasmussen *On Law and Policy in the ECJ* (1986).

One clear example of this was the approach of the Court in the ERTA case (*EC Commission* v *EC Council* (1971). In this case, the Court had to decide whether Member States required the participation of the European Community in order to enter into an international agreement with non-Community states regarding transport policy in Europe. In determining the competence of the Community to enter into international agreements, the Court examined Article 210 which confers legal personality on the European Community. This provision could not, according to the

Court, be given effect unless the objectives of the Community as a whole were taken into account. The objectives of the Community are defined in Part I of the EEC Treaty. Since the Community must have competence to pursue its fundamental objectives, the Court held that, in conducting its external affairs, the Community enjoyed capacity to establish international obligations with third countries over the whole field of objectives defined in Part I of the Treaty.

The immediate consequence of this judgment was a dramatic growth in the external competence of the Community. The Court had ruled that the capacity of the Community extended to those matters contained within its objectives. Member States therefore no longer retained competence to enter into international obligations concerning such issues without the participation or consent of the European Community. Such a radical extension of the powers of the Community was achieved by the European Court adopting a teleological approach to the interpretation of the Community treaties.

A similar approach to interpretation was demonstrated by the European Court in the *Woodpulp Case* (1988). The Community Treaties make no comment on the possible extra-territorial application of Community competition policies to undertakings resident outside the Community. However, a number of firms in Finland, Sweden and Canada entered into a cartel to fix the prices of woodpulp charged to customers inside the Community. The only way of preventing these undertakings from maintaining the cartel was to apply Community law to their activities even although their head offices were outside the Community.

In order to achieve this objective, the European Court examined Article 85 of the EEC treaty which deals with unfair competitive practices and declared that in order to prevent circumvention of Article 85, Community law had to be applied extraterritorially. The basis for this decision was pragmatism. If the applicability of the prohibitions laid down under the Community competition law were made to depend on the place an agreement was formed, the result would be to give commercial enterprises an easy means of evading their Community obligations. In other words, if the Court did not accept the principle of the extra-territorial application of competition law, the purpose of Article 85 would be significantly undermined.

The European Communities Act 1972 specifically requires that any question relating to the meaning or effect of a provision of Community law before a court or tribunal in the United Kingdom shall be treated as a question of law and determined in accordance with the provisions laid down by relevant decisions of the European Court. British courts and tribunals are therefore obliged to adopt this style of interpretation when applying Community law, whether in the form of Treaty provisions, directives or regulations.

A teleological approach to interpretation also means that measures of Community law adopted into UK law must be construed to give effect to the Community directives: see *Von Colson* v *Land Nordrhein-Westfalen* (1984); and *Elefanten Schuh GmbH* v *Jacqmain* (1982). Therefore, legislation incorporating Community directives must be interpreted in the light of the original measure. This principle was clearly endorsed in

Litster v *Forth Estuary Engineering Ltd* [1989] 1 All ER 1134. The plaintiffs brought an action for compensation based on a claim of unfair dismissal. They had been employed by a ship repairing company which fell into receivership and was subsequently sold. The employees were dismissed by the company in receivership one hour prior to the transfer of ownership in the yard to the purchasers. No compensation for redundancy was paid to the employees on the basis that no money was available to pay wages. One hour after the dismissal notices were served the transfer to the new owners took effect.

According to the terms of the Transfer of Undertakings (Protection of Employment) Regulations 1981, transfers of ownership do not automatically terminate contracts of employment if the employees were employed 'immediately before the transfer' of the business. The statutory instrument containing these regulations implemented a Community directive designed to protect the rights of workers unfairly dismissed. The plaintiffs claimed that, despite being dismissed by the company in receivership, the new owners were obliged to pay compensation for the statutory period of notice since the pursuers were immediately employed before the takeover. The Employment Regulations were silent on this particular matter.

The Industrial Tribunal upheld the claim and ordered the new owners to pay compensation and this decision was upheld on appeal to the Employment Appeal Tribunal. The new owners appealed this decision and the appellant court allowed the appeal on the grounds that the pursuers were not employed immediately before the transfer of business. The case was referred to the House of Lords on an appeal against this decision. The House of Lords applied a purposive construction to the relevant regulation in order to give effect to the terms of the Council directive, the objective of which was to protect the rights of employees in the event of a change of employer. Consequently, the pursuers were entitled to seek compensation from the new owners and the appeal was allowed.

British courts and tribunals are therefore bound to give a teleological construction to provisions of Community law. Further, in construing legislation implementing Community directives, the courts are also required to refer to the terms of the original directive in order to give effect to its objectives, even although the implementing legislation makes no reference to the subject.

Question 4

John, a UK national married with two children, and Laura, a UK national married with two children, move from Glasgow to Brussels and enter the service of the Commission of the European Communities. When both receive their salary slips, Laura notices that she has not been given the expatriate allowance which John has received. Upon enquiry, she is told by the Commission Personnel Administration office that such expatriate allowances are given to 'heads of households', that is, to husbands only. Laura would like to seek a remedy. Advise.

University of Glasgow LLB Examination
1987 Q8

General comment

A problem involving the application of the principle of non-discrimination on the ground of gender.

Skeleton solution

- Article 119 of the EEC Treaty.
- Jurisprudence of the Court: *Defrenne.*
- Definition of pay.

Suggested solution

Laura will be able to claim equal pay with John on the basis of Article 119 of the Treaty of Rome. This Article prohibits discrimination when men and women receive unequal pay for equal work carried out at the same establishment of service, be it private or public.

In the *Second Defrenne Case* (1976), the European Court held Article 119 prohibited direct and overt discrimination, a concept which was identified by reference to the criteria of equal work and equal pay specified in the article. Unfortunately, the effect of this provision was limited because, according to the Court, the provision could only support claims relating to pay periods after the date of judgment.

Article 119 of the EEC Treaty is based on the related concepts of equal pay and equal work. Equal pay is defined as 'the ordinary basic or minimum wage or salary and any other consideration, whether in cash or kind, which the worker receives, directly or indirectly, in respect of his [or her] employment from his [or her] employer'. The Court has tended to define pay in broad terms. Thus a special travel allowance, discriminatory retirement dates, discriminatory pension allowances, and discriminatory redundancy payments, have all been held as pay within the meaning of the article. A right to equal pay would be limited in value unless linked to a means of determining a comparable employment position and a Council Directive specifies the procedure for making this determination.

The principle of gender non-discrimination applies to both public and private entities. Equally, since the principle of sexual equality at work is an element of Community social policy, it applies regardless of a transborder element. In order to establish discrimination, it is not necessary that two people are performing the same employment functions simultaneously. Where a man began employment with a company and is replaced by a women in the same position or vice versa, there would be discrimination if the pay of the latter employee was below that of the former. The Court has however been willing to examine factors unconnected with sexual discrimination for an explanation of any discrepancies.

Directives have also been adopted by the Community to add substance to the general obligation of non-discrimination on the basis of gender in the workplace. For example, Council Directive 75/117 related to the approximation of the laws of the Member States relating to the application of the principle of equal pay for men and women.

Presuming that Laura is engaged in equal work with John, the fact that John receives an 'expatriate allowance' appears to be gender discrimination despite the fact that the payment is made to heads of household, since this is merely a synonym for men. As an immediate consequence of this discrepancy, Laura's contract of employment is less favourable that John's. The House of Lords decision in *Hayward* v *Cammel Laird Shipbuilders Ltd* (1988) considered this question in the context of s1(2)(c) of the Equal Pay Act 1970 which was enacted to implement Article 119. The court held that the principle of equal pay entitled women to equality where a woman's contract of employment contained a term that was less favourable than a similar term in a man's contract. This would be the case even if the contract conferred an additional benefit upon her which was not conferred on the man.

Laura should therefore be entitled to a similar allowance. However Laura will only be able to rely directly on Article 119 insofar as the discrimination against her is direct and overt. Where this is not the case, she must have recourse to the national law that implements Directive 75/117. This directive is an expansion of the principle of equal pay for work of equal value. If the national law has failed to correctly implement this directive, she will still not be able to rely on it as against private citizens: see *Foster* v *British Gas* (1987).

Question 5

To what extent has the principle of non-discrimination on the grounds of nationality evolved into an embryonic Community citizenship for the peoples of Europe?

Question prepared by the Author
February 1991

General comment

A general narrative question requiring a descriptive answer.

Skeleton solution

- Scope of Article 7 of the EEC Treaty.
- Jurisprudence of the Court.
- The decision of the Court in *Cowan*.
- Conclusions.

Suggested solution

Article 7 of the EEC Treaty establishes the fundamental principle that 'any discrimination on the grounds of nationality shall be prohibited'. This obligation extends to all activities within the scope of the Treaty and, in particular, to the exercise of rights of free movement of goods, persons, services and capital. In a number of cases, this general principle has been given direct effect, although frequently in conjunction with other specific prohibitions on discrimination: *Kenny* v *National Insurance Commissioner* (1978).

The principle of non-discrimination is expressly reformulated in the Treaty provisions regulating the free movement of persons where a positive obligation is placed on Member State to eradicate this form of discrimination. But, the right to non-discriminatory treatment essentially applies to persons as factors of production and not individuals per se. Thus, nationals of Member States are entitled to the same degree of employment protection as nationals, the same conditions of employment as well as the same social and tax advantages. Notwithstanding the scope of these rights, migrant workers are not, however, entitled to the benefits which nationality confers, such as voting rights in governmental elections or to stand for election. The fact that Member States have opened their national territory to the migration of workers within the Community does not exclude the power of the individual states to regulate the movement of foreign nationals.

A substantial encroachment into these limitations was recently made by the European Court in relation to the access of foreign nationals to judicial processes. The case in question involved a British national who, while visiting his son in Paris, was assaulted and robbed outside a Metro station by a number of assailants, thereby sustaining severe injuries: *Cowan* v *Tresor Public* (1990). The assailants were never apprehended and as a result a claim was initiated for compensation under the appropriate provision of the French Penal Code. This provision, however, specified that victims of violent attacks must either be French nationals or holders of a French identity card in order to claim compensation. The claimant was therefore disqualified from making a claim. An action was brought in the French Commission D'Indemnisation Des Victims D'Infractions (the equivalent of the Compensation Board for Victims of Crime) in order to review this decision. The Commission referred the matter to the European Court for a preliminary ruling on the question of whether foreign nations of Member States are entitled to claim compensation for criminal injuries.

The European Court held that the non-discrimination provisions of the Treaty of Rome extend to the free movement of services and in particular the freedom to receive services. Since the victim was a tourist, and thereby a recipient of services in France, he was entitled to protection from harm, and compensation in the event of an infraction, on the same basis as nationals. Since it is virtually impossible for a foreign national to enter another country without taking advantage of local services, this decision extends the protection of the law of each Member State to nationals of other states. Procedural safeguards for non-residents are, however, permitted in certain circumstances. Thus, a rule requiring a non-resident pursuer to lodge security for costs as a condition for continuing a suit was held by the European Court to be justified discrimination on the grounds that the rule was designed to allow the enforcement of judicial orders: *Berkeley Administration Inc* v *Arden McClelland* (1990).

However, even this decision is far short of the basic concept of Community citizenship. While this decision extends the civil rights of nationals in foreign Member States, access to the democratic process of government remains an unaccomplished objective of the European Community.

Question 6

Assess the jurisprudence of the European Court in relation to the incorporation of human rights into Community law.

Question prepared by the Author
February 1991

General comment

A typical question requiring discussion of the jurisprudence of the European Court in relation to human rights.

Skeleton solution

- The effect of European Convention.
- Human rights before the Court.
- Direction of the Court's jurisprudence.

Suggested solution

The European Convention on Human Rights 1950 is not an agreement established by the European Community, but an autonomous regime operated by another European organisation, the Council of Europe. Each Member State of the European Community also participates in the European Convention on Human Rights which includes a number of non-Community states. Judicial machinery to examine infringements by contracting parties of the obligations enshrined in the agreement and the subsequent protocols was specifically created under the Convention.

The European Commission on Human Rights and the European Court of Human Rights both investigate complaints from petitioners and decide whether or not infringement has occurred. The European Convention has not been incorporated into British law by statute and consequently cannot be enforced in national courts or tribunals: *R* v *Secretary of State for the Home Department, ex parte Brind* (1990). A separate procedure has been established to receive complaints and, unlike reference to the European Court of Justice, a national court may not directly refer an issue of human rights law to the European Court of Human Rights.

Although the European Court of Justice and the European Court of Human Rights are autonomous bodies, in many areas they exercise overlapping jurisdiction. In order to avoid a conflict in jurisprudence, numerous suggestions have been made that the European Convention on Human Rights should be adopted into Community law. This would give effect to the terms of the European Convention by way of the European Court of Justice and would in fact result in the indirect incorporation of the European Convention in British law through the medium of Community law. However, no proposal to subsume the Convention has in fact been successful and, as a result, the European Court of Justice has been compelled to develop principles of human rights law without being able to rely directly on the European Convention as a source of principles.

Human rights issues have often arisen before the European Court of Justice. Indeed, the Court has acknowledged that 'the fundamental rights generally recognised by the Member States form an integral part of our Community system'; *Nold* v *EC Commission* (1974). In the past, the European Court has considered issues of human rights including the right to privacy (*National Panasonic (UK) Ltd* v *EC Commission* (1980)), the freedom to practice a religion (*Prais* v *EC Council* (1976)), the right to possess property (*Hauer* v *Land Rheinland-Pfalz* (1979); *Ferriera Valsabbia SpA* v *EC Commission* (1980)), the right to lawyer-client privacy (*AM & S Europe* v *EC Commission* (1982)), issues of procedural and substantive due process of law (*Precastaing* (1980); *Musique Diffusion Francaise SA* v *EC Commission* (1985)), the non-retroactivity of criminal law provisions (*R* v *Kirk* (1984)), the principle of legal review (*Heylens* (1987)), the right to refrain from self-incrimination. Further, on a number of occasions, the Court has specifically referred to the terms of the European Convention.

Notwithstanding the Court's jurisprudence on human rights law, no allegation that Community measures have infringed fundamental human rights has yet been accepted by the European Court as a sufficient ground for declaring a rule of Community law null and void. In part, this reflects a desire on the part of the Court to uphold the principle of the supremacy of Community law. Claims that the actions on Member States infringe fundamental human rights could not be upheld in the absence of a connection with Community law.

7 THE APPLICATION OF COMMUNITY LAW IN THE UNITED KINGDOM

7.1 Introduction

Community law does not function detached from the legal systems of the Member States, but forms an integral part of each of these individual systems. Principles of Community law may be enforced in the national courts and tribunals of each of the Member States of the Community, including the courts and tribunals of the United Kingdom. Further, within the United Kingdom, even accepted constitutional doctrines and precepts require modification in order to facilitate the reception of Community law. This chapter deals with the attitude of the British government towards its Community obligations and the reaction of British courts and tribunals to Community law.

7.2 Key points

a) *Incorporation of Community law into the United Kingdom*

Community law became part of the law of the United Kingdom by virtue of the European Communities Act 1972 (1972 c68). Section 2(1) of this statute provides:

'All rights, powers, liabilities, obligations and restrictions from time to time created or arising by or under the Treaties, and all such remedies and procedures from time to time provided for by or under the Treaties, as in accordance with the Treaties are without further enactment to be given legal effect or used in the United Kingdom shall be recognised and available in law, and be enforced, allowed and followed accordingly.'

The European Communities Act 1972 was amended by the European Communities (Amendment) Act 1986 (1986 c58) in order to give force to the changes to the Community Treaties made by the Single European Act 1986.

b) *The effect of the European Communities Act 1972, as amended*

The European Communities Act makes no distinction between Community law enacted before the entry into force of the statute and Community law established after this date. Consequently, in legal proceedings before national courts and tribunals in the United Kingdom, the jurisprudence of the European Court may be invoked regardless of whether the decision in question was rendered before or after 1972. Similarly, Community legislation has force within the United Kingdom regardless of the date of adoption by the Council or Commission.

All of the fundamental principles of Community law have become part of British law by virtue of the 1972 Act. Both the principle of the supremacy of Community law and the doctrine of the direct effect of Community treaty provisions (and unimplemented Directives) have been expressly acknowledged by the English courts.

Judicial notice of all decisions of the European Court has also been taken and matters concerning the interpretation and application of Community law are to be treated as questions of law and not questions of fact, as would be the case if Community law was to be considered 'foreign law' under English conflict of law principles: s3(2) 1972 Act.

c) *Ministerial powers to implement subordinate legislation*

Section 2(2) of the 1972 Act allows designated Ministers to make subordinate legislation for the purposes of implementing Community obligations. This provision allows Ministers to fulfil the obligations of the United Kingdom as a consequence of Community directives. In addition, Ministers may provide criminal sanctions in order to enact certain Community measures.

This prerogative is restricted by a number of limitations on the prerogatives of Ministers to enact subordinate legislation. Ministers are not allowed to enact measures which:

i) impose or increase taxation;

ii) create new criminal offences punishable by more than two years of imprisonment;

iii) sub-delegate legislative authority to other bodies or persons; or

iv) introduce subordinate legislation having a retroactive effect.

Power to enact subordinate legislation may only be exercised by the Minister responsible for the administration of the particular Community subject-matter.

d) *Parliamentary control over Community secondary legislation*

Primary control over Community legislation is exercised by Parliamentary Committees which examine and comment on draft proposals for Community legislation. Each House of Parliament has established select committees to evaluate the implications and ramifications of Community legislation on the political and legal constitution of the United Kingdom.

i) The House of Commons Select Committee on European Secondary Legislation

The House of Commons Select Committee on European Legislation is better known as the 'Scrutiny Committee'. This committee has been given the following mandate by resolution of the House of Commons:

'To consider draft proposals by the Commission of the European Communities for legislation and other documents published for submission to the Council of Ministers or to the European Council whether or not such documents originate from the Commission.'

The Scrutiny Committee reports on whether or not such proposals raise issues of significant legal or political importance and gives reasons for its opinion.

ii) The House of Lords Select Committee on the European Communities

The House of Lords has established a parallel body known as the Select Committee on the European Communities. The mandate of this body has been given in the following terms:

'To consider Community proposals, whether in draft or otherwise, to obtain all necessary information about them, and to make reports on those which, in the opinion of the committee, raise important questions of policy or principle, and on other questions to which the committee consider that the special attention of the House should be drawn.'

The House of Lords Committee functions through a number of sub-committees which deal with individual subjects of relevance to the Community such as finance, law and external relations. On a number of occasions, the House of Lords Committee has produced reports of exceptional quality and detail concerning the functions of the Community.

iii) Authority of the Select Committees

Neither the House of Commons nor the House of Lords Select Committees has direct influence over the Community decision-making processes. Control over the final content of Community legislation is maintained on the basis of the principle of ministerial responsibility: see the Second Report from the Select Committee on European Secondary Legislation, HC 463-I, xii-xv (1972-73).

The Council of Ministers of the Community is composed of one representative from each Member State. In the case of the United Kingdom representative, he or she will be the Minister of the Crown with responsibility for the particular subject-matter upon which Community legislation is being passed. As a consequence of the Parliamentary convention of ministerial responsibility, the same Ministers participating in the Council are also answerable to the British Parliament. This dual responsibility ensures that the scrutiny of Parliament over Community secondary legislation continues.

e) *The reception of Community law by the British courts*

The courts and tribunals of the United Kingdom have adopted a positive attitude towards the reception of Community law. Courts have been willing to utilise the procedures established for preliminary references to the European Court. Equally, these courts have been prepared to embrace the accepted fundamental principles of Community law, with reservations only towards the principle of the supremacy of Community law.

7.3 Relevant cases

Bulmer v *Bollinger SA* [1974] 2 All ER 1226: Lord Denning's much criticised attempt to formulate rules to regulate the discretion of British courts to refer questions of Community law to the European Court.

Bourgoin SA v *Ministry of Agriculture* [1985] 3 All ER 585: An attempt to obtain damages for a failure on the part of the British government to observe Community law.

Hagen v *Fratelli & Moretti* [1980] 3 CMLR 253: In the event that leave to appeal to the House of Lords is refused, the Court of Appeal would be subject to the obligation of Article 177(3) and must refer the matter to the European Court for a preliminary reference.

Litster v *Forth Dry Dock & Engineering Co* [1989] 1 All ER 1134: Application by the House of Lords of the teleological approach to interpretation adopted by the European Court.

R v *Secretary of State, ex parte Factortame* [1989] 2 WLR 997: Qualified acceptance by the House of Lords of the doctrine of the supremacy of Community law.

7.4 Relevant materials

L Collins, *European Community Law in the United Kingdom* (fourth edition, 1990).

L Gormley, 'The Application of Community Law in the United Kingdom' (1986) 23 CML Rev, 287.

N Green & A Barav, 'Damages in the National Courts for Breach of Community Law' (1986) 6 YEL, 55.

Lord Fraser, 'Scrutiny of Community Legislation in the United Kingdom Parliament' in J Bates (ed), *In Memoriam JDB Mitchell* (1983) 29.

A Campbell, 'The Single European Act and the Implications' (1986) 35 ICLQ, 932.

7.5 Analysis of questions

Questions concerning this subject often focus attention on the implication of the reception of Community law within the English legal system and the possibility of enforcing Community rights within English courts and tribunals. Students should therefore be familiar with the relationship between Community law and the British Parliament as well as the jurisprudence of the English courts concerning questions of Community law.

7.6 Questions

Question 1

'The way Regulations and Directives are implemented in the United Kingdom shows that the United Kingdom Parliament is no longer totally sovereign.' Discuss.

University of Glasgow LLB Examination
1989 Q6

General comment

A general question requiring an answer which describes the relationship between the British legal system and Community law.

Skeleton solution

- Enactment of Community Directives and Regulations.
- Force of these instruments in the United Kingdom.
- Parliamentary controls on the content of Community law.
- Impact of the Single European Act.

Suggested solution

Community law takes two main forms - Regulations and Directives. A Regulation is binding in its entirety and is directly applicable in all Member States without legislative intervention. In other words, it may be enforced before a national court without the necessity for any statutory authority, either in the form of an Act of Parliament or a statutory instrument (such as an Order-in-Council). A Directive, on the other hand, is also binding, but only upon the Member State to whom it is addressed, and the method of implementation is left to the discretion of the individual Member State. However, this is subject to the doctrine of the direct effect of Community Directives, according to which Directives that have not been implemented by a Member State within the requisite period may be given vertical direct effect: *Marshall* v *Southampton and Hampshire Area Health Authority* (1986).

The fact that Community Regulations and, under certain circumstances, Directives may have direct effect within the United Kingdom has given rise to the charge that the British Parliament is no longer sovereign. This allegation is also often supported by reference to the principle that Community law prevails over the national laws of the Member States: *Costa* v *ENEL* (1964). Since the European Community has power to enact measures which are automatically enforceable within the United Kingdom, and since these measures take precedence over national law, this argument has a certain degree of cogency.

However, the assertion that the British Parliament is no longer sovereign because of this competence on the part of the Community ignores a number of critical points concerning the relationship between the European Community and the British legal system.

European Community law has force of law within the United Kingdom legal system merely by virtue of the European Communities Act 1972, as amended. This is an ordinary statute of Parliament with no additional legal significance, although it has considerable political implications. This statute may be repealed or amended by subsequent Acts of Parliament. In fact, the 1972 Act was amended by the European Communities (Amendment) Act 1986, which gave effect to the changes instituted by the Single European Act. A later Act of Parliament which expressly repealed the 1972 Act would be interpreted by the English courts as effective and would be applied by them according to its terms: *Shields* v *E Coomes (Holdings) Ltd* (1979).

The British Parliament therefore retains ultimate authority to repeal the 1972 Act and to reacquire total and absolute sovereignty over national legal affairs.

However, while the 1972 Act remains in force, in practice the British Parliament has deliberately delegated some of its sovereignty to the European Community, notwithstanding the authority of Dicey's principle of absolute parliamentary sovereignty. The concept of sovereignty is relative. Only once a state has divested itself of its organic powers, and placed itself under the authority of another state, can it be said that it has lost its sovereignty.

Even the authority which has been delegated to the Community by virtue of the 1972 Act has not been unconditionally conferred. A number of safeguards remain which allow the British Parliament to control the content of Community legislation.

Most importantly, the principal legislative body of the Community is the Council of Ministers, which is composed of representatives from the Member States. Each British government Minister whose portfolio contains a subject of Community concern represents the interests of the United Kingdom in the Council of Ministers. Since Ministers of the Crown are also responsible to the British Parliament in accordance with the constitutional convention of ministerial responsibility, the British Parliament can influence the behaviour of Ministers voting in the Council.

This influence is exercised through a number of procedural devices. In particular, each House of Parliament has established Committees to supervise the implementation of Community secondary legislation such as Regulations and Directives. The purpose of these bodies is to examine and comment on draft proposals for Community legislation and to evaluate the implications and ramifications of the legislation on the political and legal constitution of the United Kingdom.

Parliamentary influence over the content of Community secondary legislation has actually been consolidated by virtue of the Resolution of the House of Commons, made on 30 October 1980. This resolution declares that no Minister of the Crown should consent to any proposal for Community legislation in the Council of

Ministers before the House of Commons Select Committee has had an opportunity to examine the proposal.

This general rule is subject to two exceptions. First, where the Committee has indicated that such consent need not be withheld, such as in the case of matters of trivial relevance, the approval of the Committee is not necessary. Second, where the Minister, for special reasons, decides that consent should not be withheld, approval may also be given to a proposed measure. In the latter case, the Minister in question is obliged to explain his or her decision to the House of Commons at the first available opportunity.

This scrutiny procedure does, however, suffer from a number of defects. Theoretically, not all Regulations and Directives require unanimous approval in the Council of Ministers. The adoption of some proposals only requires unanimity. Therefore, measures may be adopted by the Council in the face of opposition from the British representative. But, under the formula adopted by the Luxembourg compromise, where the very important interests of a Member State are at stake, that Member State may require unanimous voting in the Council, notwithstanding the express terms of the Treaty. This requirement is, however, qualified as regards voting requirements concerning the implementation of the internal market programme under the amendments made by the Single European Act since these amendments were adopted without reservation of the right of Member States under the Luxembourg compromise.

Another gap in this system of supervision is the practice of the Council to delegate responsibility for the implication of certain policies to the Commission. Often, this authority includes power to enact subordinate legislation. However, while in theory this represents a limitation on the sovereignty of the United Kingdom, in practice such grants of authority are confined to enacting administrative measures which do not have significant legal or political implications.

The fact that certain measures of Community law have direct applicability within the United Kingdom and prevail over inconsistent measures of national law, does not imply that the British Parliament is no longer sovereign. The enactment of the 1972 Act establishes no more significant fetters on the exercise of the powers of Parliament than a number of the constitutional conventions which already restrict the sovereignty of Parliament. The fact that Parliament can repeal the legislation, and continues to effectively supervise the exercise of the powers conferred on the Community under the 1972 Act, adequately demonstrates that Parliament continues to remain sovereign.

Question 2

Among all the Member States of the European Community, the United Kingdom has demonstrated the greatest reluctance to observe the obligations imposed by the Community Treaties and the duties created thereunder. Discuss.

Question prepared by the Author
February 1991

General comment

A narrative question requiring a descriptive answer.

Skeleton solution

- The nature of the obligation to respect Community law; Article 5 EEC Treaty.
- The record of the United Kingdom.
- Examples of deviance from the principles of Community law.
- The record of the United Kingdom in contrast to other Member States.

Suggested solution

Violations of Community obligations may arise from both positive acts and omissions on the part of Member States. Article 5 of the EEC Treaty requires Member States to take all appropriate measures to ensure respect for Community obligations and to 'abstain from any measure which could jeopardise the attainment of the objectives of this Treaty'. Acts and omissions by Member States may also contravene the express provisions of the Community Treaties or may infringe the contents of measures of secondary legislation lawfully enacted under the Community Treaties.

A common ground of action against a Member State is the existence of national legislation which is incompatible with either the Community Treaties or Community legislation. For example, in 1988, the United Kingdom enacted the Merchant Shipping Act 1988 which requires that a number of conditions must be satisfied before a fishing vessel can be registered as British. A fishing vessel is eligible for registration only if the vessel is British-owned, is managed or operated from the United Kingdom, or is owned by a British company.

The European Commission took the view that this legislation constituted discrimination on the basis of nationality, contrary to Articles 7, 52 and 221 of the EEC Treaty. After entering into unsuccessful discussions with the United Kingdom, the Commission initiated proceedings against the United Kingdom for enacting legislation which contravenes the terms of the Community Treaties: see *EC Commission* v *United Kingdom* (1990).

Member States may also be held to have infringed Community law as a result of the enactment of secondary legislation. Thus, in *France* v *United Kingdom* (1979), the European Court held that the United Kingdom had violated its Community obligations by enacting a Order-in-Council which imposed a minimum mesh size for fishing. This requirement was held to contravene Community law on the ground that appropriate consultations had not been held prior to the enactment of the measure.

Administrative practices may also be held to contravene Community law. Customs measures and practices are most susceptible to action by the Commission for failure to observe Community law. For example, in *Conegate* v *HM Customs & Excise* (1986), the United Kingdom customs authorities took the view that inflatable dolls manufactured in Germany could not be imported into the United Kingdom on the ground that they were indecent and therefore contrary to the rules established for the administration of imports. The European Court held that such practices contravened Community law because the United Kingdom did not prohibit the manufacture of such products within the United Kingdom and consequently such practices constituted a measure having an equivalent effect to a quantitative restrict.

Proceedings are also frequently initiated against Member States for failing to implement measures of Community law, and in particular Directives. The United Kingdom has often been taken to the European Court for failing to implement directives, particularly in relation to gender discrimination; for example, *Marshall* v *Southampton and South-West Hampshire Area Health Authority* (1986). However, in part this possibility has been mitigated by the doctrine of vertical direct effect adopted by the Court.

Since the internal market programme instituted by the Single European Act involves a considerable number of proposed Directives, the significance of acts to enforce Community obligations upon Member States which have failed to implement Directives will increase in the near future. This is necessary to ensure that all Member States have implemented their obligations in time for 1992.

Neither the constitutional structure of a Member State nor pre-existing provisions of national law constitute a defence against a Member State for the enforcement of Community law. This is so even when a constituent part of a Member State - such as a region or a province - exercises exclusive authority over a particular subject-matter, independently of the control of the central government: *EC Commission* v *Belgium* (1989). As the Court itself has pointed out, responsibility for the performance of Community obligations rests with Member States. Consequently, the liability of a Member State arises whatever the agency of the state whose action or inaction is the cause of the failure to fulfil its obligations, even in the case of a constitutionally independent institution.

A Member State may even theoretically be liable for the acts of judicial bodies or tribunals for rendering decisions which are contrary to Community law. Thus a refusal of a national court of final instance to refer a question of Community law under the preliminary reference procedure could constitute a violation of Community law, unless the conduct of the court could be justified under the criteria established in *CILFIT*. This applies despite the fact that the constitutions of a number of Member States rest on the doctrine of the separation of powers.

During the 10 year period between 1980 and 1990, the United Kingdom and Denmark had the least enforcement actions initiated against them. While Denmark had less than 20 actions brought against it in the European Court, the United Kingdom had less than 25. These statistics contrast extremely favourably against those of a number of the original Member States of the Community. Italy was the Member State which was the subject of most actions, with approximately 200 actions initiated against it. France and Belgium maintained equally unimpressive records with around 100 enforcement actions during the same 10 year period. Consequently, it is completely inaccurate to suggest that the United Kingdom is the worst offender in respecting its

Community obligations. (Statistics: LN Brown, *The Court of Justice of the European Communities* (third edition, 1989 p94).

Further, the United Kingdom also maintains an impeccable record as regards implementing the adverse decisions of the European Court when cases are decided against its favour. Since the European Community is an organisation based on the rule of law, it is wholly appropriate that disputes between the United Kingdom and the Commission be settled through litigation. It is, however, indefensible that some states refuse to implement the decisions of the Court in full knowledge that they are contravening their Community obligations. The fact that the United Kingdom rarely, if ever, adopts such a policy is a reflection of the true commitment of the United Kingdom to the spirit and idea of the Community.

Question 3

In *Bulmer SA* v *Bollinger* [1974] 2 All ER 1226, Lord Denning MR elaborated a number of guidelines to assist English courts and tribunals in respect of their obligations under Article 177 of the EEC Treaty. Outline the scope and nature of these guidelines and comment on their influence on the evolution of English jurisprudence on this point.

Question prepared by the Author
February 1991

General comment

A difficult question requiring a detailed knowledge of the jurisprudence of the courts in respect of Article 177 of the EEC Treaty.

Skeleton solution

- The nature of the guidelines.
- Implications of the guidelines.
- Criticism of the guidelines.

Suggested solution

Immediately following the accession of the United Kingdom to the European Community, a need was felt among the English judiciary to specify the rules regulating applications for preliminary rulings under Article 177 of the EEC Treaty. Article 177 does not elaborate on the occasions and conditions under which English courts and tribunals exercising a discretion to refer a question for a preliminary ruling should make an application to the European Court. In order to fill this gap, Lord Denning elaborated a number of guidelines in *Bulmer* v *Bollinger* (1974), in an attempt to establish consistency among the English courts when referring a case for a preliminary reference.

Four primary guidelines were laid down. First, before a reference is made, the point of Community law upon which there is doubt must be conclusive of the case. In other words, the case must turn on the point of Community law invoked. Where Community law is immaterial to a decision, no application should therefore be made.

Second, account must be taken of the previous jurisprudence of the European Court on the matter. Thus, if the European Court has decided the point in a previous case, there would be no need to make a reference. Third, the acte clair doctrine applies insofar as it is unnecessary to refer a question of Community law to the European Court if the answer is reasonably clear and free from doubt. Fourth, the facts of the case should be decided before any reference is made.

Lord Denning also indicated that a number of subsidiary factors should be taken into account prior to a court exercising discretion to refer a case. In particular, the time required to obtain a ruling from the Court and the importance of not overburdening the Court should be considered in the context of the case. Also, the difficulty and importance of the point of Community law involved are relevant considerations as is the expense of obtaining a preliminary ruling. Finally, the wishes of the parties are important considerations in deciding whether or not a case should be referred.

These guidelines have been repudiated by academics and criticised by the European Court as wholly inappropriate. They symbolise the resistance of the English judiciary to the reception of Community law. Article 177 does not instruct the courts of the Member States to formulate rules to regulate its application. As the European Court has pointed out 'Article 177 is essential for the preservation of the Community character of the law established by the Treaty and has the object of ensuring that in all circumstances this law is the same in all States of the Community': *Rheinmuhlen* (1974).

By establishing rules to regulate applications under Article 177, Lord Denning deviated from this important principle of Community law. If the English judiciary applied the guidelines established in *Bollinger*, this could create chaos, since the courts of other Member States may decide to apply different criteria. The result could easily be the non-uniform application of Community law throughout the Community.

In the absence of common rules to regulate preliminary references, the Community legal system itself may be liable to fragment and could even be submerged by principles of national law. The function of regulating the discretion of the courts of Member States to refer a question is a matter which is best left to the European Court.

The European Court has already made it clear that a court exercising discretion to refer a case need only consider two factors: that the reference is necessary to decide the case and that a judgment cannot be rendered without deciding the point of Community law. Discretion to decide these two points resides with the court or tribunal itself. Only if the exercise of this discretion was completely wrong, based on these two factors, could a decision based on this discretion be reversed on appeal: *Rheinmuhlen*, above. Further, in a hierarchical legal system based on the doctrine of precedent, no superior court can bind a lower court to follow guidelines which fetter the discretion of the lower court by compelling it to consider factors other than the two stated in Article 177 itself.

Notwithstanding this criticism, the English judiciary have shown no intention of abandoning these guidelines laid down by Lord Denning. For example, in *English-Speaking Union of the Commonwealth* v *Commissioners for Customs and Excise* (1981), the London VAT Tribunal stated that, although it had been inclined to seek a ruling from the European Court, it had declined to do so after having regard to the guidelines expressed in *Bollinger*. In particular, the fact that the sums involved were small had been a decisive factor in persuading the court to decline the reference.

Similarly, in *Customs and Excise Commissioners* v *ApS Samex* (1983), Bingham J expressly applied the guidelines laid down by Lord Denning in deciding that a reference should be made to the European Court to decide whether or not certain practices of the commissioners of customs and excise infringed Community law. However, ironically, Bingham J applied the guidelines in a manner which favoured an application to the European Court as opposed to declining such a reference. Indeed, Bingham expressly referred to the advantages enjoyed by the European Court in interpreting questions of Community law and clearly considered that the guidelines expressed by Lord Denning should be applied with this factor in mind.

The guidelines laid down by Lord Denning are a clear example of how national courts can interfere with the functioning of the Community legal system. By meddling in areas outside their competence, national courts and tribunals can severely affect the uniform interpretation and application of Community law throughout the common market. The responsibility for elaborating rights and duties under Community law resides exclusively with the European Court.

Question 4

In 1990, the British government imposed restrictions on the import of beer from Germany on the ground that, since German beer products contain no additives or preservatives, such imports contravene statutory requirements providing that beer must have a shelf-life of over a year. In order to sustain a shelf-life of one year, additives and preservatives are required. This legislation prima facie contravenes Community law and, in particular, the principle of the free movement of goods.

Ridley Beer GmbH is a German manufacturer of beer, whose sales to the United Kingdom have been decimated by the introduction of these new requirements. The company seeks your advice regarding its remedies compensation from the British government. Advise Ridley as to its remedies under English law.

Question prepared by the Author
February 1991

General comment

A problem-type question requiring the application of the relevant law to hypothetical facts.

Skeleton solution

- Right to a remedy against the British government.
- Application of English law.

- Rights under Community law.

Suggested solution

The rights of an individual to sue a national government of a Member State for damages in respect of injuries sustained as a consequence of its breach of Community law are not firmly established. Since individuals have no direct right of action against a Member State in the European Court, such an action would have to be raised in the national court of the infringing state. In such an eventuality, a plaintiff would have to establish that either: (a) a remedy for such a breach existed in English law and could be enforced in the English courts; or (b) that Community law establishes such a remedy and that the English courts would have to recognise this remedy. The jurisprudence of the European Court to date strongly suggests that no such remedy has yet been recognised in Community law: *Asteris and Ors* v *Hellenic Republic* (1990).

Whether or not Ridley GmbH can obtain a remedy against the British government is therefore a matter of English law. Community law creates no new remedies within national legal systems and no special procedural steps are necessary to raise a matter of Community law in a national court. The normal English law remedies are therefore available to Ridley GmbH.

Under English law, judicial review may be granted for any breach by a public authority of national law. Therefore, similarly, such review must also be competent in respect of allegations of breach of Community law. In *R* v *Inland Revenue Commissioners, ex parte ICI* (1987), the plaintiff successfully obtained judicial review of an arrangement between the Inland Revenue and one of its competitors on the ground that a tax concession granted to the company by the Inland Revenue amounted to an unlawful state aid under the relevant provisions of the EEC Treaty.

Actions based on tort may also be available to Ridley GmbH, which would allow for damages in the event that the plaintiff was successful. Proceedings in tort exist on two grounds. First, the tort of breach of statutory duty could be invoked for failure to give effect to Community law under s2 of the European Communities Act 1972 as amended. Alternatively, the plaintiff might try to establish that a violation of a duty under Community law is analogous to the position as regards a United Kingdom statute.

The second ground on which a claim in tort could be based is on the basis of misfeasance in a public office. This tort is designed to afford a remedy for wrongs perpetrated by those holding public office. As a private tort concerned solely with public authorities, it is accordingly a remedy of restricted scope in English law.

The House of Lords has acknowledged that a contravention of the Community Treaties may give rise to a cause of action for breach of statutory duty, and a right to damages and injunction: *Garden Cottage Foods* v *Milk Marketing Board* (1984). However, in *An Bord Bainne* v *Milk Marketing Board* (1984), the Court of Appeal held that the Crown was not liable in damages for breach of Community law if this violation was caused by legislation, quasi-legislative measures, or administrative action involving the exercise of a discretion. Ridley GmbH would therefore be well advised to seek a remedy in private law as opposed to the public domain.

The application of the private tort of misfeasance in a public office was tested in *Bourgoin* v *Ministry of Agriculture* (1986). This case involved an action for damages brought by a French turkey producer after trade between the United Kingdom and France had been suspended because the Minister of Agriculture withdrew a general import licence permitting the importation of turkeys ostensibly on the ground on trying to stop the spread of Newcastle disease. The European Commission challenged this decision in the European Court, and the United Kingdom was held to have acted contrary to Article 30 by enacting a ban that was more severe than necessary in the circumstances.

The plaintiffs sought damages against the Minister of Agriculture based on the tort of misfeasance in a public office, claiming that the Minister knowingly acted unlawfully and inflicted severe economic damages on them. As a preliminary question, the Court of Appeal held that if the allegations could be sustained, liability for damages could result, even although the acts complained of were governmental actions which fell within the public law domain. However, it should be observed that, in order for Ridley GmbH to be successful on this ground, there will need to be a deliberate and conscious violation of Community law calculated to inflict damage on Ridley GmbH.

Therefore Ridley GmbH would be well advised to initiate proceedings in the English courts against the Minister responsible for the measures on the grounds of both a breach of statutory duty and misfeasance in a public office. Since there is no indication that the measures were taken on the basis of legislation, there is no reason to rule out action on the basis of a breach of statutory duty.

8 THE FREE MOVEMENT OF GOODS

8.1 Introduction

The creation of a more efficient market through the reduction of obstacles to transnational commerce has always been a fundamental aim of the European Community. The need to achieve the free movement of goods, persons, services and capital throughout the Community was recognised as an express goal of the EEC Treaty and was reaffirmed by the Single European Act. Of these freedoms, the free movement of goods has traditionally been acknowledged as being of paramount significance. The free movement of goods implies that goods can move from one Community country to another without having to pay customs duties or charges having an equivalent effect to customs duty and also that goods will not be subject to quantitative restrictions when moving from one Community country to another.

8.2 Key points

a) *Elimination of customs duties between Member States*

The six original Member States of the Community agreed to a series of progressive reductions in the customs duties which existed between them prior to the EEC Treaty, culminating in the elimination of all customs duties on both import and export transactions; Articles 13-16 EEC Treaty. Customs duties were officially eliminated between the original six on 1 July 1968.

States acceding to the Community are obliged, as a condition of membership, to eliminate all customs duties between them and the other Member States over negotiated transitional periods. The United Kingdom, Ireland, Denmark, and Greece have all eliminated customs duties for intra-Community trade in goods, while Spain and Portugal are obliged to remove such restrictions by 1 January 1993. Goods passing between the United Kingdom and other Members of the

Community are therefore no longer liable to customs duties on either import or export.

Article 12 of the EEC Treaty expressly prohibits the re-introduction of any custom duties on imports and export for goods passing between Community states.

b) *Elimination of charges having an equivalent effect to customs duties*

Member States are also obliged to eliminate all 'charges having an equivalent effect to customs duties' on imports and exports and to refrain from re-introducing such charges on intra-Community transactions. No definition of 'charges having an equivalent effect' is elaborated in the EEC Treaty and interpretation of this term has been left to the European Court. While the Court has elaborated on the nature of this concept in a number of cases, it has most recently stated that:

'[A]ny pecuniary charge, whatever its designation and mode of application, which is imposed unilaterally on goods by reason of the fact that they cross a frontier, and is not a customs duty in the strict sense, constitutes a charge having equivalent effect to a customs duty': *EC Commission* v *Germany (Re Customs Inspection Fees)* [1990] 1 CMLR 561.

Not all charges imposed on goods crossing a frontier between Member States will be deemed to have an equivalent effect to a customs duty. In particular, an expense will not be prohibited as a charge having an equivalent effect in three separate circumstances:

i) If the charge relates to a general system of internal dues applied systematically within a Member State without discrimination between domestic and imported products: *Denkavit* v *France* [1979] ECR 1923.

ii) If the charges constitute payment for a service in fact rendered and the charge is proportionate to the costs of receiving that service: *EC Commission* v *Denmark* [1983] ECR 3573.

iii) If the charges are levied in accordance with the terms of a Community measure. In this case, a number of conditions must be satisfied: *Bauhuis* v *Netherlands* [1977] ECR 5.

Charges levied under the authority of Community legislation for services actually rendered (category (iii) above) do not constitute charges of equivalent effect if four conditions are satisfied:

i) the charges do not exceed the actual costs of the services rendered in connection with the charge;

ii) the inspections are obligatory and uniform for all products throughout the Community;

iii) the charges are prescribed by Community law in the general interest of the Community; and

iv) the service promotes the free movement of goods by neutralising obstacles which arise from unilateral measures of inspection.

c) *Elimination of quantitative restrictions between Members*

A quantitative restriction is a national measure that restrains the volume or amount of imports or exports, not by artificially raising the costs of importing or exporting (as would be the case with a tariff or export tax), but by placing direct or indirect limits on the physical quantity of the imports or exports that may enter or leave the market. The most common example of a quantitative restriction is a quota.

Quantitative restrictions between the original six Member States were gradually phased out and acceding Members must observe a similar obligation: Articles 30-36 EEC Treaty. Article 30 of the EEC Treaty prohibits the re-introduction of quantitative restrictions on imports while Article 34 imposes the same obligation for exports.

The explicit prohibition on the introduction of quotas is periodically violated. For example, in 1978, the United Kingdom restricted imports of Dutch potatoes while France imposed an embargo on sheepmeat from the United Kingdom. Similarly, in 1982, the United Kingdom limited imports of French UHT milk by establishing a quota. Each of these actions resulted in litigation before the European Court: *EC Commission* v *United Kingdom (Re Imports of Dutch Potatoes)* [1979] ECR 1447; *EC Commission* v *France (Re Sheepmeat from the UK)* [1979] ECR 2729; and *EC Commission* v *United Kingdom (Re Imports of UHT Milk)* [1983] ECR 230.

d) *Measures having an equivalent effect to quantitative restrictions*

Article 30 of the EEC Treaty also prohibits all measures having an equivalent effect to quantitative restrictions. The concept of 'measures having an equivalent effect to quantitative restrictions' should be distinguished from that of 'charges having an equivalent effect to customs duties'. Charges having an equivalent effect to customs duties impose direct costs on imported products while measures having an equivalent effect to quantitative restrictions are national measures - either legislative or administrative - which affect the amount (quantity or volume) of products imported.

Again the EEC Treaty contains no definition of the concept of measures having an equivalent effect. In order to fill this vacuum, the European Court has adopted the following definition:

'All trading rules enacted by Member States which are capable of hindering directly or indirectly, actually or potentially, intra-Community trade are to be considered as measures having an effect equivalent to quantitative restrictions': *Procureur du Roi* v *Dassonville* [1974] ECR 837; reaffirmed in *Dansk Denkavit* v *Ministry of Agriculture* [1990] 1 CMLR 203.

The term 'measures having an equivalent effect' includes all laws and practices attributable to public authorities as well as government funding of activities which have the effect of restricting imports. For example, in 1982, the Irish government was held responsible for infringement of Article 30 because it financed a 'Buy

Irish' campaign which encouraged consumers to purchase goods produced in Ireland in preference over competitive goods from Community countries: *EC Commission* v *Ireland (Re Discriminatory Promotional Policies)* [1982] ECR 4005.

The first Community Directive enacted to reduce measures having an equivalent effect was clearly intended to eliminate measures discriminating between domestic and imported products: Commission Directive 70/50, OJ Sp Ed 17 (1970). This Directive addressed measures, other than those equally applicable to domestic and imported products, which hinder imports that would otherwise have taken place, including measures which make importation either more difficult or most costly than the disposal of domestic production. Practices deemed unlawful under this Directive included:

i) measures designed to specify less favourable prices for imports than for domestic prices;

ii) practices which establish minimum or maximum prices below or above which imports are prohibited or reduced;

iii) standards which subject imports to conditions relating to shape, size, weight or composition and which cause imported products to suffer in competition with domestic products; and

iv) laws which restrict the marketing of imported products in the absence of an agent or representative in the territory of the importing Member State.

e) *Exceptions to restrictions on quantitative restrictions and measures having an equivalent effect*

Specific exceptions to Article 30 of the EEC Treaty are made by Article 36. Quantitative restrictions and measures having equivalent effect on either imports or exports may be permitted in four circumstances:

i) The protection of public morality, public policy and public security

Restrictions justified on the basis of public morality have frequently been upheld by the European Court. In fact, the Court allows a considerable degree of discretion (or 'margin of discretion') on the part of Member States to make such determinations: see *R* v *Henn & Darby* [1979] ECR 3795.

The concept of public policy is capable of a greater application than public morality, although surprisingly few measures have been justified on this ground. The leading case is *R* v *Thompson* [1978] ECR 2247, where the European Court upheld convictions for fraudulently importing gold coins into the United Kingdom on the basis that such practices circumvented the right of a state to mint coinage for circulation, a prerogative traditionally recognised as involving the fundamental interests of the state.

ii) The protection of the health and life of humans, animals or plants

Restrictions for the protection of the life and health of humans, animals and plants are permitted if two conditions are satisfied:

- the restriction must be necessary for the protection of public health and not a disguised form of discrimination: *EC Commission* v *Germany* [1979] ECR 2555; and
- the degree of regulation imposed by the measure must be proportionate to the need to maintain the effective protection of the health and lives of human beings: *Centrafarm* [1976] ECR 613.

The principle of proportionality requires that the power of a Member State to prohibit or restrict imports should be restricted to measures necessary to attain the legitimate aim of protecting health: *Officier van Justitie* v *Sandoz BV* [1983] ECR 2445.

iii) The protection of national heritage

Member States can maintain restrictions necessary to protect national treasures which have artistic, historic, or archaeological value. This exception, however, only applies to treasures which remain in the public domain. As a general rule, only works of art which have not been placed on the market may benefit from this exception. Thus, in *EC Commission* v *Italy (Re Protection of National Treasures)* [1968] ECR 423, the European Court held that an export tax introduced by the Italian government could not be justified as a measure intended to protect national heritage because the items in question had entered the commercial market and had become sources of revenue for the national authorities.

iv) Protection of industrial and commercial property

National legislation may be maintained to protect the intellectual property rights of patent holders, licensees and copyright holders. The European Court has held that measures to protect patent holders may only be maintained if the products have been manufactured without the permission of the holder of the intellectual property right: *Centrafarm*, above. Such protection cannot be afforded where the imported product has been lawfully placed in circulation by the property right holder, or with his consent, in the Member State from which it has been imported.

f) *Discriminatory domestic taxation*

Article 95 of the EEC Treaty expressly prohibits Member States from imposing - directly or indirectly - internal taxes of any kind on Community products if such taxes exceed those imposed on identical or similar domestic products. This provision only applies to the levying of internal taxes where imported goods compete with domestic products. If there are no similar products, or no products capable of being protected, the prohibition in Article 95 is inapplicable. The products must therefore be in actual or potential competition.

The degree of competition required was illustrated in *EC Commission* v *United Kingdom (Re Wine and Beer Tax)* [1983] ECR 2265, which concerned British internal taxation policy on wines and beer. The United Kingdom imposed greater taxes on wine products, which were almost exclusively imported, than on beer products, which were mainly domestically produced. The Commission argued that, since wine and beer were conceivably interchangeable products, this tax differential created an artificial separation of the market which had the effect of de facto discrimination. The European Court agreed with this submission and held that beer and wine were competing products and therefore the United Kingdom was guilty of discrimination by levying different levels of tax.

g) *Harmonisation of barriers to trade*

Measures having an equivalent effect to quantitative restrictions form the greatest obstacles to the free movement of goods within the Community. These measures fall into three categories:

i) physical barriers to trade - for example, the systematic stopping and checking of goods and people at national frontiers;

ii) technical barriers to trade - for example, national legislation regulating product standards, conditions of marketing, or the protection of public health or safety;

iii) fiscal barriers to trade - for example, the divergence in types and rates or indirect taxes levied on goods within the Community.

The EEC Treaty specifically identifies the harmonisation (or approximation) of the laws of the Member States in order to remove these obstacles as an objective of the Community: Article 3(h) EEC Treaty. Articles 100, 100A and 235 of the EEC Treaty confer authority on the Community to enact legislation to harmonise such measures and standards throughout the Community. A number of Community measures have been adopted to eliminate such barriers through harmonisation. Products which satisfy such standards are entitled to unimpeded entry into the markets of all Member States.

The internal market programme initiated by the Single European Act aims to further eradicate such barriers to trade by introducing a substantial programme of Community legislation designed to harmonise such laws throughout the Community. Realisation of the internal market would create 'an area without internal frontiers in which the free movement of goods ... is ensured in accordance with the provisions of the [EEC Treaty]': Article 8A EEC Treaty. The deadline for achieving this goal has been set for 31 December 1992.

h) *Trade in goods from non-Community states*

Goods entering the Community from non-Community countries are subject to the Common Customs Tariff (CCT) which is a comprehensive Community-wide regime for assessing customs duties on non-EEC goods. The CCT supersedes the individual tariff schedules and customs laws of the Member States, although the

Community relies on national customs officials to enforce its provisions. The present CCT is based on Council Regulation 2658/87 OJ L256/1 (1987).

Article 10(1) of the EEC Treaty provides that products from third countries shall be considered to be in 'free circulation' within the Community if:

i) the relevant import formalities have been completed;

ii) any customs duties or charges having an equivalent effect have been levied; and

iii) the goods have not benefited from a total or partial drawback of such duties or charges.

According to Article 9(2) of the EEC Treaty, once foreign goods are in free circulation, they may not be subject to customs duties, quantitative restrictions or measures having an equivalent effect during intra-Community trade; see *Grandes Distilleries Paureux* v *Directeur des Services Fiscaux* [1979] ECR 975.

8.3 Relevant cases

EC Commission v *Germany (Re Customs Inspection Fees)* [1990] 1 CMLR 561: Definition of the concept of 'charges having an equivalent effect to customs duties'.

EC Commission v *Italy (Re Customs Administrative Charges)* Case 340/87, not yet reported: Where customs inspection charges are levied, this will not constitute a charge having equivalent effect if the importer obtains a 'definite and specific benefit'.

EC Commission v *Ireland (Re Preferential Purchasing Policies)* [1982] ECR 4005: Measures having an equivalent effect to quantitative restrictions include government funding of projects or practices which have the effect of restricting imports.

Dansk Denkavit v *Ministry of Agriculture* [1990] 1 CMLR 203: Definition of the concept of 'measures having an equivalent effect to quantitative restrictions'.

R v *Henn and Darby* [1979] ECR 3795: Exception to the restrictions on quantitative measures for reasons of public morality.

Oberkreisdirecktor Des Kreises Borken v *Handelsonderneming Moormann BV* [1990] 1 CMLR 656: Where Community Directives provide for the harmonisation of measures to ensure public health, the exceptions contained in Article 36 cannot be relied upon and checks must be carried out within the framework of the Directives.

8.4 Relevant materials

D Lasok, *The Law of the Economy of the European Community* (1980) 63-91.

L W Gormley, *Prohibiting Restrictions on Trade Within the EEC* (1985).

P Oliver, *Free Movement of Goods in the EEC* (1988).

P Oliver, 'A Review of the Case Law of the European Court of Justice on Articles 30-36' (1986) 23 CML Rev, 325.

M Quinn & N MacGowan, 'Could Article 30 Impose Obligations on Individuals?' (1987) 12 EL Rev 163.

8.5 Analysis of questions

Students should be familiar with the basic principles behind the concept of the free movement of goods, including the prohibitions on customs duties, charges having an equivalent effect to customs duties, as well as the elimination of quantitative restrictions and the abolition of measures having an equivalent effect to quantitative restrictions. In addition, an understanding of the relationship between these principles and the objectives of the internal market programme initiated by the Single European Act is desirable.

8.6 Questions

Question 1

ABC Ltd is the major French producer of goat cheese. It sends a shipment of cheese to a distributor in the United Kingdom, but the shipment is refused entry at the port of Dover. The reasons given by the Customs Inspector for refusing entry are, firstly, that the cheese is not labelled in English; secondly, that it is packed in cubic containers and therefore does not satisfy United Kingdom standards of consumer protection; and, thirdly, that it contains additives which are not allowed in cheese marketed in the United Kingdom.

Advise ABC Ltd as to its rights, if any, under European Community law.

University of London LLB Examination
(for External Students) European Community Law 1990 Q6

General comment

A problem requiring the student to apply the relevant principles of law to a hypothetical factual situation.

Skeleton solution

- Principles relating to the free movements of goods.
- Restrictions on the use of quantitative restrictions and measures having an equivalent effect.
- Remedies available to ABC Ltd.

Suggested solution

Article 30 of the EEC Treaty prohibits quantitative restrictions on imports from one Member States into another, along with all measures having an equivalent effect to quantitative restrictions. A quantitative restriction is a national measure that inhibits the volume or amount of imports by requiring that foreign goods satisfy more onerous conditions than those imposed on domestic goods in order to become merchantable within the particular state. Measures having an equivalent effect to quantitative restrictions have been defined as '[a]ll trading rules enacted by Member States which are capable of hindering directly or indirectly, actually or potentially, intra-Community trade': *Procureur du Roi* v *Dassonville* [1974]; reaffirmed in *Dansk Denkavit* v *Ministry of Agriculture* (1990). Therefore, all rules enacted by a Member State to regulate trade, and which hinder commerce, may contravene Article 30 unless they can benefit from the exceptions made to this rule under Article 36.

Three customs practices appear, ex facie, to constitute measures having an equivalent effect to quantitative restrictions: the requirement that cheese must be labelled in English; the packaging requirements; and the prohibition of certain additives in cheese.

The most important case concerning the legitimacy of national measures to protect consumers is the *Cassis de Dijon Case* (1979). In this case, the Court accepted the contention that, in the absence of Community measures of harmonisation, Member States retain authority to pass laws and regulations relating to products, but only 'in so far as those provisions may be recognised as being necessary in order to satisfy mandatory requirements relating in particular to ... the protection of public health, the fairness of commercial transactions and the defence of the consumer'. A qualitative restriction, or a measure equivalent to a quantitative restriction, could not be justified on any other ground unless it could benefit from the exceptions contained in Article 36 of the EEC Treaty.

Whether a restriction is justified under the conditions elaborated in the *Cassis de Dijon Case* depends on whether the measure serves 'a purpose which is in the general interest and such as to take precedence over the requirements of the free movement of goods, which constitutes one of the fundamental rules of the Community'; ibid. In determining whether a measure is in the public interest, it must be acknowledged that such rules reflect certain political and economic choices and, in the present state of Community law, regulation is a matter for Member States: *Torfaen Borough Council* v *B & Q* (1990).

In applying the second test - whether the goal is sufficiently important to prevail over the principle of the free movement of goods - the Court has stressed the importance of the principle that the measures in question must not produce discriminatory effects: *Quietlynn Ltd* v *Southend Borough Council* (1990). Restrictions of a discriminatory character are not compatible with the principle of the free movement of goods unless 'any obstacle to Community trade thereby created did not exceed what was necessary in order to ensure the attainment of the objective in view and unless that objective was justified with regard to Community law': *Torfaen*, above. The onus is therefore on the party relying on the mandatory requirement to prove that the application of the measure in question is necessary in the circumstances of the case.

As regards the requirement that the cheese is labelling in English, it must be ascertained whether or not the measure is in the public interest and also whether the measure is sufficiently important to outweigh the principle of the free movement of goods throughout the Community. Where a product imported from another country has been lawfully produced and marketed in one Member State, there is a presumption that the product satisfies both these conditions and must, in principle, be admitted to the markets of other Member States: see Commission Practice Note Concerning

Import Prohibitions, OJ C 256/2 (1980). In the case of the cheese, ABC is the major producer of goats cheese in France. It must therefore be presumed that the English labelling requirement is contrary to Article 30, and the onus is on the British government to prove otherwise.

The requirement that the cheese is packed in cubic containers clearly infringes the tests established in the *Cassis de Dijon Case*. Such a requirement is neither in the public interest nor of sufficient importance to override the principle of free movement of goods. Commission Directive 70/50, which relates to the abolition of measures which have an effect equivalent to quantitative restrictions on imports, states that measures which subject imported products to conditions, in respect of a particular shape, size, weight, composition, presentation, or conditions which are different from those for domestic products and more difficult to satisfy, are measures of equivalent effect to quantitative restrictions. Nor could such a requirement be exempt under the exception made for measures relating to the protection of the public under Article 36: *EC Commission* v *Italy (Re Imported Vinegar)* (1981).

The final restriction on the import of cheese concerns the allegation that it contains additives which are not allowed in cheese marketed in the United Kingdom. This measure is prima facie a measure having an equivalent effect to a quantitative restriction under Article 30 and could only be permitted if it was exempt under Article 36 on the grounds of protecting public health. The principles concerning the application of the exception under Article 36 on the grounds of the protection of public health were laid down in *EC Commission* v *Germany (Re German Beer Purity)* (1988). The Court laid down the general principle that insofar as there are uncertainties concerning the safety of food additives, it is for the Member States, in the absence of harmonising legislation, to decide what degree of protection should be afforded to the public, having regard to the requirement of the free movement of goods within the Community.

This principle is subject to two broad qualifications. First, where products satisfy the health and safety requirements of one Member State, there is a presumption that they will also satisfy those of other Member States. Second, if the Community has enacted standards regulating the use of such additives, Member States are not permitted to enact more stringent measures.

In this particular case, in view of the similarities in the eating habits between British and French consumers, such a restriction could only be maintained if scientific research could be adduced to support the ban. Consequently, in all probability, by refusing to allow the shipment of cheese to enter the United Kingdom, the United Kingdom is in violation of its obligations.

ABC Ltd has two alternative course of action in order to obtain a remedy for this breach of Community law. First, it could complain to the EC Commission that the British measures contravene Community law. If the Commission adopts ABC's arguments, an action could be brought before the ECJ against the United Kingdom. Second, ABC could pursue a remedy in the British courts on the basis that the measures contravene Community law. In such an action, a claim for compensation for injury sustained as a consequence of the measure may be competent: see *Bourgoin SA* v *Ministry of Agriculture, Fisheries and Food* (1986). In such a case, a reference to the European Court under Article 177 would be expedient.

Question 2

Hillfarm plc, a British company which exports lamb, wishes to enter the French market. Its principal product is lamb chops, packed in cube-shaped packages designed for supermarkets. It is convinced that it can compete with French producers with regard to the quality and price of the product. It hesitates to invest, however, because it has been advised that French law requires that all lamb sold in France, regardless of its place of production, must satisfy three requirements:

a) it must undergo a health inspection for which a small charge is made;

b) it must be packed in triangular-shaped packages, because tests conducted at major universities have shown that this form of packaging tends to prolong the shelf-life of meat and to be associated generally by consumers with meat of the highest quality; and

c) it must be sold only in supermarkets offering equal space to French lamb, because in the view of the French government, such a policy is necessary to encourage local production and to protect the rural environment in the mountainous regions of the country.

Advise Hillfarm plc as to its position under EEC law, assuming that there is no relevant legislation under the Common Agricultural Policy.

University of London LLB Examination
(for External Students) European Community Law 1989 Q6

General comment

Another problem-type question requiring the application of legal principles to a factual situation.

Skeleton solution

- The concept of charges having an equivalent effect to customs duties.
- Measures having an equivalent effect to quantitative restrictions.
- Compatibility of these actions with EEC law.

Suggested solution

Three particular practices impede Hillfarm from penetrating the French market: health inspection charges; packaging requirements; and preferential purchasing requirements.

Article 12 of the EEC Treaty expressly prohibits the re-introduction of any customs duties, or any charges having equivalent effect to customs duties, on imports and exports. This provision has been given direct effect and may be founded upon by individuals before national courts: *Van Gend en Loos* v *Netherlands* (1963). Charges having an equivalent effect to customs duties have been defined by the European Court as 'any pecuniary charge, whatever its designation and mode of application, which is imposed unilaterally on goods by reason of the fact that they cross a frontier, and is not a customs duty in the strict sense, constitutes a charge having an equivalent effect to a customs duty': *EC Commission* v *Germany (Re Inspection Fees)* (1990). A charge imposed on goods in transit across a frontier which discriminates between domestic and foreign goods, and which is not justified by provisions in the EEC Treaty or Community legislation will therefore amount to a charge having an equivalent effect.

Charges having an equivalent effect may only be justified in three circumstances: (a) if the charges relate to a general system of internal dues applied systematically within a Member State, without discrimination between domestic and imported products; (b) if the charges constitute payment for a service in fact rendered and are in proportion to the costs of receiving that service; or (c) if the charges are levied in order to fulfil obligations imposed by Community law.

In this particular case, the health charges levied by the French government may be lawful under Community law since the charge is made for a service actually incurred, and the service is rendered on both domestic and imported lamb products. However, Hillfarm must receive a specific benefit from the charge. A direct benefit will not accrue to an importer if the charges are made in the interests of the state *(EC Commission* v *Italy (Re Customs Administrative Charges)* (1989)), or if the charge has been levied to ensure the health of animals in transit for public policy reasons: *EC Commission* v *Belgium (Re Health Inspection Charges)* (1984).

Package requirements are prima facie measures which have an equivalent effect to quantitative restrictions. Such measures may only be lawful if they satisfy two conditions: (a) the purpose of the measure is in the general interest of the public; and (b) the interest of the public takes precedence over the requirement of the free movement of goods, which constitutes one of the fundamental rules of the Community: *Cassis de Dijon Case* (1979). Commission Directive 70/50 expressly identifies measures which subject imported products to conditions regarding shape as a measure of equivalent effect to a quantitative restriction. However, the fact that the particular measure under examination is applied without discrimination between foreign and French lamb products may mitigate the application of this provision: *Oosthoek Case* (1982). Nevertheless it may be possible to have the measure declared incompatible with Community law on the basis that the measure constitutes an obstacle to Community trade because it exceeds what is necessary to ensure the attainment of the objective which is sought by the measure: *Torfaen Borough Council* v *B & Q* (1990).

Preferential purchasing policies are also prima facie measures which have an equivalent effect to quantitative restrictions: *EC Commission* v *Ireland* (1982). The French government are pursuing a policy of promoting French goods over imported goods by requiring that lamb sold in supermarkets must be 50 per cent French lamb. Such policies, even although they may be in the general public interest, do not prevail over the principle of the free movement of goods since they result in discrimination between imported and domestic goods. Commission Directive 70/50 clearly prohibits measures which 'hinder the purchase by individuals of imported products, or encourage, require or give preference to the purchase of domestic products'. Clearly the French policy of imposing a mandatory requirement of 50 per cent French meat contravenes this rule.

Question 3

'At the end of the transition period between 1958 and 1970, the free movement of goods was expected to be a completed reality. In 1986, however, the Member States promised that the internal market would be accomplished by 1992 with the elimination of invisible barriers still affecting the free movement of goods, and doubts are already being expressed whether such a promise is realistic.'

Discuss.

University of Glasgow LLB Examination
1987 Q3

General comment

An essay-type question requiring a narrative answer commenting on the success of the freedom of movement of goods within the Community.

Skeleton solution

- Objectives of the EEC Treaty as regards goods.
- Structure of the Treaty as regards these objectives.
- Single European Act.
- Internal market programme.

Suggested solution

Article 9 of the EEC Treaty declares that the European Community is based on a customs union which extends to all trade in goods. Within a custom union, all tariffs and non-tariff barriers to trade in goods are removed and a common tariff erected to assess duties on foreign goods entering the customs union. In order to create a customs union, the EEC Treaty removed all tariffs and quantitative restrictions on intra-Community trade and introduced a common customs tariff to regulate the flow of goods from foreign countries into the Community. Prohibitions have been placed on the introduction of new tariffs and quotas on intra-EEC trade and these provisions are vigorously enforced by the European Commission in the European Court.

The EEC Treaty also provides the procedures and mechanisms through which the eradication of these barriers to trade is to be achieved. These provisions have been supplemented by Community legislation requiring the harmonisation of national customs laws and the elimination of national quantitative restrictions along with measures having a similar effect. Measures having an equivalent effect to quantitative restrictions form the main impediments to the free movement of goods between Member States. The EEC Treaty specifically identifies the harmonisation (or approximation) of national laws in order to eradicate such restrictions as an objective of the Community: Article 3(h) EEC Treaty. Articles 100, 100A and 235 of the EEC Treaty provide authority for enacting Community legislation to harmonise national laws. Community measures were adopted to harmonise technical barriers to the flow of goods by creating common Community-wide standards for the manufacture, production and marketing of goods. Products which satisfy such standards are entitled to unimpeded entry into the markets of all Member States.

Barriers to the free movement of goods may be classified according to whether they are physical barriers to trade, fiscal barriers to trade, or technical barriers to trade. Physical barriers involve the systematic stopping and checking of goods at national frontiers to regulate entry into a particular territory. These barriers are required to regulate the flow of goods from outside the Community into the internal market, to enforce national quotas on certain products, for the inspection of documents and certificates, or to ensure compliance with transportation regulations. Fiscal barriers are caused by the divergence in types and rates of indirect taxes levied on goods, in particular Value Added Tax and excise duties.

Throughout the evolution of the Community, technical barriers to trade in goods have present the most formidable obstacles to the creation of a single market within the Community: *Cecchini Report* Commission of the European Community (1988) 4. Technical barriers are legal measures or administrative practices which inhibit or obstruct trade by creating standards or conditions which impede the exercise of the right of free movement of goods. The most common forms of technical barriers to trade are national regulations and standards for marketing goods, and measures for the protection of public health and safety.

By the early 1980s, it had become clear that Community attempts to eradicate these invisible barriers to trade in goods had been unsuccessful. While the Community had been reasonably successful in erecting a common customs tariff and in implementing the common commercial policy, it had failed to achieve the transition towards a true common market in which the free movement of factors of production existed: see *Completing the Internal Market*, White Paper from the Commission to the European Council COM (85) 310 Final (1985). This lack of progress was generally attributed to the cumbersome decision-making processes within the Community which obstructed the adoption of measures to eradicate barriers and impediments to the free movement of goods. This failure led to a revaluation of the organisation structure and general goals of the Community, culminating in the adoption of the Single European Act in 1986.

The primary objective of the Single European Act (SEA) is the creation of the 'internal market' which is defined as 'an area without internal frontiers in which the free movement of goods, persons, services and capital is ensured in accordance with the provisions of the [EEC Treaty]': Article 8A EEC Treaty. The deadline for the achievement of this goal has been set as 31 December 1992.

Articles 13 to 15 of the Single European Act amended the original EEC Treaty by adding Articles 8A, 8B and 8C, which define the internal market and which lay down the rules through which this goal will be achieved. Articles 18 and 19 of the SEA introduce two new EEC Treaty Articles for the adoption of harmonising measures for the achievement and functioning of the internal market (Article 100A) and for what shall happen at the end of the period for establishing the internal market (Article 100B).

The internal market programme is designed to remove all major physical, technical and fiscal barriers to trade. The programme entails extensive and substantial alterations to national legal provisions relating to customs, tax, public procurement, capital movements, company law, intellectual property, employment, transport and investment. This is because the existing disparities, inconsistencies and variations in each Member State in these areas constitute impediments to the creation of a single, consistent and predictable economic environment for the production of goods and the conduct of commerce.

Within the Community, physical barriers to the flow of goods are administered in order to: (1) enforce national quotas in certain products; (2) to collect VAT and excise duties; (3) to carry health checks; (4) to operate the Community system of compensation under the Common Agriculture Policy; (5) to ensure compliance with transportation regulations; and (6) to gather statistical information. In order to facilitate the free movement of goods, simplified customs procedures are to be adopted. In particular, the adoption of the Single Administrative Document (SAD) is designed to replace the multiple processing of customs forms. The introduction of common border posts (banalisation) where all formalities are confined to a single stopping point between each Member State has also been proposed to pave the way for the eventual removal of all systematic controls at frontiers and the introduction of a policy which makes use of occasional spot checks. This is to be accompanied by a reduction, and eventual elimination, of national trade quotas. Issues such as the spread of rabies within the United Kingdom still remain to be tackled.

From a legal perspective, technical barriers to the construction of the internal market will involve the greatest volume of Community legislation. These barriers create standards or conditions which retard the practical exercise of these rights. Technical barriers to trade in goods include: (a) the diversity of national regulations and standards for testing products or for the protection of the safety of the consumer; (b) the duplication of product testing and certificate (particularly pronounced in the pharmaceutical industry); and (c) the reluctance of the public authorities in certain Member States to open public procurement to the nationals of other Member States.

The Commission has proposed a number of ways of eliminating technical barriers to the proper functioning of the free movement of goods. In relation to the free movement of goods, two alternative methods of reducing technical barriers have been promoted:

a) The so-called 'principle of equivalence' or 'mutual recognition' approach which requires that, once a product has been manufactured in one Member State, it should be sold without restriction throughout the Community. In other words, if a product meets the technical standards of one member, it is presumed that it will meet the same requirements in other Members. This test was sanctioned by the

ECJ in the *Cassis de Dijon Case* (1979) and was also referred to in the *German Beer Purity Case* (1988).

b) The harmonisation approach which requires that measures standardising technical standards within the Community are adopted at the Community level. This process of harmonisation normally requires the passing of Community legislation. The SEA ensures that such legislation will receive an expedited passage by requiring that the Council of Ministers adopts majority voting for the implementation of harmonising legislation on technical matters.

Where harmonisation legislation is not absolutely required, the Commission intends that the mutual recognition principle will continue to be applied by the ECJ thereby reducing such barriers.

Substantial Community legislation pertaining to the harmonisation of technical standards, mostly in the form of directives, has been passed to approximate technical standards on products ranging from the alcoholic content of certain wines to the technical specifications required to regulate noise emissions from lawn cutting equipment and to regulate the amount of research and development assistance that can be granted by a Member State: see *Fifth Progress Report of the Commission on the Completion of the Internal Market* COM 90 (90) Final (1990). The most heavily-regulated manufacturing industries will be food and drink, pharmaceuticals and chemicals.

The problem of fiscal barriers is mainly confined to the various types and rates of indirect tax particularly in relation to Value Added Tax (VAT) and excise duties. At the moment VAT is collected in the country where the goods are finally consumed. While the exporter exports goods VAT free, an importer pays VAT and excise duties in the country of importation. VAT rates throughout the Community vary between 0 per cent to 38 per cent while excise duties range from zero to 10,5 ECU per bottle of alcohol. As long as these taxes vary within Member States, frontier controls will be necessary to ensure the collection of due taxes. A more technical complaint raised against this variation in rates of VAT is that it creates artificial price differences between countries to the detriment of consumers and represent an obstacle to the free movement of goods and limit competition.

The Commission has concluded that a uniform system of indirect taxation is not a prerequisite to the abolition of fiscal controls at frontiers. Nevertheless partial harmonisation was considered essential. The Commission favours a system which would allow a margin of plus or minus 2.5-3.0 per cent on either side of a target rate of tax. This would require the United Kingdom to abandon its zero rates of VAT on certain products such as books and food, and it is estimated that Denmark would suffer a fall of approximately 10 per cent on its total tax revenues.

In respect of excise duty, by chance, the products which are covered by such a tax are similar throughout the Community, ie, cigarettes and tobacco products, alcohol, diesel and petroleum. Some exceptions do exist and no duty is levied in Greece or Italy for wine. The proposals envisaged by the Commission would include: (a) harmonisation of rates of tax on cigarettes, tobacco products, alcohol and mineral oils;

(b) proposals in relation to less significant goods and products on which excise is levied and the interlinking of Community bonded warehouses. This would allow such exercisable goods to circulate freely in the internal market without payment of duty until they are finally consumed; (c) abolition of duty-free concessions.

While the Community failed to realise the concept of a common market in which goods flowed from one Member State to another without being impeded by barriers, the internal market programme, being a less ambitious project, has a significantly greater chance of being successful. Even if the complete programme is not in place by 1992, the momentum built up towards the elimination of a significant number of barriers to trade will ensure that the internal market programme will produce tangible results.

Question 4

'The free movement of goods, as a foundation of the Common Market is subject to exceptions, but these exceptions will gradually lose their importance as integration proceeds, particularly with the completion of the internal market in 1992.' Discuss.

University of Glasgow LLB Examination
1989 Q4

General comment

A question requiring detailed knowledge of the principle of the free movement of goods and the exceptions thereto.

Skeleton solution

- Article 30.
- Exceptions to Article 30 (Article 36).
- The effect of harmonisation legislation.
- Internal market programme.
- Conclusions.

Suggested solution

The principle of the free movement of goods is embodied in two EEC Treaty provisions. First, Article 12 prohibits the introduction of any customs duties or any other charge having equivalent effect on imports and exports between Member States. Second, Article 30 forbids the creation of quantitative restrictions on import and all measures having an equivalent effect, while Article 34 imposes the same obligation for exports.

Specific exceptions to Article 30 were also created by Article 36 of the EEC Treaty. Quantitative restrictions and measures having equivalent effect on either imports or exports may be permitted where the purpose of the restriction is to protect: (a) public morality, public policy or public security; (b) the health and life of humans, animals or plants; (c) national treasures having artistic, historic, or archaeological value; or (d) industrial or commercial bodies. In addition, restrictions to protect the essential security interests or the security of Member States concerned with production or trade in arms, munitions or war material may be justified: Article 223(1)(b) EEC Treaty.

The application of these permitted exceptions is subject to a number of general principles. In the first place, prohibitions or restrictions authorised under Article 36 cannot constitute a means of arbitrary discrimination or a disguised restriction on trade between Member States. Further, since Article 36 is an exception to Article 30, it is strictly construed and the party seeking to rely on an exception has the burden of proving the applicability of the exception: *EC Commission* v *France* (1983). Finally, whether a measure is justified is an objective test and the reasonableness of the measure is decided according to whether it is effective for the purpose claimed and proportionate to the state purposes.

Restrictions justified on the basis of public morality have frequently been upheld by the Court. In fact, the Court allows a considerable degree of discretion (or the 'margin of discretion') on the part of the Member State to make such value judgments. For example, in *R* v *Henn and Darby* (1979), a prohibition on the importation of pornographic material from Community countries into the United Kingdom was upheld by the Court despite the free availability of identical material in a number of other Member States. However, this discretion is circumscribed if the national measure being reviewed by the Court procures discrimination. Thus, where the importation of erotic inflatable dolls manufactured in the Community was prevented by British customs authorities, the Court held that the absence of legislation prohibiting the manufacture of such items within the United Kingdom created discrimination: *Conegate Ltd* v *HM Customs and Excise* (1986). Consequently, a Member State may not rely on the ground of public morality to prohibit the importation of goods from other Member States when its legislation contains no similar prohibition on the manufacturing or marketing of the same goods within its territory.

Although the ground of public policy, being of a more nebulous character, is capable of a greater application than public morality, surprisingly few cases have arisen under this exception. The leading case is *R* v *Thompson and Ors* (1978), in which the European Court upheld convictions for fraudulently importing gold coins into the United Kingdom on the basis that such practices circumvented the right of states to mint coinage for circulation in the realm, a prerogative traditionally recognised as involving the fundamental interests of the State. Restrictions justified on the grounds of public security have also been upheld in the past by the Court: *R* v *Goldstein* (1983) (House of Lords).

Legislation which restricts the free movement of goods is frequently justified on the basis that it is intended to protect the lives and health of consumers. Two main principles determine whether such measures may be allowed under Community law. First, the restriction must be necessary for the protection of public health and not a disguised form of discrimination: *EC Commission* v *Germany* (1979). Second, the degree of regulation imposed by the measure must be proportionate to the need to maintain the effective protection of the health and lives of human beings: *Centrafarm Case* (1976). The principle of proportionality therefore requires that the power of the

Member State to prohibit imports of the product in question should be restricted to what is necessary to attain the legitimate aim of protecting health.

An illustration of the application of these tests by the Court occurred in *EC Commission* v *Italy* (1981). The Italian government introduced legislation which required that products labelled as 'vinegar' must be made from wine. If vinegars were manufactured from other agricultural products they were prohibited from using the description 'vinegar'. The intention of the Italian government in adopting this measure was to protect Italian wine and vinegar producers. The Court rejected that such a measure could be lawful since its application was not proportionate to a threat to the health of consumers. The interests of the consumer could be protected by listing ingredients on the packaging of vinegar products. The Court concluded that the Italian legislation was not part of a seriously considered health policy and therefore contrary to Article 30.

Another important case relating to legislation alleged to protect the health of consumers was the *German Beer Purity Case* (1988). German legislation governing the production of beer prohibited the mixing of additives to beer. To substantiate this restriction the German government: (a) prohibited the designation 'bier' for beers containing additives; and (b) maintained an absolute prohibition on the importation of beers containing additives. These measures protected German beer manufacturers because, while foreign beers could not be sold as beer in Germany, all German beer production satisfied the requirements of the legislation. The Court considered the facts of the case and concluded that 'in so far as there are uncertainties at the present stage of scientific research it is for the Member States, in the absence of harmonisation, to decide what degree of protection of the health and lives of humans they intend to assure, having regard however to the requirement of the free movement of goods within the Community.

However, this discretion was qualified by the condition that the prohibition on additives which are authorised in the Member State of production is permissible only insofar as it satisfies the requirements of Article 36 as interpreted by the Court. In particular prohibitions must be restricted to what is necessary to secure the protection of public health. Where products satisfy the health and safety requirements of one Member State, there is a presumption that they will also satisfy those of other Member States. In the case of additives, the Court held in the *German Beer Purity Case*, that in view of the similarity in the eating habits prevailing in the importing state and the state of manufacture, as well as the findings of international scientific research, such a ban could not be maintained. Consequently, the German ban on additives was declared contrary to Community law.

The third exception to the general rule of free movement of goods concerns national measures designed to protect national heritage. A number of cases have arisen concerning national measures designed to prevent, obstruct, or impede the export of works of art from Member States, particularly Italy. The exception created under Article 36 for the protection of national heritage does not permit the imposition of export taxes to protect such objects. In *EC Commission* v *Italy* (1968), the European Court held that Italy could not impose an export tax on works of art under Article 36.

The export of rare or valuable items could not be prevented or obstructed once they have entered the commercial market or have become a source of revenue for national authorities. As a general proposition, only works of art which have not been placed on the commercial market may benefit from this exception to Article 30.

Finally, Article 36 authorises measures for the protection of industrial and commercial property. National legislation may protect the rights of patent holders, licences and copyright holders. Participation in the European Community may actually erode such rights. The main problem in this respect arises where the price of a product which has been manufactured under an intellectual property right varies in different Member States. The existence of price discrimination normally encourages parallel imports whereby goods lawfully manufactured under licence in one Member State are exported to the Member State of a licence holder where the price is greater. The European Court has declared that measures to protect patent holders are legitimate if the products originate from a Member State in which the patent is being abused: *Centrafarm BV* v *Sterling Drug Inc* (1974). However, such protection cannot be afforded where the product has been put into the market in a legal manner, by the patentee himself or with his consent, in the Member State from which it has been imported.

The significance of these exceptions has declined over the last two decades and will be substantially limited by the completion of the internal market programme. This is because the Community has adopted a number of measures to harmonise the various laws of the Member States regarding the protection of the consumer, the protection of public health and safety, as well as protection for art treasures. Once Community-wide measures have been introduced, Member States will be unable to invoke the exceptions stated in Article 36 to the principle of the free movement of goods. The existence of Community measures also removes the need to have additional national measures to regulate a subject: *Schumacher* v *Hauptzollamt Frankfurt Am Main* (1990); and *Dansk Denkavit* v *Ministry of Agriculture* (1990).

Where Community legislation provides for the harmonisation of measures to ensure the protection of animal or human health, or establish Community-wide procedures to ensure observation, the exceptions created by Article 36 can no longer be relied upon and appropriate checks must be carried out within the framework of the Directive: *Oberkreisdirecktor Des Kreises Borken* v *Handelsonderneming Moormann BV* (1990). But, at the same time, where harmonising legislation only partially harmonises a subject-matter, or is intended only to achieve progressive harmonisation, this is insufficient to exclude the application of Article 36: *Schumacher* v *Hauptzollamt Frankfurt Am Main* (1990). If a product is marketed within another Member State in compliance with the appropriate safety or health regulations, there is a presumption that such procedures provide an adequate guarantee of its quality and safety. This presumption is irrebutable when the product in question has been manufactured to Community-wide specifications.

Question 5

Outline the principles which apply to goods entering the Community from non-Community countries or origin, paying particular attention to the system established under the Common Customs Tariff (CCT).

Question prepared by Author
February 1991

General comment

A general question relating to the treatment of non-Community goods within the Community.

Skeleton solution

- The concept of the CCT.
- Tariff rates, classification of goods, and valuation.
- Quotas, rules of origin.
- The concept of goods in free circulation.

Suggested solution

Goods entering the Community from non-Community states are subject to the Common Customs Tariff (CCT) which is a comprehensive Community-wide regime for the calculation of duties on non-EEC goods. The CCT supersedes the individual tariff schedules and customs laws of the Member States, although the Community relies on national customs officials to enforce its provisions. The Community has exclusive competence to regulate the CCT and measures enacted by Member States which conflict with its provisions are void: *Sociaal Fonds voor de Diamantarbeiders* v *NV Indiamex* (1973). The present CCT is based in Council Regulation 2658/87 (1987), as amended by Council Regulation 2886/89 (1989), which adopted the Combined Nomenclature system negotiated by the Customs Cooperation Council.

The Common Customs Tariff specifies a tariff rate for each item imported into the Community determined according to its description. Tariffs may be fixed, ad valorem, or mixed. A fixed tariff is a duty which is levied according to the quantity of volume of the product imported, regardless of value. An ad valorem tariff is calculated as a percentage of the value of the imported goods. Mixed tariffs are applied by formulae which combine fixed and ad valorem elements. The most common tariffs are ad valorem tariffs.

Rates of duty are assessed according to the origin of the imported product. Where the country of origin is a member of the General Agreement on Tariffs and Trade (GATT), the Most-Favoured-Nation (MFN) rate is applicable, unless the country may benefit from a rate specified for developing countries (see Lome Conventions and GSP rates). If the country of origin is not a member of the GATT or entitled to a preferred status, the standard rate of duty is applied. Rates of duty may be altered on a country-by-country basis by the negotiation of a free trade or association agreement.

Tariffs are amended each year by Council Regulation under the authority set out in the common commercial policy and common agricultural provisions. Agricultural products attract higher rates of duty than industrial products, reflecting the comparative strength of the Community in the manufacturing sectors. Rates may be altered as a result of multilateral tariff negotiations (MTNs) held under the auspices of the GATT, or unilaterally lowered below the MFN rate by special arrangement, usually with developing or associated countries.

Liability to duties depends on the classification of the goods in the scheme of the Common Customs Tariff, which in turn depends on the description given to the goods. The nomenclatures stated in the Tariff do not invariably correspond to the imported goods. In such cases, 'products which are not covered by any tariff heading must be classified under the heading for the products for which they are most analogous'. This assessment should be made on the basis not only of the physical characteristics of the goods but also their intended purpose and their commercial value: *Huber* v *Hauptzollamt Frankfurt Am Main-Flughafen* (1988).

Where customs duties are calculated on an ad valorem basis, the value attributed to the goods is important in order to determine liability to customs duty. The principles for the valuation of goods for the purposes of assessing duty have been embodied in Council Regulation 1224/80. The fundamental principle is that goods should be given their actual commercial value at the port of entry into the Community. This is known as the 'arm's length sales' price. Where a export sale is made to a Community purchaser, and the parties are unconnected, the sale price represents the value of the goods so long as: (a) the buyer remains free to dispose of the goods at his or her discretion without restrictions other than those imposed by law; (b) no additional payment is required as part of the transaction; and (c) no part of the consideration is unquantifiable.

Additions and subtractions may be made, where required, to the sales price to arrive at the final valuation. Where costs are incurred by the purchase, these must be added to the sales price. Such costs would include sales commission, royalties payable on resale of the goods, the costs of transport and insurance to the Community frontier, as well as loading and handling charges. Charges made for the non-return of returnable containers upon which duty has been assessed are part of the price of the goods and must be added to the sales price: *Schmid* v *Hauptzollamt Stuttgart-West* Case 357/87, unreported. Subtractions from the sales price include customs duties and taxes, transport charges following import, costs of installation and maintenance, purchase commissions and interest payments.

Where the parties entering the transactions are not at arm's length, such as a parent sale to a subsidiary, the transaction value may be used if it can be verified that the importer had no influence over the final sales price. If this fact cannot be established, or if the goods passed for no consideration, a number of alternative methods of valuation become applicable. A valuation may be made on the basis of: (a) the sale price of identical goods; (b) the sale price of similar goods; (c) a constructed value; of (d) in accordance with the default method which calculates the price on the basis of standard accounting principles.

Quantitative restrictions, or quotas, on imports from non-Community countries do not conflict with the obligations of Article 30 of the EEC Treaty which relate only to intra-Community trade. Quotas on goods from foreign sources are subject only to the rules of international economic law as specified in the GATT. As a general rule, quotas are prohibited by the international trading rules, but the exceptions to this general rule are so great that the Community has little difficulty in justifying the implementation of quotas on non-EEC goods.

The decision to impose quotas is made at the Community level and individual quotas allocated to Member States which administer their respective allocations. In *EC Commission* v *EC Council* Case 51/87, not yet reported, the Court annulled a regulation which apportioned quotas to Member States on the ground that the Council has acted improperly in rejecting Commission proposals for the management of quotas by the Community. Community management of quotas is anticipated with the completion of the internal market programme.

Determination of the origin of goods is essential for the proper application of the Common Customs Tariff since rates vary according to the country from which the goods came. For this purpose, the country of origin is the state which produced the goods and not the country from which the goods were shipped into the Community. The principles behind the rules of origin are not to be found in the EEC Treaty, but in secondary Community legislation.

Regulation 802/68 (1969), as amended, specified the general rule for establishing the origin of goods. Goods originate in the customs territory if they were wholly obtained or produced there, or, alternatively, where the last economically justified and substantial processing took place. Goods which are wholly produced in a territory include mined products, commodities grown in the territory, animal products, sea products from vessels registered in the territory, and products from the sea, subsoil or continental shelf over which the country has exclusive rights of exploitation.

Goods which are substantially produced in a territory present a greater problem. On the whole, the most relevant factor is the last substantial economic process which occurred to the goods resulting in either a transformation of the product or a major stage of manufacturing. However, the Community regulation specifically prohibits goods being given a country of origin where the economic processes responsible for the transformation of the product were undertaken simply for the purpose of circumventing the Common Customs Tariff. The Commission has passed numerous regulations to provide a greater degree of clarity. Further, the European Court has subjected these regulations to a test of objectivity and, at least in one case, has held that a stricter concept of origin was required in the circumstances: *SR Industries* v *Administration des Douanes* (1988).

The rules of origin are often modified when the Community enters into an international trade agreement with another country or group of countries. For example, in the agreement between the Community and the EFTA, special rules are established to facilitate reciprocal acceptance of certificates of origin and to allow for simplified procedures in certain circumstances. The distribution of certificates of origin for Community goods is governed by Council Regulation 553/81. Chambers of commerce are frequently authorised to administer such certificates to goods being exported.

Article 10(1) of the EEC Treaty states that products from a third country shall be considered to be in free circulation within the Community if the import formalities have been satisfied and any customs duties or charges having an equivalent effect payable have been levied. According to Article 9(2) once foreign goods are in free circulation, they may not be subject to quantitative restrictions or measures having an equivalent effect of the purposes of intra-Community trade. This has important consequences. Thus, no additional import requirements may be imposed on goods originating from third states but in free circulation in another Member State.

9 THE FREE MOVEMENT OF PERSONS

9.1 Introduction

The free movement of labour is recognised by the EEC Treaty as essential to achieve the goal of a common market. The essence of this freedom is the abolition of discrimination between nationals and workers from other Community Member States as regards employment, remuneration and other conditions of work. In the realisation of this object, a distinction is made between 'workers' and self-employed persons'. 'Workers' enjoy the freedom of movement, while 'self-employed persons' enjoy the freedom of establishment. Both freedoms serve the same purpose - the liberalisation of the supply of labour.

9.2 Key points

a) *The freedom of movement of workers*

Article 48 of the EEC Treaty regulates the free movement of workers. It creates four rights which are inherent in the exercise of this freedom:

i) the right to accept offers of employment actually made;

ii) the right to move freely within the territory of Member States for this purpose;

iii) the right to reside in a Member State for the purpose of employment in accordance with the provisions governing the employment of nationals of that State as laid down by law, regulations or administrative action;

iv) the right to remain in the territory of a Member State after having been employed in that State, subject to conditions laid down by the European Commission.

Article 49 authorises the Council of Ministers to issue regulations and directives to implement Article 48. However, this has not prevented the European Court from declaring that Article 48 has direct effect; see *EC Commission* v *France* [1974] ECR 359 and *Van Duyn* v *Home Office* [1974] ECR 1337.

Acting in pursuance of the authority vested by Article 49, the Council introduced the concept of the free movement of workers in three stages:

i) Council Regulation 15/61 (1961): This established the principle that every national of the Community was free to take employment in another Member State provided that no suitable employee was available among the work force of that State.

ii) Council Regulation 38/64 (1964): This reduced the level of preference enjoyed by workers with the national labour force.

iii) Council Regulation 1612/68 (1968): This legislation, which continues to remain in force in an amended form, eliminated preferences and established the full freedom of movement for workers.

b) *Definition of 'worker' under Community law*

The right to the freedom of movement is expressly restricted to 'workers' under Article 48. Whether a person qualifies as a worker depends on whether or not he or she satisfies the relevant criteria laid down in Community law. See *Lawrie-Blum* v *Land Baden-Wurttemberg* [1986] ECR 2121.

In order to qualify as a worker under Article 48, a person must be employed. The essential feature of an employment relationship is that, for a certain period of time, a person performs services for and under the direction of another person in return for which he or she receives remuneration. The term 'worker' therefore includes all persons engaged in a contract of employment, including executives, salaried employees and manual workers.

The definition of 'worker' is not restricted to full-time employees. A person who is employed on a part-time basis may acquire the right of freedom of movement provided that he or she pursues an activity as an employed person which is 'effective and genuine': *Levin* v *Staatssecretaris van Justitie* [1982] ECR 1035. Even a worker who is engaged in part-time employment, and who receives public assistance to supplement his or her income, may exercise this right: *Kempf* v *Staatssecretaris van Justitie* [1986] ECR 1741.

A person must be a national of a Community country in order to qualify as a worker for the purposes of Article 48. To determine whether a person is a national of a Member State - and thereby entitled to this right - the law of that Member State must be applied. As far as the United Kingdom is concerned, all individuals who have the right of abode within the United Kingdom by virtue of the British Nationality Act 1981 are British nationals and entitled to exercise the right of freedom of movement.

c) *Prohibitions on discrimination*

Council Regulation 1612/68 (1968) is intended to harmonise national legislation regulating employment by removing any measures discriminating between national and Community workers. This objective is achieved by creating the following rights and duties:

i) Any national of a Member State may, irrespective of his place of residence, exercise the right to take up an activity as an employed person, and to pursue such activity within the territory of another Member State in accordance with the employment law of that State.

ii) A worker has the right to take up available employment in a Member State with the same priority as a national of that State.

iii) National employment legislation will be inapplicable if it limits applications for employment or offers of employment in a discriminatory manner, or is designed to exclude Community nationals from employment positions.

iv) A worker who seeks employment in a foreign Member State shall receive the same assistance there as afforded to nationals by the employment offices of that State.

v) A worker who is a national of a Member State may not be treated differently from national workers by reason of his nationality in respect of conditions of employment, including remuneration and tenure.

vi) Spouses and dependants are entitled to accompany the worker to the place where he or she intends to exercise the right of free movement.

However, although Community countries have created the principle of the free movement of persons, Community law has not excluded the power of Member States to adopt measures enabling the national authorities to have an exact knowledge of population movements affecting their territory: *Watson* v *Belmann* [1976] ECR 1185.

d) *Rights of workers exercising the freedom of movement*

Council Directive 68/360 (1968) abolishes restrictions on the movement and residence of workers within the Community. Under this Directive, workers may exercise the freedom of movement on production of a valid identity card or passport.

Also, workers taking up employment in another Member State are entitled to a Residence Permit as proof of the right of residence: Article 4(2). This permit must be renewed unless justified reasons may be given for not doing so: Article 10.

A valid residence permit may not be withdrawn from a worker solely on the ground that he is no longer in employment due to illness or involuntary unemployment.

e) *Employment in the public service*

Article 48(4) exempts employment in the public sector from the scope of the free movement of workers. The Member States of the Community all vary from each other in their characterisation of public service. For the purposes of the application of this exemption, whether or not a position constitutes employment in the public service depends on whether or not:

'the posts in question are typical of the specific activities of the public service in so far as the exercise of powers conferred by public law and responsibilities for safeguarding the general interests of the State are vested in it': *EC Commission* v *Belgium (Re Public Service Employment)* [1980] ECR 3881.

Therefore, in order for this exemption to apply, it must be shown that the persons employed are charged with the exercise of powers conferred by public law or, alternatively, have been given responsibility for protecting the special interests of the state. See also *EC Commission* v *Italy (Re Public Service Employment)* [1987] ECR 2625.

f) *Derogations*

Article 48(3) limits the exercise of the free movement of workers on the grounds of public policy, public security and public health. Council Directive 64/221 (1964) creates rules to regulate the exercise of discretion conferred on Member States.

i) Public policy

Restrictions on the right of a Community worker to enter the territory of another Member State, to reside there, or to move around that state, cannot be imposed unless his or her presence or conduct constitutes a genuine and serious threat to public policy: *Rutili* v *Minister of the Interior* [1975] ECR 1219. If the conduct of a worker poses a threat to public policy, the reasons for this conclusion must be given to the worker in order to allow him or her decide whether or not such a judgment may be challenged.

This restriction applies not only to workers crossing frontiers, but may also allow a Member State to restrict the movements of a national within its own territory. In *R* v *Saunders* [1979] ECR 1129, the European Court held that the United Kingdom could lawfully require a British national to reside outside England and Wales for three years as a condition of a suspended sentence for theft.

Measures taken on the ground of public policy (as well as public security) shall be based exclusively on the conduct of the individual concerned and no other grounds. Further, previous criminal convictions are not in themselves sufficient grounds for the adoption of such measures: Article 3(2) Council Directive 64/221 (1964).

ii) Public security

The exception on the ground of public security implies that restrictions may be imposed on the free movement of persons for the purpose of securing the safety of the state and society in the face of violence, disturbances and threats to the peace, whether they emanate from within or outside the Member State.

iii) Public health

Restrictions on the movement of persons based on the ground of public health have been codified in Directive 64/221. This lists the only diseases and disabilities which justify refusing entry into a territory or a refusal to issue a residence permit. Diseases or disabilities occurring after a residence permit has been issued do not justify a refusal to renew the permit.

Diseases which are considered to constitute a danger to the pubic health include tuberculosis of the respiratory system, syphilis, and other infectious diseases or contagious parasitic diseases. Disabilities which constitute a threat to public health include drug addiction and profound mental disturbance.

g) *Rights of the family of a Community worker*

Under Article 10 of Council Regulation 1612/68 (1968), a worker is entitled to take his or her spouse, together with their dependants, to the country where the right of free movement is being exercised. In addition, the right to take up employment is extended to the family of the worker.

A number of other rights are granted to the family of a worker exercising the right of free movement:

i) The worker and his family are entitled to all the benefits and rights accorded to national workers in relation to housing matters.

ii) The children of the worker are entitled to education and vocational training as nationals of the Member State concerned.

iii) The children of Community workers are entitled to access to further education on the same basis as nationals. This right extends to grants for tertiary education: see *Brown* v *Secretary of State for Scotland* [1988] ECR 3205.

iv) Council Directive 77/486 (1977) provides for special free tuition to facilitate the initial reception of children into the new Member State, including training in the official languages of the state.

Council Directive 68/360 (1968) supplements these rights by requiring the abolition of restrictions on the movements and residence of workers and their families.

h) *Social security*

Article 51 of the EEC Treaty instructs the Council of Ministers to draw up legislation in the field of social security in order to facilitate the free movement of workers. In the pursuit of this objective, Community legislation should ensure two primary objectives:

i) aggregation of all periods of employment in which contributions had been made to social security funds; and

ii) payment of benefits to persons resident in the territories of Member States.

A substantial number of Community measures have been introduced in order to regulate the social security of migrant workers. Council Regulation 1408/71 (1971) applies to sickness benefit, maternity benefit, invalidity benefit, old age and survivor's benefits, workmen's compensation, occupational illness benefit, death grants, unemployment benefit and family benefit. However, the Regulation applies only to social security schemes and not public assistance benefits. This Regulation has been extended by Council Regulation 1390/81 (1981) to self-employed persons and their families.

i) *Freedom of establishment - EEC Treaty provisions*

Article 52 of the EEC Treaty provides that 'restrictions on the freedom of establishment of nationals of a Member State in the territory of another Member State shall be abolished by progressive stages'. The freedom of establishment is the right to take up and pursue activities as a self-employed person. The right of establishment also includes the right of Community nationals to participate in existing firms and businesses as the nationals of the host state.

Article 52 has been given direct effect insofar as it prohibits discrimination on the basis of nationality: *Reyners* v *Belgium* [1974] ECR 631. Thus Article 52 is intended to ensure that self-employed persons are treated in another Member State in the same way as nationals of that Member State. The rules regarding the freedom of establishment not only extend to the self-employed person, but also to his or her family.

Article 53 prohibits Member States from introducing new restrictions on the right of establishment, unless such restrictions are justified by other provisions of the Treaty. Article 54 provides the authority for the Council of Ministers to enact Community legislation to abolish the existing restrictions on the freedom of establishment within the Community.

j) *The freedom of establishment - secondary legislation*

The general programme for the implementation of the right of establishment programme requires considerable Community legislation to harmonise qualifications throughout the Community. Since the practice of most professions requires the possession of relevant qualifications, a failure to recognise equivalent qualifications obtained in one Member State can amount to an effective obstacle to the exercise of the freedom of establishment in another Member State.

Community legislation equating professional qualifications has been introduced on a profession-by-profession basis.

i) Lawyers

No Community legislation has yet entered into force regarding the mutual recognition of legal qualifications. However, the European Court has held that a Community national cannot be excluded from the legal profession of a Member State merely by virtue of the fact that he or she possesses a nationality other than that of the Member State in which the individual wishes to practice: *Reyners* v *Belgian State* [1974] ECR 631.

ii) Architects

Professional qualifications regarding architecture have been harmonised by Council Directive 85/384 (1985).

iii) Doctors

A number of measures have been passed by the Council to implement the freedom of establishment of doctors, including Council Directives 75/362, 75/363 and 86/457.

iv) Veterinary surgeons

Veterinary surgeons have a right to establishment by virtue of Council Directives 78/1026 and 78/1027.

All these Directives deal with the mutual recognition of formal qualifications to facilitate the effective exercise of the right of establishment. A number of other Directives have been adopted in relation to other professions under the single internal market programme.

9.3 Relevant cases

Kempf v *Staatssecretaris van Justitie* [1986] ECR 1741: A person who pursues part-time employment, and who receives supplementary benefits to his income, is still a worker for the purposes of the freedom of movement of workers.

EC Commission v *France* [1974] ECR 359: Article 48 of the EEC Treaty is capable of having direct effect.

Watson v *Belmann* [1976] ECR 1185: Member States still retain the prerogative of scrutinising the movements of foreign nationals despite the Community principle of free movement.

Rutili v *Minister of the Interior* [1975] ECR 1219: Definition of the concept of 'public policy' as contained in the exception to Article 48.

9.4 Relevant materials

F Jacob, 'The Free Movement of Persons Within the EEC' (1977) 30 Current Legal Problems, 123.

F Wooldridge, 'Free Movement of EEC Nationals: The Limitation Based on Public Policy and Public Security' (1977) 2 EL Rev 190.

D Edwards, 'Establishment and Services: An Analysis of the Insurance Cases' (1987) 12 EL Rev 231.

A Evans, 'Entry Formalities in the European Community' (1981) 6 EL Rev 3.

D Pickup, 'Reverse Discrimination and the Free Movement of Workers' (1986) 23 CMLR 135.

J Hardoll, 'Article 48 of the EEC Treaty and Non-National Access to Public Employment' (1988) 13 EL Rev 223.

9.5 Analysis of questions

The free movement of workers is a common subject for examination. Issues which frequently arise within this topic include the scope of the right itself, exceptions to the general rules, and the right of establishment. Although this topic is not particularly complex, students should be aware that questions from this area of the syllabus generally take the form of problem-type questions.

9.6 Questions

Question 1

The 'Today's Radical' is a right-wing extremist newspaper published weekly in the United Kingdom. Pierre, a French national, has been offered a position as a journalist with the newspaper and intends to accept this offer. Pierre has been widely associated with a radical European terrorist organisation, although he has never been prosecuted for any offence connected for this association or otherwise. The British government requests advice on its rights under Community law to prevent Pierre from entering the United Kingdom to accept this position. Advise the British government.

Question prepared by the Author
February 1991

General comment

A problem-type question requiring the application of the law to the facts of the question.

Skeleton solution

- Principle of the free movement of workers.
- Exceptions to the general rule.
- Rights of the government to prevent entry.
- Conclusions.

Suggested solution

For the purpose of the question, it is assumed that Pierre is to be employed by the newspaper rather than work for them as a freelance journalist (in which case Article 59 of the EEC Treaty would be relevant).

Pierre is entitled, by virtue of Article 48 of the EEC Treaty, which lays down the principle of the free movement of workers, to accept an offer of employment made from a potential employer in another Member State and to remain in that Member State for the purposes of that employment. Council Directive 68/380 also provides for the abolition of restrictions on the movement and residence of workers of Member States and their families.

Both Articles 48 of the EEC Treaty and Directive 68/380 have been declared by the European Court to have direct effect; see *Van Duyn* v *Home Office* (1974) and *Rutili* v *French Minister of the Interior* (1975). This means that any inconsistent provision of national law will not be applicable.

In accordance with Article 48(3) of the Treaty, Directive 68/360 places a duty upon Member States to extend the right of free movement to workers able to produce a valid identity card or passport, and confirmation of engagement from an employer or certificate of employment; Article 4, Directive 68/380. A residence permit is to be issued to the worker as proof of his right of residence.

Pierre may, however, be prevented from taking up employment in Britain on the grounds of the public policy proviso made under Article 48(3), which limits the right of entry in cases of public policy, public security and public health. In this instance, the British government may rely on the fact that Pierre intends to work for a radical magazine and that he has expressed sympathy with European terrorist organisations.

Article 3(1) of the Directive provides that the reasons for the exercise of the proviso must be based on the personal conduct of the individual concerned. This was confirmed in the case of *Bonsignore* v *Oberstadt-Direcktor of the City of Cologne* (1975), which also is authority for the proposition that the public policy provision, and its related exceptions to the principle of the free movement of workers, must be given a strict and narrow construction. Accordingly, the personal conduct that has taken place must be such that would lead the authorities to suppose that Pierre poses a present threat to public policy, unless his past conduct was of such a repugnant nature that it justified his departure without any evidence of possible future misbehaviour: *R* v *Bouchereau* (1977).

The British government would not be able to exclude Pierre from the United Kingdom merely on the basis that he is about to assume a position as a journalist with the magazine. Any attempt to do so would amount to discrimination between Community nationals and British nationals. Since British nationals are not prohibited from taking up such positions, Pierre could not be excluded from the United Kingdom because he wishes to assume a similar post.

As regards his past conduct, it is clear from two cases - *Addoui Case* (1982) and *Bouchereau Case* above - that the conduct of a foreign national may only be grounds for a refusal of entry if the Member State has seen fit to enact repressive measures to combat such conduct on the part of its own nationals. Further, while association with an organisation whose activities are contrary to the public good may justify exclusion, association must include participation in the activities of the organisation as well as identification with its aims or designs. An admission of sympathy for the cause of an organisation will not extend to association.

In addition, the British government is precluded from conducting an interrogation of Pierre by immigration officials at the port of entry. The European Court held in the *PIECK Case* (1980), that the public policy proviso was not a condition precedent to acquiring a right of entry and residence that justified frontier controls. It was merely a possibility where restrictions may be placed on the exercise of Treaty rights in individual cases.

The attention of the British government should also be drawn to the fact that Pierre would be entitled to challenge any exclusion decision in the national courts: see *Van Duyn* v *Home Office* above. The national court must decide whether or not the decision was made in accordance with Community law, and a reference to the European Court may be in order. Also, Pierre is entitled to the same legal remedies as are available to British nationals under Article 8 of Directive 68/360: *Santillo Case* (1980).

One final point is in order. The European Court has held that a person challenging a deportation order must be afforded the chance of lodging an appeal and thereby obtaining a stay of execution before the order is carried out: *Procureur du Roi* v *Royer* (1976). Therefore, Pierre would be entitled to remain in the United Kingdom for this purpose.

Question 2

In 1987, Sabena, a German national, accepted a position as a translator in a British bank in London. Over the course of the next three years, Sabena developed an addiction for cocaine. After a raid on her flat in London, the police recovered a small amount of cocaine and she was subsequently convicted for the unlawful possession of drugs. The Home Office has refused to renew Sabena's residence permit and have threatened her with deportation in the event that she does not leave the United Kingdom of her own free will.

Advise Sabena of her rights under Community law.

Question prepared by the Author
February 1991

General comment

A variation on the general theme of the free movement of workers.

Skeleton solution

- Right of free movement of workers.
- Exceptions on the grounds of public policy.
- Relevance of convictions.
- Right to challenge the decision to refuse renewal.

Suggested solution

Based on the presumption that Sabena is a 'worker' for Community purposes, she would normally be entitled to exercise the right of freedom to work in any Member State by virtue of her German nationality. This applies even if she works part-time so long as her work is not simply 'marginal': *Kempf* v *Staatssecretaris Van Justitie* (1987). Even although her residence permit has expired, it should be automatically renewable under Article 6(1) of Council Directive 68/360. However, Council

Directive 64/221 does allow a Member State to refuse to issue or renew a residence permit in certain circumstances, or to expel the holder of a residence permit on the grounds of public policy, public security or public health. This right is subject to the condition that such grounds are not invoked to serve economic ends: Article 2(2).

Article 3 of Directive 64/221 states that measures taken on grounds of public policy shall be based exclusively on the personal conduct of the individual involved. In this case, we shall assume that the refusal by the Home Office to renew the residence permit is based on criteria of public policy.

However, this article continues to the effect that previous criminal convictions do not, ipso facto, justify the taking of such measures. Thus, in *Bonsignore* v *Oberstadt-Direcktor for the City of Cologne* (1975), the European Court considered the case of an Italian worker in Germany who had been convicted and fined for the unlawful possession of a pistol. The plaintiff had accidentally shot another person and, upon conviction, was ordered to be deported by the German authorities. The Court held that exceptions to the principle of the free movement of workers had to be construed strictly. Deportation (which obviously prevents such freedom of movement for the person concerned), should be consequent on the behaviour of the individual, not for the purpose of deterring others from unlawful behaviour.

Although previous convictions alone will not automatically justify the deportation of a worker, such convictions may indicate a propensity to behave in a manner contrary to public policy or security. Thus, in *R* v *Bouchereau* (1977), a French worker who had been convicted of possessing dangerous drugs for the second time, was lawfully expelled from the United Kingdom. However, the European Court did point out that to justify expulsion, the threat to public safety must be genuine and serious: see also *Santillo* [1980] ECR 1585.

It is even possible that a worker can be refused admittance to a Member State, and therefore presumably expelled from such a state, even although he or she has not committed any offence, if the work in which they are engaged in the host state, although not unlawful, is regarded by the host state as being socially harmful and thus contrary to public policy: *Van Duyn* v *Home Office* (1975).

In the present case, Sabena can certainly argue that her conviction for the unlawful possession of cocaine is not sufficient to justify her expulsion from the United Kingdom. For example, she could claim that her drug problem was under control and she was undertaking drug rehabilitation. It could then be argued that her past drug problems do not indicate any harmful future propensity.

It should also be noted that even if Sabena has become a drug addict, this disability would not, by itself, justify her exclusion. The Annex to Directive 64/221 does indeed set out a list of diseases and disabilities including drug addiction, from which a Member State is entitled to protect its citizens by prohibiting entry to a worker from another Member State who is suffering from such a disease or disability. However, Article 4(2) of this Directive states that, where such diseases or disabilities occur in respect of a worker from another Member State after a residence permit has been obtained, such an eventuality will not justify a refusal to renew the permit or the expulsion of the worker affected by the disease or disability.

Clearly, therefore, Sabena will have grounds for challenging the Home Office's decision in the English courts. Also, in accordance with Article 9 of Regulation 64/221, except in the case of urgency, if there is no substantive right of appeal to a court, or where the appeal cannot have suspensory effect, the administrative authorities of the host state cannot expel a national of another Member State, or refuse to renew a residence permit, until those administrative authorities have sought an opinion from the 'competent authorities' of the host state, this body being independent of the administrative authorities and before which the person concerned must have an opportunity to argue their case as are allowed by the domestic law of the host state.

Question 3

To what extent is it true to say that once a person is qualified to practise law in one European Community country, he or she may practice law in any other European Community country?

University of London LLB Examination
(for External Students) European Community Law 1990 Q8

General comment

A popular question requiring consideration of the implications of the right of establishment for the legal profession.

Skeleton solution

- The complexities of the present legal position.
- The primary legislation.
- Case law.
- Proposed amendments.

Suggested solution

It is not yet possible to make a categorical statement that once a person is qualified to practise law in one Community Member State, he or she may practise law in another Member State. This lack of clarity is partially due to the uncertain scope of Article 52 of the EEC Treaty which establishes the right of establishment and Article 59 which regulates the right to provide services, which implies a more temporary arrangement. The European Court has, however, stressed the parallels between Articles 48 (free movement of workers), 52 and 59 and that the three Articles comprise an integrated whole: *Procureur de Roi* v *Royer* (1976).

Council Directive 77/249 has helped to clarify the matter. It is concerned with the recognition of the lawyer coming from another Member State as a lawyer, and to offer him the opportunity of acting as a lawyer in the host state. It is thus only concerned with the freedom to provide services (although it has been introduced as a result of

Articles 57 and 66 of the EEC Treaty) and has no effect on the right of establishment in a host state, with all the consequent benefits for the immigrant's family. This would require mutual recognition of qualifications which has not yet been achieved (in contrast see Directives 75/362 and 75/363 on the mutual recognition of medical qualifications).

A lawyer is permitted to practise in another Member State under the Directive but this freedom is subject to various conditions. First, under Article 4(1), activities of representing a client in legal proceedings or before public authorities in a Member State must be carried out under the conditions laid down for lawyers established in that state, but there are exceptions against requirements for a residence qualification and the necessity for registration with any organisational body. Article 5 of the Directive also permits supplementary conditions to be imposed on the foreign lawyer with respect to procedural details consequent to legal representation. Actual appearance before a foreign court is, however, likely to be hampered by linguistic difficulties. Second, when giving legal advice, certain basic rules of the host state are imposed on foreign lawyers in addition to the professional rules of the Member State of origin: Article 4(4). Third, the foreign lawyer can be excluded from making wills in the host country and can be refused the right to represent an employer if he is a salaried lawyer-employee: Article 6.

The effects of this Directive have been largely superseded by the development of a considerable body of jurisprudence by the Court which is intended to offer greater freedom to the foreign lawyer. In *Reyners* v *Belgian State* (1974), the leading case in this area, the plaintiff was a Dutch national resident in Belgium. He had been born in Belgium, educated there, and taken his Docteur en Droit Belge, only to be finally refused admission to the Belgian bar on the grounds of his Dutch nationality. The European Court held that the prohibition of discrimination contained in Article 52 of the EEC Treaty, concerned the right to establishment, was directly applicable as of the end of the transitional period, despite the opening words of the text of the Article. The Court expressed the view that the aim of Article 52 was intended to be facilitated by the Council of Ministers through the introduction of a legislative programme, but the direct effect of the provision was not made dependent on the initiation of such a programme.

The European Court went one stage further in *Thieffery* v *Paris Bar Council* (1977). That case showed that even in the absence of Directives under Article 57, recognition of foreign legal qualifications may be required under Article 52 which prohibits discrimination on the grounds of nationality. Thieffery, a Belgian national, held a Belgian law degree recognised by the University of Paris as equivalent to a French law degree. He also acquired the qualifying certificate for the profession of advocate, but the Paris Bar Council refused to allow him to undergo practical training on the ground that he did not possess a French law degree. The European Court held that such a refusal could amount to discrimination under Article 52 of the EEC Treaty.

The next case, *Ordre des Advocats* v *Klop* (1985) appears to put foreign lawyers in a better position than national lawyers. Article 52 of the EEC Treaty et seq were held by the European Court to preclude the denial to a national of another Member State the right to enter and to exercise the profession of advocate solely on the ground that he maintains chambers in another Member State (a national lawyer can only maintain one set of chambers within the national territory). The host state's rules of conduct, however, apply to the foreign lawyer providing they do not discriminate between the national and the foreign lawyer: *Gulleng* v *Ordre des Advocats* (1988).

Directly applicable rights derived from Article 52 secure the foreign lawyer a greater degree of freedom to practise, while dodging the pitfalls arising from rights derived from the Directive. Naturally, the derogations to Article 52 also apply to the freedom of establishment of lawyers. The 'official authority' exception in Article 55 was raised in the *Reyners Case*, above. The European Court, while tacitly acknowledging that the occasional exercise of judicial power by an advocate would amount to the exercise of an official authority, declared that this would not be the case with respect to the advocate's other responsibilities and so the part of the EEC Treaty relating to establishment was applicable. Certain functions of notaries public might fall within the ambit of Article 55.

Council Directive 89/48, which establishes a general system for the mutual recognition of higher education diplomas, was adopted by the Council of Ministers on 21 December 1988. By 1 January 1991, lawyers qualified in the United Kingdom and in the rest of the Community will, in principle, be able to practise anywhere in the Community, provided they have obtained a diploma following a minimum of at least three years university training, the completion of the relevant professional training and some relevant professional experience in the country of origin or host country.

The Directive permits derogations to this basic principle if there are major differences in the education and training of the migrant and the training received by people qualified in the intended host state. The legal profession is specifically identified as falling into this category so that the 'compensatory mechanism' provisions apply. In the case of lawyers, the Member State can choose whether the migrant lawyer should satisfy an adaptation period, extending to a maximum of three years duration, or should pass an aptitude test.

Question 4

Grunhild, who recently graduated from university in Germany with a degree in biochemistry, seeks employment in England. She receives an offer of employment with a public-sector company in Manchester, which is willing to employ her part-time on a monthly salary and also to offer her regular freelance work as a technical consultant. While she is considering this offer, she is informed by the British immigration authorities that she is not eligible for either the salaried employment or the freelance work, because:

a) United Kingdom legislation provides that the company in question may employ only British nationals;

b) the part-time salaried position is considered to be employment in the public service, as it involves frequent meetings with government officials in London;

c) according to the company's rules, the rate of pay for freelance consultants varies according to the gender of the consultant, with the daily rate for women being approximately 80 per cent of that for men, and the United Kingdom government does not wish to put pressure on the company to change its rules as a change in its salary structure might increase its operating costs.

Advise Grunhild as to her position under EEC law.

University of London LLB Examination
(for External Students) European Community Law 1989 Q7

General comment

Another problem-type question requiring the student to demonstrate knowledge of the principles behind the free movement of workers.

Skeleton solution

- Rights of part-time workers under Community law.
- Prohibitions on discrimination.
- Public service exception.
- Gender discrimination issue.

Suggested solution

For the purposes of the question, it is assumed that Grunhild is a citizen of Germany, and therefore a national of a Community country. Article 48 of the EEC Treaty establishes the right of free movement throughout the Community for the purpose of obtaining employment. In particular, Community workers are entitled to accept offers of employment actually made and to reside within a Member State for the purpose of exercising this right.

Whether or not Grunhild is a worker entitled to the right of free movement is a question of Community law. Grunhild has received an offer of part-time employment together with a supplementary offer of freelance work. A person employed part-time may qualify as a worker under Community law so long as he or she pursues an activity as an employed person and so long as that employment is both genuine and effective. In *Levin* v *Staatssecretaris van Justitie* (1982), the European Court held that the concept of worker must be interpreted in order to allow activities on a part-time basis to be included within its scope.

Further, even if Grunhild is paid less than at subsistence level, she would still qualify as a worker for the purposes of the right to free movement. The European Court has held that a person in genuine and effective part-time employment cannot be excluded from the sphere of application of Article 48 merely because the remuneration derived is below the minimum level of subsistence: see *Kempf* v *Staatssecretaris van Justitie* (1986).

As a worker under Community law, Grunhild is entitled to the rights conferred by Article 48, as supplemented by Community legislation. As Article 1 of Council

Regulation 1612/68 (1968) states, any national of a Member State may, irrespective of his or her place of residence, exercise the right to take up an activity as an employed person, and to pursue such activity in accordance with the provisions of the national law of that Member State.

However, the immigration authorities have suggested that national legislation provides that the company may only employ British nationals. Such a measure infringes two Community provisions. First, Article 48(2) of the EEC Treaty requires the abolition of any discrimination based on nationality between the workers of the Member States as regards remuneration and other conditions of employment. Further, this provision has been given direct effect by the European Court: *EC Commission* v *France* (1974). The absolute nature of this prohibition has the effect of rendering inapplicable legislation which impedes equal access to employment to the nationals of all Member States.

Second, Article 3 of Council Regulation 1612/68 declares that any national law which excludes Community nationals from applying for positions within the Member State is inapplicable if it discriminates between nationals and foreign Community workers. This prohibition applies particularly to laws which restrict the number or percentage of foreign nationals in any company or firm.

However, the company offering the position to Grunhild functions in the public sector. Article 48(1) expressly excluded employment in the public service from the scope of the freedom of movement of workers. The question which arises is whether employment within this company constitutes employment in the public sector.

Although there is no definition of 'public service' either in the EEC Treaty or in secondary legislation, the European Court has held that whether or not a position is within the public sector depends on whether the post in question is typical of the specific activities of the public service and involves either the exercise of the powers conferred by public law or responsibility for safeguarding the general interests of the state: *EC Commission* v *Belgium* (1980).

The immigration officials have asserted that the position falls within the public sector because it involves frequent meetings with government officials. However, this does not imply that the position which was offered to Grunhild involved the exercise of powers conferred by public law. This is extremely unlikely considering that Grunhild is a biochemist. Equally, it seems unlikely that the post entails a responsibility for safeguarding the interests of the state. Such an allegation could only be sustained if the research in which Grunhild was about to engage was of a secret nature.

In these circumstances, it is extremely unlikely that the British authorities could successfully claim that the position offered to Grunhild was exempt from the scope of Article 48 by virtue of the fact that it constituted employment in the public service.

Nor could the fact that the company indulges in discrimination justify the refusal of the British authorities to grant Grunhild a Residence Permit. In fact such practices constitute a violation of Article 119 of the EEC Treaty which states the principle that men and women should receive equal pay for equal work. Grunhild would therefore be able to claim that she was a victim of gender discrimination on the basis that Article 119 of the EEC Treaty has direct effect and Community secondary legislation has created additional rights.

The United Kingdom could also be guilty of failing to observe its obligations under Article 5 of the EEC Treaty by allowing a public sector company to indulge in discrimination. The European Court has consistently upheld the direct effect of Article 119 and the failure on the part of the British government to implement Community legislation preventing such discrimination may render the United Kingdom liable. In this situation, the appropriate course of action is for the European Commission to bring proceedings against the United Kingdom before the European Court for failing to observe its Community obligations.

Grunhild is also entitled to exercise the right of establishment. The right of establishment is a separate right from the right to free movement. It applies to self-employed persons establishing businesses in another Member State. The offer of freelance work could allow Grunhild to claim that she is a self-employed person and entitled to the right of establishment.

If such a claim was successful, Grunhild could rely on Article 52(2) of the EEC Treaty to establish her right to take up and pursue activities as a self-employed person. The same provision requires Member States to extend the same treatment to foreign community nationals as is given to their own nationals as regards conditions of employment. Not only are Member States obliged to abolish existing discriminatory provisions, but under Article 53, Member States may no longer introduce new restrictions on the exercise of the right of establishment by foreign Community nationals. The British legislation clearly prevents Grunhild from exercising her right of establishment, and is therefore also challengeable on that basis. Consequently, it appears that Grunhild would be successful in challenging these restrictions on the employment of Community nationals, either on the basis of the right of free movement or because they infringe the right of establishment.

10 FREEDOM TO PROVIDE SERVICES

10.1 Introduction

The freedom to provide services allows individuals and companies to move throughout the Community and, at least in theory, to supply their services without being prevented from doing so by national legislation or administrative practices. This requires the abolition of the numerous technical barriers to foreign suppliers of services. In particular, the removal of regulatory mechanisms which require suppliers of services to maintain a presence in a Member State is necessary, along with the harmonisation of company law throughout the Community and the creation of rules to regulate public procurement.

10.2 Key points

a) *The scope of the freedom to supply services*

Article 59 of the EEC Treaty requires Member States to progressively abolish restrictions on the freedom to provide services in respect of suppliers who are established in a State of the Community other than that of the person for whom the services are intended.

Services are deemed to include activities of an industrial character, activities of a commercial character, the services of craftsmen, and the supply of professional services.

Article 63 of the EEC Treaty confers upon the Council of Ministers, acting on the proposals the Commission, authority to enact Community legislation to achieve the abolition of existing restrictions on the freedom to provide services within the Community. Substantial Community legislation has been passed to achieve the harmonisation of the national rules governing the supply of services. This legislation has been supplemented by a number of important decisions of the European Court.

b) *The right to receive services*

Although the EEC Treaty contains no express right, the European Court has held that Article 59 also entails the right to receive services. Thus, the freedom to provide services includes the freedom of a recipient of services to go to another Member State in order to receive a service: *Luisi and Crabone* v *Ministero del Tesoro* [1984] ECR 377. This right may be exercised without obstruction from restrictions based on discrimination between domestic and foreign recipients.

The right to receive services has important ramifications, particularly as regards the rights of tourists. If Community law guarantees a person the freedom to enter another Member State for the purposes of receiving services, this right must be exercised in accordance with Article 7 of the EEC Treaty which prohibits discrimination on the basis of nationality. Recipients of services are therefore entitled to the full protection of the law of the Member States, including the right to compensation in the event of a criminal assault: *Cowan* v *Tresor Public* [1990] 2 CMLR 613.

Procedural safeguards for non-residents are, however, permitted for the administration of justice in certain circumstances. Thus a rule requiring a non-resident plaintiff to lodge security for costs as a condition for continuing an action was held to be justifiable discrimination by the European Court on the ground that the rule was designed to allow the enforcement of judicial orders: *Berkeley Administration Inc* v *Arden McClelland* [1990] 2 CMLR 116.

c) *Community legislation implementing free movement of services*

The Community has adopted the instrument of Community Directives for achieving the establishment of the free movement of services. Since the purpose of these directives is to harmonise national legislation, these measures have been passed on an activity-by-activity basis. The aim is to eliminate all national measures causing discrimination between national suppliers of services and foreign Community suppliers.

The most common national restriction on the free movement of services is the requirement that the supplier must be resident within the Member State in order to lawfully provide a service. Generally, this requirement is justified on the basis of the needing to regulate certain services, such as banking, insurance, investment and telecommunications.

The European Court has taken the view that Article 59 has direct effect and abolishes all discrimination against a person providing a service by reason of his or her nationality or the fact that he or she is resident in another Member State, although exceptions to this rule do exist: *Maria van Binsbergen* v *Bedrijfsvereniging voor de Metaalnijverheid* [1974] ECR 1299. A requirement of residence is not, however, incompatible with the EEC Treaty where it has as its purpose 'the application of professional rules justified by the general good'.

Rules relating to the organisation, qualifications, professional ethics, supervision or liability of suppliers of services may therefore be justified where the person who is supplying the services would escape from the ambit of these rules by being established in another Member State. But, the requirement of residence in the territory of the Member State where the service is provided can only be allowed as an exception where the Member State is unable to apply other, less restrictive, measures to ensure respect for these rules: *Gerardus Coenen* v *Sociaal Economische Raad* [1975] ECR 1547.

d) *Community regulation of the supervisory powers of Member States*

While the European Court has recognised the abilities of Member States to supervise certain commercial activities for the public interest, such supervision must be administered in a non-discriminatory manner. Article 59 has been held to abolish all discrimination against the person providing the service by reason of his or her nationality or place of residence. Therefore, a Member State may not impose more onerous obligations on foreign suppliers of services than on national suppliers. Thus, the issue of a licence or supervision by competent authorities must be made available to both foreign and domestic suppliers of services on an equal basis: *Ministere Public* v *Waesmael* [1979] ECR 35; *Alfred John Webb* [1981] ECR 3305.

Restrictions based, directly or indirectly, on discrimination between foreign and domestic suppliers of services will rarely be upheld by the European Court. Further, restrictions of an administrative nature cannot justify any derogation from the principle of the free movement of services, since such restrictions prevent the exercise of one of the fundamental freedoms of the EEC Treaty: *EC Commission* v *Germany (Re Regulation of the Insurance Sector)* [1987] 2 CMLR 69.

e) *Non-discriminatory access to public procurement*

Public procurement is the process through which national governmental agencies such as the central government, or local authorities, place contracts for the supply of goods or services. The Department of Trade and Industry estimates that over 15 per cent of the gross domestic product of each Member State of the Community consists of purchases of goods and services by governments and associated bodies and agencies. If these contracts were excluded from the scope of the right to supply services throughout the Community, a serious limitation would be placed on the exercise of this right.

The Community has adopted a number of Directives to provide access to public procurement contracts by Community suppliers of services not resident in the Member State where the services are to be performed. These rules vary according to whether the contract relates to public supply contracts or public work contracts:

i) Public supply contracts: These relate to the provision of goods for the use of governmental organs and are regulated by Council Directive 77/62 (1977), as amended by Council Directive 80/767 (1980) and Council Directive 88/295 (1980).

ii) Public works contracts: These are contracts relating to the construction of buildings and premise and are regulated by Council Directive 71/305 (1971), as amended by Council Directive 89/440 (1989).

A number of additional proposed Directives have been drafted by the European Commission in order to achieve the objective of the internal market programme. The proposed Community legislation aims to liberalise public procurement to the same extent as the supply of goods, and the legislation is scheduled for implementation in 1992.

f) *Harmonisation of company law*

One of the principal restrictions on the freedom to provide services is the requirement that a supplier must establish a legal presence, generally in the form of an incorporated body, prior to engaging in the supply of services. The harmonisation of company law has therefore been assumed as a primary goal for the achievement of the free movement of services as well as the freedom of establishment.

According to Article 66 of the EEC Treaty, companies formed in accordance with the law of a Member State and having their registered office, central administration or principal place of business within the Community shall be treated in the same way as natural persons who are nationals of Member States. While in theory this principle seems simple enough, in practice companies are creatures of the legislation of Member States and are subject to different rights and duties in different states of incorporation. It is difficult to see how a company formed under British law could move its operations to France and still be able to exercise its legal rights and duties under UK law. Rights and duties of companies are, on the whole, non-transferable and companies shifting operations would generally be required to reform under the law of the state to which they are relocating.

In order to approximate the company laws of the Member States for the purpose of harmonising the rights and obligations of companies throughout the Community, a convention, together with a number of regulations and directives has been adopted.

The Convention on the Mutual Recognition of Companies and Bodies Corporate 1968 was negotiated to give effect to the mutual recognition of companies but, as yet, it has not entered force. In essence it provides that companies formed under the law of one contracting party shall be recognised in another as having the capacity accorded to them by the law under which they were formed, subject to certain derogations.

In addition, a considerable number of directives have been adopted to harmonise company law throughout the Community:

i) Council Directive 68/151 (1968): Requires companies operating in the Community to disclose certain information in the annual accounts.

ii) Council Directive 77/91 (1977): Concerns the formation and maintenance of capital.

iii) Council Directive 78/855 (1978): Relates to mergers between companies incorporated in the same Member State.

iv) Council Directive 78/660 (1978): Regulates the contents of the annual accounts of public and private companies.

v) Council Directive 83/349 (1983): The presentation of consolidated accounts.

vi) Council Directive 84/253 (1984): Deals with the professional qualifications of statutory auditors.

vii) Council Directive 88/627 (1988): Specifies the information which must be published when a major holding in a listed company is acquired.

Each of these Directives requires national legislation to incorporate them into the domestic laws of the individual Member States.

g) *The European Company Statute*

The Council of Ministers has also enacted Council Regulation 268/89 (1989), the European Company Statute. The purpose of this legislation is to allow companies to establish an incorporated body which has identical rights and duties in all Member States.

At the moment, the right to incorporate a European company is limited to three situations:

i) Two or more public limited companies may form a European company (known by the initial SE for the French acronym) by merging if at least two of them have their central administrations in different Member States;

ii) Two or more public limited companies having their offices in at least two different Member States may create a European company by forming a holding company;

iii) Under a similar geographical criteria, two or more public limited companies may form a European company by creating a joint subsidiary.

Only companies already incorporated in the Community can form a European company, but this right is also extended to European subsidiaries of third country parent companies.

The main benefit of a European company is that such companies are allowed to provide services in all Community countries.

h) *Free movement of capital*

Article 67 of the EEC Treaty instructs the Member States to progressively abolish all restrictions on the movement of capital between Member States, but only to the extent necessary to ensure the proper functioning of the common market. This provision is designed to remove any discriminatory barriers to the movement of capital which might inhibit freedom to invest capital, particularly for the purpose of providing services.

The free movement of capital is less developed that the other freedoms (free movement of goods, free movement of workers, freedom of establishment and freedom to provide services). Article 67 does not have direct effect and therefore cannot be relied upon by individuals to establish directly enforceable rights: *Casati* [1981] ECR 2595. The European Court has observed that, although Article 67 is considered one of the four fundamental freedoms, its function is closely linked with the economic and monetary policies of the Member States. Since Community cooperation in these fields, particularly monetary union, has been less spectacular than in other areas, the provision cannot, at the moment, be given direct effect.

At present, only the United Kingdom, Germany, the Netherlands, Denmark and France have abolished all exchange controls on the movement of capital. Belgium and Luxembourg maintain no exchange controls other than those used to distinguish current account transactions from capital account transactions. Other Member States maintain various degrees of exchange control.

In fulfilment of the internal market programme, a Council Directive on Capital Movements was adopted in June 1988 and applies to most Member States from 1 July 1990. However, Spain, Ireland, Greece and Portugal have been given extensions until 31 December 1992, to complete the transition.

The objective of the Directive is the liberalisation of capital movements by eliminating exchange controls. No limits will be placed on the amount of capital transferred between Member States after the transition period. All restrictions on the actual transfer of capital are to be abolished, as are all measures which limit the carrying out of underlying transactions (such as trade in goods or the payment of services).

Member States faced with economic problems may be allowed to re-impose restrictions on the movement of capital in exceptional circumstances such as the short-term movement of capital on an exceptional scale, causing disruption of monetary and exchange rate policies.

Member States are also urged to endeavour to attain the same degree of liberalisation in their transactions with third countries as in their transactions with other Member States.

10.3 Relevant cases

Binsbergen v *Bedrijfsvereniging voor de Metaalnijverheid* [1974] ECR 1299: Scope of the right of Member States to restrict the supply of services to those resident within the territory of the Member State.

EC Commission v *Germany [Re Regulation of the Insurance Sector]* [1987] 2 CMLR 69: Considerations of an administrative nature cannot justify derogations from the application of Article 59.

The Queen v *HM Treasury and Commissions of Inland Revenue, ex parte Daily Mail and General Trust plc* [1988] 3 CMLR 713: Neither Article 52 nor 58 of the EEC

Treaty confer rights on a company incorporated in one Member State to transfer its central management and control to another Member State without re-incorporating.

Casati [1981] ECR 2595: Article 67 of the EEC Treaty relating to the free movement of capital does not have direct effect.

10.4 Relevant materials

D Edward, 'Establishment and Services: An Analysis of the Insurance Cases' (1987) 12 EL Rev 231.

L Gormley, 'Public Works Contracts and Freedom to Supply Services' (1983) 133 NLJ 533.

R Hodgin, 'Case Law of the Court of Justice' (1987) 24 CML Rev 273.

10.5 Analysis of questions

The free movement of services is an area of the syllabus which incorporates an extensive number of seemingly divergent subjects. Students must acquaint themselves thoroughly with all aspects of this topic before attempting a question relating to the free movement of services. Among the more popular areas with examiners are the harmonisation of company law, the legal effect of Article 59 and the problem of discrimination between domestic and Community suppliers of services.

10.6 Questions

Question 1

Michelle is a British national. She travels to France as a tourist and is mugged by a gang of French youths. Her passport and money are stolen and her holiday is ruined. She discovers that in France there exists a criminal injuries compensation scheme, but is shocked to discover that, as a non-French national, she is not entitled to recover any financial damages from the scheme. Advise Michelle.

University of Glasgow LLB Examination
1989 Q9

General comment

A problem-type question requiring the application of Community law to a set of hypothetical facts.

Skeleton solution

- Limitations on the rights of individuals under the free movement of workers principle.
- The right to supply services and the right to receive services.
- Decision of the Court of Justice in *Cowan*.
- Limitations of this decision.

Suggested solution

Article 7 of the EEC Treaty establishes the general principle that any discrimination on the grounds of nationality shall be prohibited, but this prohibition is expressly restricted to those subjects which fall within the scope of the Treaty itself. In other words, the prohibition on discrimination does not apply by virtue of the fact that a person is a Community national, but only if the discrimination is perpetrated against an individual exercising his or her rights under Community law.

The principle of non-discrimination is also expressly reformulated in the Treaty provisions regulating the free movement of workers where a positive obligation is placed on Member State to eradicate this form of discrimination. But, the right to non-discriminatory treatment essentially applies to persons as factors of production and not individuals per se. Thus, nationals of Member States are entitled to the same degree of employment protection as nationals, the same conditions of employment as well as the same social and tax advantages: *Wurttembergische Milchverwertung-Sudmilch AG* v *Salvatore Ugliola* (1969). Further, this principle has been extended to the provision of further education on a non-discriminatory basis: *Blaizot* v *University of Liège* (1989).

Notwithstanding the scope of these rights, migrant workers are not, however, entitled to the benefits which nationality confers, such as voting rights in governmental elections or to stand for election. The fact that Member States have opened their national territory to the migration of workers within the Community does not mean that they are obliged to extend the benefits of citizenship to migrant workers. In fact, the European Court has expressly held that Member States continue to exercise their powers to regulate the movement of foreign nationals: *Watson* v *Belmann* (1976).

Since the principle of the free movement of workers would not confer any rights on Michelle in her circumstances, the alternative is to seek redress through the application of Article 59 which establishes the right to provide services. The European Court has, in the past, held that the right to provide services also implies the right to receive services: *Luisi and Carbone* v *Ministero del Tesoro* (1984). Thus, consumers are entitled to receive services from suppliers of services and, in the exercise of this right, the principle of non-discrimination on the basis of nationality prohibits discrimination between foreign and domestic consumers.

Since tourists are recipients of services, Michelle can claim that, in exercising her right to receive services in France, she is entitled to protection from the French legal system on a non-discriminatory basis. The freedom to travel to receive services therefore implies that the tourist is entitled to the same protection of the law as nationals of that Member State.

The European Court elaborated on the doctrine of non-discrimination as it applies to recipients of services in *Cowan* v *Tresor Public* (1990). This case involved a British national who, while visiting his son in Paris, was assaulted and robbed outside a Metro station by a number of assailants, thereby sustaining severe injuries. The assailants were never apprehended and as a result a claim was initiated for compensation under the appropriate provision of the French Penal Code. This provision, however, specified that victims of violent attacks must either be French nationals or holders of a French identity card in order to claim compensation. The claimant was therefore disqualified from making a claim.

An action was brought in the French Commission D'Indemnisation Des Victims D'Infractions (the equivalent of the Compensation Board for Victims of Crime) in order to review this decision. The Commission referred the matter to the European Court for a preliminary ruling on the question of whether foreign nationals of Member States are entitled to claim compensation for criminal injuries.

The European Court held that the non-discrimination provisions of the Treaty of Rome extend to the free movement of services and in particular the freedom to receive services. Since the victim was a tourist, and thereby a recipient of services in France, the Court held that that he was entitled to protection from harm, and compensation in the event of an infraction, on the same basis as nationals.

Since it is virtually impossible for a foreign national to enter another country without taking advantage of local services, this decision extends the protection of the law of each Member State to nationals of other states. Procedural safeguards for non-residents are, however, permitted in certain circumstances.

Michelle would therefore be entitled to make a claim for compensation before the appropriate French compensation, and would be entitled to any remedy available to a French national. Whether or not such compensation extends to financial damage and not merely physical injury depends on the terms of the French Penal Code itself.

Question 2

Wren Construction plc has recently become aware of the existence of an advertisement soliciting tenders for the construction of a local town hall outside Paris. In addition, the advertisement also tenders a contract for the supply of office furniture after the completion of the construction project. Snug Bug, a British subsidiary of Wren Construction, manufactures office equipment. The director of Wren Construction seeks your advice on the following points:

a) What rights does Community law confer on Wren Construction and Snug Bug if they decide to tender for these contracts?

b) Can the French local authority responsible for the construction of the building discriminate in favour of French contractors? and

c) What remedies are available to Wren Construction and Snug Bug in the event that the contracts are awarded contrary to Community law.

Advise Wren Construction and Snug Bug on their rights under Community law.

Question prepared by the Author
February 1991

General comment

Another problem-type question, this time dealing with the complexities of public procurement.

Skeleton solution

- The Community Directives on public works contracts.
- The Community Directives on public supply contracts.
- Principles behind these instruments of Community law.

Suggested solution

The rules relating to public procurement vary according to whether the contract relates to public supply contracts or public works contracts.

Public supply contracts relate to the provision of goods for the use of governmental organs and are regulated by the Directive of 1977 on Public Procurement (77/62), as amended by Directive 80/767 (1980) and Directive 88/295 (1988). Public works contracts are regulated by Council Directive 71/305 (1971), as amended by Council Directive 89/440 (1989). These are contracts relating to offers for construction of buildings and premises.

The Directives for the public procurement of goods and services all have the same objective: the gradual elimination of discrimination among suppliers for governmental agencies. Three common themes run throughout this legislation: transparency, increasing the scope of applications and compliance.

Supply contracts for governmental bodies must be published in the appropriate section of the Official Journal. Such contracts must refer to European standards which avoids the possibility of introducing discriminating national standards.

Sectors which were formerly excluded from the ambit of earlier Community procurement requirements are opened up to foreign tendering, including water, energy, transport, and for supplies, telecommunications. Proposals before the European Parliament would further reduce excluded sectors.

In addition, a complaints procedures have been established in order to provide remedies against public bodies discriminating in favour of local suppliers. An Enforcement Directive (Council Directive 89/665 (1989)) has been adopted to ensure the proper compliance of these requirements. This permits unsuccessful applicants to petition the Commission to investigate a matter and also provides for the review procedure in local courts ultimately culminating in compensation for parties which have been unlawfully discriminated against.

The contract which Wren Construction seeks to tender for is a public works contract. Council Directive 71/305, as amended, requires governmental agencies to tender such contracts to Community suppliers of services when two conditions are satisfied: the government agency falls within the scope of the Directive; and the contract is valued over the minimum required.

The Directive applies to all State, regional and local, authorities governed by public law. A body established by public body means any body established for the specific purpose of meeting the needs of the general public and not having an industrial or commercial character. A list of bodies to which the Directive applies forms Annex I to the Directive. For present purposes, it can be assumed that the construction of the local town hall is a function of either the local or regional government, both of which fall within the scope of the Directive.

The second condition relates to the value of the contract. As amended, the threshold for the public tendering of works contracts has been raised to 5 million ECU. Such contracts have to be advertised in the Official Journal for tender by any supplier from any Member State. All the legislation required to implement this scheme has been passed.

If these two conditions are satisfied, the substantive provisions of Directive 89/440 are applicable to the contract. A specific procedure must be followed for the tendering of the contract. First, the contract must be advertised in the Official Journal of the Community. Second, any supplier who submits an offer which is rejected must be informed of the reasons why the offer was rejected. Third, a number of criteria are established for the award of the contract. An acceptance by the government agency must be on the basis of the lowest price or, the most economically advantageous tender. In determining the most economically advantageous tender, the government agency is required to consider a number of criteria including price, period of completion, running costs, profitability and technical merit.

Aggregation rules are also specified which prevent governmental agencies from breaking down contracts into lesser amounts in order to fall below the thresholds. In particular, these rules concentrate on renewal contracts and sub-divided contracts. By dividing public works contracts, the governmental authorities may be able to create a number of individual contracts which fall below the five million ECU threshold for tendering public supply contracts.

The contract for the supply of office furniture which is sought by Snug Bug is also subject to Community legislation, and in particular Council Directive 77/62. Again this Directive is applicable only to certain governmental agencies and according to minimum price thresholds. Again the Directive is applicable to government agencies regulated by Annex I to the Directive, which would again include the local or regional authorities in this case.

However, in this case, two thresholds are applicable. A minimum threshold of 200,000 ECU is specified for supply contracts subject only to the Community rules, while a threshold of 130,000 ECU is required for supply contracts also subject to the rules embodied in the GATT Government Procurement Code. These limits are, however, presently being revised to take into account inflation.

Again, if a public supply contract fulfils these criteria, a number of obligations must be satisfied by the tendering authority. First, the contract must be published. Second, specifications must be given in European standards where possible. Third, the same criteria for awarding contracts must be observed as was the case in public works contracts.

The aim of these Directives is to eliminate discrimination between domestic and other Community suppliers of services. Therefore, if the contracts fall within the scope of these Directives, the governmental authorities or agencies cannot indulge in discrimination against Wren Construction or Snug Bug.

These Directives also establish complaints procedures which unsuccessful tenderers can utilise in order to obtain redress in the event that discrimination has been perpetrated. However, in general, remedies will be sought through national courts, according to national standards and procedures, and this gives rise to the problem that complete harmonisation in this field has not be achieved.

As regards the supply of services other than for the performance of public works contracts, the Community has failed to adopt any concrete measures. However, proposed Community legislation aims to liberalise this aspect of public procurement to the same extent as the supply of goods, and the legislation is scheduled for adoption in 1991 and implementation in 1992. However, it is extremely likely that forthcoming community legislation on services will be similar to that for the supply of goods.

Question 3

The Commission has embarked on an extensive programme of harmonisation of company law and many Directives it has proposed have been adopted. However, proposals for granting employees certain rights to participate in the corporate decision-making process is proving to be one of the stumbling blocks on the way to complete harmonisation. Discuss.

University of Glasgow LLB Examination
1989 Q4

General comment

A narrative question requiring an answer outlining the main features of the Community company law harmonisation programme.

Skeleton solution

- The harmonisation programme.
- Directives on company law.
- The proposed Fifth Directive.
- British objections to the Fifth Directive.

Suggested solution

The field of company law is no stranger to Community law. However, since in the past Community law relating to companies has taken the form of Directives which have been incorporated into the United Kingdom by domestic legislation, this has not been a completely visible phenomenon. The First EC Directive of 1968 (68/151) required that companies operating within the Community were obliged to disclose certain information in the annual accounts and was implemented in the Companies Act 1980 and the Companies Act 1985.

The Second Directive of 1976 (77/91) was also implemented by this legislation and in fact to date a total of nine directives have been adopted [Third Directive of 1978 (78/855); Fourth Directive of 1978 (78/660); Sixth Directive of 1982 (82/891); Seventh Directive of 1983 (83/349); Eighth Directive of 1984 (84/253); Eleventh Directive of 1989 (89/528); and Twelfth Directive of 1989 (89/101)].

In addition two directives have been adopted in relation to the banking industry [Bank Branches Directive of 1989 (89/117); Bank Accounts Directive of 1986 (86/635)].

While these directives have been mainly confined to information and data in the accounts of public bodies, the remaining directives which have been proposed are not so restrictive and in fact, if adopted, would signal a radical transformation in existing UK company law.

The Fifth Directive of 1983 (83/185) forms the core of the proposed harmonisation of European company law and, at this moment, the proposals are under discussion at the Second Reading Stage of the Council Working Group. As it stands at present, this tentative Directive proposes to introduce a two-tier management structure for companies, a scheme which is already familiar to most continental Member States. Instead of a company being under the direction of one managing body - the Board of Directors - there would be two different bodies: the Management Organ (or Executive Organ) which would make the management decisions of the corporation; and the Supervisory Organ, which would supervise the actions of the Management Organ.

The Supervisory Organ would have the power to authorise certain actions by the Management Organ including transfers of business, mergers, closures and structural changes and it would be entitled to receive a written report of the company's affairs every three months. It would have exclusive power to appoint and dismiss members of the Management Organ.

In relation to the appointment and dismissal of members of the Supervisory Organ, a number of alternative procedures would be possible where the company has more than 1,000 employees: appointment and dismissal could be carried out by the shareholders and employees, by the shareholders acting alone, or by co-option (which, in some cases, would be subject to veto by employees).

In the face of British opposition to this proposal, a short-term concession has been made. Where this two-tier structure would be impractical to enforce then, as a short term measure, a single-tier structure based on the Management Organ could be adopted provided that different members undertake distinct management and supervisory roles.

The British government also opposes this harmonised company structure on a number of other grounds. First, the participation of workers in the management of companies, while common in continental companies, is alien to the British conception of management within limited liability companies.

Second, the Directive requires detailed disclosure of information in the minutes of meetings held at the management level.

Third, in order to secure the independence of auditors, company accounts can only be audited by the same accounting firm after a certain period of time has elapsed. Auditors cannot be retained for periods longer than one year unless the required period has elapsed since the company inspected the accounts.

As a result of this opposition, it is unlikely that the harmonised community company legislation will be passed by 31 December 1992. A similar fate also awaits the Ninth Directive of 1984 which relates to the structure of companies containing a plc as a subsidiary and the Tenth Directive which relates to mergers between plcs in different Member States.

Question 4

Describe the formation, structure and main features of a European Company as incorporated under the European Company Statute 1989.

Question prepared by the Author
February 1991

General comment

A difficult question requiring detailed knowledge of recent developments within the Community company law programme.

Skeleton solution

- The European Company Statute.
- Methods of forming a European Company.
- Features of a European Company.
- Problems over the constitutional basis of the Statute.

Suggested solution

As an immediate consequence of the absence of consensus over harmonisation, the Council of Ministers has concentrated on the creation of the European Company Statute as a substitute for Community-wide unanimity on harmonising legislation. The intention was to create a limited liability company which would be regulated by Community law and which would be registered in one Member State and also a central agency. The draft statute has recently been completed and takes the form of proposed Council Regulation 268/89 (1989).

No direct right to incorporate a European company has been established in a similar manner as is possible under national legislation. European companies must be formed by the coming together of existing companies in different Member States. This can take three forms.

First, two or more public limited companies may form a European company by merging if at least two of them have their central administrations in different Member States. Second, two or more public limited companies having their offices in at least two in different Member States may create a European company by forming a holding company. Third, under similar geographical criteria, two or more public limited companies may form a plc by forming a joint subsidiary.

Consequently, only companies already incorporated can form a European company, but this right is also extended to European subsidiaries of third-country parent companies.

A European company, which could have its registered office in any Member State would have a number of distinctive features. The structure of the company would conform to the proposed structure under the harmonisation legislation, ie a two-tier management structure. Also employees would be actively involved in the decision-making process, particularly in relation to decisions having a direct effect on employment.

A European company has no constraints on the form of its shares. Such a company could raise capital in any Member State, and in the form of equities, shares or debentures.

The profits of permanent establishment of a European company in any Member State would be taxable in that Member State alone.

Finally, a European company could be converted into a limited company under the law of the Member State in which effective management was located.

This company structure is based on the Dutch and German models of limited liability, particularly in relation to worker-participation.

However, the constitutional basis for the creation of the European company statute is questioned by the British delegates to the Council. Article 235 of the EEC Treaty provides that, if action is necessary to achieve one of the objectives of the Common Market, and the Treaty has not provided the necessary powers, the Council may adopt the appropriate course of action acting unanimously. The United Kingdom believes that this is the appropriate course of action for the adoption of the Statute.

The Commission takes a different view. Acting under the authority of Articles 100A and Article 54, a Regulation and a Directive respectively have been proposed for the creation of the Statute. Adoption of these measures as part of the Single European Act package requires merely a qualified majority. Consequently, until the constitutional issue is settled and the United Kingdom agrees to the proposal, complete implementation of the Statute will be delayed.

11 EUROPEAN COMPETITION LAW - ARTICLE 85 EEC TREATY

11.1 Introduction

Articles 85 and 86 of the EEC Treaty are the pillars of the Community competition policy. Each of these articles addresses different forms of anti-competitive behaviour. Article 85 (the subject of this chapter) prohibits agreements and concerted practices among private commercial bodies if they affect trade between Member States and distort, prevent or restrict competition. Article 86 (the subject of the next chapter) prohibits commercial practices by one or more enterprises where such practices amount to an abuse of a dominant position with the Community. These two provisions therefore seek to achieve separate objectives. Article 85 attempts to eradicate unfair commercial practices which result from collaboration between enterprises while Article 86 strikes at companies taking advantage of dominant or monopoly positions in the market-place.

11.2 Key points

a) *The subjects of European Community law*

Both Articles 85 and 86 apply to 'undertakings' although this term is not expressly defined. The European Court has, however, defined an undertaking as:

'a single organisation of personal, tangible and intangible elements, attached to an autonomous legal entity and pursuing a long-term economic aim': *Mannesmann* v *High Authority* [1962] ECR 357.

This definition embraces all natural and legal persons engaged in commercial activities, whether profit-making or otherwise. The fact that an entity is a non profit-making organisation is irrelevant for the purpose of identifying an undertaking: *Heintz van Landewyck Sarl* v *EC Commission* [1980] ECR 3125. The critical characteristic is whether or not the entity is engaged in economic or commercial activities.

The application of European competition law is not restricted to undertakings located within the Community, but extends to undertakings whose registered offices are situated outside the Community: ***Beguelin* v *GL Imports Export*** [1971] ECR 949. This is because European competition law is not concerned with the behaviour of entities but rather the effects of such behaviour on the competitive environment within the Community. See the *Woodpulp Cartel Case* [1988] 4 CMLR 901.

b) *Commercial practices prohibited by Article 85 EEC Treaty*

Article 85(1) of the EEC Treaty addresses different forms of concerted behaviour between two or more undertakings and specifically provides:

'The following shall be prohibited as incompatible with the common market: all agreements between undertakings, decisions by associations of undertakings, and concerted practices which may affect trade between Member States and which have as their object or effect the prevention, restriction or distortion of competition within the Common Market, and in particular those which:

a) directly or indirectly fix purchase or selling prices or any other trading conditions;

b) limit or control production, markets, technical development, or investment;

c) share markets or sources of supply;

d) apply dissimilar conditions to equivalent transactions with other trading parties, thereby placing them at a competitive disadvantage;

e) make the conclusion of contracts subject to acceptance by the other parties of supplementary obligations which, by their nature or according to commercial usage, have no connection with the subject of such contracts.'

All agreements, decisions and practices prohibited under Article 85(1) are automatically void unless exempt from the scope of this subsection by virtue of Article 85(3).

The Article itself specifically enumerates a number of examples of anti-competitive behaviour in order to illustrate the types of conduct which the provision is intended to limit.

i) Price fixing

Practices which have the effect of directly or indirectly fixing buying or selling prices for products are incompatible with competition policy. This includes arrangements whereby undertakings agree on the particular trading conditions which are applicable to their business dealings, such as discounts or credit terms.

ii) Limitation or control of production

Quotas on production and supply cartels are contrary to competition policy, as are arrangements to control marketing, technical development or investment.

iii) Allocation of markets

Practices which allow potential competitors to apportion a market in a particular product amongst each other on a mutually exclusive basis are prohibited.

iv) Application of dissimilar conditions

By applying dissimilar sales conditions to identical transactions one undertaking may place another at a competitive disadvantage. For example, an agreement to provide one purchaser with more advantageous purchasing conditions than another purchaser would result in unfair discrimination.

v) Imposition of supplementary obligations

Agreements requiring the fulfilment of supplementary obligations which, by their nature or commercial usage, have no connection with the original subject matter of a contract, are prohibited. For example, agreements which require a buyer of one product or service to purchase another product or service unconnected with the first transaction would amount to the imposition of a supplementary obligation.

This list of anti-competitive behaviour is intended to illustrate the most common forms of conduct which will infringe Article 85(1) and is not intended to be exhaustive.

c) *Agreements, decisions by associations of undertakings and concerted practices*

Article 85 identifies three separate arrangements which may contravene competition law: agreements, decisions, and concerted practices. Each of these concepts refers to a different form of commercial practice among undertakings.

i) Agreements

The term 'agreements' includes all contracts in the sense of binding contractual obligations, whether written, verbal, or partly written and partly verbal. Further, an arrangement between two or more parties may constitute an agreement for the purposes of Article 85(1) even although the arrangement in question has no binding legal effect: see *Atka A/S* v *BP Kemi A/S* [1979] CMLR 684.

Unrecorded understandings, the mutual adoption of common rules, and so-called 'gentlemen's agreements' are also agreements for the purposes of competition law: *Boehringer* v *EC Commission* [1970] ECR 769.

Agreements which prevent, distort or restrict competition are classified either as horizontal agreements or vertical agreements. Horizontal agreements are arrangements made between competitors or potential competitors while vertical agreements are arrangements between undertakings at the differing stages of process through which a product or service passes from the manufacturer to the final consumer.

Illustrations of horizontal agreements include agreements dividing markets among competitors, price fixing, export and import bans, cartels, and boycotts. Examples of vertical agreements include exclusive distribution agreements, exclusive patent licensing agreements, exclusive purchasing agreements, and tying.

ii) Decisions of associations of undertakings

The concept of decisions of associations of undertakings refers to the creation of rules establishing trade associations, as well as any other formal or informal decisions or recommendations made under such rules.

Prohibited decisions of trade associations would include recommending prices, fixing discounts, collective boycotts and the negotiation of restrictive contract clauses. A recommendation by a trade association may constitute a decision, even although such acts are not binding under the constitution of the association in question: see *Vereeniging van Cementhandelaren* v *EC Commission* [1972] ECR 977.

iii) Concerted practices

The term 'concerted practice' refers to commercial cooperation in the absence of a formal agreement. The European Court has defined a concerted practice as:

'a form of coordination between enterprises that has not yet reached the point where it is a contract in the true sense of the word but which, in practice, consciously substitutes practical cooperation for the risks of competition': *Imperial Chemical Industries* v *EC Commission* [1972] ECR 619.

Manufacturers and producers are, of course, entitled to take into consideration prices set for similar goods by competitors. It is only when potential competitors deliberately and intentionally agree to coordinate pricing policy that a concerted practice arises.

Commercial cooperation will likely amount to a concerted practice if it enables the entities under investigation to consolidate their market positions to the detriment of the principle of free movement of goods within the Community and the freedom of consumers to select products: *Cooperatieve Vereeniging 'Suiker Unie' UA* v *EC Commission* [1975] ECR 1663.

It is contrary to the rules on competition contained in Article 85 for a producer to cooperate with its competitors in order to determine a coordinated course of action relating to pricing policy, particularly if this cooperation ensures the elimination of all uncertainty among competitors as regards matters such as price increases, the subject matter of increases, and the date and place of increases.

d) *Effect on trade between Member States*

No agreement, decision or concerted practice may be held contrary to Community competition law unless it affects patterns of trade between Member States. As the European Court has observed:

'It is only to the extent to which agreements may affect trade between Member States that the deterioration in competition falls under the prohibition of Community law contained in Article 85; otherwise it escapes the prohibition': *Consten and Grundig* v *EC Commission* [1966] ECR 299.

This requirement is intended to enable a distinction to be drawn between unfair commercial practices which have only national ramifications and those practices which have Community implications.

The effect of an agreement on trade between Member States is ascertained by reference to the principle of free movement of goods and, in particular, the realisation of the objective of creating a single market among all the Member States of the Community. An agreement, decision or practice will affect trade between Member States if it is capable of constituting a threat, either direct or indirect, actual or potential, to the freedom of trade between Member States in a manner which might harm the attainment of the objective of a single market between states: *Remia BV* v *EC Commission* [1985] ECR 2545.

Actual harm need not be established. It is sufficient that the agreement is likely to prevent, restrict or distort competition to a sufficient degree: *Société Technique Minière* v *Maschinenbau Ulm GmbH* [1966] ECR 235.

There is no violation of Article 85 if an agreement or practice has only a negligible effect on trade between Member States. Early in the jurisprudence of competition law, the European Court held that:

'[A]n agreement falls outside the prohibition in Article 85 when it has only an insignificant effect on the markets, taking into account the weak position which the persons concerned have on the market of the product in question': *Frans Volk* v *Vervaercke* [1969] ECR 295.

Insignificant agreements escape the prohibition of Article 85 because their relative effect on trade between Member States is negligible.

e) *The object or effect of preventing, restricting or distorting competition within the Community*

Agreements, decisions and practice are only prohibited under Article 85 if, in addition to satisfying all other relevant criteria, they have as their object or effect the prevention, restriction or distortion of competition within the Community. Such arrangements may have either the object or the effect of distorting competition. These options are clearly intended to be alternative, not cumulative, tests.

An agreement will have the object of distorting competition if, prior to its implementation, it can be determined that the agreement would prevent or restrict competition which might take place between the parties to the agreement: *Consten and Grundig* v *EC Commission* [1966] ECR 299. If an agreement does not have the object of restricting competition, whether or not an agreement has the effect of distorting competition may be determined by market analysis.

f) *Activities outside the scope of Article 85(1)*

An agreement, decision or practice may be excluded from the scope of Article 85(1) on four principal grounds: (i) where an agreement has been given negative clearance by the Commission; (ii) where an agreement is of minor importance; (iii) where an agreement regulates relations between undertakings to which the competition rules are inapplicable; and (iv) where agreements and practices benefit from the exemptions under Article 85(3).

i) Negative clearance

An undertaking proposing to enter into an agreement or engage in a practice which might be considered to restrict, prevent or distort competition may apply to the Commission for negative clearance in respect of the arrangement. Negative clearance is a determination made by the Commission that, on the basis of the facts in its possession, it believes that there are no grounds under Article 85(1) (or Article 86) for action to be taken against the submitted agreement, decision or practice.

In order to obtain negative clearance, the undertakings submitting the application must prove that the agreement, decision or practice is excluded from the scope of the applicable competition provision. Negative clearance is therefore not strictly a separate ground for exclusion from the competition provisions of the EEC Treaty, but rather certification that an agreement or practice, in the opinion of the Commission, falls outside Community competition law.

Frequently, instead of making a formal decision on a matter, the Commission may notify the undertaking by correspondence that no action is required to conform to the terms of Article 85(1). Such correspondence is known as a 'comfort letter'. It offers no absolute protection from investigation by the Commission, particularly where the facts submitted by the undertaking vary from the true facts of the case. But, if an investigation is subsequently initiated, the statement may be pleaded in mitigation should an infringement be established.

ii) Agreements of minor importance

Agreements which would otherwise be caught by Article 85(1) may nevertheless be exempt from its scope if they are incapable of affecting trade between Member States or restricting competition to any appreciable extent. This principle is known as the de minimus rule and was originally conceived by the European Court in the *Volk Case* above. Agreements fall outside the prohibition of Article 85(1) if they have an 'insignificant effect' on the market in such products.

The Commission has published a notice intended to establish guidelines for the application of the de minimus rule, the basis of which is the jurisprudence of the European Court in this subject. The Commission has indicated that, in normal circumstances, agreements would fall outside Article 85(1) by virtue of the de minimus rule, if two conditions can be established:

- market share: the goods or services which are the subject of the agreement and its immediate substitutes do not constitute more than 5 per cent of the total market for such goods or services in the area of the common market affected by the agreement; and
- turnover: the aggregate annual turnover of the undertakings participating in the arrangement does not exceed 200 million ECU (approximately £150 million): Commission Notice Concerning Agreements, Decisions and Concerted Practices of Minor Importance (1986).

The intention of the notice is to allow small and medium sized undertakings to benefit from the rule exempting minor agreements from the rigours of Article 85(1).

iii) Commercial relations to which competition rules do not apply

The competition rules established under Article 85 do not apply to two particular commercial relationships: between principals and agents; and between parents and subsidiaries.

From the beginning of Community competition policy administration contracts entered into between principals and commercial agents have been traditionally excluded from the scope of Article 85(1) so long as the agent is concerned with the simple negotiation of transactions on behalf of the principal: Commission Notice Relating to Exclusive Dealing Contracts with Commercial Agents (1962). While the non-application of Article 85(1) to such relationships legally has the form of a group negative clearance, the application of competition rules to such relations is clearly contrary to the policy of promoting competition throughout the Community.

A subsidiary which is under the control of a parent company is not considered to be capable of anti-competitive behaviour in relation to its parent since it has no autonomous decision-making capacity. Restrictive agreements and anti-competitive concerned practices between parents and non-autonomous subsidiaries are therefore not subject to the rules of Community competition law. As the European Court has explicitly ruled:

'Article 85 is not concerned with agreements or concerted practices between undertakings belonging to the same concern and having the status of parent company and subsidiary, if the undertakings form an economic unit within which the subsidiary has no real freedom to determine its course of action on the market, and if the agreements or practices are concerned merely with the internal allocation of tasks as between the undertakings': *Hydrotherm Geratebau* v *Andreoli* [1984] ECR 2999.

Two conditions are therefore required in order to avoid the application of Article 85(1) on this basis:

- The subsidiary cannot have any real freedom to dictate its own course of action in the market place. Control over the conduct of a subsidiary is determined by reference to the size of the shareholding held by the parent.
- The restrictive agreement itself must relate only to the allocation of responsibilities and tasks between the parent and the subsidiary.

iv) Exempt agreements and practices

Article 85(3) specifically creates criteria for exempting agreements, decisions and concerted practices from the effects of Article 83(1). Agreements and practices which satisfy the exemption criteria established by Article 85(3) are not void under Article 85(2) nor subject to the imposition of fines. Two positive and two negative tests must be satisfied for an agreement to be exempt and the onus is on the applicant to establish these conditions are present:

- the agreement, decision or practice must contribute to improving the production or distribution of goods or promoting technical or economic progress;
- a fair share of the resulting benefit must accrue to the consumer;
- the agreement or practice must not impose any restrictions which go beyond the positive aims of the agreement or practice; and
- these restrictions must not create a possibility of eliminating competition in respect of a substantial part of the products in question.

Two types of exemption are granted on the basis of the authority of this provision: (1) individual exemptions which are issued on the basis of an individual application; and (2) block exemptions which are applicable to categories of agreements. Subject to review by the Court of First Instance and thereafter the European Court itself, the European Commission has exclusive authority to create exemptions on the basis of Article 85(3).

The procedure for obtaining an individual exemption is specified in Council Regulation 17/62. Individual exemptions are granted in the form of Commission decisions. These decisions are issued for a limited period and may be conditional on the fulfilment of certain obligations. A decision may be renewed if the relevant conditions continue to be satisfied. The Commission may revoke or amend a decision granting an individual exemption in the event of a change of circumstances. Naturally an individual exemption will only be granted if the four conditions on Article 85(3) are satisfied.

To reduce the bureaucratic burdens imposed by applications for individual exemption, the Commission is empowered to establish group exemption categories: Council Regulation 19/65 and Council Regulation 2821/71. The

Commission has enacted a number of Regulations in order to grant group exemption to a number of types of agreements including exclusive distribution agreements, exclusive purchasing agreements, patent licensing agreements, motor vehicle distribution and servicing agreements, specialisation agreements, research and development agreements, franchising agreements, and know-how agreements.

If an agreement falls within the scope of a group exemption under a Commission regulation, the parties to the agreement are not required to notify the Commission of the agreement and the parties cannot be fined by the Commission for violating competition law on that basis.

11.3 Relevant cases

ICI v *EC Commission* [1972] ECR 619: Definition of the concept of concerted practice, together with the identification of the requisite criteria.

Remia BV v *EC Commission* [1985] ECR 2445: Decision of the European Court applying the test necessary to identify whether or not an agreement has an effect on trade between Member States.

Metro v *SB-Grossmarkte GmbH* v *EC Commission (No 2)* [1986] ECR 3021: Identification of the scope of the requirement that an agreement must have the effect of distorting competition before contravening Community competition law.

Woodpulp Cartel Case [1988] 4 CMLR 901: An example of the application of the principle of extraterritoriality to Community competition law by the European Court.

11.4 Relevant materials

D G Goyder, *EEC Competition Law* (1988).

I Van Bael & J-F Bellis, *European Community Law* (1987).

V Korah, *EEC Competition Law and Practice* (1986).

C W Bellamy et al, *Common Market Law and Competition* (1987).

R Goebel, 'Metro II's Confirmation of the Selective Distribution Rules' (1987) 24 CMLR 605.

S Hornsby, 'Competition Policy for the 1980s: More Policy, Less Competition' (1987) 12 EL Rev 79.

J Shaw, 'Group Exemptions and Exclusive Distribution and Purchasing Agreements' (1985) 34 ICLQ 190.

11.5 Analysis of questions

European competition law is perhaps the most complex element of the Community law syllabus, not only due to the nature of the subject-matter, but also because the principles of competition law have been mainly developed by the European Commission and the ECJ. However, it is an extremely popular area for examiners.

Students should therefore be familiar with the terms of Article 85(1), the types of agreement prohibited by Article 85, and the exceptions to Article 85.

11.6 Questions

Question 1

Article 85(1) of the EEC Treaty is designed to prohibit certain types of agreements, decisions and concerted practices between private parties within the Community. Identify the essential features of the agreements, decisions and concerted practices which the Article is designed to combat, and distinguish each of these arrangements from the others.

Question prepared by the Author
February 1991

General comment

A general question requiring a narrative description of one particular aspect of competition law.

Skeleton solution

- Types of agreements covered by Article 85(1).
- Concept of decisions by associations of undertakings.
- Essential elements of a concerted practice.

Suggested solution

Article 85(1) is directed against three separate types of arrangements made between undertakings: agreements between undertakings, decisions by associations of undertakings, and concerted practices among undertakings. These commercial practices may contravene Community competition law if their object or effect is to prevent, restrict or distort competition within the Community.

Naturally the term 'agreements' includes all contracts in the sense of binding contractual obligations, whether written, verbal, or partly written and partly verbal. An arrangement between two or more parties can constitute an agreement for the purposes of Article 85(1) even although the arrangement in question has no binding legal effect. In *Atka A/S* v *BP Kemi A/S* (1979), the Commission ruled that an understanding between two petrochemical product manufacturers constituted an agreement under Article 85 notwithstanding the fact that the relevant document had not been signed by the parties nor dated and could not be enforced in the national courts of the Member State where the agreement was negotiated. The mere fact that two separate and independent commercial entities maintained identical prices in the same market during the same period provided sufficient evidence of an agreement, particularly where identical pricing of the product was unlikely in the prevailing market conditions.

Unrecorded understandings, the mutual adoption of common rules, and so-called 'gentlemen's agreements' are also agreements for the purposes of competition law. In *Boehringer* v *EC Commission* (1970), the practices under investigation were based on a contract which established a cartel fixing the world prices for certain products. Although the European Community was expressly excluded from the application of the contract, the parties had negotiated a separate written 'gentlemen's agreement' to extend the application of this arrangement to the European Community. The European Court upheld the determination by the Commission that this arrangement constituted an agreement under Article 85, even although the parties had agreed among themselves to suspend the application of that part of the arrangement applicable to the Community.

The concept of decisions of associations of undertakings refers to the creation of rules establishing trade associations, as well as any other formal or informal decisions or recommendations made under such rules. Prohibited decisions of trade associations would include recommending prices, fixing discounts, collective boycotts and the negotiation of restrictive contract clauses. A recommendation by a trade association may constitute a decision, even although such acts are not binding under the constitution of the association in question: *Vereeniging van Cementhandelaren* v *EC Commission* (1972).

Agreements between trade associations may also contravene Article 85, even although the agreement itself is not enforceable, if the participating associations have authority to require their members to comply with the terms of the agreement: *NV IAZ International Belgium* v *EC Commission* (1983).

The concept of a 'concerted practice' refers to a particular form of commercial behaviour which occurs in the absence of a formal agreement. The European Court has defined a concerted practice as 'a form of coordination between enterprises that has not yet reached the point where it is a contract in the true sense of the word but which, in practice, consciously substitutes practical cooperation for the risks of competition': *Imperial Chemical Industries* v *EC Commission* (1972). Manufacturers and producers are entitled to take into consideration prices set for similar goods by competitors. It is only when potential competitors deliberately and intentionally agree to coordinate pricing policy that a concerted practice arises.

Commercial cooperation will amount to a concerted practice if it enables the entities under investigation to consolidate their market positions to the detriment of the principle of free movement of goods within the Community and the freedom of consumers to select products. It is contrary to the rules on competition contained in Article 85 for a producer to cooperate with its competitors in order to determine a coordinated course of action relating to pricing policy, particularly if this cooperation ensures the elimination of all uncertainty among competitors as regards matters such as price increases, the subject matter of increases, and the date and place of increases.

In order to ascertain the existence of a concerted practice, it is necessary to compare the actual market conditions for a product with the normal conditions of that market. In the *Dyestuffs Case* above, the European Court held that the similarity in price rises and the timing of such rises could not be explained by reference to the normal market conditions for a product since such conditions rarely produced parallel yet independent price rises prior to the ones under investigation.

A concerted practice need not involve the detailed calculation of a plan. Thus, in the *Sugar Case* (1975), the European Court examined a number of allegations of anti-competitive behaviour among Dutch sugar producers and declared that, in order to constitute a concerted practice, the economic cooperation under investigation need not amount to the working out of an actual plan. However, since each undertaking independently determines commercial policy, direct or indirect contact between undertakings with the object of influencing an actual or potential competition is necessary to establish a concerted practice. This amounts to a requirement of positive contact between the parties and may take the form of negotiations, conferences, discussions, meetings or exchanges of information.

Evidence of concerted practices among producers is generally circumstantial, there being generally no documents to evidence the intended practice. The Commission has adopted the practice of requiring parties accused of concerted practices to provide a suitable explanation for the facts which infer the existence of a concerted practice: see for example, *Compagnie Royal Asturienne des Mines and Rhienzink* v *EC Commission* (1984). This is also illustrated by the *Woodpulp Cartel Case* (1985). In this case, the Commission established evidence of collusion among producers based on the fact that the prices of certain products bore no relation to either supply or demand. Since commodity prices fluctuate wildly in relation to variations in supply and demand, this behaviour suggested collusion.

Question 2

British Breweries plc is an important producer of beer in the United Kingdom. Statistics show that British Breweries account for some 12 per cent of all beer sold in the United Kingdom but that its British Brewlite is especially successful and accounts for 40 per cent of all non-alcoholic beer consumed in the UK.

British Breweries want to establish a German subsidiary but have been advised that most retailers in Germany have agreed to purchase non-alcoholic beer only from the German Brewers' Association. The Association checks the quality of its members' products. However, there is a two-year trading requirement in Germany before a new brewery can be admitted to the Association.

Advise British Breweries as to the significance, if any, of EEC law for each of the above aspects of its business.

adapted from University of London LLB Examination
(for External Students) European Community Law 1990 Q7

General comment

A problem-type question involving the application of Article 85 to hypothetical circumstances.

Skeleton solution

- Is there a prohibited practice?
- Does this practice affect trade between Member States and distort competition?

- Application of individual or group exemption.
- Alternative methods of challenge.

Suggested solution

In order to ascertain whether or not a practice infringes Community competition policy, three separate determinations must be made: (1) the activity in question must constitute an agreement, decision or concerted practice as prescribed by Article 85(1); (2) the practice must affect trade between Member States; and (3) the practice must prevent, restrict or distort competition.

Both the German beer retailers and the German Brewers Association (GBA) are undertakings for the purpose of Article 85(1). All natural and legal persons engaged in economic activities constitute undertakings, regardless of whether or not they are profit-making or otherwise. The fact that the GBA is a non-profit making organisation would be irrelevant for the purpose of identifying it as an undertaking.

Article 85(1) addresses decisions of associations of undertakings, whether formal or informal. Therefore any decision made by the GBA - as an association of undertakings - is subject to review under Community competition law. Further, its decisions need not be legally binding. In the case, *Re Fire Insurance* Case 45/85, the Commission applied Article 85 to a 'recommendation', described as 'non-binding' by an association of insurers in Germany, that premiums for various classes of policy be raised by a stipulated percentage. The conclusive factor is the ability of the association, in fact if not in law, to determine the conduct and behaviour of its members.

It is also immaterial whether the GBA is publicly or privately established. Competition law makes no distinction between public and private commercial bodies for the purpose of identifying undertakings. The term applies to all state bodies engaged in commercial activities: *IAZ* v *EC Commission* (1983). Furthermore, GBA's rules themselves are a product of an agreement and thus potentially contravene Article 85.

Naturally, the decisions of the GBA affect trade between Member States. A decision will affect trade between Member States if it is capable of constituting a threat, either direct or indirect, actual or potential, to the freedom to trade between Member States in a manner which might harm the attainment of the objectives of a single market: *Remia BV* v *EC Commission* (1985). The fact that the GBA effectively prevents foreign sellers from entering the German non-alcoholic beer market is more than sufficient to establish that its decisions affect trade between Member States.

Article 85(1) refers to decisions which 'have as their object or effect the prevention, restriction or distortion of competition' within the common market, to an appreciable degree. It is sufficient that a decision of an association of undertakings has as its object the restriction of competition without this necessarily representing the common intention of the parties: see *Consten & Grundig* v *EC Commission* (1966).

Competition is clearly severely restricted if not prevented by the two year trading requirement imposed in Germany by the GBA. Since most retailers purchase non-alcoholic beer only from members of the GBA, any brewery attempting to enter the market would have to trade for two years, selling to a very limited number of retailers - a venture which would not be commercially viable. The two year trading requirement acts as a disincentive to new competitors entering the market and effectively closes the market to new entrants to the market. It is immaterial that the arrangement is a vertical agreement between undertakings operating at different levels.

Since the two year trading requirement does not appear to be covered by any of the block exemptions, and presumably has not been granted an individual exemption, only the de minimus rule would apply. However, the sheer magnitude of the domination of the market suggests that the de minimus defence would be inapplicable.

British Breweries should therefore be advised to make a complaint to the Commission under Regulation 17/62, Articles 3(1) and 3(2). British Breweries is a party with a sufficient legitimate interest. If the Commission decides not to initiate proceedings and notifies British Breweries accordingly, British Breweries will have sufficient locus standi to bring an action for annulment under Article 173. Further, if the Commission takes no action British Breweries can bring Article 175 proceedings.

GBA could seek an exemption under Article 85(3) for the decision, primarily on the ground that the two year trading requirement ensures that any new brewer is a reliable, quality producer of non-alcoholic beers. This supervision process, it could be argued, contributes to improved production which inevitably benefits the consumers and retailers.

However, these arguments are likely to fail for three reasons. First, the benefit of the two year trading requirement is not strictly economic. Second, a two year requirement goes substantially beyond what is absolutely necessary to achieve the objectives regarded as beneficial. Third, the measure has resulted in the elimination of a substantial degree of competition.

British Breweries could also challenge the decision of the GBA on the ground that it breaches the right of an undertaking to establish itself anywhere in the Community under Article 52 of the EEC Treaty.

Question 3

Outline the origins and evolution of the de minimus rule which exempts small businesses from the application of Article 85 of the EEC Treaty.

Question prepared by the Author
February 1991

General comment

A narrative question requiring a descriptive answer.

Skeleton solution

- Origins of the de minimus rule - effect on trade between Member States.
- Jurisprudence of the Court.

- Commission regulations.

Suggested solution

No agreement, decision or concerted practice may be held contrary to Community competition law unless it affects patterns of trade between Member States. Commercial practices are capable of infringing Article 85 only to the extent to which they affect trade between Member States. This requirement is intended to enable a distinction to be drawn between unfair commercial practices which have only national ramifications and those practices which have Community implications.

Consequently, there is no violation of Article 85 if an agreement or practice has only a negligible effect on trade between Member States. Early in the jurisprudence of competition law, the European Court held that an agreement falls outside the prohibition in Article 85 when it has only an insignificant effect on the markets, taking into account the weak position which the persons concerned have in the market for the product in question: *Frans Volk* v *Veraercke* (1969). Insignificant agreements therefore escape the prohibition of Article 85 because their relative effect on trade between Member States is negligible.

In order to benefit from this de minimus ruling two conditions have to be satisfied by an agreement, decision or practice. First, the products covered by the agreement must constitute an insignificant part of the market for identical and similar products. Second, the turnover of the undertakings involved must not exceed limits which would allow them to exercise a strong influence over the market in the product: *Distillers Co* v *EC Commission* (1980).

'Insignificant effect' has not been defined by the Court, but in *Miller* v *EC Commission* (1978), an agreement extending to approximately 5 per cent of the total market in sound recordings in Germany was held to be sufficient to be caught by Article 85(1). See also *AEG* v *EC Commission* (1983).

In addition, undertakings entering into agreements which concern volumes of sales which might qualify under the de minimus rule will not escape the prohibition if one or more of the undertakings involved are of sufficient importance for their behaviour to be considered capable of influencing patterns of trade. The Court has tended to refuse to apply the de minimus rule, even though the market share of the products involved in the agreement is relatively small, if large undertakings are concerned. In *Musique Diffusion Française* v *EC Commission* (1983), the Court held that, although the two undertakings involved maintained market shares of less than 4 per cent in the relevant markets, the agreement was not excluded from Article 85(1) under the de minimus rule because the relevant market in the products was fragmented and the market shares of the applicants by brand were greater than their competitors.

Similarly, in *Distillers Co* v *EC Commission* above, the Court refused to apply the de minimus rule to a product which constituted a mere fraction of the market in spirits in the UK but which was manufactured by a large undertaking involved in the marketing of a variety of other spirits.

The European Commission has in fact codified the jurisprudence of the European Court by publishing guidelines which establish specific thresholds for the application of Article 85. The Commission has published a notice intended to establish guidelines for the application of the de minimus rule, the basis of which is the jurisprudence of the European Court in this subject: Commission Notice Concerning Agreements, Decisions and Concerted Practices of Minor Importance (1986).

The Commission has indicated that, in normal circumstances, agreements would fall outside Article 85(1) by virtue of the de minimus rule, if two conditions can be established:

a) market share: the goods or services which are the subject of the agreement and its immediate substitutes do not constitute more than 5 per cent of the total market for such goods or services in the area of the common market affected by the agreement; and

b) turnover: the aggregate annual turnover of the undertakings participating in the arrangement does not exceed 200 million ECU (approximately £150 million).

The intention of the notice is to allow small and medium sized undertakings to benefit from the rule exempting minor agreements from the rigours of Article 85(1).

In order to calculate the market share of a product, it is necessary to determine the relevant market. This implies the identification of both a relevant product market and a relevant geographical market. The relevant product market consists of the market for the particular product together with the market for products which are identical or substantially equivalent to the particular product. Identical and substantially equivalent products must be interchangeable with the original product. Whether or not this requirement is satisfied must be judged from the perspective of the consumer, normally taking into account the characteristics, price and intended use of the products. However, in certain cases it is perfectly possible that a particular product can constitute a separate market by itself: *United Brands* v *EC Commission* (1978).

The relevant geographical market is the area within the Community in which the agreement produces its effects. There is a presumption that this area is the whole territory of the Community if the products which are the subject of the agreement are regularly bought and sold in all Member States. Where the products cannot be bought or sold in a particular part of the Community, or are bought and sold only in limited quantities or at irregular intervals in a part of the Community, that part is disregarded for the purposes of ascertaining the geographical market.

The relevant geographical market will be narrower than the whole Community if: (a) the nature and characteristics of the product (such as prohibitive transport costs) restrict its mobility; or (b) the free movement of the product within the Community is hindered by barriers to entry into national markets resulting from state intervention and non-tariff barriers. In such cases the relevant geographical territory is the national territory of origin.

Question 4

Examine any one of the block exemptions adopted by the Commission and, in particular comment on the problems which it is designed to solve, the benefits which the exemption brings and any difficulties created by this procedure.

Question prepared by the Author
February 1991

General comment

A difficult question requiring the student to demonstrate detailed knowledge of the application of competition law.

Skeleton solution

- Authority for the creation of block exemptions.
- Description of a block exemption - one vertical, one horizontal.
- Functions of block exemptions.

Suggested solution

Article 85(3) specifically creates criteria for exempting agreements, decisions and concerted practices from the effects of Article 85(1). Agreements and practices which satisfy the exemption criteria established by Article 85(3) are not void under Article 85(2) nor subject to the imposition of fines.

Two types of exemption are granted on the basis of the authority of this provisions: (1) individual exemptions which are issued on the basis of an individual application; and (2) block exemptions which are applicable to categories of agreements. Subject to review by the Court of First Instance and thereafter the European Court itself, the European Commission has exclusive authority to create exemptions on the basis of Article 85(3).

To reduce the bureaucratic burdens imposed by applications for individual exemption, the Commission is empowered to establish group exemption categories: Council Regulation 19/65 (1965). The Commission has enacted a number of Regulations in order to grant group exemption to a number of agreements including exclusive distribution agreements (Commission Regulation 1983/83 (1983)), exclusive purchasing agreements (Commission Regulation 1984/83 (1983)), patent licensing agreements (Commission Regulation 2349/84 (1984)), motor vehicle distribution and servicing agreements (Commission Regulation 123/85 (1985)), specialisation agreements (Commission Regulation 417/85 (1985)), research and development agreements (Commission Regulation 518/85 (1985)), franchising agreements (Commission Regulation 4087/88 (1988)), and know-how agreements (Commission Regulation 556/89 (1989)). If an agreement falls within the scope of a group exemption under a Commission regulation, the parties to the agreement are not required to notify the Commission of the agreement and the parties cannot be fined by the Commission for violating competition law on that basis.

Each block exemption contains specific and particular criteria which must be satisfied in order for an agreement to take advantage of the exemption. Many of the exemptions are mutually exclusive and occasionally an agreement will fail to qualify as an exempt agreement because it falls within two mutually exclusive categories. At the same time a number of exemptions overlap and reliance may be placed on one or other option to obtain exemption for an agreement.

Group exemptions have been created for both horizontal and vertical agreements. An example of group exemption applicable to a horizontal agreement is the specialisation agreement block exemption. Specialisation agreements are agreements whereby the parties agree among themselves who should manufacture certain products. By relinquishing production of certain goods, the participating undertakings can concentrate on manufacturing those products which remain on their respective production lines. Competition is restricted because the parties refrain from independently manufacturing certain items.

In order to qualify for exemption under this provision, an agreement must satisfy all the following conditions: (a) the agreement must be between small and medium sized undertakings, measured on the basis of market share and turnover; (b) the commitment to specialise must be reciprocal which means that an obligation on only one of the parties to refrain from production of a certain item would not qualify for group exemption; (c) the commitment must refer only to the nature of the products, so any quantitative limitation of production does not fall within the group exemption; (d) certain additional clauses must be agreed which are essential to implement the commitment to specialise, including a non-competition clause and exclusive purchasing and distribution commitments; and (e) commitments with regard to prices are not allowed in the context of the group exemption.

The purpose of this group exemption is to allow small and medium-sized firms to improve their production processes and thereby strengthen their competitive positions in relation to larger firms.

Vertical agreements may also be the subject of group exemptions. A typical example of such a group exemption is the exclusive distribution agreements block exemption. This group exemption applies to three situations: (i) where the supplier and the distributor agree that the distributor should supply a certain area; (ii) where the distributor agrees to purchase goods exclusively from the supplier; and (iii) where the supplier agrees to supply the distributor exclusively, and the distributor agrees to purchase exclusively from the supplier.

In order to be exempt, such agreements must fulfil the following principal conditions: (a) the agreement can involve only two parties; (b) the products must be supplied for resale; (c) the sales area must be either a defined part of the Common Market or the entire Common Market; (d) the only permitted restriction on the supplier is the obligation not to sell to other resellers in the sales area allocated to the exclusive distributor; (e) the distributor must agree to purchase all his requirements from the supplier; (f) the agreement must not involve competing manufacturers, since this might lead to market sharing; and (g) there must be no effort by the parties to create absolute territorial protection for the distributor. In other words, parallel imports of the goods must remain possible.

Although agreements which satisfy these conditions are automatically exempt, the Commission retains the right to withdraw the benefit of the group exemption in particular cases such as, for example, a distributor abusing an exemption by charging unreasonable prices.

12 EUROPEAN COMPETITION LAW AND MERGER CONTROL - ARTICLE 86 EEC TREATY

12.1 Introduction

This chapter will deal mainly with the restraints imposed on commercial practices by Article 86 of the EEC Treaty and also the regulation of mergers within the Community by competition law. In addition, a number of other matters of general competition law will be considered in order to provide a comprehensive description of the Community competition policy scheme. This includes the proper procedure for the initiation of a complaint, the determination of infringements, the powers of the Commission to investigate complaints, and the imposition of fines. These matters are equally relevant to the application of Article 85 as well as Article 86, but are included in this chapter to avoid duplication and repetition.

12.2 Key points

a) *Commercial practices prohibited by Article 86 EEC Treaty*

Article 86 of the EEC Treaty prohibits practices which constitute an abuse of a dominant position within the Community market. Article 86 expressly provides:

'Any abuse by one or more undertakings of a dominant position within the common market or in a substantial part of it shall be prohibited as incompatible with the common market in so far as it may affect trade between Member States. Such abuse may, in particular, consist in:

a) directly or indirectly imposing unfair purchase or selling prices or other unfair trading conditions;

b) limiting production, markets or technical developments to the prejudice of consumers;

c) applying dissimilar conditions to equivalent transactions with other parties, thereby placing them at a competitive disadvantage;

d) making the conclusion of contracts subject to acceptance by the other parties of supplementary obligations which, by their nature and according to commercial usage, have no connection with the subject of such contracts.'

Article 85(1) and 86 are not mutually exclusive. The Commission has discretion in selecting the appropriate instrument to enforce competition policy. Consequently, the possibility that both Articles 85 and 86 may be applicable to a particular case cannot be ruled out: *Ahmed Saeed* v *Zentrale zur Bekampfung* Case 66/86, Judgment of 11 April 1989, not yet reported.

The existence of a dominant position per se is not prohibited under Article 86, only any abuse of the market power which usually accompanies such a position. Article 86 is not intended to penalise or punish efficient forms of economic behaviour. On the contrary, Article 86 seeks to discourage the acquisition or maintenance of a dominant position through anti-competitive practices which create artificial competitive conditions.

b) *The existence of a dominant position*

The concept of dominant position is not defined in the EEC Treaty but, in effect, is analogous to the existence of a monopoly in a particular sector of the economy. The European Court has defined dominant position in the following terms:

'Undertakings are in a dominant position when they have the power to behave independently, which puts them in a position to act without taking into account their competitors, purchasers or suppliers. That is a position when, because of their share of the market, or of their share of the market combined with the availability of technical knowledge, raw materials or capital, they have power to determine prices or to control production or distribution for a significant part of the products in question': *Continental Can Co* v *EC Commission* [1973] ECR 215.

The two key relevant concepts in establishing the existence of a dominant position are: (i) the definition of the market; and (ii) the calculation of market share.

i) Definition of the relevant market

The relevant market is defined in terms of both the relevant product market and the relevant geographical market.

To identify a product market it is necessary to isolate the product under investigation from similar products in the market. For this purpose, the Commission identifies the relevant product together with all other products which may be perfectly substituted for the product under investigation. Jointly these products constitute the relevant product market. The test for ascertaining substitutable products depends on whether or not:

'there is a sufficient degree of interchangeability between all the products forming part of the same market in so far as a specific use of such products is concerned': *Hoffmann-La-Roche & Co AG* v *EC Commission* [1979] ECR 461.

The relevant geographical market has been defined by the European Court as the area:

'where the conditions are sufficiently homogeneous for the effect of the economic power of the undertaking concerned to be evaluated': *United Brands* v *EC Commission* [1978] ECR 207.

In general, the relevant geographical market will be assumed to be the whole of the Community. Only if the existence of impediments to cross-border trade, such as physical, technological, legal or cultural non-tariff barriers, can be established will the relevant geographical market be reduced. Further, as the single internal market programme proceeds, it is less likely that such artificial barriers will be permitted to reduce the geographical market from the whole territory of the Community.

ii) Calculation of market share

No particular share of a market is required to prove the existence of a dominant position. In the *United Brands Case* above, the European Court stated that the fact that an undertaking possessed around 40 per cent of the relevant market was not itself sufficient to establish market dominance. Other factors contributed to the determination that United Brands maintained a dominant position, including the facts that the company controlled its own shipping fleet, could regulate the volume of the product entering the Community regardless of weather conditions and subjected distributors to rigorous restrictive covenants.

On the other hand, in the *Continental Can Case*, the Commission decided that a company with a share of approximately 50 per cent of the relevant market occupied a dominant position.

c) *Abuse of a dominant position*

Abuse is an objective concept which relates to the behaviour of the undertaking alleged to be in a dominant position. It is behaviour which modifies the structure of a market in such a way as to reduce the levels of competition or retard the growth of competition in a particular economic area.

Article 86 lists a number of practices which are specifically identified as perpetrating such abuse, including:

i) Directly or indirectly imposing unfair purchase or selling prices or other unfair trading conditions: see for example, *Bodson* v *Pompes Funebres*, Case 30/87, Judgment of 4 May 1989, not yet reported.

ii) Limiting production, markets or technical development to the prejudice of consumers.

iii) Applying dissimilar conditions to equivalent transactions with other trading parties, thereby placing them at a competitive disadvantage: see *San Pellegrino SpA* v *Coca-Cola Export Corp* [1989] 4 CMLR 137.

iv) Making the negotiation of contracts subject to acceptance by the other parties of supplementary obligations which, by their nature or according to commercial usage, have no connection with the subject of such contracts.

This catalogue is intended to be illustrative and, in common with the list elaborated in relation to Article 85(1), is not exhaustive.

d) *Merger control in the European Community - the original provisions*

The Community competition provisions make no express reference to the control of mergers among undertakings in the Community. Notwithstanding this omission, the Commission has been prepared to apply both Articles 85(1) and 86 to mergers and takeovers. For example:

i) The acquisition of a competitor by a company which maintains a dominant position in a field may amount to an abuse of that position contrary to Article 86: *Continental Can* v *EC Commission* [1972] ECR 157. Such behaviour will be presumed when the acquisition is intended to eliminate effective competition in the particular market.

ii) Article 85(1) may be applied to acquisitions of shareholdings where a company acquires a minority stake in a competitor as leverage for the coordination of marketing strategy between the two undertakings: *British American Tobacco & RJ Reynolds Industries Inc* v *EC Commission* [1986] ECR 1899.

iii) Article 85(1) may also be infringed if a company enters into a joint venture or acquires an interest in a third company where the other principal shareholder is in a related field of business.

iv) Consortium bids may also violate Article 85 if the consortium involves competitors seeking to acquire a competitor or attempting to influence its behaviour.

Notwithstanding the application of these provisions to individual cases, until 1990, the European Commission had no specific mandate to investigate mergers or acquisitions within the Community.

e) *Merger control in the European Community - the Merger Control Regulation 1990*

After a series of controversial takeovers in the early 1980s, the Council of Ministers agreed to adopt Community legislation conferring authority on the Commission to investigate takeovers and mergers above a certain threshold. Council Regulation 4064/89 (1989) was enacted for this purpose and came into force in September 1990.

The Regulation uses the term 'concentration' to refer to mergers and takeovers. A concentration arises where either: (a) two or more previously independent undertakings merge into one; or (b) one or more persons already controlling at least one undertaking acquire, whether by purchase of securities or assets, direct or indirect control of the whole or part of one or more other undertakings.

Article one of the Regulation confers regulatory jurisdiction upon the Commission over all mergers involving a 'Community dimension'. A concentration has a 'Community dimension' where:

i) the aggregate worldwide turnover of all the undertakings concerned is more than ECU 5,000 million; and

ii) the aggregate Community-wide turnover of each of the undertakings concerned is more than ECU 250 million.

Aggregate turnover is calculated on the basis of amounts derived by the undertakings concerned in the preceding financial year from the sale of goods or the supply of services during the course of ordinary trading activities. Deductions are permitted for sales rebates, value added tax and other taxes directly related to turnover.

Certain types of mergers are expressly excluded from the jurisdiction of the Commission by virtue of the regulation itself. A concentration has no Community dimension where, despite satisfying both the necessary criteria, all of the undertakings involved make more than two-thirds of its aggregate Community-wide turnover within one and the same Member State. In such cases, the concentration has no Community dimension.

Even if a merger is approved by the Commission, Member States retain a veto over mergers in particularly sensitive sectors of their national economies. Member States may take appropriate measures to protect legitimate national interests such as public security, the plurality of the media and the maintenance of prudent rules for the conduct of commerce. However, such measures are subject to the requirement that they must be compatible with the general principles and other provisions of Community law.

Concentrations with a Community dimension must be notified to the Commission not more than one week after the conclusion of the agreement, or the announcement of a public bid, or the acquisition of the necessary controlling interest. If a merger is by consent, the notification must be made jointly by all the parties involved. In all other cases, including contested acquisitions, the notification to the Commission must be made by the acquiring undertaking.

The Commission is empowered to impose fines on persons, undertaking or associations of undertakings if they intentionally or negligently fail to notify the Commission of a concentration with a Community dimension. These fines can range from ECU 1,000 to ECU 50,000.

Once a concentration with a Community dimension is notified, two options are available to the Commission:

i) The commission can conclude that the concentration does not fall within the scope of the Regulation and must record such a finding by means of a decision.

ii) it can find that the concentration falls within the scope of the Regulation. In such a case, it may adopt one of two alternative courses of action:

- declare that the concentration, while within the scope of the Regulation, is not incompatible with the common market and will not therefore be opposed; or
- find that the concentration falls within the Regulation and is incompatible with the common market in which case it is obliged to initiate proceedings.

In each of these cases, the Commission must make its decision within one month of the notification.

To appraise the compatibility of a concentration with the common market, the Commission must evaluate the implications of the concentration in the light of the need to preserve and develop effective competition within the common market, taking into account, inter alia, the structure of all the relevant markets concerned and the actual or potential competition from other undertakings both within and outside the Community. In making this assessment, the Commission must consider the market position of the undertakings concerned, their economic and financial power, the opportunities available to both suppliers and consumers, access to supplies and markets, the existence of legal or other barriers to the entry of the product into particular markets, the interests of intermediate and ultimate consumers, as well as technical and economic development and progress.

f) *Determination of infringements of European Competition law*

The Commission may investigate alleged anti-competitive behaviour either on an ex proprio motu basis, or at the instance of interested parties. Interested parties permitted to notify the Commission of anti-competitive behaviour include Member States, undertakings and individuals who are affected by the alleged infringement of the competition rules; see *BMW Belgium SA* v *EC Commission* [1979] ECR 2435.

Although the Commission has discretion whether or not to pursue an investigation after allegations have been made by interested parties, it is obliged to notify a petitioner if no action is to be taken.

In conducting its investigations, the Commission has a right to obtain all necessary information from the competent authorities of Member States as well as from undertakings and associations subject to investigation. The owners of undertakings or, in the case of companies, the persons authorised by the articles of association to represent incorporated bodies, are obliged to supply such information.

Generally, the Commission exercises its power to request information in two stages. Initially, an informal request is made to the undertaking which states the legal basis and purpose of the request and specifying a time limit for a response. At this stage an undertaking is under no legal obligation to reply. If the undertaking fails to respond to the informal request, the Commission makes a formal decision under the authority of Article 11(5) of Regulation 17/62 to require the information. Failure to respect such a decision will result in the imposition of penalties.

After adopting a decision to investigate, the Commission is authorised to examine books and business records, to take copies from such documents, to demand oral explanations, and to enter premises: see *Hoechst AG* v *EC Commission*, Cases 46/87 and 227/88, not yet reported. Prior to exercising these powers, Community officials must produce authorisation in writing specifying both the subject-matter and purpose of the investigation and the penalties for non-compliance. Officials of the competent authorities in Member States may assist the Commission, if the Commission makes such a request.

Before the Commission renders a decision on a matter of competition policy after an investigation, undertakings and associations of undertakings have a right to be heard on the matters to which the Commission has taken objection. The Commission has issued Regulation 99/63 (1963) specifying the procedure for conducting such hearings. The Commission will inform undertakings of objections raised against their conduct and they will be given an opportunity to make their views known in writing. In addition, any natural or legal person with a sufficient interest is also entitled to make their views known. After all written correspondence has been submitted, the Commission will convene a hearing at which time all interested parties shall have an opportunity to submit oral arguments.

g) *Power to fine*

According to Article 15 of Council Regulation 17/62, as amended, the Commission may impose fines ranging from ECU 1,000 to ECU 1,000,000 or a sum in excess of this limit but not exceeding 10 per cent of the turnover, against any undertakings found in violation of Articles 85(1) and 86. In addition, fines can be imposed for the supply of false or misleading information, for the submission of incomplete books or other documents or for refusal to submit to an investigation.

The Commission also has authority to require undertakings to adopt particular courses of action including:

i) discontinuing infringements of Articles 85(1) and 86;

ii) discontinuing action prohibited under Article 8(3) of Regulation 17/62;

iii) supplying completely and truthfully any information requested under Article 11(5); and

iv) submitting to any investigation ordered under the investigative powers of the Commission.

While the Commission has authority to fix the amount of the fine, the national authorities concerned enforce the decision by virtue of Article 192 EEC Treaty in accordance with their rules of civil procedure.

12.3 Relevant cases

United Brands v *EC Commission* [1978] ECR 207: Identification of the criteria applied in order to determine the relevant product market.

Cooperatieve Vereniging 'Suiker Unie' v *EC Commission* [1975] ECR 1663: The relevant geographic market is the whole of the Community unless the pattern and volume of production allow for a determination otherwise.

Hoffman La Roche v *EC Commission* [1979] ECR 451: Illustration of the practices deemed to be dominant.

Continental Can v *EC Commission* [1975] ECR 495: Description of the concept of abuse.

Sacchi [1974] ECR 409: Public bodies and corporations may be considered undertakings for the purpose of competition law.

12.4 Relevant materials

D R Price, 'Abuse of a Dominant Position' (1990) 3 ECLR 80.

L Gyselden et al, 'Article 86 EEC: The Monopoly Power Measurement Issue Revisited' (1986) 11 EL Rev 134.

M Siragusa, 'The Application of Article 86 to the Pricing Policy of Dominant Companies' (1979) 16 CML Rev 179.

V Korah & P Lasok, 'Philip Morris and Its Aftermath: Merger Control?' (1988) 25 CMLR 333.

J S Venit, 'The "Merger" Control Regulation: Europe Comes of Age ... or Caliban's Dinner' (1990) 27 CMLR 7.

W Elland, 'The Mergers Control Regulation (EEC) No 4064/89' (1990) 3 ECLR 111.

12.5 Analysis of questions

In common with the regulation of commercial practices under Article 85, the application of the concept of abuse of a dominant position is particularly complex. The following examples consider some of the more complex issues, but, at a minimum, students should understand basic concepts such as 'abuse' and the 'relevant market'. Familiarity with the investigation procedure is also extremely important.

12.6 Questions

Question 1

British Breweries plc is an important producer of beer in the United Kingdom. Statistics shown that British Breweries account for some 12 per cent of all beer sold in the United Kingdom but that its British Brewlite is especially successful and accounts for 40 per cent of all non-alcoholic beer consumed in the UK.

a) British Breweries has been negotiating with County Beers Ltd with a view to merger. County Beers is the principal other producer of non-alcoholic beers and after merger the new company, British County Breweries, will control 65 per cent of the market in non-alcoholic beer.

b) British Breweries includes in its standard supply contract a requirement that pubs and other purchasers must display prominently its non-alcoholic beer and advertising materials. The advertising materials offer consumers 'healthy drinking discounts' whereby the more non-alcoholic beer they buy, the lower the price they have to pay. Since the healthy drinking discounts were introduced two years ago, British Breweries' sales have doubled and several small-scale producers of non-alcoholic beers have gone out of business.

Advise British Breweries as to the significance, if any, of EEC law for each of the above aspects of its business.

adapted from University of London LLB Examination
(for External Students) European Community Law 1990 Q7

General comment

A problem question requiring the application of Article 86 to hypothetical facts.

Skeleton solution

- British Breweries as an undertaking.
- Do the practices affect trade between Member States?
- Application of Article 86 - dominant position and abuse.

Suggested solution

a) British Breweries is clearly an undertaking for the purposes of Article 86, as is County Beers Ltd. Further, Article 86 covers all sectors of the economy and the sale of drink is not covered by any derogation to the Treaty. Therefore, whether the proposed merger amount would to an abuse of a dominant position depends on whether the criteria established under Article 86 are satisfied.

The acquisition of a competitor by a company which maintains a dominant position in the market may infringe Article 85 if the merger results in an abuse of a dominant position, and this abuse affects trade between Member States.

British Breweries could feasibly argue that, since its activities only take place in the United Kingdom, trade between Member States is not affected. In this case,

British law would apply and not Community competition law. However, in *Hugin* v *EC Commission* (1979), the European Court stated that the test for effect on trade is whether the practice constitutes a threat to the freedom of trade between Member States in a way that might harm the attainment of a single market. In other words, it is only necessary that it is possible to foresee with a sufficient degree of probability that the practice in question would influence, directly or indirectly, actually or potentially, the pattern of trade between Member States.

The broad wording of this test means that it is not difficult for the Commission to establish that an effect on trade exists. Activities by an undertaking which create artificial divisions of the national market have been found to have an indirect effect on trade, for example, by making it harder for imports to penetrate the market; see *Cementhandelaren* v *EC Commission* (1972). Specifically, under Article 86, the European Court has held that where a dominant company refused to sell chemicals to the smaller company which sold almost all of its production outside the common market, that the requirement of an effect on trade was satisfied by the impairment of the competitive structure in the Community. A similar test was applied in the *Woodpulp Case*. Thus, it would seem likely that Community law would apply to the activities of British Breweries, unless it could prove that its activities fell within the de minimus standard. In view of the market share held by British Breweries, this argument is likely to fail.

Next, it is necessary to ascertain whether British Breweries holds a dominant position, a term not defined in the EEC Treaty, but which has been interpreted to mean an overall independence of behaviour on the market 'which puts [undertakings] in a position to act without taking into account their competitors, purchasers or suppliers': *Continental Can* v *EC Commission* (1975). Absolute domination is not necessary.

There are two tests to establish a dominant position: (a) the identification of the relevant market; and (b) the assessment of the strength of the undertaking in question on the market.

It would be in British Breweries' interest to define the relevant market as broadly as possible, such as the market for all drinks, alcoholic and non-alcoholic, or at least the market for non-alcoholic drinks. In *United Brands* v *EC Commission* (1978), the Court had to decide whether bananas should be regarded as an independent market in themselves or, alternatively, part of the general market for fresh fruit. In this case, the Court adopted the test of limited interchangeability and decided that the banana could be 'singled out by such special features distinguishing it from other fruits that it is only to a limited extent interchangeable with them and it is only exposed to their competition in a way that is hardly perceptible'.

The same agreement may be used to distinguish alcoholic beer from non-alcoholic beer, the latter being developed expressly for its non-alcoholic content. Following the Court's reasoning in *Michelin* v *EC Commission* (1983) which distinguished the market in retreaded tyres from the market in replacement tyres, it could be argued that although other soft drinks are to some extent interchangeable with non-alcoholic beer, and hence in competition with such beer, sales of soft drinks do not sufficiently undermine the sales of non-alcoholic beer, which has been specifically developed for its similarity to beer and not just as another soft drink.

In assessing the strength of an undertaking in a market, the most important factor is the size of the undertaking's share of the relevant market. Market shares have normally been relatively high. In the *Continental Can Case,* above, the undertaking accounted for 50-60 per cent of the market in Germany for meat tins, 80-90 per cent of fish tins and 50-55 per cent for metal closures for glass jars. In *Hoffman La Roche* v *EC Commission* (1979), the undertaking held an 80 per cent share of the vitamin market. However, in *United Brands,* above, the Court was content to hold a figure of 40-45 per cent of the relevant market as constituting a dominant position. The Commission has said that a dominant position will usually be found once a market share of the order of 40-45 per cent is reached, but cannot be ruled out even as regards shares of between 20 and 40 per cent.

Furthermore, the rest of the market is likely to be fragmented - County Beers holds a 25 per cent share and the remaining 35 per cent is likely to belong to smaller producers. This factor underlines British Breweries' dominance.

Although nothing is known about British Breweries' financial resources or its performance, these factors suggest that the Commission would have a strong case for establishing the existence of a dominant position after merger.

However, to violate Article 86, British Breweries must be abusing their dominant position. One possible abuse is the takeover of competitors. The EEC Treaty does not contain any explicit merger control provision equivalent to Article 66 of the ECSC Treaty. However, in the *Continental Case*, above, the European Court established the principle that a merger which causes the strengthening of a dominant position may amount to abuse. In that case the undertakings under investigation had acquired control of two other companies. The Commission decided that the merger with one amounted to an abuse of a dominant position because it was a potential competitor and the effect of the acquisition was to practically wipe-out competition. Although the decision of the Commission was subsequently annulled on the ground that the facts had not been adequately analysed, the Court confirmed that Article 86 would be applicable in such circumstances.

For a merger to fall within the prohibition of Article 86, two conditions must be satisfied. First there must be a pre-existing dominant position to be abused - this has already been shown to be probable in *British Breweries' case.* It is possible that Article 86 also includes the case where a single merger operation between two leading firms results in the creation of a dominant position of such magnitude as to substantially fetter competition. If British Breweries are not deemed to hold a dominant position, its merger with County Beers would mean that the combined forces of the two undertakings would constitute a dominant position, although whether a 65 per cent share of the market is of sufficient magnitude is debatable.

Article 86 cannot apply to mergers falling short of dominance even if these seriously affect competition.

Also, in the *Continental Can Case*, the Court spoke of strengthening an undertaking's position to a point where all the remaining operators in the market are dependent upon it. In the light of developments in cases such as *Michelin* and *Hoffman La Roche*, it is unlikely that the Court would insist that a merger would have such a drastic effect before it would qualify as abuse.

Given this reasoning, it seems likely that the proposed merger would attract the prohibition in Article 86. British Breweries would therefore be well advised to notify the Commission of the proposed merger under Regulation 17 and seek a negative clearance under Article 2 to be assured that there are no grounds for intervention.

Two further matters should also be noted. First, since *BAT and Reynolds* v *EC Commission*, transfers of ownership and in particular minority acquisitions which result in the coordination of the behaviour of independent companies constitute a breach of Article 85. This reasoning could be applied to the British Breweries and County Beers merger. Second, Regulation 4064/89 has come into force and requires prior notice to the Commission of mergers and acquisitions. The language of this regulation reflects the existing law and the pre-existing law will continue to be used extensively.

b) Tying arrangements may also constitute an abuse of a dominant position. As illustrated by Article 86(d), where a person is required to accept, as a condition of entering into a contract, 'supplementary obligations which, by their nature or according to commercial usage, have no connection with the subject of such contracts', a prima facie infringement of competition law arises. The requirement that public houses and other purchasers must display British Breweries products and also advertisements in a prominent position appears to fall inside Article 86(d).

Such conditions may, however, be sanctioned by commercial usage. For example, the inclusion of a meal in the price of an airline ticket is an accepted use of tying. The onus would therefore be on British Breweries to establish that such conditions are an accepted commercial practice.

But, in this particular case the advertising goes beyond describing the attributes of the non-alcoholic beer by offering financial incentives towards its purchase, thus locking the consumer into the purchase of a single brand name, to the exclusion of other products. The main objection to tying is that it enables an undertaking with a dominant position in the market to gain a competitive advantage. Therefore, it is likely that the practices of British Breweries as regards the ancillary conditions for purchasers would fall foul of Article 86.

Even if British Breweries are not deemed to be abusing a dominant position, these contract terms may fall foul of Article 85(1)(e). The Brewers could, however, try to bring themselves within one of the existing exceptions to Article 85(1). By arguing that these contractual terms were necessary to establish non-alcoholic beer on the market, using the analogies drawn from two cases - *Société Technique Minière* v *Maschinenbau Ulm* (1966) and *Pronuptia* (1986) - such contractual terms might escape possible contravention of the competition provisions.

Alternatively, British Breweries could seek an exemption from liability under Article 85(3) by arguing that the contractual terms contribute to improving the production or distribution of goods. British Breweries is likely to be on weaker ground here since the Commission insists that the gain to welfare must exceed what could have been achieved without the restriction on competition: see *Re Ford Werke* (1984). In British Breweries' case, competition has clearly been restricted since several small-scale producers have gone out of business.

Question 2

Amalgamated Drinks Ltd and Acme Spirits Ltd are both private companies which produce whisky and other spirits for the United Kingdom market. Amalgamated Drinks has captured 50 per cent of the market in whisky products, while Acme Spirits maintains a market share of approximately 20 per cent. However, Amalgamated Drinks has initiated a takeover bid for the White Heather Co which possesses around 15 per cent of the whisky market in the United Kingdom.

Acme Spirits wish to prevent the merger of these two companies on the grounds that such a development would threaten its position in the market. An employee has recently been hired by Acme Spirits after having worked for Amalgamated Drinks for the last ten years. He has acquired a number of confidential documents regarding the future marketing strategies of Amalgamated Drinks after the takeover, much of which suggests that Amalgamated Drinks seek to reap monopoly profits from this venture. However, Acme are also concerned that the Commission's investigation may require them to reveal confidential information at the inquiry.

Advise Acme on the Community aspect of this situation.

Question prepared by the Author
February 1991

General comment

Another problem question requiring students to apply Article 86 to set of hypothetical facts.

Skeleton solution

- Possibility of an interim injunction against the proposed merger.
- Application of Article 86.
- Possibility of complaining to the Commission.
- Treatment of confidential information.
- Remedy for failing to observe this obligation.

Suggested solution

It is clear that Acme Ltd can base an application for interlocutory relief on an alleged breach of Article 86 of the EEC Treaty. Community law is part of the law of the Member States so that liability will arise where one person, acting in contravention of Community law, causes loss to another person. In these circumstances, a national court can grant an injunction where this is considered to be the appropriate remedy.

The leading case on this subject is *Garden Cottage Foods Ltd* v *Milk Marketing Board* (1983). In this case, the defendant, who produced all the bulk butter in England and Wales, pursuant to a new policy, decided to limit the number of distributors to whom it was prepared to sell its butter. The plaintiffs had previously been one of the Board's distributors, but were not included on the new, reduced list. The plaintiffs, who had resold butter obtained from the Board to a customer in the Netherlands, argued that the Board was abusing a dominant position and this affected trade between Member States contrary to Article 86 of the EEC Treaty. The plaintiffs, accordingly, applied to the English High Court for an interim injunction to restrain the defendants from withholding supplies of butter.

In the High Court, Parker J, took the view that while it was arguable that a breach of Article 86 had occurred, injunctive relief was not appropriate since, if such a breach was confirmed by the Commission, damages would be an adequate remedy. Although on appeal from this ruling the Court of Appeal was, indeed, prepared to grant an interim injunction, this decision was reversed by the House of Lords (Lord Wilberforce dissenting), since whether or not injunctive relief is granted in any given case is a matter for the trial judge's discretion.

In the instant problem, therefore, whether or not Acme Ltd will be granted the interlocutory injunction sought is a matter for the judge's discretion as to whether it would be the appropriate remedy in the circumstances. No doubt because of the alleged threat posed to Acme Ltd's survival, a strong case can be made to the judge that an interlocutory injunction would be the most appropriate remedy in the circumstances.

Article 86 of the EEC Treaty states that any abuse by one or more undertakings of a dominant position within the common market or in a substantial part of it shall be prohibited as incompatible with the common market insofar as it may affect trade between Member States. The article then goes on to give illustrations of such abuse.

In deciding whether a prima facie breach of Article 86 has taken place in this case, it must first be considered whether Amalgamated Drinks Ltd holds a dominant position in the relevant geographical and product market. The United Kingdom would be regarded as a 'substantial part' of the common market for this purpose: *Michelin* v *EC Commission* (1983). The relevant product market would be alcoholic spirits. A product market determination must take into account product-substitutes. In this case, there are a number of product substitutes for whisky; although barriers to entry to the relevant market must also be considered.

A continuing market share of 50 per cent of whiskies would be important, but not per se decisive, as to market dominance. One important factor to be taken into consideration in this regard would be the market share of the nearest rival in the market. Thus in *United Brands* v *EC Commission* (1978), the undertaking under consideration was held to have a dominant position in the banana market in several Community countries when it had approximately 45 per cent of the market, about twice the share of its nearest rival.

Assuming that the Commission (always subject to the Court's ruling if there is an appeal against the decision of the Commission) concludes that Amalgamated Drinks Ltd does hold a dominant position in the relevant market, it would then have to decide whether it was guilty of abusing that position and whether such abuse may affect trade between Member States. Article 86 provides a number of examples of abusive activities and it is clear that the range of abusive activity for the purpose of that provision is very wide. The Commission has certainly held that predatory pricing (eg selling goods at excessively low prices to damage rivals) by a dominant undertaking can amount to abusive conduct for this purpose: see *Akzo* v *EC Commission* (1987).

There would probably be no difficulty in concluding that the abuse complained of would have the potential to affect trade between Member States, since, in particular, the elimination of the White Heather Company by Amalgamated Drinks would obviously give it a freer hand with regards to pricing policy. It could, therefore, probably be concluded that the facts given in this question do indicate a prima facie breach of Article 86.

The Commission must reach conclusions concerning violations of competition law on the basis of the information available to it. Regulation 17/62 empowers the Commission, under Articles 11 and 14, to obtain information from business undertakings, in the case of Article 11 on the basis of a written request and, in the case of Article 14 by an actual investigation, with or without prior warning. In addition to information gathered under Articles 11 and 14 above, the Commission will use information which comes from either source, even from prior communications from undertakings applying for exemption or negative clearance. Furthermore, information may be sent to the Commission by those who are complaining to the Commission about the activities of other enterprises.

Difficulties arise when an organisation claims that information concerning it has been stolen or otherwise obtained from breaches of confidence by a third party and then passed to the Commission. This point in fact arose in *Hoffman La Roche* v *EC Commission* (1979). Although in this case an allegation was made that the Commission had obtained confidential information in an irregular manner, the allegation was denied by the Commission and later withdrawn by the undertaking concerned. Thus, the European Court was not called upon to rule on the matter but it appears highly likely that in a case where it could be shown that information has reached the Commission as a result of an irregularity, the Court would forbid its use in any proceedings by the Commission.

All the institutions of the Community and their staff are under a duty not to disclose information of the kind covered by the obligation of professional secrecy: Article 214 of the EEC Treaty. Further, Regulation 17/62, in several articles, also deals with the question of professional secrecy with regard to information acquired by the Commission in the exercise of its information-gathering powers granted by the Regulation. Thus, in particular, Article 20 provides, inter alia, that the Commission and its staff shall not disclose information covered by the obligation of professional secrecy.

The duty of the Commission to protect the business secrets of undertakings it is investigating was considered in *Akzo* v *EC Commission* (1986). In this case, the Court stated that the Commission might, under Article 19(2) of Regulation 17/62, provide third-party complainers with certain information covered by the obligation of professional secrecy, to the extent to which it might be necessary 'to smooth the conduct of the investigation'. However, the Court also stressed that Regulation 17/62 requires that in publishing information the Commission must have regard to the legitimate interests of undertakings in the protection of their business secrets. Accordingly, the Court pointed out that in no circumstances might documents containing business secrets be disclosed to third-party complainers.

If Acme wishes to challenge the Commission's decision concerning Amalgamated Drinks, under Article 173 of the EEC Treaty, it will clearly have standing to do so since, although the decision will be addressed to Amalgamated Drinks, it will be of direct and individual concern to Acme Ltd. Amalgamated Drinks could also challenge the decision on the basis of the alleged infringement of an essential procedural requirement if no hearing was held on the matter. Article 19(2) of Regulation 17/62 entitles complainers to put their arguments to the Commission. Amalgamated Drinks could claim that the failure of the Commission to convene a hearing prejudiced its effective participation in the proceedings, with the consequence that an incorrect decision was adopted.

However, while this would be a ground for challenging the Commission's decision in favour of Amalgamated Drinks, it is submitted that the Commission's defence, based on its duty to keep confidential the business secrets of undertakings it is investigating, would be successful: *Akzo* v *EC Commission*, above.

Question 3

Two American airline corporations, together with two other airline companies - one Canadian and one Swiss - have negotiated an agreement to fix the price of airline tickets for transatlantic flights from London. The purpose of this agreement is to put a British airline company, which offers transatlantic flights at a substantially discounted rate, out of business.

This agreement was submitted to the European Commission who, after an investigation, issued a comfort letter. This assurance was subsequently withdrawn after the Commission had realised the full implications of the agreement. No hearing was held by the Commission prior to the withdrawal of the comfort letter.

What are the legal implications of this situation under Community competition law?

Question prepared by the Author
February 1991

General comment

A question requiring a description of the rights and duties of undertakings as regards competition law.

Skeleton solution

- Effect of a comfort letter.
- Right to challenge the decision of the Commission.
- Extra-territorial application of Community law.
- Breach of an essential procedural requirement.

Suggested solution

Article 15(5) of Regulation 17/62 provides that fines for infringement of Community competition policy shall not be imposed in respect of acts taking place after notification to the Commission following an application for exemption and before the decision of the Commission has been reached regarding the application. However, Article 15(6) of Regulation 17/62 then specifies that the above provision shall not have effect where the Commission has informed the undertakings concerned that after a preliminary examination it has formed the view that the practices infringe Community competition policy.

It is now clear that notification by the Commission, as above, since it defines the legal position of the parties involved, will be regarded by the European Court as a decision: *Cimenteries* v *EC Commission* (1967). Because a notification by the Commission of its conclusion is tantamount to a decision by the Commission, the parties affected by it can apply to the Court under Article 173, within the prescribed period, to have it quashed. Since decisions, inter alia, must specify the reasons on which they are based, such reasons must, consequently, be set out in any decisions made under Article 15(6) of Regulation 17/62. Otherwise this will be a ground for annulment of the decision by the Court.

All four parties to the agreement under consideration in this question will have standing to seek a review of the decision contained in the letter. Article 173(2) of the EEC Treaty provides that any legal or natural person may institute proceedings in the Court against a decision addressed to that person. Clearly then, the actual addressee of the decision has standing to challenge it before the Court.

Further, Article 173(2) provides that a natural or legal person shall have standing to challenge a decision, inter alia, addressed to another person where that decision is of direct and individual concern to the first person. There can be no doubt that the airline companies, though not addressees of the letter-decision, would also, by passing the test laid down by the Court in *Plaumann* v *EC Commission* (1963), have standing to initiate proceedings before the Court to annul the Commission's decision. The

Plaumann test, in regard to the problem under consideration, is whether the decision affects the applicant 'by reason of circumstances in which they are differentiated from all others so that they are individually distinguished'. Clearly, the decision does affect them.

The four non-Community organisations must be advised that the Commission does not hesitate to apply Community competition law to undertakings situated outside the territory of the Community if the operations of such undertakings have an unlawful effect within that territory: see the *Woodpulp Cartel Case* (1988). The European Court has resolutely supported the Commission in its attempts to acquire the extra-territorial application of competition law. Clearly therefore any argument raised before the Court questioning the competence of the Commission in this regard will be dismissed.

However, the four companies will be on much firmer ground in claiming that the Commission has sought no comments or advice from them. Article 19 of Regulation 17/62 provides that before taking certain decisions, including a decision under Article 3, which requires undertakings to terminate infringements of competition law, the Commission shall give the undertakings involved an opportunity to be heard on the matters under consideration. If the non-Community undertakings can convince the Court that the letter-decision of the Commission amounts to a decision of the type covered by Article 19, and that they were denied an opportunity to be heard, this would be a ground for the Court to quash the decision.

Where the European Court has reviewed the legality of an act under Article 173 of the EEC Treaty, such actions may be held void if the action is well founded. Accordingly, if the act concerned in this problem - the Commission's decision that the notified agreement does not qualify for exemption - is annulled by the Court, then presumably the application for exemption will be reinstated and given continued immunity from fines unless and until the Commission adopts a valid final decision to reject the application.

Question 4

Describe the powers of the European Commission to conduct investigations into alleged violations of Community competition policy.

Question prepared by the Author
February 1991

General comment

A general essay type question on the powers of the Commission to conduct investigations.

Skeleton solution

- Authority of the Commission's powers - Regulation 17/62.
- Power to compel evidence.
- Sanctions for refusal to cooperate.

- Fines and penalties.

Suggested solution

The basic provision that governs investigations against undertakings for breaches of Articles 85 and 86 is Council Regulation 17/62 (1962). The Commission may initiate proceedings on its own initiative or in respect to a complaint by a 'natural or legal person claiming a legitimate interest' or in response to a notification by the undertaking in question.

During investigation proceedings, the Commission has certain fact finding powers to determine whether or not the undertaking is in breach of Community competition law. These are of a two-fold nature, as provided for in Articles 11 and 14 of Regulation 17/62.

Under Article 11, the Commission may obtain all necessary information from the governments and competent authorities of the Member States and from undertakings and associations of undertakings. This is effected by means of an informal request being made with a specified date for reply. Despite the non-compelling nature of this request, an undertaking may still be fined should it be subsequently discovered that the undertaking gave an incorrect response to a question posed by the Commission.

If an undertaking refuses to reply, the Commission may adopt a decision ordering the supply of information under Article 11(5) of Regulation 17. If the undertaking continues to refuse to comply, it may again be fined under Article 15(1)(b), or it will be made the subject of a periodic payment under Article 16(1)(c).

By virtue of Article 14, the Commission may enter the premises of an undertaking, examine and take copies of, or extracts from, books and business records and ask for oral explanations on the spot.

Once the Commission has acquired authority to conduct an investigation, an undertaking is subject to an obligation to cooperate fully with the Commission. If an undertaking fails to cooperate, the Commission can adopt a decision under Article 14(3) requiring an undertaking to cooperate. Refusal risks a fine or a periodic payment.

The Commission has an option whether to proceed on the basis of Article 14(2) or 14(3). It is not a two stage procedure as is the case under Article 11. Such investigatory action may also be taken against subsidiaries of undertakings if they are deemed to be a single economic unit.

Undertakings are entitled to claim legal professional privilege with regard to certain documents. This right was recognised by the European Court in *AM & S* v *EC Commission* (1982). It relates to communications made for the purposes and in the interests of the client's right of defence and extends to earlier written communications which have a relationship to the subject-matter of the procedure. However, this privilege may only be claimed for communications emanating from independent lawyers established in the Community. This excludes in-house lawyers and lawyers from non-EEC countries.

If the status of a document is disputed, the Commission may adopt a decision ordering disclosure. This decision may, of course, be challenged under Article 173 of the EEC Treaty.

Once the Commission considers that it has collected sufficient material to initiate proceedings, it will do so by sending the undertaking a statement of objections. It will inform the undertaking of the basis and the facts which the Commission consider violate Articles 85 or 86. After the statement of objections has been issued, the undertaking may examine the Commission files relating to the case, except for business secrets and internal documents.

The undertaking will be invited to reply to the statement within a specified period, normally about three months. It may request an oral hearing, which is governed by Commission Regulation 99/63 (1963). This would enable it to further develop its written submissions.

Where the Commission has decided that an undertaking has indeed infringed Articles 85 or 86, under Article 3(1) of Regulation 17/62, it may order this state of affairs to be terminated and specify the steps to be taken, which may even include an order to supply.

If the Commission believes that the infringement of the competition rules was negligent or intentional, it may fine an undertaking between 1,000 and 1,000,000 ECU or up to 10 per cent of the previous year's turnover. The quantum of the fine will depend on such factors as the duration and gravity of the infringements and the degree of cooperation by the undertaking throughout the course of the investigation: see *Chemiefarma* v *EC Commission* (1970).

Proceedings may also be terminated by means of a comfort letter. This will state that the file on an investigation is closed pending a change of legal or factual circumstances (such as the existence of fresh evidence). Such a letter is of no legal import and it is questionable whether even the Commission is bound by such a letter even in the absence of a change of circumstances: see *Frubo* v *EC Commission* (1975).

If an undertaking wishes to appeal the decision of the Commission, recourse lies to the Court of First Instance, which exercises jurisdiction in this particular field.

13 THE COMMON AGRICULTURAL POLICY

13.1 Introduction

The Common Agricultural Policy has been the most successful, and most controversial, policy of the European Community. Expenditure on this policy accounts for a considerable portion of the Community budget. However, the Common Agricultural Policy has been responsible for moving the Community from the position of being a net importer of agricultural products to that of a net exporter. This has been achieved by a complex system of domestic and export subsidies, administered by an equally complex bureaucracy. Article 3(d) of the EEC Treaty instructs the Community to establish a common market in agricultural products, while Articles 38 to 47 define the scope of the Common Agricultural Policy. Considerable Community legislation is also required to give effect to the policy.

13.2 Key points

a) *The scope of the Common Agricultural Policy*

According to Article 38 of the EEC Treaty, the common market extends to all agricultural trade and trade in agricultural products. Agricultural products are products of the soil, of stockfarming and of fisheries, as well as products which have undergone first-stage processing directly related to these products.

Products which qualify as agricultural products are enumerated in Annex II to the EEC Treaty. This list has been amended on a number of occasions, but most importantly by Council Regulation 7/59 (1959). Any product which does not appear on this list is not an agricultural product for the purposes of Article 38 and is therefore not regulated by the Common Agricultural Policy.

b) *The objectives of the Common Agricultural Policy*

The objectives of the CAP are set out in Article 39 of the EEC Treaty. This provision identifies five primary aims of the policy:

i) To increase agricultural productivity by promoting technical progress and by ensuring the rational development of agricultural production and the optimum utilisation of the factors of production, particularly labour.

ii) To ensure a fair standard of living for the agricultural community, in particular, by increasing the individual earnings of persons engaged in agriculture.

iii) To stabilise product markets.

iv) To assure the availability of supplies.

v) To ensure that supplies reach consumers at reasonable prices.

The Treaty also requires that a number of factors must be taken into account in formulating the CAP, including:

i) the particular nature of the agricultural activity, which results from the social structure of agriculture and from structural and natural disparities between the various agricultural regions;

ii) the need to effect appropriate adjustments by degrees; and

iii) the fact that in the Member States agriculture constitutes a sector closely related to the economy as a whole.

In the event of a conflict among these objectives and factors, preference is given to the interests of the farming community: *W Beaus GmbH & Co* v *Hauptzollamt Muchen* [1968] ECR 83.

c) *Evolution of the Common Agricultural Policy*

A number of guidelines were drawn up in 1960 by the Council of Ministers, based on the proposals of the Commission, for the purposes of implementing the CAP. These guidelines implemented four main principles: the free movement of agricultural products; a joint agricultural and commercial policy; a common price level for agricultural products throughout the Community; and the co-ordination of structural reform.

Legislation was progressively adopted to achieve these goals. Article 43 provides that the Council of Ministers shall, acting on a proposal from the Commission, make regulations, issue directives and take decisions to implement the CAP.

d) *The creation of European market organisations*

Article 40(2) of the EEC Treaty provides that, in order to achieve the objectives set out in Article 39, a common organisation of agricultural markets is to be established for individual agricultural products. These organisations were to take one of three structures:

i) Common rules on competition;

ii) Compulsory coordination of the various national market organisations; or

iii) A European market organisation.

The European market organisation has been the preferred instrument for controlling the vast majority of products and nearly all agricultural products are now covered by such an organisation.

A European market organisation facilitates the concept of an open market to which every producer has access and is designed to remove all barriers to intra-Community trade, to create a common system of border regulations for import and export, and to establish common rules for the regulation of competition.

Market organisations are also intended to prevent discrimination between producers on the ground of nationality. Where a common organisation has been established for a product, Member States are required to refrain from introducing national measures which would derogate from the functioning of the organisation: *Pigs and Bacon Commission* v *McCarren & Co* [1979] ECR 2161 and *EC Commission* v *Germany* [1989] 2 CMLR 733.

e) *The structure of European market organisations*

While the exact structure of market organisations varies from one particular organisation to another, each organisation functions on two main principles: the creation of a price policy; and the establishment of a trading system.

i) Price policy

A typical price policy consists of the setting of two prices: the target (or guide) price; and the intervention price.

Target prices are set annually by the Council for each agricultural product based on the prices which the Council believes producers will receive for their produce during the marketing seasons for which the prices are fixed. These prices are not binding, and are designed to assist producers budget for the forthcoming year. However, Member States are not permitted to enact measures which could prevent producers from achieving a price which approximates to the target price. See *Galli* [1975] ECR 47 and *Russo* [1976] ECR 45.

The intervention price is the price at which the Community guarantees that it will purchase agricultural products from farmers. These are fixed below the target price and are designed to ensure that farmers will be able to dispose of their produce. It is this practice which results in wine lakes and butter mountains since the Community is obliged to purchase produce regardless of supply and demand.

Intervention agencies have been established in all Member States in order to facilitate this policy. Within the United Kingdom, the Intervention Board for Agricultural Products undertakes this task. The intervention prices are also fixed annually by the Council of Ministers, based on a proposal from the Commission.

ii) The establishment of a trading system

There are five elements to the administration of a trading system: threshold prices, levies, refunds, import licences and export licences.

Threshold prices are prices set for imports of agricultural products into the Community from third countries. These are also fixed by the Council at a level which makes the selling price of the product equal to the target price within the Community. This mechanism is designed to protect Community producers from cheap imports from third countries.

Levies are duties charged on imports or exports of agricultural products. They are intended to compensate for the difference between world prices and prices within the Community. Their function is to protect and stabilise the market within the Community from the fluctuations which occur in world markets: *Frecassetti* v *Italian Finance Administration* [1976] ECR 983.

Import levies are fixed daily by the Commission at a rate which ensures that the price of Community produce is the same, or less than, the price of the imported product. Export levies have been introduced to regulate trade in those few agricultural products which have a higher value on the world market than within the Community.

Export refunds are payments made to producers on the export of their goods from the Community. These are intended to compensate farmers for the difference between Community prices and generally lower world prices for agricultural products. The purpose of export refunds is to encourage the export of agricultural produce to foreign markets and thereby lowering the volume or quantity of surplus agricultural production.

Import and export licences are generally required for all transactions between the Community and third states involving agricultural products. In the United Kingdom, such licences are issued by the Intervention Board for Agricultural Produce. A number of exceptions have been made to the general requirement that an import or export licence must be obtained. Licences are not required in respect of products:

- which are placed in free circulation within the Community;
- in respect of which export is effected under a customs procedure which allows imports free from customs duties or charges having an equivalent effect;
- which are placed in free circulation under provisions governing the treatment of returned goods; or
- which are re-exported and the exporter provides proof of the repayment or remission of import duties.

f) *Products not subject to European market organisations*

Agricultural products which are not subject to European market organisations nevertheless continue to be regulated by the general rules of the EEC Treaty. Therefore, provisions relating to the removal of customs duties and charges having an equivalent effect apply unless marketing organisations have been established: *EC Commission* v *Ireland* [1985] ECR 1761. Further, Member States are also required to eliminate state trading monopolies in respect of agricultural products not subject to market organisations.

In practice, few agricultural products are not covered by market organisations, the most notable exceptions being cotton, peas, ethyl alcohol and sweet potatoes.

g) *The application of Community competition policy to agricultural products*

By virtue of Article 42 of the EEC Treaty, principles of Community competition policy are applicable to agricultural products 'only to the extent determined by the Council within the framework of Article 43(2) and (3)', account being taken of the objectives set out in Article 39 itself.

Council Regulation 26/62 (1962) applies Articles 85 to 90 of the EEC Treaty to agricultural products, subject to a number of derogations set out in Article 2(1) of the Regulation. In particular, Article 85(1) is inapplicable to:

i) agreements, decisions and concerted practices which form an integral part of a national (not European) market organisation;

ii) agreements which are necessary to attain the objectives set out in Article 39; and

iii) agreements, decisions and concerted practices which concern the production or sale of agricultural products or the use of joint facilities for the storage, treatment or processing of agricultural products.

h) *Structure and guidance provisions*

One of the fundamental objectives of the CAP is to increase agricultural productivity by promoting technical progress and by ensuring the rationale development of agricultural production and the optimum utilisation of the factors of production: Article 39(1)(a) EEC Treaty. In order to achieve this objective, the small inefficient farms which existed when the CAP was first conceived were to be amalgamated into larger, more productive units. This was to be achieved by providing finance for farmers wishing to leave the land.

In 1968, the Commission proposed a Memorandum on the Reform of Agriculture in the EEC (known as the Mansholt Plan). The aim of this programme was to produce larger, more efficient farms. This was to be achieved by adopting a number of measures.

i) Member States were required to introduce an aid scheme to set aside arable land.

ii) States were also obliged to promote the conversion of production to areas in which surpluses did not exist.

iii) Aid was made available to farmers who wished to improve their occupational skills and competence.

iv) Agricultural groups were encouraged to engage in mutual assistance projects and joint ventures.

v) Specific measures were introduced to assist mountain and hill farming and farming in less-favoured areas.

vi) Early retirement among the farming community was to be promoted.

vii) Special aid schemes were introduced to facilitate protection of the environment.

13.3 Relevant cases

Hauptzollamt Bielefeld v *Konig* [1974] ECR 607: Definition of the concept of 'products of first stage processing'.

W Beus GmbH v *Hauptzollamt Muchen* [1968] ECR 83: The paramount objective of the Common Agricultural Policy is the principle of Community preference in favour of farmers.

Pig Marketing Board v *Redmond* [1978] ECR 2347: Discussion on the principal attributes of European market organisations.

Firma Walter Rau Lebensmittel Werke v *European Community* [1988] 2 CMLR 704: European market organisations are based on the fundamental principle of the prohibition of discrimination on the ground of nationality.

EC Commission v *Germany*, [1989] 2 CMLR 733: Unilateral national measures are void if they derogate from the principles of the CAP even if they are designed to assist achieve its goals.

EC Commission v *Ireland* [1985] ECR 1761: Products not covered by European market organisations still remain subject to the general obligations of the EEC Treaty.

13.4 Relevant materials

J Usher, *The Common Agricultural Policy of the European Community* (1989).

D Lasok, *The Law of the Economy of the European Communities* (1980) 283-322.

13.5 Analysis of questions

Since the Common Agricultural Policy is such a controversial subject, students must be aware of the problems which the policy has caused. This involves keeping up to date with developments within the Community itself and the GATT. A detailed knowledge of the vast volume of detailed legislation concerning the day-to-day administration of the policy is not necessary, but familiarity with the general structure and content of the policy should be acquired. Since this topic is relatively finite, it can often provide a solid basis for achieving reasonable marks during examinations.

13.6 Questions

Question 1

What are the objectives of the Common Agricultural Policy (CAP); how is it structured and what results has it achieved? Discuss.

University of Glasgow LLB Examination
June 1987 Q7

General comment

A general question requiring a description of the main principles behind the policy.

Skeleton solution

- The five objectives specified in Article 39 of the EEC Treaty.
- Structure: common market organisations; price policy; trading systems.
- Structure and guidance provisions.

Suggested solution

Article 39 of the EEC Treaty establishes five separate objectives of the Common Agricultural Policy. First, the policy should promote increased productivity by encouraging technical progress, the development of agricultural production and the optimum utilisation of all the factors of production. Labour is specifically identified as a factor of production which should be most efficiently employed.

Second, the policy should ensure a fair standard of living among the agricultural community by increasing the individual earnings of farmers. Third, the policy should stabilise markets in agricultural produce. Fourth, supplies of produce to the market place should be ensured. Finally, supplies to consumers at reasonable prices should be ensured. The Common Agricultural Policy seeks to achieve each of these objectives through a number of different means.

Agricultural productivity is stimulated by two separate aspects of the policy. Farmers are guaranteed payment for the agricultural products which they cultivate and, in addition, the Community provides structural assistance to allow farmers to purchase modern machinery to maximise efficiency.

Payments to farmers are guaranteed through the creation of European market organisations for individual agricultural products. These organisations set price policies which ensure that, regardless of the factors of supply and demand, the European Community will purchase the produce. These price policies are supported by a complex system which allows the market organisations to regulate supply and demand - between certain parameters - within the Community.

Price policies for agricultural products are based on two separate prices; the target price and the intervention price. Each year the Council of Ministers establishes target prices for agricultural products. These are prices which the Council believes will be met for agricultural products in the forthcoming year. These estimates are based on projected supply and demand for each commodity. Target prices do not create legal obligations on the part of the Council; they are merely guide prices to allow farmers to calculate their budgets.

Target prices also function to encourage trade between markets within the Community. Where, for example, prices in the United Kingdom for particular cereals are well below the target prices in other parts of the Community, this implies a surplus of goods. Therefore, farmers in the United Kingdom are encouraged to sell their produce in other areas of the Community where there is a deficit in production and comparatively higher prices. Target prices allow the producer to calculate whether or not transportation to the other market is a viable alternative.

Intervention prices, on the other hand, do establish legal obligations on the part of the Community. The intervention price for a particular agricultural product is the price set annually at which the Community will reimburse producers who are unable to sell their produce on the open market. Since farmers are guaranteed the intervention price at a minimum price for their produce, naturally they are encouraged to grow as much agricultural produce as possible. This is the main incentive to maximise production.

Although the target price is uniform throughout the Community, intervention prices vary from region to region according to the circumstances of the area. Further, the intervention price is invariably lower than the target price to encourage farmers to try to sell their produce on the market rather than to the Community.

In order to maintain price policies, the Community also allows market organisations to regulate the supply and demand for a product within the Community by regulating the flow of goods into and out of the Community. Market organisations establish systems to regulate trade by setting threshold prices, by imposing levies, by administering refunds, and by administering import and export licences. Each of these mechanisms regulates the supply and demand for goods and are therefore useful to support prices.

The threshold price for a commodity is the price fixed by the Community for imports into the Community from third countries. This price is calculated at or above the target price to prevent foreign produce from undermining the price structure set by the Community for the particular agricultural goods. In effect, this mechanism prevents foreign agricultural products from competing with Community goods, regardless of the efficiency of the foreign producers, or more disturbingly, the inefficiency of Community producers.

Further, while the Community protects agricultural markets within the Community, it also distorts the international markets for agricultural products by granting export subsidies through its refund systems. Thus, if the world price for a particular agricultural good is below the intervention price for the product in the Community, the farmer can obtain a refund equal to the difference between the Community price and the world price. These export subsidies, particularly those made on wheat and wheat products, are a constant source of controversy throughout the world trading system where they are perceived as unfair commercial prices.

In addition, control of the supply of agricultural products is maintained by allowing market organisations the powers to impose quotas and to require that licences are obtained for both imports and exports of commodities. The techniques allow the Community to control the quantity or volume of agricultural products within the Community. Since supply and demand are related to price, in effect this is an indirect means of regulating prices within the Community.

In conjunction with controlling prices to achieve greater efficiency, the Community has also embarked on a programme of structure reform. Reform of the agricultural sector of the Community has been based on the so-called Mansholt Plan of 1968. This proposal formed the main elements of the Council Resolution adopted in 1971 to reform agriculture. The main problems of agriculture were perceived to be the existence of too many small farms and over-employment in the industry. The Community therefore sought to increase the average size of farms within the Community and to reduce the number of people employed in agriculture.

Grants were given to farmers to alleviate the problems which would be encountered by those wishing to leave the land. Farmers over 55 could enter schemes for retraining and placement. Modernisation of agricultural machinery was also introduced, and grants to purchase machinery were introduced. Undoubtedly, over the last two decades, the average size of farms in the Community has increased and the number of people employed in agriculture has significantly decreased. But the costs of this programme, both social and financial, have been considerable.

The European market organisation structure also partially fulfils a number of the other objectives of the Common Agricultural Policy. It ensures that farmers are guaranteed a minimum standard of living by providing minimum returns for produce through the intervention price mechanism. Individual earnings can be increased by setting intervention prices at a level which provides a minimum standard of living.

The target price and intervention price mechanisms also allow the Community to provide certainty of supplies to consumers at reasonable prices. Reasonable prices are maintained because the supply of agricultural products would naturally increase if no farmer took advantage of the intervention price mechanism. This would increase the volume of produce on the market thereby ensuring that prices remain at a reasonable level.

Finally, markets may be stabilised by controlling the flow of agricultural goods into and out of the Community. In the event that prices increase dramatically, the Community can allow supplies to increase by preventing exports of the product out of the Community and by lowering threshold prices to allow foreign produce into the Community. Conversely, if prices are excessively low, the Community can prohibit imports from foreign countries into the Community and can encourage exports from the Community by increasing export subsidies.

Question 2

Agricultural products and goods have been included in the system of the EEC common market and the common agricultural policy has been very successful; but it needs to be reformed. Discuss.

University of Glasgow LLB Examination
June 1986 Q5

General comment

A narrative question requiring a descriptive answer.

Skeleton solution

- The main features of the CAP.
- The primary problems in the functioning of the system: budget, surpluses.
- Reforms proposed by the Member States.

Suggested solution

The objectives of the Common Agricultural Policy are undoubtedly desirable in themselves. The promotion of productivity by encouraging technical progress and by ensuring optimum utilisation of the factors of production, ensuring a fair standard of living for the agricultural community, the stabilisation of markets, and the guarantee of supplies at reasonable prices, are all commendable goals. However, the methods which have been selected to achieve these objectives have been a source of constant controversy.

Prior to the CAP, the Community was a net importer of agricultural products. Since the early 1970s, the Community has been a net exporter of agricultural goods. However, a price has had to be paid for this achievement, and a number of Member States, particularly the United Kingdom, have asked whether or not this price has been excessive in relation to the results achieved.

The Community has chosen to establish European market organisations to achieve the objectives of the CAP. These organisations set target prices for farmers and buy produce at intervention prices. The main defect of this structure is that, by intervening to purchase produce, the market organisations substantially distort the relationship between supply and demand on the one hand, and price on the other hand. Agricultural prices are therefore set at artificial prices which bear no relation to the volume or amounts of produce which are being grown.

The immediate result of guaranteeing to purchase agricultural produce at the intervention price is that farmers are encouraged to over-produce goods. Surpluses of agricultural goods are therefore common, and in the past have taken the form of butter mountains and wine lakes. The Community is legally obliged to purchase these surpluses. This results in charges to the Community budget, not only in respect of the intervention prices paid for the produce, but also for costs incurred as a result of storing the excess produce.

Further, the Community often disposes of excess surpluses by releasing the products into the world markets. This has three adverse effects. First, it requires the Community to incur the expenses of purchasing the produce at the intervention price, storing it, and then releasing it at a lower price to ensure that sales of the product can be made. Second, the release of enormous surpluses onto the world market destablises global prices for agricultural products. This can cause injury to non-Community states that are unable to compete with the reduced prices.

Third, the Community frequently 'dumps' agricultural produce on the world market. Dumping is perceived to be an unfair commercial practice and involves a country selling a product to another at a price less than the price of the identical good on the domestic market. In the event that dumping can be proven, and injury is caused to the industry of a third state, that third state is entitled to impose anti-dumping duties on the imports of the agricultural surplus from the Community. The ultimate consequence is a perversion of the factors of supply and demand in the world market.

As formulated in the CAP, the regime established to ensure the free movement of agricultural products suffers from the principal defect that competition is not encouraged in the agricultural sector. Healthy competition promotes efficiency and discourages the production of excessive stockpiles of goods. However, in agriculture, the existence of a guaranteed intervention price discourages competition since farmers are guaranteed a market for all their production. The result is that supply and demand no longer bear any correlation with price. The lack of competition among producers discourages reductions in price and although efficiency increases, this is artificial because subsidisation acts as a substitute for competition.

At the end of the day, it is the Community budget which must bear the costs of financing the CAP. Costs are incurred throughout the structure of the CAP. Charges to the budget occur as a result of intervention purchasing, subsidisation of exports, and the financing of the structural adjustment programme. The CAP accounts for around 75 per cent of the annual Community budget. This figure disregards the costs paid to the Community consumers as a result of being prevented from purchasing cheaper non-Community agricultural produce.

Reform is also required because the costs of agricultural products within the Community no longer bear any relationship to the world market prices. The protection the CAP offers to Community farmers has insulated the Community market from the effects of competition in the world market. A bilevel price has therefore emerged. One price is the Community price, the other is the world market price. For most products, the Community price is invariably higher than the world market price.

Reform of the CAP is necessary because the costs of protecting the farming community inside the EEC have now greatly exceeded the benefits of such protection. The agricultural sector now functions on an artificial basis, with no true relationship to the factors of competition, supply or demand. Consumers are forced to pay the costs of purchasing more expensive Community produce. The expense of the CAP has crippled the Community budget. Projects which are more worthy than protectionism cannot be financed because of the massive expenditure on the CAP. And, perhaps most importantly of all, the CAP has caused a crisis in the international agricultural market place.

Reform of the CAP must be comprehensive. Efficiency and productivity should replace protectionism as the main objective of the CAP. This would probably require the abolition of intervention prices, and export subsidies. Agriculture within the Community must address the phenomenon of competition from foreign farmers. The Community budget must be brought back under control within the framework of a reform package.

In fact, even the claim that the CAP has had limited success cannot wholly be sustained. No benefit to the consumer has emerged from the CAP. Inefficiency in the agricultural community within the EEC is rife. The surpluses that have been created bear no relationship to efficiency; it is only proportional to the amount of money that has been wasted on the CAP. Even the farming community itself constantly complains that its standard of living has been undermined. Without comprehensive reform, the CAP threatens to destroy the very fabric of the Community itself.

Question 3

The European Economic Community would have developed better without the success and problems of the Common Agricultural Policy. Discuss.

University of Glasgow LLB Examination
June 1988 Q2

General comment

A question which requires the student to give an opinion on the success or otherwise of the CAP.

Skeleton solution

- The place of the CAP within the framework of the Community.
- The costs of the CAP: internally.
- Costs of the CAP: externally.
- Future direction of the CAP.

Suggested solution

Trade in agricultural products forms a substantial part of the trade in goods between Member States of the Community. It was therefore essential that trade in agricultural products should be covered by the EEC Treaty. However, what can be questioned is whether the agricultural sector forms an area of economic importance which deserves separate treatment from trade in other products.

The EEC Treaty itself recognises that agriculture is an area of special concern. Agriculture formed an individual, and independent title of the EEC Treaty (Articles 38 to 47). Within this title, different objectives were established for agricultural products than for the rest of the economies of the Community. The promotion of the standards of living for employees in this activity, the stabilisation of markets and the rational development of production are all objectives which are not expressly stated for other economic areas. Consequently, although it was deemed essential to bring agriculture within the scope of the EEC Treaty, this was done with full recognition that agriculture was an activity which requires special consideration.

While the original Member States of the Community, and in particular France and Germany, maintained a consensus as regards the objectives of the CAP, the addition of subsequent Member States has resulted in speculation as to the direction of the CAP. The United Kingdom has constantly questioned the structure of the CAP and its costs in relation to the Community budget. Serious divisions have emerged between the northern European members and the Mediterranean members as regards the treatment of citrus fruits. But most importantly, divisions have emerged between the Community and the rest of the trading system as regards the structure and function of the CAP.

Since the inauguration of the CAP, the trading partners of the Community have consistently opposed the principles which form the infrastructure of the CAP. At the GATT, the United States challenged the formation of the Community on the grounds that the CAP represented a retreat from the policy of trade liberalisation which that organisation seeks to promote. Trade disputes between the United States and the Community have centred around the issue of the treatment of agriculture by the Community. In 1982, the United States challenged the Community system for refunds on wheat and wheat products. In both cases the Community was found to have failure to respect its obligations under the GATT. Subsequent disputes have also focussed on matters of agricultural concern.

However, it has been during the Uruguay Round of GATT multilateral trade negotiations that the divisions among the world community as regards the CAP have become most visible. Since 1982, the GATT has been conducting discussions and negotiations concerning the reduction of subsidies, quantitative restrictions, tariffs and non-tariff barriers to trade (such as import and export licences). International agreements have been drafted to implement the international obligations which have been framed. These form a package. Ratification of one requires ratification of all as regards the important trading nations of the world.

However, in 1990, these negotiations broke down as a result of the failure of the Community to reform certain aspects of the CAP. In particular, the United States, strongly supported by Australia, Canada and New Zealand, demanded reductions in export subsidies on Community agricultural products. The Community failed to agree on substantial reductions in these subsidies, and the negotiations broke down. This episode is instructive as regards the CAP for two reasons.

First, the European Community was unable to agree on cuts in exports subsidies because such reforms require unanimity among the Member States. Certain Member States, most notably German and France, refused to consent to the requested cuts, despite encouragement from other Member States to do so. While the United

Kingdom supported cuts of around 70 per cent in export subsidies, no such reform was forthcoming. This highlights the deep divisions which the CAP has caused within the Community and the political importance of the agricultural community to certain Member States. These factors decrease the likelihood that the CAP will be successfully reformed.

Second, the CAP is the cause of substantial friction in the international trading community. The Community has been alienated from the GATT negotiations because of the CAP. This means not only that liberalisation of the agricultural sector may not occur throughout the world. It means that the benefits which the Community has sought through these discussions must be forsaken because of the CAP. The CAP is therefore a major liability to the Community, and one which is not compensated by any benefits which accrue internally to either consumers or the farming community within the EEC.

It cannot be doubted that the CAP has retarded the development of the Community. Internally, the CAP has been the source of bitter diplomatic confrontations as regards both structure and costs. Internationally, the Community has been isolated because of the CAP. Reform of the CAP may only partially remedy this situation. The CAP should not, however, be allowed to threaten the progressive development of the Community. Once the CAP has this effect, then it has served any useful purpose it may ever have had, if it ever had one.

14 EUROPEAN COMMUNITY POLICIES

14.1 Introduction

To ensure that the objectives of the European Community are achieved, the EEC Treaty authorises the creation of a number of Community policies. These policies facilitate economic integration among the Member States and ensure that the purposes of the common market are not undermined or eroded by the existence of inconsistent national policies. Although some of the Community policies were originally specified in the Community Treaties, a number of other policies, including environmental protection policy and monetary policy, have evolved as a consequence of the functions of the Community. This chapter will deal with the principal Community policies other than competition policy and the common agricultural policy, which form independent chapters of the WorkBook, and the common commercial policy, which forms a substantial portion of the chapter dealing with the external relations of the Community.

14.2 Key points

a) *The Community transport policy*

The adoption of a common policy in the sphere of transportation is sanctioned by Article 3(e) of the EEC Treaty and Articles 74 to 84 provide the guidelines for the implementation of this policy. The common transport policy extends to carriage of goods and persons by road, rail and inland waterways.

Article 75 allows the Council, acting on a proposal from the Commission, to establish:

i) common rules applicable to international transport to or from the territory of Member States or passing across the territory of one or more Member States;

ii) conditions under which non-resident carriers may operate transport services within a Member State; and

iii) any other appropriate provisions.

The implementation of a common transport policy is, of course, an essential element in achieving the goal of the free movement of goods.

i) Carriage of goods by road

Council Regulation 1018/68 (1968) allocated quotas of Community-wide permits among Member States. These permits enable the holders to convey goods by road between Member States. This system has been revised with substantial increases in the levels of quotas. At present, Council Regulation 3621/84 (1984) contains the relevant allocations.

The Council has also adopted common rules for certain types of vehicles which are exempt from requiring a permit.

ii) Road passenger transport

The basic measure regulating the carriage of passengers is Council Regulation 117/66 (1966). This establishes common definitions for international services and a system largely free from bureaucracy.

Both the carriage of goods and passengers are subject to rules relating to the maximum permitted number of hours for drivers. Council Regulation 3820/85 (1985) now governs the maximum number of permitted hours, although the actual figures have been altered from time to time. Criminal penalties may be imposed under the authority of Community Regulations in the event that drivers exceed maximum permitted daily driving periods or are not allowed compulsory rest periods: see *Anklagemyndigheden* v *Hausen and Son I/S*, Case 326/88, Judgment of 14 August 1990, not yet reported. Other Regulations concern matters such as drivers' qualifications and minimum levels of training.

iii) Railway transportation

Although in theory the Community transport policy extends to railway transportation, in practice, national railway systems do not often extend beyond the boundaries of Member States. Nevertheless, a number of Regulations have been passed to deal with issues such as competition between railways and other forms of transportation, the fixing of rates for the international carriage of goods by rail, and investment in railway network systems.

iv) Inland waterways

A number of important rivers, including the Rhine and the Danube, flow through Europe and pass through a number of Member States. Council Directive 76/135 (1976) provides for the mutual recognition of navigation licences issued for vessels using inland waterways. This regulation requires that a certain minimum amount of information is set out in the licence.

v) Air transportation

A number of cases before the European Court have confirmed that air transport falls within the scope of the common transport policy: *EC Commission* v *France (Re Air Transport)* [1974] ECR 35; and *Ministère Public* v *Asjes* [1986] ECR 1425. Matters such as competition, tariffs, noise emission and airline schedules are subject to the Community transport policy.

The Community has also introduced a number of measures designed to create a common air transportation policy. Three Council measures form the core of this policy:

- Council Regulation 3975/87 (1987) which specifies the implementation of Community competition policy in this economic sector: see *Ahmed Saeed Flugreisen* v *Zentrale zur Bekampfung Unlauteren Wettbewerbs* [1990] 4 CMLR 102;
- Council Regulation 3976/87 (1987) which exempts certain agreements under Article 85(3) of the EEC Treaty; and
- Council Decision 87/602 (1987) which deals with the sharing of passenger capacity and access of carriers to scheduled air routes within the Community.

Other recent Council measures deal with the sharing of revenues, computer reservation systems and ground handling services.

b) *The Community social policy*

Title III of Part Three of the EEC Treaty (Articles 117 to 128) deals with the social policy of the Community, together with the related matter of the European Social Fund. In general, the Community social policy is mainly confined to matters relating to the treatment of Community workers, including the elimination of gender discrimination and equal pay. Article 118 obliges the Commission to promote closer cooperation between Member States as regards employment, labour law, working conditions, vocational training, social security, the prevention of occupational accidents, and the related rights of association and collective bargaining.

The Single European Act augmented this provision with Article 118A which requires the Council to enact Directives harmonising national measures concerning improvements in conditions relating to the health and safety of workers.

c) *The Community fisheries policy*

The EEC Treaty does not expressly sanction the creation of a common fisheries policy (CFP). However, since Article 38 of the Treaty defines agricultural products to include the products of fisheries, the common fisheries policy was developed as a subsection of the common agricultural policy. However, in practice it is organised on an independent basis: see *France* v *United Kingdom [Re Fishing Mesh]* [1979] ECR 2923.

The territorial scope of the common fisheries policy extends to the fishing zones of all the Member States. A Council Resolution of 1976 urged Member States to adopt a 200 mile fishing limit along the Atlantic and North Sea coasts and Council Regulation 507/81 (1981) provides the legal authority to extend exclusive fishing zones.

The essence of the common fisheries policy is the principle of non-discrimination on the ground of nationality. Council Regulation 101/76 (1976) extended the principle of non-discrimination to access to the fishing grounds of Member States by vessels registered in other Member States. This general principle is subject to four exceptions:

i) Member States are entitled to maintain an exclusive fishing zone for their own nationals up to a maximum of 12 nautical miles;

ii) Previously existing arrangements made between Member States prior to the CFP in reserved waters can be continued;

iii) Special restrictions are imposed on large fishing vessels in the 'Orkney/Shetlands box'; and

iv) Unlimited access to Portuguese and Spanish waters will not be established until 2002.

The Community regulates fishing activities within Community waters by limiting fish catches, introducing measures of price support and quality control, establishing measures for conservation, and negotiating access agreements with third countries. These matters now fall within the exclusive competence of the Community: *EC Commission* v *United Kingdom* [1981] ECR 1045.

i) Total allowable catches

Council Regulation 170/83 (1983) grants authority to the Council to set total allowable catches on an annual basis. The total allowable catch is calculated on the basis of scientific research into the volume and quantity of fishing stocks. Mathematically, the allowable catch is determined on a global basis, then by reference to species of fish and area, and then this allowance is allocated among the Member States.

ii) Price support and quality control

The Council sets guide prices annually according to the species of fish, taking into account market conditions, as well as the supply and demand for the product. An intervention price is also established, but in the context of the CFP this is known as the 'withdrawal price'. The withdrawal price is the price at which the Community will purchase fish products by way of intervention buying.

Quality control is maintained by a Community scheme to facilitate the mutual recognition of producer organisations within Member States: Council Regulation 105/76 (1976). Producer organisations generally purchase the products from fishermen and adopt measures designed to improve product quality.

iii) Conservation

Conservation of fishing resources is achieved through three Council Regulations: 3440/84 (1984), 1866/86 (1986) and 3094/86 (1986). These regulations specify technical measures designed to conserve fishing stocks. Conservation measures include minimum mesh sizes, restrictions on types of fishing gear, restrictions on the size of vessels, minimum fish sizes, and the designation of closed areas and closed seasons.

iv) Access agreements

Access agreements allowing non-Community vessels to fish in Community waters fall within the scope of the common commercial policy. The Community has exclusive authority to enter into agreements with third states to regulate access by foreign fishermen: *Kramer* [1976] ECR 1279.

In the pursuit of this policy, the Community has entered a number of international agreements to regulate access, including the Northwest Atlantic Fisheries Convention 1978 and the Northeast Atlantic Fisheries Convention 1981.

d) *The Community environmental policy*

A Community policy for the protection of the environment was not originally included in the EEC Treaty. However, the Single European Act amended the Treaty by adding Title VII to Part Three (Articles 130r to 130t) which regulates environmental policy.

According to Article 130r, Community action relating to the environment should have three main objectives:

i) to preserve, protect and improve the quality of the environment;

ii) to contribute towards protecting human health; and

iii) to ensure a prudent and rational utilisation of natural resources.

Community measures relating to the environment are to be based on a number of principles, including the principle that preventative action should be taken, that environmental damage should be rectified at source, and that the polluter should pay for damage to the environment.

The Council of Ministers has authority, acting on the proposals of the European Commission, to adopt measures on behalf of the Community to tackle issues of environmental protection.

To date, Community measures relating to the environment have been confined to three main areas: public health, atmospheric pollution, and the disposal of waste. Regulations in the field of public health deal, for example, with the quality of drinking water and the cleanliness of beaches. A number of Directives also deal with allowable levels of emissions from industrial plants. Finally, Community legislation has been introduced to regulate the acceptable levels of by-products from waste disposal processes.

e) *Monetary and fiscal policy*

Once again the EEC Treaty makes no explicit reference to the concept of monetary and fiscal policy among the Members of the Community, other than providing a framework for the free movement of capital. However, in 1979 the European Monetary System (EMS) was launched to create a common unit of account and to coordinate monetary policy among Member States. The EMS was formed by a Resolution of the European Council and does not formally amend the EEC Treaty. In fact, the actual legal status of the Resolution itself is uncertain.

At present, 10 of the 12 Members of the Community participate in the EMS, including the United Kingdom which entered the system in 1990. The two main elements of the European Monetary System are the European Currency Unit (ECU) and the Exchange Rate Mechanism (ERM).

The European Currency Unit is a composite unit of currency, made up of a basket of the currencies of all the Members of the Community. It is composed of fixed amounts of currency rather than a percentage of each and has been redefined twice since its formation in 1979 - in September 1984 and September 1989.

The ECU is designed to enable a zone of monetary stability to be created in Europe. It serves four main functions:

i) as a denominator for the functioning of the exchange rate mechanism;

ii) as a basis of a divergence indicator;

iii) as the denominator for operations on the intervention and credit mechanisms of the ERM; and

iv) as a means of settling debts between the monetary authorities of the European Community.

The Exchange Rate Mechanism is a system where the currencies of the participating Member States are pegged against each other to establish bilateral exchange rates. The effect of this process is to stabilise exchange rates, thereby adding certainty to international transactions involving different Community currencies.

All of the participating states, with the exception of the United Kingdom, Italy and Portugal, adhere to a fluctuation margin of plus or minus 2.25 per cent. The British pound functions within a margin of 6 per cent. If a currency exceeds a certain level of fluctuation from its fixed exchange rates, the central banks of the Member States are required to intervene in order to redress the imbalance.

Notwithstanding the existence of the European Monetary System, little substantial progress has been made towards monetary union within the Community despite the fact that the Single European Act amended the EEC Treaty to facilitate monetary union. Article 102a, as amended, specifically creates power to establish a Monetary Union within the Community.

However, true monetary union within the Community requires two further changes in the existing structure:

i) the complete liberalisation of capital movements throughout the Community; and

ii) the inauguration of a Central European Bank.

At present, discussions are being held at the inter-governmental level to decide the best course to follow regarding monetary and fiscal union.

14.3 Relevant cases

EC Commission v *France (Re Air Transportation Policy)* [1974] ECR 359: Member States no longer possess capacity to enact measures which regulate subjects which fall within the competence of the Community.

R v *Kirk* [1984] ECR 2689: The European Court quashed the conviction of a Danish fisherman on the ground that unilateral quotas could not be introduced by a Member State even when the Council had failed to agree on revised terms for a common fisheries policy.

Pesca Valentia v *Ministry of Fisheries and Forests* [1988] 1 CMLR 888: Member States are entitled to require that a specified minimum proportion of the crews of ships registered in the Member State are nationals of that state.

EC Commission v *Denmark (Re Returnable Containers)* [1989] 1 CMLR 619: Environmental considerations may justify limitations on the free movement of goods so long as the objectives to be achieved are not disproportionate to the restrictions imposed.

Knichem Base and Others v *Commune di Cinisello Balsamo*, Case 380/87, not yet reported: Directives enacted to implement the policy of environmental protection may be given direct effect.

14.4 Relevant materials

D Lasok, *The Law of the Economy of the European Communities* (1981) 335-392.

J Usher, 'Legal Regulation of the European Currency Unit' (1988) 37 ICLQ 249.

J-V Louis, 'Monetary Capacity in the Single European Act' (1988) 25 CML Rev 9.

Delors, *Report on Economic and Monetary Union in the European Community* (1989).

14.5 Analysis of questions

Questions relating to the common policies of the Community rarely refer to particular decisions of the European Court. Instead, knowledge of general concepts and principles is usually required. Students should therefore be familiar with the general scope and framework of the various Community policies. In particular, an understanding of any recent events or changes within the structure or content of each particular policy is desirable.

14.6 Questions

Question 1

What contribution can the European Community make to the development of Community wide measures to protect the environment?

University of Glasgow LLB Examination
1989 Q8

General comment

A narrative question requiring an answer describing the present state of the Community environmental policy.

Skeleton solution

- The provisions of the EEC Treaty relating to the protection of the environment.
- The subjects regulated by Community measures.
- Future content of the policy.
- Impact of the policy on the protection of the environment.

Suggested solution

Protection of the environment is an apt illustration of the growing competence of the Community in areas which were, for some considerable time, presumed to be outside the scope of the economic nature of the EEC Treaty. Prima facie, the protection of the environment is an issue which is only remotely related to the regulation of economic activities. However, the Community has vigorously assumed the duty of protecting the environment, on the ground that such activities will improve the quality of life within the Community.

Prior to the Single European Act of 1986, the Community had been involved in regulating certain aspects of environmental protection under the guise of consumer protection. However, the Single European Act conferred unambiguous authority on the Community to regulate issues of environmental concern by amending the EEC Treaty to contain a whole section dealing with the environment. This section consists of three articles (Articles 130r to 130t).

Article 130s authorises the Council of Ministers to pass legislation, acting on a proposal from the Commission, to protect the environment. Further, Article 130t provides that the adoption of such measures shall not preclude Member States from introducing more stringent protective measures so long as these are compatible with the EEC Treaty. In other words, measures enacted in pursuit of a common environmental policy are intended to be minimum standards and do not remove the power to legislate on such matters from the individual Member States. In fact the Community has been given a wide mandate to harmonise laws throughout the Community to protect the environment, and the potential for protecting the environment is significant.

The wide scope of the competence of the Community in this field is clear from Article 130r. The Council is authorised to enact legislation to achieve three separate goals. First, a policy of preserving, protecting and improving the quality of the environment is to be vigorously pursued. Second, measures to protect human health are to be introduced. Third, the prudent and rational utilisation of natural resources is to be encouraged.

Further, in enacting such provisions, a number of principles are to be borne in mind, including the principle that prevention is better than cure, that environmental damages should be rectified at source, and that polluters should be held financially responsible for their unlawful acts. The discretion of the Council to enact measures in this field is therefore substantially unfettered.

The Community has already made a substantial contribution to the protection of the environment by targeting three areas of concern: public health, atmospheric pollution, and the disposal of waste.

Measures designed to protect the health of consumers from dangers stemming from pollution in drinking water were enacted as early as 1975. Council Directive 75/440 (1975) regulated the standards for drinking water and, in particular, the maximum permissible levels of harmful substances. This Directive was subsequently replaced by Council Directive 80/778 (1980) which expanded on these minimum requirements. Annex I to the Directive lists the substances which are considered harmful along with maximum admissible concentrations in drinking water. Deviation from these standards must be justified by an emergency and can only be sustained for the minimum amount of time necessary to restore the quality of water: see *Criminal Proceedings Against Persons Unknown* Case (1989).

A number of other Directives have been passed in connection with the pollution of water. Thus, Directive 76/160 (1976) concerns the quality of bathing waters and the standard of beaches, the latter being a subject which the United Kingdom has frequently been threatened with prosecution in the European Court. Other Directives deal with the maximum permissible amounts of pollutants which can be discharged into the environment.

The regulation of air pollutants is a matter which has been controlled by more recent measures. Council Directive 88/609 (1988) identified the most toxic substances and limits the emission of these substances from combustion plants. Other Directives tackle the problems of emissions from incinerating plants and the quality of air. The problem of exhaust emissions from vehicles has not escaped the rigors of regulation. Member States are required to ensure that unleaded petrol is freely available throughout their respective territories and limits on emissions from new cars have been set. A comprehensive measure has been recently adopted to limit the volume of emissions from new cars with less than 1.4 litre cylinder capacity: see Council Directive 89/458 (1989).

Also, the disposal of waste and unwanted bi-products is considered by the Community to fall within the scope of its mandate to protect the environment. Council Directive 75/442 (1975) established standards of the protection of public health during waste disposal processes and has been given direct effect by the European Court: see *Knichem Base* v *Commune di Cinisello Balsamo* (1989). Community legislation regulates the amount of noxious substances that can be released into the atmosphere during this process, in terms of both volume and chemical composition. The transportation of dangerous chemicals, spillage from which would endanger the environment, has also been controlled. However, as yet a comprehensive Community regime for the reduction of noxious emissions has not been adopted.

Strictly speaking, the subject of noise pollution does not fall within the scope of the Community policy of environmental protection. However, the Community has been relatively successful in introducing standards to regulate the sound emissions from certain products including the exhausts of motor vehicles and motorcycles, the noise of garden tools and agricultural machinery, industrial machinery, and even the noise levels emitted from subsonic aircraft.

While the Community has authority to embark on a comprehensive programme of environmental protection, it has preferred to tackle the issue on an industry-by-industry, or subject-by-subject basis, the result being a somewhat piecemeal approach to the issue. A number of critical issues continue to remain unregulated at the Community level, including the levels of permissible radiation from nuclear power stations and the maximum levels of pollutants which can be discharged into the seas and oceans surrounding the Community. While the Community was widely expected to make a substantial contribution to the protection of the environment, progress has not been dramatic. The length of time taken to introduce measures has also been the subject of criticism.

The contribution made by the Community to the protection of the environment will ultimately depend on the willingness of the Member States to impose restrictions on their industries. Inevitably, such requirements will affect the profitability of industries. To date, Member States have appeared unwilling to burden their domestic industries with these extra costs and the immediate consequence has been an environmental protection programme of limited impact.

Question 2

The prospects for monetary union within the European Community have been greatly enhanced by the recent decision of the British government to participate in the European Monetary System.

Do you agree with this assessment?

Question prepared by the Author
February 1991

General comment

Another question requiring a narrative answer, but also involving knowledge of contemporary developments.

Skeleton solution

- The nature of the European Monetary System.
- The policy of the British government towards EMS.
- The limitations of the existing system.
- Possibilities for reform.

Suggested solution

The EEC Treaty was designed to promote economic integration among the Member States of the European Community. This involves the continuous modification of the structure of the Community in the light of its successes and failures. Limits are effectively placed on the objectives of the Community by its failure to achieve monetary union. The use of 11 different currencies by the 12 Member States complicates even the most simple transactions between undertakings in different Member States. Fluctuations in exchange rates add a significant degree of uncertainty and expense in such transactions.

The creation of a monetary union among the Member States and the introduction of a single currency throughout the Community would allow the Community to achieve a significantly greater degree of economic integration. However, these benefits are counterbalanced by arguments that participation in a monetary union requires the transfer of a significant degree of sovereignty to the Community. In the past, the policy of the United Kingdom has been to resolutely oppose such a transfer of sovereignty. However, recently the policy has undergone a significant modification with the membership of the United Kingdom in the European Monetary System.

The European Monetary System was established in 1979, and consists of two main elements: the creation of the European Currency Unit (ECU); and the formation of the Exchange Rate Mechanism (ERM).

The ECU is a composite currency which is made up of a certain amount of the currencies of each Member State. It performs a number of important functions within the Community, although its use for transactions in the private sector has been limited. The ECU is not designed to be a single currency for the Community, but rather a unit which can be used as a denominator to regulate foreign exchange within the Community. As an immediate consequence of its composition, the ECU is designed to appreciate less than the strongest of its participants currencies and conversely to depreciate less than the weakest of these currencies. The result is a unit of account with a strong degree of stability.

The Exchange Rate Mechanism, on the other hand, is a system whereby the currencies of the participants in the EMS can be tied to each other at certain levels, thereby eradicating the possibility of wild fluctuations in exchange rates. Currencies are permitted to float relative to each other, but this must be confined to the parameters set at the date of entry into the mechanism. For most of the participants in the ERM, fluctuations of plus or minus 2.25 per cent are permissible. The United Kingdom has, however, participated in a system with a deviation level of 6 per cent. This will subsequently be reduced in line with the rest of the Member States.

Fluctuations in currency levels are regulated by interventions by central banks. Thus, if the exchange rate between the pound Sterling and the German Deutschmark exceed 6 per cent, the Bundesbank will intervene to purchase British pounds if the pound is weak against the mark, and the Bank of England will intervene to buy marks if the mark is weak against the pound.

Notwithstanding the existence of the EMS, progress towards monetary union has been slow. While the Single European Act amended the EEC Treaty to create Article 102A, this provision merely requires Member States to 'cooperate' to achieve monetary union, bearing in mind the experience gained from the EMS and in developing the ECU. However, Article 102A(2) did establish a Monetary Committee to investigate the prospects for monetary union.

While the use of multiple currencies within the Community unquestionably hinders full realisation of an integrated European market, since monetary and economic policy is vital to the maintenance of national sovereignty, the issue of monetary union has become a sensitive subject. Opposition has been voiced, particularly in the United Kingdom, against the next phase of monetary union which would ultimately involve a single European currency and a single European central bank. Further, it is unclear whether or not such a central bank would be independent, such as the German Bundesbank, or subject to political control, such as the Bank of England. However, attainment of these two goals is remote when it is remembered that not all Member States of the Community participate in the EMS itself.

In 1988, the European Council appointed a Committee for the Study of Economic and Monetary Union to discuss concrete steps towards monetary union. The President of the European Commission, Jacques Delors, was appointed Chairperson of this Committee, and a report was produced in June 1989 outlining proposals for the achievement monetary union [hereinafter the Delors Report].

This Report outlined three stages towards monetary union. The first stage requires the removal of obstacles to financial integration and the promotion of intensified cooperation on monetary policy. This would involve the creation of a single financial area in which all monetary and financial instruments circulate freely. In addition, all Member States would be required to participate in the ERM and all impediments to the private use of the ECU would be removed.

The second stage would involve the creation of the basic organs and structure of the economic and monetary union. This would, in turn, entail amendments to the Community Treaties, and perhaps even the negotiation of a new treaty to establish a monetary union.

The third, and final, stage would require the irrevocable fixing of exchange rates and the transition towards a single monetary policy. At this stage, all the national currencies of the Member States would be replaced by a single European currency. This single European currency could in fact be developed from the ECU.

At the European Council meeting held in Rome in November 1990, 11 of the 12 Member States agreed that the transition towards monetary union was inevitable and although they did not embrace the Delors Report completely, these Member States expressed their commitment to full monetary union. The United Kingdom expressed its strong opposition to this proposal, mainly on the basis that, while monetary union itself may be a desirable objective, expressing the desire to achieve monetary union without agreeing on the steps of this process was a short-sighted policy.

The European Council meeting in Rome in 1990 does however mark a significant watershed in the progress towards monetary union. At least 11 of the 12 Member States have declared their willingness to enter into a process towards monetary union. Naturally, these states are free to enter into such a process without the United Kingdom.

While the entry of the United Kingdom into the EMS is a significant development in the process towards monetary union, events have moved quickly to overtake the significance of this event. Therefore, it cannot be said that membership of the United Kingdom in this system is a significant development in the road to monetary union. In fact, this event by itself only serves to expose the divisions which exist within the Community regarding the direction of the Community as regards European monetary policy.

Question 3

The masters of two German fishing vessels were prosecuted for offences committed under the West Coast Herring (Prohibition of Fishing) Order 1981, a statutory instrument enacted under the authority of a British statute. Both masters were convicted for violating prohibitions on fishing in designated waters off the British coast and their catches confiscated. In addition, a fine of £30,000 was imposed on both masters.

Advise the fishermen of their rights under Community law with a view to appealing both the fines and the confiscation of their catches.

Question prepared by the Author
February 1991

General comment

A rare problem-type question requiring the student to understand the fundamental nature of one particular Community policy.

Skeleton solution

- Authority of the Prohibition Order - Community or national law?
- Competence of the Community in this field.

- Compatibility of the convictions with Community law.
- Possible appeal to the ECJ under Article 177.

Suggested solution

Since the creation of the common fisheries policy, competence to regulate fishing in the exclusive economic zones of the Member States has been exercised at the Community level. In other words, the Council of Ministers, acting on proposals from the European Commission, enacts Community measures to regulate such matters as total allowable catches, quotas, access by foreign fishermen, conservation and structural policy.

Member States no longer maintain capacity to enact measures of domestic law which affect matters which fall within the competence of the common fisheries policy unless such measures have been promulgated with the consent of the Community: *Gewiese & Mehlich* v *MacKenzie* (1984). Therefore, if the Order in Council has been passed under the authority of a British statute, the Order may be challenged on the ground that it infringes a principle of Community law.

The basis of the Community common fisheries policy is the principle of non-discrimination between nationals of Member States in Community fishing waters. Community legislation has also been passed to implement this obligation: Council Regulation 101/76 (1976). However, at the same time the Community has responsibility for regulating fishing within Community waters and may therefore pass legislation to conserve fishing stocks, which could involve a ban on fishing in certain areas: see *EC Commission* v *United Kingdom* (1981). In particular, the Community is empowered to establish total allowable catches which establish limits on the quantity of fish which may be caught in certain areas.

While the Community is responsible for setting quotas, enforcement of these measures usually falls within the competence of the individual Member States. Thus, even although the German fishermen have been prosecuted under British law, it is possible that this national legislation has been promulgated to incorporate a measure of Community law, such as Regulations and Directives, into British law. In these circumstances, the authorities of the United Kingdom are allowed to conduct prosecutions to uphold the Community rule of law.

If the Order in Council was enacted as enabling legislation for a Community measure, it must satisfy a number of criteria. First, the legislation must satisfy all the obligations incumbent upon the Member States and partial implementation is insufficient. For example, in *EC Commission* v *United Kingdom (Re Tachographs)* (1979) the British government was held to have violated Community law by not passing legislation making non-compliance with a Community regulation a criminal offence. The European Court held the United Kingdom liable for a breach of Community law and declared inconceivable the implementation of a regulation by a Member State 'in an incomplete and selective manner so as to render abortive certain aspects of Community legislation which it opposed or which it considered contrary to its national interests'.

Therefore, the German captains may challenge the convictions on the basis that the Order in Council is a measure of national law which contravenes Community law, but if the Order has been introduced with the consent of the Community, or if it implements a Community measure, the convictions may not be overturned on the basis of a European defence.

Further, where a Community measure specifies that Member States have discretion as to the type of criminal penalty which may be imposed upon those found to have violated the measure in question, it is not possible to challenge the implementing legislation on the ground that different Member States have applied different criminal sanctions. Thus, in *Anklagemyndigheden* v *Hausen and Son I/S* (1990), the European Court held that the fact that some Member States imposed strict criminal liability to enforce a Regulation while others did not constitute a ground to challenge the implementing instrument of national legislation. This conclusion was reached because the regulation in question left considerable discretion to Member States for its implementation. Naturally, where a regulation specifies particular criminal penalties, such provisions must be strictly observed. However, it is rare for Community legislation to require particular criminal sanctions.

The two German captains should therefore be advise to appeal their convictions to the superior criminal courts if it can be established that the Order in Council infringes Community measures implementing the common fisheries policy. In particular, a reference from the European Court under Article 177 of the EEC Treaty would be most appropriate in these circumstances. In this respect it should be remembered that preliminary references may be made from both criminal and civil courts to the European Court.

15 THE EXTERNAL RELATIONS OF THE EUROPEAN COMMUNITY

15.1 Introduction

The Member States of the European Community have transferred considerable external sovereignty to the Community for the purpose of conducting economic and commercial relationships with non-Community states. The European Community, on behalf of the individual Member States, negotiates trade and economic agreements with third countries and administers the various trade protection mechanisms to protect industry within the Community from unfair foreign competition. The European Commission and the Council of Ministers are the bodies responsible for the conduct of the Community's external affairs. Authority to exercise powers to regulate external affairs is vested in the Community by virtue of Common Commercial Policy (CCP) provisions of the EEC Treaty.

15.2 Key points

a) *The international legal personality of the European Community*

The European Community has limited international personality and has entered a substantial number of bilateral and multilateral agreements with third states. In addition, the Community participates in a number of international organisations, including the General Agreement on Tariffs and Trade (GATT).

Article 210 of the EEC Treaty expressly declares that '[t]he Community shall have legal personality'; see also Article 75 ECSC Treaty and Article 101 Euratom.

b) *Types of international agreements entered into by the Community*

Express capacity to enter international agreements is granted under Articles 113 and 238 of the EEC Treaty. In addition, Article 228 specifies the procedure for the negotiation of such agreements. Agreements between the Community and third states may be classified according to form and content into four groups:

i) multilateral trade agreements, primarily negotiated within the context of the General Agreement on Tariffs and Trade;

ii) bilateral free trade agreements;

iii) association agreements, which are usually concluded with states about to become members of the Community; and

iv) development and assistance agreements with developing states.

These agreements vary, in both content and legal structure, according to the relationship which is to be regulated by a particular agreement.

c) *Capacity of the European Community to enter into international obligations*

The Community does not exercise unlimited capacity to enter into international agreements on behalf of its Member States. Where the subject matter of an agreement is unrelated to the objectives and purpose of the Community, the Community has no competence to act. Unfortunately, the distinction between those subjects which concern the Community under the terms of the three Community Treaties and other issues of international concern is not clear cut. Often an international agreement will regulate issues of Community concern as well as unrelated issues: for example the United Nations Convention on the Law of the Sea 1982.

If the subject matter of an international agreement falls completely within the competence of the Community, the Community has exclusive capacity to negotiate the agreement and the individual Member States have no authority to negotiate. Such agreements are known as 'Community Agreements'.

Where an international agreement contains provisions relating to matters within the competence of the Community, and also issues which fall outside the scope of the Community Treaties, both the Member States and the Community participate in the negotiating process and ratify the final agreement. Such agreements are known as 'mixed agreements'.

The Member States of the Community may be parties to international treaties, in their own right, concerning matters not related to the Community. Even although all the Member States participate in such agreements, if the subject matter bears no relation to issues of Community concern, the obligations are assumed by the Member States alone. These agreements are known as 'International Agreements Assumed by the Member States'. An example of such an agreement is the European Convention on Human Rights 1950 which, despite participation by all Community Member States, is not an agreement of Community concern.

i) Community agreements

The Community has express capacity to enter into two forms of international agreements without the participation of the Member States in the negotiating process:

- Article 113 of the EEC Treaty authorises the Community to enter commercial agreements relating to tariff and trade matters for the purpose of achieving the objectives of the Common Commercial Policy. This authority expressly extends to export aids, credit and finance, and matters relating to multilateral commodity agreements.
- Article 238 authorises the Community to negotiate with third states, unions of states or international organisations, association agreements creating reciprocal rights and obligations, and facilitating common action through special procedures.

While the capacity to enter association agreements under Article 238 is relatively defined, the exercise of power under Article 113 has a potentially greater application since no explicit parameters have been set in relation to its application.

In order to define the scope of the Community's power under Article 113, the European Commission has sought a number of opinions from the European Court. In *EC Commission* v *EC Council [Re ERTA]* [1971] ECR 263, the Court held that authority to enter international agreements not only arose from the express provisions, but also provisions of the EEC Treaty which require the negotiation of international agreements for their achievement. As a result, the Court decided that:

'the Community enjoys the capacity to establish contractual links with third countries over the whole field of objectives defined in Part One (Articles 1 to 8) of the [EEC] Treaty.'

The rationale for extending the competence of the Community was the need for the Community to assume and carry out contractual obligations towards third states affecting the whole sphere of the application of the Community legal system.

This decision, along with a number of subsequent judgments of the Court, established the doctrine of implied powers. These implied powers supplement the express powers of the Community to enter into international agreements. Whether an agreement with a third state in negotiated by the Community on the basis of an express power or an implied power makes no difference to its status as a 'Community Agreement'.

ii) Mixed agreements

Since Member States have not conferred upon the Community their absolute sovereignty to negotiate treaties and in fact continue to exercise those powers not transferred to the Community, a conflict may arise where an international agreement contains provisions which fall within the competence of both the Community and the individual Member States. Implementation of such agreements requires joint action and such agreements are concluded simultaneously by the Community and the Member States.

In these mixed agreements, each party acts in its own name, undertaking to perform the obligations which fall within its competence. Mixed agreements may be concluded by the Community, acting with the participation of the Member States, under either Article 113 or Article 238.

Mixed agreements have been used extensively to implement the numerous treaties between the Community and developing countries, namely Yaounde I (1964), Yaounde II (1969), Lome I (1975), Lome II (1979), Lome III (1984) and Lome IV (1989).

iii) International obligations assumed by the Member States

The Member States of the Community were parties to a number of international agreements prior to the conclusion of the treaties forming the Community, including the European Convention on Human Rights 1950 and the General Agreement on Trade and Tariffs.

The Community is deemed to succeed to treaties concluded before the Community Treaties only if they contain matters within the competence of the Community. In one case relating to the status of the GATT in Community law, the Court declared that:

'in so far as under the EEC Treaty the Community has assumed the powers previously exercised by the Member States in the area governed by the GATT, the provisions of that agreement have the effect of binding the Community': *International Fruit Company* v *Produktschap voor Groenten en Fruit* [1972] ECR 1219.

Treaties concluded after the Community Treaties by the Member States on subjects within the competence of the Community are probably void, although in practice this is an unlikely eventuality because of the propensity of the Community to participate in all agreements which might conceivably relate to its affairs.

d) *Incorporation of treaties into European Community law*

The EEC Treaty itself does not specify the status and effect of international agreements within the Community legal order, nor does it identify the means through which such obligations are incorporated into Community law. Although the practice of the Council is to enact a decision or a regulation to approve an agreement, it appears that the actual instrument of approval itself is not the source of authority for an agreement in Community law. Rather, an international agreement concluded by the Community, by its mere conclusion and approval by the Council, and subsequent publication in the Community Official Journal, is incorporated into Community law: see *Haegemann* v *Belgian State* [1973] ECR 125.

e) *Effect of treaties in Community law*

Treaties concluded by the Community exercising its express or implied treaty-making powers are 'binding on the institutions of the Community and the Member States' by virtue of Article 228(2) of the EEC Treaty.

Community treaties form an integral element of Community law and have been given direct effect by the European Court. In other words, individuals may rely upon the terms of treaties negotiated by the Community. In order to have direct effect, a particular provision of a Treaty must satisfy two main criteria:

i) an individual may only rely on such a provision if it is 'capable of creating rights of which interested parties may avail themselves in a court of law': *International Fruit*, above; and

ii) in order to ascertain whether a Community agreement confers rights upon individuals, regard must be had to the 'purpose and nature of the agreement itself' to determine if the provision in question 'contains a clear and precise obligation which is not subject, in its implementation or effects, to the adoption of any subsequent measure': *Demirel* v *Stadt Schwabisch Gmund* [1989] 1 CMLR 421.

If these conditions are satisfied, then direct effect may be given to the terms of a Community agreement: see *Hauptzollamt Mainz* v *Kupferberg* [1983] 1 CMLR 1.

f) *The contents and effect of the Common Commercial Policy*

The Community Common Commercial Policy is founded on the uniform application of principles relating to tariff rates, the conclusion of tariff and trade agreements, the attainment of uniformity in measures of trade liberalisation, the formulation of a consistent export policy and the adoption of measures to protect against unfair trade practices: Article 113(1) of the EEC Treaty.

The process for the formulation of the CCP is similar to the normal decision-making procedures within the Community. The European Commission drafts proposals after consultations with interested parties, or third states in the case of negotiating agreements. These proposals are submitted to the Council of Ministers, which must adopt proposals by a qualified majority: Article 148 EEC Treaty. The Council has authority to enact regulations, directives and decisions in the pursuit of the Common Commercial Policy.

g) *European Community trade protection laws*

The Community has a number of powers to impose measures on imports from third countries in order to protect industry and commerce within the Community from unfair foreign trade practices. These measures may be classified into four categories: (i) anti-dumping measures; (ii) countervailing (or anti-subsidy) measures; (iii) safeguard measures; and (iv) measures under the New Commercial Policy Instrument.

i) Anti-dumping actions

The Community authorities are authorised to impose anti-dumping duties on foreign products which are deemed to have been 'dumped' within the Community and which have caused injury to a Community industry: Council Regulation 2423/88 (1988). A foreign product has been 'dumped' inside the Community if it has been introduced into the internal market at a price less than the comparable price for the identical product in the country of manufacture.

Protection against dumped products is the most common form of trade protection measure employed by the European Community.

ii) Countervailing duty (or anti-subsidy) actions

Countervailing duties are imposed by the Community on foreign products that have benefited from subsidies from foreign governments during their manufacture, distribution or export, if such products cause injury to Community industries producing similar goods. Such duties are infrequently imposed by the Community on foreign products. The authority under which the Community imposes countervailing duties is also contained in Council Regulation 2423/88 (1988).

iii) Safeguard actions

Imports into the Community from third countries may also be subject to safeguard measures under the relevant provisions of Council Regulations 288/82 (1982) and 1765/82 (1982). If foreign products are being imported into the Community in such increased quantities as to cause, or threaten to cause, serious injury to a Community industry, safeguard measures may be imposed to protect the Community industry, regardless of the cause or source of the increase in the volume of imports.

If the existence of increased imports can be established, and if such imports cause serious injury, the Community may impose additional duties, tariffs or quotas on the importation of such products to protect the Community industry.

iv) The new Commercial Policy Instrument

The Community authorities are also empowered to adopt measures designed to combat the 'illicit commercial practices' of third countries under Council Regulation 2641/84 (1984), the so-called New Commercial Policy Instrument. This measure is designed to protect the interests of Community industries and exports to foreign markets which are being obstructed by illicit practices on the part of the governments of the third state. The Policy Instrument allows individuals within the Community to complain to the Community authorities regarding foreign commercial practices and, after investigation, if these practices are found to be illicit, retaliatory measures may be adopted in order to coerce the foreign state into desisting in such practices.

15.3 Relevant cases

EC Commission v *EC Council [Re ERTA]* [1971] 1 CMLR 335: Development by the Court of the doctrine of the implied powers of the Community.

Hauptzollamt Mainz v *Kupferberg* [1983] 1 CMLR 1: A decision relating to the direct effect of treaties negotiated by the Community within the Community legal system

International Fruit Company v *Produktschap voor Groenten en Fruit* [1972] ECR 1219: The direct effect of treaties negotiated by the Member States prior to the adopting of the three founding Community Treaties.

Polydor v *Harlequin Record Shops* [1982] ECR 329: The effect of free trade agreements between the Community and third states in Community law.

Demirel v *Stadt Schwabisch Gmund* [1989] 1 CMLR 421: The direct effect of the EEC-Turkey association agreement.

15.4 Relevant materials

P Pescatore, 'Treaty-making by the European Communities' in FG Jacobs & S Roberts (eds), *The Effect of Treaties in Domestic Law* (1987) 171-195.

D O'Keefe & HG Schermers (eds), *Mixed Agreements* (1983).

G Bebr, 'Agreements Concluded by the Community and Their Possible Direct Effect' (1983) 20 CML Rev 35.

M Hilf et al (eds), *The European Community and the GATT* (1986).

I Van Bael & J-F Bellis, *International Trade Law and Practice of the European Community* (Second edition, 1990).

EA Vermulst, *Anti-Dumping Law and Practice in the United States and the European Community* (1987).

J Cunnane & C Stanbrook, *Dumping and Subsidies in the European Community* (1983).

15.5 Analysis of questions

The subject of the external relations of the European Community is a specialist field which explains the relative scarcity of questions relating to this topic among examiners. However, the external relations of the Community has acquired a greater degree of significance in light of the Community participation in the Uruguay Round of GATT multilateral trade negotiations and the decisions of the European Court giving direct effect to terms of certain types of international agreements negotiated between the Community and third states. Not surprisingly, the following questions focus on these issues together with the matter of Community trade protection laws.

15.6 Questions

Question 1

What role has the Court of Justice played in defining the extent of the Community's powers in the external relations field?

University of Glasgow LLB Examination
1989 Q9

General comment

A general question on the function of the European Court in determining the scope of the external competence of the Community.

Skeleton solution

- Express powers of the Community to negotiate treaties.
- Implied powers imputed by the Court.
- Development of the doctrine through the jurisprudence of the Court.

Suggested solution

The Community has capacity to enter international agreements between itself and third states without the participation of the Member States in the negotiating processes. Express treaty-making capacity is conferred in the EEC Treaty for two particular forms of agreement.

Article 113 authorises the Community to conclude commercial agreements relating to tariff and trade matters for the purposes of achieving the objectives of the common commercial policy. This authority expressly extends to export aids, credit and finance, and matters relating to multilateral commodity agreements.

Article 238 of the EEC Treaty also authorises the Community to negotiate with third states, unions of states or international organisations, association agreements creating reciprocal rights and obligations, and facilitating common action through special procedures. Association agreements perform two functions. In the case of certain European countries the purpose of this form of agreement is to act as a preliminary procedure prior to membership of the Community. Other association agreements establish free trade status between the products of the Community and the third state in each others markets.

Agreements under Article 238 are supplemented by a special form of association agreement under Articles 131 to 136 of the EEC Treaty which provide for agreements between the Community and overseas countries and territories. These territories are listed in Annex IV to the Treaty and were originally dependencies of the Member States. The purpose of such agreements is to promote the economic and social development of these territories by establishing 'close economic relations' between the Community and the territory.

The exercise of power under Article 113 of the EEC Treaty has a potentially greater application. Two developments have significantly expanded the powers of the

Community under Article 113 to the exclusion of the participation of the Member States: the development of a broad interpretation by the Court of the concept of the common commercial policy; and the creation, also by the Court, of the 'theory of parallelism'.

The intention of the European Court to interpret the concept of the CCP in broad terms was made clear in the *International Agreement on Rubber Case* (1979), which was an advisory opinion from the European Court on a reference by the Commission under Article 228(1). The case concerned the participation of the Community in the negotiation of an international commodity agreement to regulate the supply of rubber. The Court stressed that a coherent common commercial policy would not be feasible if the Community was unable to exercise its treaty-making powers in relation to those international agreements which, alongside traditional commercial agreements, form an important element of the international economic environment. A broad interpretation of this provision was supported by the fact that the enumeration of the individual subjects covered by the article was conceived in a non-exhaustive fashion.

However, at the same time the Court believed that an important factor in deciding whether the Community had exclusive competence in this matter was the financial burden of participating in an agreement. In the case of a commodity agreement, if the burden of financing the agreement is placed on the Community budget, the Community has exclusive jurisdiction. Alternatively, if the charges are to be borne directly by the Member States, this factor implies the participation of the Member States in the negotiation of the agreement. The effect of this decision was in fact to expand the concept of the CCP itself, and also, in turn, the powers of the Community.

While the *Rubber Case* confirms that the Community has express authority to achieve those objectives specified for the achievement of the common commercial policy, the European Court has gone much further in developing the theory of implied powers, not only for the purposes of achieving a common commercial policy, but in fact to attain the objectives set out in Part One of the EEC Treaty. This has been achieved by the development of the theory of parallelism by the Court which was originally elaborated *EC Commission* v *EC Council [Re ERTA]* (1971).

In 1967 the Member States entered into negotiations with other European states to establish a European Road Transport Agreement. During these negotiations, the Council enacted a regulation which covered substantially the same subject-matter, but the Member States, anxious to include third states within the scope of the agreement continued negotiations on the subject. In 1970 the Council decided that negotiations would continue on an individual Member State basis without the participation of the Commission in the process. The Commission objected to this situation and brought an action before the European Court to annul the Council resolution deciding to conduct the negotiations on a Member State basis.

The Court held that authority to enter international agreements not only arose from those provisions which granted express authority, but also from other provisions of the Treaty which require international agreement for their achievement. In particular, each time the Community adopts legislation for the purpose of implementing a common policy envisaged by the Treaty, the Member States no longer have the right, acting individually or even collectively, to undertake obligations with third countries which would affect those rules. The doctrine of parallelism therefore requires that if the Community exercises an internal power, it simultaneously acquires a parallel external power to government the subject-matter.

In other words, the exercise of the internal capacity of the Community over a particular subject-matter deprives the Member States of individual authority to regulate the matter by international agreement. The basis for this determination was the need for the Community to assume and carry out contractual obligations towards third states affecting the whole sphere of the application of the Community legal system. This rationale was later confirmed in *Hauptzollamt Mainz* v *Kupferberg* (1983).

One qualification was, in fact, made to the functioning of the theory of parallelism under the EEC Treaty. The mere existence of internal legislative competence within the scheme of the Treaty was not ipso facto conclusive of the inability of the Member States to conclude international agreements bearing on such matters. Not only must legislative competence exist, but this power must be exercised by the Community. This restriction stems from the construction given by the Court to the rationale behind the theory - the desirability of avoiding conflicts between internal Community legislative and the international obligations of the Member States.

The Court has elaborated upon the doctrine of parallelism in a number of subsequent cases, one of the most significant being the *North-East Atlantic Fisheries Convention Case* (1975). Seven of the nine Member States entered into a convention to conserve fishing stocks in the North-East Atlantic and the Netherlands promulgated legislation implementing the provisions of the convention which provided inter alia for criminal prosecutions. A number of Dutch fishermen were prosecuted in a Dutch court for violating this statute. In their defence, the fishermen alleged that the Member States had no authority to enter international agreements on this subject since competence to regulate fishing policy had been passed to the Community. The Dutch legislation therefore infringed Community law.

The Community had in fact passed two regulations dealing with a common fishing policy but neither concerned the issue of conservation. Therefore, no Community legislation had been passed and no express authority to enter fishing conservation agreements had been conferred by the EEC Treaty. The Court held that the Community had authority to enter international commitments for the conservation of the resources of the sea, even although the Community had not passed legislation in exercise of this internal capacity. However, since the Community had not yet exercised its powers for this purpose, concurrent authority over this matter existed between the Community and the Member States and the Dutch legislation was upheld.

The Court later abandoned these restrictions on the implied powers of the Community to enter international agreements in the *Inland Waterway Vessels Case* (1977). In this case, the Community had no express treaty-making power to regulate inland waterway administration, although it did have authority to pass internal legislation in pursuit of a common transport policy under Articles 74 and 75 of the EEC Treaty. This internal legislative power had not been exercised.

Nevertheless, the European Court declared that the theory of parallelism extended not only to cases in which internal legislative power had been exercised by the Community but also to those cases which the Treaty creates an internal legislative capacity and the participation of the Community in the negotiation of an agreement 'is necessary for the attainment of one of the objectives of the Community'. In this decision, the Court conferred upon the Community authority to negotiate all agreements which fell within the competence of the Community by virtue of the EEC Treaty.

The European Court has therefore played a significant role in the expansion of the powers of the Community in the field of external relations. This has, in turn, resulted in a restriction of the powers of the Member States to conduct international affairs. The Court has achieved this expansion primarily through the teleological interpretation of the terms of the EEC Treaty.

Question 2

What criteria does the Court of Justice apply in deciding whether a provision of an international agreement has direct effects?

University of Glasgow LLB Examination
1988 Q1

General comment

A difficult question requiring detailed knowledge of the recent jurisprudence of the European Court.

Skeleton solution

- Legal effect of agreements within the Community.
- Rights of individuals.
- Criteria for establishing direct effect.
- Examples of the application of the principle.

Suggested solution

Treaties concluded by the Community within the powers vested by the EEC Treaty are 'binding on the institutions of the Community and the Member States' by virtue of Article 228(2) of the EEC Treaty. The European Court has taken the view that treaties to which the Community is a party, either by succession or direct negotiation, are an 'integral element of community law': *Haegemann* v *Belgian State* (1973). The Court has taken this view to ensure that international obligations assumed by the Community are consistently respected by the Member States.

In *Hauptzollamt Mainz* v *Kupferberg* (1983), the Court held that in order to 'ensure respect for treaty obligations concluded by the Community institutions, the Member States fulfil an obligation not only in relation to the non-Member country concerned but also and above all in relation to the Community which has assumed responsibility for the due performance of the obligation'. However, naturally a Community Treaty may be binding on both the Community and the Member States without conferring rights on individuals.

While a Community treaty may form an integral element of Community law, the Court has not automatically granted directly enforceable rights to individuals to vindicate this aspect of community law in the national tribunals of the Member States. The jurisprudence of the Court establishes a number of conditions which must be satisfied before an individual may exercise rights created under a Community agreement.

First, an individual may only contest the validity of a Community Regulation or a national rule of law if the treaty provision is 'capable of creating rights of which interested parties may avail themselves in a court of law': *International Fruit Company* v *Produktschap voor Groenten en Fruit* (1975); *Schluter* v *Hauptzollamt Lorrach* (1973).

Second, in order to ascertain whether a Community agreement confers rights upon individuals, regard must be had to 'the purpose and nature of the agreement itself' to determine whether the provision in question 'contains a clear and precise obligation which is not subject, in its implementation or effects, to the adoption of any subsequent measure: *Demirel* v *Stadt Schwabisch Gmund* (1989). If these conditions are satisfied, then direct effect may be given to the terms of a Community agreement under Community law.

The Court has demonstrated a greater reluctance to construe treaties to which the Community has succeeded as conferring individual enforceable rights than under treaties which the Community has negotiated itself. In *Bresciani* v *Amministrazione Italiana delle Finanze* (1976), the Court was prepared to accept that certain provisions of the Yaounde Convention of 1963 were directly enforceable after ascertaining that the purpose and nature of the provisions being relied upon was the automatic abolition of charges having an equivalent effect. Also, in *Pabst & Richarz* v *Hauptzollamt Oldenberg* (1982), the Court was willing to give direct effect to certain provisions of the EEC-Greece Association Agreement.

While the plaintiff in the *Kupferberg Case* above, was unsuccessful in invoking the EEC-Portugal Free Trade Agreement as a defence, nevertheless the Court made a number of important points in defining the direct enforcement of Community agreements. The Court elaborated on the nature of the obligations assumed by the Community under Community agreements. On the one hand, it was the Community which was internationally responsible for the execution of the international obligations, while on the other hand, the obligation extended to the third state. A refusal by a national court to implement an obligation assumed by the Community did not invariably constitute an infringement of a reciprocal obligation since such agreements did not always require incorporation into national law. The full performance of an obligation might leave a party free to determine the legal means necessary within its legal system to pursue the objectives agreed.

Since this distinction existed, it was impossible to allow individuals to enforce rights at the national level unless the Member States in question would be failing to conform to its international obligations assumed through the Community. This was the ultimate rationale for distinguishing between the enforceable and unenforceable exercise of rights by individuals under Community treaties. In *R* v *Secretary of State, ex parte Narin* (1990), the English High Court applied this rationale in rejecting the argument that provisions of the EEC-Turkey association could be given direct effect in English law.

In an earlier case relating to the direct effect of the provisions of the EEC Treaty, the European Court acknowledged that 'the vigilance of individuals concerned to protect their rights amounts to an effective supervision in addition to the supervision by other states or by international organs': *Van Gend en Loos* v *Netherlands* (1963). Where EEC Treaty provisions were capable of clear, unqualified and unconditional application then they were capable of being directly effective as a source of Community law. The Court has not adopted a similar policy with regard to the enforceability of treaties in Community law.

This aims and purposes standard established for the direct enforceability of such agreements, while perhaps more rigorous than the test for the direct enforcement of EEC Treaty provisions, is eminently sensible. First, the EEC Treaties and the related founding agreements are the constitution of the Community and should enjoy a preferred status to agreements negotiated under authority of them. Second, a dramatic expansion of enforceable rights would arise if every Community treaty was capable of conferring directly enforceable rights. Third, direct enforcement of Community treaties as an element of Community law would represent a usurpation of those legal systems which maintain a dualist legal tradition such as the United Kingdom. Fourth, considerable opposition has been manifested by a number of Member States to this limited inroad into the direct enforceability of Community treaties by the Court.

Question 3

Describe the processes which are involved in the formulation and administration of the common commercial policy within the European Community and comment on the extent to which the scope of this policy is limited by international regulations.

Question prepared by the Author
February 1991

General comment

A narrative question requiring a descriptive answer.

Skeleton solution

- The scope of Articles 110-116 EEC Treaty.
- Procedure for the formulation of the CCP.
- An illustration of the tensions involved.
- The existence of international restraints and their effects.

Suggested solution

The creation of a consistent trade policy among the Member States of the European Community has been achieved by the delegation of decision-making authority over this subject-matter to the centralised agencies of the Community. Both the EEC Treaty and the ECSC Treaty reserve exclusive competence to the Community for the conduct of 'commercial policy': Articles 110-116 EEC Treaty; Articles 71-75 ECSC Treaty. Individual Member States no longer retain competence to legislate or enter into international obligations relating to these matters, in the absence of specific authorisation from the Community: *Donckerwolke* v *Procureur de la Republique* (1976). While the exact scope of the right to formulate commercial policy has not been clearly defined, the European Commission has consistently adopted an aggressive interpretation of this authority and on the whole, this policy has been supported by the ECJ.

From an international trade policy perspective, the European Community is a customs territory which is erected on the establishment of a common customs tariff and the creation of a common commercial policy towards third countries. The common customs tariff has replaced individual national tariff schedules with a harmonised and comprehensive scheme to facilitate the levying of duties on goods and products entering the Community. The Community common commercial policy is founded on the uniform application of principles relating, inter alia, to tariff changes, the conclusion of tariff and trade agreements, the achievement of uniformity in measures of trade liberalisation, the formulation of a consistent export policy and the adoption of measures to protect against unfair trade practices.

The procedure for the formulation of the common commercial policy is similar to the normal decision-making processes within the Community. The European Commission drafts proposals after consultations with various foreign representatives and forwards these initial draft texts to working groups composed of national representatives which negotiate a minimum acceptable proposal for submission to the Council of Ministers. The final content of the policy is the product of a continuous process of negotiation between the Commission and the Council of Ministers on the one hand, and where international agreements are involved, between the Commission and third states on the other hand. Although ultimate authority for Community legislation rests with the Council of Ministers, the powers of that organ are circumscribed by the requirement that the Council may only act on the basis of a proposal from the Commission.

This separation of powers in the adoption of trade policy is a hallmark of the institutional structure of the Community legislative process. The Commission is the initiator of policy, both within the Community itself and in relation to agreements with foreign states. The Council is compelled to act upon a formal proposal from the Commission as the basis for its final policy position. A tension has developed between the Council and the Commission, since the Member States demonstrate a propensity to attempt to preserve national control over the conduct of foreign policy.

The final content of Community trade policy is the compromise reached between the Council and the Commission, tempered by the need to accommodate international obligations assumed by the Community in the exercise of its external affairs competence.

The tension between the interests of the Member States, as manifested in the Council of Ministers, and the objectives of the Community, as advocated by the Commission, surfaced during the Tokyo Round of Multilateral Tariff Negotiations held under the auspices of the GATT, and again during the European Community - United States steel dispute in the early 1980s. After the conclusion of the 1979 GATT Code on Non-Tariff Barriers to Trade, a number of Member States of the Community argued that the subject-matters of certain agreements fell within the jurisdiction of the Member States and outside that of the Community. During the steel dispute, a number of Member States pointed to the less rigorous Community provisions in the ECSC Treaty in contrast to the comparable provisions in the EEC Treaty. The final resolution of this dispute required the negotiation of an extensive mandate between the Member States to allow the Commission to settle the issue with the United States government.

Despite the expiry of the transition periods for the completion of the objectives of the EEC Treaty, and the renewed impetus towards the creation of an internal market by the Single European Act, Member States continue to express a reluctance to transfer complete authority to the Community to formulate a comprehensive and coherent common commercial policy. This reluctance may be attributed to two separate factors. First, the institutional structure established for the creation of a commercial policy is insufficient. Second, the objectives of the common commercial policy are fragmented and not comprehensively stated to a degree which would encourage transfer of competence to the Community.

Consistent commercial policy requires a centralised agency to express policy objectives. Within the Community, the Council of Ministers, which is the organ with ultimate responsibility for commercial policy, indulges in extensive internal debate and bargaining before a mandate is given to the Commission to present the policy at the global level. Since the final position within the Council is the embodiment of an internal political compromise, the final Community policy is rigid and inflexible. The internal decision-making processes, by allowing for the continued voicing of national concerns, are not suitable for consistent policy formulation.

Also the objectives of the common commercial policy are organically integrated with the success of other Community policies. The ineffective control of the Community over certain areas of the Community economy, such as agriculture, has undermined even this weak policy position. While the Community has failed to adopt legislation standardising technical requirements for intra-Community trade, it is unlikely that it will succeed in doing so for foreign goods. The failure of the Community at this level, ultimately exacerbates the problems at the international level. For example, the Member States of the Community continue to negotiate voluntary export restraints with foreign nations even although this matter is an issue for Community regulation.

The ultimate consequence of the fragmented approach to policy formulation is the reluctance of Member States to transfer regulatory authority to the Community.

Community external policy depends on the Common Customs Tariff (CCT) and the Common Commercial Policy (CCP). Each of these is subject to the international regulations established under the GATT and assumed by the Community on behalf of the individual Member States. Non-adherence or violation of such rules would therefore ex facie give rise to a presumption of protectionism. The existence of international rules negotiated in the GATT does limit the scope of the Community to formulate the CCP, but this effect is minimised by the fact that international rules regulating economic matters are generally vague and imprecise. As a result, the normative effect of such rules is strictly circumscribed. This is particularly true as regards the international legal restraints on the use of trade protection measures such as anti-dumping duties.

The European Community appears to have tightened its legislation in the field of trade protection laws in order to take advantage of the relative laxity of the international rules. A number of trade remedy provisions do in fact seem to violate the international rules. But greater concern must be raised by the volume of actions taken under the authority of trade protection laws. One disconcerting illustration of this problem is the adoption of anti-dumping measures by the Community. Before the accession to the Tokyo Round Agreement on Anti-Dumping in 1979, the European Community first enacted anti-dumping legislation in 1968. In the next 10 year intervening period, a total of 60 anti-dumping investigations were initiated. But, in the 10 year period between 1979 and 1989, this average has climbed dramatically: IV Bael & J-F Bellis, *International Trade Law and Practice of the European Community* (second edition, 1990).

Although a number of reasons have been offered to explain this phenomenon, at least one commentator is prepared to acknowledge that these trends may be attributed to two factors: the economic recession within the Community prompted an increase in the number of actions, coupled with the realisation that anti-dumping duty actions constituted an effective instrument of economic coercion: I Van Bael, 'EEC Anti-Dumping Law and Practice Revisited' (1990) 24 JWT 5.

Despite recognition that the abuse of measures of contingent protection represents a serious threat to the stability of the global trading system - a fact acknowledged during the Tokyo Round of Multilateral Tariff Negotiations - the introduction of Community legislation to implement the 1979 Anti-Dumping Code has done nothing to stem the growth of anti-dumping duty actions. The conclusion must therefore be reached that the Code itself is ineffective.

At the same time, subsequent amendments to the 1979 legislation have attempted to close any loopholes in the law which may facilitate abuse. The general theme of this process has been a tightening of the regulations against the interests of foreign producers and importers. As the subject of dumping has been increasingly regulated, it has become progressively easier for a complainer to be successful in its action, or at least to harass the importer or foreign producer.

Question 4

The Mitsubishi Corporation of Japan has been accused of dumping Video Cassette Recorders in the European Community by the Government of France. This allegation is denied by Mitsubishi who seek advice from you in relation to the nature of the investigation by the Commission into the allegation of dumping. The French government has also alleged that Mitsubishi has established a manufacturing plant in Sunderland, England, in order to circumvent the payment of earlier anti-dumping duties by importing the component parts for final assembly in Sunderland.

Advise Mitsubishi of the nature of the investigation which will be carried out by the Commission and of the legitimacy its activities in Sunderland.

Question prepared by the Author
February 1991

General comment

A problem-type question requiring the student to apply Community anti-dumping procedure to a hypothetical factual situation.

Skeleton solution

- The Anti-Dumping Regulation.
- The elements of a dumping action - procedure and substantive.
- Screwdriver Regulation.

Suggested solution

Dumping is the practice by which goods are introduced into the Community at a price lower than the price of equivalent goods on the domestic market of the exporting country. It is deemed to be an unfair trade practice and most states, including the Community, have legislation which allows anti-dumping duties to be levied in order to prevent injury to domestic industries competing with the foreign products.

The European Commission has responsibility for investigating the facts surrounding an anti-dumping petition and determines whether or not there is sufficient evidence to justify an investigation: Council Regulation 2423/88 OJ L209/1 (1988). It is also empowered under certain conditions to impose provisional anti-dumping duties for a maximum period of six months and to accept undertakings by foreign exporters.

However, the Council of Ministers has sole competence to order definitive anti-dumping duties.

A dumping complaint may be lodged by any legal person (an individual or company) or by an association not having legal personality, acting on behalf of a Community industry. According to the Council Regulation, investigations of anti-dumping must normally be completed within a period of not less than six months immediately prior to the initiation of the complaint.

The complaint itself must contain 'sufficient evidence' of the existence of both dumping and injury to a Community industry. In general, this requires information relating to: (a) the nature of the allegedly dumped product; (b) the origin of the exporting country; (c) the names of the country of origin, the producer and the exporter of the product in question; and (d) evidence of dumping and injury resulting therefrom from the industry which considers itself injured or threatened. Upon receipt of a complaint setting forth such facts, the Commission will begin its investigation.

The Commission investigates the question of dumping until its final determination. If this is negative, the investigation terminates, but where the finding is positive, definitive anti-dumping duties may be imposed. This is done by way of a report submitted to the Council of Ministers which has the discretion to accept, modify or reject the Commission's proposal. Where duties are imposed, this is achieved by the adoption of a Regulation (or a Decision) sanctioning the imposition of duties.

The basic substantive elements of an anti-dumping action are the existence of dumping, injury and 'Community interests' requiring intervention.

The procedure for determining the existence of dumping in the Community is deceptively simple. it involves four basic steps: (a) the determination of 'normal value'; (b) the determination of 'export price'; (c) a comparison of the normal value to export price; and (d) the calculation of the 'margin of dumping' (the normal price minus the export price). Each of these determinations allows considerable latitude for interpretation.

Normal value is the price of the goods in the country of origin, while the export price is the price of the goods inside the Community. The margin of dumping is the difference between these two figures and is also the quantum of the anti-dumping duty which will be levied to neutralise the unfair competitive advantage enjoyed by the foreign product.

In addition to establishing the existence of actual dumped products, it is also necessary to prove that these products have caused material injury to an industry within the Community. This involves proof of actual material injury, the threat of material injury or the material retardation of an industry. In addition, the investigation must reveal that the dumped products have caused the material injury. If it cannot be shown that the dumped products are the cause of the injury, no anti-dumping duties can be imposed.

Finally, before anti-dumping duties can be assessed, a third condition must be met; it must be decided that 'the interests of the Community call for intervention'. No list of definitive Community interests is provided in the Regulation concerning the imposition of dumping duties. However, the concept of Community interests will cover a wide range of factors, but the most important concern the interests of the consumer and processors of imported products and the need to have regard to the competitive equilibrium within the Community market.

If all these elements are established during the Commission investigation, Mitsubishi may be subject to anti-dumping duties in respect of its VCR products.

The Community has also adopted legislation to prevent foreign importers from circumventing the application of anti-dumping duties by breaking down their products into their component parts and then importing these for reassembly inside the Community. Anti-dumping duties may be imposed on the finished product even if assembled in a factory within the Community, at the rate applicable to the finished product but by reference to the CIF value of the parts imported for assembly in this manner. The relevant legislation which achieves this goal is known as the 'Screwdriver Regulation'.

Three conditions must be satisfied in order to attract this form of anti-dumping duty: (a) the assembly must be carried out by a person related to the exporter of the like products subject to the anti-dumping duties; (b) the assembly has started or substantially increased after the anti-dumping investigation leading to the imposition of duties had commenced; and (c) the value of the parts or materials used in the finished product which have come from the country concerned constitutes at least 60 per cent of the parts and materials used.

The Screwdriver Regulation has in fact been held to be unlawful by a recent GATT panel report and the Regulation itself will most likely be amended or repealed in the near future. Until then, it is likely that Mitsubishi may be subject to additional duties in respect of VCRs if the component parts for the finished product have entered the Community for assembly for the purpose of avoiding the imposition of duties.

HLT GROUP PUBLICATIONS FOR THE LLB EXAMINATIONS

Our publications, written by specialists, are used widely by students at universities, polytechnics and colleges throughout the United Kingdom and overseas.

Textbooks
These are designed as working books to provide students with a valuable framework on which to base their studies. They are updated each year to reflect new developments and changing trends.

Casebooks
These are designed as companion volumes to the Textbooks and incorporate important cases, statutes as appropriate, and other material, together with detailed commentaries.

Revision WorkBooks
For first degree law students, these provide questions and answers for all topics in each law subject. Every topic has sections on key points, recent cases and statutes, further reading etc.

Suggested Solutions
These are available to past London University LLB examination papers and provide the student with an invaluable revision aid and an insight into the techniques essential to examination success.

The books listed below can be ordered through your local bookshops or obtained direct from the publisher using this order form. Telephone, Fax or Telex orders will also be accepted. Quote your Access or Visa card numbers for priority orders. To order direct from the publisher please enter the cost of the titles you require, fill in the despatch details and send it with your remittance to the HLT Group Ltd.

ORDER FORM

LLB PUBLICATIONS	Textbooks		Casebooks		Revision WorkBooks		Sug. Sol. 1984/88		Sug. Sol. 1989	
	Cost £	£	Cost £	£	Cost £	£	Cost £	£	Cost £	£
L01 Criminal Law	12.95		16.95		9.95		14.95		3.95	
L02 Constitutional Law	12.95		16.95		9.95		14.95		3.95	
L03 English Legal System	12.95		14.95				*6.95		3.95	
L04 Law of Contract	12.95		15.95		9.95		14.95		3.95	
L05 Law of Tort	12.95		16.95				14.95		3.95	
L06 Law of Trusts	12.95		16.95		9.95		14.95		3.95	
L07 Land Law	12.95		18.95		9.95		14.95		3.95	
L08 Jurisprudence	14.95				9.95		14.95		3.95	
L09 Administrative Law	15.95		18.95				14.95		3.95	
L10 Law of Evidence	17.95		14.95		9.95		14.95		3.95	
L11 Commercial Law	17.95		18.95		9.95		14.95		3.95	
L13 Pub. Int. Law	16.95		14.95		9.95		14.95		3.95	
L14 Succession	14.95		15.95		9.95		14.95		3.95	
L16 Family Law	14.95		18.95				14.95		3.95	
L17 Company Law	16.95		18.95		9.95		14.95		3.95	
L18 Revenue Law	14.95		18.95		9.95		14.95		3.95	
L20 European Community Law	15.95									

Cut along dashed line

* 1987 and 1988 only

DETAILS FOR DESPATCH OF PUBLICATIONS

Please insert your full name below

Please insert below the style in which you would like correspondence to be addressed to you

TITLE Mr, Miss etc.	INITIALS	SURNAME/FAMILY NAME

Address to which study material is to be sent (please ensure someone will be present to accept delivery of your College Publications.)

POSTAGE & PACKING

You are welcome to purchase study material from the College at 200 Greyhound Road W14 9RY, during normal working hours.

If you wish to order by post this may be done direct from the College. Postal charges are as follows:

UK - all orders over £25 - no charge; orders below £25 - £1.50.

OVERSEAS - all orders are sent by airmail and the charge is £6 for the first item, an additional £4 for the second item and an additional £3 for the third and for every additional item. If ordering *Suggested Solutions 1989 only* add 30% to the charge for the Suggested Solutions ordered.

The College cannot accept responsibility in respect of postal delays or losses in the postal systems.

DESPATCH All cheques must be cleared before material is despatched.

SUMMARY OF ORDER

Date of order: / /

Cost of publications ordered:	£
Add: Postage and packing United Kingdom (see above) Overseas Air Mail: First item at £6; Second item at £4; Additional items at £3; Suggested Solutions only: 30%	£
Total cost of order:	£

Please ensure that you enclose a cheque or draft payable to The HLT Group Ltd for the above amount, or charge to ☐ Access ☐ Visa

Card Number

Expiry Date / / Signature ______________________

Your completed form and remittance should be sent to :

The HLT Group Ltd, Despatch Department, 200 Greyhound Road, London W14 9RY.

Telephone: (01) 385 3377 Telex: 266386 Fax: (01) 381 3377.